T0202927

# Lecture Notes in Computer Science 12151

More information about this series at http://www.springer.com/series/7407

Ponnuswamy Sadayappan ·
Bradford L. Chamberlain ·
Guido Juckeland · Hatem Ltaief (Eds.)

# High Performance Computing

35th International Conference, ISC High Performance 2020
Frankfurt/Main, Germany, June 22–25, 2020
Proceedings

Editors
Ponnuswamy Sadayappan
School of Computing
University of Utah
Salt Lake City, UT, USA

Guido Juckeland ⓘ
Helmholtz-Zentrum Dresden-Rossendorf
Dresden, Germany

Bradford L. Chamberlain
Cray, a Hewlett Packard Enterprise Company
Seattle, WA, USA

Hatem Ltaief ⓘ
Extreme Computing Research Center
King Abdullah University of Science
and Technology
Thuwal, Saudi Arabia

ISSN 0302-9743          ISSN 1611-3349 (electronic)
Lecture Notes in Computer Science
ISBN 978-3-030-50742-8          ISBN 978-3-030-50743-5 (eBook)
https://doi.org/10.1007/978-3-030-50743-5

LNCS Sublibrary: SL1 – Theoretical Computer Science and General Issues

# Preface

ISC High Performance, formerly known as the International Supercomputing Conference, was founded in 1986 as the Supercomputer Seminar. Originally organized by Hans Meuer, Professor of Computer Science at the University of Mannheim, Germany, and former director of its computer center, the seminar brought together a group of 81 scientists and industrial partners who shared an interest in high-performance computing. Since then, the annual conference has become a major international event within the HPC community and, accompanying its growth in size over the years, the conference has moved from Mannheim via Heidelberg, Dresden, Hamburg, and Leipzig to Frankfurt. Over recent years, we have seen a steady increase in the number of submissions of high-quality research papers to the conference and in the number of conference attendees. A record-setting attendance was anticipated for ISC-HPC 2020 in Frankfurt, but as with all other conferences in summer 2020, the global coronavirus pandemic forced it to be a digital event.

For ISC-HPC 2020, the call for participation was issued in Fall 2019, inviting researchers and developers to submit the latest results of their work to the Program Committee. In all, 87 papers were submitted from authors all over the world. The Research Papers Program Committee consisted of **88** members from **22** countries throughout the world. After initial reviews were completed, a rebuttal process offered authors an opportunity to respond to reviewers' questions and help clarify issues the reviewers might have had. To come to a final consensus on the papers, a face-to-face Program Committee meeting was held in Frankfurt to discuss the papers. Finally, the committee selected 27 papers for publication.

For the past several years, the ISC-HPC conference has presented an ISC-sponsored award to encourage outstanding research in high-performance computing and to honor the overall best research paper submitted to the conference. Two years ago, this annual award was renamed the Hans Meuer Award in memory of the late Dr. Hans Meuer, general chair of the ISC-HPC conference from 1986 through 2014, and a co-founder of the TOP500 benchmark project. In recent years, from all research papers submitted, the Research Papers Program Committee nominated two papers as finalists for the award and then selected the best paper based on the final presentations during the conference. Because ISC-HPC 2020 became an all-digital event without physical attendance and live presentations, both nominated papers were bestowed with the Hans Meuer Award:

- "Load-balancing Parallel Relational Algebra" by Sidharth Kumar and Thomas Gilray
- "Time Series Mining at Petascale Performance" by Amir Raoofy, Martin Schulz, Carsten Trinitis, Dai Yang, and Roman Karlstetter

The Gauss Centre for Supercomputing sponsors the Gauss Award. This award is assigned to the most outstanding paper in the field of scalable supercomputing and went to:

- "Solving Acoustic Boundary Integral Equations Using High Performance Tile Low-Rank LU Factorization" by Noha Al-Harthi, Rabab Alomairy, Kadir Akbudak, Rui Chen, Hatem Ltaief, Hakan Bagci, and David Keyes

We would like to express our gratitude to our colleagues for submitting papers to the ISC-HPC scientific sessions, and the area chairs and members of the Technical Papers Program Committee for organizing this year's program.

June 2020

Ponnuswamy Sadayappan
Bradford L. Chamberlain
Guido Juckeland
Hatem Ltaief

The original version of the book was revised: For detailed information see correction chapter. The correction to the book is available at
https://doi.org/10.1007/978-3-030-50743-5_28

# Organization

## Research Papers Program Committee

### Research Paper Chairs

Saday Sadayappan      University of Utah and Pacific Northwest National Laboratory, USA
Bradford L. Chamberlain      Cray, HPE, USA

## Architectures, Networks and Infrastructure

Jonathan Beard      ARM Inc., USA
Ron Brightwell      Sandia National Laboratories, USA
Nectarios Koziris      National Technical University of Athens, Greece
Arthur Maccabe      Oak Ridge National Laboratory, USA
Satoshi Matsuoka      Riken Center for Computational Science, Tokyo Institute of Technology, Japan
Dhabaleswar Panda      Ohio State University, USA
John Shalf      Lawrence Berkeley National Laboratory, USA
Tor Skeie      Simula Research Laboratory, Norway
Guangming Tan      Institute of Computing Technology (ICT), China
Carsten Trinitis      Technical University of Munich, Germany

## Artificial Intelligence and Machine Learning

Woongki Baek      UNIST, South Korea
Thomas Brettin      Argonne National Laboratory, USA
Xiaowen Chu      Hong Kong Baptist University, Hong Kong
Judy Fox      Indiana University, USA
Mohammad Ghasemzadeh      Apple, USA
David Gregg      Trinity College Dublin, Ireland
Bingsheng He      National University of Singapore, Singapore
Xiaosong Ma      Qatar Computing Research Institute, Qatar
Dimitrios Nikolopoulos      Queen's University Belfast, UK
Martin Schultz      Forschungszentrum Jülich, Germany
Ana Lucia      Varbanescu University of Amsterdam, The Netherlands
Yu Wang      Tsinghua University, China
Zeyi Wen      The University of Western Australia, Australia

## Data, Storage and Visualization

| | |
|---|---|
| Suren Byna | Lawrence Berkeley National Lab, USA |
| Philip Carns | Argonne National Laboratory, USA |
| Yong Chen | Texas Tech University, USA |
| Tanzima Islam | Texas State University, USA |
| Preeti Malakar | Indian Institute of Technology Kanpur, India |
| Suzanne McIntosh | New York University, USA |
| Kathryn Mohror | Lawrence Livermore National Laboratory, USA |
| Talita Perciano | Lawrence Berkeley National Laboratory, USA |
| Venkatram Vishwanath | Argonne National Laboratory, USA |

## Emerging Technologies

| | |
|---|---|
| Guang Hao | Low Microsoft, USA |
| Sriram Krishnamoorthy | Pacific Northwest National Laboratory, USA |
| Mathias Soeken | EPFL Lausanne, Switzerland |
| Robert Wille | Johannes Kepler University Linz, Austria |

## HPC Algorithms

| | |
|---|---|
| Anne Benoit | ENS Lyon, France |
| Umit Catalyurek | Georgia Institute of Technology, USA |
| Aurélien Cavelan | University of Basel, Switzerland |
| Anshu Dubey | Argonne National Laboratory, University of Chicago, USA |
| Sascha Hunold | TU Wien, Austria |
| Ananth Kalyanaraman | Washington State University, USA |
| Kamer Kaya | Sabancı University, Turkey |
| Hatem Ltaief | KAUST, Saudi Arabia |
| Veronika Sonigo | University of Franche-Comté, FEMTO-ST Institute, France |
| Didem Unat | Koç University, Turkey |
| Ana Lucia Varbanescu | University of Amsterdam, The Netherlands |

## HPC Applications

| | |
|---|---|
| Edouard Audit | CEA, France |
| Xing Cai | Simula Research Laboratory, Norway |
| Carlo Cavazzoni | CINECA, Italy |
| Anne C. Elster | University of Texas, USA, and Norwegian University of Science and Technology (NTNU), Norway |
| Erwin Laure | KTH, Sweden |
| Erik Lindahl | SciLifeLab, Sweden |
| Hatem Ltaief | KAUST, Saudi Arabia |
| A. Cristiano I. Malossi | IBM Research, Switzerland |

Gabriel Noaje                  NVIDIA, Singapore
Dirk Pleiter                   Forschungszentrum Jülich, Germany
Filippo Spiga                  Arm, Arm Ltd., UK
Tjerk Straatsma                ORNL, USA

## Performance Modeling and Measurement

Sudheer Chunduri               Argonne Leadership Computing Facility, USA
I-Hsin Chung                   IBM Research, USA
Florina Ciorba                 University of Basel, Switzerland
Georg Hager                    University of Erlangen-Nuremberg, Erlangen Regional
                               Computing Center, Germany
Daniel Holmes                  EPCC, The University of Edinburgh, UK
Guillaume Mercier              Bordeaux INP, France
Bernd Mohr                     Jülich Supercomputing Centre, Germany
Miwako Tsuji                   RIKEN, Japan
Michele Weiland                EPCC, The University of Edinburgh, UK
Felix Wolf                     Technical University of Darmstadt, Germany
Jidong Zhai                    Tsinghua University, China

## Programming Models and Systems Software

Abhinav Bhatele                University of Maryland, USA
Ron Brightwell                 Sandia National Laboratories, USA
Huimin Cui                     Institute of Computing Technology, CAS, China
Angeles Gonzalez Navarro       Universidad de Malaga, Spain
Clemens Grelck                 University of Amsterdam, The Netherlands
Jaejin Lee                     Seoul National University, South Korea
Naoya Maruyama                 Lawrence Livermore National Laboratory, USA
Satoshi Matsuoka               Riken Center for Computational Science,
                               Tokyo Institute of Technology, Japan
Simon McIntosh-Smith           University of Bristol, UK
Swaroop S. Pophale             ORNL, USA
Sven-Bodo Scholz               Radboud University, The Netherlands
Martin Schulz                  Technical University of Munich, Germany
Xuanhua Shi Huazhong           University of Science and Technology, China
Daisuke Takahashi              University of Tsukuba, Japan
Christian Terboven             RWTH Aachen University, Germany
Chenxi Wang                    UCLA, USA
Qing Yi                        University of Colorado at Colorado Springs, USA
Jidong Zhai                    Tsinghua University, China

## BoFs Committee

Marc Baboulin                  Université Paris-Saclay, France
Claudia Blaas-Schenner         TU Wien, VSC Research Center, Austria

| Joshua Booth | University of Alabama in Huntsville, USA |
| Nahid Emad | University of Versailles, France |
| Dominik Göddeke | University of Stuttgart, Germany |
| Mozhgan Kabiri Chimeh | NVIDIA, UK |
| Harald Köstler | FAU Erlangen-Nuremberg, Germany |
| Carola Kruse | Centre Européen de Recherche et de Formation Avancée en Calcul Scientifique (CERFACS), France |
| Simon McIntosh-Smith | University of Bristol, UK |
| Iosif Meyerov | Lobachevsky State University of Nizhni Novogorod, Russia |
| Lubomir Riha | IT4Innovations National Supercomputing Center, Technical University of Ostrava, Czech Republic |
| Marie-Christine Sawley | Intel, France |
| Masha Sosonkina | Old Dominion University, USA |
| Vladimir Stegailov | Higher School of Economics, JIHT RAS, Russia |
| Dave Turner | Kansas State University, USA |
| Roman Wyrzykowski | Czestochowa University of Technology, Poland |

## PhD Forum Committee

| Eishi Arima | The University of Tokyo, Japan |
| Dorian Arnold | Emory University, USA |
| Hans-Joachim Bungartz | Technical University of Munich, Germany |
| Florina Ciorba | University of Basel, Switzerland |
| Christian Engelmann | Oak Ridge National Laboratory, USA |
| Karl Fuerlinger | Ludwig Maximilian University Munich (LMU), Germany |
| Georgios Goumas | National Technical University of Athens, Greece |
| Katherine Isaacs | University of Arizona, USA |
| Tanzima Islam | Texas State University, USA |
| Alice Koniges | University of Hawaii, Maui High Performance Computing Center, USA |
| Stefan Lankes | RWTH Aachen University, Germany |
| Valerie Maxville | Curtin University, Australia |
| Mi Sun Min | Argonne National Laboratory, USA |
| Shinobu Miwa | The University of Electro-Communications, Japan |
| Cosmin Eugen | Oancea University of Copenhagen, Denmark |
| Olga Pearce | Lawrence Livermore National Laboratory, USA |
| Amanda Randles | Duke University, USA |
| Bettina Schnor | University of Potsdam, Germany |
| Martin Schulz | Technical University of Munich, Germany |
| Sean Smith | NCI Australia, Australia |
| Leon Song | The University of Sydney, Australia |

# Project Posters Committee

| | |
|---|---|
| Jean-Thomas Acquaviva | Data Direct Networks, France |
| Alexander Breuer | Fraunhofer ITWM, Germany |
| Apostolos Evangelopoulos | University College London, UK |
| Derek Groen | Brunel University, UK |
| Ludek Kucera | Charles University, Czech Republic |
| Sebastian Kuckuk | Friedrich-Alexander-University Erlangen-Nuremberg (FAU), Germany |
| Michael Kuhn | Universität Hamburg, Germany |
| Hatem Ltaief | KAUST, Saudi Arabia |
| Hitoshi Murai | RIKEN, Japan |
| Philipp Neumann | Helmut-Schmidt-University Hamburg, Germany |
| Christian Perez | Inria, France |
| Erwan Raffin | Atos Bull, France |
| Martin Schreiber | Technical University of Munich, Germany |
| Hiroyuki Takizawa | Tohoku University, Japan |
| Yu-hang Tang | Lawrence Berkeley National Laboratory, USA |
| Ben van Werkhoven | Netherlands eScience Center, The Netherlands |

# Research Posters Committee

| | |
|---|---|
| Ritu Arora | Texas Advanced Computing Center, UT Austin, USA |
| Sridutt Bhalachandra | Lawrence Berkeley National Laboratory, USA |
| Marc Casas | Barcelona Supercomputing Center, Spain |
| Irina Demeshko | Los Alamos National Laboratory, USA |
| Ryusuke Egawa | Tohoku University, Cyberscience Center, Japan |
| Christian Engelmann | Oak Ridge National Laboratory, USA |
| Kei-ichiro Fukazawa | Kyoto University, Japan |
| Ana Gainaru | Vanderbilt University, USA |
| Lin Gan | Tsinghua University, National Supercomputing Center in Wuxi, China |
| Wilfried Gansterer | University of Vienna, Austria |
| Dominik Göddeke | University of Stuttgart, Germany |
| Patricia González | University of A Coruña, Spain |
| José Gracia | University of Stuttgart, HLRS, Germany |
| Ryan E. Grant | Sandia National Laboratories, University of New Mexico, USA |
| Sara Hamouda | Inria, France |
| Toshihiro Hanawa | The University of Tokyo, Japan |
| Oguz Kaya | Universite Paris-Saclay, LRI, France |
| Kazuhiko Komatsu | Tohoku University, Japan |
| Ignacio Laguna | Lawerence Livermore National Laboratory, USA |
| Seyong Lee | ORNL, USA |
| Jiajia Li | Pacific Northwest National Laboratory, USA |
| Hitoshi Murai | RIKEN, Japan |

| Takeshi Nanri | Kyushu University, Japan |
| Swaroop S. Pophale | ORNL, USA |
| Kento Sato | RIKEN, Japan |
| Keita Teranishi | Sandia National Laboratories, USA |
| Jesmin Jahan Tithi | Intel, USA |
| Vadim Voevodin | RCC MSU, Russia |
| Jeffrey Young | Georgia Institute of Technology, USA |

## Tutorials Committee

| Damian Alvarez | Forschungszentrum Jülich, Germany |
| Katie Antypas | Lawrence Berkeley National Laboratory, USA |
| Rosa M. Badia | Barcelona Supercomputing Center, Spain |
| Pavan Balaji | Argonne National Laboratory, USA |
| Janine Bennett | Sandia National Laboratories, USA |
| Jong Choi | Oak Ridge National Laboratory, USA |
| Dan Ellsworth | Colorado College, USA |
| Kevin Huck | University of Oregon, USA |
| Mozhgan Kabiri Chimeh | NVIDIA, UK |
| Michael O. Lam | James Madison University, Lawrence Livermore National Laboratory, USA |
| David Lecomber | Arm, Arm Ltd., UK |
| Kelvin Li | IBM, Canada |
| Simon McIntosh-Smith | University of Bristol, UK |
| C. J. Newburn | NVIDIA, USA |
| Dhabaleswar Panda | Ohio State University, USA |
| Ojas Parekh | Sandia National Laboratories, USA |
| Olga Pearce | Lawrence Livermore National Laboratory, USA |
| Christian Plessl | Paderborn University, Germany |
| Harald Servat | Intel, Spain |
| Michela Taufer | University of Tennessee, USA |

## Workshops Committee

| Emmanuel Agullo | Inria, France |
| Hartwig Anzt | Karlsruhe Institute of Technology, Germany, and University of Tennessee, USA |
| Richard Barrett | Sandia National Laboratories, USA |
| Roy Campbell | Department of Defense, USA |
| Florina Ciorba | University of Basel, Switzerland |
| Anthony Danalis | University of Tennessee, USA |
| Manuel F. Dolz | Universitat Jaume I, Spain |
| Nick Forrington | Arm, Arm Ltd., USA |
| Karl Fuerlinger | Ludwig Maximilian University Munich (LMU), Germany |
| Judit Gimenez Lucas | Barcelona Supercomputing Center, Spain |

| Thomas Gruber | University of Erlangen-Nuremberg, Erlangen Regional Computing Center, Germany |
| Joachim Hein | Lund University, Sweden |
| David Henty | University of Edinburgh, UK |
| Marc-Andre Hermanns | RWTH Aachen University, Germany |
| Kevin Huck | University of Oregon, USA |
| Sascha Hunold | TU Wien, Austria |
| Heike Jagode | University of Tennessee, USA |
| Eileen Kühn | Karlsruhe Institute of Technology, Germany |
| Diana Moise | Cray, HPE, Switzerland |
| Tapasya Patki | Lawrence Livermore National Laboratory, USA |
| Jelena Pjesivac-Grbovic | Verily Life Sciences LLC, Google LLC, USA |
| Philip Roth | Oak Ridge National Laboratory, USA |
| Ana Lucia Varbanescu | University of Amsterdam, The Netherlands |

## Proceedings Chairs

| Guido Juckeland | Helmholtz-Zentrum Dresden-Rossendorf (HZDR), Germany |
| Hatem Ltaief | KAUST, Saudi Arabia |

# Contents

## Performance Modeling and Measurement

## Programming Models and Systems Software

# Architectures, Networks and Infrastructure

# FASTHash: FPGA-Based High Throughput Parallel Hash Table

Yang Yang[1]([✉]), Sanmukh R. Kuppannagari[2], Ajitesh Srivastava[2],
Rajgopal Kannan[3], and Viktor K. Prasanna[2]

[1] Department of Computer Science, University of Southern California,
Los Angeles, CA, USA
yyang172@usc.edu
[2] Ming Hsieh Department of Electrical and Computer Engineering,
University of Southern California, Los Angeles, CA 90089, USA
{kuppanna,ajiteshs,prasanna}@usc.edu
[3] US Army Research Lab, Playa Vista, Adelphi, CA 90094, USA
rajgopal.kannan.civ@mail.mil

**Abstract.** Hash table is a fundamental data structure that provides
efficient data store and access. It is a key component in AI applications
which rely on building a model of the environment using observations
and performing lookups on the model for newer observations. In this
work, we develop FASTHash, a "truly" high throughput parallel hash
table implementation using FPGA on-chip SRAM. Contrary to state-
of-the-art hash table implementations on CPU, GPU, and FPGA, the
parallelism in our design is data independent, allowing us to support $p$
parallel queries ($p > 1$) per clock cycle via $p$ processing engines (PEs) in
the worst case. Our novel data organization and query flow techniques
allow full utilization of abundant low latency on-chip SRAM and enable
conflict free concurrent insertions. Our hash table ensures relaxed eventual consistency - inserts from a PE are visible to all PEs with some
latency. We provide theoretical worst case bound on the number of erroneous queries (true negative search, duplicate inserts) due to relaxed
eventual consistency. We customize our design to implement both static
and dynamic hash tables on state-of-the-art FPGA devices. Our implementations are scalable to 16 PEs and support throughput as high as
5360 million operations per second with PEs running at 335 MHz for
static hashing and 4480 million operations per second with PEs running at 280 MHz for dynamic hashing. They outperform state-of-the-art
implementations by 5.7x and 8.7x respectively.

**Keywords:** Hash table · Parallel processing · FPGA

## 1 Introduction

Artificial Intelligence (AI) has played a central role in pushing the frontiers of
technology. There has been a significant progress in several domains due to AI,

© Springer Nature Switzerland AG 2020
P. Sadayappan et al. (Eds.): ISC High Performance 2020, LNCS 12151, pp. 3–22, 2020.
https://doi.org/10.1007/978-3-030-50743-5_1

including computer vision [3], robotics [21], machine learning on graphs [32], and games [8]. Conceptually, AI algorithms use observations to *learn* a model for the task, which is then consulted (searched, looked-up) to reason about new observations and update the model. To enable fast look-up during training as well as inference, hash table has been widely adopted in the implementation of many AI algorithms [10,13,27,28,32]. For example, Graph Convolution Neural Network (GCN) uses hash tables in the graph sampling operation to determine whether the currently sampled vertex or edge exists in the sampled set or not [32]. Similarly, in Approximate Nearest Neighbor (ANN), hashing is used to determine the neighbor (point) closest to the current observation [28]. Hashing plays a central role in text-mining for creating and maintaining bag-of-words models [4]. Therefore, a parallel high throughput hash table is imperative to accelerate a wide range of AI applications.

Several works have developed high-throughput hash table implementations by "parallelizing" the hash table. The "parallelization" in these works implies exploiting certain features of the hash table, such as the availability of multiple partitions [22], to increase the number of parallel queries that can be supported. However, this does not imply *true parallelism* as the parallelism is highly data dependent and the worst case performance - for example, when all queries belong to the same partition - is similar to a serial implementation. In contrast, our focus in this work is to develop a parallel implementation of hash table that supports $p$ parallel queries ($p > 1$) in each clock cycle even in the worst case.

Field Programmable Gate Arrays (FPGA) have proved successful in applications which require energy-efficient acceleration of complex workloads such as AI due to their high energy-efficiency and the availability of fine grained parallelism [18]. Their dense logic elements (up to 5.5 million), abundant user-controllable on-chip SRAM resources (up to 500 MB, up to 38 TB/s bandwidth), and interfaces with various external memory technologies such as High Bandwidth Memory (HBM) make them a logical choice for accelerating computationally intensive time critical AI applications in an energy-efficient manner [14,30]. Cloud platforms are increasingly being augmented with FPGAs to accelerate computation with offering such as Amazon EC2 F1, Microsoft Catapult, Alibaba Faas, etc. The versatility of FPGAs is evident from their widespread deployment in high performance cloud and data-centre platforms [30] as well as in low-powered edge applications [12].

In this work, we develop FASTHash: FPGA-based High Throughput Parallel Hash Table. FASTHash supports $p$ queries ($p > 1$) in each clock cycle, where $p$ is the number of parallel Processing Engines (PEs). To enable such an implementation, we exploit the fact that AI applications are approximate in nature and can tolerate small errors in observations or computations. Thus, we allow the semantic of relaxed eventual consistency i.e. a query inserted by a PE is visible to all the other PEs with a maximum delay of $O(p)$ clock cycles and provide worst case bounds on the erroneous queries (true negative search and duplicate insertion). We implement our hash table entirely using FPGA on-chip SRAM. On-chip SRAM has a very low access latency (1 cycle) compared to external memory (range of 10 s of cycles). Extremely high bandwidth of up to 38 TB/s is supported by state-of-the-art FPGA devices [30]. Moreover, the abundant on-chip SRAM allows implementation of hash table with entries ranging from several hundred thousands to more than a million.

The key contributions of our paper are:

- To the best of our knowledge, we develop the first "truly" parallel implementation of a hash table on FPGA which supports $p$ operations ($p > 1$) in each clock cycle, thus achieving a throughput of $p$ per clock cycle. The parallel queries in each clock cycle can be any combination of search and insert.
- To fully utilize the abundant low latency on-chip SRAM, we develop novel data organization and query flow techniques. Our techniques allow each of the $p$ PEs to perform hash table search and insert without memory conflicts.
- Our hash table uses relaxed eventual consistency model, i.e. an element inserted from a PE is visible to all the other PEs with some latency. We provide theoretical worst case bounds on the number of queries that are incorrectly served (true negative search or duplicate inserts) due to the relaxed eventual consistency semantics of our hash table.
- Our architecture is flexible and device agnostic. We implement both static and dynamic hash tables on state-of-the-art Xilinx and Intel FPGAs.
- Our hash table designs are scalable to 16 PEs with the static hash table reaching a throughput of 5360 million operations per second at 335 MHz, and the dynamic hash table achieving a throughput of 4480 million operations per second at 280 MHz. They outperform state-of-the-art implementations by 5.7x and 8.7x respectively.

## 2 Related Work

### 2.1 Hash Table Implementation on CPU and GPU

Many parallel hashing approaches have been proposed on CPU and GPU platforms. On CPU, significant effort has focused on designing concurrent and lock-free hash table through shared memory and message passing [19,20,24]. With the emergence of many-core architectures, several researches have investigated hash table implementations on GPU [1,9,16]. Essentially, these works divide a hash table into partitions, either coarse or fine grained, and extract parallelism by processing queries to each partition concurrently. In the event that all the queries go to the same partition, they are intrinsically serialized. Recent work by Shankar et al. [25] investigated accelerating Cuckoo hash table using modern CPUs' SIMD instructions, such as Intel AVX2 and AVX-512 extensions. However, their study is limited to lookups, and the complexity incurred by simultaneous lookups and insertions is not considered.

### 2.2 Hash Table Implementation on FPGA

A number of FPGA-based high performance hash table implementations have been proposed in the community. Among these works, Bando et al. [2] proposed a hash table based IP lookup technique. Their architecture achieves a lookup throughput of 250 Mops/s. Istvn et al. [15] described a pipelined hash table on FPGA for MemcacheD applications that sustain 10 Gbps throughput. To reduce unnecessary hash table accesses, Cho et al. developed an efficient hash table implementation with bloom filter [6]. Tong et al. [26] developed a data forwarding unit to overcome the data hazards during dynamic hash table updates. Their proposed architecture achieves up to 85 Gbps throughput. Cuckoo hashing implementation of [29] is based on an efficient memory layout. They incorporate a decoupled key-value storage that enables parallel computation of hash values with low overhead. However, all the above works focus on improving performance for a single processing pipeline, which is not sufficient to fully exploit the high bandwidth on-chip SRAM in state-of-the-art FPGAs.

Pontarelli et al. presented an FPGA-based Cuckoo hash table with multiple parallel pipelines [22]. To increase throughput, each pipeline has a different entry point, each of which corresponds to a different hash function. Therefore, the parallelism of their design is limited by the number of hashing functions in a given Cuckoo hash table. Furthermore, due to access conflicts to the same hash function, the achieved throughput with 4 parallel pipelines is only 1.6 queries per clock cycle.

### 2.3  Novelty of Our Work

State-of-the-art works improve the throughput of hash table by one of the following three techniques: (i) pipelining the implementation to increase the clock frequency, (ii) parallel atomic access to a shared hash table, and (iii) partitioning of hash table to enable parallel access. Technique (i) while improving throughput is clearly not a parallel implementation. Techniques (ii) and (iii) lead to high parallelism if the parallel queries do not need atomic access to the same portion of the hash table or if they map to different partition of the hash table. However, this is highly data dependent and in the worst case all the parallel queries will be serialized leading to reduced throughput similar to a sequential implementation.

In contrast, our implementation processes $p$ parallel queries in each clock cycle, with $p$ being the degree of parallelism. Our implementation is data independent and supports any combination of parallel searches and inserts.

## 3  Hash Table Overview

### 3.1  Definition of Hash Table

Hash table is a fast and compact data structure that stores a set $S$ of keys from a much larger universe $U$. Usually the size of $S$ is much smaller than the size of $U$. Hash function is used to perform hash table lookup operations. Assume the size of hash table is $M$, which is usually in the same order as $|S|$, a hash function $h, h : U \rightarrow \{0, ..., M - 1\}$, maps a key $k$ in $U$ to an index of $M$.

The hash table operations supported by our design are:

- SEARCH $(k)$: Return $\{k, v\} \in S$ or $\varnothing$. Retrieve the value associated with the input key if the key exists in the hash table, or empty if not found.
- INSERT $(k, v)$: $S \leftarrow S \cup \{k, v\}$. Insert a new key-value pair to the hash table if the key does not exist in the hash table at the time of insertion.

There are two forms of hash table, *Static Hash table* and *Dynamic Hash table*. We briefly explain the concept below.

*Static Hash Table.* In a static hash table, $S$ is a fixed priori, and is immutable during runtime. Therefore, the only operation allowed is search. Perfect hashing is one of the methods to construct static hash tables without collision [7]. One method to construct such hash table using perfect hashing is by employing two levels of hash functions. The first level hash table, in this method, is created using a hash function from the universal hash function family $H$ [5]. For each bucket that has more than 1 item in the first level hash table, i.e. producing some collisions, it creates a second level hash table with $O(n_i^2)$ entries, where $n_i$ is the number of items in bucket $i$ $(n_i > 1)$. The second level hash function is also randomly selected from $H$. A hashing constructed using this method does not have collisions.

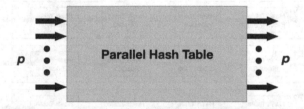

**Fig. 1.** A hash table that is capable of processing $p$ operations in parallel.

*Dynamic Hash Table.* As its name suggests, dynamic hashing allows search operations while data is incrementally added to a hash table. As a result, dynamic hash table is a mutable object. When a new key is inserted but its respective entry is already occupied, collision is said to occur. On FPGA, collision is usually handled through multiple level of hash functions or linear chaining [15,17,29].

## 3.2  Parallel Hash Table

In the context of parallel hash table, instead of searching or inserting one key at a time, each query can contain $p$ $(p > 1)$ independent operations. The $p$ operations can be in any combination of search and insert. Figure 1 shows the high level concept of parallel hash table. In this case, hash table can complete at most $p$ operations per clock cycle. Designing a parallel architecture on FPGA to efficiently access hash table is a challenging research problem. The primary issue is resource contentions such as on-chip memory conflicts between concurrent hash table operations. Our proposed architecture guarantees $p$ operations per clock cycle.

## 4   FASTHash: An FPGA-Based Parallel Hash Table

In this section, we first introduce the novel data organization and query flow in our proposed architecture, to allow concurrent accesses with mixed operation types, and efficiently scale to $p$ parallel processing engines on FPGA. Then we show the architecture details of our design. We also present the extensions to support static hash tables.

### 4.1   Hash Table Data Organization

Our design goal is to support $p$ hash table accesses per clock cycle with $p$ processing engines. To achieve the desired target, we require a data organization that can perform $p$ parallel operations without stalling.

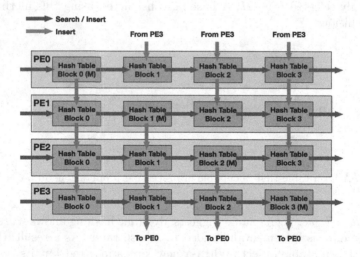

**Fig. 2.** Data organization and high level architecture of a 4 PEs design. "(M)" indicates the Master Hash Table Block from which a PE initiates insert operation.

The proposed hash table architecture is implemented using on-chip SRAM (BRAM, URAM, or M20K), which is an abundant resource in modern FPGAs [14,30]. Since such memory block is dual-ported, and supports one read and one write per clock cycle, implementing a hash table that guarantees $p$ operations per clock cycle is challenging.

In our proposed design, we assign a copy of the hash table content to each PE. Inside each PE, the hash table is further split into multiple Hash Table Blocks to enable concurrent hash table insert operations. Each Hash Table Block is mapped to one or more BRAM, URAM, or M20K blocks. To ensure data consistency across PEs, we design an efficient and conflict-free *Inter-PE Dataflow* that connects each Hash Table Block across PEs. With the *Inter-PE Dataflow*, an insert that is made by one PE is visible to all the other PEs with up to $O(p)$ clock cycle delays.

Figure 2 shows an example of our proposed hash table data organization with 4 PEs. Each row represents a PE and the *Inter-PE Dataflow* connects Hash Table Blocks that are in the same column. With this data organization, hash table operations can be performed independently by each processing engine without any memory conflict.

**Query Flow.** Our hash table architecture supports search and insert operations defined in Sect. 3.2. Before we discuss the query flow of the supported operations, we need to introduce an auxiliary structure called *Master Hash Table Block*.

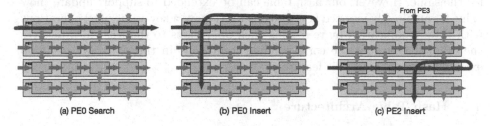

(a) PE0 Search          (b) PE0 Insert          (c) PE2 Insert

**Fig. 3.** Query flow in a 4 PEs design.

*Master Hash Table Block (MHTB):* As we mentioned earlier, we store our hash table in FPGA on-chip SRAM. The split data organization increases the parallelism of our hash table, but it inevitably poses challenges when performing insert to the hash table. This is because we need to keep all the Hash Table Block synchronized in order to return consistent queries. Essentially, an all-to-all communication between PEs would be required during an insert event. To reduce the wiring overhead, we assign block $i$ to PE $i$ – if PE $i$ receives an insert request for a key that does not already exist, it will be inserted by PE $i$ in Hash Table Block $i$, and subsequently to the whole column $i$ to enable concurrent reads. We refer this Hash Table Block as *Master Hash Table Block (MHTB)*, as shown in Fig. 2. This design guarantees that at any given clock cycle there can only be one insert for any Hash Table Block.

The query flow of our hash table, i.e. mapping of search and insert operations to our parallel architecture, is described below:

*Search:* Searching for a specific key in our hash table is similar to traditional hash table. Once a PE receives a search query, it goes through a *Lookup Pipeline* that sequentially looks for the key in each Hash Table Block inside the PE. If input key is found, search query flow returns the key-value pair back to application. If no matching key is found, we return empty.

*Insert:* To insert a key-value pair into our hash table, the operation needs to enter *Lookup Pipeline* first. This ensures the uniqueness of keys in our hash table. If the input key is not found, PE sends the request to *Insert Pipeline* in its MHTB. *Insert Pipeline* connects the MHTB in one PE to non-Master Hash Table Blocks in the other PEs. They receive the same to-be-inserted key-value pair as data flows through the *Insert Pipeline*. Collision is handled by reserving multiple slots for each hash table entry. Figure 3 shows an example of search and insert operations' data flow in a 4 PEs design. As depicted in Fig. 3(b) and Fig. 3(c), upon a simultaneous insert from PE0 and PE2, insert operations are performed by writing to different Hash Table Blocks (columns), thus they never introduce memory conflicts.

*Remarks on Supporting Other Hash Table Operations.* We focus on a high throughput implementation of hash table suitable for AI applications. As search and insert are the two key operations in such applications, our design is optimized for the same. However, our hash table can be extended to support update (new value for an already inserted key) and delete (remove a key-value pair) operations with little modification by re-routing such operations to the PE which receives the original insert for the corresponding input key. In this work, we make no extra effort to support this feature.

## 4.2  Hash Table Architecture

**Design Overview.** As shown in Fig. 2, our proposed design consists of $p$ processing engines (PEs). Each PE can receive input queries independently and with different operation types. Search operations can be completed within each PE itself. For insert operations, each PE needs to propagate changes to the hash table of the other PEs to ensure data consistency. This is achieved by the *Inter-PE Dataflow*. Enforced by our architecture model, inserts initiated by one PE never intervene with inserts by other PEs. Therefore, we can guarantee $p$ parallel accesses per clock cycle in our design.

**Processing Engine Design.** Figure 4 shows the architecture of our PE design. It contains three key components: *Hashing Unit, Data Processing Unit,* and *Collision Handling Unit*. When an input query arrives, it is sent to the *Hashing Unit* to compute the entry index for each hash table block to lookup. *Data Processing Unit* receives the output from *Hashing Unit*. It performs hash table lookup by reading each hash table block sequentially, keeps track of metadata information, and initiates hash table insert if necessary. Both *Hashing Unit* and *Data Processing Unit* are pipelined in order to achieve high operating frequency on FPGA.

*Hashing Unit.* Hash functions from the Class $H_3$ [5] has been demonstrated to be effective on distributing keys randomly among hash table entries. The hash function is defined as follows [23]:

**Definition 1.** Let $i$ denote the number of bits for input key, and $j$ denote the number of bits for hash index. Furthermore, let $Q$ denote a $i \times j$ Boolean matrix. For a given $q \in Q$, let $q(m)$ be the bit string of the $m$th row of $Q$, and let $x(m)$ denote the $m$th bit of input key. The hash function is: $h(x) = (x(1) \cdot q(1)) \oplus (x(2) \cdot q(2)) \oplus ... \oplus (x(i) \cdot q(i))$.

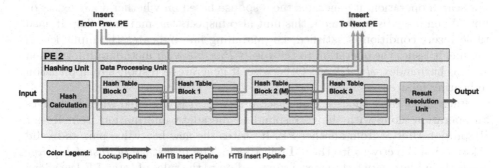

**Fig. 4.** Architecture of PE 2 in a 4 PEs design. Master Hash Table Block (MHTB) ID is 2 in this case.

We map the hash calculation into a 2-stage pipeline. The first stage simultaneously calculates the AND results for each bit of the input key. The second stage calculates the final hash value by XORing the results of the first stage. Therefore, this hash function calculation logic can be achieved with O(1) latency.

*Data Processing Unit.* The Data Processing Unit (DPU) handles operations in the order they arrive. As seen in Fig. 4, every operation goes through the *Lookup Pipeline* first; depending on the operation type and lookup result, only insert operations are required to go through *Insert Pipeline*. The entire *Lookup Pipeline* is divided into $p$ mega-stages, as illustrated in Fig. 5(a). Each mega-stage $i$ performs a read operation from hash table block $i$. Mega-stage can take

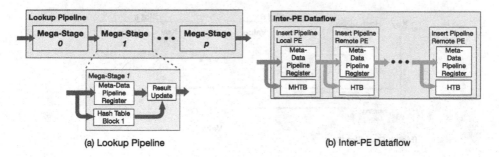

(a) Lookup Pipeline                    (b) Inter-PE Dataflow

**Fig. 5.** Implementation details of *Lookup Pipeline* and *Inter-PE Dataflow*.

multiple clock cycles and is pipelined as well. DPU has shift-registers for meta-data information that is needed in a later stage or at the end of the *Lookup Pipeline*. When a key in the hash table is found equal to the input key and the entry is valid, a matching flag is captured and stored into the metadata shift-register.

Result Resolution Unit collects the metadata information and result from the last mega-stage of *Lookup Pipeline*, and routes operations to their next hop. For search operation, it generates the response based on whether a key exists or not. When insert is performed, this unit also inspects the matching flag. If hash table insert condition is satisfied, i.e. matching flag indicates the input key is unique, it issues the operation to the *Insert Pipeline* with metadata information such as hash index, *slot ID*, etc. Otherwise, it generates a response to application indicating failure.

Each Hash Table Block has an *Insert Pipeline*. It is triggered when it receives an operation along with the corresponding metadata information from Result Resolution Unit or from another PE. It writes the new key-value pair and valid information directly to its Hash Table Block. The last stage of *Insert Pipeline* sends the update data to the next PE according to the rules of Inter-PE Dataflow, which we will describe below.

*Collision Handling Unit.* To handle collision, we design our hash table entry to have multiple slots. Each slot can be allocated to store one key-value pair. One valid field is associated with each slot to indicate if this slot has valid data or available for insertion. An operation is performed only when both the key matches and validity of the slot.

In each PE, only DPU MHTB mega-stage has extra collision handling logic. Other Hash Table Block mega-stage doesn't need collision handling because collision, if any, has already been resolved by the PE which initiates insert operations. Collision is handled by finding the first available slot to insert. We implement a parallel collision handling unit, as shown in Fig. 6. That is: we examine all the slots from a hash table entry at the same clock cycle. This collision handling logic is an extension on top of the hit/miss detection logic that already presents in each Hash Table Block. It has *s* parallel comparators to detect a matching key.

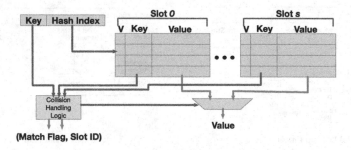

**Fig. 6.** Parallel collision handling with *s* slots per Entry. "Hit/Miss/Collision Handling Logic" outputs the outcome of lookup, and *slot ID* for MHTB based on operation type.

The *slot ID* from this stage needs to be recorded into the shift-register because this information is needed by the *Insert Pipeline* later on. Given our low collision rate with $H_3$ hash functions, we expect 2 to 4 slots per entry to be sufficient. Therefore, it can produce *slot ID* for insert with O(1) latency.

**Inter-PE Dataflow.** Figure 5(b) shows the Inter-PE communication flow. It plays a vital role in our design to ensure conflict free hash table updates, as discussed in Sect. 4.1. *Inter-PE Dataflow* connects *Insert Pipelines* that are in the neighbor PEs into a "relay network". Therefore, there are totally $p$ parallel *Inter-PE Dataflow* in our architecture. For each *Inter-PE Dataflow*, there is only one *Insert Pipeline* which is capable of initiating hash table insert operations, all the other *Insert Pipelines* in the same "relay network" simply processes the insert and passes the data to the next one, until it reaches the end.

**Relaxed Eventual Consistency.** As described above, a new key is not seen by all the PEs for up to $pt_0 + p_0 + t_0$ clock cycles, where $t_0$ is read/write latency of one Hash Table Block. This includes $pt_0$ clock cycles to search and then $p + t_0$ clock cycles to insert to all the PEs (instead of $pt_0$ due to pipelining). When the same key is referenced during this time window, our design doesn't make extra effort to forward the data. However, our design guarantees that eventually all accesses to that key will return the inserted value. We refer this behavior as relaxed eventual consistency.

### 4.3  Customization for Static Hash Table

In order to support perfect hashing with two levels of hash tables, another *Hashing Unit* is added to each PE for the second level hash table. This *Hashing Unit* is placed between the Hashing Unit for the first level hash table and the *Data Processing Unit*. Inside this unit, we use a lookup table to store the hashing functions for each entry in the first level hash table. *Collision Handling Unit* and *Inter-PE Dataflow* are removed because they are designed for insert operations.

## 5  Hash Table Guarantees and Applications Supported

### 5.1  Implications of Relaxed Eventual Consistency

An error due to relaxed eventual consistency may occur when the following hold simultaneously: (i) an insert request for a key $u$ is received for the first time; and (ii) another request of search or insert for the same key $u$ is received within $pt_0 + p + t_0$ cycles. Since, every clock cycle serves $p$ requests, we can bound this error by finding number of such issues within $p^2 t_0 + p^2 + pt_0$ requests in the sequence of all requests. Note that it is possible to create large number of such errors by having a new key inserted and searched in every clock cycle. However, such cases are unusual in practical setting. Instead, we will assume that there is a sequence of requests to be served, where the requests (search/insert) occur in small chunks of $b$ keys. The keys in two distinct chunks may be dependent, but all keys within one chunk follow

$$P(\text{one more occurrence of } u | u \text{ has occurred}) \leq P(\text{occurrence of } u) \quad (1)$$

Note that this condition is satisfied, if all the keys within one chunk are independent. For instance, when sampling a sub-graph through edge sampling, we pick edges and hash their vertices. In that case, out of the edges in $\{(u_1, v_1), (u2, v_2), \ldots (u_b, v_b)\}$, $\{u_1, u_2, \ldots, u_b\}$ are mutually independent, and $\{v_1, v_2, \ldots, v_b\}$ are mutually independent. Further, if $b$ vertices coming from $b/2$ edges were considered in the same chunk, they also satisfy the condition as occurrence of a vertex can only reduce the probability of it being selected again (in absence of self loops). Similarly, picking vertices through $b$ independent random walks ensures that vertices within the same chunk are mutually independent. For simplicity, we will pick $b = p^2 t_0 + p^2 + p t_0$.

**Theorem 1.** *Number of requests $n_{err}$ that are incorrectly served due to relaxed eventual consistency is given by $P(n_{err} \geq \theta) \leq \frac{p^2 t_0 + p^2 + p t_0}{\theta}$.*

*Proof.* As noted above, we can bound the number of errors, by counting for each key $u$, the number of times a request for $u$ is made in the same chunk after the first request for $u$.

Let $C_{i,j}$ be the event that $u$ is requested for the first time in chunk $i$ and the first occurrence is at position $j$ in the chunk. Let $n$ be the total number of requests. Let $X_u^f$ be the number of times a request for $u$ is made within the same chunk just after its first request. Let $X_{u,k}$ be the indicator function for occurrence of $u$ at position $k$ in a chunk. Then, by linearity of expectation:

$$\mathbb{E}(X_u^f) = \sum_{i=1}^{n/b-1} \sum_{j=1}^{b} \left( P(C_{i,j}) \sum_{k=j+1}^{b} \mathbb{E}(X_{u,k} | X_{u,j} = 1) \right) \quad (2)$$

$$\leq \sum_{i=1}^{n/b-1} \sum_{j=1}^{b} \left( P(C_{i,j}) \sum_{k=j+1}^{b} \mathbb{E}(X_{u,k}) \right) \quad (3)$$

$$\leq \left( \sum_{i=1}^{n/b} \sum_{j} P(C_i) \right) \left( \sum_{j=1}^{b} P(X_{u,j} = 1) \right) \qquad \leq \sum_{j=1}^{b} P(X_{u,j} = 1). \quad (4)$$

Now, $n_{err} = \sum_u X_u^f$. Therefore,

$$\mathbb{E}(n_{err}) = \sum_u \mathbb{E}(X_u^f) \leq \sum_u \sum_{j=1}^{b} P(X_{u,j} = 1) = b. \quad (5)$$

Markov Inequality leads to

$$P(n_{err} \geq \theta) \leq b/\theta = \frac{p^2 t_0 + p^2 + pt_0}{\theta}. \qquad (6)$$

$\square$

## 5.2   Applications Supported

Hash table is a widely used data structure in various AI algorithms. We list two examples of the AI algorithms and the required hash table characteristics below:

- **Graph Convolutional Neural Network (GCN):** GCN is the generalization of the CNNs to high-dimensional irregular domains represented as Graphs [32]. To tractably handle large graphs, graph sampling is performed to obtain smaller (10,000–50,000 vertices) representative graphs for training. Hashing is used in graph sampling to keep track of the sampled vertices at any given time. With relaxed eventual consistency, it is possible the that same node is sampled multiple times. This will result in an incorrect counting of total nodes sampled. However, this discrepancy is bounded by Theorem 1 and have no effect on subgraph-based graph embedding [33]. In other graph embedding methods that sample neighboring nodes for a given node, such as GraphSAGE [11], this scenario cannot arise because each neighbor is presented only once. **Hash Table Characteristics** [32]: Type: Dynamic. Key size: 32 bits. Value size: 32 bits. Hash Table size: 10,000–50,000.
- **Approximate Nearest Neighbor (ANN) Search:** Given a query point, the objective is to find the point in the dataset closest to the query. Hashing based ANN has been widely adopted in large scale image retrieval [28]. A hash table is created using each sample in the dataset before performing any lookups. Since each point is unique, it is seen only once, relaxed eventual consistency has no effect on the correctness. **Hash Table Characteristics** [28]: Type: Static. Key size: 32–128 bits. Value size: 64 bit (assuming value is memory location of the image). Hash Table Size: 10,000–100,000 entries (equal to image dataset size).

Hash tables are also used for linear function approximation in Reinforcement Learning [10], association rule mining [13], neural network classification [27], etc.

# 6   Experiments and Results

## 6.1   Experimental Methodology

We implemented both the static and the dynamic hash tables on Xilinx Alveo U250 FPGA [30] and Intel Stratix 10 MX2100 FPGA [14] using Verilog HDL. The Xilinx device has 1,728,000 LUTs, 3,456,000 Flip-flops, and 327 MB of URAM memory, while the Intel device has 702,720 ALMs, 2,810,880 ALM registers, and 134 MB of M20K memory. Post place-and-route simulations were performed using Xilinx Vivado Design Suite 2018.3 and Intel Quartus Prime 19.3 respectively. The static hash table, with two levels of hash functions, was created offline using synthetic data.

We conducted detailed analysis on the performance, power, and scalability of the proposed architecture. We evaluated the performance and resource utilization by increasing number of PEs from 2 to 16, and varying the total number of hash table entries. The key sizes we used in our experiments were 16, 32, and 64 bits; and value sizes were 32 and 64 bits. These numbers cover the most configurations in AI applications (Sect. 5.2), and they also cover a sufficiently wide range to test the scalability of our architecture. We generated uniformly distributed access patterns, which include both the operation types and the hash keys, as our stimulus. The metric for throughput analysis is million operations per second (MOPS). The utilization of FPGA resources is reported in terms of percent usage of LUTs (ALMs), flip-flops (registers), and on-chip SRAM. To reduce the extra-long duration of the post-route simulation, we used the

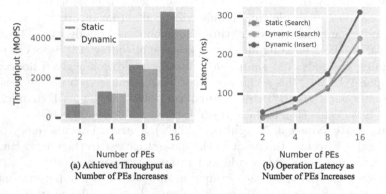

**Fig. 7.** Evaluation of static and dynamic hash tables on Xilinx U250 FPGA. Parameters: key/value length: 32-bit. 4 slots/entry (dynamic hash table).

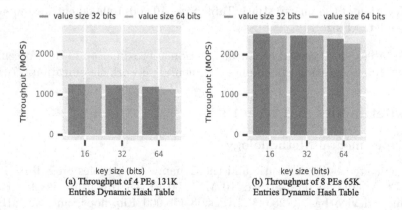

**Fig. 8.** Throughput with different key and value sizes on Xilinx U250 FPGA.

vectorless power estimation methodology provided by the EDA tools [31]. Power estimation includes leakage and dynamic power.

## 6.2 Results

**Evaluation on Xilinx U250 FPGA.** Figure 7 shows the throughput and operation latency of our hash tables from a configuration with 65K entries hash table size. The throughput matches our design goal, which is $p$ operations per clock cycle sustained. The results clearly verify the scalability of our design with the number of PEs. The throughput difference between static and dynamic hashing is due to the max clock frequency. For static hash table scheme, we are able to achieve 335 MHz clock frequency across all PE configurations. On the other hand, parallel collision handling unit and the long wires for inter-PE connections are in the critical paths of our dynamic hashing design. When the number of PEs for dynamic hash table grows, the pressure on place and route also increases. Therefore max clock rate as well as achieved throughput drop when compared with static hashing implementations. Figure 7(b) shows the operation latency increases with the number of PEs. Due to the extra clock cycles that is spent on writing new key-value pair to all PEs, insert latency is higher than search latency. With 16 PEs, search operation can be completed within 209 ns for static hashing and 243 ns for dynamic hashing; insert operation requires 311 ns.

Figure 8 illustrates the throughput as we vary the sizes of hash table keys and values on the dynamic hashing implementation. We find that key and value length have little impact on throughput until the length grows to 64-bit. The clock rate for 4 PEs and 8 PEs configurations drops to 285 MHz and 280 MHz respectively when the size of key and value are both 64-bit. This again demonstrates the scalability of our architecture.

Resource utilization of a dynamic hash table implementation is reported in Table 1. The hash table has 65K entries, 4 slots per entry, and 32-bit key and value length. We make heavy use of URAM for on-chip hash table store. Table 1(a) shows that URAM utilization increases linearly as we increase the number of PEs. This is because each PE stores an entire copy of the hash table. On the other hand, the utilization of other resources, as presented in Table 1(b), is low. Table 1 also shows the estimated power consumption. Our architecture is power efficient, with the power of 16 PEs configuration as low as 9.06 W.

**Table 1.** Resource utilization of 65K entries dynamic hash table on U250 FPGA.

| # of PEs | LUT (%) | Flip-Flop (%) | URAM(%) | Power (W) |
|----------|---------|---------------|---------|-----------|
| 2        | 0.08    | 0.08          | 10      | 3.40      |
| 4        | 0.18    | 0.31          | 20      | 4.13      |
| 8        | 0.66    | 1.21          | 40      | 5.34      |
| 16       | 2.45    | 4.82          | 80      | 9.06      |

**Table 2.** Max hash table sizes supported on Xilinx U250 FPGA.

|  | 2 PEs | 4 PEs | 8 PEs | 16 PEs |
|---|---|---|---|---|
| 2 slots per entry | 1,310K | 655K | 327K | 131K |
| 4 slots per entry | 655K | 327K | 163K | 65K |

In Table 2, we show the max hash table size—number of entries that can be implemented on Xilinx U250 FPGA, with 32-bit key and value sizes. Note that as the URAM utilization is pushed to its limit, pipeline depth for each mega-stage in the *Lookup Pipeline* has to be increased to meet optimal timing performance. Our modular design and flexible configurability give user a wide range of design options to choose from based on application requirements and available FPGA resources.

**Evaluation on Intel Stratix 10 FPGA.** Our architecture is designed as a general solution to work with various FPGA devices. To illustrate, we also implemented our hash table on Intel Stratix 10 FPGA. We used 32-bit as key and value size and used 4 slots per entry for dynamic hash table. Figure 9 shows the performance of our architecture for a hash table with 50K entries. The result

**Table 3.** Resource utilization of dynamic hash table on Stratix 10 FPGA.

| # of PEs | # of entries | ALM (%) | Register (%) | M20K (%) |
|---|---|---|---|---|
| 2 | 150,000 | 2 | 1 | 59 |
| 4 | 100,000 | 3 | 2 | 78 |
| 8 | 50,000 | 5 | 4 | 81 |
| 16 | 16,000 | 10 | 11 | 52 |

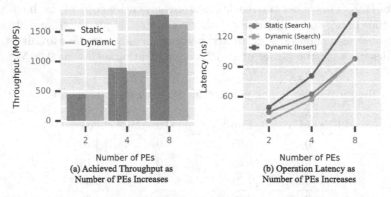

(a) Achieved Throughput as Number of PEs Increases

(b) Operation Latency as Number of PEs Increases

**Fig. 9.** Evaluation of static and dynamic hash table on Intel Stratix 10 FPGA. Parameters: key/value length: 32-bit. 4 slots/entry (dynamic hash table).

indicates that the benefits of our architecture is independent of FPGA devices. This design can process up to 1792 MOPS for static hash able and 1628 MOPS for the dynamic version, with 8 PEs. Since the number of PEs affects the max clock rate of the design, the achieved throughput doesn't scale linearly. From Table 3 we can see that the usage of ALM and register is slow, while the utilization of M20K depends on the hash table capacity and number of PEs.

## 6.3   Comparison with State-of-the-Art (SOTA) Designs

We compare the performance of our 16 PEs hash table implementation on Xilinx U250 FPGA with state-of-the-art GPU and FPGA designs. Performance metric is in term of throughput - MOPS. In [1], the design is implemented on NVIDIA Tesla K40c GPU. The GPU has 2880 CUDA cores. It operates at 745 MHz, and can be boosted up to 876 MHz. The authors report the performance for bulk build (static) and incremental inserts (dynamic) separately. We used 32-bit key/value size and random traffic pattern in the comparison, which is the same as reported by [1, 22]. Proposes a parallel Cuckoo hashing on FPGA. Hash table is stored completely on-chip. The target FPGA device is Xilinx Virtex5 XC5VLX155T. Their implementation operates at 156.25 MHz. Table 4 shows the comparison results. Comparing with SOTA GPU work, we observe speedup of 5.7x (static) and 8.7x (dynamic) respectively while running at less than half of the clock rate. Comparing with SOTA FPGA work, our design achieves up to 17x raw speedup, or up to 9.3x speedup after normalizing the clock frequency. Unlike these intrinsically sequential or less optimal parallel implementations, FastHASH fully exploits SOTA FPGA's high bandwidth on-chip SRAM using its unique parallel architecture.

**Table 4.** Throughput comparison with state-of-the-art (SOTA)

|  | SOTA GPU [1] | SOTA FPGA [22] | Our Design |
|---|---|---|---|
| Static hashing (search MOPS) | 937 (peak) | n/a | 5360 (sustained) |
| Dynamic hashing (MOPS) | 512 (peak) | 480 (sustained, normalized Fmax) | 4480 (sustained) |

## 7   Conclusion

This paper presented FASTHash, a high throughput parallel hash table using FPGA on-chip SRAM that supports $p$ parallel queries per cycle from $p$ PEs ($p > 1$). The architecture is designed to accelerate various AI applications such as graph convolution networks and approximate nearest neighbors. FASTHash uses novel data organization and query flow techniques within and between processing engines to ensure data consistency and conflict-free memory accesses. In addition, FASTHash is customized to support both static and dynamic hashing on Xilinx and Intel FPGA devices. Both architectures demonstrate high scalability with respect to the number of PEs, key/value lengths, and hash table sizes. The static hash table achieves up to 5360 MOPS throughput and the dynamic variant achieves up to 4480 MOPS, thus outperforming state-of-the-art implementations by 5.7x and 8.7x respectively.

**Acknowledgement.** This work has been supported by Xilinx and by the U.S. National Science Foundation (NSF) under grants OAC-1911229 and SPX-1919289.

# References

1. Ashkiani, S., Farach-Colton, M., Owens, J.D.: A dynamic hash table for the GPU. In: 2018 IEEE International Parallel and Distributed Processing Symposium (IPDPS), pp. 419–429, May 2018
2. Bando, M., Artan, N.S., Chao, H.J.: Flashlook: 100-Gbps hash-tuned route lookup architecture. In: 2009 International Conference on High Performance Switching and Routing, pp. 1–8 (2009)
3. Bengio, Y., et al.: Learning deep architectures for AI. Found. Trends® Mach. Lear. **2**(1), 1–127 (2009)
4. Boulis, C., Ostendorf, M.: Text classification by augmenting the bag-of-words representation with redundancy-compensated bigrams. In: Proceedings of the International Workshop in Feature Selection in Data Mining, pp. 9–16. Citeseer (2005)
5. Carter, J.L., Wegman, M.N.: Universal classes of hash functions (extended abstract). In: Proceedings of the Ninth Annual ACM Symposium on Theory of Computing, STOC 1977, pp. 106–112. ACM, New York (1977)
6. Cho, J.M., Choi, K.: An FPGA implementation of high-throughput key-value store using bloom filter. In: Technical Papers of 2014 International Symposium on VLSI Design, Automation and Test, pp. 1–4 (2014)
7. Fredman, M.L., Komlós, J., Szemerédi, E.: Storing a sparse table with 0(1) worst case access time. J. ACM **31**(3), 538–544 (1984)
8. Funge, J.D.: Artificial Intelligence for Computer Games an Introduction. AK Peters/CRC Press, Boca Raton (2004)
9. García, I., Lefebvre, S., Hornus, S., Lasram, A.: Coherent parallel hashing. In: Proceedings of the 2011 SIGGRAPH Asia Conference, SA 2011, pp. 161:1–161:8. ACM, New York (2011). https://doi.org/10.1145/2024156.2024195. http://doi.acm.org/10.1145/2024156.2024195
10. Gendron-Bellemare, M.: Fast, scalable algorithms for reinforcement learning in high dimensional domains (2013)
11. Hamilton, W.L., Ying, R., Leskovec, J.: Inductive representation learning on large graphs. In: Proceedings of the 31st International Conference on Neural Information Processing Systems, NIPS 2017, pp. 1025–1035. Curran Associates Inc., New York (2017)
12. Hao, C., et al.: FPGA/DNN co-design: an efficient design methodology for IoT intelligence on the edge. arXiv preprint arXiv:1904.04421 (2019)

13. Holt, J.D., Chung, S.M.: Mining association rules in text databases using multipass with inverted hashing and pruning. In: Proceedings 14th IEEE International Conference on Tools with Artificial Intelligence 2002, ICTAI 2002, pp. 49–56. IEEE (2002)
14. Intel: Stratix 10 MX FPGAs. https://www.intel.com/content/www/us/en/products/programmable/sip/stratix-10-mx.html
15. István, Z., Alonso, G., Blott, M., Vissers, K.: A flexible hash table design for 10 Gbps key-value stores on FPGAS. In: 2013 23rd International Conference on Field programmable Logic and Applications, pp. 1–8 (2013)
16. Khorasani, F., Belviranli, M.E., Gupta, R., Bhuyan, L.N.: Stadium hashing: scalable and flexible hashing on GPUs. In: 2015 International Conference on Parallel Architecture and Compilation (PACT), pp. 63–74, October 2015
17. Kumar, S., Crowley, P.: Segmented hash: an efficient hash table implementation for high performance networking subsystems. In: Proceedings of the 2005 ACM Symposium on Architecture for Networking and Communications Systems, ANCS 2005, pp. 91–103. ACM, New York (2005)
18. Kuppannagari, S.R., et al.: Energy performance of FPGAs on perfect suite kernels. In: 2014 IEEE High Performance Extreme Computing Conference (HPEC), pp. 1–6. IEEE (2014)
19. Metreveli, Z., Zeldovich, N., Kaashoek, M.F.: CPHash: a cache-partitioned hash table. In: Proceedings of the 17th ACM SIGPLAN Symposium on Principles and Practice of Parallel Programming, PPoPP 2012, pp. 319–320. ACM, New York (2012)
20. Michael, M.M.: High performance dynamic lock-free hash tables and list-based sets. In: Proceedings of the Fourteenth Annual ACM Symposium on Parallel Algorithms and Architectures, SPAA 2002, pp. 73–82. ACM, New York (2002)
21. Peters, J.: Machine learning for motor skills in robotics. KI-Künstliche Intelligenz 2008(4), 41–43 (2008)
22. Pontarelli, S., Reviriego, P., Maestro, J.A.: Parallel d-pipeline: a cuckoo hashing implementation for increased throughput. IEEE Trans. Comput. 65(1), 326–331 (2016)
23. Ramakrishna, M.V., Fu, E., Bahcekapili, E.: Efficient hardware hashing functions for high performance computers. IEEE Trans. Comput. 46(12), 1378–1381 (1997)
24. Shalev, O., Shavit, N.: Split-ordered lists: lock-free extensible hash tables. J. ACM 53(3), 379–405 (2006)
25. Shankar, D., Lu, X., Panda, D.K.: SimdHT-bench: characterizing SIMD-aware hash table designs on emerging CPU architectures. In: 2019 IEEE International Symposium on Workload Characterization (IISWC) (2019)
26. Tong, D., Zhou, S., Prasanna, V.K.: High-throughput online hash table on FPGA. In: 2015 IEEE International Parallel and Distributed Processing Symposium Workshop, pp. 105–112 (2015)
27. Vijayanarasimhan, S., Yagnik, J.: Large-scale classification in neural networks using hashing, US Patent 10,049,305, 14 August 2018
28. Wang, D., et al.: Supervised deep hashing for hierarchical labeled data. In: Thirty-Second AAAI Conference on Artificial Intelligence (2018)
29. Liang, W., Yin, W., Kang, P., Wang, L.: Memory efficient and high performance key-value store on FPGA using cuckoo hashing. In: 2016 26th International Conference on Field Programmable Logic and Applications (FPL), pp. 1–4 (2016)
30. Xilinx: Alveo U250 data center accelerator card. https://www.xilinx.com/products/boards-and-kits/alveo/u250.html

31. Xilinx: Vivado design suite. https://www.xilinx.com/products/design-tools/vivado.html
32. Zeng, H., Zhou, H., Srivastava, A., Kannan, R., Prasanna, V.: Accurate, efficient and scalable graph embedding. In: 2019 IEEE International Parallel and Distributed Processing Symposium (IPDPS), pp. 462–471. IEEE (2019)
33. Zeng, H., Zhou, H., Srivastava, A., Kannan, R., Prasanna, V.K.: GraphSAINT: graph sampling based inductive learning method. CoRR abs/1907.04931 (2019). http://arxiv.org/abs/1907.04931

# Running a Pre-exascale, Geographically Distributed, Multi-cloud Scientific Simulation

Igor Sfiligoi[1]($\boxtimes$), Frank Würthwein[1], Benedikt Riedel[2], and David Schultz[2]

[1] University of California San Diego, La Jolla, San Diego, CA 92093, USA
isfiligoi@sdsc.edu
[2] University of Wisconsin - Madison, Madison, WI 53715, USA

**Abstract.** As we approach the Exascale era, it is important to verify that the existing frameworks and tools will still work at that scale. Moreover, public Cloud computing has been emerging as a viable solution for both prototyping and urgent computing. Using the elasticity of the Cloud, we have thus put in place a pre-exascale HTCondor setup for running a scientific simulation in the Cloud, with the chosen application being IceCube's photon propagation simulation. I.e. this was not a purely demonstration run, but it was also used to produce valuable and much needed scientific results for the IceCube collaboration. In order to reach the desired scale, we aggregated GPU resources across 8 GPU models from many geographic regions across Amazon Web Services, Microsoft Azure, and the Google Cloud Platform. Using this setup, we reached a peak of over 51k GPUs corresponding to almost 380 PFLOP32s, for a total integrated compute of about 100k GPU hours. In this paper we provide the description of the setup, the problems that were discovered and overcome, as well as a short description of the actual science output of the exercise.

**Keywords:** Cloud · Exascale · GPU · HTCondor · IceCube · Astrophysics

## 1 Introduction

In the past couple of years, there has been a lot of activity around getting ready for the exascale computing era. At the same time, public Cloud computing has been gaining traction, including funding agencies starting to invest in this sector; examples being NSF's ECAS and CloudBank awards, and the European Cloud Initiative. Cloud computing, with its promise of elasticity is the ideal platform for prototyping, as well as urgent computing needs. We thus attempted to demonstrate an exascale, or at least a pre-exascale workload using a real application that was already running on the Open Science Grid (OSG) [1], given that most workloads there follow the distributed High Throughput Computing (dHTC) paradigm, and could thus easily transition to the Cloud. The chosen application was IceCube's photon propagation simulation [2], for technical (heavy use of GPU at modest IO) and scientific reasons (high impact science). We emphasize that this meant it would not be a purely experimental setup, but it would produce valuable and much needed simulation for the IceCube collaboration's science program.

© Springer Nature Switzerland AG 2020
P. Sadayappan et al. (Eds.): ISC High Performance 2020, LNCS 12151, pp. 23–40, 2020.
https://doi.org/10.1007/978-3-030-50743-5_2

Since no public Cloud region, or even a single Cloud provider could deliver an on-demand exascale-class compute resource, we went for a geographically distributed multi-cloud setup, while still operating it as a single compute pool. Due to our limited budget, the compute exercise was executed as a short-lived burst, with the aim of demonstrating peak performance, even if only for a short amount of time. This allowed us to exceed 51k GPUs of various kinds in the pool at peak, which provided about 380 PFLOP32s (i.e. fp32 PFLOPS) and 160M GPU cores. We ramped to $2/3^{rd}$ of the total size in about half hour from the provisioning start and then reached the peak within about two hours. The total integrated compute time was of about 100k GPU hours.

The exercise used the IceCube's standard workload management system, i.e. HTCondor [3], but on dedicated hardware. We chose not to use the existing IceCube hardware installation since we did not want risk to disrupt the normal production activities, and we also wanted to minimize the risk of failure by using a slightly tuned setup. The used setup, including the special configurations and tunings are described in Sect. 2.

Section 3 provides an overview of the experience of ramping up to the peak 380 PFLOP32s and back down, including issues encountered in the process. We also provide an overview of the type of resources we were using at peak.

Section 4 describes the science behind the simulation application as well as a summary description of the simulation code internals. The effectiveness of the various GPU types for this specific application is also presented, both in terms of relative speed and total contribution during the run.

## 1.1 Related Work

Running scientific workloads in the public Cloud is hardly a novel idea. This work is however novel in

a) the concurrent use of all three major Cloud providers,
b) the concurrent use of resources from all over the world,
c) the concurrent use of several different GPU models,
d) the total aggregate PFLOP32s at peak, and
e) in its focus on the use of GPU-providing Cloud instances.

Moreover, running an unmodified, production scientific code in such a setup is also quite unusual.

In terms of sheer size, the largest scientific Cloud run we are aware of is the 2.1M vCPU weather modeling run performed by Clemson [4]. While the paper does not provide the achieved peak FLOP32s, it is unlikely it has exceeded 100 PFLOP32s, so it was significantly smaller than what we achieved in our setup. And while not exactly an apples-to-apples comparison, the 2.1M CPU cores are almost two order of magnitude fewer than the 160M GPU cores we provisioned at peak. Finally, it is also worth noting that their setup was confined to a single Cloud provider.

In terms of multi-Cloud setups, there have been many small scale, experimental studies. We are not aware of any other large-scale multi-Cloud scientific run though.

## 2   The Workload Management System Setup

The workload management system software used for the pre-exascale, geographically distributed, multi-cloud setup was the same as normally used by IceCube to run its regular production on resources in the Open Science Grid and the European Grid Infrastructure, namely HTCondor. We saw no need to pick anything else, since HTCondor is naturally good at aggregating and managing heterogeneous resources, including when they are geographically distributed. HTCondor is also used for production activates at scales comparable to the desired peak, although mostly for CPU-focused workloads [5].

We decided to host a completely independent installation for the service processes, using dedicated hardware. We did this both to minimize the impact to IceCube's regular production environment, and to properly size it for the expected size and burst nature of the exercise, which are not typical of the abovementioned production environment. In the process we also tuned this setup to minimize the risk of failure during the actual multi-Cloud burst.

We also decided to not tackle the data movement problems to and from central storage related to such a large GPU compute burst. The IceCube jobs fetched input data from native Cloud storage and staged the results back to the native Cloud storage, too. In both cases we provisioned storage accounts close to where the jobs were actually running. For the input files we made educated guesses and used significant replication, since we did not know in advance where and how many GPU resources would be available. We fully acknowledge that this is not the ideal operations mode, but we were trying to tackle one problem at a time, namely large-scale, bursty GPU-heavy compute. We are likely to perform a more data-focused exercise in the near future.

Section 2.1 contains the summary overview of the HTCondor setup, including the reasons for the deployment choices. Section 2.2 provides the description of the changes needed to deal with Cloud native storage. Section 2.3 provides an overview of the problems encountered and the adopted solutions.

### 2.1   The Multi-cloud, Geographically Distributed HTCondor Setup

IceCube, and the Open Science Grid community at large, has a lot of experience with operating large scale HTCondor instances. None however experiences the kind of burst growth we expected at peak times. The expected total resource pool was also comparable in scale to the largest production environments. Nevertheless, our experience suggested it was a feasible proposition, assuming we made arrangements to deal with a couple well-known bottlenecks.

The design goal for the HTCondor pool used in the multi-Cloud exercise was to be able to add at least 10k GPU resources per minute continuously up to a maximum of at least 120k concurrently running GPU jobs. In addition, most Cloud providers bundle many CPU cores with the GPU in their offering. We utilize this spare capacity by running at least a couple CPU jobs alongside each GPU job. This brings the total desired peak to about 350k concurrently running jobs.

HTCondor has been used in other production setups to sustain a job load of about 300k jobs, using CPU-only resources but with similar runtime characteristics. We applied the same sizing rules as they were applied there. The limiting factor in such setups is the number of running jobs that a single HTCondor job queue process, called the schedd, can handle; approximately 12k jobs. We thus used 10 nodes for GPU jobs and 20 nodes for CPU jobs. While the job queues are handled independently, they are scheduled as a single set and each of the jobs could still run on any compute resource that matched its requirements. By treating each schedd as a different logical user, the HTCondor policy engine, namely the negotiator process, keeps approximately the same number of jobs running on each of them by virtue of its standard fair-share policy.

The other well-known HTCondor limit is the ability of the central manager, namely the collector process, to add additional resources to its pool. The total size is actually not that important. The HTCondor central manager is essentially an in-memory database, and as long as there is enough RAM available, can easily scale to millions of resources being tracked. The problem is just the initial security handshake with the HTCondor daemon managing the remote resource, the so-called startd, and high-latency WAN communication makes the problem worse. It should also be noted that only the initial handshake is expensive. Further communication (in the absence of network problems) uses a much cheaper protocol.

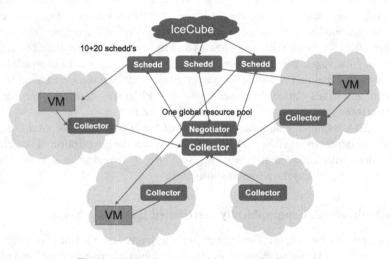

**Fig. 1.** HTCondor setup with a tree of collectors.

Fortunately, HTCondor also provides a solution to work around the above limitation, by allowing for the creation of a tree of collectors, as seen in Fig. 1. In this setup, the main collector process only ever talks to leaf collectors; it thus only has to establish a new security session at startup. Consequently, the startd processes are only aware of the leaf collectors and after picking one (at random), use it as their only connection to advertise their resources to the HTCondor pool. The leaf collectors then forward the information they receive to the main collector which thus gets a complete picture. The cost of resources joining the pool is thus distributed over many leaf nodes, and those leaf nodes can also be spread geographically to further minimize the cost inherent to high-latency WAN traffic. In our particular setup, we used one small Cloud instance running 20 leaf collector processes in each of the major Cloud regions, with startds always picking one of those collectors in the closest region. The 20-per-node ratio was chosen as a perceived safe value to serve the largest of the Cloud regions and replicated everywhere in order to keep the setup as homogeneous as possible.

For completeness, the installed HTCondor version was 8.8.4, using the RPMs packaged and provided by OSG v3.4. We also used the standard OSG provided configuration unless otherwise specified. For securing the setup we used a shared secret, also known as a HTCondor pool password.

## 2.2 Dealing with Data Handling

Given both the unknown total size and composition of the compute pool and the bursty nature of the planed experiment, we decided to not add a data handling challenge of streaming data to and from IceCube's home storage to the exercise. We thus pre-staged all the needed input files into Cloud native storage and the outputs of the simulation were also to be staged back to native Cloud storage. In both cases, the native Cloud storage used was supposed to be close to where the job was running and belonging to the same Cloud provider that had provisioned the compute resource. We used extensive replication of input files to compensate for provisioning uncertainties. Fetching data back to IceCube's home storage happened asynchronously after the compute exercise was completed.

One problem of this approach is that the application would not know what the proper native Cloud storage to use is until it was running, including location and API used to access that storage. To address this, we had to solve two problems: 1) discover where the job is running and 2) make storage access homogenous for the application.

Discovering where a job runs is quite simple, once you know what Cloud provider you are using, and we used independent worker node images for each of the three providers, so the later was trivial. All three Cloud providers expose a Metadata service that allows for any process running in the instance to discover at runtime what region it belongs to. The syntax is slightly different between the three, but in all cases it is a REST API call, and is easy to automate e.g. by means of a *curl* invocation [6–8]. Once this information is known, a simple lookup table is all that is needed to find the appropriate storage URI.

In order to minimize the changes needed to the IceCube's compute jobs, we wrapped the metadata query, table lookup and the calls to the actual Cloud provider specific tools in a couple of simpler wrappers, one for downloading the data to the local disk and one for uploading the data from local disk to the closest native Cloud storage. The application thus only had to provide the relative paths, and the scripts would do the rest, making the application itself completely unaware of the environment it was running in. From the IceCube's jobs framework point of view, it was basically a two-line change of their production workflow on the Open Science Grid.

Finally, a quick mention on how we dealt with the actual application code binaries, which are indeed quite sizable. IceCube workflow expects their application software and dependencies to be present on the resources they land on. OSG provides IceCube with a uniform runtime environment via CVMFS, which uses just-in-time fetching of the binaries and extensive caching. This is efficient when the same application is run on a worker node multiple times. Our setup was however designed to be bursty, so the penalty of populating the cache may have been excessive. We thus decided to pre-loaded all the necessary software in the image itself. From an application point of view there was no difference at all.

We fully acknowledge that this is not the ideal data handling solution if one were to run this setup multiple times and over an extended period. We do plan to have a more data-oriented exercise in the near future.

### 2.3   Unexpected Problems Encountered in the HTCondor Setup

Many of the compute resources IceCube usually runs on are behind NATs, and thus cannot be directly reached from the outside world. HTCondor has a solution for this problem, called Connection Brokering (CCB). It consists of a lightweight process that functions as a software-based router for schedds to start remote compute jobs.

Public IPs are a metered commodity subject to quotas in at least some Cloud infrastructures. We were planning to use CCB for the Cloud setup, too. Unfortunately, during the initial feasibility tests, we discovered that HTCondor with CCB enabled does not properly handle rapid job startup bursts, resulting in an unusable setup, at least for our purposes. After convincing ourselves and the HTCondor development team that this was an actual software bug and not simply a configuration issue, and that a proper solution was not promptly available, we decided to just request public IPs for all the cloud instances that were part of the test pool. This turned out to be an acceptable solution for all the involved Cloud providers. It was more an annoyance than a real problem, but a limitation to be aware of for mimicking our setup.

We also encountered an issue in the policy engine code, resulting in jobs not being properly matched to resources. This bug is only triggered in very heterogeneous setups. Given our data placement policy, each Cloud region was treated as a different entity for scheduling purposes, as only a subset of the input data was placed in each Cloud region and the requirement to fetch from "local" Cloud native storage. Our pool was thus indeed quite inhomogeneous. Fortunately, the bug was part of a code optimization base that was introduced recently and could be avoided through a (mostly undocumented) configuration parameter:

```
NEGOTIATOR_PREFETCH_REQUESTS = False
```

## 3   The Multi-cloud, Multi-region Setup

While the HTCondor workload management setup was almost identical to the production IceCube environment used on e.g. the Open Science Grid, the provisioning part of the exercise was completely ad-hoc. Nobody in our community had ever tried something similar before, so we did not have much prior art or engineering to rely upon.

On paper the problem did not seem too hard to tackle. All we needed to do was create an image containing the HTCondor binaries with proper configuration and start as many instances as we could in the shortest amount of time. The API is slightly different between the three Cloud providers, and the recommended methods and implementation limits slightly different, but apart from that the amount of work needed seemed to be very modest.

Given however the significant projected expense involved, and our relatively limited budget, we wanted to minimize the risk of hitting any technical limits during the actual GPU multi-Cloud burst. We thus spent significant time testing various aspects of the proposed setup using cheaper alternatives, namely CPU-only instances. We provide more details in Sect. 3.4.

The tests did not identify any significant issues, but they did allow us to further tune our setup before the main exercise, which is described in Sect. 3.2. It is worth noting that we did encounter unexpected problems during our actual run, which did not show up during testing. The decisive factor was likely the much higher variety of GPU Cloud instances compared to CPU Cloud instances.

We reached 65% of the maximum number of concurrently running instances in about half hour after we started the provisioning, 90% in about another half hour, and added an additional 10% over the course of the final hour. After about 2 h from the provisioning start, we initiated a controlled shutdown which lasted another good hour. In Sect. 3.3 we provide an overview of the resources provisioned at peak, as well as an analysis of the total compute integrated during the lifetime of the exercise.

The biggest hurdle we encountered during the setting up of the Cloud infrastructure for the bursty GPU run was not technology. Rather, the most time-consuming part was convincing the Cloud providers to even allow us to purchase that many GPU-enabled instances. A short summary is presented in Sect. 3.1.

Finally, in Sect. 3.5 we provide a short overview of the current Cloud pricing, with an emphasis on the resources we used during this run.

## 3.1 The Social Hurdle

Cloud computing is great, in that it allows anyone to provision resources with minimal effort and hardly any advance planning. This is however only true if your needs are small. Try provisioning any large amount of compute, and you will very fast bump into the limits imposed by the default quotas.

We can only speculate why this is the case. Our suspicion is that the Cloud providers want to minimize the risk that a user ends up with an unexpectedly large bill that they cannot pay. And as we demonstrate with our exercise, there is enough capacity out there to easily accumulate a million-dollar bill in just a couple of days!

Each Cloud provider has a different strategy on what an acceptable quota for different resources is. But in our case those quotas were universally too low. And our initial attempts at requesting sizable quota increases through standard channels were met by staff telling us that they did not have the authority to grant our requests.

We thus spent significant time reaching out to contacts at the three Cloud providers, explaining both the fact that we did have the money to pay the expected bill, were technically competent enough to not overspend and that our goal was actually worthwhile to support. We eventually got enough attention high enough in the leadership chain to get all our wishes granted, but it was a long process!

## 3.2   Provisioning the 51k GPUs Over 3 Cloud Providers Using Multiple Regions

The main objective of this exercise was to provision the maximum number of GPUs that could be rented in any public Cloud for a couple of hours. We wanted to discover what was possible without any long-term commitments and demonstrate that it could be used efficiently for scientific workloads. The overlay workload management system, namely HTCondor, was described in the previous sections, so here we limit ourselves to the description of the provisioning part alone.

Given that HTCondor was dealing with job handling and resource matchmaking, the provisioning part was strictly limited to starting up properly configured worker node instances. In order to minimize external dependencies, we created self-contained and self-configuring images that we uploaded to the native Cloud image repositories. We decided to create a slightly different image for each of the three Cloud providers, both because there is no easy Cloud-native way of sharing images between them and it was easier to deal with system level differences between the three platforms. We did however use a single image for all of the regions belonging to each Cloud provider. The region-specific details were stored in a local lookup table. We then relied on their Metadata services for region discovery [6–8] and, after proper table lookups, finished the configuration of the node at instance boot time. All of this was done ahead of the run, has taken a couple of iteration to get right, but could be used as-is for any number of runs from that point on.

With images in the proper Cloud native repositories, it was just a matter of automating the rapid startup and teardown of a large number of instances. This meant not only dealing with three separate Cloud providers, but also specifics of each region. Any region is essentially its own island, with only the Identity and Access Management (IAM) tying them together. The automation thus had to deal with 28 independent Cloud regions, using 3 different APIs.

For Amazon Web Services (AWS), we were relying on the fleet mechanism [9]. We created one fleet configuration template for each GPU instance type in every targeted Cloud region, for a total of over 40 different templates. The provisioning in AWS was just a matter of creating new fleets with the desired number of instances. Note that the AWS API supports the request of multiple instance types within a fleet, but while that seemed to work fine for CPU instances in our preliminary tests, when mixing GPU instances it resulted in some instance types never being requested, so we opted for the safer although more complex alternative.

For Microsoft Azure, we used the Azure Virtual Machine Scale Sets [10]. Conceptually, an Azure Scale Set is very similar to an AWS Fleet. There are however a few significant differences; 1) an Azure Scale Set can be resized, AWS Fleets cannot, 2) an Azure Scale set has a hard upper limit to how many instances it can manage, while AWS Fleets do not, and 3) an Azure Scale Set always manages a uniform set of instances, while AWS Fleets can be more heterogeneous. Given that Azure Scale Sets can be easily resized yet have limited maximum size, we created several ahead of time for each GPU instance type in every targeted region, enough to allow us to provision all instances in even the most optimistic projection without coming too close to the hard limits of the Azure Scale Set infrastructure. Overall, we created over 200 of them. With the Scale

Sets in place, the provisioning during the actual burst was as simple as increasing the instance count from 0 to the desired max.

In Google Cloud Platform (GCP) we used their Unmanaged Instance Groups [11]. They are conceptually very similar to the Azure Scale Set, so we used virtually the same approach; create a set of them ahead of time and then just set the instance number to the desired max during the exercise. GCP will then automatically deal with the rest.

The provisioning ramp-up went mostly smoothly. We did however encounter internal limits in a few Cloud regions that required manual intervention to recover. This can be observed in the two rapid rises in Fig. 2a; the initial provisioning request at time zero, and the additional rapid rise after the manual recovery about 50 min later. Apart from that, the whole ramp-up happened completely autonomously. All Cloud regions across providers ramped up at the same time, as can be seen from the different colors in the figure, and no-one is ever providing a dominating fraction. Unfortunately, we are not authorized to identify the various regions involved. We can show which geographical areas were being provisioned, see Fig. 2b. Here you can clearly see that instances have been joining the IceCube serving HTCondor pool from all over the world, with no single region significantly dominating the others.

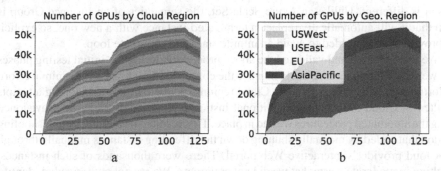

**Fig. 2.** Number of GPU instances over time (in mins) during the ramp-up period. a) grouped by cloud region. b) grouped by geographical region.

Managing a controlled shutdown turned out to be a harder problem than the provisioning. This was partially due to the desire of dynamically de-provision the instances only after the last job ran, and partially due to semantics of the provisioning tools used.

The desired sequence of the controlled shutdown was to remove all not-yet-started GPU jobs from the HTCondor queues, let the already running GPU jobs run to completion and de-provision the instance as soon as that GPU job terminated. Most instances also ran CPU jobs alongside the GPU jobs at all times. We would let CPU jobs run up until the last GPU job on the instance terminated and remove them at that point. Given the comparatively low value of the CPU-only compute, we wanted to optimize for maximum GPU utilization.

The removing of the not-yet-started GPU jobs from the HTCondor queues was obviously trivial. De-provisioning the running Cloud instances soon after the last GPU job ended was not. And we had to implement a different mechanism for each Cloud provider API.

The easiest was AWS. Since AWS Fleets were launched as ephemeral, all we had to do was to submit a set a system shutdown service jobs that would match as soon as the GPU job terminated. Unfortunately, we could not use this method for either Azure or GCP managed instances.

For Azure, the first obvious step was to set the desired numbers of instances in the Scale Set's configurations to the number of running instances at the beginning of the shutdown period, so no new instances would be started. However, instances in an Azure Scale Set have the property that just shutting down an instance at the system level will not de-provision that instance; one will still be charged for that time at the same rate as if the instance was still running [12]. The only proper way to de-provision an instance managed by an Azure Scale Set is to invoke the Azure API with the proper Scale Set and Instance ID pair. We thus wrote some service scripts that would extract that information from the instance Metadata service and automate the invocation of the proper API at the appropriate time.

For GCP, we had to follow a pattern similar to the one on Azure. First, we updated the desired number of instances for the Instance Groups, then we explicitly invoked the GCP API to de-provision each and every instance that we wanted removed from the Instance Groups. While the needed procedure is conceptually identical, the underlying reason is different. Unlike an Azure Scale Set, the semantics of an Instance Group is such that it will automatically replace a terminated instance with a new one, so explicit de-provisioning is needed to avoid an infinite start-and-terminate loop.

We had prepared and validated the above procedure during the initial testing phases and were quite confident we could manage the controlled shutdown with minimal effort. Unfortunately, we hit bugs in some Cloud regions, where our de-provisioning attempts resulted in Cloud APIs starting additional instances that could not be de-provisioned using the automated procedures we had in place. This resulted in a frantic troubleshooting session that ended by manually shutting down the offending instances manually through the Cloud provider's interactive Web portal. There were thousands of such instances, resulting in moderate waste that we did not anticipate. We are not authorized to identify neither the offending Cloud regions nor the associated Cloud provider(s). If we were to repeat such a large scale, bursty multi-Cloud exercise again, we would definitely put in place additional tools that would allow for rapid detection and cleanup of unexpected instances.

### 3.3 An Overview of the Provisioned Resources

The total runtime of the exercise was slightly over 3 h. We reached 90% of the maximum number of concurrently running instances in about 70 min after we started the provisioning. We sustained that level and added an additional 10% in the following 45 min. After which we started a controlled shutdown, which lasted just about an hour and a half. As can be seen from Fig. 3a, we peaked at about 51.5k GPU jobs running.

The provisioned instances spanned 8 generations of NVIDIA GPUs. As seen from Table 1 and Fig. 3b, the most abundant GPU types at peak were the K80 and the M60, but the most compute power was provided by the V100 and the P100 GPUs. We were also pleasantly surprised to see a significant contribution by the quite recent, and very cost effective T4.

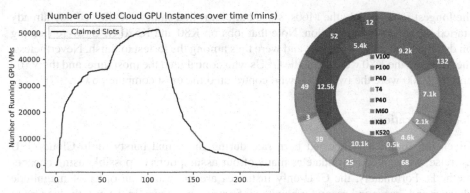

**Fig. 3.** a) Time evolution of the HTCondor pool. b) GPU composition at peak. The inner circle shows the number of instances, the outer circle the PFLOP32s contribution.

**Table 1.** Distribution of GPU types at peak.

| GPU type (NVIDIA) | Count at peak | Total PFLOP32s |
|---|---|---|
| V100 | 9.2k (18%) | 132.2 (35%) |
| P100 | 7.1k (14%) | 68.1 (18%) |
| P40 | 2.1k (4%) | 25.2 (7%) |
| T4 | 4.6k (9%) | 38.6 (10%) |
| P4 | 0.5k (1%) | 2.5 (1%) |
| M60 | 10.1k (20%) | 48.8 (13%) |
| K80 | 12.5k (24%) | 51.6 (14%) |
| K520 | 5.4k (10%) | 12.4 (3%) |
| Total | 51.5k | 379.4 |

**Table 2.** Distribution of GPU types over the total runtime

| GPU type (NVIDIA) | Total walltime in hours | Total PFLOP32 hours |
|---|---|---|
| V100 | 18.2k (19%) | 260.7 (35%) |
| P100 | 16.0k (17%) | 152.8 (21%) |
| P40 | 4.4k (5%) | 51.5 (7%) |
| T4 | 7.3k (8%) | 61.4 (8%) |
| P4 | 0.7k (1%) | 3.6 (1%) |
| M60 | 25.1k (26%) | 121.3 (16%) |
| K80 | 18.5k (19%) | 76.2 (10%) |
| K520 | 7.0k (7%) | 16.1 (2%) |
| Total | 97.3k | 734.7 |

The total integrated time of the exercise was about 100k GPU hours. As seen from Table 2, it features the same NVIDIA GPU types, but is skewed toward the GPUs that ran the longest jobs, namely the M60s, since our controlled shutdown allowed any already started job to run to completion. Note that jobs on K80 and K520 GPUs were running on drastically smaller input files and were thus among the fastest to finish. Nevertheless, the M60 and the K80 were again the GPUs who contributed the most time, and the V100 and the P100 were the two GPUs who contributed the most compute power.

### 3.4  Preparations

Given the significant expected burn rate during the actual bursty multi-Cloud GPU exercise, we wanted to validate as many of our assumptions as possible using cheaper methods. Fortunately, the CPU-only instances are more than an order of magnitude cheaper and are a good proxy for how the infrastructure works. In the months leading to the actual exercise we tested three aspects of the whole system; 1) network performance, 2) HTCondor scalability and 3) Cloud API scalability.

The network part of the setup was deemed the most critical. If we were not able to transfer data in and out fast enough, we would have had huge waste in expensive GPU time, rendering the setup not feasible. We benchmarked both access to local cloud native storage as well as WAN transfers inside the Clouds and to scientific networks. The results were beyond our most optimistic expectations, with region-local Cloud storage easily exceeding 1 Tbps and 100 Gbps being the norm in the networking between Cloud regions. More than enough to make IO latencies negligible for our workload. Connectivity to scientific networks was also generally good, with 10 Gbps being exceeded in most setups. This made pre and post exercise data movement not at all challenging. The results of the tests have been presented at the CHEP19 conference [13].

The scalability of the HTCondor setup was technically the most critical one, but we had enough experience with other large-scale setups to be fairly confident that it would be feasible. Nevertheless, we did run a few bursty CPU-only tests to validate our assumptions, and did find some unexpected issues, as explained in Sect. 2.3. While unfortunate, these tests allowed us to implement workarounds that later tests proved to be effective under conditions expected during the actual GPU burst. At peak, our largest test setup had over 80k slots, coming from the same combination of Cloud providers and regions we were planning to provision from during the exercise.

The major unknown was the performance of the Cloud APIs. We had virtually no prior experience with provisioning that many instances in any of the three Cloud providers, and we were also very eager to learn how fast these APIs could provision the resources. The preliminary tests did not show any problems, beyond the need of proper quotas being put in place, and the ramp-up speeds were very promising. Figuring out what the best APIs to use were was actually the major hurdle.

Finally, we also ran a small-scale GPU-enabled test, which tried to mimic as close as possible the final setup that would be used for the exercise. Here we discovered that AWS Fleets do not like heterogeneous GPU instance types, as mentioned in Sect. 3.2, and we adjusted accordingly.

### 3.5 Cloud Cost Analysis

Unfortunately, we are not authorized to discuss the actual price paid to carry out this exercise. We are instead providing an analysis based on the published list prices of the used Cloud providers, and in particular with a focus to opportunistic use scenarios. For clarity, the opportunistic use is called Spot pricing on AWS and Microsoft Azure, and preemptable instances in GCP. The rationale for using the opportunistic instance pricing stems from the fact that they are about three times cheaper that full price instances and dHTC workloads can gracefully recover from preemption, so there is no reason not to use them unless aiming for maximum resource pool size. Additionally, we only recorded an average preemption rate of 2% for opportunistic instances during this exercise, which is considered absolutely negligible in such setups.

Table 3 provides a list price range for instances providing each of the used GPU types. We also include an estimated hourly list cost for an experiment like ours, which turns out to be just shy of $20k/h. The table also provides a clear indication that it is much more cost effective to use the more recent GPU types; for example, the instances providing the K520 GPUs had approximately the same hourly list cost as instances providing T4 and P40 GPUs, yet they provided only a small fraction of the FLOP32s.

**Table 3.** Cloud opportunistic hourly pricing for various GPU types

| GPU type (NVIDIA) | Price range (list) | Count at peak | PFLOP32s at peak | Estimated list price at peak |
|---|---|---|---|---|
| V100 | $0.6–$1.0 | 9.2k | 132.2 | $7.2k/h |
| P100 | $0.4–$0.6 | 7.1k | 68.1 | $3.5k/h |
| P40 | $0.4–$0.6 | 2.1k | 25.2 | $1.0k/h |
| T4 | $0.2–$0.3 | 4.6k | 38.6 | $1.2k/h |
| P4 | $0.2–$0.2 | 0.5k | 2.5 | $0.1k/h |
| M60 | $0.2–$0.3 | 10.1k | 48.8 | $2.7k/h |
| K80 | $0.13–$0.3 | 12.5k | 51.6 | $2.9k/h |
| K520 | $0.2–$0.2 | 5.4k | 12.4 | $1.0k/h |
| Total | | 51.5k | 379.4 | $19.6k/h |

## 4   The IceCube Science Proposition

From the ground up, this exercise was planned with the goal of advancing science. While we were definitely interested in the technical aspect of the endeavor, we wanted primarily to demonstrate that such large-scale computation is actually useful for science. The technical participants in this group thus partnered early on with a scientific community that had a dHTC computing workload which needed significantly more compute resources than they were normally getting. This resulted in the exercise being a joint collaboration between personnel from both the Open Science Grid and the IceCube collaboration.

Section 4.1 provides an overview of the science behind IceCube. Section 4.2 provides an overview of the compute challenges involved in the IceCube science. Section 4.3 provides an overview of GPU-enabled code that was run during this exercise. Section 4.4 provides a comparison of the efficacy of the various GPU types for the purpose of IceCube, including how this skewed total contribution of various GPU types to the advancement of science objectives.

### 4.1 The IceCube Neutrino Observatory

The IceCube Neutrino Observatory [14] is the world's premier facility to detect neutrinos with energies above 1 TeV and an essential part of multi-messenger astrophysics. IceCube is composed of 5160 digital optical modules (DOMs) buried deep in glacial ice at the geographical south pole. Neutrinos that interact close to or inside of IceCube produce secondary particles, often a muon. Such secondary particles produces Cherenkov (blue as seen by humans) light as it travels through the highly transparent ice. Cherenkov photons detected by DOMs can be used to reconstruct the direction and energy of the parent neutrino. IceCube has three components: the main array, which has already been described; DeepCore: a dense and small sub-detector that extends sensitivity to ~10 GeV; and IceTop: a surface air shower array that studies O(PeV) cosmic rays.

IceCube is a remarkably versatile instrument addressing multiple disciplines, including astrophysics, the search for dark matter, cosmic rays, particle physics and geophysical sciences. IceCube operates continuously and routinely achieves over 99% up-time while simultaneously being sensitive to the whole sky. Highlights of IceCube scientific results is the discovery of an all sky astrophysical neutrino flux and the detection of a neutrino from Blazar TXS 0506 + 056 that triggered follow-up observations from a slew of other telescopes and observatories [15].

### 4.2 The Importance of Proper Calibration

Any experiment requires a fundamental level of understanding of the employed instruments. In IceCube's case, the detector is built into a naturally existing medium, i.e. glacial ice, that has been deposited over millennia. *A priori* there was only limited information regarding the optical properties of the detector.

The optical properties of the glacial ice greatly affect the pointing resolution of IceCube. Improving the pointing resolution has two effects in this case: greater chance to detect astrophysical neutrinos and better information sent to the community. While IceCube can detect all flavors and interaction channels of neutrinos, about two-thirds of the flux reaching IceCube will generate a detection pattern with a large angular error, see Fig. 4a. In the same figure you can also see that this angular error is mostly driven by systematic effects. Similarly, different optical models have a great effect on the reconstructed location of an event on the sky, see Fig. 4b. The comparatively minute field of view of partner observatories and telescopes requires IceCube to provide as accurate as information as possible. Having the best calibration possible is therefore imperative.

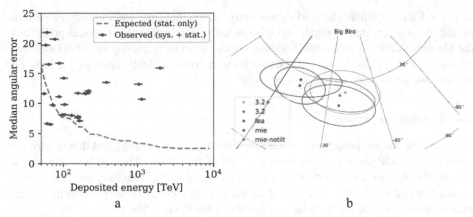

**Fig. 4.** Impact of the IceCube detector calibration on science results. a) Angular momentum vs errors in IceCube b) Pointing area based on different estimates.

## 4.3 Using GPUs for Photon Propagation Simulation

The photon propagation algorithm used by IceCube allows for massive parallelization using either a large number of CPU cores or GPUs [2]. The algorithm follows these steps. Initially a set of photons is created along the path of charged particles produced in the neutrino interaction or from *in-situ* light sources used for calibration. The number of photons inserted along the path depends on the energy loss pattern of the product. Most higher energy products will suffer stochastic energy loses due to bremsstrahlung, electron pair production, or ionization as they travel through the detector causing concentrations of light at certain points along the particle's path. For calibration sources, a fixed number of photons is inserted depending on the calibration source and its settings.

Once the location and properties of the photons have been determined, they are added to a queue. For a given device, a thread pool is created depending on the possible number of threads. If using a CPU, this typically is one thread per logical core. When using a GPU, this mapping is more complicated, but can be summarized as one to several threads per "core", and the exact mapping depends on the specific vendor and architecture. Each thread takes a photon out of the queue and propagates it. During the propagation, the algorithm will first determine the absorption length of the photon, i.e. how long the photon can travel before being absorbed. Then the algorithm will determine the distance to the next scatter. The photon is now propagated the distance of the next scatter. After the propagation, a check is performed to test whether the photon has reached its absorption length or intersected with an optical detector along its path. If the photon does not pass these checks, the photon is scattered, i.e. a scattering angle and a new scattering distance are determined, and the cycle repeats. Once the photon has either been absorbed or intersected with an optical detector, its propagation is halted and the thread will take a new photon from the queue.

The IceCube photon propagation code is distinct from others, e.g. Nvidia OptiX in that it is purpose-built. It handles the medium, i.e. glacial ice and the physical aspects of photon propagation in great detail. The photons will traverse through a medium with varying optical properties. The ice has been deposited over several hundreds of thousands of years. Earth's climate changed significantly during that time and imprinted a pattern on the ice as a function of depth. In addition to the depth-dependent optical properties the glacier has moved across the Antarctic continent and has undergone other unknown stresses. This has caused layers of constant ice properties, optically speaking, to be tilted and to have anisotropic optical properties.

### 4.4 The Science Output

The IceCube photon propagation code relies mostly on fp32 math, and this is why we focused on FLOP32s in the first three sections of this paper. There is however also a non-negligible amount of code that is needed to support the dataflow, and that cannot be directly tied to FLOPS of any kind. In the next few chapters we provide the actual measurements of how this translates in run times for the IceCube code.

**Table 4.** IceCube runtime for different GPU types.

| GPU type (NVIDIA) | Runtime in mins | Peak TFLOP32s | Correlation |
|---|---|---|---|
| V100 | 24 | 14 | 110% |
| P100 | 43 | 9.5 | 100% |
| P40 | 38 | 12 | 95% |
| T4 | 50 | 8.1 | 100% |
| P4 | 80 | 5.0 | 100% |
| M60 | 95 | 4.8 | 90% |
| K80 | 138 | 4.1 | 70% |
| K520 | 310 | 2.3 | 55% |
| GTX 1080 | 50 | 8.9 | 90% |

Before running the actual large-scale GPU burst, we benchmarked the IceCube photon propagation code, using a single representative input file, on all the various GPU-enabled instances of the various Cloud providers. Table 4 provides the observed runtimes, alongside the correlation to the nominal FLOP32s of those GPUs, relative to the performance of the recent and cost effective T4. A desktop-class GPU card, the NVIDIA GTX 1080 is also provided as a reference point. As can be seen, modern GPUs provide significantly shorter runtimes per nominal FLOP32 compared to the older ones.

The distribution of the observed run times of the jobs completed during the exercise matched very well the test data. The contribution to science results of the overall run was thus now much more skewed toward the newer GPU types, as can be seen from Fig. 5. In particular, the older K80 and K520, which together contributed about a quarter of all the walltime, contributed less than 8% of the science output. In contrast, the more modern V100 and T4 together produced over 50% of all the science output while using about the same amount of wallclock time. A similar pattern can be also observed when comparing the list price versus the science output in the same figure.

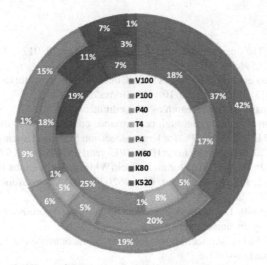

**Fig. 5.** Contribution of different GPU types during the exercise. The external ring represents the fraction of science events simulated. The intermediate ring represents the estimated list price fraction. The inner ring represents the wallclock time fraction.

## 5   Conclusions

In this paper we present our experience in provisioning a pre-exascale dHTC workload using a real science application using Cloud resources from multiple Cloud providers. The chosen application was IceCube's photon propagation simulation, both for technical (heavy use of GPU at modest IO) and scientific reasons (high impact science). We emphasize that this meant it was not a purely experimental setup, but it produced valuable and much needed simulation for the IceCube collaboration's science program.

We managed to provision almost 380 PFLOP32s distributed over 51k instances using 8 different GPU types, from all over the world, reaching 2/3$^{rd}$ of the total size in about half hour from the provisioning start and the peak within about two hours. No special arrangements or long-term commitments were needed, apart from having the quotas raised to the appropriate levels. While the raising of quotas indeed involved a non-trivial effort, as explained in Sect. 3.1, we believe pre-exascale dHTC computing using Cloud resources is today within reach of anyone with a $100k budget.

Our exercise intentionally avoided to deal with real-time data movement problems in and out of the Cloud, by keeping all networking within Cloud providers' domains during the exercise. We do plan to have a follow-on exercise which will be much more data focused.

**Acknowledgements.** This work was partially funded by the US National Science Foundation (NSF) under grants OAC-1941481, MPS-1148698, OAC-1841530, OAC-1826967 and OAC-1904444.

# References

1. Pordes, R., et al.: The open science grid. J. Phys. Conf. Ser. **78**, 012057 (2007). https://doi.org/10.1088/1742-6596/78/1/012057
2. Chirkin, D.: Photon tracking with GPUs in IceCube. Nucl. Inst. Methods Phys. Res. Sec. A. **725**, 141–143 (2013). https://doi.org/10.1016/j.nima.2012.11.170
3. HTCondor Homepage. https://research.cs.wisc.edu/htcondor/
4. Posey, B. et al: On-demand urgent high performance computing utilizing the google cloud platform. In: 2019 IEEE/ACM HPC for Urgent Decision Making (UrgentHPC), Denver, CO, USA, pp. 13–23 (2019). https://doi.org/10.1109/UrgentHPC49580.2019.00008
5. Balcas, B., et al.: Pushing HTCondor and glideinWMS to 200K+ jobs in a global pool for CMS before Run 2. J. Phys: Conf. Ser. **664**, 062030 (2015). https://doi.org/10.1088/1742-6596/664/6/062030
6. AWS Instance Identity Documents. https://docs.aws.amazon.com/AWSEC2/latest/UserGuide/instance-identity-documents.html
7. Azure Instance Metadata service. https://docs.microsoft.com/en-us/azure/virtual-machines/linux/instance-metadata-service
8. GCP Storing and retrieving instance metadata. https://cloud.google.com/compute/docs/storing-retrieving-metadata
9. Launching an EC2 Fleet. https://docs.aws.amazon.com/AWSEC2/latest/UserGuide/ec2-fleet.html
10. What are virtual machine scale sets. https://docs.microsoft.com/en-us/azure/virtual-machine-scale-sets/overview
11. Google Cloud Instance groups. https://cloud.google.com/compute/docs/instance-groups/
12. Molosky, K: Azure Virtual Machines – Stopping versus Stopping (Deallocating). https://blogs.technet.microsoft.com/uspartner_ts2team/2014/10/10/azure-virtual-machines-stopping-versus-stopping-deallocating/
13. Sfiligoi, I., Graham, J., Wuerthwein, F.: Characterizing network paths in and out of the clouds. To be published Proceedings of 24th International Conference on Computing in HEP (CHEP 2019) (2020)
14. Aartsen, M.G., et al.: The IceCube neutrino observatory: instrumentation and online systems. J. Instrum. **12**, P03012–P03012 (2017). https://doi.org/10.1088/1748-0221/12/03/P03012
15. The IceCube Collaboration, et al.: Multimessenger observations of a flaring Blazar coincident with high-energy neutrino IceCube-170922A. Science **361**(6398), eaat1378 (2018). https://doi.org/10.1126/science.aat1378

# Scalable Hierarchical Aggregation and Reduction Protocol (SHARP)™ Streaming-Aggregation Hardware Design and Evaluation

Richard L. Graham[1]([✉]), Lion Levi[2], Devendar Burredy[1], Gil Bloch[2],
Gilad Shainer[1], David Cho[1], George Elias[2], Daniel Klein[2], Joshua Ladd[1],
Ophir Maor[1], Ami Marelli[2], Valentin Petrov[2], Evyatar Romlet[2], Yong Qin[1],
and Ido Zemah[2]

[1] Mellanox Technologies, Inc., 350 Oakmead Parkway, Sunnyvale, CA 94085, USA
`richardg@mellanox.com`
[2] Mellanox Technologies, Ltd., HaKidma St 26, 2069200 Yokne'am, Israel

**Abstract.** This paper describes the new hardware-based streaming-aggregation capability added to Mellanox's Scalable Hierarchical Aggregation and Reduction Protocol in its HDR InfiniBand switches. For large messages, this capability is designed to achieve reduction bandwidths similar to those of point-to-point messages of the same size, and complements the latency-optimized low-latency aggregation reduction capabilities, aimed at small data reductions. *MPI_Allreduce()* bandwidth measured on an HDR InfiniBand based system achieves about 95% of network bandwidth. For medium and large data reduction this also improves the reduction bandwidth by a factor of 2–5 relative to host-based (e.g., software-based) reduction algorithms. Using this capability also increased DL-Poly and PyTorch application performance by as much as 4% and 18%, respectively. This paper describes SHARP Streaming-Aggregation hardware architecture and a set of synthetic and application benchmarks used to study this new reduction capability, and the range of data sizes for which Streaming-Aggregation performs better than the low-latency aggregation algorithm.

**Keywords:** In-network computing · All-reduce · Streaming reduction · Hardware collectives · InfiniBand · Mellanox SHARP

## 1 Introduction

A parallel application is a collection of independent computational elements that communicate with each other to the degree needed by the application. In tightly coupled High Performance Computing (HPC) applications the type of inter-process communication involved is either some form of point-to-point or

© The Author(s) 2020
P. Sadayappan et al. (Eds.): ISC High Performance 2020, LNCS 12151, pp. 41–59, 2020.
https://doi.org/10.1007/978-3-030-50743-5_3

collective communication. The Message Passing Interface (MPI) [1] and Open SHMEM [2] define HPC oriented APIs that provide interfaces to such capabilities. Network communication happens between end-points. In point-to-point communication, data is moved from one source to a single destination, and includes operations such as the non-blocking MPI_Isend() and MPI_Irecv() which are used to initiate sending or receiving data, respectively. Collective communication involves some form of data exchange with participation of all members of a group of endpoints, such as MPI_Barrier() which is used to synchronize a set of end-points (MPI processes), or MPI_Allreduce() which is used to gather equal-sized vectors from all members of the collective group, produce a single output vector, and return this to all members of the group.

Collective communication is used by many HPC applications. Efficient implementations of such algorithms often use a chain of point-to-point communication thus serializing algorithm communication, which tends to be scale dependent, with the number of such communication in the critical path increasing with group size. Therefore, collective communication often has a large impact on application scalability.

This scalability challenge has spawned many efforts to optimize collective communication algorithms. Most of these have used host-side logic to manage the collective algorithm as well as the necessary data manipulation with the network being used exclusively as a data pipe. Some network-hardware-based solutions have been implemented, with those relevant to the focus of this paper reviewed in Sect. 2.

Mellanox Technologies, as a provider of HPC network technology, has been moving the implementation of portions of the collective operations to the network, freeing up the computational elements, such as CPUs and GPUs, for computation. For example, CORE-Direct®[10] moved management of the communication dependencies in the chain of collective operations to network hardware in support of asynchronous progress. Mellanox is in the process of IO Processing Units (IPUs) that improve system efficiency by relocating the processing of network operations and data algorithms from the main host into the network fabric. As part of this effort the Mellanox SHARP [9] protocol has been developed to optimize collective reduction and aggregation operations. The first set of capabilities supported include those needed to implement reduction operations, including allreduce, reduce and barrier-synchronization, with a latency-optimized short vector reduction algorithm.

This paper describes and evaluates a new IPU SHARP capability added to Mellanox's HDR InfiniBand switches. This capability, called Streaming-Aggregation, moves distributed large-data reductions from the host to the network, using a bandwidth-optimized algorithm designed to handle wide radix reduction at near wire speeds. Section 3 describes the Streaming-Aggregation capability introduced in Mellanox's Quantum$^{TM}$® switch, providing support for long vector reduce, allreduce and broadcast operations. Due to space considerations, we focus only on the reduction operations, and specifically the allreduce operation. Streaming-Aggregation optimizes these often-used global reduction operations by performing the data reduction operations as it traverses a reduction tree in the network. Data from each source is injected into the network only once, and the volume of data is reduced as it goes towards the root of the tree. This is in contrast to CPU-based algorithms where data traverses the network multiple times between network endpoints, to be reduced at each stage at some node in the system. The large-radix reduction trees used provide a highly scalable algorithm and shallow reduction trees, reducing the latency of a one MByte (MB) data reduction across 64 hosts by a factor of 3.5. The effect of this optimization on overall application performance depends on the frequency of using such calls, as well as the skew in the collective initiation across the group of participating processes. The greater the skew, the less pronounced the impact. However, the latter is true for any aggregation algorithm, whether implemented in hardware or software.

Section 2 describes previous work, Sect. 3 describes the Streaming-Aggregation design and Sect. 4 provide some experimental data to demonstrate the effectiveness of this approach in improving system performance, making more CPU cycles available for computation.

## 2   Previous Work

Previous work on reduction algorithms for distributed vectors has included both algorithmic level optimization with software-based implementation as well as work on hardware acceleration of such algorithms. Most of this work is aimed at accelerating small-to-medium data reduction, with relatively little work on optimizing the reduction of longer vectors.

This algorithmic work has resulted in several algorithms in common use today. For long vector reduction Rabensiefner [14] has developed a widely used algorithm baring his name. This algorithm uses a reduce-scatter phase to compute a distributed result vector, with this vector being distributed across members of the communicator, and an allgather step to gather the full vector to all group members. A ring algorithm [14] has also been developed to optimize large vector reductions, and scales linearly with vector size.

Most of the work on hardware optimized collectives has focused on short-vector reduction, with a limited number of published efforts aiming to address large data reduction. The latter faces the challenge of handling very large amounts of data in a single collective operation while staging data across the network for performing the data reduction. In addition, for a given vector length, the total volume of data being reduced, increases with group size, further increasing the amount of data manipulated. To achieve reduction rates similar to the available network bandwidth, such data needs to be reduced efficiently as it is transferred, to form an efficient reduction pipeline. While multiple implementation of short-to-medium vector reductions have been found which offload the full operation to the network, only one reference has been identified on work that offloads the full large-vector reduction. Gao [8] implemented several tree-based reduction algorithms for FPGA-based systems, and ran experiments on a 32 node system. The latencies are reported for messages up to 140 Kbyte (KB) in size are high - on the order of milliseconds. Kumar et al. [11] developed an efficient algorithm for the Blue Gene/Q platform, which leverages the system's 5D torus with the reductions being performed by the host CPU. Adachi [6] implemented the Rabenseifner algorithm for the K-computer taking advantage its 5D network topology, segmenting the vectors into three parts which are reduced in parallel over three disjoint trees, and using the host CPU to perform the data reductions. Stern [13] developed an FPGA based methodology that is relevant for large reductions, but focuses on small-to-medium reductions.

The methodology being described in this paper offloads the full data reduction operations to the network, with the use of an efficient pipeline to achieve reduction throughput similar to the peak network bandwidth.

## 3   Streaming-Aggregation

Streaming-Aggregation [7] is a new capability introduced with Mellanox's HDR InfiniBand technology to perform reductions on data in-flight while maintaining near line-rate data transfers. This section describes the hardware enhancements made to the Mellanox SHARP protocol in support of this capability. This new protocol supplements the latency optimized reduction capabilities introduced with Mellanox srp in Switch-IB®-2 EDR switches [9].

Mellanox SHARP protocol details are described in [9], with a brief summary below. Mellanox SHARP uses reduction trees where the interior nodes of the tree and the root are instantiated in the switches. Hosts serve as the data source and data destination, and are the leaves of the reduction-trees. Figure 1a shows an example of a three-level fat tree and an aggregation group within this tree, with the hexagons representing radix-six switches which include a Collective Functional Unit (CFU) represented by a circle in the switch. Switch connectivity is shown by the edges, and the hosts connecting into the switched fabric by circles. One of several possible reduction-trees that may be defined within this network include the switches with red and cyan aggregation nodes (ANs), with the hosts that are the sources of data colored red or striped. In general, switches need not be ANs within a reduction-tree, as is reflected by the AN in the second level of the red tree on the left hand side, which is not colored.

The AN is used to support Mellanox SHARP's reduction functionality. These nodes reduce the data received from their children producing one output vector. Interior nodes forward the result to their parent and the root node initiates the result distribution phase, replicating the data to its children. Interior nodes replicate the result received from their parent to their children. The upper limit on the node radix supported by the CFU leads naturally to a hierarchical approach being used to implement collective operations, with a set of levels handling host-side aspects of the collective operations, and the switching infrastructure handling the network-side portion of these collective operations.

Reduction-trees are defined at network initialization time, and reduction groups at run-time. An aggregation-group is defined by the hosts that serve

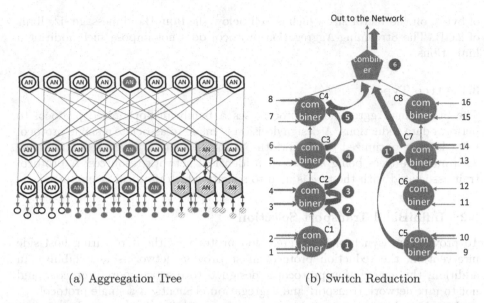

(a) Aggregation Tree                    (b) Switch Reduction

**Fig. 1.** (a) Aggregation tree and a reduction group overlaid on this tree. Switches are displayed as hexagons, nodes as circles and the edges showing switch-to-switch connectivity. (b) Switch-level reduction operation. (Color figure online)

as sources of data for a given set of collective operation. For example, an MPI implementation may create a Mellanox SHARP group at communicator initialization time or on first use. In Fig. 1a the cyan colored nodes and striped hosts define a two-level aggregation-group on the specified reduction-tree.

The following enhancements to Mellanox SHARP have been made in support of the Streaming-Aggregation capability:

- Reduction-trees have a new trait added to specify their type, supporting either low-latency reduction or Streaming-Aggregation.
- The ability to lock a Streaming-Aggregation tree for exclusive use is added. This is done with new capabilities added to the low-latency reduction-tree, with a topology that is identical to that of the Streaming-Aggregation tree.
- Switch-level support for a pipelined reduction ring.
- A single child is supported per tree per switch port. A given aggregation group supports one outstanding operation at a time, with a switch supporting operations on up to two trees at a time.
- A scalable reliable multicast is supported on the tree.

The reduction algorithms are implemented using existing InfiniBand transports, and as such inherit the characteristics of these transports. They include the message size restrictions imposed by InfiniBand and HCA capabilities, such as the gather/scatter capabilities. The low-latency aggregation protocol originally implemented imposes a protocol-specific upper limit, on the order of hundreds of bytes, on the vector size which is well below the InfiniBand message size limit of 2 GB. The Streaming-Aggregation protocol does not impose such additional limitations.

## 3.1   Tree Type

The Streaming-Aggregation protocol uses a bandwidth-optimized protocol to perform data reductions. A design decision is made to associate a single protocol (e.g., latency-optimized or bandwidth-optimized) with a given reduction-tree, with multiple trees being able to span identical network resources. A protocol trait associated with the tree is used to specify which protocol is supported.

## 3.2   InfiniBand Transport Selection

To provide an asynchronous aggregation protocol, without requiring host-side intervention, the reduction protocol must provide network-side reliability. In addition, the aggregation protocol is designed to use transport protocols, and not to mix network transport and aggregation elements in a single protocol.

It is desirable to use a reliable transport to send data between nodes towards the root of the reduction-tree and let the hardware transports handle all reliability issues. Such an approach does not slow down the aggregation by waiting on CPU cycles to become available for progressing the protocol, or for timers with long end-to-end timeout periods to expire. The InfiniBand Reliable Connection (RC) transport is favored over the Dynamically Connected (DC) transport because the number of AN-to-AN connections is small, limited by the upper limit on the AN radix, and remains constant unless the network is reconfigured. Therefore, the scalability benefits of DC, with its ability to support multiple destinations are not relevant in this case, which is why InfiniBand RC transport is used for sending data between tree nodes.

Since the result of the aggregation is destined to one or more user-space address spaces, depending on the collective operation being performed, using host-based reliability algorithms as part of an algorithm that handles missing result data is possible. Using Unreliable Datagram (UD) multicast to distribute the results within the tree provides the lowest latency method for distributing the aggregation result within the tree. However, since the protocol is unreliable, a second transmission of the same data is needed, with appropriate handling of duplicate data reception, to ensure that the result is received by each member of the reduction group. For short messages sending the results twice makes sense, once using InfiniBand's UD multicast transport and then with the reliable RC transport down the tree, as message rate, and not network bandwidth, is the limiting latency factor determining the latency of the result distribution. Duplicate data is handled by receiving data into temporary buffers and copying one result into the user buffer, thus ensuring a second copy is not received into user destination buffers after the user process has already been notified of completion and could be modifying the data. For short messages, the cost of the memory copy is small relative to the overall cost of the UD multicast data distribution, and therefore makes sense from an aggregation latency perspective. However, for large messages, sending the data twice effectively halves the available network bandwidth, doubling the latency, and making such a solution impractical from a performance perspective. Delivering the data to a temporary buffer and the copying it to the user buffer, further increases the cost of distributing the result with UD multicast. Therefore, RC transport is used to distribute the results.

With the aggregation protocols using existing transport protocols, access to these capabilities is through the standard InfiniBand network access mechanisms. Initiating a reduction operation from a given end-point is done by posting a send request. Receive requests for the results are posted to receive queues, InfiniBand completion queues are used to retrieve reduction completion notification. The send request holds an aggregation protocol-specific header as part of the user payload, with the destination address being used to indicate that a message is part of an aggregation operation. New aggregation operations are introduced for the management purposes, such as aggregation-group formation. Space considerations do not allow a discussion of these operations.

## 3.3 Tree Locking

Streaming-aggregation is designed to perform long-vector distributed data reductions, while maintaining network throughput comparable to that of point-to-point data transfers of the same length. Since data from different children needs to be buffered long enough to combine the data from different sources at a given AN, and there are no guarantees on the temporal nature of data from different sources in specifications like MPI, it is desirable to delay occupying the Streaming-Aggregation buffer resources until all aggregation-group input vectors are ready. This is because the aggregation buffers are a shared switch-level resource that should not be held indefinitely, allowing those operations that are fully ready for the reduction to proceed.

To avoid occupying reduction buffers indefinitely, a protocol for locking a tree for a specified number of streaming-aggregations has been added. This protocol runs on a low-latency aggregation tree with an identical layout to that of the Streaming-Aggregation tree. In addition, the ability to unlock the Streaming-Aggregation tree has been added. This also allows for automatic unlocking of the tree when the number of full message aggregations performed matches the number requested. It is also possible for the tree to be used with no limit on the number of aggregations. This mode is suited for systems that are used to run a single job at time. The mode of operation is set when the lock request is made.

The locking protocol is similar to a Mellanox SHARP barrier operation, with each process in the group initiating a request to lock the tree. These requests propagate up the tree, locking the resources along the way. In the event that a resource is already locked and is unavailable, the failed request is propagated up the tree, with the root sending a failed-lock notification down the tree causing locked resources to be released, and the calling host process to be notified of the failure. The cost of such a lock is similar to a barrier-synchronization operation on the same low-latency aggregation tree.

As noted above, for resource locking purposes, each reduction-tree is associated with a low-latency reduction-tree of identical layout.

## 3.4  Reduction Tree

The Streaming-Aggregation reduction-tree is very similar in nature to the low-latency reduction-trees, with respect to how the aggregation proceeds. Individual ANs receive data from a predetermined number of children and reduce the data to produce a single output vector. Interior aggregation-group nodes forward the data to their parent, and the root of the aggregation-group initiates result distribution. An important feature of the aggregation protocol is that a single result is forwarded towards the root of the tree from each AN thereby reducing the amount of data forwarded by its aggregation radix. Similarly, as data is distributed from the root, it is replicated once per child at each AN, keeping the volume of data transferred to a minimum, and generally transferring much less data than that of host-based algorithms.

## 3.5  Reduction Pipelining

To achieve high network bandwidth with long vectors while performing a data reduction, an efficient pipeline needs to be established, which supports data staging into the arithmetic units. These units are then used to operate on the data, while maintaining high end-to-end data throughput. This data motion must be maintained throughout the full distributed reduction data path.

To achieve good pipelining InfiniBand's credit-based mechanism is used as a means for the responder (e.g., the AN) to inform the producer, i.e., the source of the data, of its available buffer space. This allows data to be sent between the two at an optimal rate, while avoiding overwhelming the responder with data it must drop. The credit mechanism runs over a reliable InfiniBand transport. This synchronizes the responder and requester by sending the amount of credits in response packets from the responder and allowing sending an additional single "limited" packet when the requester runs out of credits. This is as described in the InfiniBand specification for handling end-to-end credits.

## 3.6  Switch-Level Reduction

The AN in each switch takes input from a pre-configured set of children, and then delivers the data to the pre-configured destination, as shown in Fig. 1b. There is a one-to-one mapping between children and physical ports, on a per reduction-tree basis. Switch ports are paired and assigned reduction resources. The ports are arranged in two half rings, which meet in the middle, with the top CFU producing the final result and sending it to the destination. Data is supplied to the reduction tree at MTU granularity, which enables setting up an efficient pipeline capable of achieving end-to-end reduction at near wire speed.

Figure 1b shows how a switch performs the reduction of data coming from eight sources, for a switch of radix 16. The red arrows represent the children for the reduction at the AN, with the circles representing the Streaming-Aggregation reduction unit that handles data from two ports, and the pentagon represents the CFU which produces the final result. On the left-hand branch there are five reduction steps, with the first reduction taking data from the bottom two ports forwarding the result to the second combiner.

On the left-hand side, data from ports 1 and 2 are combined by C1. The result is forwarded to C2 where it is combined with the input from port 3 with the result being combined by C2 with the input from port 4, and forwarded to C3. At C3, the forwarded data is combined with the data from port 5 and forwarded to C4, where the data is combined with the data from port 8.

On the right-hand side, data from port 10 is forwarded through the combiner in C6 to C7 where it is combined with the data from port 14. The result is forwarded through C8 to the CFU where it is combined with the data from C4, and sent out to the appropriate exit port to the next AN in the tree.

At each step through the switch, data is processed at near wire speed, providing good throughput, with sufficient switch resources to keep the pipeline busy, supporting near full wire speed reduction.

## 3.7  Result Distribution

With the reduction complete at the root of the aggregation-group, it is ready to be distributed to data recipients, be it the host in the group for an allreduce type of operation, or the root of a reduction operation. With the short message, the latency-optimized hardware multicast protocol is used to provide low-latency data distribution, and a reliable transport is used to send the result down the tree to ensure reliable data distribution. For a bandwidth-oriented protocol, distributing the result twice, with both reliable connections and UD multicast protocols, reduces the operations bandwidth by a factor of two, making it a poor option.

Therefore, a new reliable broadcast protocol has been developed to distribute the data reliably at near wire bandwidths. This protocol uses unicast messages to send data between nodes in the aggregation-group, encapsulating the Mellanox SHARP reduction-tree which is used to distribute the data. When the CFU receives the unicast message, it extracts the SHARP group handle, and uses this to look up in its local SHARP group tables the list of ports through which the data needs to be forwarded. An optimized reliable packet generator is used to replicate the data which is sent out through each of the ports constructing new RC messages, one for each of the group destinations. This is depicted in Fig. 2 for a radix-6 switch and SHARP group 0X1. The process of extracting the SHARP group handle, replicating the reliable packets and sending the data to the next nodes in the reduction-tree is continued until the data reaches the destination.

## 3.8  Aggregation Protocol Resilience

The high performance computing community has yet to converge on a set of agreed upon protocols to handle application-side error recovery. Therefore, the

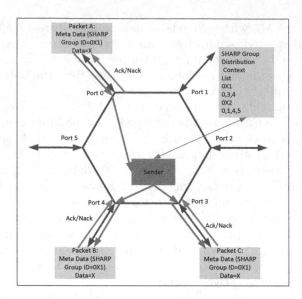

**Fig. 2.** Reliable Data Distribution. Black arrows represent ports, red arrows represent the data path and green arrow represent the control path. (Color figure online)

protocol is designed to allow users to select their own method of handling aggregation protocol failure.

With network error rates being rather low, with the average duration between unrecoverable errors being orders of magnitude higher than that of the longest aggregation protocol duration, Mellanox SHARP's mode of handling errors is limited to notifying the data sources when failure occurs, and letting the user decide how to proceed. Upon failure, the affected aggregation trees are torn down, and it is up to the host-side SHARP stack to decide if to re-initialize the SHARP resources, with a potentially new network configuration (i.e., without the failed resources).

Once the running application receives notification that a given aggregation has failed, it can decide how to proceed. It can try and re-initialize the application SHARP resources and use them again, or use an alternative host-based algorithm, which bypasses the affected resources, and restarts the affected aggregations. In addition, since successful local aggregation protocol completion does not imply success across the full reduction group, the application is free to add an agreement protocol, with the associated costs, before declaring the operation complete and returning control over the result buffers to the user.

## 4   Experiments

The Mellanox SHARP Streaming-Aggregation capability is studied using synthetic benchmarks and full applications, to explore the performance characteristics of this capability and its impact on applications.

## 4.1    Test System Configuration

The primary system used to run the synthetic benchmarks included 64 nodes of dual 18 core sockets of Intel(®) Xeon(®) Gold 6154 CPU running at 3.00 GHz. Each host uses the Red-Hat Linux version eight package and MLNX_OFED_LINUX-4.7-1.0.0.1. Each node is connected to network using a ConnectX®-6 HDR InfiniBand Mellanox HCA which were connected to HDR InfiniBand Mellanox Quantum$^{\text{TM}}$ switches. Each host is able to send data at the limit imposed by the PCIe Gen-3.0x16 bus, which is just above 100 Gbit/sec. The switches are connected in a two-level fat-tree topology, with four InfiniBand HDR Quantum$^{\text{TM}}$ L1 switches connected to one Quantum$^{\text{TM}}$ L2 switch. The HCAs used firmware version 20.26.1040, and the switches used firmware version 27.2000.2306.

The single switch scalability tests were run on a 32-node cluster. It has 16-core dual-socket Intel(®) Xeon(®) CPU E5-2697A v4 (Broadwell) running at 2.60 GHz with 256 GB of physical memory. Operating system is CentOS 7.7.1908 with kernel version 3.10.0-1062.4.1.el7.x86_64 and MLNX_OFED 4.7-1.0.0.1. Cluster nodes are connected with ConnectX-6 HDR100 InfiniBand and a Quantum$^{\text{TM}}$ switch. DL-Poly was also run on this system.

In addition, an 8-node cluster with AMD EPYC 7742 64-core Processors with MLNX OFED version 4.7 running the RDY1003B BIOS connected to a ConnectX®-6 HDR InfiniBand HCA via a PCIe Gen-4 bus was also used to measure performance on a fully enabled single-stream HDR configuration. Availability of systems with PCIe Gen-4 based CPUs has limited most of the testing to network injection bandwidths limited to just over 100 Gbit/s.

The MLPerf data was collected on an HPE Apollo 6500 configured with 8 NVIDIA Tesla V100 SXM2 with 16 GB of memory. The CPU used was a dual socket HPE DL360 Gen10 Intel Xeon-Gold 6134 (3.2 GHz/8-core/130 W) running Ubuntu 16.04, and connected via a PCIe Gen-3 PCI bus to HDR100 HCA running at 100 Gbit/sec connected to a single Mellanox Quantum$^{\text{TM}}$ switch.

The MPI from HPC-X version 2.5 [3] was used in the experiments.

## 4.2    Synthetic Benchmarks

The OSU allreduce [4] benchmark is used to study the performance of reduction capability. The test is modified to report the achieved bandwidth, in addition to the latency, where the bandwidth is computed as the message size divided by the measured latency. This is done to assess the hardware's ability to utilize available network bandwidth while performing the data reduction.

Measurements were taken to assess the efficiency at utilizing available network bandwidth, its efficiency compared to the low-latency aggregation capability and host-based distributed reduction algorithms. The host-based algorithm used is a radix-2 Rabenseifner's algorithm [14] - reduce-scatter followed by an allgather. In addition, Streaming-Aggregation's performance as a function of switch configuration and job size is studied. All the experiments described in this subsection focus on the in-network Streaming-Aggregation feature, so only a single process is used on each host.

The efficiency of the Streaming-Aggregation and its performance relative to the low-latency aggregation and host-based implementations was measured using all 64 hosts, with 16 hosts attached to each leaf switch. Ping-pong bandwidths are also reported. The results of these experiments are displayed in Fig. 3a. As this figure shows, the allreduce bandwidths obtained by the Streaming-Aggregation are close to that obtained in the ping-pong experiment which transfers data without manipulating it. The bandwidths obtained are much higher than those obtained with the host-based reduction operations, varying from a factor of about 2 higher at 4 KB message size to a factor of 4.8 higher at 256 MB message size. The bandwidth obtained is also higher than that obtained with the low-latency aggregation protocol, being similar at 8 KB message size and similar to the host-based performance at large message size. The reduction bandwidth achieved peaks out at about 96% of the ping-pong bandwidth, dropping off a bit at larger message sizes.

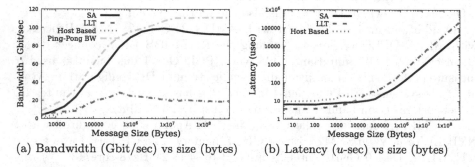

(a) Bandwidth (Gbit/sec) vs size (bytes)    (b) Latency ($u$-sec) vs size (bytes)

**Fig. 3.** (a) Streaming-aggregation (SA), low-latency aggregation (LLA), host-based MPI_Allerduce implementations and MPI ping-pong bandwidth. (b) Streaming-aggregation (SA), low-latency aggregation (LLA) and host-based MPI_Allreduce.

The Streaming-Aggregation is designed for long message aggregation, whereas the low-latency aggregation is designed to optimize for the small data reductions, which are dominated by latency effects. It is therefore important to figure out at what message size to switch from using the low-latency aggregation to the Streaming-Aggregation algorithm. Figure 3b compares the MPI_Allreduce latency obtained using Streaming-Aggregation, low-latency aggregation and the host-based algorithm. As expected, the hardware offloaded latency is better than that of the host-based algorithm, with the latency optimized algorithm performing better at small message sizes, and bandwidth optimized algorithm overtaking it in the range of 4 to 8 KB. These measurements do not take into account the cost of reserving the Streaming-Aggregation resources, for those instances in which this reservation is required. In such instances, the cross-over point will be at a larger message size. The overheads of managing multiple message data segments in the reduction pipeline, includes a credit mechanism, as well data orchestration logic within the AN, which is absent from the low-latency aggregation protocol. It is such logic that enables the high-bandwidths supported by the Streaming-Aggregation protocol, but increases the latency, and is independent of the data source.

Bandwidth was also measured on an AMD Rome cluster, supporting a PCIe Gen-4 bus, which enables full HDR throughput. The reduction bandwidth as a function of message size is displayed in Fig. 4a, peaking at close to 95% of available network bandwidth and 96% of ping-pong bandwidth, which is about 4.5 times that of the host-based algorithms, and about a factor of 7.6 better than using the low-latency aggregation capabilities.

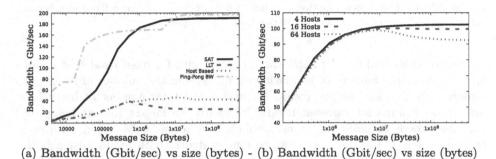

(a) Bandwidth (Gbit/sec) vs size (bytes) - (b) Bandwidth (Gbit/sec) vs size (bytes) Rome CPU

**Fig. 4.** (a) Streaming-aggregation (SA), low-latency aggregation (LLA), host-based MPI_Allerduce implementations and MPI ping-pong bandwidth - Rome CPU. (b) MPI_Allreduce Streaming-aggregation using four leaf switches and varying the number of hosts per switch.

Several other comparisons are made to further study the behavior of the Streaming-Aggregation capabilities. Single switch measurements were performed to understand how the distributing the reduction between the two reduction rings in a single switch impact performance. Since the setup available had 32 nodes per switch, 16 hosts *MPI_Allreduce()* runs were made varying the configuration from all 16 nodes on a single ring, to half and half. As expected, this showed no discernible impact on the MPI-level reduction latency and bandwidth.

Figure 5a shows the *MPI_Allreduce()* bandwidth as a function of message size with all the hosts connected to the same switch and a variable number of hosts. As this figure shows, the host count has a very small impact on the measured reduction bandwidth.

Figure 4b shows the *MPI_Allreduce()* bandwidth as a function of message size and the number of hosts per switch, for a 4 switch two-level fat-tree configuration. For this particular configuration the number of hosts has minimal impact on measured bandwidth up to about 4 MB message size, but with 16 hosts per switch we see a drop of about 7% in measured bandwidth. Host based measurements show a corresponding drop of about 12%.

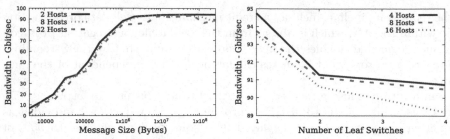

(a) Bandwidth (Gbit/sec) vs size (bytes). (b) Bandwidth (Gbit/sec) vs switch count.

**Fig. 5.** (a) Single switch MPI_Allreduce Streaming-aggregation reduction bandwidth (Gbit/sec) as a function of message size. (b) 1048576 byte message size MPI_Allreduce bandwidth (Gbit/sec) as a function number of hosts per switch, for a fixed number of total hosts. The number of switches varies from one to four.

Figure 5b showed the *MPI_Allreduce()* bandwidth for fixed total host count and an increasing number of leaf switches, decreasing the number of hosts per switch with increased switch count. Increasing the total number of hosts has only a small impact on overall bandwidth, with the largest impact being on the case where 16 hosts are in use dropping by about 4.8% going from one to four switches. The drop from two to four switches (both require using both levels of the two-level fat-tree) is only about 1.6%. The corresponding drops in performance for the host-base algorithm are 1.9% and 0.3%.

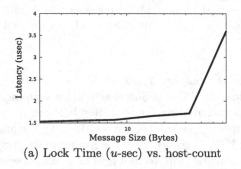

(a) Lock Time (*u*-sec) vs. host-count

**Fig. 6.** (a) Streaming-Aggregation tree lock time, as a function of host count. 2 to 32 nodes are attached to a single switch and 64 hosts are configured in a two level fat-tree.

Locking the tree for the aggregation operation can be done either for the duration of the life of the application, such as the lifetime of an MPI communicator, or for a specified number of reduction operations, thus allowing other reduction trees to use the resources. Figure 6a shows the latency of the reduction operation in the range of 2 to 64 hosts. The range of data points between 2 and 32 hosts was measured on the single switch Intel based system, and the 64-node data on the two level fat-tree configuration. The cost of the lock is indeed similar to that of the barrier operation, with a very small increase in latency for the fixed single-switch configuration and the expected increase in latency going from one to two levels in the reduction tree.

## 4.3  Application Benchmarks

The impact of the Streaming-Aggregation on the performance of two applications, DL-Poly and PyTorch is studied. These are described below.

**DL-Poly** [15] is a classical molecular dynamics code developed at Daresbury Laboratory. The bars in Fig. 7a show the total run-time of the Sodium Chloride melt with Ewald sum electrostatics and 27 K atoms (bench4) as a function of host count, with (orange bars) and without (blue bars) using the Streaming-Aggregation. The line plot represents the overall improvement in application run-time as a percent of total application run time. Measurements were taking using a host count varying between 2 and 24, with 32 processes per node. The amount of time spent in the large $MPI\_Allreduce()$ operations at 24 nodes and 32 ranks per node is 6.85 s out of a total run time of 45.02 s, or about 15%. The Streaming-Aggregation reduces this time to 4.73 s, and is used to reduce vectors of size 524288, 196608 and 98304 bytes. As the results indicate, using the Streaming-Aggregation capabilities to speedup the $MPI\_Allreduce()$ operations improved overall simulation time by as much as 4% at 22 nodes, and about 2.5% at 24 nodes. Reduction costs at these different sizes are similar, with most of the fluctuations in run-time coming from other parts of the code.

**PyTorch** [12] is a machine learning library used in computer vision and natural language processing. This was used to run the Transformer Translation model [16] MPLerf benchmark, with and without using the Streaming-Aggregation capabilities. The performance on a 4 host 8 GPU system, using one and two HDR100 interfaces is shown in Fig. 7b, with the data being reduced from the GPU buffers. The reduction capabilities are exposed through the NVIDIA Collective Communication Library (NCCL) [5] which also includes support for Mellanox's Streaming-Aggregation capabilities. As the figure shows, using the Streaming-Aggregation capabilities improves the benchmark performance relative to the default tree and ring reduction algorithms used by NCCL. The single HCA performance is improved by about 10% relative to the ring-based reduction algorithm, with the two-HCA performance improving by 3.7%. Incidentally, the GNMT MLPerf benchmark running on 24 DGX1V nodes and the VAE benchmark running on 32 DGX1V nodes, using 4 parallel HDR networks and enabling the Streaming-Aggregation improves performance by 18% in both cases, but analyzing these is beyond the scope of this paper. The vectors being reduced are long, as shown in Table 1. When NCCL's ring algorithm is used for the reduction 28% of total run time is spent in reduction, but when Mellanox SHARP is used this drops to 20% of total run time.

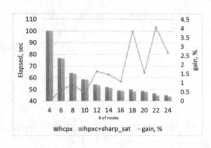 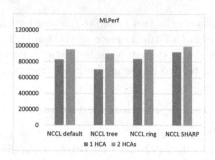

(a) DL-Poly Run-time (sec) vs. host-count          (b) ML Perf

**Fig. 7.** (a) DL-Poly run time (sec) as a function of host count, with 32 process per host using Streaming-Aggregation.Test case: Bench4 - Sodium Chloride, 27 K atoms. (b) MLPerf performance using PyTorch (Color figure online)

**Table 1.** MLPerf transformer translation model reduction message distribution. The data type is 16 bit floating point.

| # Calls | Message count | Message size (MByte) | # Calls | Message count | Message size (MByte) |
|---------|---------------|----------------------|---------|---------------|----------------------|
| 1 | 210808832 | 402 | 1100 | 46169088 | 88 |
| 2200 | 46171136 | 88 | 1100 | 72297472 | 137 |

As Mellanox SHARP Streaming-Aggregation performance optimization efforts continue, we expect to improve the performance of the aggregation operations. Improvement in application performance will depend on how this capability is used.

## 5   Summary

This paper describes the Mellanox SHARP Streaming-Aggregation capability introduced in Mellanox's HDR InfiniBand network hardware. It takes in vectors from different network end-points, reduces the data to produce a single output vector, which is then distributed to the specified nodes in the network. No software is used in the reduction path.

As the *MPI_Allreduce()* OSU benchmark results show, the efficiency of the data reduction and distribution is close to that of the point-to-point bandwidth, achieving good pipeline efficiency in reducing and forwarding data. On a 64-node HDR system using a PCIe Gen-3 bus to connect to the network a reduction efficiency of as high as 96% of ping-pong message efficiency for a 2 MByte message, and at 64 KB achieves about 80% efficiency. Peak reduction bandwidth is achieved with messages of size 8 MB. When the bandwidth limitation imposed by the PCI bus is removed, using a PCIe Gen-4 bus, the bandwidth reaches

59 Gbps ate 64 Kbyte, which is 3.5 times higher than with the host-based algorithm. With 67 GB message size it peaks at 190 Gbps, which is 95% of the network bandwidth and 4.45 times higher than with the host-based algorithm.

Comparing Mellanox SHARP Streaming-Aggregation bandwidth to that obtained using a host-based approach, a large increase in measured bandwidth using the new capabilities is observed. As the data from Fig. 3a shows, Streaming-Aggregation bandwidth is about a factor of two higher than the host-based reduction algorithm bandwidth at 4 KB message size, and close to a factor of five greater for messages of size 128 KB and above. Similarly, the Streaming-Aggregation reduction bandwidth is greater than the low-latency aggregation based reduction bandwidth, for all but the 4 KB message size.

For small message sizes, the latency of the low-latency aggregation based reductions is lower than the Streaming-Aggregation based algorithm, with both being lower than the host-based algorithm. For the 64 host configuration the cross-over point between the algorithms is between 4 and 8 KB, and when tree locking is necessary, this increases to about 16 KB. The cost of managing and pipelining multiple data segments with the Streaming-Aggregation is what makes the short message aggregation less efficient then when using low-latency aggregation. When more than two to three message segments are required using the low-latency aggregation protocol it is more efficient to use the Mellanox Streaming-Aggregation protocol.

As a basic capability, the addition of the Streaming-Aggregation functionality enables the asynchronous offloaded reduction capabilities to supersede the host-based algorithms. Also, using these capabilities with DL-Poly and PyTorch shows this to be a viable alternative to host-based reduction algorithms at the full application level, improving the application performance for the tests run by up to 7% and 10% for DL-Poly and PyTorch, respectively.

Finally, studying Streaming-Aggregation as a function of network configuration has shown that performance remains as the system size increases, albeit with some reduction in bandwidth. This is expected with a longer data path which increases the latency for the first MTU to reach the destination, thus reducing the measured bandwidth. Factors that are local to a single switch have a much smaller impact on performance relative to factors such as reduction tree depth and the width of the reduction tree. The distribution of hosts across the reduction rings in the switch had no discernible effect on the end-to-end reduction performance, while the number of hosts per switch was shown to have a small effect. The largest measured impact seems to be related to the reduction tree depth, with a smaller impact exerted by the number of switches used at a given tree depth. As larger switch configurations become available for testing, the impact of scale on overall measured bandwidth can continue to be studied. The large-radix reduction supports shallow reduction trees, with a three level tree able to support systems with over 10,000 nodes using 40 port switches as building blocks.

To summarize, the Streaming-Aggregation capability has been shown to significantly improve the distributed reduction performance of medium and large messages relative to both low-latency aggregation hardware Mellanox SHARP and host-based software reduction implementations. It provides reduction throughput similar to that of point-to-point traffic, and improves the performance of both synthetic and full applications.

# References

1. http://www.mpi-forum.org
2. http://www.openshmem.org
3. http://www.mellanox.com/page/products_dyn?product_family=189&mtag=hpc-x
4. http://mvapich.cse.ohio-state.edu/benchmarks/
5. https://github.com/NVIDIA/nccl
6. Adachi, T., et al.: The design of ultra scalable MPI collective communication on the K computer. Comput. Sci. Res. Dev. **28**, 147–155 (2006). https://doi.org/10.1007/s00450-012-0211-7
7. Elias, G., Levi, L., Romlet, E., Marelli, A.: Parallel computation network device. US Patent 16/357,356. Filed 19 March 2019
8. Gao, S., Schmidt, A.G., Sass, R.: Impact of reconfigurable hardware on accelerating MPI_Reduce. In: 2010 International Conference on Field-Programmable Technology, pp. 29–36 (2010)
9. Graham, R., et al.: Scalable hierarchical aggregation protocol (SHArP): a hardware architecture for efficient data reduction. In: 2016 First International Workshop on Communication Optimizations in HPC (COMHPC), COM-HPC 2016, pp. 1–10, November 2016
10. Graham, R.L., et al.: ConnectX-2 infiniband management queues: first investigation of the new support for network offloaded collective operations. In: Proceedings of the 2010 10th IEEE/ACM International Conference on Cluster, Cloud and Grid Computing, CCGRID 2010, pp. 53–62 (2010)
11. Kumar, S., Mamidala, A., Heidelberger, P., Chen, D., Faraj, D.: Optimization of MPI collective operations on the IBM blue Gene/Q supercomputer. Int. J. High Perform. Comput. Appl. **28**(4), 450–464 (2014)
12. Paszke, A., et. al.: PyTorch: an imperative style, high-performance deep learning library. In: Wallach, H., Larochelle, H., Beygelzimer, A., Alche-Buc, F., Fox, E., Garnett, R. (eds.) Advances in Neural Information Processing Systems 32, pp. 8024–8035. Curran Associates, Inc. (2019). http://papers.neurips.cc/paper/9015-pytorch-an-imperative-style-high-performance-deep-learning-library.pdf
13. Stern, J.A., Xiong, Q., Skjellum, A.: A novel approach to supporting communicators for in-switch processing of MPI collectives. In: Workshop on Exascale MPI (2019)
14. Thakur, R., Rabenseifner, R.: Optimization of collective communication operations in MPICH. Int. J. High Perform. Comput. Appl. **19**, 49–66 (2005)
15. Todorov, I., Smith, W., Trachenko, K., Dove, M.: J. Mater. Chem. **16**, 1911–1918 (2006)
16. Vaswani, A., et al.: Attention is all you need. CoRR abs/1706.03762 (2017). https://arxiv.org/abs/1706.03762

# Artificial Intelligence and Machine Learning

# Predicting Job Power Consumption Based on RJMS Submission Data in HPC Systems

Théo Saillant[1,2(✉)], Jean-Christophe Weill[1], and Mathilde Mougeot[2,3]

[1] CEA, DAM, DIF, 91297 Arpajon, France
[2] Université Paris-Saclay, ENS Paris-Saclay, CNRS, Centre Borelli, 94235 Cachan, France
theo.saillant@ens-paris-saclay.fr
[3] ENSIIE, 91000 Evry, France

**Abstract.** Power-aware scheduling is a promising solution to the resource usage monitoring of High-Performance Computing facility electrical power consumption. This kind of solution needs a reliable estimation of job power consumption to feed the Resources and Jobs Management System at submission time. Available data for inference is restricted in practice because unavailable or even untrustworthy. We propose in this work an instance-based model using only the submission logs and user provided job data. GID and the number of tasks per node appears to be good features for prediction of a job's average power consumption. Moreover, we extant this model to production context with online computation to make a practical global power prediction from job submission data using instances re-weighting. The performance of the online model are excellent on COBALT's data. With any doubt this model will be a good candidate for the achievement of consistent power-aware scheduling for other computing centers with similar informative inputs.

**Keywords:** RJMS · Job scheduling · Power consumption · Machine learning

## 1 Introduction

Power efficiency is a critical issue for the goal of ExaFLOP performance. It will be impossible to run applications at such a scale without a dedicated power plant if High-Performance Computing (HPC) systems are not more power-efficient [3]. Minimizing electricity consumption to reduce production costs and environmental issues is of ever increasing importance. Created in 2007, the Green500 ranks the 500 most energy-efficient computer systems to raise awareness other performance metrics.

© Springer Nature Switzerland AG 2020
P. Sadayappan et al. (Eds.): ISC High Performance 2020, LNCS 12151, pp. 63–82, 2020.
https://doi.org/10.1007/978-3-030-50743-5_4

## 1.1    Constraints for Job Scheduling

One potential direction to improve the power efficiency is to better understand user behaviors and to create incentives to reward the use of power-efficient applications using software. The Resource and Job Management System (RJMS) can be used in this case. If the RJMS is aware of the power consumption, an energy-budget scheduling policy [5] to avoid power peaks or to address the intermittent nature of renewable energies can be designed.

Nevertheless, power consumption is rarely known in advance, even by the user, so an alternative solution is to add power consumption forecasting facilities to the RJMS. Since the only job data available at the stage of submission is what the users provide to the RJMS on the resources their jobs need for allocation and running, one solution may be to use the RJMS submission data to predict the power consumption of the submitted jobs before scheduling, as already proposed by [2]. Many studies have been carried out on job power consumption estimations [17,18], however these have often made use of application type data. Application type data is not generally available due to confidentiality issues and can also be untrustworthy, because users may falsify data (e.g. by renaming the executable file) to take advantage of the scheduling policy, for power-aware scheduling.

A particularly useful functionality would be to use only the RJMS submissions data to predict the power consumption of a job. The power consumption of the whole computer center can then easily be monitored.

## 1.2    Related Work

The use of RJMS data in this type of problem has already been investigated; using application types [3] or symbol information [20] to make predictions. In these works, the data is not restricted to submission data.

Online model to forecast the elapsed time of the job using only the data given at submission and the current user's usage is proposed by [7] so that the RJMS can use backfilling more efficiently [13]. This estimation is designed for backfilling and may not be good for power-aware scheduling. An estimate for memory usage and run time using only submission data has been proposed [19]. Although these papers did not estimate power consumption, the used inputs suggest that user information is needed to provide a practical estimate when application types are not available.

Except in a few cases, the instantaneous power consumption of a user and the whole computer center can be predicted with workload information as the number of nodes, components used by the user's jobs and runtime [16]. In our case, the time evolution of power consumption within a job is not available in the log files. In a further study [17], submission data to predict job duration, and not power consumption, are used with the executable name as input data.

## 1.3    Contributions

The main contributions presented in this paper are first an instance-based model to predict average power consumption of a job per node using only the data submitted to the SLURM RJMS. An online model is then proposed, easy to use and to maintain in production while a weighted model is introduced to predict the global power consumption of all jobs.

Moreover this work shows how it is possible to build an efficient model to forecast the power consumption based on the exploitation of a historical log database from the SLURM RJMS data collected from the industrial computer center COBALT that is only composed of user inputs of jobs and associated energy consumption measures.

Submitted data appears to be sufficient to provide a good estimate of job power consumption for the RJMS. This can be used in power-aware scheduling with our generic model because job submission is redundant. This model may be used in other industrial HPC facilities for power-aware scheduling because it uses only the data that is necessary for scheduling and because it is easy to maintain, but further tests must be made using data from other computing centers.

The paper is organized as follows: we first extract and pre-process log data from SLURM RJMS [21] and we introduce an instance-based model to process the submitted data as categorical inputs. The model is then adapted to remove biases and to handle streamed data. The final section presents the results.

## 2 Extracted Data and Preprocessing

### 2.1 The COBALT Supercomputer and The SLURM RJMS

The data used for this application are collected from the COBALT[1] supercomputer, more precisely, from its main partition which is composed of 1422 nodes ATOS-BULL with Intel Xeon E5-2680V4 2.4 GHZ processors that have 2 CPUs per node and 14 cores per CPU. The Thermal Design Power of each CPU is equal to 120 W.

The energy accounting and control mechanisms are implemented within the open-source SLURM [21] Resource and Job Management System (RJMS) [8]. The data are recorded from accounting per node based on the IMPI measuring interfaces [8]. IMPI collects data on the consumed power from all the components (e.g. CPU, memory, I/O, ...) of the node, temporally aggregates it and returns the consumed energy during an elapsed time to SLURM. As it is impossible to differentiate between jobs running on the same node, so it was decided to exclude jobs that did not have exclusivity on a node.

The collected dataset is the resulting logs of SLURM submission data of 12476 jobs run on the supercomputer over 3 months at the beginning of 2017 and their respective consumed energy. The jobs that do not have exclusive usage of a node or for which the consumed energy is null are filtered out.

### 2.2 From Raw Data to Relevant Features

There are two potential outputs to predict: the elapsed time and the total consumed energy which are both available once the job is finished. For various

---

[1] https://www.top500.org/system/178806.

reasons (e.g. failure of jobs or sensors), null value can be sometimes returned for energy consumption. Only non-zero values of energy consumption are here considered.

Three groups of information provided to SLURM may be used to predict the output (a summary is provided in Table 1)

1. **Information on the user:**

   **User Identifier (or UID)** is a number identifying the user that submits the job. 200 separate UIDs were observed over the 3 month period.

   **Group Identifier (or GID)** characterizes the users that belong to the same company or community sharing the same group. This number allows the inclusion of an *a priori* on what type of job the user runs. 30 unique GIDs were observed over the selected period.

2. **Type of resources required by the job:**

   **Quality of Service (QoS)** sets the maximum timelimit, and discriminates between test and production jobs.

   **Timelimit** can be set by the user to benefit from backfilling. This is a continuous system variable, but only 520 distinct values were used over the 3 month period (430 by the same user), showing that users often reuse the same value. Hence, we chose to discretize this variable by taking only the number of hours that are needed (c.f. Table 1).

3. **Computing power quantities required by a job:**

   **Number of tasks in parallel** is defined by SLURM with option -n (e.g. the number of MPI processes if MPI is used)

   **Number of cores per task** is defined by SLURM with option -c and is used for threading models or if an MPI job needs more memory than is available per core. This information is combined with the number of tasks to form the number of nodes required and is not stored.

   **Number of nodes:** SLURM combines the number of tasks and the number of cores per task to define the number of nodes needed but the user may specifying this directly.

SLURM logs may also be useful for prediction:

**Date of submission** of the job. This cannot be used directly as input since no future job will have the same date. However, some features can be computed based on the time of day the submission was made (c.f. Table 1).

**Final number of nodes** that the SLURM allocated for the job. This is the same as the number of nodes required in our data.

**Start date** of the job can differ from the submission date if the job has to wait to be run, but it is set by SLURM and not the user, so it is not used. The same holds for the **end date**.

**Executable name** could be used in some cases to identify the type of application the job is running. However, it can be irrelevant ('python' or 'a.out' are extreme examples) and users may take advantage to manipulate SLURM if it is used to define scheduling policy. Hence, it was decided to ignore this in our model.

Table 1 summarizes the model's inputs and the potential outputs of interest. Although the number of cores per task is unavailable as it is not memorized by SLURM, it is an interesting value. The average number of tasks per node (tasks/node in Table 1) can be computed as an equivalent quantity. Redundant features, such as the required number of nodes that is given by the SLURM RJMS but is almost always equal to the final number of nodes, are removed.

**Table 1.** Synthesis of the relevant handcrafted input features and outputs of SLURM for the studied model.

| Feature | Meaning | Comment |
|---|---|---|
| | **Potential raw inputs** | Information before allocation |
| UID | User IDentifier | Anonymized and unique identifier |
| GID | Group IDentifier | Project membership identifier |
| QoS | Quality of Service | Indicates if job is in test/production |
| #nodes | Number of nodes allocated | Redundant with requested number |
| #tasks | Number of tasks in parallel | E.g. number of MPI processes |
| submit | Date of submission by the user | Cannot be used directly |
| timelim | Time limit before a job is killed | Cannot be used directly |
| | **Computed features** | Knowledge incorporation |
| tasks/node | Number of tasks per node | Manually created features |
| submit_h | Hour of submission in the day | Relevant information from submit |
| timelim_h | Limit duration in hours | Relevant information from timelim |
| | **Outputs** | Given after the job is finished |
| elapsed | Time elapsed | True duration of the job (wall time) |
| energy | Total consumed energy by the job | Aggregate temporally and by nodes |
| | **Target** | Model output |
| meanpow | Average power consumption per node | Computed as Eq. (1) |

## 2.3  Target and Problem Formalization

The elapsed time and the power consumption are the two unknown values needed before the job runs to improve the management of power consumption by the RJMS.

The elapsed time inference which has been a subject of interest in several papers [7,13,17] improves the backfilling of the scheduling policy so that resource usage is maximal at any time.

The energy usage value returned by SLURM is the total consumed energy used by all the nodes for the entire job duration. The energy consumption increases by definition if the elapsed time increases or if the number of nodes that a job uses increases. The total energy grows approximately linearly with the number of nodes and elapsed time. However, this assumption has some limitations, as it implicitly means that the power consumption remains constant when the job is running and each node uses the same amount of resources over time. Although this assumption is strong, it is not far from reality for the majority of jobs, as shown by [1], and it can be removed only with time-evolving data inside jobs that is not available.

If the number of nodes and elapsed time are not provided, the meaningful consumption statistic able to be predicted given the information collected by SLURM is the average power per node. The average power per node, denoted by meanpow, is defined and computed as:

$$\text{meanpow} = \frac{\text{energy}}{\text{elapsed} \times \#\text{nodes}} \tag{1}$$

Once a model returns the average power per node, the job's power consumption can be computed by multiplying it by the number of nodes and used in a monitoring policy as the estimation $\tilde{P}_{comp}$ for budget control [5] or powercapping. If the elapsed time is given (by other models like [7]), the consumed energy can also be predicted under the linearity assumption.

Most of the previously proposed methods use standard machine learning models from the SciKit-Learn python library [14], such as decision tree, random forest for [3] or SVR for [16]. Those models provide interesting results, but all of these rely on several parameters known to be difficult to tune and they assume regularity in the input space that may not exist in our case. Our first motivation and our contribution are to propose an alternative model that requires fewer assumptions and that works at the same time efficiently.

## 3    Instance Based Regression Model

### 3.1    Inputs as Categorical Data

Using all the available data, Fig. 1 shows four empirical distributions of the approximated average power per node for jobs with the same number of cores per task. We observe that the distributions are well separated with respect to the power. It shows that the number of cores per task is already an efficient criterion to estimate average power per node for certain jobs. This is particularly the case for the most power consuming jobs (reaching 300 W/nodes), which most likely use one core for each task, and those using 7 cores per task, which mainly use half of the full power. This is in fact expected as the number of cores assigned to the same tasks generally depends on the threading model of the application, which implies a different power consumption. The Gaussian like distributions contain interesting and useful information. Hence we infer that a low complexity model may be useful for modeling. Combined with other inputs, such as UIDs, we expect a good discrimination of power usage for any submitted job can be made based on a few internal parameters.

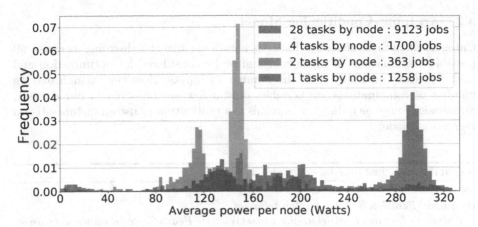

**Fig. 1.** Distributions of average power per node. Each histogram is computed for jobs using the same number of tasks by node. Full MPI jobs use 28 tasks by node.

In our application, the input features are either categorical or numerical, for example:

- The metadata related to the chosen QoS, the user and group identifiers (UID, GID) are categorical and thus their values (numerical or not) cannot be ordered.
- Other features are numerical and describe two types of information; discrete (the number of nodes or tasks) or continuous related to date or time (submit, start, end date of the job, duration and timelimit).

However, the discrete numerical features (number of nodes, tasks, or their ratio) may also be considered as categorical variables. For example, an application's performance depends on the number of cores and is sometimes optimal when the number of cores verifies arithmetic properties, e.g. LULESH 2.0 should be used with a number of MPI processes that is a perfect cube [11]. An application running with $27 = 3^3$ cores is likely to be different to a plausible OpenMP application using 28 cores (28 is the number of cores on a COBALT's node). Full MPI jobs use one task for each core while full OpenMP jobs use one task for the whole node. It shows that the threading model imposes the number of tasks per node.

It then seems more relevant to consider the number of nodes or tasks as a class of job or a category. Only 55 unique values were observed for requested nodes in the data when the range of possibilities is theoretically ≃1000, which confirms the discrete and categorical behavior of the number of nodes or tasks. Although time related data is continuous by nature, we choose to discretize it at an hour level to have categories.

In the end, we transform all available inputs as categorical. We then propose a data-model to predict the average power consumption per node (meanpow) of any job, using only categorical inputs.

## 3.2   An Input-Conditioning Model

Categorical data is generally hard to handle in machine learning because all possible combinations of input values must be considered for optimization and this grows exponentially with the number of inputs. However, though a large number of combinations are possible, only a few are observed in our dataset. Submissions may be redundant and this is a motivation to use an instance-based regression model.

---

**Algorithm 1.** instance-based model Training

---
instance-based model Training

**Require:** $FeatSelected, Estimator, trainset$
$\quad Values \leftarrow Unique(FeatSelected(trainset))$    ▷ $FeatSelected$'s values in $trainset$
$\quad$ **for all** $val \in Values$ **do**      ▷ Group by jobs' value of $FeatSelected$
$\qquad \mathcal{J}_{val} \leftarrow \emptyset$
$\qquad$ **for** $j \in trainset$ **do**     ▷ $\mathcal{J}_{val}$ = Jobs where $FeatSelected$ match $val$
$\qquad\quad$ **if** $FeatSelected(\{j\}) = val$ **then**
$\qquad\qquad \mathcal{J}_{val} = \mathcal{J}_{val} \cup \{j\}$
$\qquad\quad$ **end if**
$\qquad$ **end for**
$\qquad OutputDict(val) \leftarrow Estimator(\mathcal{J}_{val})$   ▷ Estimate output value for $val$ input
$\quad$ **end for**
$\quad$ **return** $OutputDict$

---

---

**Algorithm 2.** instance-based model Prediction

---
instance-based model Prediction

**Require:** $FeatSelected, OutputDict, job$
$\quad$ **return** $OutputDict(FeatSelected(\{job\}))$   ▷ $OutputDict$ for $FeatSelected$ of $job$

---

An instance-based model computes a prediction by searching comparable instances in a historical training set. The simplest case of instance-based learning is Rote-Learning [15] as the nearest neighbor approach with a trivial distance [4]. The prediction for a given job is an estimator computed on the subset of the training instances that share some inputs as already proposed in [17].

Let $\mathcal{J}$ denotes our job training dataset. Each job $j \in \mathcal{J}$ is a combination of observed values for the features described in Table 1. Rote-Learning is a supervised problem for data as $(X_j, Y_j)_{j \in \mathcal{J}}$. $X_j$ is the vector containing selected input features (i.e. a subset of the submission data as seen by SLURM) of job $j$ used to predict $Y_j$. $X_j$ is referred as the "job profile". $Y_j$ is the target output of job $j$ computed with any available features. In our case, it is the average power per node called meanpow as defined by (1). This is a regression task of $Y_j$ given $X_j$ since $Y_j$ is real valued.

Common regression models make assumptions regarding the behavior of $Y$ given $X$ through a linear hypothesis or a kernel method like SVR in SciKit-Learn [14] and assume implicitly that $X$ is either a continuous or a binary variable. In our case $X$ is discrete and these models can be used consistently with "dummy indicators" for each possible modality of a categorical variable. However, the input space dimension grows at the rate of the number of unique values for categories, which makes these models impractical.

On the contrary, the Rote-Learning regression model computes an estimator of the target for the jobs in the training set that have the same job profile as described in the pseudo-code 1 for training and 2 for prediction. We introduce two functions to tune how the predictions are computed. $FeatSelected()$ is a function that extracts job profiles $(X_j)_{j \in \mathcal{J}}$ that are the values from a fixed subset of inputs from job set $\mathcal{J}$. $Estimator()$ is a function that takes a list of jobs with the same profile $X_j$ and computes a chosen estimator as prediction. After training, we return $OutputDict()$ as a mapping or dictionary that returns the prediction of any job $j$ having the profile $X_j$ extracted with $FeatSelected()$. When the job has a profile $X_j$ that is not found in the training set, a prediction for a subset of the profile $X_j$ can be made by another Rote-Learner to handle this case or a default value can be returned.

It is well-known that the Rote-Learner is the best unbiased estimator as discussed by [12]. This means that if no prior knowledge is incorporated into another model, the Rote-learner has a smaller loss. Despite this strength, the Rote-learner is rarely used in machine learning because of memory issues and for statistical reasons: the number of samples for each combination of inputs must be sufficiently large and this is rarely the case.

In our case, the number of unique observed inputs is limited in our dataset because the number of samples for a combination of inputs is large enough, hence there are no memory issues. Training time is then short because it is basically the time taken to compute the $Estimator()$ multiplied by the number of unique job profiles in the training set.

In the sequel, we use the arithmetic mean of average power per node as $Estimator()$. This minimizes the Root Mean Square Error (RMSE) for average power per node, which is then the loss function used to evaluate the possible models. In our framework, $Estimator()$ is defined as:

$$OutputDict(val) = Estimator(\mathcal{J}_{val}) = \frac{1}{\text{card } \mathcal{J}_{val}} \sum_{j \in \mathcal{J}_{val}} \frac{\text{energy}_j}{\text{elapsed}_j \times \#\text{nodes}_j}$$

with $\mathcal{J}_{val} = \{j \in \mathcal{J} | FeatSelected(\{j\}) = X_j = val\}$ for the job profile $val$.

## 3.3  Variable Selection

The number of internal parameters that the Rote-Learner has to learn during training is the number of unique job profiles in the training dataset. For a fixed training dataset, this number depends of the choice of subset of inputs that defines the job profile. If this number increases, the model complexity also increases. The model complexity is a statistical concept that quantifies the ability of the model to fit complex phenomena, even in the case of simple noise. But a low complexity model is able to generalize for new data. For this reason, complexity and then the job profile $FeatSelected()$ definition must be carefully chosen.

In our application there are less than 10 features, so the number of possible input feature combinations needed to define $FeatSelected()$ is quite low, and we can exhaustively test all the features subsets one by one and retain only the best one. In this work, a cross-validation procedure is used to find the best inputs: we split our data into two parts, the training set is the first two months of data and the test set is the last month.

This procedure allows the identification of SLURM information pieces which are meaningful. However the computations can be time consuming. Once we empirically find the best inputs, we use only these for the following models as job profiles without repeating the process of finding the most relevant inputs. We discuss the performance results in the experimental part of Sect. 5.

At its best, the resulting model predicts the average power consumption per node of any job. Nevertheless, this objective is not monitoring the global power consumption. Certain jobs matter more than others and they are presented one by one in practice with no training time, which motivates the improvements of the following section.

## 4   Global Consumption Practical Estimation

### 4.1   Weighted Estimator for Global Power Estimation

In practice, jobs that run for the longest on many nodes contribute the most to the global power consumption of a computer center. Moreover, we observe a correlation between the duration of the jobs and the average power per node. The scatter plot in Fig. 2 shows that jobs running for less than one minute consumed less power than the others. A possible reason is that the jobs are first setting up parallelism and reading data from disks. This phase is not generally compressible and does not consume significant amounts of power. If a job is short (test, debug job or crashed), perhaps less than one minute, this phase becomes non-negligible and may then lower the average power consumption, which explains the observed bias.

However, each job has the same contribution to the mean estimate used in the previous section. Short jobs disproportionately lower the mean estimate that is defined in Sect. 3.2, despite their limited contribution to the global consumption. This is why jobs should be weighted by their total consumed node-time (number of nodes multiplied by elapsed time) when computing the mean for global consumption estimation. One method is to sum the total consumed energies then divide by the sum of their total node-time instead of dividing consumed energies individually then taking the mean. More formally, $Estimator()$ must be chosen as:

$$Estimator(\mathcal{J}) = \frac{\sum_{j \in \mathcal{J}} \text{energy}_j}{\sum_{j \in \mathcal{J}} \text{elapsed}_j \times \#\text{nodes}_j} \qquad (2)$$

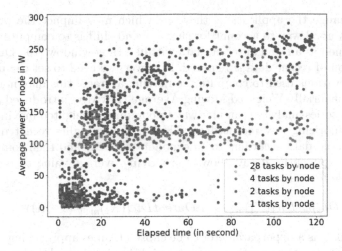

**Fig. 2.** Scatter plot of jobs less than two minutes long, short jobs consume less power.

## 4.2    Online Computations

Previous section has presented a model which computes offline the estimation of the arithmetic mean: training and prediction are two distinct and successive steps. Once training is done, the model is fixed and used to predict the power consumption of the job.

In the case of job scheduling, data is presented to SLURM as a stream of logs containing information on submitted jobs and the previous two step approach has a major flaw. A model used for prediction does not continue to learn: for a job's profile that was not present in the training data, it can only return a default value at best every time it appears. The whole model can be regularly retrained but it is then necessary to memorize all the recent data seen by SLURM in prevision of the next training round. This approach has other drawbacks: if the rounds are too frequent, a training set may be too small and if they are too rare, a lot of data has to be memorized and the prediction may be worse before the rounds.

Thankfully, the arithmetic mean used as $Estimator()$ can be straightforward to compute online and lots of approaches exist in the literature [10].

If $OutputDict(X_i)_m$ is the mean estimator at the $(m + 1)^{th}$ occurrence of a job with inputs $X_i$ and average power per node $Y_i$, it can be updated independently once the job is finished as $OutputDict(X_i)_{m+1} = \frac{m}{m+1}OutputDict(X_i)_m + \frac{1}{m+1}Y_i$. The counter $m$ and current value $OutputDict(X_i)_m$ only should be maintained to compute the next value when a job ends. This is called a cumulative moving average or CUMSUM [10]. This is referred to as an online model because the model is continuously training itself, and a training round is not required.

However, this CUMSUM model gives equal weight to old and recent observations of a job profile $X_i$, and thus the expected job average power per node is expected to always be the same. This is not always true: a group of users may suddenly change the applications they use which may impact the power consumption. A good way to account for such a trend-shift is to compute a moving average defined as a mean of recent data within a time-window [10]. Once again, memorization of recent data is required. However, we need to set the number of recent observations used to compute the moving average, this may not be easy.

An Exponentially Weighted Moving Average (EWMA) introduced in [9] and [10] for time series analysis is an nice way to compute a weighted moving average without memorizing any recent data. This method weights recent data more heavily than old data according to an exponential decay and then computes the mean. The exponential decay allows the moving average value to be updated with a simple formula:

$$OutputDict(X_i)_{m+1} = \alpha OutputDict(X_i)_m + (1 - \alpha)Y_i \tag{3}$$

where $\alpha \in [0, 1]$ is a hyperparameter to be chosen (values approaching 0 indicate lesser influence from the past). A custom weighting is required to remove underestimation of the computed estimator for global power consumption estimation.

### 4.3   Exponential Smoothing for Weighted and Streamed Update

As stated before, EWMA has the big advantage of memoryless updating but it must be weighted in the update formula (3) for global power consumption estimation. Previous online estimators were initially designed and used for time series analysis [9,10]. To weight them consistently, as in Sect. 4.1 and keep them online, we formally define their associated time series and modify it slightly.

At any time, the value of $OutputDict(X_i)$ is the last estimation of meanpow for a job with the profile $X_i$ since a job with profile $X_i$ ended. The value of the estimate $OutputDict(X_i)$ changes only when a job with profile $X_i$ ends. As it is an evolving mean, it behaves like a trend estimation of the series of meanpow of jobs with profile $X_i$ ordered by end date. Each job contributes in the same way to the future estimation. The contribution to the estimation of a job with profile $X_i$ depends only on which rank it ends. The job's contribution to the online estimation does not depend on its node-time contrary to Sect. 4.1. An example of the series and its estimation by EMWA are given in Fig. 3. We observe that the EWMA is lowered by the low node-time jobs with low meanpow that have the same weight the highest node-time jobs because the series is agnostic to this quantity.

We propose a novel way to account for the needed weighting of the job without changing much our online estimation. The idea is to generalize and compute trend estimate on another series that is irregular. It is the same previous series of the average power per node of jobs with given profile $X_i$ ordered by end date but the intervals between two successive finished jobs is the node-time of the first job, as if a job must wait the node-time of the last before starting. The resulting estimator is a continuous smoothing of this irregular time series parametrized by a node-time constant and can be used as before for online estimation but jobs with lowest node-time will not change the trend estimation as

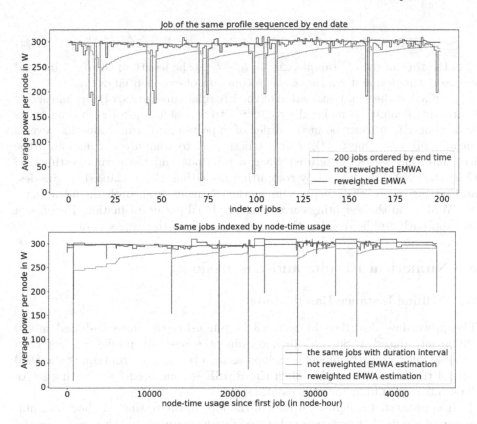

**Fig. 3. Up:** Series of the average power per node of 200 jobs with the same profile and its estimation by classical and reweight EWMA. **Bottom:** The associated irregular series used to weight the jobs according to node-time and the same EMWA estimations series. EWMA hyperparameters are $\alpha = \exp(\log(0.5)/20)$ (a job contribution is halved after the 20 next ended jobs) in regular case and $\tau = 4000$ node-hour in irregular case.

much as the ones with highest node-time. The adaptation of CUMSUM replaces $m$ by the sum of the previous jobs node-time with inputs $X_i$, and in the moving average case the recent job are weighted by their node-time for example. The irregular series deduced from the previous example are given in Fig. 3. The short jobs have almost no influence on the current re-weighted estimate even if their meanpow value are extreme. On the contrary, it is clear that the classical EWMA strongly underestimate the irregular series meanpow because of them.

We propose to apply this adaptation to EWMA so that our estimation is memoryless and weighted correctly. We compute directly the weighted estimator without computing the irregular series by slightly modifying the previous estimator formula (3) to take into account of the node-time of the current ending job. EWMA is generalized as exponential smoothing and computed for irregular time series in [22] or [6], the update formula uses variable $\alpha$ to account for the irregular time interval thanks to the memoryless property of exponential:

$$\text{EMWA}(Y)_{t_n} = e^{-\Delta t_n/\tau}\text{EWMA}(Y)_{t_{n-1}} + (1 - e^{-\Delta t_n/\tau})Y_{n-1} \tag{4}$$

$t_n$ is the time of the $n^{th}$ sample, $\Delta t_n = t_n - t_{n-1}$ the length of the $n - 1$ interval between samples, and $\tau$ a chosen time constant of exponential decay.

Applied to the trend estimation of the irregular time series, (4) formula shows that $\alpha$ in (3) must be replaced by $e^{-\Delta t_i/\tau}$ to weight the job $i$ according to its node-time $\Delta t_i$. $\tau$ must be in the order of expected node-time value for several meaningful jobs. Due to (4), it is not necessary to compute and maintain the irregular time series, (4) is used when a job ends and the current estimation $OutputDict(X_i)$ is updated by computing node-time $\Delta t_i = \text{elapsed}_i \times \#\text{nodes}_i$ and setting $\alpha = e^{-\Delta t_i/\tau}$ in (3). Our method benefits from both the advantages of EWMA and the weighting correction for global power estimation. Benefits of our approach are discussed in the last experiment of the next section.

## 5    Numerical Results and Discussion

### 5.1    Offline Instance-Based Model

The proceeding described in Sect. 3.3 is run using the instance-based model offline introduced in Sect. 3.2 to determine the best job profile $X_i$. For each possible job profile, the model is trained using a training set containing the 8000 jobs of the first two months. Then the RMSE is computed for a testing set of 4000 future jobs from the next month.

It appears that a significant part of the jobs in the testing set show a combination of inputs that were never observed during training. In this case the model does not return an output value if the job profile is not seen previously in the training set. For a fair evaluation of any choice of job profile, we need to avoid handling the case where a pretrained model does not return an output because the profile is not known by the model. For that, we first extract a small test subset from the initial testing set composed of 1022 jobs for which their profiles are present in the training set. This is so that any model returns an output value no matter what job profile it uses.

We illustrate the bias-variance trade-off by showing the best choice of job profile that has a given number length with the lowest score (here the RMSE) and the number of unique job profile values observed in training set is shown as "diversity". Diversity is a simple way to approximate the complexity of the model to highlight bias-variance trade-off. We present the results for the small testing set in the first column of Table 2. In the special case where the job profile has zero inputs, the model always returns the mean of the average power per node of all jobs in the training set.

The best prediction requires features that identify the user, because users tend to submit the same jobs. UID is first chosen but the number of tasks per node improves power estimation and is more general when combined with GID instead of UID. Indeed, diversity is lower when the model uses GID instead of UID, and GID still indicates well enough that the jobs may be similar as

**Table 2.** Variable selection by cross-validation and results. The score is the RMSE (lower is better). Diversity is the number of memorized instances after training.

| | Results on small test | | | Results on large test | |
|---|---|---|---|---|---|
| # | Best combination | Score | Diversity | Best combination | Score |
| 0 | (returns the mean) | 78.04 | 1 | (returns the mean) | 89.87 |
| 1 | UID | 46.17 | ≃150 | UID | 44.85 |
| 2 | GID, task/node | 43.98 | 48 | GID, task/node | **43.31** |
| 3 | GID, task/node, timelim_h | **43.63** | 217 | GID, task/node, QoS | 43.83 |
| 4 | Add QoS | 43.78 | 232 | Add timelim_h | 44.16 |
| 5 | GID, QoS, #nodes, #tasks | 45.09 | 245 | Add UID (all features) | 45.49 |
| 6 | Add timelim_h | 45.53 | 475 | (no more features) | – |
| 7 | Add UID (All but submit_h) | 47.55 | 578 | (no more features) | – |
| 8 | All features | 52.84 | 1981 | (no more features) | – |

part of the same project given they have the same number of tasks per node. Surprisingly, adding the hour part of timelimit improves the results although it drastically increases the diversity. However, adding more inputs to the job profiles worsens the results, and the effect of over-fitting is stronger as diversity increases. In particular, the number of nodes and tasks by themselves seem to be not relevant for prediction of the power consumption as these parameters are always selected together. QoS does not seem to be informative on power usage. The hour of submission is the last selected feature showing that the type of job is the same no matter what the hour in the day is, which can be explained by auto-submissions.

The number of nodes, tasks and the submitted hour can have a large range of unique values that substantially increase the diversity which means they tend to produce over-fitting. In our experiment, this is observed when the result does not improve if these values are accounted for. But the reduced testing set is constructed only with jobs that have a combination of all these inputs values in the training set. To get more robust results about other choices of input features we reduce the space of possible job profiles which increases the number of jobs in the testing set with a profile in the training set. As these parameters seem not to be relevant for prediction, they are removed, and a larger testing set of 2216 jobs is constructed with the combination of inputs without these omitted values. The results are given in Table 2 in the second column.

The RMSEs are of the same order of magnitude as they do not depend on the size of the dataset. The same behavior in variable selection is observed, except that timelimit is no longer relevant, even selected after the QoS (and we can only choose up to 5 features as the others are removed). This difference may be explained by the strong selection of which jobs are included in the small testing set slightly favoring over-fitting.

From these observations we conclude that the GID and the ratio of number of tasks and nodes are the best choice of features to predict the average power consumption per node with any model for data on COBALT. The resulting model of this choice of features will be called IBmodel for Instance-Based model in the next sections.

## 5.2   Comparison with the Offline IBmodel

We compare the IBmodel with models currently in use and proposed by [3] and [19]. We focus on models based on trees, Decision Tree Regression (DTR) and Random Forest (RF), that are well-known to handle better inputs from categorical features. We also add the Gradient Boosted Regression Trees (GBRT). For these last two models, we increment the number of tree estimators and retain only the best results. We also compare the IBmodel with results from Support Vector Regression (SVR), as used by [17], choosing the best SVR parameters by manual tuning. The SciKit-Learn library [14] is used to run and train the models.

**Table 3.** Comparison with other models. Score is RMSE (lower is better). **Score (all):** result with all the input features for the large test set. **Score (selected):** results with input features being GID and task/node. As RF training is not deterministic, it is run 100 times, then the mean score and standard deviation are given.

| SciKit models | Tested parameters | Score (all) | Score (selected) |
|---|---|---|---|
| DTR | Pure leaves, MSE criterion | 48.80 | 43.31 |
| RF | Pure leaves, 0 to 50 trees | 45.79 (0.15) | **43.14 (0.07)** |
| GBRT | max-depth 5, 0 to 300 trees | 44.40 | **43.10** |
| SVR | rbf kernel, C = 1000, $\gamma = 0.01$ | 53.58 | 45.79 |
| **IBmodel** | $X_i = (\text{GID}_i, \text{task/node}_i)$ | **43.31** | 43.31 |

At this stage, the IBmodel is not designed to return an output in case of unknown job profile. So our tests are run on the large testing set of 2216 jobs previously selected and we drop the same features (number of nodes, tasks and the submitted hour) to avoid unknown job profile during testing. In a first test run, all the features used to obtain the second columns of Table 2 are the model inputs. In a second test run, the chosen features are only GIDs and task/node, which are the best choices for average power per node prediction found with the IBmodel (hence it keeps same score). We point out to the reader that this favours competing models, especially the ones based on trees for which only the best is retained.

Table 3 presents the results with a range of parameters. It is observed that the IBmodel outperforms all other models when the input space is large. This underlines that there may be no variable selection in the other models. However,

RF and GBRT outperform when we explicitly force the selection of the relevant inputs we have computed previously for all the models. DTR also provides the same results as the IBmodel as it becomes similar to an instance-based model when the dimension is low and the decision tree's leaves may be pure (they can have only one sample in training).

The interpretability of the instance-based models, in particular the selection of explicit features, is a strong advantage as this improves also the other models. Although RF and GBRT are the best performers once the most effective inputs for prediction are known, we do not think they are the most suitable for our application. First, the IBmodel can be updated online whereas RF and GBRT must be completely and regularly retrained in order to handle a job's stream, second, the IBmodel can weight the observations of average power per node of jobs with minimal modification, and finally, it is not easy to explain how RF and GBRT built their predictions.

## 5.3   Online IBmodel

For practical monitoring of global power consumption through the RJMS it is necessary to provide online and instance weighted models, as already presented in Sect. 4. To demonstrate this claim we compare predictions of future global power consumption available at the submission date of a job by the IBmodel with and without these two improvements. We first construct a reference target with an oracle estimation over time. At any time $t$, the oracle value is the sum over all running jobs at time $t$ of the jobs' average power consumption. The oracle value is not the true global power consumption as a job's consumption can vary when running, but it is the best approximation following the hypothesis made in [5] and Sect. 2.3 (consumption is constant over the job's entire duration).

With the data from the same period of two months used in the previous section, the IBmodel is trained with only improved weighting (2), only online updating (3) with $\alpha = \exp(\log(0.5)/20)$ (job's contribution is divided by 2 after the 20 next ended jobs with the same profile) and also both (4) with $\tau = 4000$ node hours, then the results are compared to the oracle value of the test set. To compute the estimated value of global power consumption available to SLURM, the list of jobs is converted to a list of events ordered by their time $t$ of three types:

- **Submission event:** The job $j$ is submitted at time $t$, its average power consumption per node is estimated with the models and buffered for a future event. If models cannot return an estimation (unknown input values), we return the default value 292.89 Watts per node as it is the global average power per node of all the jobs we have.
- **Starting event:** The job $j$ starts at time $t$, and its average power consumption per node that is estimated at submission is multiplied by the number of nodes to get its power consumption, which is added to the current global power consumption (same for oracle but with true average power per node).

– **Ending event:** Job $j$ ends at time $t$, then we update the online models and we remove the job's power consumption estimation from the current global power consumption estimation (same with oracle for the latter).

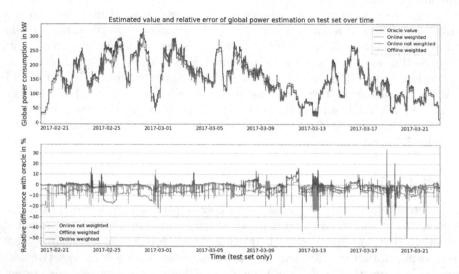

**Fig. 4. Up:** Evolution of global electrical consumption in Watts over the test period for the offline and online, weighted or not, models. The black curve is the oracle estimation i.e. the evolution's estimate if meanpow of each job is known in advance. **Bottom:** Difference between values predicted by the three models and the oracle

The upper plot of Fig. 4 shows the global power estimation results over time, and the lower plot shows the relative error of the different models compared to the oracle. The online IBmodel (3) without weight adaptation of the jobs underestimates the global consumption given by the oracle by 5% to 10%. The errors of the weighted offline IBmodel (2) peak many times. This suggests that some jobs have profiles that the model did not see enough during training and that they impact the estimation randomly in high proportions. The model needs to be retrained using more recent historical data to improve its estimation, although the spikes will reappear as soon as training stops.

On the contrary, the online and weighted model (4) gives a much more consistent estimation, as the distribution of the relative differences with the oracle are more symmetrical with respect to 0 due to weighting adaptation. The online estimation seems to have stabilized the errors. The peaks in the error patterns may be due to bad default values for new unknown inputs, but as the model is still learning, it only sets a meaningful value for those inputs once a job has ended. Thus, the error remains low even after some time. The absolute deviation of the predictions compared to the oracle is 99% of the time under 12.7 kW, with a mean of 2.40 kW. The relative deviation for 99% of the time is under 10.4%

with a mean of 1.68%. The relative errors approach the measurement precision of the IMPI interface that was used to collect the data.

# 6   Conclusion

This work shows that it is possible to compute an accurate estimation of the average consumption per node of the submitted jobs using the redundancy of the information provided to SLURM by users. Predictions are computed by an instance-based model which brings several advantages. It is interpretable and shows that jobs on the COBALT computing center have a power consumption that is well predicted by the GID and the number of tasks per node. We show that instance re-weighting and online computations implemented in the IBmodel are necessary to provide a prediction of the global power consumption at submission time that is not underestimated and to stabilize the relative error. The proposed model has a relative error that is of the order of the relative measurement error of the data, which indicates that the IBmodel's performance is already satisfactory.

The next step of this work is to evaluate the capability of the instances model for other computing centers with different behavior of users. This work should be extended by studying the instantaneous power consumption of jobs with time evolving data. Accounting for instantaneous power consumption will allow regulation of each job with a power cap and will enable jobs to be redistributed with more precision.

# References

1. Borghesi, A., Bartolini, A., Lombardi, M., Milano, M., Benini, L.: Predictive modeling for job power consumption in HPC systems. In: Kunkel, J.M., Balaji, P., Dongarra, J. (eds.) ISC High Performance 2016. LNCS, vol. 9697, pp. 181–199. Springer, Cham (2016). https://doi.org/10.1007/978-3-319-41321-1_10
2. Borghesi, A., Bartolini, A., Lombardi, M., Milano, M., Benini, L.: Scheduling-based power capping in high performance computing systems. Sustain. Comput.: Inform. Syst. **19**, 1–13 (2018)
3. Bugbee, B., Phillips, C., Egan, H., Elmore, R., Gruchalla, K., Purkayastha, A.: Prediction and characterization of application power use in a high-performance computing environment. Stat. Anal. Data Min.: ASA Data Sci. J. **10**(3), 155–165 (2017)
4. Cover, T., Hart, P.: Nearest neighbor pattern classification. IEEE Trans. Inf. Theory **13**(1), 21–27 (1967)
5. Dutot, P.F., Georgiou, Y., Glesser, D., Lefevre, L., Poquet, M., Rais, I.: Towards energy budget control in HPC. In: Proceedings of the 17th IEEE/ACM International Symposium on Cluster, Cloud and Grid Computing. IEEE Press (2017)
6. Eckner, A.: Algorithms for unevenly-spaced time series: moving averages and other rolling operators (2012)
7. Gaussier, E., Glesser, D., Reis, V., Trystram, D.: Improving backfilling by using machine learning to predict running times. In: SC 2015 Proceedings, pp. 1–10. IEEE (2015)

8. Georgiou, Y., Cadeau, T., Glesser, D., Auble, D., Jette, M., Hautreux, M.: Energy accounting and control with SLURM resource and job management system. In: Chatterjee, M., Cao, J., Kothapalli, K., Rajsbaum, S. (eds.) ICDCN 2014. LNCS, vol. 8314, pp. 96–118. Springer, Heidelberg (2014). https://doi.org/10.1007/978-3-642-45249-9_7

9. Holt, C.C.: Forecasting seasonals and trends by exponentially weighted moving averages. Int. J. Forecast. **20**(1), 5–10 (2004)

10. Hunter, J.S.: The exponentially weighted moving average. J. Qual. Technol. **18**(4), 203–210 (1986)

11. Karlin, I., Keasler, J., Neely, J.: Lulesh 2.0 updates and changes. Technical report, Lawrence Livermore National Lab. (LLNL), Livermore, CA, USA (2013)

12. Mitchell, T.M.: The need for biases in learning generalizations (1980)

13. Mu'alem, A.W., Feitelson, D.G.: Utilization, predictability, workloads, and user runtime estimates in scheduling the IBM SP2 with backfilling. IEEE Trans. Parallel Distrib. Syst. **12**(6), 529–543 (2001)

14. Pedregosa, F., et al.: Scikit-learn: machine learning in Python. J. Mach. Learn. Res. **12**(Oct), 2825–2830 (2011)

15. Russell, S.J., Norvig, P.: Artificial Intelligence - A Modern Approach, 3 Internat. edn. Pearson Education, London (2010)

16. Sîrbu, A., Babaoglu, O.: Power consumption modeling and prediction in a hybrid CPU-GPU-MIC supercomputer. In: Dutot, P.-F., Trystram, D. (eds.) Euro-Par 2016. LNCS, vol. 9833, pp. 117–130. Springer, Cham (2016). https://doi.org/10.1007/978-3-319-43659-3_9

17. Sîrbu, A., Babaoglu, O.: A data-driven approach to modeling power consumption for a hybrid supercomputer. Concurr. Comput.: Pract. Exp. **30**(9), e4410 (2018)

18. Storlie, C., Sexton, J., Pakin, S., Lang, M., Reich, B., Rust, W.: Modeling and predicting power consumption of high performance computing jobs. arXiv preprint arXiv:1412.5247 (2014)

19. Tanash, M., Dunn, B., Andresen, D., Hsu, W., Yang, H., Okanlawon, A.: Improving HPC system performance by predicting job resources via supervised machine learning. In: Proceedings of the PEARC, p. 69. ACM (2019)

20. Yamamoto, K., Tsujita, Y., Uno, A.: Classifying jobs and predicting applications in HPC systems. In: Yokota, R., Weiland, M., Keyes, D., Trinitis, C. (eds.) ISC High Performance 2018. LNCS, vol. 10876, pp. 81–99. Springer, Cham (2018). https://doi.org/10.1007/978-3-319-92040-5_5

21. Yoo, A.B., Jette, M.A., Grondona, M.: SLURM: simple Linux utility for resource management. In: Feitelson, D., Rudolph, L., Schwiegelshohn, U. (eds.) JSSPP 2003. LNCS, vol. 2862, pp. 44–60. Springer, Heidelberg (2003). https://doi.org/10.1007/10968987_3

22. Zumbach, G., Müller, U.: Operators on inhomogeneous time series. Int. J. Theor. Appl. Financ. **4**(01), 147–177 (2001)

# HyPar-Flow: Exploiting MPI and Keras for Scalable Hybrid-Parallel DNN Training with TensorFlow

Ammar Ahmad Awan$^{(\boxtimes)}$, Arpan Jain, Quentin Anthony, Hari Subramoni, and Dhabaleswar K. Panda

The Ohio State University, Columbus, OH 43210, USA
{awan.10,jain.575,anthony.301,subramoni.1,panda.2}@osu.edu

**Abstract.** To reduce the training time of large-scale Deep Neural Networks (DNNs), Deep Learning (DL) scientists have started to explore parallelization strategies like data-parallelism, model-parallelism, and hybrid-parallelism. While data-parallelism has been extensively studied and developed, several problems exist in realizing model-parallelism and hybrid-parallelism efficiently. Four major problems we focus on are: 1) defining a notion of a distributed model across processes, 2) implementing forward/back-propagation across process boundaries that requires explicit communication, 3) obtaining parallel speedup on an inherently sequential task, and 4) achieving scalability without losing out on a model's accuracy. To address these problems, we create **HyPar-Flow**—a model-size and model-type agnostic, scalable, practical, and user-transparent system for hybrid-parallel training by exploiting MPI, Keras, and TensorFlow. HyPar-Flow provides a single API that can be used to perform data, model, and hybrid parallel training of any Keras model at scale. We create an internal distributed representation of the user-provided Keras model, utilize TF's Eager execution features for distributed forward/back-propagation across processes, exploit pipelining to improve performance and leverage efficient MPI primitives for scalable communication. Between model partitions, we use *send* and *recv* to exchange layer-data/partial-errors while *allreduce* is used to accumulate/average gradients across model replicas. Beyond the design and implementation of HyPar-Flow, we also provide comprehensive correctness and performance results on three state-of-the-art HPC systems including TACC *Frontera* (#5 on Top500.org). For ResNet-1001, an ultra-deep model, HyPar-Flow provides: 1) Up to 1.6× speedup over Horovod-based data-parallel training, 2) 110× speedup over single-node on 128 Stampede2 nodes, and 3) 481× speedup over single-node on 512 Frontera nodes.

**Keywords:** Hybrid parallelism · Model parallelism · Keras · TensorFlow · MPI · Eager Execution · Deep Learning · DNN training

This research is supported in part by NSF grants #1931537, #1450440, #1664137, #1818253, and XRAC grant #NCR-130002.

© Springer Nature Switzerland AG 2020
P. Sadayappan et al. (Eds.): ISC High Performance 2020, LNCS 12151, pp. 83–103, 2020.
https://doi.org/10.1007/978-3-030-50743-5_5

# 1  Introduction and Motivation

Recent advances in Machine/Deep Learning (ML/DL) have triggered key success stories in many application domains like Computer Vision, Speech Comprehension and Recognition, and Natural Language Processing. Large-scale Deep Neural Networks (DNNs) are at the core of these state-of-the-art AI technologies and have been the primary drivers of this success. However, training DNNs is a compute-intensive task that can take weeks or months to achieve state-of-the-art prediction capabilities (*accuracy*). These requirements have led researchers to resort to a simple but powerful approach called *data-parallelism* to achieve shorter training times. Various research studies [5,10] have addressed performance improvements for data-parallel training. As a result, production-grade ML/DL software like TensorFlow and PyTorch also provide robust support for data-parallelism.

While data-parallel training offers good performance for models that can completely reside in the memory of a CPU/GPU, it *can not* be used for models larger than the memory available. Larger and deeper models are being built to increase the accuracy of models even further [1,12]. Figure 1 highlights how *memory consumption* due to larger images and DNN depth limits the compute platforms that can be used for training; e.g. ResNet-1k [12] with the smallest possible batch-size of one (a single $224 \times 224$ image) needs 16.8 GB memory and thus *cannot* be trained on a 16 GB Pascal GPU. Similarly, ResNet-1k on image size $720 \times 720$ needs 153 GB of memory, which makes it out-of-core for most platforms except CPU systems that have 192 GB memory. These *out-of-core* models have triggered the *need for model/hybrid parallelism*.

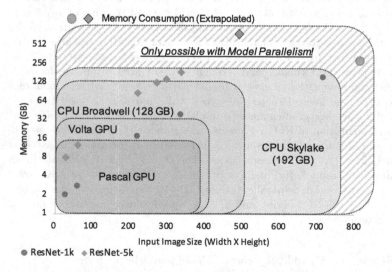

**Fig. 1.** The need for model/hybrid-parallelism

However, realizing *model-parallelism*—splitting the model (DNN) into multiple partitions—is non-trivial and requires the knowledge of best practices in ML/DL as well as expertise in High Performance Computing (HPC). We note that model-parallelism and layer-parallelism can be considered equivalent terms when the smallest partition of a model is a layer [7,15]. Little exists in the literature about model-parallelism for state-of-the-art DNNs like ResNet(s) on HPC systems. Combining data and model parallelism, also called hybrid-parallelism has received even less attention. Realizing model-parallelism and hybrid-parallelism efficiently is challenging because of *four major problems*: 1) defining a distributed model is necessary but difficult because it requires knowledge of the model as well as of the underlying communication library and the distributed hardware, 2) implementing distributed forward/back-propagation is needed because partitions of the model now reside in different memory spaces and will need explicit communication, 3) obtaining parallel speedup on an inherently sequential task; forward pass followed by a backward pass, and 4) achieving scalability without losing out on a model's accuracy.

**Proposed Approach:** To address these four problems, we propose HyPar-Flow: a scalable, practical, and user-transparent system for hybrid-parallel training on HPC systems. We offer a simple interface that does not require any model-definition changes and/or manual partitioning of the model. Users provide four inputs: 1) A model defined using the Keras API, 2) Number of model partitions, 3) Number of model replicas, and 4) Strategy (data, model, or hybrid). Unlike existing systems, we design and implement all the cumbersome tasks like splitting the model into partitions, replicating it across processes, pipelining over batch partitions, and realizing communication inside HyPar-Flow. This enables the users to focus on the science of the model instead of system-level problems like the creation of model partitions and replicas, placement of partitions and replicas on cores and nodes, and performing communication between them. HyPar-Flow's simplicity from a user's standpoint and its complexity (hidden from the user) from our implementation's standpoint is shown in Fig. 2.

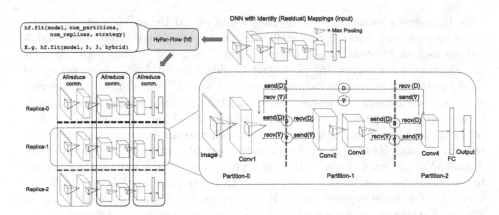

**Fig. 2.** Proposed user-transparent hybrid-parallel training approach (HyPar-Flow)

## 1.1  Contributions

From a research and novelty standpoint, our proposed solution is both model-size as well as model-type agnostic. It is also different compared to all existing systems because we focus on high-level and abstract APIs like Keras that are used in practice instead of low-level tensors and matrices, which would be challenging to use for defining state-of-the-art models with hundreds of layers. HyPar-Flow's solution to communication is also novel because it is the first system to exploit standard Message Passing Interface (MPI) primitives for inter-partition and inter-replica communication instead of reinventing single-use libraries. To the best of our knowledge, there are very few studies that focus on hybrid-parallel training of large DNNs; especially using TensorFlow and Keras in a user-transparent manner for HPC environments where MPI is a dominant programming model. We make the following key contributions in this paper:

- Analyze various model-definition APIs and DL frameworks and highlight why *Keras* APIs and custom-built training loops using TensorFlow Eager's *GradientTape* are well suited for realizing user-transparent hybrid-parallelism.
- Propose, design, and implement HyPar-Flow to enable parallel training of any Keras model (with consecutive as well as non-consecutive layer connections [7]) on multiple processes under any parallelization <strategy>, i.e. data, model, and hybrid.
- Thoroughly verify the correctness of the HyPar-Flow framework by training the models to state-of-the-art published accuracy.
- Evaluate HyPar-Flow's performance using a variety of models including VGG-16, ResNet-110, ResNet-1001, and AmoebaNet on three HPC systems
- Report up to 3.1× speedup over sequential training for ResNet-110 and up to 1.6× speedup over data-parallel training for ResNet-1001 on a single node.
- Report 110× speedup over single-node on 128 Stampede2 nodes and 481× speedup over single-node on 512 Frontera nodes for ResNet-1001.

## 2  The Design Space for Parallel Training Frameworks

Alex Krizhevsky introduced model-parallelism on GPUs in [15] using a single-tower design that used data-parallelism in convolutional layers but model-paralle-lism in fully-connected layers. Simulation-based results about various parallelization strategies are presented in [9]. The LBANN team presented model-parallel solutions including support for spatial convolutions split across nodes in [8]. However, model-parallelism in LBANN is not yet publicly available so we cannot compare its performance with HyPar-Flow. MXNet-MP [2] also offers model-parallelism support but no working examples are available at the time of writing. GPipe [13] enables the training of extremely large models like AmoebaNet [19] on Google TPUs and accelerators. GPipe is publicly available but we found no examples and/or documentation to train models like ResNet(s) with model-parallel support on an HPC system. FlexFlow [14] searches parallelization strategies using simulation algorithms and highlights different dimensions of parallelism in DNNs. FlexFlow uses Legion [6] for communication within the node and GASNet across nodes. Unfortunately, FlexFlow only works on GPUs so we cannot offer a direct comparison. Also, we were unable to configure FlexFlow for multiple nodes. Mesh-TensorFlow (MTF) [20] is a language for distributed DL with an emphasis on tensors distributed across a processor mesh. MTF only works with the older TF APIs (sessions, graphs, etc.). Furthermore, the level at which MTF distributes work is much lower compared to HyPar-Flow, i.e., tensors vs. layers. Users of MTF need to re-write their entire model to be compatible with MTF APIs. Unlike MTF, HyPar-Flow works on the existing models without requiring any code/model changes. We summarize these related studies on data, model, and hybrid-parallelism and their associated features in Table 1. Out-of-core methods like [4,17] take a different approach to deal with large models, which is not directly comparable to model/hybrid-parallelism. Several data-parallelism only studies have been published that offer speedup over sequential training [3,5,10,18,21]. However, all of these are only limited to models that can fit in the main memory of the GPU/CPU.

**Table 1.** Features offered by HyPar-flow compared to existing frameworks

| Existing and proposed studies | Features and supported platforms | | | | | |
|---|---|---|---|---|---|---|
| | User transparent | Speedup over data-parallel | Communication runtime Runtime e/library | Publicly available MP support | Compatible w/Keras | Compatible w/TF Eager |
| AlexNet [15,16] | ✗ | ✔ | CUDA | ✗ | ✗ | ✗ |
| MXNet-MP [2] | ✗ | Unknown | MPI | ✔ | ✔ | ✗ |
| LBANN [8] | ✔ | ✔ | MPI/Aluminum | ✗ | ✗ | ✗ |
| Mesh TensorFlow [20] | ✗ | ✔ | MPI | ✔ | ✗ | ✗ |
| Gpipe [13] | ✗ | ✗ | gRPC/TF | ✔ | ✗ | Unknown |
| PipeDream [11] | ✗ | ✔ | ZeroMQ | Unknown | ✗ | ✗ |
| FlexFlow [14] | ✔ | ✔ | Legion/GASNet | ✔ | ✗ | ✗ |
| **Proposed (HyPar-Flow)** | ✔ | ✔ | MPI | Planned | ✔ | ✔ |

# 3   Background

We provide the necessary background in this section.

**DNN Training:** A DNN consists of different types of *layers* such as convolutions (*conv*), fully-connected or dense (*FC*), pooling, etc. DNNs are usually trained using a labeled dataset. A full pass over this dataset is called an *epoch* of training. Training itself is an iterative process and each iteration happens in two broad phases: 1) Forward pass over all the layers and 2) Back-propagation of loss (or error) in the reverse order. The end goal of DNN training is to obtain a model that has good prediction capabilities (*accuracy*). To reach the desired/target *accuracy* in the fastest possible time, the training process itself needs to be efficient. In this context, the total training time is a product of two metrics:

1) the number of epochs required to reach the target accuracy and 2) the time required for one epoch of training.

**Data-Parallelism:** In data-parallel training, the complete DNN is replicated across all processes, but the training dataset is partitioned across the processes. Since the model replicas on each of the processes train on different partitions of data, the weights (or parameters) learned are different on each process and thus need to be synchronized among replicas. In most cases, this is done by averaging the *gradients* from all processes. This synchronization is performed by using a collective communication primitive like allreduce or by using parameter servers. The synchronization of weights is done at the end of every batch. This is referred to as *synchronous parallel* in this paper.

**Model and Hybrid-Parallelism:** Data-parallelism works for models that can fit completely inside the memory of a single GPU/CPU. But as model sizes have grown, model designers have pursued aggressive strategies to make them fit inside a GPU's memory, which is a precious resource even on the latest Volta GPU (32 GB). This problem is less pronounced for CPU-based training as the amount of CPU memory is significantly higher (192 GB) on the latest generation CPUs. Nevertheless, some models can not be trained without splitting the model into partitions; Hence, model-parallelism is a necessity, which also allows the designers to come up with new models without being restricted to any memory limits. The entire model is partitioned and each process is responsible only for part (e.g. a layer or some layers) of the DNN. Model-parallelism can be combined with data-parallelism as well, which we refer to as hybrid-parallelism.

## 4   Challenges in Designing Model and Hybrid-Parallelism

We expand on *four problems* discussed earlier in Sect. 1 and elaborate specific challenges that need to be addressed for designing a scalable and user-transparent system like HyPar-Flow.

*Challenge-1: Model-Definition APIs and Framework-Specific Features*
To develop a practical system like HyPar-Flow, it is essential that we thoroughly investigate APIs and features of DL frameworks. In this context, the design analysis of execution models like Eager Execution vs. Graph (or Lazy) Execution is fundamental. Similarly, analysis of model definition APIs like TensorFlow Estimators compared to Keras is needed because these will influence the design choices for developing systems like HyPar-Flow. Furthermore, the granularity of interfaces needs to be explored. For instance, using tensors to define a model is very complex compared to using a high-level model API like Keras and ONNX that follow the layer abstraction. Finally, we need to investigate the performance behavior of these interfaces and frameworks. Specific to HyPar-Flow, the main requirement from an API's perspective is to investigate a mechanism that allows us to perform user-transparent model partitioning. Unlike other APIs, Keras seems to provide us this capability via the *tf.keras.Model* interface.

*Challenge-2: Communication Between Partitions and Replicas*
Data-parallelism is easy to implement as no modification is required to the forward pass or the back-propagation of loss (error) in the backward pass. However, for model-parallelism, we need to investigate methods and framework-specific functionalities that enable us to implement the forward and backward pass in a distributed fashion. To realize these, explicit communication is needed between model partitions. For hybrid-parallelism, even deeper investigation is required because communication between model replicas and model partitions needs to be well-coordinated and possibly overlapped. In essence, we need to design a distributed system, which embeds communication primitives like *send*, *recv*, and *allreduce* for exchanging partial error terms, gradients, and/or activations during the forward and backward passes. An additional challenge is to deal with newer DNNs like ResNet(s) [12] as they have evolved from a linear representation to a more complex graph with several types of skip connections (shortcuts) like identity connections, convolution connections, etc. For skip connections, maintaining dependencies for layers as well as for model-partitions is also required to ensure deadlock-free communication across processes.

*Challenge-3: Applying HPC Techniques to Improve Performance*
Even though model-parallelism and hybrid-parallelism look very promising, it is unclear if they can offer performance comparable to data-parallelism. To achieve performance, we need to investigate if applying widely-used and important HPC techniques like 1) efficient placement of processes on CPU cores, 2) pipelining via batch splitting, and 3) overlap of computation and communication can be exploited for improving performance of model-parallel and hybrid-parallel training. Naive model-parallelism will certainly suffer from under-utilization of resources due to stalls caused by the sequential nature of computation in the forward and backward passes.

## 5   HyPar-Flow: Proposed Architecture and Designs

We propose HyPar-Flow as an abstraction between the high-level ML/DL frameworks like TensorFlow and low-level communication runtimes like MPI as shown in Fig. 3(a). The HyPar-Flow middleware is directly usable by ML/DL applications and no changes are needed to the code or the DL framework. The four major internal components of HyPar-Flow, shown in Fig. 3(b), are 1) Model Generator, 2) Trainer, 3) Communication Engine (CE), and 4) Load Balancer. The subsections that follow provide details of design schemes and strategies for HyPar-Flow and challenges (**C1–C3**) addressed by each scheme.

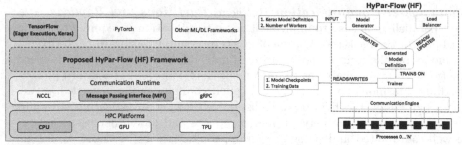

(a) Overview of the Execution Stack          (b) Major Components of HyPar-Flow

**Fig. 3.** HyPar-Flow: a middleware for hybrid-parallel training

## 5.1 Designing Distributed Model Representation (Address C1)

The *Model Generator* component is responsible for creating an internal representation of a DNN (e.g. a Keras model) suitable for distributed training (Fig. 2). In the standard single-process (sequential) case, all trainable variables (or weights) of a model exist in the address space of a single process, so calling *tape.gradients()* on a *tf.GradientTape* object to get gradients will suffice. However, this is not possible for model-parallel training as trainable variables (weights) are distributed among model-partitions. To deal with this, we first create a local model object on all processes using the *tf.keras.model* API. Next, we identify the layers in the model object that are local to the process. Finally, we create dependency lists that allow us to maintain layer and rank dependencies for each of the local model's layers. These three components define our internal distributed representation of the model. This information is vital for realizing distributed back-propagation (discussed next) as well as for other HyPar-Flow components like the *Trainer* and the *Communication Engine*.

## 5.2 Implementing Distributed Back-Propagation (Address C1,C2)

Having a distributed model representation is crucial. However, it is only the first step. The biggest challenge for HyPar-Flow and its likes are: "How to train a model that is distributed across process boundaries?". We deal with this challenge inside the *Trainer* component. First, we analyze how training is performed on a standard (non-distributed) Keras model. Broadly, there are two ways to do so: 1) *model.fit(..)* and 2) *model.train_on_batch(..)*. Second, we explore how we can design an API that is very similar to the standard case. To this end, we expose a single *hf.fit(..)* interface that takes parallelization strategy as an argument. The value of the *strategy* argument can be model, data, or hybrid. Third, we design a custom training loop for distributed back-propagation for the model/hybrid parallel case. For data-parallel, it is not needed because the model is replicated on all processes instead of being distributed across processes.

We show a very simple DNN in Fig. 4 to explain back-propagation and highlight what needs to be done for realizing a distributed version. In addition to

Fig. 4, we use Eqs. 1–7 to provide a more detailed explanation. There are three key data elements in DNN Training: 1) The input $X$, 2) The predicted output $Y'$, and 3) The actual output (or label) $Y$. The intermediate output from the hidden layer is denoted as $V$. The difference between $Y$ and $Y'$ is called error or loss labeled as $L$ (Eq. 2).

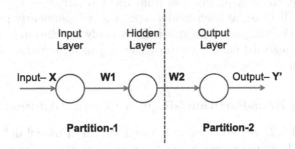

**Fig. 4.** A neural network with a single hidden layer

$$Y = ActualOutput, Y' = PredictedOutput \tag{1}$$

$$L(Loss) = loss\_function(Y, Y') \tag{2}$$

$$V(HiddenLayer) = W_1(Weight - on - hidden - layer) * X(Input) \tag{3}$$

$$Y'(PredictedOutput) = W_2(Weight - on - output - layer) * V \tag{4}$$

$$D2 = \frac{\partial L}{\partial W_2} = \frac{\partial L}{\partial Y'} * \frac{\partial Y'}{\partial W_2} \tag{5}$$

$$D1 = \frac{\partial L}{\partial W_1} = partial\_error * \frac{\partial V}{\partial W_1} \tag{6}$$

$$partial\_error = \frac{\partial L}{\partial Y'} * \frac{\partial Y'}{\partial V} \tag{7}$$

To realize distributed back-propagation, we need 1) partial derivative (D1) of Loss $L$ with respect to the weight $W1$, and 2) partial derivative (D2) of Loss $L$ with respect to the weight $W2$. The challenge for multi-process case is that the term called "partial error" shown in Eqs. 6 and 7 can only be calculated on *Partition-2* (Fig. 4) as $Y'$ only exists there. To calculate D1, *Partition-1* needs this "partial error" term in addition to D1. Because we rely on accessing gradients using the DL framework's implementation, this scenario poses a fundamental problem. TensorFlow, the candidate framework for this work, does not provide a way to calculate gradients that are not part of a layer. To implement this functionality, we introduce the notion of *grad layer* in HyPar-Flow, which acts as a pseudo-layer inserted before the actual layer on each model-partition. We note that TensorFlow's *GradientTape* cannot be directly used for this case.

*Grad layers* ensure that we can call *tape.gradients()* on this *grad layer* to calculate the partial errors during back-propagation. Specifically, a *grad layer* is required for each *recv* operation so that partial error can be calculated for each preceding partition's input. A call to tape.gradients() will return a list that contains gradients as well as partial errors. The list is then used to update the model by calling *optimizer.apply_gradients()*.

We note that there is no need to implement distributed back-propagation for the data-parallel case as each model-replica is independently performing the Forward and Backward pass. The gradients are only synchronized (averaged) at the end of the Backward pass (back-propagation) using *allreduce* to update the model weights in a single step.

### 5.3   Realizing Inter-Partition/-Replica Comm. (Address C2,C3)

In Sects. 5.1 and 5.2, we discussed how the distributed model definition is generated and how back-propagation can be implemented for a model that is distributed across processes. However, *Trainer* and *Model Generator* only provide an infrastructure for distributed training. The actual communication of various types of data is realized in HyPar-Flow's *Communication Engine (CE)*. The CE is a light-weight abstraction for internal usage and it provides four simple APIs: 1) send, 2) recv, 3) broadcast and 4) allreduce.

**HyPar-Flow CE Basic Design:** For pure data-parallelism, we only need to use allreduce. However, for model-parallelism, we also need to use point-to-point communication between model-partitions. In the forward pass, the send/recv combination is used to propagate *partial predictions* from each partition to the next partition starting at *Layer 1*. On the other hand, send/recv is used to back-propagate the *loss* and *partial-errors* from one partition to the other starting at *Layer N*. Finally, for hybrid-parallelism, we need to introduce allreduce to accumulate (average) the gradients across model replicas. We note that this is different from the usage of allreduce in pure data-parallelism because in this case, the model itself is distributed across different partitions so allreduce cannot be called directly on all processes. One option is to perform another p2p communication between model replicas for gradient exchange. The other option is to exploit the concept of MPI communicators. We choose the latter one because of its simplicity as well as the fact the MPI vendors have spent considerable efforts to optimize the allreduce collective for a long time. To realize this, we consider the same model-partition for all model-replicas to form the *Allreduce communicator*. Because we only need to accumulate the gradients local to a partition across all replicas, allreduce called on this communicator will suffice. Please refer back to Fig. 2 (Sect. 1) for a graphical illustration of this scheme.

**HyPar-Flow CE Advanced Design:** The basic CE design described above works but does not offer good performance. To push the envelope of performance further, we investigate two HPC optimizations: 1) we explore if the overlap of computation and communication can be exploited for all three parallelization strategies and 2) we investigate if pipelining can help overcome some of the limitations that arise due to the sequential nature of the forward/backward passes. Finally, we also handle some advanced cases for models with non-consecutive layer connections (e.g. ResNet(s)), which can lead to deadlocks.

*Exploiting Overlap of Computation and Communication:* To achieve near-linear speedups for data-parallelism, the overlap of computation (forward/ backward) and communication (allreduce) has proven to be an excellent choice. Horovod, a popular data-parallelism middleware, provides this support so we simply use it inside HyPar-Flow for pure data-parallelism. However, for hybrid-parallelism, we design a different scheme. We create one MPI communicator per model partition whereas the size of each communicator will be equal to the number of model-replicas. This design allows us to overlap the allreduce operation with the computation of other partitions on the same node. An example scenario clarifies this further: if we split the model across 48 partitions, then we will use 48 allreduce operations (one for each model-partition) to get optimal performance. This design allows us to overlap the allreduce operation with the computation of other partitions on the same node.

*Exploiting Pipeline Stages within Each Minibatch:* Because DNN training is inherently sequential, i.e., the computation of each layer is dependent on the completion of the previous layer. This is true for the forward pass, as well as for the backward pass. To overcome this performance limitation, we exploit a standard technique called pipelining. The observation is that DNN training is done on batches (or mini-batches) of data. This offers an opportunity for pipelining as a training step on samples within the batch is parallelizable. Theoretically, the number of pipeline stages can be varied from 1 all the way to batch size. This requires tuning or a heuristic and will vary according to the model and the underlying system. Based on hundreds of experiments we performed for HyPar-Flow, we derive a simple heuristic: use the largest possible number for pipeline stages and decrease it by a factor of two. In most cases, we observed that $num\_pipeline\_stages = batch\_size$ provides the best performance.

*Special Handling for Models with Skip Connections:* Figure 5 shows a non-consecutive model with skip connections that requires communication 1) between adjacent model-partitions for boundary layers and 2) non-adjacent model-partitions for the skip connections. To handle communication dependencies among layers for each model-partition, we create two lists: 1) Forward list and 2) Backward list. Each list is a list of lists to store dependencies between layers as shown in Fig. 5. "F" corresponds to the index of the layer to which the current layer is sending its data and "B" corresponds to the index of the layer from which the current layer is receiving data. An arbitrary sequence of sending and receiving messages may lead to a deadlock. For instance, if *Partition-1* sends the partial predictions to *Partition-3* when *Partition-3* is waiting for predictions from *Partition-2*, a deadlock will occur as *Partition-2* is itself blocked (waiting for results from *Partition-1*). To deal with this, we sort the message sequence according to the ranks so that the partition sends the first message to the partition which has the next layer.

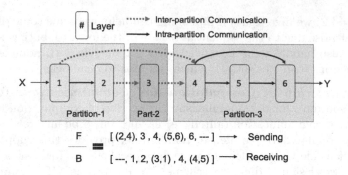

**Fig. 5.** Avoiding deadlocks for models with non-consecutive connections

## 5.4   Load Balancer

The models we used did not show any major load imbalance but we plan to design this component in the future to address emerging models from other application areas that require load balancing capabilities from HyPar-Flow.

# 6   Performance Characterization and Correctness Testing

We have used three HPC systems to evaluate the performance and test the correctness of HyPar-Flow: 1) **Frontera** at Texas Advanced Computing Center (TACC), 2) **Stampede2** (Skylake partition) at TACC, and 3) **Epyc**: A local system with dual-socket AMD EPYC 7551 32-core processors.

**Inter-connect:** Frontera nodes are connected using Mellanox InfiniBand HDR-100 HCAs whereas Stampede2 nodes are connected using Intel Omni-Path HFIs.

**DL Framework:** All experiments have been performed using TensorFlow v1.13.

**MPI Library:** MVAPICH2 2.3.2 was used on Frontera, Intel MPI 2018 was used on Stampede2, and MVAPICH2 2.3.1 was used on Epyc.

**Model Definitions:** We use and modify model definitions for VGG and ResNet(s) presented in Keras Applications/Examples [1].

**Note about GPUs:** The design schemes proposed for HyPar-Flow are architecture-agnostic and can work on CPUs and/or GPUs. However, in this paper, we focus only on designs and scale-up/scale-out performance of many-core CPU clusters. We plan to perform in-depth GPU-based HyPar-Flow studies in the future.

*We now present correctness related experiments followed by a comprehensive performance evaluation section.*

## 6.1    Verifying the Correctness of HyPar-Flow

Because we propose and design HyPar-Flow as a new system, it is important to provide confidence to the users that HyPar-Flow not only offers excellent performance but also trains the model correctly. To this end, we present the correctness results based on two types of accuracy-related metrics: 1) Train Accuracy (train_acc)- Percentage of correct predictions for the training data during the training process and 2) Test Accuracy (test_acc)- Percentage of correct predictions for the testing data on the trained model. Both metrics are covered for small scale training using **VGG-16** on the CIFAR-10 dataset. We train VGG-16 for 10 epochs using 8 model-partitions on two Stampede2 nodes with a batch size of 128 and 16 pipeline stages as shown in Fig. 6(a). Next, we show test accuracy for **ResNet-110-v1** in Fig. 6(b) and **ResNet-1001-v2** in Fig. 6(c). The learning rate (LR) schedule was used from Keras Applications [1] for both ResNet(s) and was kept similar for sequential as well as parallel training variants. Training for ResNet-110 and ResNet-1001 was performed for 150 and 50 epochs, respectively. The following variants have been compared:

1) **SEQ (GT)** - Sequential using tf.GradientTape (GT).
2) **SEQ (MF)** - Sequential using model.fit (MF).
3) **SEQ (MF-E)** - Sequential using model.fit (MF) and (E)ager Execution.
4) **HF-MP (2)/(56)** - HyPar-Flow model-parallel with 2/56 model-partitions.

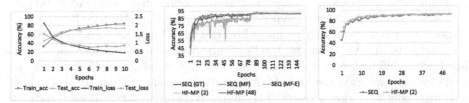

(a) VGG-16 Training (all metrics) for 10 epochs with BS=128 and LR=0.0002    (b) ResNet-110-v1 Test Accuracy for 150 Epochs with BS=32    (c) ResNet-1001-v2 Test Accuracy for 50 epochs with BS=32

**Fig. 6.** Testing the correctness of HyPar-Flow using different models

**Discussion:** Clearly, model-parallel training with HyPar-Flow is meeting the accuracy of the sequential model for 150 and 50 epochs of training for ResNet-110 and ResNet-1001, respectively. We note that training is a stochastic process and there are variations in earlier epochs whether we use the sequential version or the model-parallel version. However, the significance is of the end result, which in this case peaks at 92.5% for all the configurations presented. We ran multiple training jobs to ensure that the trends presented are reproducible.

## 6.2  Experimental Setup for Performance Evaluation

We use the term "process" to refer to a single *MPI Process* in this section. The actual mapping of the process to the compute units (or cores) varies according to the parallelization strategy being used. *Images/second* (or Img/sec) is the *metric* we are using for performance evaluation of different types of training experiments. Number of images processed by the DNN during training is affected by the *depth* (number of layers) of the model, batch size (*bs*), image size (W × H), and number of processes. Higher *Img/sec* indicates better performance. Some important terms are clarified further:

**Batch Size (BS):** # of samples in the batch (mini-batch)
**Effective Batch Size (EBS)** = BS × num_replicas for data/hybrid parallelism
**Effective Batch Size (EBS)** = BS for model-parallelism
**Image Size:** Dimension of the image (Width × Height).

**Legend Entries for Graphs** in Sects. 6.3 and 6.4 are:

- **Sequential:** Single-process DNN training using default TF/Keras APIs.
- **HF (MP):** DNN training using *hf.fit (..,strategy=model-parallel)*.
- **HF (DP):** DNN training using *hf.fit(..,strategy=data-parallel)*.
- **Horovod (DP):** DNN training using Horovod directly (data-parallel).

## 6.3  Model Parallelism on a Single Node

We train various models on a single Stampede2 node– dual-socket Xeon Skylake with 48 cores and 96 threads (hyper-threading enabled). The default version of TensorFlow relies on underlying math libraries like OpenBLAS and Intel MKL. On Intel systems, we tried the Intel-optimized version of TensorFlow, but it failed with different errors such as "function not implemented" etc. For the AMD system, we used the OpenBLAS available on the system. Both of these platforms offer very slow sequential training. *We present single-node results for VGG-16, ResNet-110-v1, and ResNet-1001-v2.*

  **VGG-16** has 16 layers so it can be split in to as many as 16 partitions. We try all possible cases and observe the best performance for num_partitions = 8. As shown in Fig. 7(a), we see that HF (MP) offers better performance for small batch sizes and HF/Horovod (DP) offers better performance for large batch sizes. HF (MP) offers better performance compared to sequential (1.65× better at BS 1024) as well as to data-parallel training (1.25× better at BS 64) for VGG-16 on Stampede2.

  **ResNet-110-v1** has 110 layers so we were able to exploit up to 48 model-partitions within the node as shown in Fig. 7(b). We observe the following: 1) HF (MP) is up to 2.1× better than sequential at BS = 1024, 2) HF (MP) is up to 1.6× better than Horovod (DP) and HF (DP) at BS = 128, and 3) HF (MP) is 15% slower than HF (DP) at BS = 1024. The results highlight that model-parallelism is better at smaller batch sizes and data-parallelism are better only when large batch-size is used. Figure 8(a) shows that HF (MP) can offer up to

3.2× better performance than sequential training for ResNet-110-v1 on *Epyc* (64 cores). *Epyc* offered better scalability with increasing batch sizes compared to Stampede2 nodes (Fig. 7(b) vs. 8(a)) The performance gains suggest that HF (MP) can better utilize all cores on *Eypc* compared to sequential training.

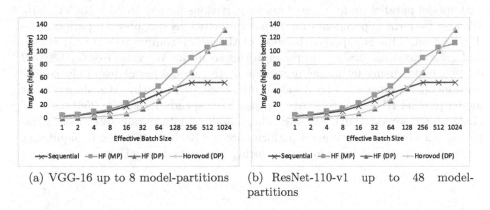

(a) VGG-16 up to 8 model-partitions    (b) ResNet-110-v1 up to 48 model-partitions

**Fig. 7.** HyPar-Flow's model-parallelism vs. sequential/data-parallelism (one node)

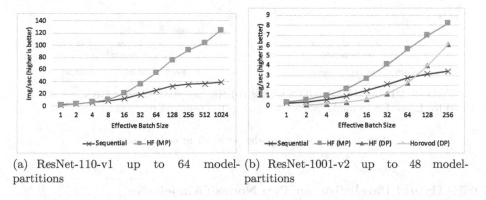

(a) ResNet-110-v1 up to 64 model-partitions    (b) ResNet-1001-v2 up to 48 model-partitions

**Fig. 8.** HyPar-Flow's model-parallelism vs. sequential/data-parallelism (one node)

**ResNet-1001-v2:** To push the envelope of model depth and stress the proposed HyPar-Flow system, we also perform experiments for ResNet-1001-v2, which has 1,0001 layers and approximately 30 million parameters. Figure 8(b) shows the performance for ResNet-1001-v2. It is interesting to note that data-parallel training performs poorly for this model. This is because the number of parameters increases the synchronization overhead for HF (DP) and Horovod (DP) significantly. Hence, even for large batch sizes, the computation is not enough to amortize the communication overhead. Thus, HF (MP) offers much better performance compared to sequential (2.4× better at BS = 256) as well as to data-parallel training (1.75× better at BS = 128).

### 6.4    Model Parallelism on Two Nodes

Two-node results for model parallelism are presented using VGG-16 and ResNet-1001-v2. Figure 9(a) shows the performance trends for VGG-16 training across two nodes. As mentioned earlier, we are only able to achieve good performance with model-parallelism for up to 8 model-partitions for the 16 layers of VGG-16. We also perform experiments for 16 model-partitions but observe performance degradation. This is expected because of the lesser computation per partition and greater communication overhead in this scenario. We scale ResNet-1001-v2 on two nodes using 96 model-partitions in the model-parallelism-only configuration on Stampede2. The result is presented in Fig. 9(b). We observe that model-parallel HF (MP) training provides 1.6× speedup (at BS = 256) over HF (DP) and Horovod (DP). On the other hand, a data-parallel-only configuration is not able to achieve good performance for ResNet-1001 due to significant communication (allreduce) overhead during gradient aggregation.

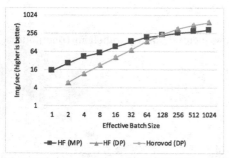 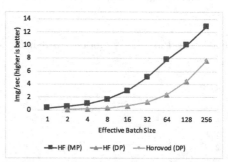

(a) VGG-16: MP Good for Small BS vs. DP Good for Large BS (8 model-partitions)    (b) ResNet-1001-v2: MP Good for All BS (up to 96 model-partitions).

**Fig. 9.** HyPar-Flow model-parallelism on two nodes

### 6.5    Hybrid Parallelism on Two Nodes (AmoebaNet)

Emerging models like AmoebaNet [19] are different compared to VGG and ResNet(s). In order to show the benefit of HyPar-Flow as a generic system for various types of models, we show the performance of training a 1,381-layer AmoebaNet variant in Fig. 10. We provide results for four different conditions: 1) Sequential training using Keras and TensorFlow on one node, 2) HF (MP) with 4 partitions on one node, 3) HF (MP) with 8 partitions on two nodes, and 4) HF (HP), where HP denotes hybrid parallelism on two nodes. As shown in Fig. 10, we observe that hybrid parallelism offers the best possible performance using the same set of nodes.

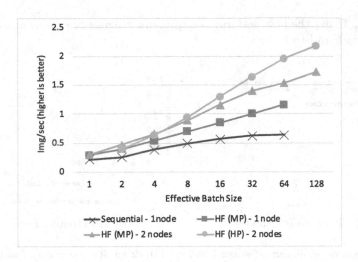

**Fig. 10.** Hybrid parallelism for AmoebaNet on two nodes

## 6.6  Hybrid Parallelism at Scale: Up to 28,762 Cores on 512 Nodes

The most comprehensive coverage of HyPar-Flow's flexibility, performance, and scalability are presented in Fig. 11(a). The figure shows performance for various combinations of hybrid-parallel training of ResNet-1001-v2 on 128 Stampede2 nodes. The figure has three dimensions: 1) the number of nodes on the X-axis, 2) Performance (Img/sec) on Y-axis, and 3) Batch Size using the diameter of the circles. The key takeaway is that hybrid-parallelism offers the user to make trade-offs between high-throughput (Img/sec) and batch size. From an accuracy (convergence) standpoint, the goal is to keep the batch-size small so model updates are more frequent. However, larger batch-size delays synchronization and thus provides higher throughput (Img/sec). HyPar-Flow offers the flexibility to control these two goals via different configurations. For instance, the large blue circle with diagonal lines shows results for 128 nodes using 128 model-replicas where the model is split into 48 partitions on the single 48-core node. This leads to a batch-size of just 32,768, which is 2× smaller than the expected 65,536 if pure data-parallelism is used. It is worth noting that the performance of pure data-parallelism even with 2× larger batch-size will still be lesser than the hybrid-parallel case, i.e., 793 img/sec (=6.2 × 128 – considering ideal scaling for data-parallel case presented earlier in Fig. 8(b)) vs. 940 img/sec (observed value– Fig. 11(a)). This is a significant benefit of hybrid-parallel training, which is impossible with pure model and/or data parallelism. In addition to this, we also present the largest scale we know of for any model/hybrid-parallel study on the latest Frontera system. Figure 11(b)) shows near-ideal scaling on 512 Frontera nodes. Effectively, every single core out of the 28,762 cores on these 512 nodes is being utilized by HyPar-Flow. The ResNet-1001 model is split into 56 partitions as Frontera nodes have a dual-socket Cascade-Lake Xeon processor for a total of 56 cores/node. We run one model-replica per node with a batch size of 128. To get the best performance, pipeline stages were tuned and the best number was found to be 128.

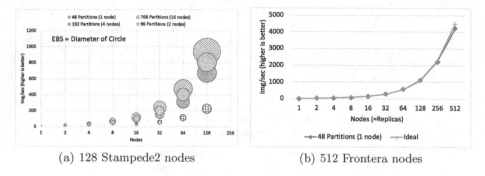

(a) 128 Stampede2 nodes          (b) 512 Frontera nodes

**Fig. 11.** Hybrid-parallelism at scale: ResNet-1001-v2 on Stampede and Frontera with different batch sizes, number of replicas, and number of partitions

## 6.7  Next-Generation Models: ResNet-5000?

Today, designers develop models accounting for the restriction of memory consumption. However, with HyPar-Flow, this restriction no longer exists, and designers can come up with models with as many layers as needed to achieve the desired accuracy. To illustrate this, we present ResNet-5000, an experimental model with 5000 layers. ResNet-5000 is massive and requires a lot of memory so we were able to train it with a batch-size of 1 only. Beyond that, it is not trainable on any existing system. We stress-test HyPar-Flow to scale the training of ResNet-5000 to two nodes and were able to train for bigger batch sizes. We note that training ResNet-5000 and investigation of its accuracy and finding the right set of hyper-parameters is beyond the scope of this paper. The objective is to showcase HyPar-Flow's ability to deal with models that do not exist today.

## 6.8  Discussion and Summary of Results

Model and data-parallelism can be combined in a myriad of ways to realize hybrid-parallel training. E.g. model-parallelism on a single node with multiple cores with data-parallelism across nodes. There are non-trivial and model-dependent trade-offs involved when designing hybrid schemes. Model-parallelism and data-parallelism have different use cases; model-parallelism is beneficial when we have a large model, or we want to keep a small effective batch size for training. On the other hand, data-parallelism gives a near-linear scale-out on multiple nodes but it also increases batch size. In our experiments, we observe that single-node model-parallelism is better than single-node data-parallelism. Theoretically, the number of model-partitions can not be larger than the number of layers in the model; we can not have more than 110 partitions for ResNet-110. In practice, however, we observe that one layer per model-partition will not be used because it suffers from performance degradation. To conclude, HyPar-Flow's flexible hybrid-parallelism offers the best of both worlds; we can benefit from both model and data parallelism for the same model. We summarize the key observations below:

- Models like ResNet-110 offer better performance for model-parallelism on smaller batch sizes (<128).
- Newer and very-deep models like ResNet-1001 benefit from model-parallelism for any batch size (Fig. 8(b)).
- HyPar-Flow's model-parallel training provides up to 3.2× speedup over sequential training and 1.6× speedup over data-parallel training (Fig. 8(a)).
- HyPar-Flow's hybrid-parallel training offers flexible configurations and provides excellent performance for ResNet-1001; 110× speedup over single-node training on 128 Stampede2 (Xeon Skylake) nodes (Fig. 11(a)).
- HyPar-Flow's hybrid-parallel training is highly scalable; we scale ResNet-1001 to 512 Frontera nodes (28,762 cores) as shown in Fig. 11(b).

## 7  Conclusion

Deep Learning workloads are going through a rapid change as newer models and larger, more diverse datasets are being developed. This has led to an explosion of software frameworks like TensorFlow and approaches like data and model-parallelism to deal with ever-increasing workloads. In this paper, we explored a new approach to train state-of-the-art DNNs and presented HyPar-Flow: a unified framework that enables user-transparent and parallel training of TensorFlow models using multiple parallelization strategies. HyPar-Flow does not enforce any specific paradigm. It allows the programmers to experiment with different parallelization strategies without requiring any changes to the model definition and without the need for any system-specific parallel training code. Instead, HyPar-Flow Trainer and Communication Engine take care of assigning the partitions to different processes and performing inter-partition and inter-replica communication efficiently. For ResNet-1001 training using HyPar-Flow, we were able to achieve excellent speedups: up to 1.6× over data-parallel training, up to 110× over single-node training on 128 Stampede2 nodes, and up to 481× over single-node on 512 Frontera nodes. We also tested the ability of HyPar-Flow to train very large experimental models like ResNet-5000, which consists of 5,000 layers. We believe that this study paves new ways to design models. We plan to publicly release the HyPar-Flow system so that the community can use it to develop and train next-generation models on large-scale HPC systems.

## References

1. Keras (2019). https://keras.io/
2. Model parallelism in MXNet (2019). https://mxnet.apache.org/api/faq/model_parallel_lstm

3. Akiba, T., Suzuki, S., Fukuda, K.: Extremely large minibatch SGD: training resnet-50 on ImageNet in 15 minutes (2017). CoRR abs/1711.04325. http://arxiv.org/abs/1711.04325
4. Awan, A.A., Chu, C., Subramoni, H., Lu, X., Panda, D.K.: OC-DNN: exploiting advanced unified memory capabilities in CUDA 9 and volta GPUs for out-of-core DNN training. In: 2018 IEEE 25th International Conference on High Performance Computing (HiPC), pp. 143–152, December 2018. https://doi.org/10.1109/HiPC.2018.00024
5. Awan, A.A., Hamidouche, K., Hashmi, J.M., Panda, D.K.: S-Caffe: co-designing MPI runtimes and caffe for scalable deep learning on modern GPU Clusters. In: Proceedings of the 22nd ACM SIGPLAN Symposium on Principles and Practice of Parallel Programming PPoPP 2017, pp. 193–205. ACM, New York (2017). https://doi.org/10.1145/3018743.3018769
6. Bauer, M., Treichler, S., Slaughter, E., Aiken, A.: Legion: expressing locality and independence with logical regions. In: Proceedings of the International Conference on High Performance Computing, Networking, Storage and Analysis SC 2012, pp. 66:1–66:11. IEEE Computer Society Press, Los Alamitos (2012). http://dl.acm.org/citation.cfm?id=2388996.2389086
7. Ben-Nun, T., Hoefler, T.: Demystifying parallel and distributed deep learning: an in-depth concurrency analysis (2018). CoRR abs/1802.09941. http://arxiv.org/abs/1802.09941
8. Dryden, N., Maruyama, N., Benson, T., Moon, T., Snir, M., Essen, B.V.: Improving strong-scaling of CNN training by exploiting finer-grained parallelism (2019). CoRR abs/1903.06681. http://arxiv.org/abs/1903.06681
9. Gholami, A., Azad, A., Jin, P., Keutzer, K., Buluc, A.: Integrated model, batch, and domain parallelism in training neural networks. In: Proceedings of the 30th on Symposium on Parallelism in Algorithms and Architectures SPAA 2018, pp. 77–86. ACM, New York (2018). https://doi.org/10.1145/3210377.3210394
10. Goyal, P., et al.: Accurate, large minibatch SGD: training ImageNet in 1 hour (2017). CoRR abs/1706.02677. http://arxiv.org/abs/1706.02677
11. Harlap, A., et al.: PipeDream: fast and efficient pipeline parallel DNN training (2018). CoRR abs/1806.03377. http://arxiv.org/abs/1806.03377
12. He, K., Zhang, X., Ren, S., Sun, J.: Identity mappings in deep residual networks (2016). CoRR absscaffe,/1603.05027. http://arxiv.org/abs/1603.05027
13. Huang, Y., et al.: GPipe: efficient training of giant neural networks using pipeline parallelism (2018). CoRR abs/1811.06965. http://arxiv.org/abs/1811.06965
14. Jia, Z., Zaharia, M., Aiken, A.: Beyond data and model parallelism for deep neural networks (2018). CoRR abs/1807.05358. http://arxiv.org/abs/1807.05358
15. Krizhevsky, A.: One weird trick for parallelizing convolutional neural networks (2014). CoRR abs/1404.5997. http://arxiv.org/abs/1404.5997
16. Krizhevsky, A., Sutskever, I., Hinton, G.E.: ImageNet classification with deep convolutional neural networks. In: Pereira, F., Burges, C.J.C., Bottou, L., Weinberger, K.Q. (eds.) Advances in Neural Information Processing Systems, vol. 25, pp. 1097–1105. Curran Associates, Inc. (2012). http://papers.nips.cc/paper/4824-imagenet-classification-with-deep-convolutional-neural-networks.pdf
17. Markthub, P., Belviranli, M.E., Lee, S., Vetter, J.S., Matsuoka, S.: DRAGON: breaking GPU memory capacity limits with direct NVM access. In: Proceedings of the International Conference for High Performance Computing, Networking, Storage, and Analysis SC 2018, pp. 32:1–32:13. IEEE Press, Piscataway (2018). http://dl.acm.org/citation.cfm?id=3291656.3291699

18. Mikami, H., Suganuma, H., Chupala, U.-P., Tanaka, Y., Kageyama, Y.: Imagenet/resnet-50 training in 224 seconds (2018). CoRR abs/1811.05233. http://arxiv.org/abs/1811.05233
19. Real, E., Aggarwal, A., Huang, Y., Le, Q.V.: Regularized evolution for image classifier architecture search (2018). CoRR abs/1802.01548. http://arxiv.org/abs/1802.01548
20. Shazeer et al.: Mesh-TensorFlow: deep learning for supercomputers. In: Bengio, S., Wallach, H., Larochelle, H., Grauman, K., Cesa-Bianchi, N., Garnett, R. (eds.) Advances in Neural Information Processing Systems, vol. 31, pp. 10414–10423. Curran Associates, Inc. (2018). http://papers.nips.cc/paper/8242-mesh-tensorflow-deep-learning-for-supercomputers.pdf
21. Sun, P., Feng, W., Han, R., Yan, S., Wen, Y.: Optimizing network performance for distributed DNN training on GPU clusters: Imagenet/alexnet training in 1.5 minutes (2019). CoRR abs/1902.06855. http://arxiv.org/abs/1902.06855

# Time Series Mining at Petascale Performance

Amir Raoofy[1(✉)], Roman Karlstetter[1,2], Dai Yang[1,3], Carsten Trinitis[1],
and Martin Schulz[1]

[1] Computer Architecture and Parallel Systems,
Technical University of Munich, Garching, Germany
{amir.raoofy,roman.karlstetter,carsten.trinitis,martin.w.j.schulz}@tum.de
[2] IfTA GmbH, Puchheim, Germany
[3] NVIDIA, Munich, Germany
daiy@nvidia.com

**Abstract.** The mining of time series data plays an important role in modern information retrieval and analysis systems. In particular, the identification of similarities within and across time series has garnered significant attention and effort over the last few years. For this task, the class of matrix profile algorithms, which create a generic structure that encodes correlations among records and dimensions—the matrix profile—is a promising approach, as it allows simplified post-processing and analysis steps by examining the resulting matrix profile structure. However, it is expensive to create a matrix profile: it requires significant computational power to evaluate the distance among all subsequence pairs in a time series, especially for very long and multi-dimensional time series with a large dimensionality. Existing approaches are limited in their scalability, as they do not target High Performance Computing systems, and—for most realistic problems—are suited only for datasets with a small dimensionality.

In this paper, we introduce a novel MPI-based approach for the calculation of a matrix profile for multi-dimensional time series that pushes these limits. We evaluate the efficiency of our approach using an analytical performance model combined with experimental data. Finally, we demonstrate our solution on a 128-dimensional time series dataset of 1 million records, solving 274 trillion sorts at a sustained 1.3 Petaflop/s performance on the *SuperMUC-NG* system.

## 1 Introduction

State-of-the-art physical systems, such as monitoring infrastructures or operational logs of industrial machines, often generate a time-tagged series of data points in a given order. A collection of such data points over time, which is called a *time series*, is crucial to understanding the underlying behavior of the physical system that produces it. Such time series are usually provided in the form of

---

D. Yang—This research is completed at TU Munich.

© Springer Nature Switzerland AG 2020
P. Sadayappan et al. (Eds.): ISC High Performance 2020, LNCS 12151, pp. 104–123, 2020.
https://doi.org/10.1007/978-3-030-50743-5_6

a *collection* of individual time series, which together form a *multi-dimensional time series.*

One important aspect in understanding multi-dimensional time series is the explorative discovery of similar and repeating patterns in a (potentially large) dataset [4]. Recent advances in data mining techniques enable the extraction of complex pattern structures in multi-dimensional time series. They generally rely on computing generic similarity data structures, e.g., correlation information from the individual time series.

One prominent example for time series data mining is the *matrix profile* approach, which has been introduced by Yel et al. [24] and has been successfully applied to many datasets from various fields. A matrix profile is a generic meta series, i.e., a time series itself that provides information about the input series by summarizing correlations and nearest neighbor indices among subsequences in a set of given time series. A matrix profile also enables easier in-depth studies of patterns and anomalies, and with that many data mining tasks, such as the discovery of frequent patterns, correlations, and clusters in a dataset.

State-of-the-art algorithms for the computation of a matrix profile mostly target one-dimensional time series, i.e., a single time series covering one sensor input. Only recently, the first algorithms for multi-dimensional time series appeared [23] offering detailed insights into repeating patterns across different time series, significantly increasing the ability to understand multi-dimensional time series. However, these approaches are significantly more compute-intensive than one-dimensional matrix profile algorithms and hence are no longer feasible on standard systems, which they currently target, for realistic workloads. They have not been shown to scale to larger systems nor that they can be used on anything but small datasets.

However, multi-dimensional time series with large numbers of records in each time series are typical in many disciplines. One example is the operation of *industrial gas turbines.* Such systems are monitored by more than 100 different sensors and generate millions of records[1] per month [10]. The analysis of this data can generate new insights about correlations among different sensors and operational modes, which can be used to optimize the operation of a gas turbine for more stable operation, better fuel efficiency, and consequently less air pollution. Another real-world example is monitoring of HPC infrastructures. Netti et al. [14] use up to 3176 sensors per node to monitor multiple production HPC systems at the *Leibniz Supercomputing Centre* and have shown that the collected monitoring data contains valuable information on the system's behavior, and can be used, eg., in the characterization of applications running on it.

To apply the concept of the matrix profile to large-scale multi-dimensional time series and hence to such real-world problems, we require new approaches to scale the computation of matrix profiles both to larger computational resources and to larger datasets. In this work, we provide a novel approach of calculating the matrix profile for large multi-dimensional time series in parallel on HPC systems. We build our approach on the observation that the calculation of a matrix

---

[1] In this case, a record is a collection of samples of all sensors at a specific time.

profile is highly memory bound [15], and therefore can benefit from horizontal scaling of memory bandwidth and throughput. In addition, parallel computation of the matrix profile requires the aggregation of final results, i.e., a series of reduction operations, which can exploit high performance interconnects. However, in order to achieve efficiency, a series of algorithmic advances and optimization steps are needed, which we introduce in this work and verify with an analytical performance model.

In particular, the contributions in this paper are:

- We introduce a new highly-parallel algorithm to compute the matrix profile for multi-dimensional time series.
- We provide an analytical and experimental model for the performance of our algorithm.
- We provide a scalable implementation of our algorithm to compute a multi-dimensional matrix profile efficiently on a *Petascale* HPC system.

Using our novel algorithmic approach, we demonstrate the computation on a 128-dimensional time series dataset of 1 million records on the *SuperMUC-NG* Petascale system, solving 274 trillion sorts at sustained 1.3 Petaflop/s performance.

The remainder of this paper is organized as follows: Sect. 2 introduces the concept of matrix profile, existing algorithms to compute it, and the challenges to running this computation on HPC systems. Section 3 discusses our approach for parallel computation of the matrix profile. Section 4 describes our MPI implementation, and Sect. 5 presents a performance model to describe the workload of matrix profile computation for a multi-dimensional time series on a parallel system. Section 6 explains and analyzes our experiments, Sect. 7 discusses related work, and Sect. 8 provides conclusions and final discussions.

## 2 Background on Matrix Profile

A matrix profile is a generic similarity indexing approach for the analysis of one- or multi-dimensional time series, in particular, the investigation and quantification of similar patterns. This analysis relies on the study of similarities (or correlations) among local chunks—i.e., subsets of continuous values—of the time series, referred to as subsequences. A matrix profile summarizes a complete correlation matrix (or equivalently distance matrix) of all the subsequences of a time series, the distance matrix, into mainly two data structures:

- A *matrix profile P*, which is a meta series encoding the distance of a subsequence to its nearest neighbor, and
- A *matrix profile index I*, which is an indexing structure storing pointers to the nearest neighbor of a subsequence in the time series.

The terminology introduced above, i.e., matrix profile and matrix profile index, in principle, also applies to multi-dimensional time series. However, for a multi-dimensional time series, the notion of similarity is generalized so that the

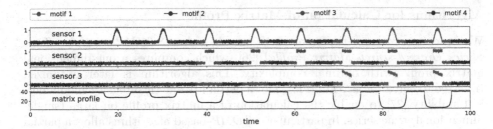

**Fig. 1.** Illustration of automatic semantic segmentation using a multi-dimensional matrix profile. We show a synthetic time series of three sensors, the corresponding matrix profile, and we group the patterns in the time series based on matrix profile into four clusters denoted by colors. Each sensor consists of 20 000 samples. The subsequence length for the analysis is set to 4 s, and we use k-means with 4 clusters on the 3D matrix profile to distinguish the clusters. (Color figure online)

analysis takes the correlation among subsequences in different dimensions into account. Moreover, the resulting matrix profile (and index) for a time series with the dimensionality of $d$ consists of $d$ matrix profiles. These profiles are presented in a single matrix with $d$ rows where the $k$-th $(k \leq d)$ row of the matrix profile provides information about the nearest neighbors of subsequences in the best matching $k$ dimensions.

To illustrate the matrix profile, we present a simple scenario in Fig. 1 and show how a matrix profile can be used for automatic semantic segmentation of a multi-dimensional time series[2]. Our synthetic example uses a set of 3 sensors: the first carries $sin(x)$-wavelets starting at $+20$ s; the second carries square-wavelets starting at time $+40$ s; and the third carries a sawtooth-wavelet starting at $+70$ s; all wavelets are repeated every 10 s. This introduces four phases in the presented sensor data during which the correlations among the sensors are *unique*. The generated matrix profile highlights and distinguishes these phases by summarizing the correlation structure among the sensors in the time series.

We perform a multi-dimensional matrix profile analysis on this example. The resulting matrix profile (only the last row in the matrix profile corresponding to the nearest neighbors of 3D patterns) is presented in the lower graph colored in black in Fig. 1. We use a *k-means* algorithm to cluster this matrix profile and group the corresponding motifs—which are patterns with a unique correlation structure among all three sensors—based on their distances in the matrix profile (see Fig. 1, color-coded time series segments). This analysis results in meaningful clusters corresponding to the respective phases in the original data.

---

[2] We choose this example in favor of a real-world one for simplicity. Moreover, our goal is to show the capabilities of the approach without binding it to a specific domain. For more illustrative examples, we refer to Yeh et al. [22,24] and Gharghabi et al. [7].

## Algorithms for Calculation of Matrix Profile

We base our work on the state-of-the-art algorithm *STOMP (Scalable Time Series Ordered-search Matrix Profile)* [26], which computes a one-dimensional matrix profile with optimal complexity. This algorithm is later optimized (referred to hereafter as $STOMP_{opt}$) for a better arithmetic intensity and numerical stability [27] to enable the calculation of a matrix profile on large (single-dimensional) time series. In particular, *STOMP*-based algorithms allow a partial storage of the *distance matrix*—a matrix of, e.g., Euclidean distances among all subsequences—using an *ordered* iterative solver for matrix profiles by computing a so-called *distance profile*. The distance profile is one row within the distance matrix (see Eq. 8 and Fig. 2 right), which is computed in a given iteration to update the matrix profile data structure.

For the calculation of a matrix profile over a multi-dimensional time series, Yeh et al. [23] introduce *mSTAMP*. It uses *STOMP*-based formulations for the computation of the distance profile. *mSTAMP* iteratively computes the matrix profile by independent calculation of distance profiles for all dimensions. Unlike *STOMP*, in each iteration, before updating the resulting intermediate state of the matrix profile, *mSTAMP* sorts the distance profiles in each record separately. However, this method has three significant drawbacks: (a) it does not exploit the numerically stable formulation for computation of a matrix profile, (b) it is only available as a scripted prototype in Python and Matlab, and (c) it exists only in a sequential version. Consequently, it is currently insufficient for computing a matrix profile on a large-scale multi-dimensional real-world dataset.

## 3   Multi-dimensional Parallel Matrix Profile: $(MP)^N$

To overcome the limitations stated above, we introduce a new approach to compute multi-dimensional matrix profiles. Building on top of the existing *mSTAMP* concepts, we introduce $(MP)^N$ (stands for Multi-dimensional Parallel Matrix Profile), which is designed to exploit the computational power, high performance interconnect, and I/O capabilities of HPC systems to calculate matrix profiles of multi-dimensional datasets within realistic execution times.

For this, the *mSTAMP* formulations can be adapted for parallel processing, allowing the distribution of computational workload among multiple workers with minimum communication during the computation phase. By partitioning the time series along records, we can distribute the workload across multiple processing elements, e.g., cores of a multiprocessor. This workload consists of (1) the computation of the distance profile, (2) the sorting of the distance profile, and (3) the updates on the resulting matrix profile. Finally, the results residing in the memory of the various machines are merged by performing reduction operations. This way, we can scale the computation of a multi-dimensional matrix profile to a large number of nodes.

## 3.1   Overview of the $(MP)^N$ Algorithm

The foundation of our algorithm is an adapted version of $mSTAMP$ based on $STOMP_{opt}$ kernels. Its mathematical representation is given in Table 1, which provides us good numerical stability and a better single thread arithmetic performance for the evaluation of the distance matrix [27].

For a multi-dimensional time series with $d$ dimensions, each of length (number of records) $n$, and considering a subsequence length $m$, we evaluate a total of $d$ distance matrices, one for each dimension. A distance matrix is a symmetric matrix storing the Euclidean distance among all subsequence pairs of the input time series separately for every dimension.

In contrast to $mSTAMP$, we explicitly take the symmetric structure of the distance matrices into account to avoid redundant computations. Further, we consider the fact that there is a significant semantic difference between one- and multi-dimensional motifs: in multi-dimensional motifs, subsequences can correlate with any other subsequences in any $k$-dimensional ($k \leq d$) subspace across all dimensions. This results in a matrix profile that is defined as the minimum value of each column in the distance matrices after sorting and partial aggregation of resulting distance profiles of the $d$ dimensions. The resulting matrix profile represents the nearest neighbors of a subsequence with the best matching $k$ ($k \leq d$) dimensions. To achieve this with minimal overhead, we sort the distances across the dimensions for all records in the distance profile using an optimized memory layout combined with a high-performance sorting kernel. Accordingly, the matrix profile index is defined as the $argmin^3$ pointing to the closest neighbor of each subsequence (Eq. 10).

In the case of a self-join[4], we exclude the trivial matches, i.e., a subsequence matching a given region including itself or its neighboring subsequences. These regions correspond to the proximities of the diagonal entries in the distance matrices. $(MP)^N$ invalidates these trivial matches in so-called "exclusion zones" when merging the calculated intermediate profiles into the final result.

At the end of each iteration, $(MP)^N$ merges the sorted and aggregated distance profiles into the final matrix profile and its index using element-wise $min$ and $argmin$ operations (see Eq. 10).

## 3.2   Iterative Computation of the Matrix Profile

We use the formulas in Table 1 for the iterative computation of the distance matrix and its distance profile (Algorithm 1), which can be summarized in the following steps (see Fig. 2 right):

---

[3] Given two distance values $a$ and $b$, and associated neighboring indices $i_a$ and $i_b$, the $argmin$ operation is defined as following: the output ($i_{out}$) is set to $i_a$ if $a < b$ and is set to $i_b$ otherwise.

[4] Similarity join—also known similarity indexing in the literature—is an operation that combines two input (multi-dimensional) time series and finds similarities. Self-join is the case with two identical input series. For simplicity and without losing generality, we restrict the formulations and discussions to self-joins.

---

**Algorithm 1:** Procedure for computing the multi-dimensional matrix profile based on $STOMP_{opt}$;

**Input:** d-dim. time series $T \in \mathbb{R}^{d \times n}$ and subsequence length $m \in \mathbb{N}$ ;

**Output:** multi-dimensional matrix profile $P \in \mathbb{R}^{d \times n-m+1}$ and matrix profile index $I \in \mathbb{Z}^{d \times n-m+1}$

---

1  $\mu$, $d^{-1}$, $df$, $dg$ ← precompute statistics (T, m)                    ▷ Eqs. 1–4
2  $QT$ ← initialize streaming dot product                              ▷ see [27]
3  **for** $idx \leftarrow 0$ **to** $n - m$ **do**
4  |  **for** $dim \leftarrow 0$ **to** $d - 1$ **do**
5  |  |  **for** $i \leftarrow idx$ **to** $n - m$ **do**
6  |  |  |  $\delta_{i,dim}$ ← compute distance profile               ▷ see Fig. 2 right
7  |  |  **end**
8  |  **end**
9  |  invalidate entries of $\delta$ in exclusion region          ▷ see [24] and [23]
10 |  **for** $i \leftarrow idx$ **to** $n - m$ **do**
11 |  |  $\delta'_i$ ← sort $i$-th row of $\delta$                              ▷ Eq. 9
12 |  **end**
13 |  **for** $dim \leftarrow 0$ **to** $d - 1$ **do**
14 |  |  $\delta''$ ← column-wise aggregate and normalize($\delta'$)        ▷ see [23]
15 |  |  $P, I$ ← element-wise argmin($P, \delta''$)                ▷ matrix updates
16 |  |  tmp ← row-wise minimum ($\delta''$)
17 |  |  $P_c[idx], I_c[idx]$ ← element-wise argmin($P_c[idx], tmp$) ▷ vector updates
18 |  **end**
19 **end**
20 $P, I \leftarrow combine(P, I, P_c, I_c)$;

---

1. First, we (pre-)compute statistics of all subsequences using Eqs. 1–4 in all $d$ dimensions (Line 1, Algorithm 1).
2. In Line 2, Algorithm 1, we initialize the streaming dot product (see the formulation developed by Zimmerman et al. [27]) with the distance between the *first* subsequence in the time series and all other subsequences and (pre-)compute the distance profiles for all $d$ dimensions.
3. We use Eqs. 5–8 to iteratively—and in-situ—update the distance profile $\delta$ (Line 3, Algorithm 1), by calculating the Euclidean distances between subsequence $idx$ and all the other subsequences $i$. This, in turn, is done for all $d$ dimensions (Lines 4–8, Algorithm 1). Further, in each iteration $idx$, we. . .
   (a) . . . invalidate the entries in the exclusion zone of $\delta$ (Line 9, Algorithm 1).
   (b) . . . sort the distance profile $\delta$ in each record and across the dimensions (Eq. 9 and Lines 10–12, Algorithm 1).
   (c) . . . combine the sorted distance profile with the matrix profile for all $d$ dimensions using element-wise *min* and *argmin* operations, i.e., the matrix profile and its index are updated according to the distance profile (Eq. 10, Lines 13–18, Algorithm 1 and Fig. 2 right).

## 3.3  Algorithmic Optimizations in $(MP)^N$

As discussed in Sect. 3.1, we only compute the upper triangular part of the distance matrix and then compensate for this by updating the matrix profile accordingly. For that, we introduce an additional set of matrix profiles $P_c$ and matrix profile indices $I_c$. $P_c$ and $I_c$ represent column-wise (for column $c$) matrix profiles and indices (similar to the definitions by Zimmerman [27]), and are both multi-dimensional (Fig. 2 right). We compute the partial results $P_c$ and $I_c$ from already computed distance profiles using the transpose of the distance matrix instead of computing the lower triangular part of the distance matrix. We then compute $P_c$ and $I_c$ using $min$ and $argmin$ operations per dimension at each iteration on the distance profile $\delta$. Finally, we construct the final matrix profile and its index by merging the results of $P_c$ to $P$, and $I_c$ to $I$ (Line 20, Algorithm 1). This optimization and merging scheme are parallelizable, as we demonstrate below in our MPI implementation of $(MP)^N$.

## 3.4  Data Layout Considerations

For optimal data-locality, we use a column-wise in-memory data layout for most data structures, as most kernels access the data structures in a column-wise data layout (see Fig. 2 left). Only for the distance profile $\delta$, we use a double buffering scheme, where data is accessed row-wise as well. This way, vectorized sorting kernels can exploit a more efficient access pattern to $\delta$.

**Table 1.** Iterative $STOMP_{opt}$ formulation extended for multi-dim. matrix profiles

| | | |
|---|---|---|
| Average of samples in a subsequence starting at record i in dimension k | $\mu_{i+1,k} = \mu_{i,k} + (T_{i+m,k} - T_{i,k})/m$ | (1) |
| Inverse of norm-1 of samples in a subsequence starting at record i in dimension k | $d_{i,k}^{-1} = (\sum_{z=0}^{m} T_{i+z,k} - \mu_{i,k})^{-1}$ | (2) |
| Intermediate values used in mean-centered streaming dot product formulation 5 | $df_{i+1,k} = (T_{i+m,k} - T_{i,k})/2$ | (3) |
| Intermediate values used in mean-centered streaming dot product formulation 5 | $dg_{i+1,k} = (T_{i+m,k} - \mu_{i+1,k}) + (T_{i,k} - \mu_{i,k})$ | (4) |
| Streaming dot product of samples in subsequences i and j in k-th dimension [27] | $\overline{QT}_{i+1,j+1,k} = \overline{QT}_{i,j,k} + df_{i,k} \times dg_{j,k} + df_{j,k} \times dg_{i,k}$ | (5) |
| Pearson correlation matrix among subsequences starting at records i and j in dimension k | $\rho_{i,j,k} = \overline{QT}_{i,j,k} \times d_{i,k}^{-1} \times d_{j,k}^{-1}$ | (6) |
| Euclidean distance matrix among subsequences starting at records i and j in dimension k | $D_{i,j,k} = \sqrt{2 \times m \times (1 - \rho_{i,j,k})}$ | (7) |
| i-th distance profile in dimension k | $\delta_{i,k} = D_{i,*,k}$ | (8) |
| Sort i-th distance profile along dimensions | $\delta_i' = sort(\delta_i)$ | (9) |
| Matrix profile and its index | $P_{i,k} = min(\delta_{i,k}'), \quad I_{i,k} = argmin(\delta_{i,k}')$ | (10) |

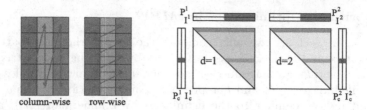

**Fig. 2.** Illustration of the column- and row-wise layouts for storage of the distance profile $\delta$ (left). Each column with a unique color represents one dimension, and rows represent records. Besides, the red arrows indicate the data layout. On the right, the iterative computation of the matrix profile in all dimensions is visualized. The active distance profiles in a specific iteration are colored in green. These two distance profiles are sorted and partially aggregated, and the corresponding elements in the matrix profile and its index are updated—colored in brown and magenta. (Color figure online)

### 3.5 Partitioning and Aggregation Scheme

Apart from the pre-computation of the first row of each *local* distance matrix, the iterative computation of the distance matrix and matrix profile, as introduced in Sect. 3.2, is an *embarrassingly-parallel* workload. Therefore, each process has to compute the first iteration using a naive sliding dot product formulation [24] (Fig. 2 right). Figure 3 left illustrates the partitioning scheme used in $(MP)^N$ for a two-dimensional problem by decomposing the problem into four independent subproblems. Here, the iterative evaluation of the two distance matrices—one for each dimension—in a two-dimensional problem is distributed among four processing units. Note that $(MP)^N$ computes the matrix profile by evaluating only the upper triangular parts of the partitioned distance matrix. In addition, we introduce an additional final step to aggregate the partial results from different processing units (cf. the merging scheme in Sect. 3.3). Due to the symmetry of the distance matrix, the following property for all resulting matrix profiles in the partitions holds: $P^{(i,j)} = P_c^{(j,i)}$—where $(i, j)$ is the index of a process in the virtual topology. Given this property, the partial matrix profiles are merged according to the following equation (see Fig. 3 left):

$$P_{merged}^{(0,0)} = merge(P^{(0,0)}, P^{(0,1)}) = merge(P^{(0,0)}, P_c^{(1,0)}) \qquad (11)$$

By generalizing Eq. 11, we can formulate this merging step for aggregation of partial matrix profiles in partitions (cf. Fig. 3). The merge operation in Eq. 11 represents element-wise reduction similar to Lines 15 and 17, Algorithm 1.

## 4    MPI-Based Parallelization and Optimization

We have implemented the parallel version of our $(MP)^N$ algorithm using the Message Passing Interface (MPI), which allows us to exploit the performance advantages in tightly coupled HPC systems. In particular, we replace a

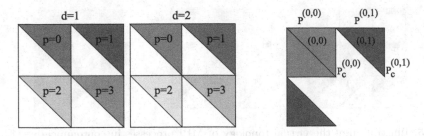

**Fig. 3.** (Left) Illustration for the partitioning scheme of the distance matrix in $(MP)^N$ for a two-dimensional matrix profile (cf. Fig. 2): we use four partitions in this illustration. (Right) Aggregation scheme: the parts of the distance matrix with a similar color are computed on the same partition, e.g., partitions colored in pink are computed in the processing element with id $(0, 1)$. (Color figure online)

filesystem-based final aggregation [27] with high-performance reduction operations, utilize fast communication and scalable I/O functionality for massively-parallel pre- and post-processing, and enable unprecedented scaling, all of which have been bottlenecks in existing cloud-based parallel matrix profile algorithms.

## 4.1  Phases of $(MP)^N$

Our $(MP)^N$ implementation includes six phases (see Fig. 4):

1. *Setup Phase*: We first build a virtual topology of processes (see Fig. 5). Using this topology, we create the MPI communicators required for reading and writing input and output time series from the file system, as well as the MPI communicators required for the distribution of time series and the aggregation of the matrix profile. Finally, we distribute the data and workload among all MPI processes according to our partitioning algorithm (see Sect. 3.5).
2. *File Read Phase:* We read the time series from the file, using a "row-wise" layout for storing data, i.e., the data points from different data streams with a given timestamp are stored consecutively in the file. This simplifies the partitioned read operation when using a large number of processes.
3. *Data Distribution Phase:* Processes that participate in the *File Read Phase* broadcast the input time series via the MPI communicators created during the setup.

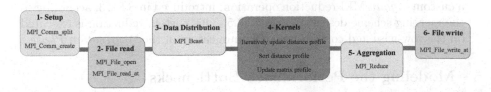

**Fig. 4.** Illustration of all phases in our approach on a distributed memory HPC system.

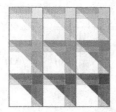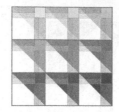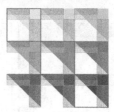

**Fig. 5.** Illustration of the virtual topology of MPI processes in communicators. Each triangle with a distinct color represents a separate MPI process working on a distinct part of the distance matrix. The red boxes represent exclusive process sets in communicators. The left and middle figures represent communicators used in *Data Distribution* and *Aggregation* phases, and the right figure shows the communicator used in I/O phases. The small boxes in each process represent data buffers associated with a local matrix profile and its index to be reduced in the *Aggregation* phase. Buffers depicted with the same colors within the same process group are reduced. (Color figure online)

4. *Kernel Execution Phase:* We execute the necessary kernels to compute a local multi-dimensional matrix profile for a subset (partition) of the input series using the iterative algorithm introduced in Sect. 3.
5. *Aggregation Phase:* We aggregate and merge the final results (see Eq. 11 and Fig. 5). This is done using reduction operations over MPI communicators created in the *Setup Phase*. After this phase, the final results are available on all processes that participate in the *Write Phase*.
6. *Write Phase:* A subset of MPI processes responsible for parallel-write operations outputs the final matrix profile and its index using MPI I/O (Fig. 5).

## 4.2    MPI Communicators in $(MP)^N$

We use three communicators in various phases presented in Fig. 4. These communicators are illustrated in Fig. 5 and are as follows:

- For reading and writing, we use only MPI processes responsible for the diagonals on the virtual topology (Fig. 5 right). This allows us to reduce the pressure on the parallel file system caused by the large amount of I/O operations $(IOP)$, which would otherwise degrade the I/O performance.
- We use both column- and row-wise communicators for the *Distribution* of data and the reduction of the final result in the *aggregation* phase. We further use a custom *argmin* MPI reduction operation, introduced in Sect. 3, according to the merging scheme described in Sect. 3.5. This custom reduction is executed on the row-wise and column-wise communicators in the *Aggregation Phase*.

## 5    Modeling the Performance Bottlenecks

To understand the scaling behavior of our algorithm, we introduce an analytical performance model for $(MP)^N$. We base our model on two inputs: the number of processes and the problem size. Our model includes all phases in the computation of our algorithm as introduced in Sect. 4.1. We decompose the execution in shares of execution time for these phases[5]:

$$T_{Execution} = T_{Setup} + T_{Read} + T_{Distribution} + T_{Kernel} + T_{Aggregation} + T_{Write} \quad (12)$$

We consider a time series of size $n$ with $d$ dimensions resulting in $n \times d$ as the input size, and we assume a total of $p$ MPI processes. Using these notations, the following equations describe the scaling behavior of each phase in $(MP)^N$:

$$T_{Setup} = C_{Setup} \cdot p \cdot log_2 p \quad (13)$$

$$T_{Read} = C_{Read} \cdot n \cdot d / \sqrt{p} \quad (14)$$

$$T_{Broadcast} = C_{Broadcast} \cdot \sqrt{p} \cdot log_2 \sqrt{p} \cdot n \cdot d \quad (15)$$

$$T_{Kernel} = C_{Kernel} \cdot n^2 \cdot d \cdot log_2 d / p \quad (16)$$

$$T_{Aggregation} = C_{Aggregation} \cdot \sqrt{p} \cdot log_2 \sqrt{p} \cdot n \cdot d \quad (17)$$

However, to simplify our discussions regarding the scaling bottlenecks of $(MP)^N$, we only present our model for dominant portions of the runtime, which are $T_{Setup}$ and $T_{Kernel}$ (cf. Sect. 6.4). We consider a linearithmic growth of $T_{Setup}$ with respect to $p$ (see Moody et al. [12]), and the growth of $T_{Kernel}$ is driven from the parent algorithm $mSTAMP$, and is modified for $(MP)^N$. This results in the final model of:

$$T_{Execution} \approx T_{Setup} + T_{Kernel} = C_{Setup} \cdot p \cdot log_2 p + C_{Kernel} \cdot n^2 \cdot d \cdot log_2 d / p \quad (18)$$

## 6    Evaluation

To demonstrate the performance of our implementation, we conduct a wide set of experiments. All our experiments are carried out on the $SuperMUC\text{-}NG$[6] system at the Leibniz Supercomputing Centre (LRZ). Each SuperMUC-NG node features two 24-core Intel Xeon Platinum 8174 Processors (*Skylake*) running at 2.69 GHz and 96 GB main memory. Our code is implemented in $C{+}{+}$ and uses double-precision floating-point values in the kernels. We use the Intel $C{+}{+}$ compiler v19.0 update 4.0 for compilation, and unless otherwise noted, we use Intel MPI.

All our scaling experiments are executed using 48 MPI processes per node and each MPI process is mapped to one physical core. Thus, we use the terms *cores* and *processes* interchangeably in the remainder of this paper. Moreover, all input sets are randomly generated sequences, as the performance is agnostic to the input data used.

---

[5] Synchronization between the phases is implied by MPI operations used in implementation of $(MP)^N$.

[6] https://doku.lrz.de/display/PUBLIC/SuperMUC-NG.

## 6.1  Correctness and Numerical Stability

To validate the correctness and stability of $(MP)^N$, we compare the matrix profile and its indices calculated with different numbers of processes, as sequential baseline executions are infeasible for our target input datasets. For that, we fix the setup to $n = 524\,288$, $d = 128$ and $m = 512$, and execute $(MP)^N$ on 512 MPI processes to create a baseline. We then repeat the analysis using $1\,024$, $4\,096$, $16\,384$, and $65\,536$ processes. In all experiments, $L_1$ and $L_\infty$[7] norms of the resulting matrix profiles are accurate on up to 15 significant digits and the matrix profile index fully matches the baseline. This confirms the numerical stability of our solution with respect to double-precision floating-point numbers.

## 6.2  Single-Core Performance

We evaluate how the problem size parameters and the difference in sorting kernels affect the execution time on a single-core setup. In the following, each experiment is repeated 5 times, and we show the average result.

For the sorting-kernel used during construction of the complete matrix profile, we use existing standard libraries. In particular, we compare three leading libraries for their performance:

- *AVX-512-bitonic* [3], which is a high performance sorting kernel for small- and mid-sized arrays optimized for the Intel *Skylake* architecture
- *Intel Integrated Performance Primitives* (*IPP*) library [19], as a vendor-specific alternative
- `qsort` from *C++-stdlib*-based [9] as a basic Quicksort implementation

First, we analyze the effect of the *dimensionality* parameter $d$. Figure 6 top illustrates our result. Different colors represent the sorting kernels used in a given experiment. We confirm an expected linear growth in execution time for all three kernels, which validates our proposed model presented in Sect. 5. While all three kernels complete in similar time for smaller dimensionality, *AVX-512-bitonic* provides the best performance with an increasing dimensionality, which is our target. The superiority of *AVX-512-bitonic* is in accordance with the results of an existing study by Bramas et al. [3]. Therefore, we fix the *AVX-512-bitonic* kernel for all further experiments.

Second, we analyze the effect of the *number of records* $n$ on execution time. Figure 6 middle shows a quadratic growth of time with respect to the number of records matching our model in Sect. 5 as well as a previous study by Yeh et al. [23]. The *subsequence length* $m$ has a limited effect on execution time (see Fig. 6 bottom), which is also confirmed by Yeh et al. [23].

Overall, we confirm that the single-node performance of our adapted algorithm is preserved in relation to the *STOMP*-based *mSTAMP* [23], and we validate our execution time model against the obtained experimental data.

---

[7] Taxicab norm $(L_1)$ and Infinity norm $(L_\infty)$.

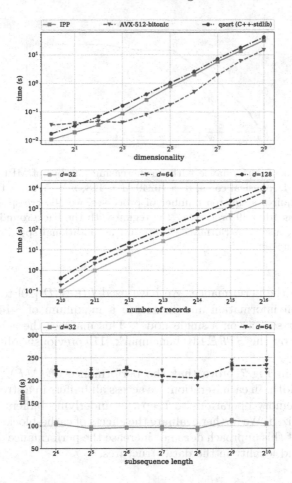

**Fig. 6.** (Top) Linearithmic growth of execution time vs. increasing dimensionality parameter $d$, with $n = 2^{14}$ samples and $m = 2^9$. (Middle) Quadratic growth of execution time vs. increasing number of records $n$, with $d = 2^5$, $m = 2^9$. (Bottom) Near-constant execution time with increasing subsequence length $m$, with $n = 2^{14}$, $d = 2^5$.

## 6.3  Single-Node Performance

Next, we present results from single-node execution. We execute $(MP)^N$ with I_MPI_PIN_ORDER=scatter to pin the MPI processes within NUMA nodes[8]. This ensures optimal sharing of the available memory bandwidth across all cores.

As shown in Fig. 7, we can see the expected performance saturation pattern for a memory bound application. We further observe a performance increase with an increasing number of cores on a single node, but hyper-threading does not

---

[8] For details on mapping MPI processes to cores see https://software.intel.com/en-us/mpi-developer-reference-linux-interoperability-with-openmp.

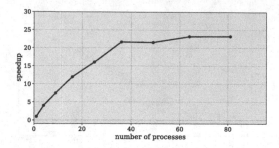

**Fig. 7.** Saturation of performance with an increasing number of MPI processes on a single node with 48 physical cores, $n = 10240$, $d = 128$, $m = 512$. As the structure of the algorithm requires a squared number of processes, we observe speedups up to 36 processes. Starting from 49 processes—the region with the background color of red—hyper-threading causes a performance drop and no additional speedup can be seen. (Color figure online)

further improve the performance. We have used *LIKWID* [20] to collect bandwidth utilization information and measured a maximum of $\sim$140 GB/s using 36 cores (18 per socket) on a single node[9]. This matches the achievable bandwidth reported by the *STREAM* benchmark [11] previously obtained on this machine[10].

The results in Fig. 7 prove that the performance of $(MP)^N$ is bound by memory bandwidth. In each iteration, we access all buffers in a streaming fashion and perform memory operations to keep the underlying buffers with different layout synchronized. We further evaluate the effects of cache-blocking by utilizing smaller tiles, but this approach does not increase the performance due to the lack of reusability and locality in the data structures.

### 6.4  Scalability

Figure 8 illustrates the speedup and efficiency (top) as well as the runtime decomposition (bottom) for strong scaling experiments. We select a random time series of size $n = 524\,288$, $d = 128$ and $m = 512$, and run these experiments on SuperMUC-NG using 6 to 1 366 nodes (256 cores to 65 536 cores). We observe a linear speedup and throughput of the kernel execution time, using the 6-node configuration as the baseline. However, the time for problem setup—mainly time for creating communicators—increases drastically. This reduces the parallel efficiency to 64% for the experiment with 1 366 nodes.

Similarly, Fig. 9 shows our results for weak scaling experiments. Here, we fix the workload per core $n_{core}$ to 2 048. This results in a global problem size of $n = 2\,048$ on 1 node with 1 core, scaling up to $n = 1M$ on 5 462 nodes

---

[9] $(MP)^N$ requires a quadratic number of MPI processes.

[10] We achieved a maximum bandwidth of 185.9 GB/s using *STREAM* benchmark for copy operation using 48 cores.

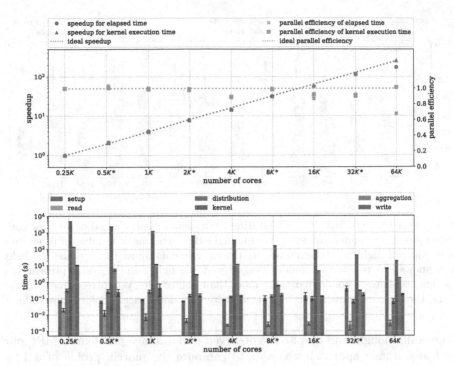

**Fig. 8.** Results of strong scaling experiments for computing the matrix profile. We show speedup and parallel efficiency (Top) and a detailed breakdown of time spent in various phases of the application (Bottom). Note that the measurements denoted by * on the x-axis are executed with exclusive access to the system .

with 262 144 cores. This setup results in weak scaling experiments with kernel execution time of roughly 20 s, which is sufficient for discussions in this paper, and enough to characterize the performance of $(MP)^N$ and illustrate dominating overheads. Again, we observe an ideal scaling of kernel execution time. However, we again encounter a significant increase ($\sim$58%) in time spent on the creation of communicators. In contrast to the strong scaling results, though, this lies within an acceptable range, as setup time is problem independent and scales only with the number of MPI processes.

Even though the setup overheads can be absorbed by the runtime in the more common weak scaling scenario, it clearly represents a performance problem. Further, by comparison with our performance model, we also see that this is not a property of the algorithm, but rather of the system. Upon further investigation, we trace the overhead back to the creation of the column- and row-wise communicators using `MPI_Comm_split` in the *Setup* phase when using the default Intel MPI implementation. Subsequent experiments with alternative MPI implementations have shown significantly better scaling for the `MPI_Comm_split` operation, indicating a non-scalable implementation, which needs to be resolved.

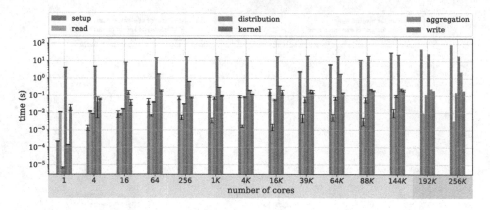

**Fig. 9.** Weak scaling of $(MP)^N$, illustrating time spent in kernels and other time consuming phases vs. number of cores. We highlight three regions of number of processes: the region with light red color represents the experiments limited to 1 node; the light green shows experiments in middle ranges; and the light blue region represent the experiments that are conducted using more than half of the system resources. Unlike others, the large experiments in blue regions are only done once. (Color figure online)

Overall, though, and despite the observed performance problem in MPI, our novel algorithmic approach was able to compute the matrix profile of a 128-dimensional time series dataset of 1 million records on the SuperMUC-NG Petascale system. This corresponds to a projected performance (using measurements from Intel Advisor) of 1.3 Petaflop/s for $(MP)^N$ kernels.

### 6.5   Validation of $(MP)^N$ Against Our Model

As can be observed from the presented results in this section (Figs. 7, 8, and 9), Eq. 16 well represents $T_{Kernel}$, however, this is not the case for Eq. 13, which represents $T_{Setup}$. We conduct a number of experiments to evaluate the models that we presented in Sect. 5. We execute $(MP)^N$ with 283 different combinations of various parameters on the SuperMUC-NG and evaluate $C_{Setup}$ and $C_{Kernel}$ to $(8.8 \pm 0.4)$e-06 and $(5.644 \pm 0.020)$e-09 respectively. As the suggested analytical model for $T_{Setup}$ does not properly fit to our experimental data, we used Extra-P[11] to investigate $T_{Setup}$, which suggests quadratic growth with the number of MPI processes. This growth corresponds to the performance problem with MPI_Comm_split discussed above.

## 7   Related Work

There is extensive literature on mining time series, including several survey papers [5,6,16]. Esling et al. [5] introduce dimensionality as a fundamental problem in time series mining, and most of the techniques exploit a dimensionality reduction step to address this problem, leaving only limited methods that

---

[11] https://www.scalasca.org/software/extra-p.

address similarity search in all dimensions. Matrix profile is superior to alternative approaches like Balasubramanian et al. [1], Tanaka et al. [18] and Vahdatpour et al. [21] in mining similar patterns and provides semantically meaningful multi-dimensional motifs [23].

There are a number of studies on scalable solutions for time series mining: Huang et al. [8] target the use of Apache Spark for speeding discord discovery in time series, however, the conducted experiments in this work are limited to 10 nodes. Berard et al. [2] scale time series similarity search to 20 nodes on a Hadoop cluster. Sart et al. [17] and Zhu et al. [26] use accelerators for speeding time series mining workloads. Movchan et al. [13] study time series similarity search on the Intel Many-core Accelerators, utilizing *OpenMP*. However, none of the above studies address multi-dimensional datasets, and the analysis is very limited to specific targets of similarity search. Overall, there is a large gap in investigation of scalable multi-dimensional time series mining methods.

Yeh et al. [23–26] previously developed various algorithms for the calculation of matrix profiles. Their evaluation shows good performance for their solutions in the construction of matrix profiles, but the datasets in the mentioned articles are limited to one-dimensional datasets and/or small problem sizes. The existing work by Yeh et al. [23–26] is not suited for large dimensionality in such large datasets. To target the high demand of computational power, Zimmerman et al. developed *SCAMP* [27], a cloud-based framework for the parallel calculation of one-dimensional matrix profiles on multiple GPU-based accelerators. However, the multi-dimensional time series problem is also not covered in their solution.

# 8   Conclusion

In this work, we present a first scalable solution—$(MP)^N$—for the mining of large-scale multi-dimensional time series targeting CPU-based HPC systems. It comprises optimizations and parallelization of the *mSTAMP* algorithm. For the first time, this enables the computation of large matrix profiles—as a modern data mining approach—on an HPC system and makes it thereby applicable to large-scale real-world problems. Our parallelization scheme enables scaling up to 256K cores, providing highly scalable throughput and accuracy. With that, we confirm the scalability of the matrix profile approach in mining time series. In our experiments, we performed the fastest and largest ($1M \times 128$) multi-dimensional matrix profile ever computed with a projected kernel performance of 1.3 Petaflop/s.

**Acknowledgments.** This work is funded by Bayerische Forschungsstiftung under the research grant *Optimierung von Gasturbinen mit Hilfe von Big Data* (AZ-1214-16).

The authors gratefully acknowledge the Gauss Centre for Supercomputing e.V. (https://www.gauss-centre.eu) for funding this work by providing computing time on the GCS Supercomputer SuperMUC-NG at Leibniz Supercomputing Centre (LRZ). Also, we would also like to thank LRZ's staff for their valuable support.

# References

1. Balasubramanian, A., Wang, J., Prabhakaran, B.: Discovering multidimensional motifs in physiological signals for personalized healthcare. IEEE J. Sel. Topics Signal Process. **10**(5), 832–841 (2016). https://doi.org/10.1109/JSTSP.2016.2543679
2. Berard, A., Hebrail, G.: Searching time series with Hadoop in an electric power company. In: Proceedings of the 2nd International Workshop on Big Data, Streams and Heterogeneous Source Mining: Algorithms, Systems, Programming Models and Applications BigMine 2013, pp. 15–22. ACM, New York (2013). https://doi.org/10.1145/2501221.2501224
3. Bramas, B.: A novel hybrid Quicksort algorithm vectorized using AVX-512 on Intel Skylake. Int. J. Adv. Comput. Sci. Appl. **8**(10) (2017). https://doi.org/10.14569/IJACSA.2017.081044
4. Chakrabarti, S., et al.: Data mining curriculum: a proposal (version 1.0). In: Intensive Working Group of ACM SIGKDD Curriculum Committee 140 (2006)
5. Esling, P., Agon, C.: Time-series data mining. ACM Comput. Surv. **45**(1), 12:1–12:34 (2012). https://doi.org/10.1145/2379776.2379788
6. Fu, T.C.: A review on time series data mining. Eng. Appl. Artif. Intell. **24**(1), 164–181 (2011). https://doi.org/10.1016/j.engappai.2010.09.007
7. Gharghabi, S., et al.: Domain agnostic online semantic segmentation for multidimensional time series. Data Min. Knowl. Discov. **33**, 96–130 (2018)
8. Huang, T., et al.: Parallel discord discovery. In: Bailey, J., Khan, L., Washio, T., Dobbie, G., Huang, J.Z., Wang, R. (eds.) PAKDD 2016. LNCS (LNAI), vol. 9652, pp. 233–244. Springer, Cham (2016). https://doi.org/10.1007/978-3-319-31750-2_19
9. Josuttis, N.M.: The C++ Standard Library: A Tutorial and Reference. Addison-Wesley, Boston (2012)
10. Karlstetter, R., et al.: Turning dynamic sensor measurements from gas turbines into insights: a big data approach. In: Proceedings of the ASME Turbo Expo: Power for Land, Sea, and Air, Volume 6: Ceramics; Controls, Diagnostics, and Instrumentation; Education; Manufacturing Materials and Metallurgy, June 2019. https://doi.org/10.1115/GT2019-91259. v006T05A021
11. McCalpin, J.D.: Memory bandwidth and machine balance in current high performance computers. IEEE Comput. Soc. Tech. Comm. Comput. Archit. (TCCA) Newsl. **2**, 19–25 (1995)
12. Moody, A., Ahn, D.H., de Supinski, B.R.: Exascale algorithms for generalized MPI_Comm_split. In: Cotronis, Y., Danalis, A., Nikolopoulos, D.S., Dongarra, J. (eds.) EuroMPI 2011. LNCS, vol. 6960, pp. 9–18. Springer, Heidelberg (2011). https://doi.org/10.1007/978-3-642-24449-0_4. http://dl.acm.org/citation.cfm?id=2042476.2042480
13. Movchan, A., Zymbler, M.: Time series subsequence similarity search under dynamic time warping distance on the intel many-core accelerators. In: Amato, G., Connor, R., Falchi, F., Gennaro, C. (eds.) SISAP 2015. LNCS, vol. 9371, pp. 295–306. Springer, Cham (2015). https://doi.org/10.1007/978-3-319-25087-8_28
14. Netti, A., et al.: From facility to application sensor data: modular, continuous and holistic monitoring with DCDB. In: Proceedings of the International Conference for High Performance Computing, Networking, Storage and Analysis SC 2019, pp. 64:1–64:27. ACM, New York (2019). https://doi.org/10.1145/3295500.3356191
15. Pfeilschifter, G.: Time series analysis with matrix profile on HPC systems. Master thesis, Technische Universität München (2019)

16. Roddick, J.F., Spiliopoulou, M.: A survey of temporal knowledge discovery paradigms and methods. IEEE Trans. Knowl. Data Eng. **14**, 750–767 (2002)
17. Sart, D., Mueen, A., Najjar, W., Keogh, E., Niennattrakul, V.: Accelerating dynamic time warping subsequence search with GPUs and FPGAs. In: 2010 IEEE International Conference on Data Mining, pp. 1001–1006, December 2010
18. Tanaka, Y., Iwamoto, K., Uehara, K.: Discovery of time-series motif from multidimensional data based on MDL principle. Mach. Learn. **58**, 269–300 (2005)
19. Taylor, S.: Optimizing Applications for Multi-Core Processors, Using the Intel Integrated Performance Primitives. Intel Press, Santa Clara (2007)
20. Treibig, J., Hager, G., Wellein, G.: LIKWID: a lightweight performance-oriented tool suite for x86 multicore environments. In: Proceedings of PSTI2010, the First International Workshop on Parallel Software Tools and Tool Infrastructures, San Diego, CA (2010)
21. Vahdatpour, A., Amini, N., Sarrafzadeh, M.: Toward unsupervised activity discovery using multi-dimensional motif detection in time series. In: Proceedings of the 21st International Joint Conference on Artifical Intelligence IJCAI 2009, pp. 1261–1266. Morgan Kaufmann Publishers Inc., San Francisco (2009). http://dl.acm.org/citation.cfm?id=1661445.1661647
22. Yeh, C.M., Herle, H.V., Keogh, E.: Matrix profile III: the matrix profile allows visualization of salient subsequences in massive time series. In: 2016 IEEE 16th International Conference on Data Mining (ICDM), pp. 579–588, December 2016. https://doi.org/10.1109/ICDM.2016.0069
23. Yeh, C.M., Kavantzas, N., Keogh, E.: Matrix profile VI: meaningful multidimensional motif discovery. In: 2017 IEEE International Conference on Data Mining (ICDM), pp. 565–574, November 2017. https://doi.org/10.1109/ICDM.2017.66
24. Yeh, C.M., et al.: Matrix profile I: all pairs similarity joins for time series: a unifying view that includes motifs, discords and shapelets. In: 2016 IEEE 16th International Conference on Data Mining (ICDM), pp. 1317–1322, December 2016. https://doi.org/10.1109/ICDM.2016.0179
25. Zhu, Y., Yeh, C.M., Zimmerman, Z., Kamgar, K., Keogh, E.: Matrix profile XI: SCRIMP++: time series motif discovery at interactive speeds. In: 2018 IEEE International Conference on Data Mining (ICDM), pp. 837–846, November 2018. https://doi.org/10.1109/ICDM.2018.00099
26. Zhu, Y., et al.: Matrix profile II: exploiting a novel algorithm and GPUs to break the one hundred million barrier for time series motifs and joins. Knowl. Inf. Syst. **54**(1), 203–236 (2018)
27. Zimmerman, Z., et al.: Scaling time series motif discovery with GPUs: breaking the quintillion pairwise comparisons a day barrier. In: Proceedings of the ACM Symposium on Cloud Computing (2018)

# Data, Storage and Visualization

# Shared-Memory Parallel Probabilistic Graphical Modeling Optimization: Comparison of Threads, OpenMP, and Data-Parallel Primitives

Talita Perciano[1]([✉])([iD]), Colleen Heinemann[1,2], David Camp[1], Brenton Lessley[3], and E. Wes Bethel[1]

[1] Lawrence Berkeley National Laboratory, Berkeley, USA
{tperciano,dcamp,ewbethel}@lbl.gov
[2] University of Illinois at Urbana-Champaign, Champaign, USA
heinmnn2@illinois.edu
[3] Verb Surgical, Inc., Santa Clara, USA

**Abstract.** This work examines performance characteristics of multiple shared-memory implementations of a probabilistic graphical modeling (PGM) optimization code, which forms the basis for an advanced, state-of-the art image segmentation method. The work is motivated by the need to accelerate scientific image analysis pipelines in use by experimental science, such as at x-ray light sources, and is motivated by the need for platform-portable codes that perform well across many different computational architectures. The primary focus of this work and its main contribution is an in-depth study of shared-memory parallel performance of different implementations, which include those using alternative parallelization approaches such as C11-threads, OpenMP, and data parallel primitives (DPPs). Our results show that, for this complex data-intensive algorithm, the DPP implementation exhibits better runtime performance, but also exhibits less favorable scaling characteristics than the C11-threads and OpenMP counterparts. Based upon a set of experiments that collect hardware performance counters on multiple platforms, the reason for the runtime performance difference appears to be due primarily to algorithmic efficiency gains: the reformulation from the traditional C11-threads and OpenMP expression of the solution into that of data parallel primitives results in significantly fewer instructions being executed. This study is the first of its type to do performance analysis using hardware counters for comparing methods based on VTK-m-based data-parallel primitives with those based on more traditional OpenMP or threads-based parallelism. It is timely, as there is increasing awareness of the need for platform portability in light of increasing node-level parallelism and increasing device heterogeneity.

**Keywords:** Probabilistic graphical models · Modeling optimization · Markov random fields · Image segmentation · Computer vision · Data parallel primitives · Shared-memory parallel · Platform portability

© Springer Nature Switzerland AG 2020
P. Sadayappan et al. (Eds.): ISC High Performance 2020, LNCS 12151, pp. 127–145, 2020.
https://doi.org/10.1007/978-3-030-50743-5_7

# 1   Introduction

Image segmentation is a computationally intensive task, influencing scientific analysis pipelines as a critical element, particularly those that work with large image-based data obtained by experiments and advanced instruments, such as the X-ray imaging devices located at the Advanced Light Source at Berkeley Lab[1]. As such instruments continually update in spatial and spectral resolution, there is an increasing need for high-throughput processing of large collections of 2D and 3D image data for use in time-critical activities such as experiment optimization and tuning [3]. Our work here is motivated by the need for image analysis tools that perform well on modern platforms, and that are expected to be portable to next-generation hardware (Fig. 1).

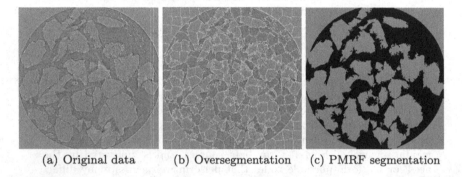

(a) Original data        (b) Oversegmentation        (c) PMRF segmentation

**Fig. 1.** Going from a raw image obtained by experiment to a segmented image suitable for quantitative analysis involves multiple processing stages. This example shows a single 2D slice from a 3D image stack obtained by x-ray microscopy at the Advanced Light Source. Here, the original data (left) undergoes an image oversegmentation to produce coarse regions (middle), which then undergo an additional processing stage to produce a highly accurate segmentation (right). The focus of this paper is on the method for the final processing stage, which uses a probabilistic graphical model that is optimized using a Markov Random Field formulation.

This work centers on evaluating the viability of specific approaches for achieving platform portability and performance on multi- and many-core platforms. We focus on a specific data-intensive problem for this study known as probabilistic graphical model (PGM) optimization using a Markov Random Field (MRF) formulation to tackle image segmentation problems. Such methods are known for their high degree of accuracy, and, thanks to recent advances, their amenability to parallelization. We focus on shared-memory parallel performance in this study, with an eye towards future hybrid-parallel implementations that build on our previous works [11,17,18,30].

We parallelize this unsupervised, graph-based learning method applied to scientific image segmentation using three different approaches, and perform an

---

[1] Advanced Light Source website: http://als.lbl.gov/.

in-depth performance analysis of each of the three: first by using C11-threads, then using the Open Multi-Processing (OpenMP) API, and finally using data-parallel primitives (Sort, Scan, Reduce, etc.). The C11-threads implementation is the most coarse in terms of workload decomposition, where $N$ pixel neighborhoods are spread across $P$ threads, where each thread receives $N/P$ of the work. The OpenMP implementation uses loop parallelization over the $N$ neighborhoods, which is a finer-grained distribution than the C11-threads version, and also benefits from better load balance due to OpenMP's dynamic scheduling capabilities. The DPP implementation is the finest level of workload decomposition, where the $K$ operations in a given DPP are divided in chunks of size $C$ across $P$ execution threads.

In this work, we evaluate the key performance characteristics of each implementation using strong scalability measures and runtime performance. We also analyze the factors that lead to these performance characteristics by examining hardware performance counters for metrics like code vectorization, number of instructions executed, and memory cache utilization. The main contributions of this paper are: (1) to compare performance of a PGM optimization algorithm implemented with VTK-m-based data parallel primitives with ones based on explicit threading and OpenMP; (2) to give insight into performance characteristics of PGM optimization using VTK-m-based data parallel primitives; (3) the first use of hardware performance counters to examine the performance of a VTK-m-based code, where previous works looking at visualization and rendering measure and report runtime only (e.g., [15–17,19,23,28]).

## 2   Background and Previous Work

In the following sections, we summarize works relating to image segmentation, graph-based methods including MRF, and approaches for performance and portability using C11-threads, OpenMP, and data parallel primitives.

### 2.1   MRF-Based Image Segmentation

The process of segmenting an image involves separating various phases or components from a picture using photometric information and/or relationships between pixels/regions representing a scene. This essential step in an image analysis pipeline has been given great attention recently when studying experimental data [29]. There are several different types of image segmentation algorithms, which can be divided into categories, such as: threshold-based, region-based, edge-based, clustering-based, graph-based, and learning-based techniques. Of these, the graph- and learning-based methods tend to achieve the highest accuracy, but at the highest computational cost.

Graph-based methods are well-suited for image segmentation tasks due to their ability to use contextual information contained in the image, i.e., relationships among pixels and/or regions. The probabilistic graphical model (PGM) known as Markov random fields (MRF) [22] is an example of one such method.

MRFs represent discrete data by modeling neighborhood relationships, thereby consolidating structure representation for image analysis [21].

Despite their high accuracy, MRF optimization algorithms have high computational complexity (NP-hard). Strategies for overcoming the complexity, such as graph-cut techniques, are often restricted to specific types of models (first-order MRFs) [14] and energy functions (regular or submodular) [14]. For higher-order MRFs and non-submodular functions, some strategies using parallelized graph cuts and parallelized Belief Propagation have also been proposed [7,10,12,32]. These approaches, though, typically depend on orderly reduction or submodular functions [34], which are undesirable constraints when dealing with complex and large image datasets because they limit the contextual modeling of the problem.

In order to circumvent such drawbacks, recent works [24,25] have proposed theoretical foundations for distributed parameter estimation in MRF. These approaches make use of a composite likelihood, which enable parallel solutions to subproblems. Under general conditions on the composite likelihood factorizations, the distributed estimators are proven to be consistent. The Linear and Parallel (LAP) [26] algorithm parallelizes naturally over cliques and, for graphs of bounded degree, its complexity is linear in the number of cliques. It is fully parallel and, for log-linear models, it is also data efficient. It requires only the local statistics of the data, i.e., considering only pixel values of local neighborhoods, to estimate parameters.

Perciano *et al.* [30] describe a graph-based model, referred to as Parallel Markov Random Fields (PMRF), which exploits MRFs to segment images. Both the optimization and parameter estimation processes are parallelized using the LAP method, and the implementation is based on C11 multithreading. The first attempt to reimplement the PMRF algorithm is described in [11], where a distributed-memory version of the algorithm is implemented using MPI. Lessley *et al.* [18] reformulates the PMRF algorithm using data parallel primitives implemented in the VTK-m library. This work takes advantage of a new implementation of the maximal cliques problem also using DPPs [19].

Although the previous works study the computational performance of the reimplemented versions of the PMRF algorithm, the correctness of the new versions is emphasized. In the work we present here, we describe a detailed study of shared-memory scalability, as well as collecting hardware performance counters, such as FLOPS/vectorization, memory utilization, instruction counts, and so forth, and use these to perform an in-depth analysis of three shared-memory parallel implementations of the PMRF algorithm: C11-threads, OpenMP, DPP. In the long term, these shared-memory parallel methods would be paired with our distributed-memory parallel implementation [11] to produce a scalable, hybrid-parallel implementation that is portable across HPC platforms and processors.

## 2.2   Performance and Portability

**Open Multi-Processing (OpenMP).** OpenMP has been used before to accelerate graph-based algorithms. Recently, Meng *et al.* [24] proposed a parallelization of graph-based machine learning algorithms using OpenMP. The authors also use LAPACK [2] and BLAS [4], which are highly vectorized and multi-threaded using OpenMP, to optimize intensive linear algebra calculations.

Sariyuce *et al.* [31], describe a hybrid implementation of graph coloring using MPI and OpenMP. Ersoy *et al.* [9] proposed a parallel implementation of a shortest path algorithm for time dependent graphs using OpenMP and CUDA. Time dependent shortest path problem (TDSPP) is another example of an NP-hard problem, as the one we tackle in this paper.

We reformulate the PMRF algorithm using OpenMP by targeting loop parallelization over neighborhoods, which is relatively coarse-grained when compared to "inner-loop" parallelization. Load balancing is enabled through OpenMPs dynamic scheduling algorithms.

**Data Parallel Primitives (DPP).** The primary motivation of using DPPs, particularly those that are amenable to vectorization, is because this approach appears promising for achieving good performance on multi- and many-core architectures. Levesque and Voss, 2017 [20], speculate that vectorized codes may achieve performance gains of as much as 10–30 fold compared to non-vectorized code, with the added benefit of using less power on multi- and many-core architectures. DPPs are amenable to vectorization, and in turn, are capable of high performance on multi- and many-core architectures. This idea is not new, but goes over 20 years to early work by Blelloch [5], who proposed a vector-scan model for parallel computing.

Lessley, et al., 2018 [18] present an implementation of the PMRF algorithm using DPPs. The DPP form of PMRF required a non-trivial reformulation of the reference C++/OpenMP implementation, where reformulation is required to map traditional loop-based computations onto data parallel primitives such as Sort, Scan, Reduce, etc. That work compared performance and scaling differences of DPP-PMRF and C++/OpenMP parallel versions by measuring runtime performance.

The DPP-PMRF implementation relies on the VTK-m library [28], which is a platform-portable framework that provides a set of key DPPs, along with back-end code generation and runtime support for the use of GPUs (CUDA) and multi-core CPUs (TBB [6]) from a single code base [27]. VTK-m achieves parallelization by distributing the work of its DPPs across "threads" using a chunking/blocking model, where a larger collection of work is distributed in chunks or blocks across threads. This basic concept applies to both CPU and GPU implementations.

For the work we present here, we are using the implementation of DPP-PMRF from Lessley et al., 2018 [18], but building upon that previous work in a significant way. Namely, the 2018 study measured only runtime, whereas in the work we present here, we are measuring several different types of hardware performance counters to gain a better understanding of the factors contributing to absolute runtime performance differences and relative scaling characteristics, and compare those measures with those obtained from traditional OpenMP and threads-parallel implementations of the PMRF algorithm.

## 3   Design and Implementation

We begin by presenting the baseline, serial MRF-based image segmentation algorithm (Sect. 3.1). The subsequent subsections cover three different parallel implementations: C11-threads (Sect. 3.2), OpenMP (Sect. 3.3), and DPP (Sect. 3.4). Each of these parallel subsections will focus on key parallelization topics, namely work decomposition and the parallel algorithm implementation, with an emphasis on highlighting differences from the baseline implementation.

### 3.1   The Baseline MRF Algorithm

The baseline MRF algorithm, along with a threads-parallel variant, are described in more detail in Perciano *et al.*, 2016 [30]. The input consists of a grayscale image, an oversegmentation of the input image, and a parameter indicating the desired number of output labels (classes). The oversegmented image is a preliminary segmentation based upon a low-cost computational estimate. For example, a threshold operator can produce an oversegmented image. The oversegmented image is known to be inaccurate, but is inexpensive to compute. It is inaccurate in that it has "too many" segments, or regions, hence the name "oversegmented". The oversegmented image serves as the starting point for MRF optimization, which will merge and change oversegmented regions into a more accurate segmentation.

The pseudocode for the Baseline MRF algorithm is shown in Algorithm 1. It consists of a one-time initialization phase, followed by a compute-intensive, primary parameter estimation optimization phase. The output is a segmented image.

---

**Algorithm 1.** Baseline MRF

---

**Require:** Original image, oversegmentation, number of output labels
**Ensure:** Segmented image and estimated parameters
1: Initialize parameters and labels randomly
2: Create graph from oversegmentation
3: Find maximal cliques of the graph
4: Construct $k$-neighborhoods for all maximal cliques
5: **for** each EM iteration **do**
6:     **for** each neighborhood of the subgraph **do**
7:         Compute MAP estimation
8:     **end for**
9:     Update parameters and labels
10: **end for**

---

The goal of the initialization phase is the construction of an undirected graph of pixel regions, each with statistically similar grayscale intensities among member pixels. Starting with the original image and the oversegmented version of that image, the algorithm then builds a graph from the oversegmented image, where each vertex $V$ represents a region in the oversegmented image (i.e., a spatially connected region of pixels having similar intensity), and each edge $E$ indicates spatial adjacency of regions.

Next, in the main computational phase, we define an MRF model over the set of vertices, which includes an energy function representing contextual information of the image. In particular, this model specifies a probability distribution over the $k$-neighborhoods of the graph. Each $k$-neighborhood consists of the vertices of a maximal clique, along with all neighbor vertices that are within $k$ edges (or hops) from any of the clique vertices; in this study, we use $k = 1$.

The MRF algorithm then performs energy function optimization over each of these neighborhoods. This optimization consists of an iterative invocation of the expectation-maximization (EM) algorithm, which performs parameter estimation using the maximum *a posteriori* (MAP) inference algorithm [13]. The goal of the optimization routine is to converge on the most-likely (minimum-energy) assignment of labels for the vertices in the graph; the mapping of the vertex labels back to pixels yields the output image segmentation.

## 3.2   The C++/Threads Algorithm

The C++/Threads implementation uses the same input and parameters as the Baseline implementation and performs the same types of computations. The computation is parallelized by dividing the $N$ neighborhoods evenly across each of the $T$ threads. In this case, the first group of $N/T$ neighborhoods is assigned to the first thread, the second $N/T$ to the second thread, and so forth. Processing consists of optimizing a set of neighborhoods using MAP and estimating the parameters for the desired labels (classes). In this implementation, a shared-memory array that hold results from the optimization process is used by all threads on subsequent EM iterations. This shared-memory array is a vector that carries the estimated classes for each vertex of the graph. During the parallel optimization process, the threads are synchronized every time the shared-memory is updated with new estimated values for each vertex.

This threads-based model is coarse-grained parallelism: each thread is responsible for a rather sizeable amount of work, with relatively little interaction between threads. Also, the way the algorithm distributes the work across threads does not take into account the size of the neighborhoods. This can potentially lead to load imbalance, given that the neighborhoods can vary considerably depending on the input and oversegmentation.

---

**Algorithm 2.** C++/Threads: Threaded implementation of parallel MRF

---

**Require:** Original image, oversegmentation, number of output labels
**Ensure:** Segmented image and estimated parameters
 1: Initialize parameters and labels randomly
 2: Create graph from oversegmentation
 3: Find maximal cliques of the graph
 4: Construct $k$-neighborhoods for all maximal cliques
 5: Partition into T groups of size N/T
 6: **for** *In parallel*: each thread processes its N/T group **do**
 7:     **for** each EM iteration **do**
 8:         **for** each neighborhood of the subgraph **do**
 9:             Compute MAP estimation
10:         **end for**
11:         Update parameters and labels
12:     **end for**
13: **end for**

---

### 3.3   The C++/OpenMP Algorithm

The OpenMP-parallel version of the MRF algorithm, shown in Algorithm 3, uses the same input and parameters as the Baseline implementation and performs the same types of computations. This version is finer-grained in terms of workload distribution as compared to the C++/Threads version: the inner loop of Algorithm 3 iterates over neighborhoods, of which there are typically many (thousands for 2D images to millions for 3D volumes). We parallelize that neighborhood-iteration loop using OpenMP, and use OpenMP's dynamic thread scheduling algorithms to achieve more even load balance across all threads. The challenge in this problem is that the amount of computation required for each neighborhood varies as a function of the size of the neighborhood and its connectivity to adjacent regions.

---

**Algorithm 3.** C++/OpenMP: Parallelization with OpenMP

---

**Require:** Original image, oversegmentation, number of output labels
**Ensure:** Segmented image and estimated parameters
 1: Initialize parameters and labels randomly
 2: Create graph from oversegmentation
 3: Find maximal cliques of the graph
 4: Construct $k$-neighborhoods for all maximal cliques
 5: **for** each EM iteration **do**
 6:     **for** *OpenMP parallel* each neighborhood of the subgraph **do**
 7:         Compute MAP estimation
 8:     **end for**
 9:     Update parameters and labels
10: **end for**

---

Compared to the threads implementation, the OpenMP design targets a finer granularity so as to achieve better load balance across threads. One of the objectives of our performance study is to better understand the performance impact of these different design choices.

## 3.4 VTK-m/DPP

Our VTK-m/DPP implementation [18] is a complete reformulation of the MRF algorithm using data-parallel primitives. To make use of DPPs, the implementation recasts the algorithm into a sequence of DPP-based processing steps, e.g, sequences of operations like Scan, Sort, and Reduce.

Algorithm 4 shows pseudocode for the VTK-m/DPP algorithm. Each of these steps is a complex seqeuence of DPP calls. For example, from [18], the line that reads"Construct k-neighborhoods from maximal cliques in parallel" consists of several DPP operations:

---

**Algorithm 4.** VTK-m/DPP: Data parallel primitive version of Markov Random Field algorithm

---

**Require:** Original image, oversegmentation, number of output labels
**Ensure:** Segmented image and estimated parameters
 1: *DPP in parallel:* Create graph from oversegmentation
 2: *DPP in parallel:* Enumerate maximal cliques of graph
 3: Initialize parameters and labels randomly
 4: *DPP in parallel:* Construct $k$-neighborhoods from maximal cliques
 5: *DPP in parallel:* Replicate neighborhoods by label
 6: **for** each EM iteration **do**
 7:     *DPP in parallel:* Gather replicated parameters and labels
 8:     **for** each vertex of each neighborhood **do**
 9:         *DPP in parallel:* MAP estimation
10:     **end for**
11:     *DPP in parallel:* Update parameters and labels
12: **end for**

---

1. A Map operator finds the count of neighbors that are within 1 edge from the vertex and not a member of the vertex's maximal clique;
2. A Scan operator adds the counts of neighbors for the purpose of allocating a neighbors array work buffer;
3. A Map operator populates the newly created neighbors array;
4. The SortByKey and Unique operators remove duplicate neighbors.

There are several significant differences between the VTK-m/DPP, C++/-OpenMP, and C++/Threads implementations of this method. One is the level of granularity in parallelization. The C++/Threads is the coarsest decomposition, C++/OpenMP in the middle, and the VTK-m/DPP is the finest level of granularity of parallelization. Each of the DPPs is distributed in chunking fashion across each of the $T$ available execution threads. Another key difference is in the relative level of "verboseness" of the algorithm itself. While we did not count the number of lines of code, as we shall see in the Results section (Sect. 4.3), there is a significant difference in the number of instructions executed by each of these implementations.

# 4    Experiment and Results

The experiments in this section serve to answer two primary questions. First, we are interested in how well the different implementations perform on a single-socket study: what are the key performance characteristics of each version? Second, we collect hardware performance counters to understand how well each implementation vectorizes and makes use of the memory hierarchy: what are the factors that lead to these performance characteristics? Sect. 4.1 describes the source datasets and the computational platform that we use for the experiments. Sect. 4.2 presents results of the study, which we discuss in Sect. 4.3.

## 4.1    Datasets, Computational Platforms, and Software

**Datasets.** We are using an experimental dataset that was generated by the Lawrence Berkeley National Laboratory Advanced Light Source X-ray beamline 8.3.2[2] [8] for all tests. This dataset contains cross-sections of a geological sample and conveys information regarding the x-ray attenuation and density of the scanned material as a gray scale value. The scanned samples are pre-processed using a separate software that provides reconstruction of the parallel beam projection data into a 1 GB stack of 500 image slices with dimensions of $1290 \times 1305$.

For our experiments, we use two augmented versions of this dataset, where we replicate the data of each cross-section by mirroring in both the X and Y dimensions of the data, resulting in one 3.3 GB stack of 500 image slices with dimensions of $2580 \times 2610$ (referred to as the 'Sandstone2K' dataset), and one 6.6 GB stack of 500 image slices with dimensions of $5160 \times 5220$ (referred to as the 'Sandstone5k' dataset).

**Hardware Platforms**
*Intel Xeon Phi.* Cori.nersc.gov is a Cray XC40 system comprised of 2,388 nodes containing two 2.3 Ghz 16-core Intel Haswell processors and 128 GB DDR4 2133 MHz memory, and 9,688 nodes containing a single 68-core 1.4 GHz Intel Xeon Phi 7250 (Knights Landing) processor and 96 GB DDR4 2400 GHz memory. For our experiments, we use the KNL processor.[3] Compiler: Intel ICC 19.0.3.199.

---

[2] http://microct.lbl.gov.
[3] Cori configuration page: http://www.nersc.gov/users/computational-systems/cori/configuration/.

*Ivy Bridge.* `Allen.lbl.gov` is an Intel(R) Xeon(R) CPU E5-2609 v2 containing two 2.5 GHz 4-core Intel Xeon Ivy Bridge EN/EP/EX processors and 32 GB of memory. Compiler: Intel ICC 19.1.0.166.

**Software Environment.** The software environment in these tests consists of several different codes, each of which we describe below.

*Oversegmentation.* We use a custom implementation of the Simple Linear Iterative Clustering (SLIC) method [1]. This implementation will take as input 2D images or 3D volumes of scalar values (gray-level images), and output 2D images or 3D volumes at the same resolution as the input data, but where output pixels/voxels are region label values, rather than pixel/voxel luminosity. We prepare using the input images/volumes described above, and process them using the following SLIC parameters: superpixel size = 80, compactness = 10.

*C++/OpenMP and C++/Threads.* The C++/Threads version of PMRF is implemented using C11 multithreading for parallelization. The C++/OpenMP algorithm is implemented with OpenMP 4.5. We take advantage of OpenMP loop parallelism constructs to achieve outer-parallelism over MRF neighborhoods, and make use of OpenMP's dynamic scheduling algorithm in the performance studies.

*VTK-m/DPP.* The VTK-m/DPP algorithm is implemented using the platform-portable VTK-m toolkit [27], and coded to VTK-m API version 1.3.0. In our experiments, we configured VTK-m for parallelism on the CPU by enabling an OpenMP backend, and set the VTK-m index integer (vtkm::Id) size to 64 bits.

*Hardware Performance Counters.* For measuring hardware performance counters on CPU platforms, we made use of `likwid-perfctr`, which is part of the LIKWID toolsuite [33]. LIKWID is a collection of command line programs that facilitate performance-oriented program development and production in x86 multicore environments under Linux. Using LIKWID 4.3.4 on Allen/Ivy Bridge and 4.3.0 on Cori/KNL, we collected and analyzed several different performance counters and restricted these measures to the PGM graph optimization phase only by using LIKWID's marker API:

- Counts of total number of double-precision scalar and vector instructions executed (`FLOPS_DP`), as well as total number of all scalar and vector instructions executed (`UOPS_RETIRED_*`).
- Measures related to L2 cache: L2 request rate, miss rate, and miss ratio (`L2CACHE`).
- Vectorization ratio. On Ivy Bridge, LIKWID reports this directly. On KNL, we compute this ratio to be $V/(V + S)$, where $V$ is the count of vector ("packed") operations, and $S$ is the count of scalar operations.

## 4.2    Performance and Scalability Studies: Parallel MRF

Here, we present the results of performance and scaling studies of the three different PMRF implementations (VTK-m/DPP, C++/OpenMP, C++/Threads) on two different platforms (KNL, Ivy Bridge). The primary objective is to compare their runtime performance and scalability, and to examine hardware counters to gain deeper insight into the performance characteristics of each method. The discussion and analysis of these results appears in Sect. 4.3, which follows.

*Runtime.* The first performance study question we examine is a comparison of runtimes among the implementations used. We executed all the codes at varying levels of concurrency on the KNL platform and Ivy Bridge platforms using two different datasets (sandstone2k and sandstone5k). The speedup plots for the datasets on both platforms are shown in Fig. 2 and Fig. 3.

Speedup is defined as $S(n,p) = \frac{T^*(n)}{T(n,p)}$ where $T(n,p)$ is the time it takes to run the parallel algorithm on $p$ processes with an input size of $n$, and $T^*(n)$ is the time for the best serial algorithm on the same input.

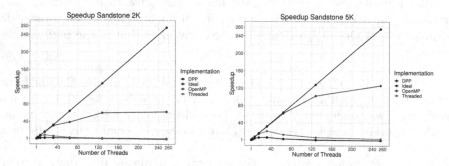

**Fig. 2.** Speedup of the Sandstone2K and Sandstone5K datasets on Cori. The horizontal axis is the concurrency level and the vertical axis measures the speedup.

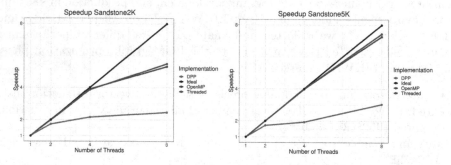

**Fig. 3.** Speedup of the Sandstone2K and Sandstone5K datasets on the Ivy Bridge platform. The horizontal axis is the concurrency level and the vertical axis measures the speedup.

Examining these two speedup plots, we notice that although the VTK-m/DPP version presents much faster runtimes at lower concurrencies, this implementation shows the worst speedups for both platforms. On the Ivy Bridge platform, both the C++/Threads and C++/OpenMP versions present the best speedup values with very similar results. On the other hand, on the KNL platform, the C++/Threads version presents a similar speedup compared to the VTK-m/DPP version.

*Hardware Performance Counters.* To gain a deeper understanding into code performance, we collect hardware performance counters using LIKWID on the KNL and Ivy Bridge platforms for the three different implementations. Table 1 shows the results of the three different implementations run on the KNL platform. Here, we vary concurrency across the range of 1, 2, ..., 256. Using LIKWID, we record the counts for the FLOPS_DP and L2CACHE performance counter groups. Results for the Ivy Bridge platform tests are shown in Table 2, where concurrency varies across 1, 2, ..., 8.

**Table 1.** KNL Platform and Hardware Performance Counters for the Sandstone5K Dataset. Legend for counters: FLOPS: FLOPS_DP ($*10^9$); Vector%: Vectorization Ratio (Proxy); L2 Miss Ratio: average % across all threads at a given concurrency.

| Counter | Code ver. | Concurrency | | | | | | | | |
|---|---|---|---|---|---|---|---|---|---|---|
| | | 1 | 2 | 4 | 8 | 16 | 32 | 64 | 128 | 256 |
| Runtime (secs) | VTK-m/DPP | 5.78 | 3.93 | 3.01 | 1.33 | 0.94 | 0.90 | 1.84 | 6.65 | 27.39 |
| | C++/OpenMP | 143.56 | 72.75 | 36.48 | 18.25 | 9.14 | 4.58 | 2.31 | 1.40 | 1.13 |
| | C++/Threads | 140.16 | 70.24 | 35.48 | 18.09 | 9.89 | 6.73 | 10.92 | 21.60 | 43.23 |
| | | 1 | 2 | 4 | 8 | 16 | 32 | 64 | 128 | 256 |
| FLOPS | VTK-m/DPP | 0.85 | 0.86 | 0.86 | 0.86 | 0.86 | 0.86 | 0.86 | 0.88 | 0.88 |
| | C++/OpenMP | 49.32 | 49.32 | 49.32 | 49.32 | 49.32 | 49.32 | 49.32 | 49.32 | 49.32 |
| | C++/Threads | 45.39 | 45.49 | 45.59 | 45.79 | 46.19 | 47.00 | 48.62 | 51.84 | 57.66 |
| | | 1 | 2 | 4 | 8 | 16 | 32 | 64 | 128 | 256 |
| L2 Miss Ratio % | VTK-m/DPP | 0.01 | 0.20 | 0.39 | 0.97 | 2.86 | 7.72 | 24.79 | 61.05 | 64.66 |
| | C++/OpenMP | 0.01 | 0.01 | 0.02 | 0.09 | 0.09 | 0.05 | 0.11 | 1.22 | 8.12 |
| | C++/Threads | 0.01 | 0.01 | 0.06 | 0.16 | 0.28 | 0.36 | 0.42 | 0.94 | 1.57 |
| | | 1 | | | | | | | | |
| Vector % | VTK-m/DPP | 43.48% | | | | | | | | |
| | C++/OpenMP | 51.44% | | | | | | | | |
| | C++/Threads | 46.89% | | | | | | | | |

## 4.3  Discussion and Analysis

*The VTK-m/DPP code is executing far fewer floating point instructions than its C++/OpenMP and C++/Threads counterparts.* For all the test results we present, the runtime difference between the DPP (VTK-m/DPP) and non-DPP

140     T. Perciano et al.

(C++/OpenMP, C++/Threads) versions appears to be proportional to the difference in the amount of floating point instructions being executed. While the DPP code is solving the same set of numerical equations as the non-DPP code (for the MRF optimization), it does so using a completely different algorithmic formulation. The DPP code design involved a significant refactorization of the MRF optimization algorithm to map it to data parallel primitives [18]. This reordering has resulted in significantly fewer operations being required to perform the computation, and is one of the primary findings of this study.

*Vectorization Ratios.* In both Table 1 and Table 2, we report a Vectorization Ratio only for the serial configuration because this value does not change in a significant way with increasing concurrency: the algorithm's complexity is primarily dependent upon problem size.

On the KNL platform, we see vectorization ratios that are comparable across all three implementations, in the range of about 43%–51%. This result suggests that the looping structures in all three implementations are amenable to a reasonable level of automatic vectorization by the compiler on the KNL platform.

On the Ivy Bridge platform, the C++/OpenMP and C++/Threads versions show vectorization ratios above 70%, while the VTK-m/DPP version shows a much lower vectorization ratio of about 18%. There are two likely factors

**Table 2.** Ivy Bridge Platform and Hardware Performance Counters for the Sandstone5K Dataset. Legend for counters: FLOPS: (Double Precision Scalar FLOPS + Double Precision Vector FLOPS) / ($10^9$); Vector%: Vectorization Ratio; L2 Miss Ratio: average % across all threads at a given concurrency.

| Counter/Measure | Code version | Concurrency | | | |
|---|---|---|---|---|---|
| | | 1 | 2 | 4 | 8 |
| Runtime (secs) | VTK-m/DPP | 2.51 | 1.46 | 1.30 | 0.83 |
| | C++/OpenMP | 13.34 | 6.66 | 3.35 | 1.83 |
| | C++/Threads | 13.94 | 7.00 | 3.51 | 2.16 |
| | | 1 | 2 | 4 | 8 |
| FLOPS ($*10^9$) | VTK-m/DPP | 0.47 | 0.33 | 0.33 | 0.33 |
| | C++/OpenMP | 7.14 | 7.13 | 7.13 | 7.13 |
| | C++/Threads | 7.25 | 7.26 | 7.26 | 7.27 |
| | | 1 | 2 | 4 | 8 |
| L2 Miss Ratio % | VTK-m/DPP | 0.26 | 0.26 | 0.25 | 0.25 |
| | C++/OpenMP | 0.05 | 0.07 | 0.05 | 0.05 |
| | C++/Threads | 0.04 | 0.06 | 0.06 | 0.06 |
| | | 1 | | | |
| Vector % | VTK-m/DPP | 18.16% | | | |
| | C++/OpenMP | 73.31% | | | |
| | C++/Threads | 70.43% | | | |

contributing to this difference. The first is in the code itself: the C++/OpenMP and C++/Threads codes implement their computations using C++ vector objects, and these are likely easier for the compiler to auto-vectorize compared to code that performs explicit blocking and chunking, as is the case with VTK-m internals, which will take a large DPP operation and decompose it into smaller chunks, which are then executed in parallel by one of several backends (TBB, OpenMP, or CUDA). With explicit blocking and chunking, there may be an adverse interplay between how VTK-m blocks and chunks and what the compiler needs for a given architecture. This particular issue merits further study to better understand this interplay.

The second reason concerns variation in how the compiler auto-vectorizes code for each architecture. What works well on one architecture may not work so well on a different architecture: we see this with the VTK-m/DPP code base where the Intel compiler auto-vectorizes code to produce 43.48% vectorization on the KNL platform, but is able to manage only 18.16% on the Ivy Bridge platform. With the hardware performance counters we have access to with LIKWID, we are unable to discern precisely which type of vector instructions are being executed (e.g., SSE, AVX, AVX512) on each platform, which would in term provide more useful insights.

At the outset of this study, we had the expectation that the VTK-m/DPP code would have significantly better vectorization characteristics, which would then account for its significantly faster runtime, particularly as we observed in earlier studies [18]. Instead, what we see are comparable levels of vectorization on the KNL (43%–51%), and a lower vectorization level on Ivy Bridge (18%).

It turns out that there are other factors that, in this study, have much more impact on code performance than vectorization, namely the absolute number of instructions executed. One of the primary findings of this study is that our refactoring a complex graph algorithm (PMRF) to use DPPs results in significantly fewer instructions being executed compared to implementations using C++/OpenMP and C++/Threads.

*Scalability.* These studies show differing levels of scalability, as evidenced in the speedup charts shown in Fig. 2. The VTK-m/DPP code on the KNL platform shows decreasing runtime up to about 32 cores, after which it increases in runtime. Looking at the performance counters in Table 1, we see a corresponding increase in the L2 Cache Miss ratio. The L2 cache misses are due to how KNL shares L2 cache across hardware threads, where increasing the number of threads to exceed the number of cores causes the amount of L2 cache available to each core to be reduced. In other words, if there is one thread per core, it will use all of the L2 cache, if two threads share a core, each thread has one-half of the L2 cache, and if three or four threads share a core, then each thread has access to 1/4 of the L2 cache.

On the KNL, the C++/Threads implementation shows decreasing runtime up to about 32 cores, after which point the runtime increases significantly. Whereas the VTK-m/DPP code shows significant L2 cache misses at higher concurrency, the C++/Threads version does not. Instead, this performance difference between C++/Threads and C++/OpenMP at higher concurrency is most likely the result of a highly optimized OpenMP loop parallelization that is provided by the compiler, an effect that does not become readily apparent until higher degrees of node-level concurrency on the KNL platform.

On the Ivy Bridge platform, all implementations exhibit better scalability than on the KNL platform. This is most likely the result of a large L3 cache that is shared across all cores, something that is not present on the KNL platform. However, the Ivy Bridge study only goes up to 8 threads, and the declined in speedup shown in the KNL study (Fig. 2) does not begin until higher levels of concurrency. Therefore, while we may see a decline in speedup on the Ivy Bridge at higher concurrency, since that platform has only 8 cores, our study only goes up to 8-way concurrency.

*Platform Portability Issues.* One of the objectives of OpenMP and VTK-m is to provide platform portability, so that a given code implementation can be run, without modification, on CPU and GPU platforms. We have demonstrated in previous work [18] that the VTK-m/DPP is capable of running on the GPU platform. For the C++/OpenMP implementation, there are significant restrictions and limitations on OpenMP in terms of what kind of code can be processed successfully to emit device code. At the present time, our C++/OpenMP implementation would require significant changes, including, but not limited to, eliminating the use of "ragged arrays", which are not naturally supported by OpenMP on the GPU. This will be the subject of future work. Meanwhile, the KNL platform in these studies allows us to go to 256-way parallel for the purposes of performance analysis. This degree of node-level concurrency is expected to be commonplace on future platforms.

## 5   Conclusion and Future Work

One of the objectives of this work has been to understand the performance characteristics of three different approaches for doing shared-memory parallelization of a probabilistic graphical modeling optimization code, which serves as the basis for a highly accurate, and scalable method for scientific image segmentation. The work is motivated by the need to improve throughput of scientific analysis tools in light of increasing sensor and detector resolution. The three parallelization methods consist of two that are "traditional" (C++/OpenMP and C++/Threads) and one that is "non-traditional" (VTK-m/DPP).

At the outset of this work, we expected that the VTK-m/DPP implementation was running faster than the other two due to better vectorization characteristics. The results of our performance study point to a different reason for the performance difference: the VTK-m/DPP version executes many fewer instructions. The reason is because the process of reformulating a complex, graphical model optimization code to use sequences of DPPs results in runtime code that is more terse and efficient in terms of number of computations needed to produce the same answer as the corresponding C++/Threads and C++/OpenMP formulations. This bit of insight, and the performance analysis methodology we used, is the primary contribution of this paper. To our knowledge, this study is the first of its kind: an in-depth performance analysis of codes based on DPPs, OpenMP, and threads.

Future work will include pressing deeper into the topic of platform portability. While our VTK-m/DPP implementation can run on both CPU and GPU platforms, owing to the capabilities of the underlying DPP implementation, which is based on VTK-m, our OpenMP codes are not yet capable of running on GPU platforms. For OpenMP to emit code that runs on a GPU, the application must conform to a strict set of memory access patterns. Future work will include redesigning our code so that it does conform to those limitations.

The topic of platform portability and performance is of significant concern as computational platforms increase in concurrency, particularly at the node level. For that reason, this particular study is timely, for it sheds light on the performance characteristics of a non-trivial, data-intensive code implemented with three different methodologies, one of which is relatively new and holds promise.

**Acknowledgment.** This work was supported by the Director, Office of Science, Office of Advanced Scientific Computing Research, of the U.S. Department of Energy under Contract No. DE-AC02-05CH11231, through the grant "Scalable Data-Computing Convergence and Scientific Knowledge Discovery," program manager Dr. Laura Biven, and the Center for Applied Mathematics for Energy Related Applications (CAMERA). We also thank the LBNL ALS division for the data and NERSC for the computational resources.

# References

1. Achanta, R., Shaji, A., Smith, K., Lucchi, A., Fua, P., Süsstrunk, S.: Slic superpixels compared to state-of-the-art superpixel methods. IEEE Trans. Pattern Anal. Mach. Intell. **34**(11), 2274–2282 (2012). https://doi.org/10.1109/TPAMI.2012.120. https://ieeexplore.ieee.org/document/6205760
2. Anderson, E., et al.: Lapack: a portable linear algebra library for high-performance computers. In: Proceedings of the 1990 ACM/IEEE Conference on Supercomputing, pp. 2–11. Supercomputing 1990, IEEE Computer Society Press, Los Alamitos, CA, USA (1990)
3. Bethel, E.W., Greenwald, M., van Dam, K.K., Parashar, M., Wild, S.M., Wiley, H.S.: Management, analysis, and visualization of experimental and observational data - the convergence of data and computing. In: Proceedings of the 2016 IEEE 12th International Conference on eScience. Baltimore, MD, USA, October 2016
4. Blackford, L.S., et al.: An updated set of basic linear algebra subprograms (BLAS). ACM Trans. Math. Softw. **28**(2), 135–151 (2002). https://doi.org/10.1145/567806. 567807
5. Blelloch, G.E.: Vector Models for Data-parallel Computing. MIT Press, Cambridge (1990)
6. Corporation, I.: Introducing the Intel Threading Building Blocks, May 2017. https://software.intel.com/en-us/node/506042

7. Delong, A., Boykov, Y.: A scalable graph-cut algorithm for n-d grids. In: IEEE Conference on Computer Vision and Pattern Recognition (2008)
8. Donatelli, J., et al.: Camera: the center for advanced mathematics for energy research applications. Synchrotron Radiation News 28(2), 4–9 (2015)
9. Ersoy, M.A., Özturan, C.: Parallelizing shortest path algorithm for time dependent graphs with flow speed model. In: 2016 IEEE 10th International Conference on Application of Information and Communication Technologies (AICT), pp. 1–7, October 2016. https://doi.org/10.1109/ICAICT.2016.7991833
10. Eslami, H., Kasampalis, T., Kotsifakou, M.: A GPU implementation of tiled belief propagation on markov random fields. In: 2013 Eleventh ACM/IEEE International Conference on Formal Methods and Models for Codesign (MEMOCODE 2013), pp. 143–146 (Oct 2013)
11. Heinemann, C., Perciano, T., Ushizima, D., Bethel, E.W.: Distributed memory parallel markov random fields using graph partitioning. In: Fourth International Workshop on High Performance Big Graph Data Management, Analysis, and Mining (BigGraphs 2017), in conjunction with IEEE BigData 2017, December 2017
12. Jamriska, O., Sykora, D., Hornung, A.: A cache-efficient graph cuts on structured grids. In: IEEE Conference on Computer Vision and Pattern Recognition, pp. 3673–3680 (2012)
13. Koller, D., Friedman, N.: Probabilistic Graphical Models: Principles and Techniques - Adaptive Computation and Machine Learning. MIT Press, Cambridge (2009)
14. Kolmogorov, V., Zabin, R.: What energy functions can be minimized via graph cuts? IEEE Trans. Pattern Anal. Mach. Intell. 26(2), 147–159 (2004)
15. Larsen, M., Labasan, S., Navrátil, P., Meredith, J., Childs, H.: Volume rendering via data-parallel primitives. In: Proceedings of EuroGraphics Symposium on Parallel Graphics and Visualization (EGPGV), pp. 53–62. Cagliari, Italy, May 2015
16. Larsen, M., Meredith, J., Navrátil, P., Childs, H.: Ray-tracing within a data parallel framework. In: Proceedings of the IEEE Pacific Visualization Symposium, pp. 279–286. Hangzhou, China, April 2015
17. Lessley, B., Moreland, K., Larsen, M., Childs, H.: Techniques for data-parallel searching for duplicate elements. In: Proceedings of IEEE Symposium on Large Data Analysis and Visualization (LDAV), pp. 1–5. Phoenix, AZ, October 2017
18. Lessley, B., Perciano, T., Heinemann, C., Camp, D., Childs, H., Bethel, E.W.: DPP-PMRF: rethinking optimization for a probabilistic graphical model using data-parallel primitives. In: 8th IEEE Symposium on Large Data Analysis and Visualization (LDAV). Berlin, Germany, October 2018
19. Lessley, B., Perciano, T., Mathai, M., Childs, H., Bethel, E.W.: Maximal clique enumeration with data-parallel primitives. In: IEEE Large Data Analysis and Visualization. Phoenix, AZ, USA, October 2017
20. Levesque, J., Vose, A.: Programming for Hybrid Multi/Many-core MPP Systems. Chapman & Hall, CRC Computational Science, CRC Press/Francis&Taylor Group, Boca Raton, November 2017, preprint
21. Lezoray, O., Grady, L.: Image Processing and Analysis with Graphs: Theory and Practice. CRC Press, Boca Raton (2012)
22. Li, S.Z.: Markov Random Field Modeling in Image Analysis (2013). https://doi.org/10.1007/978-1-84800-279-1
23. Li, S., Marsaglia, N., Chen, V., Sewell, C., Clyne, J., Childs, H.: Achieving portable performance for wavelet compression using data parallel primitives. In: Proceedings of EuroGraphics Symposium on Parallel Graphics and Visualization (EGPGV), pp. 73–81. Barcelona, Spain, June 2017

24. Meng, Z., Wei, D., Wiesel, A., Hero, A.O.: Distributed learning of gaussian graphical models via marginal likelihoods. In: The Sixteenth International Conference on Artificial Intelligence and Statistics, pp. 39–47 (2013)
25. Meng, Z., Wei, D., Wiesel, A., Hero, A.O.: Marginal likelihoods for distributed parameter estimation of gaussian graphical models. IEEE Trans. Signal Process. **62**(20), 5425–5438 (2014)
26. Mizrahi, Y.D., Denil, M., de Freitas, N.: Linear and parallel learning of markov random fields. Proc. Int. Conf. Mach. Learn. **32**, 1–10 (2014)
27. Moreland, K.: VTK-m website, May 2017. http://m.vtk.org
28. Moreland, K., et al.: VTK-m: accelerating the visualization toolkit for massively threaded architectures. IEEE Comput. Graph. Appl. (CG&A) **36**(3), 48–58 (2016)
29. Perciano, T., et al.: Insight into 3D micro-CT data: exploring segmentation algorithms through performance metrics. J. Synchrotron Radiat. **24**(5), 1065–1077 (2017)
30. Perciano, T., Ushizima, D.M., Bethel, E.W., Mizrahi, Y.D., Parkinson, D., Sethian, J.A.: Reduced-complexity image segmentation under parallel markov random field formulation using graph partitioning. In: 2016 IEEE International Conference on Image Processing (ICIP). pp. 1259–1263, September 2016
31. Sariyuce, A.E., Saule, E., Catalyurek, U.V.: Scalable hybrid implementation of graph coloring using MPI and OPENMP. In: Proceedings of the 2012 IEEE 26th International Parallel and Distributed Processing Symposium Workshops & Ph.D. Forum, pp. 1744–1753. IPDPSW 2012, IEEE Computer Society, Washington, DC, USA (2012). https://doi.org/10.1109/IPDPSW.2012.216
32. Shekbovstov, A., Hlavac, V.: A distributed mincut/maxflow algorithm combining augmentation and push-relabel. In: International Journal of Computer Visualization (2012)
33. Treibig, J., Hager, G., Wellein, G.: Likwid: a lightweight performance-oriented tool suite for x86 multicore environments. In: Proceedings of the 2010 39th International Conference on Parallel Processing Workshops, pp. 207–216. ICPPW 2010, IEEE Computer Society, Washington, DC, USA (2010). https://doi.org/10.1109/ICPPW.2010.38
34. Wang, C., Komodakis, N., Paragios, N.: Markov random field modeling, inference, learning in computer vision and image understanding: a survey. Comput. Vis. Image Understand. **117**(11), 1610–1627 (2013)

# Opportunities for Cost Savings with In-Transit Visualization

James Kress[1,2]($\boxtimes$), Matthew Larsen[3], Jong Choi[1], Mark Kim[1], Matthew Wolf[1], Norbert Podhorszki[1], Scott Klasky[1], Hank Childs[2], and David Pugmire[1]

[1] Oak Ridge National Laboratory, Oak Ridge, TN 37830, USA
{kressjm,choij,kimmb,wolfmd,pnorbert,klasky,pugmire}@ornl.gov
[2] University of Oregon, Eugene, OR 97403, USA
hank@uoregon.edu
[3] Lawrence Livermore National Laboratory, Livermore, CA 94550, USA
larsen30@llnl.gov

**Abstract.** We analyze the opportunities for in-transit visualization to provide cost savings compared to in-line visualization. We begin by developing a cost model that includes factors related to both in-line and in-transit which allows comparisons to be made between the two methods. We then run a series of studies to create a corpus of data for our model. We run two different visualization algorithms, one that is computation heavy and one that is communication heavy with concurrencies up to 32, 768 cores. Our primary results are in exploring the cost model within the context of our corpus. Our findings show that in-transit consistently achieves significant cost efficiencies by running visualization algorithms at lower concurrency, and that in many cases these efficiencies are enough to offset other costs (transfer, blocking, and additional nodes) to be cost effective overall. Finally, this work informs future studies, which can focus on choosing ideal configurations for in-transit processing that can consistently achieve cost efficiencies.

## 1 Introduction

In situ visualization is increasingly necessary to address I/O limitations on supercomputers [2,3]. That said, the processing paradigm for in situ visualization can take multiple forms. With this study, we consider two popular forms. In the first form, which we refer to in this paper as in-line visualization, the visualization routines are embedded into the simulation code, typically via a library which is linked into the simulation binary. In this case, the visualization routines directly access the memory of the simulation code. When it is time to perform visualization tasks, the simulation pauses, and the visualization tasks use the same nodes that were being used for the simulation. With the second form, which we refer to in this paper as in-transit visualization, extra compute nodes run concurrently to the simulation. In this case, the simulation runs on the primary compute nodes (the "simulation nodes") and the visualization runs, as a separate program, on the extra compute nodes (the "in-transit nodes"). The simulation

© Springer Nature Switzerland AG 2020
P. Sadayappan et al. (Eds.): ISC High Performance 2020, LNCS 12151, pp. 146–165, 2020.
https://doi.org/10.1007/978-3-030-50743-5_8

shares data with the visualization program by sending data over the network. In this scenario, the simulation and visualization are both running at the same time.

In-line and in-transit both have beneficial aspects [6]. For example, in-transit naturally lends itself to fault tolerance, while in-line saves on usage of primary memory. In short, there are good reasons motivating the use of either technique. However, one factor has a special importance, namely cost. With this study, we define cost to be in units of "node seconds," i.e., using ten compute nodes for one second or one compute node for ten seconds are both "ten node seconds." Cost directly informs the size of the request needed on a supercomputer to perform the simulation. Therefore, we believe understanding the relative costs of in-transit and in-line is critical in helping scientists determine which paradigm to use. While other factors (fault tolerance, memory usage, etc.) may play a role in the decision, we believe cost will be a critical factor.

In-transit visualization incurs new costs that do not exist with in-line visualization. There are additional resources for the in-transit nodes, and a new activity to perform: transferring the data from the simulation nodes to the in-transit nodes. Further, if the in-transit nodes are not able to perform their tasks quickly enough, they can block the simulation from advancing. While blocking the simulation is not the only possible decision for this scenario, it is the decision we consider in the context of this paper.

Despite these additional costs, in-transit also has a potential cost advantage that in-line does not have. The number of in-transit nodes is typically much less than the number of simulation nodes. Further, when algorithms exhibit poor scaling, fewer nodes are more efficient. In effect, in-transit has the potential to reduce costs that result from poor scaling of visualization algorithms. Consider a scenario: if a visualization algorithm takes 1 s on 1000 nodes running in-line, but the same algorithm takes 50 s on 10 nodes running in-transit, then the visualization cost is 1000 node seconds for in-line and 500 node seconds for in-transit. We define a term to capture this phenomenon: **Visualization Cost Efficiency Factor (VCEF)**. $VCEF$ is the in-line visualization cost divided by the in-transit visualization cost. In the scenario just described, the $VCEF$ would be 1000/500 or 2—the cost to perform in-line is 2X more than in-transit. Of course, $VCEF$ is just one consideration for in-transit, and must be considered alongside its other factors, including, extra resources, transfer costs, and blocking, which impose barriers to cost savings.

Our hypothesis entering this study is that there are configurations of in-transit visualization such that the cost to reach the final solution are less in-transit than in-line. To that end, for this study, we consider the topic of relative costs between in-transit and in-line visualization. What makes our study novel is the identification and usage of $VCEF$. We observe that $VCEF$ is a significant phenomenon; our communication-heavy algorithm regularly yields a $VCEF$ of four or above, and even our computation-heavy algorithm yields such values at very high concurrency. This high $VCEF$ value in turn allows in-transit to become cost effective overall in many scenarios, as the savings are enough to offset other costs (extra resources, transfer costs, and blocking). We also provide a model for reasoning about this space, and a corpus of data that reflects experiment times for currently popular software. Overall, this study provides significant evidence that in-transit can be cost effective.

## 2  Related Works

In recent years, some application teams have began seeing the need to adopt the in situ approach for visualization and analysis of large-scale simulations [10]. One strength of in situ methods is the ability to access all of the data during the course of a simulation, and only save what is interesting. This means, in situ is not just a tool for visualization, but also for processing of data such as reduction, explorable feature extractions, simulation monitoring, and the generation of statistics [11]. The choice then, comes down to which in situ approach is appropriate for a given application.

To aid in making that choice, several studies have looked at in-transit and in-line from the perspective of time. Morozov et al. [16] describes a system for launching in situ/in-transit analysis routines, and compares each in situ technique based on time to solution for two different analysis operations. They find there were times when in-transit analysis was faster due to how the analysis code scaled. Friesen et al. [5] describes a setup where in-line and in-transit visualization are used in conjunction with a cosmological code to run two different analysis routines. They analyze the time to solution using both in situ techniques, finding that there are configurations where in-transit is faster to use, due to the inter-node communication overhead of the analysis routines. These and other studies have largely focused on analysis pipelines which can have different communication and computation scaling curves than visualization pipelines. Further, they do not do an in depth analysis of the trade-offs associated with in-transit or in-line methods.

Our work takes a different view than these past works. First, we concentrate on in situ visualization pipelines. Second, we focus specifically on in-line in situ vs. in-transit in situ from the perspective of visualization frequency, resource requirements, and how different combinations of these factors impact the final cost of the simulation and visualization for research scientists.

There are three highly relevant works preceding this work:

- Oldfield et al. [17] also considered in-transit and in-line costs. The main difference between their work and our own is that they focused on analysis tasks which did not benefit from a $VCEF$ speedup. As such, their findings differ from ours.
- Malakar et al. did twin studies on cost models, one for in-line [12] and one for in-transit [13]. Once again, these studies did not consider $VCEF$. Further, they considered optimizing allocation sizes and analysis frequencies which is a complementary task to our effort.

– Work by Kress et al. [7] considered trade-offs between in-transit and in-line
  for isosurfacing at high concurrencies. This study was the first to show evidence of $VCEF$. However, the algorithm considered was computation-heavy,
  so the extent of the effect was smaller and only appeared at very high concurrency. Further, that paper lacked a cost modeling component, rather just
  observing that the phenomenon was possible. Our paper focuses exclusively
  on cost savings, providing a model and considering both computation- and
  communication-heavy visualization algorithms. Finally, we note the corpus of
  data for our study in part draws on runs from the Kress et al. study.

## 3  Cost Model

This section defines a cost model for determining when in-transit visualization
can cost less than in-line visualization. First, terms are introduced for the operations that occur in both in-line and in-transit visualization. Next, we use those
terms to demonstrate when in-transit will cost less than in-line visualization, and
provide a discussion for when and how this occurs. Finally, we derive a formulation to determine the degree of scalability of in-transit over in-line, ($VCEF$),
that is required for in-transit to be cost effective.

### 3.1  Definition of Terms

Below we define terms for both in-line and in-transit visualization operations.

– Let $T$ be the time for the simulation to advance one cycle.
– Let $N$ be the number of nodes used by the simulation code.
– Let $Res_p$ be the proportion of nodes (resources) used for in-transit visualization. E.g., if the number of nodes for the simulation ($N$) is 10,000
  and the number of nodes for in-transit visualization is 1,000, then $Res_p =
  1,000/10,000$, which is 0.1.
– Let $Vis_p$ be the proportion of time spent doing visualization in the in-line
  visualization case. E.g., if $T$ is 5 s and the in-line visualization time is 1 s,
  then $Vis_p = 1/5$, which is 0.2.
– Let $Block_p$ be the proportion of time that the simulation code is blocking
  while waiting for in-transit visualization to complete. E.g., if $T$ is 5 s and
  the simulation has to wait an additional 2 s for the in-transit resources to
  complete, then $Block_p = 2/5$, which is 0.4. If the in-transit visualization
  completes and does not block the simulation, then $Block_p$ is 0.
– Let $VCEF$ be the term identified earlier in this paper that captures the efficiency achieved by running at lower concurrency. E.g., if in-line visualization
  took 1 s on 10,000 nodes, but in-transit visualization took 5 s on 1,000 nodes,
  then $VCEF$ would be $\frac{1 \times 10,000}{5 \times 1,000}$, which is 2.

We have two terms for transferring data because sending data from the simulation side may be faster than receiving it on the in-transit side. For example, if
8 simulation nodes send to 1 visualization node, then that 1 visualization node
will need to unserialize eight times as much data as each of the simulation nodes
serialized.

- Let $Send_p$ be the proportion of time by the simulation code sending data to in-transit visualization resources. E.g., if $T$ is 5 s and the send time is 2 s, then $Send_p = 2/5$, which is 0.4.
- Let $Recv_p$ be the proportion of time spent receiving data on the in-transit visualization resources. E.g., if $T$ is 5 s and the transfer time is 2 s, then $Recv_p = 2/5$, which is 0.4.

### 3.2   Base Model Defined

We define our base cost model below. This cost model will be refined in Sect. 3.4 as we consider the implications of blocking. The cost for in-transit visualization will be lower than in-line visualization when:

$$\begin{gather} \text{(total resources with in-transit)} \times \text{(time per cycle for simulation with in-transit)} \\ < \\ \text{(total resources with in-line)} \times \text{(time per cycle for simulation with in-line)} \\ \implies \\ \text{(\#in-transit nodes + \#simulation nodes)} \times \\ \text{(simulation cycle time + transfer time + block time)} \\ < \\ \text{(\#simulation nodes)} \times \text{(simulation cycle time + in-line vis time)} \end{gather} \tag{1}$$

Using the terms defined above in Sect. 3.1, this becomes:

$$(N \times Res_p + N) \times (T + T \times Send_p + T \times Block_p) < (N) \times (T + T \times Vis_P) \tag{2}$$

This equation can be simplified by dividing both sides by the simulation cycle time $(T)$ and number of nodes $(N)$:

$$(1 + Res_p) \times (1 + Send_p + Block_p) < (1 + Vis_P) \tag{3}$$

If Eq. 3 is true, then in-transit costs less than in-line.

### 3.3   Base Model Discussion

In-transit visualization has three different costs that do not occur with in-line. (1) In-transit visualization requires data transfer, which slows down the simulation nodes. (2) In-transit visualization requires dedicated resources beyond those required for in-line. If the in-transit visualization finishes quickly, these additional resources sit idle, and yet still incur cost. (3) In-transit can block the simulation if the visualization is not finished before the simulation is ready to send data for the next cycle. This is very harmful since it slows down the simulation nodes. There are alternatives to blocking, for example skipping cycles, and only visualizing the latest. In this study, our focus is on blocking, and we do not consider the alternatives.

Given the three additional costs incurred by in-transit, the *only* way for it to cost less than in-line is for the visualization to run faster at lower concurrency. In other words, the cost savings with in-transit can *only* occur if the benefit of

($VCEF$) outweighs the combined effects of the three additional costs described above. The fact that certain operations are more efficient at lower levels of concurrency provides an opporunity for a more cost effective solution.

That said, there are scenarios where any value of $VCEF$ is insufficient to achieve cost savings. Examples where in-transit can never be more cost effective, regardless of $VCEF$, are discussed below:

- If blocking takes longer than in-line visualization (e.g., $Block_p = 0.3, Vis_p = 0.2$), it is impossible to be more cost efficient. For example, even if $T = \epsilon$, then $(1 + \epsilon) \times (1 + \epsilon + 1.3) < (1 + 1.2)$ is not possible.
- Further, even if $Block_p = 0$ (no blocking), then some in-transit configurations will still always be less efficient:
  - if the simulation transfer cost is bigger than the in-line visualization time (e.g., $Send_p = 0.4, Vis_p = 0.2$), then: $(1 + \epsilon) \times (1 + 0.4 + 0) < 1.2$
  - if there are many in-transit nodes (e.g., $Res_p = 0.5$) and the in-line visualization time is sufficiently fast (e.g., $Vis_p = 0.5$), then: $(1 + 0.5) \times (1 + \epsilon + 0) < 1 + 0.5$

## 3.4   When Does Blocking Occur?: Replacing $Block_p$ via $VCEF$

In this section we expand the model by using the $VCEF$ term to determine when blocking will occur. We then present two new equations that define when in-transit will cost less if blocking does or does not occur.

Consider what it means to block. Blocking occurs when in-transit resources are taking longer to do their job than the simulation resources are taking to do their job. Similarly, "not blocking" means that the in-transit resources are doing their job faster than the simulation resources take to do their job. So, what does "time to do their job" mean? For the simulation side, this means the time to advance the simulation plus the time to send the data, i.e., $T + T \times Send_p$. For the in-transit side, this means the time to receive data ($T \times Recv_p$) plus the time to do the visualization task. This latter time is explored below.

Nominally, assuming that visualization scaled perfectly as a function of concurrency, the cost (number of node seconds) to do the visualization task can be directly calculated from the in-line case: $N \times (Vis_p \times T)$. However, a key premise of this study is that in-transit has an advantage at lower concurrency because of $VCEF$. Because in-transit is running at a lower concurrency, the cost is scaled by the $VCEF$ term: $\frac{N \times (Vis_p \times T)}{VCEF}$. Finally, the time to carry out the visualization task on the in-transit nodes would be the $VCEF$-reduced cost divided by the resources ($N \times Res_p$). Thus, the in-transit visualization time is:

$$\frac{N \times (T \times Vis_p)}{VCEF \times N \times Res_p} \tag{4}$$

Canceling out N gives a simpler form:

$$\frac{Vis_p \times T}{VCEF \times Res_p} \tag{5}$$

Restating, blocking occurs with in-transit when the time to receive data plus the visualization time is greater than the simulation time plus the time to send data:

$$Recv_p \times T + \frac{Vis_p \times T}{VCEF \times Res_p} > T \times (1 + Send_p) \tag{6}$$

This means that blocking *does not* occur if:

$$Recv_p \times T + \frac{Vis_p \times T}{VCEF \times Res_p} \leq T \times (1 + Send_p) \tag{7}$$

The terms in Eq. 7 can be rearranged to find the $VCEF$ values when blocking *does not* occur:

$$\frac{Vis_p}{Res_p \times (1 + Send_p - Recv_P)} \leq VCEF \tag{8}$$

This analysis on blocking informs the original question: when does in-transit incur less cost than in-line? This can be answered using a combination of Eq. 3 and our observations about blocking in this section. If blocking does not occur, then $Block_p$ drops out as zero, and Eq. 3 is simplified:

$$(1 + Res_p) \times (1 + Send_p) < (1 + Vis_P) \tag{9}$$

If blocking does occur, then the simulation advances only as fast as the in-transit resources can take new data. This means that the time term for the left-hand side of Eq. 3, which was previously $1 + Send_p$, is replaced with the in-transit time. Using the relationship in Eq. 6, we get:

$$(1 + Res_p) \times (Recv_p + \frac{Vis_p}{VCEF \times Res_p}) < (1 + Vis_P) \tag{10}$$

## 3.5   Cost Model Discussion

The basis of the cost model are described above in Eqs. 3, 8, 9, and 10. This model allows the relative costs of in-line and in-transit visualization for a particular configuration to be analyzed. The first step is to determine the cost feasibility of in-transit. Equation 3 serves as a threshold for determining when this is *possible*. If Eq. 3 is false, in-line visualization is the cost-effective solution. Otherwise, when Eq. 3 is true, Eqs. 8, 9, and 10 are used to determine cost feasibility based on blocking, as follows:

- The $VCEF$ value necessary to prevent blocking is given by Eq. 8:
  $VCEF \geq \frac{Vis_p}{Res_p \times (1 + Send_p - Recv_P)}$

- For cases when there is no blocking, using Eq. 9 shows that in-transit is cost efficient if:
  $(1 + Res_p) \times (1 + Send_p) < (1 + Vis_P)$
- Otherwise, for cases where blocking occurs, using Eq. 10 shows that in-transit is cost efficient if:
  $(1 + Res_p) \times (Recv_p + \frac{Vis_p}{VCEF \times Res_p}) < (1 + Vis_P)$

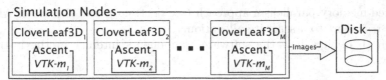

(a) In-line visualization setup. The simulation and visualization alternate in execution, sharing the same resources.

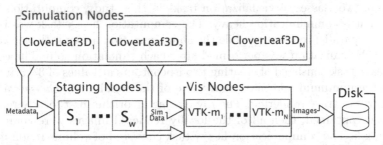

(b) In-transit visualization setup. The simulation and visualization operate asynchronously, and each have their own dedicated resources.

**Fig. 1.** Comparison of the two workflow types used in this study.

# 4   Corpus of Data

In this section we detail the experimental setup, methods, and software used to generate our corpus of data, as well as a cursory overview of the data we collected.

## 4.1   Experiment Software Used

To generate data for this study, we use CloverLeaf3D [1,14], a hydrodynamics proxy-application. Cloverleaf3D spatially decomposes the data uniformly across distributed memory processes, where each process computes a spatial subset of the problem domain. To couple CloverLeaf3D with both in-transit and in-line in situ, we leveraged existing integrations with Ascent [8].

In-line visualization is accomplished with Ascent which uses VTK-m [15] for visualization operations. The visualization is described through a set of actions which Ascent turns into a data flow graph, and then executed. Figure 1a depicts how the software components interact in the in-line workflow.

In-transit visualization used Ascent's integration with the Adaptable I/O System (ADIOS) [9] to transport data from the simulation nodes to the in-transit nodes using its RDMA capabilities [4,18]. ADIOS requires the use of dedicated staging nodes to hold the metadata necessary to service RDMA requests. Once the data are transported, the visualization tasks are performed using VTK-m. To be clear, the same VTK-m code was being used for both in-line and in-transit visualization. The only differences are the number of nodes used for visualization, the shared-memory parallelism approach (see Sect. 4.5), and the use of ADIOS for data transport to a separate allocation.

Figure 1b depicts how the software components interact in the in-transit workflow.

## 4.2 Visualization Tasks Studied

There were two classes of visualization tasks in this study, computation heavy and one that is communication heavy. The computation heavy task was isocontouring and parallel rendering, while the communication heavy task was volume rendering. Visualization was performed after each simulation step. The computation heavy task consisted of creating two isocontours at values of 33% and 67% between the minimum and maximum value of the simulations *energy* variable, followed by ray trace rendering. The ray tracing algorithm first locally rendered the data it contained, then all of the locally rendered images were composited using radix-k. The communication heavy task consisted of volume rendering the simulations *energy* variable. Compositing for volume rendering is implemented as a direct send.

## 4.3 Application/Visualization Configurations

In this study we used five different in situ configurations of the application and visualization:

- **Sim only:** Baseline simulation time with no visualization
- **In-line:** Simulation time with in-line visualization
- **Alloc(12%):** In-transit uses an additional 12% of simulation resources
- **Alloc(25%):** In-transit uses an additional 25% of simulation resources
- **Alloc(50%):** In-transit uses an additional 50% of simulation resources

For in-transit visualization, predetermined percentages of simulation resources for visualization were selected. These percentages, were selected based off of a rule of thumb where simulations typically allow up to 10% of resources for visualization. 10% was our starting point, and we then selected two additional higher allocations to explore a range of options. We initially considered in-transit allocations that were below 10%, but due to the memory limitations on Titan (32 GB per node), the visualization nodes ran out of memory. We leave a lower percentage study as future work on a future machine. Finally, we ran each one of these configurations with weak scaling with concurrency ranging between 128 and 32,768 processes, with $128^3$ cells per process (268M cells to 68B cells).

CloverLeaf3d uses a simplified physics model, as such, it has a relatively fast cycle time. This fast cycle time is representative for some types of simulations, but we also wanted to study the implications with simulations that have longer cycle times. We simulated longer cycle times by configuring CloverLeaf3D to pause after each cycle completes, using a sleep command. This command was placed after the simulation computation, and before any visualization calls were made. We used three different levels of delay:

- **Delay(0):** simulation ran with no sleep command.
- **Delay(10):** a 10 s sleep was called after each simulation step.
- **Delay(20):** a 20 s sleep was called after each simulation step.

Lastly, we ran each test for 100 time steps using a fixed visualization frequency of once every time step. This frequency ensures that fast evolving structures in simulation data are not missed. Also, very frequent visualization gives us an upper bound for how visualization will impact the simulation.

### 4.4 Hardware

All runs in this study were performed on the Titan supercomputer deployed at the Oak Ridge Leadership Computing Facility (OLCF). Because the mini-app we used for our study runs on CPUs only, we restricted this study to simulations and visualizations run entirely on the CPU.

### 4.5 Launch Configurations

The configuration for each experiment performed is shown in Table 1. Isosurfacing plus rendering was run on up to 16K cores, volume rendering was run on up to 32K cores. Because CloverLeaf3D is not an OpenMP code, the in-line in situ and the simulation only configurations were launched with 16 ranks per node. The in-transit configurations used 4 ranks per visualization node and 4 OpenMP threads to process data blocks in parallel. Therefore, in-transit and in-line both used 16 cores per node. Additionally, the in-transit configuration required the use of dedicated staging nodes to gather the metadata from the simulation in order to perform RDMA memory transfers from the simulation resource to the visualization resource. These additional resources are accounted for in Table 1 and are used in the calculation of all in-transit results.

**Table 1.** Resource configuration for each experiment in our scaling study.

| Test Configuration | Sim Procs<br>Data Cells | 128<br>$648^3$ | 256<br>$816^3$ | 512<br>$1024^3$ | 1024<br>$1296^3$ | 2048<br>$1632^3$ | 4096<br>$2048^3$ | 8192<br>$2592^3$ | 16384<br>$3264^3$ | 32768<br>$4096^3$ |
|---|---|---|---|---|---|---|---|---|---|---|
| In-line | Total Nodes | 8 | 16 | 32 | 64 | 128 | 256 | 512 | 1024 | 2048 |
| In-transit<br>*Alloc*(12%) | Vis Nodes | 1 | 2 | 4 | 8 | 16 | 32 | 54 | 128 | 256 |
|  | Staging Nodes | 1 | 2 | 2 | 4 | 4 | 8 | 8 | 16 | 16 |
|  | Total Nodes | 10 | 20 | 38 | 76 | 148 | 296 | 584 | 1168 | 2320 |
| In-transit<br>*Alloc*(25%) | Vis Nodes | 2 | 4 | 8 | 16 | 32 | 64 | 128 | 256 | 512 |
|  | Staging Nodes | 1 | 2 | 2 | 4 | 4 | 8 | 8 | 16 | 16 |
|  | Total Nodes | 11 | 22 | 42 | 84 | 164 | 328 | 648 | 1296 | 2576 |
| In-transit<br>*Alloc*(50%) | Vis Nodes | 4 | 8 | 16 | 32 | 64 | 128 | 256 | 512 | 1024 |
|  | Staging Nodes | 1 | 2 | 2 | 4 | 4 | 8 | 8 | 16 | 16 |
|  | Total Nodes | 13 | 26 | 50 | 100 | 196 | 392 | 776 | 1552 | 3088 |

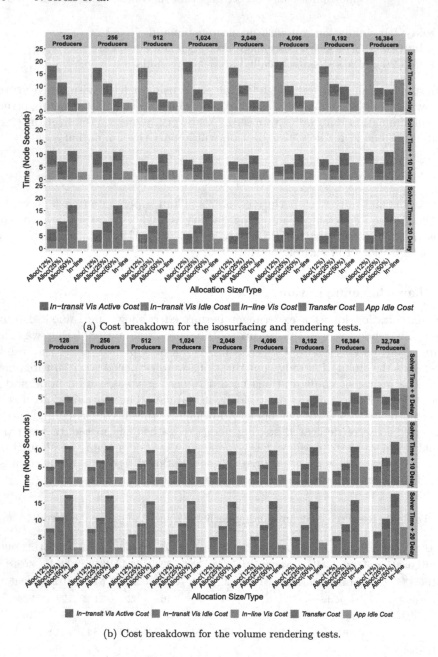

(a) Cost breakdown for the isosurfacing and rendering tests.

(b) Cost breakdown for the volume rendering tests.

**Fig. 2.** Stacked bar charts comparing the total cost per step for using in-transit and in-line visualization. In-transit visualization is broken down into cost for the time that the visualization is actively working, cost for the time that it is idle, cost for the time it is receiving data from the simulation, and cost associated with blocking the application. The application active cost is excluded from this chart as it is the same for each level of Delay, and obfuscates the times for visualization and data transfer.

An important detail from these configurations is that the in-line tests have one core per MPI task, while the in-transit tests have four cores per MPI task. Where the in-line tests were restricted to the MPI approach of the simulation code, the in-transit tests were not, enabling shared-memory parallelism. As a result, in-transit had even fewer participants in communication, which will boost its $VCEF$ factor.

### 4.6  Overview of Data Collected

In total, we ran 255 individual tests, each for 100 time steps. From each of these tests we collected the total time for each time step from both the simulation and visualization resources, as well as more fine grained timers placed around major operations. After the runs were complete, the total cost was calculated by multiplying the total time by the total number of nodes listed in Table 1. Figure 2a shows the total cost per time step we observed for each of the isosurfacing plus rendering tests and Fig. 2b shows the total cost per time step we observed for each of the volume rendering tests. These charts break down the cost of each step associated with each of our runs, showing if the simulation was blocked by the visualization and how much that blocking cost, how much it cost to transfer data from the simulation to the in-transit resources, how long the visualization resources were active and their cost, how long they were idle and that cost, and how long the in-line visualization operation took and its associated cost.

There are marked differences in the performance of the isosurfacing and rendering runs versus the volume rendering runs. The isosurfacing tests have large periods of blocking whereas the volume rendering runs have very little. One reason for that blocking was that on average, isosurfacing and rendering took twice as long per step as volume rendering. Finally as the simulation cycle time increased, isosurfacing and rendering benefited more than volume rendering, showing that the isosurfacing tests were compute bound on the in-transit resources.

## 5  Results

In this section we use the model described in Sect. 3 to analyze the data collected from our experiments. In particular, we follow the discussion detailed in Sect. 3.5. In Sect. 5.1, we discuss and analyze the magnitude of $VCEF$ (Eq. 8) for each experiment. In Sect. 5.2 we use Eq. 3 from our model to determine the in-transit cost savings feasibility for each experiment. Finally, in Sect. 5.3, we combine these two and discuss the experiments that are feasible and have sufficient $VCEF$ to produce cost savings using in-transit for both non-blocking and blocking cases (Eqs. 9 and 10).

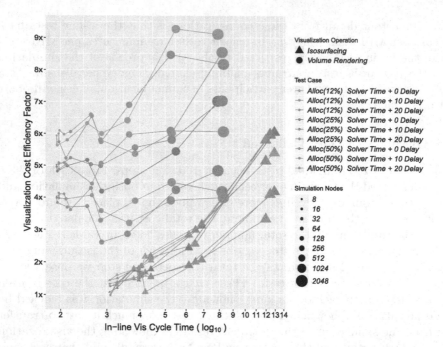

**Fig. 3.** This plot shows in-transit $VCEF$ as a function of the in-line cycle time. Iso-surfacing experiments are denoted with a triangle glyph and volume rendering with a circle glyph. Each glyph is scaled by the concurrency of the experiment (isosurfacing 8-1024; volume rendering: 8-2048). Experiments are group by color (configuration) and connected by lines (concurrency sequence).

## 5.1 $VCEF$ Magnitude Across Experiments

Figure 3 shows the $VCEF$ for each experiment. We felt the most surprising result was how large $VCEF$ values were as a whole. Many of the experiments had values above $4X$, which creates significant opportunities for the cost effectiveness of in-transit. Surprisingly, volume rendering experiments where the in-transit resources were 50% of the simulation ($Alloc(50\%)$) were able to achieve $VCEF$ values of about $4X$. Putting this number in perspective, if an $Alloc(50\%)$ experiment runs in the same amount of time as its in-line counterpart using half the concurrency, then its $VCEF$ would be 2. This is because it would have run using half the resources while taking the same amount of time as in-line. Higher values indicate that the runtime has decreased at smaller concurrency, i.e., 4X cost efficiency via using half the resources and running 2X faster. Further, we note this volume rendering algorithm has been extensively optimized and is used in a production setting. This result highlights the significant advantage that $VCEF$ provides. Algorithms with poor scalability (i.e., heavy communication) are able to run at lower levels of concurrency, and therefore achieve better performance.

As expected, $VCEF$ is heavily dependent on the type of algorithm. The volume rendering experiments were communication-heavy, lending itself to higher cost efficiency when running at lower concurrency. The isosurfacing experiments were computation-heavy—first, an isosurface is calculated, and then it was rendered. The isosurface calculation is embarrassingly parallel, so there is no reason to expect a high $VCEF$. That said, the parallel rendering became very slow at high concurrency, as evidenced by the high in-line times ($>10$ s). This was due to the communication required to perform the image compositing and the final reduction using the radix-k algorithm. In these cases, the $VCEF$ values increased from $3X$ to $6X$.

While the main takeaway of Fig. 3 is high $VCEF$ values, a secondary takeaway looks ahead to our analysis of cost savings, and in particular establishing intuition about which configurations will be viable for cost savings. All volume rendering experiments had high $VCEF$ values, while only isosurfacing experiments at very high concurrency had high $VCEF$ values. The isosurfacing experiments at lower concurrencies had smaller $VCEF$ values, which makes them less likely to offset the additional costs incurred for in-transit (transfer times, blocking, idle).

## 5.2   Feasibility of Cost Savings

Equation 3 from our model is used to determine the feasibility of cost savings for in-transit visualization. When Eq. 3 is true, then cost feasibility is possible. Figure 4a uses this equation to show the feasibility for each experiment. The black line shows where in-line and in-transit costs are identical, and the region above the black line is cost feasibility for in-transit. This figure follows discussion from Sect. 3.3. For example, if the in-line cost is less than the transfer cost, then no $VCEF$ value can make in-transit cost effective. Or if the resources devoted to in-transit are very large, then they will likely sit idle and be a incur cost at no gain. About half of our experiments were in this category, incapable of achieving cost savings with in-transit, because the transfer and resource costs exceeded the in-line costs. In the remaining half of the experiments, our choice for the number of in-transit nodes created a potentially feasible situation—the resources dedicated to in-transit and the cost of transferring data was less than the in-line visualization cost. That said, only some of these experiments actually led to cost savings with in-transit. This is because the feasibility test for Fig. 4a placed no consideration on whether the in-transit resources were sufficient to perform the visualization task. In some cases, $VCEF$ was enough that the in-transit resources could complete its visualization task within the allotted time. In others cases, $VCEF$ was not sufficient, and this caused the in-transit resources to block. Figure 4b takes this blocking into account, and faithfully plots the terms from Eq. 3 from Sect. 3.2. The difference between Fig. 4a and 4b, then, is whether blocking is included when considering in-transit costs.

A final point from Fig. 4a is the trend as concurrency increases—in-line visualization increases at a much higher rate than transfer costs. Consider the example of isosurfacing, with $Alloc(50\%)$ and $Delay(0)$ i.e., the blue lines on the right of Fig. 4a with triangle glyphs. These experiments have in-line costs that go from 0.6X of the simulation cycle time at the smallest scale to 2.2X for the largest

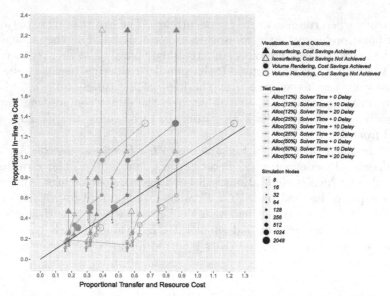

(a) In this plot, blocking is not considered. Some glyphs above the line are hollow however due to $VCEF$ being insufficient to achieve overall cost savings.

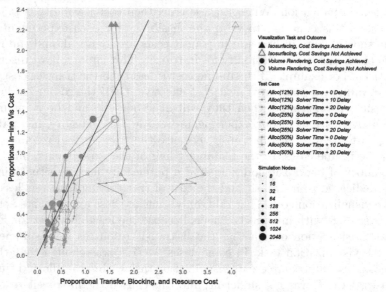

(b) Updating Figure 4a to include blocking costs. This plot demonstrates that our cost model is able to perfectly infer when cost savings can be achieved with in-transit, as only solid glyphs appear above the line.

**Fig. 4.** Plot of cost savings feasibility for each test case. Each glyph denotes the in-line cost as a function of transfer and resource costs. Glyph size represents the number of simulation nodes used in each test (isosurfacing: 8-1024; volume rendering: 8-2048). Hollow glyphs indicate in-line was more cost efficient and solid glyphs indicate that in-transit was more cost efficient. The black line marks where in-line and in-transit costs are equal. Above the line is where in-transit can be cost effective.

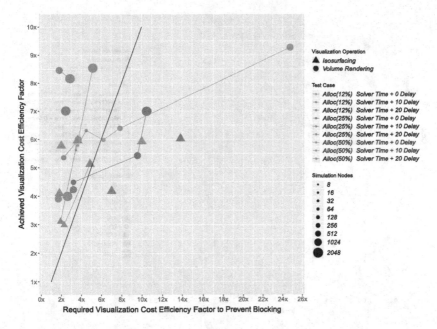

**Fig. 5.** This plot takes the points from experiments in Fig. 4b where in-transit was cost effective and plots the achieved $VCEF$ as a function of the required $VCEF$ to prevent blocking. The black line is Eq. 8. Points above the line did not block, while those below did block. This plot shows two things: first, the necessary $VCEF$ speedup required to prevent blocking, and second, that cost feasibility is possible even with simulation blocking.

scale. Further, the x-values (i.e., transfer cost and resource cost) change in a much more modest way (0.75X to 0.85X, with this representing only a variation in transfer since the resource cost is fixed at 0.5 for this case). This is a critical point to bring up for in-line visualization: It can be very difficult to scale some algorithms up to the scale of the simulation without incurring huge penalties. All of the other families of experiments exhibit a similar trend, with little variation in X (transfer and resource) and significant increases in Y (in-line visualization) as scale increases. Extrapolating forward, the opportunities demonstrated in our experiments will only become greater as supercomputers get larger and larger.

## 5.3  Achieved Cost Savings

Figure 5 extends Fig. 4b by plotting the results of Eq. 8 for each of the points that did provide cost savings. Equation 8 calculates the required $VCEF$ value for a in-transit experiment to not block the simulation. While blocking the simulation is certainly not an ideal configuration, it is still possible to achieve cost savings if the cost savings gained through $VCEF$ is greater than the cost of the blocked simulation. About a third of the experiments that provided cost savings from Fig. 4b actually blocked the simulation (points to the right of the black line).

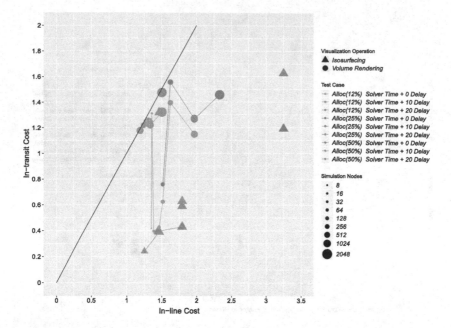

**Fig. 6.** This plot takes the points from experiments in Fig. 4b where in-transit was cost effective and plots the in-transit cost as a function of the in-line cost using Eq. 9 (if no blocking occurred), or Eq. 10 (otherwise). The black line indicates where costs are equal.

The main takeaway from this plot though, is the rate at which $VCEF$ allowed in-transit visualization to achieve cost savings and prevent blocking. About two thirds of the cases that achieved cost savings did so by not blocking the simulation. This was in large part due to the high values for $VCEF$ that were achieved in those cases.

Looking back to the intuition we established in Sect. 5.1 about which experiments would be viable from a cost savings standpoint, we see that our intuition was correct. Our intuition was that volume rendering would lead to more experiments with cost savings vs. isosurfacing due to its high $VCEF$ values across all concurrencies, whereas isosurfacing only had high $VCEF$ values at high concurrency. Looking at Fig. 5, we see that the majority of the points are for volume rendering, 19 cases were more cost efficient, vs. isosurfacing, 9 cases being more cost efficient. This trend indicates two important things: first, at even higher concurrency we should expect to see larger values for $VCEF$, with even more cases where in-transit is more cost efficient, and second, in future as more algorithms are studied, those with even more communication than volume rendering should see even greater cost savings due to $VCEF$.

Figure 6 takes all of the cases that achieved cost savings from Fig. 4b and shows what the observed in-transit and in-line costs were in each case. The further the points are from the black line the larger the in-transit cost savings.

This chart shows that 30 cases out of a possible 58 cases from Fig. 4a were able to achieve cost savings. Meaning that overall, out of our 153 in-transit tests, we demonstrated high $VCEF$ values and cost savings in 30, or 20%, of our cases. We note that these test cases were originally conceived for a study on the fastest time to solution, not cost savings, so seeing 20% of cases costing less is encouraging. Stated differently, our experiments did not focus on optimizing over resources, and so it is possible that more success could have been found. By focusing on smaller allocations, these studies should see a much higher percentage of cases where in-transit is the most cost efficient choice.

# 6 Conclusion

The primary results from this paper are three-fold: (1) VCEF values are surprisingly high, and in particular high enough to create opportunities for in-transit to be cost effective over in-line, (2) a model for considering the relative costs between in-transit and in-line that incorporates $VCEF$, and (3) consideration of that model over a corpus of data that demonstrated that VCEF-based savings do in fact create real opportunities for in-transit cost savings. We feel this result is important, since it provides simulation teams a valuable metric to use in determining which in situ paradigm to select. Combined with in-transit's other benefits (such as fault tolerance), we feel this new information on cost could be impactful in making a decision. In our studies, our communication-heavy algorithm showed more promise for in-transit cost benefit than the computation-heavy algorithm. This observation speaks to an additional role for in-transit: sidestepping scalability issues by offering the ability to run at lower concurrency. This is particularly important as the visualization community considers critical algorithms like particle advection, topology, connected components, and Delaunay tetrahedralization.

The results of this study open up several intriguing directions for future work:

The first direction is in selecting an in-transit allocation that is likely to create cost benefits. Our corpus of data was originally conceived for a study on time savings. This is why it included configurations like $Alloc(50\%)$, which have very little chance of providing cost savings. Saying it another way, although we put little effort into choosing configurations that could achieve cost savings, we still found these cost savings occurred 20% of the time. If we put more effort into choosing such configurations, perhaps by incorporating the work of Malakar [12,13], who had complementary ideas on choosing allocation sizes and analysis frequencies, this proportion could rise significantly. A twin benefit to choosing an appropriately sized in-transit allocation is that potentially more nodes would be available for simulation use, as over allocating an in-transit allocation can limit the maximum size of a simulation scaling run.

The second direction is in further understanding of $VCEF$. For our study, we ran production software for two algorithms. We were able to observe $VCEF$ factors after the run, but we are not able to predict them. Predicting $VCEF$ is hard—it will vary based on algorithm, data size, architecture, and possibly due to data-dependent factors. However, being able to predict $VCEF$ would have great benefit in being able to choose cost effective configurations. Further, our test configuration had in-line experiments that were restricted to the MPI approach of our studied simulation code (one core per MPI task). While this configuration reflects an advantage of in-transit (i.e., freedom to select the optimal configuration), this likely boosted $VCEF$, and future work should evaluate the extent of $VCEF$ when in-transit runs does not have such an advantage.

The third direction is in considering more alternatives to blocking. Making the choice to block simplified our cost model and study. A twin choice was to ignore idle time—we could have tried to do "more visualization" when the in-transit resources completed their initial task and went idle. Making a system that is more dynamic (not blocking and instead visualizing data from the next time step and/or also adding tasks when there is idle time) would be an interesting future direction. Such a system would be able to realize cost savings compared to in-line, provided $VCEF$ can offset transfer costs.

**Acknowledgments.** This manuscript has been authored by UT-Battelle, LLC under Contract No. DE-AC05-00OR22725 with the U.S. Department of Energy. The United States Government retains and the publisher, by accepting the article for publication, acknowledges that the United States Government retains a non-exclusive, paid-up, irrevocable, world-wide license to publish or reproduce the published form of this manuscript, or allow others to do so, for United States Government purposes. The Department of Energy will provide public access to these results of federally sponsored research in accordance with the DOE Public Access Plan (http://energy.gov/downloads/doe-public-access-plan). This work was partially performed under the auspices of the U.S. Department of Energy by Lawrence Livermore National Laboratory under contract DE-AC52-07NA27344 (LLNL-CONF-805283).

# References

1. Cloverleaf3d. http://uk-mac.github.io/CloverLeaf3D/. Accessed 19 Dec 2018
2. Bauer, A.C., et al.: In Situ methods, infrastructures, and applications on high performance computing platforms, a state-of-the-art (STAR) report. In: Proceedings of Eurovis Computer Graphics Forum, vol. 35(3) (2016)
3. Childs, H., et al.: In situ visualization for computational science. IEEE Comput. Graph. Appl. (CG&A) **39**(6), 76–85 (2019)
4. Docan, C., et al.: Dataspaces: an interaction and coordination framework for coupled simulation workflows. Cluster Comput. **15**(2), 163–181 (2012)
5. Friesen, B., et al.: In situ and in-transit analysis of cosmological simulations. Comput. Astrophys. Cosmol. **3**(1), 4 (2016)
6. Kress, J., et al.: Loosely coupled in situ visualization: a perspective on why it's here to stay. In: Proceedings of the First Workshop on In Situ Infrastructures for Enabling Extreme-Scale Analysis and Visualization, pp. 1–6. ISAV2015, ACM, New York (2015). https://doi.org/10.1145/2828612.2828623
7. Kress, J., et al.: Comparing the efficiency of in situ visualization paradigms at scale. In: ISC High Performance, Frankfurt, Germany, pp. 99–117, June 2019
8. Larsen, M., et al.: The ALPINE in situ infrastructure: ascending from the ashes of strawman. In: Workshop on In Situ Infrastructures on Enabling Extreme-Scale Analysis and Visualization (ISAV), pp. 42–46 (2017)

9. Liu, Q., et al.: Hello ADIOS: the challenges and lessons of developing leadership class I/O frameworks. Concurr. Comput. Pract. Exp. **26**(7), 1453–1473 (2014)
10. Ma, K.L.: In situ visualization at extreme scale: challenges and opportunities. IEEE Comput. Graphics Appl. **29**(6), 14–19 (2009)
11. Ma, K.L., et al.: In-situ processing and visualization for ultrascale simulations. In: Journal of Physics: Conference Series, vol. 78, p. 012043. IOP Publishing (2007)
12. Malakar, P., et al.: Optimal scheduling of in-situ analysis for large-scale scientific simulations. In: Proceedings of the International Conference for High Performance Computing, Networking, Storage and Analysis, p. 52. ACM (2015)
13. Malakar, P., et al.: Optimal execution of co-analysis for large-scale molecular dynamics simulations. In: Proceedings of the International Conference for High Performance Computing, Networking, Storage and Analysis, p. 60. IEEE Press (2016)
14. Mallinson, A., et al.: Cloverleaf: preparing hydrodynamics codes for exascale. In: The Cray User Group 2013 (2013)
15. Moreland, K., et al.: VTK-m: accelerating the visualization toolkit for massively threaded architectures. Comput. Graphics Appl. **36**(3), 48–58 (2016)
16. Morozov, D., Lukic, Z.: Master of puppets: cooperative multitasking for in situ processing. In: Proceedings of the 25th ACM International Symposium on High-Performance Parallel and Distributed Computing, pp. 285–288. ACM (2016)
17. Oldfield, R.A., Moreland, K., Fabian, N., Rogers, D.: Evaluation of methods to integrate analysis into a large-scale shock shock physics code. In: Proceedings of the 28th ACM International Conference on Supercomputing, pp. 83–92. ACM (2014)
18. Zhang, F., et al.: In-memory staging and data-centric task placement for coupled scientific simulation workflows. Concurr. Comput. Pract. Exp. **29**(12), 4147 (2017)

# Semi-automatic Assessment of I/O Behavior by Inspecting the Individual Client-Node Timelines—An Explorative Study on $10^6$ Jobs

Eugen Betke[1][✉] and Julian Kunkel[2]

[1] DKRZ, Hamburg, Germany
betke@dkrz.de
[2] University of Reading, Reading, UK
j.m.kunkel@reading.ac.uk

**Abstract.** HPC applications with suboptimal I/O behavior interfere with well-behaving applications and lead to increased application runtime. In some cases, this may even lead to unresponsive systems and unfinished jobs. HPC monitoring systems can aid users and support staff to identify problematic behavior and support optimization of problematic applications. The key issue is how to identify relevant applications? A profile of an application doesn't allow identifying problematic phases during the execution but tracing of each individual I/O is too invasive.

In this work, we split the execution into segments, i.e., windows of fixed size and analyze profiles of them. We develop three I/O metrics to identify three relevant classes of inefficient I/O behaviors, and evaluate them on raw data of 1,000,000 jobs on the supercomputer Mistral. The advantages of our method is that temporal information about I/O activities during job runtime is preserved to some extent and can be used to identify phases of inefficient I/O.

The main contribution of this work is the segmentation of time series and computation of metrics (Job-I/O-Utilization, Job-I/O-Problem-Time, and Job-I/O-Balance) that are effective to identify problematic I/O phases and jobs.

## 1 Introduction

Modern HPC systems are processing many thousands of jobs every day. Some of them can misbehave for some reasons (e.g., due to poor programming practices, I/O intensive tasks, or bugs) and can slow down the whole system performance and affect other jobs that are running on the same system in parallel. This bad behavior must be identified and brought under control. Before we can think about what to do with these jobs, we need to find a way to detect them.

It is important to detect inefficient I/O patterns. Monitoring systems are employed to solve this problem. However, the amount of time needed by humans to identify inefficient usage grows with the system size and the runtime of jobs.

© Springer Nature Switzerland AG 2020
P. Sadayappan et al. (Eds.): ISC High Performance 2020, LNCS 12151, pp. 166–184, 2020.
https://doi.org/10.1007/978-3-030-50743-5_9

To overcome this, the monitoring system must provide tools aiding the analysis. It needs to produce more compact representation of data providing meaningful metrics and allow for deeper analysis.

There are a variety of data-intensive parallel applications that run on HPC-systems solving different tasks, for example, climate applications. Depending on the application, we can observe different data and metadata characteristics such as parallel/serial I/O, check-pointing behavior, or I/O bursts in write/read phases. Efficient patterns are critical for I/O performance of file systems and application runtime. Checking every application manually is not possible for the support. We believe that focusing on relevant jobs is important, hence we need meaningful metrics tailored to parallel jobs and are sensitive to specific I/O behaviors.

After the related work section, the theoretical part follows. Then, we evaluate the approach on a real HPC system.

## 2   Related Work

There are many tracing and profiling tools that are able to record I/O information [6]; we will discuss a selection of them in more detail in the following. The issue of performance profiles is that they remove the temporal dimension and make it difficult to identify relevant I/O phases. As the purpose of interesting applications is the computation and I/O is just a byproduct, applications often spend less than 10% time with I/O. Tracing tools, however, produce too much information that must be reduced further.

The Ellexus tools[1] include `Breeze`, a user-friendly offline I/O profiling software, an automatic I/O report generator `Healthcheck`, and command line tool `Mistral`[2] which purpose is to report on and resolve I/O performance issues when running complex Linux applications on high performance compute clusters. Mistral is a small program that allows you to monitor application I/O patterns in real time, and log undesirable behaviour using rules defined in a configuration file called a contract. Ellexus tools support POSIX and MPI (MPICH, MVAPICH, OpenMPI) I/O interfaces.

Darshan [2,3] is an open source I/O characterization tool for post-mortem analysis of HPC applications' I/O behavior. Its primary objective is to capture concise but useful information with minimal overhead. Darshan accomplishes this by eschewing end-to-end tracing in favor of compact statistics such as elapsed time, access sizes, access patterns, and file names for each file opened by an application. These statistics are captured in a bounded amount of memory per process as the application executes. When the application shuts down, it is reduced, compressed, and stored in a unified log file. Utilities included with Darshan can then be used to analyze, visualize, and summarize the Darshan log information. Because of Darshan's low overhead, it is suitable for system-wide deployment on large-scale systems. In this deployment model, Darshan can be used not just to investigate the I/O behavior of individual applications but also

---

[1] https://www.ellexus.com/products/.
[2] Not to confuse with the DKRZ supercomputer Mistral!.

to capture a broad view of system workloads for use by facility operators and I/O researchers. Darshan is compatible with a wide range of HPC systems.

Darshan supports several types of instrumentation via software modules. Each module provides its own statistical counters and function wrappers while sharing a common infrastructure for reduction, compression, and storage. The most full-featured modules provide instrumentation for POSIX, MPI-I/O and standard I/O library function calls, while additional modules provide limited PNetCDF and HDF5 instrumentation. Other modules collect system information, such as Blue Gene runtime system parameters or Lustre file system striping parameters. The Darshan eXtended Tracing (DXT) module can be enabled at runtime to increase fidelity by recording a complete trace of all MPI-I/O and POSIX I/O operations.

Darshan uses *LD_PRELOAD* to intercept I/O calls at runtime in dynamically linked executables and link-time wrappers to intercept I/O calls at compile time in statically linked executables. For example, to override POSIX I/O calls, the GNU C Library is overloaded so that Darshan can intercept all the read, write and metadata operations. In order to measure MPI I/O, the MPI libraries must be similarly overridden. This technique allows an application to be traced without modification and with reasonably low overhead.

LASSi tool [7] was developed for detecting, the so called, victim and aggressor applications. An aggressor can steal I/O resources from the victim and negatively affect its runtime. To identify such applications, LASSi calculates metrics from Lustre job-stats and information from the job scheduler. One metric category shows file system load and another category describes applications I/O behavior. The correlation of these metrics can help to identify applications that cause the file system to slow down. In the LASSi workflow this is a manual step, where a support team is involved in the identification of applications during file system slow down. Manual steps are disadvantageous when processing large amounts of data and must be avoided in unsupervised I/O behavior identification. LASSi's indicates that the main target group are system maintainers. Understanding LASSi reports may be challenging for ordinary HPC users, who do not have knowledge about the underlying storage system.

The Ellexus tool set includes, `Breeze`, an offline I/O profiling software, an automatic I/O report generator `Healthcheck`, and command line tool `Mistral`, which purpose is to report on and resolve I/O performance issues when running complex Linux applications on high performance compute clusters. Mistral is a small download that allows you to monitor application I/O patterns in real time, and log undesirable behaviour using rules defined in a configuration file called a contract. Another powerful feature of Mistral is the ability to control I/O for application individually. Ellexus tools currently support POSIX and MPI (MPICH, MVAPICH, OpenMPI) I/O interfaces.

Another branch of research goes towards I/O prediction. Some methods work with performance data from storage systems, application side and hybrids. Application runtime prediction, efficient scheduling, I/O performance improvement. The methods work in a dynamically changing environment. They didn't tell much about the application.

The discussed limitations are well known, and many projects investigate new solutions for I/O assessment of behaviour.

In [5], the authors utilized probes to detect file system slow-down. A probing tool measures file system response times by periodically sending metadata and read/write requests. An increase of response times correlates to the overloading of the file system. This approach allows the calculation of a slow-down factor identification of the slow-down time period.

In [4], the authors run HPC applications in monitored containers. Depending on metric values captured during application runtime, the I/O management can increase or decrease the number of containers, or even take them offline, if insufficient resources are available.

In [8], a performance prediction model is developed by developers that aims to improve job runtime estimation for better job scheduling. The authors use the property of static iterative scientific code to produce near constant I/O burst, when considered over a longer period of time.

## 3    Methodology

The methodology of this work relies on (1) the segmentation of I/O traces for jobs, i.e., the generation of performance profiles for fixed length time windows. This operation results in a set of segments over job runtime that (2) are analyzed individually and aggregated on node level or job level. (3) Finally, the development of metrics for scoring the segments, i.e., the mapping from segment data to meaningful scores. The thresholds for those metrics can be semi-automatically determined and learned. In this section, we introduce the methodology in a generic manner, without giving any numbers or using metrics. We apply and evaluate the approach on a real HPC system in Sect. 5.

### 3.1    Segmentation and Timeline Aggregation

Let us assume the following as a starting situation. A data collector runs on all compute nodes, captures periodically metrics, and sends them to a centralized database. Database stores each metric as a time series together with information like node name, file system, job ID.

As the resolution of the sampling is too fine-grained (the default sampling interval is 5 s), we split the timeline obtained on a client node into segments of equal length.

To illustrate the approach, consider the fictive example: a job runs on 4 nodes and a monitoring system collects data for 4 different metrics at time points $t_X$, with $0 \leq X < 9$. By grouping 3 samples of each metric into one segment, we obtain 3 segments.

Node and job segments are collections of metric segments that aggregate this information for each node or for each job. The example is illustrated in Fig. 1. A segment can be related to an individual metric (green), a node (red), or the job data (blue).

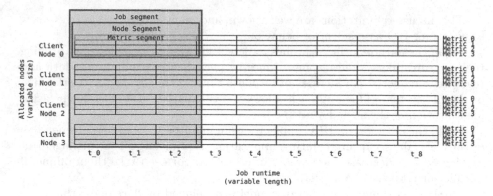

**Fig. 1.** Monitoring data structure and segmentation. In the example, 4 metrics are captured on 4 client nodes at time points $t_i$. Three sequential samples are aggregated to metric segments (green box). Node and job segments are collections of metric segments (red and blue boxes). (Color figure online)

### 3.2   Training

The training step produces statistics, which describe the overall I/O performance of the HPC system. Ideally, the analyzed dataset should contain peak performance values, achievable on an HPC, for all metrics. Similar performance values form categories (e.g., low, medium, and high performance).

There are several alternative ways to form categories: by manual selection, by using statistics like quantiles, and by using machine learning algorithms. We tried all the three mentioned methods, but quantiles worked robustly for our purpose. Furthermore, it allows to determine the percentage of jobs that the support team can investigate. For example, for the one million jobs investigated in this study (covering a period of 3 month), DKRZ could inspect 1000 - 10k jobs closer, hence looking at the 0.1% of jobs that are most I/O demanding.

We want to take a closer look at the computation of quantiles. Tabe 1 illustrates the idea. First of all, we define two quantiles qX and qY, and use them to determine the limits for each metric individually (in our case X = 99 and Y = 99.9). For simplification, we use the same quantiles for all metrics. After definition of the limit, the metric segments can be categorized and we count the number of segments that falls into each category in the following way:

LowIO        smaller than qX        $c_{0,X} = count(value(\text{metric}_X) \leq \text{limit}_{0,X})$
HighIO       between qX and qY      $c_{1,X} = count(\text{limit}_{0,X} > value(\text{metric}_X) \leq \text{limit}_{1,X})$
CriticalIO   larger than qY         $c_{2,X} = count(value(\text{metric}_X) > \text{limit}_{1,X})$

**Table 1.** Generic limits and category statistics.

| Metric | Limits | | Number of occurrences | | |
|---|---|---|---|---|---|
| Name | qY | qX | LowIO | HighIO | CriticalIO |
| $metric_0$ | $limit_{0,0}$ | $limit_{1,0}$ | $c_{0,0}$ | $c_{1,0}$ | $c_{2,0}$ |
| $metric_1$ | $limit_{0,1}$ | $limit_{1,1}$ | $c_{0,1}$ | $c_{1,1}$ | $c_{2,1}$ |
| ... | | | | | |
| $metric_N$ | $limit_{0,N}$ | $limit_{1,N}$ | $c_{0,N}$ | $c_{1,N}$ | $c_{2,N}$ |

## 3.3 Scores

Our categories are labeled manually. The scoring strategy is based on the following considerations:

Since, LowIO represents low I/O utilization, it gets a score of 0. This category will be mostly ignored in derived metrics. HighIO contains no outliers but may generate a mixed workload or be inefficient and needs to be taken into account. Therefore, it gets a score of 1. CriticalIO is a weight factor, larger than HighIO. We suggest to compute CriticalIO/HighIO, and to take the smallest value for Z (this is summarized in Table 2a).

**Table 2.** Summary of the scoring

| Category name | MScore |
|---|---|
| LowIO | 0 |
| HighIO | 1 |
| CriticalIO | Z |

*(a) Category scores*

| Score name | Definition |
|---|---|
| MScore | = category scores |
| NScore | $\sum$ MScore |
| JScore | $\sum$ NScore |

*(b) Segment scores*

Based on the individual metrics scores, further scores are derived. The node score is the sum of all individual metrics scores for a segment, i.e., it indicates if there is an I/O issue at all in this segment and on this node. The job level aggregation is the sum of the node score (see Table 2b).

## 3.4 Job Assessment

Once the system is trained and a configuration file with the statistics generated, a single job can be analyzed and assessed automatically. To understand the behavior of the job I/O, we exploit the knowledge about the timeline and analyze the temporal and spatial I/O behavior of the segments in coarse-grained fashion. This is achieved by introducing new metrics that reduce the complexity into relevant scores that show potential for optimization: the Job-I/O-Problem-Time, Job-I/O-Utilization, and Job-I/O-Balance. These values must be considered together.

*Job-I/O-Problem-Time.* This metric is the fraction of job runtime that is I/O-intensive; it is approximated by the fractions of segments that are considered problematic (JScore > 1). I/O problem time is the amount of problematic, I/O-intensive job segments (IOJS) divided by the total number of job segments (JS) (see Eq. (1)).

$$\text{Job-I/O-Problem-Time} = \frac{\text{count (IOJS)}}{\text{count (JS)}} \tag{1}$$

*Job-I/O-Utilization.* While most phases may not do any I/O, these might have extraordinary I/O activity during such phases. Large jobs with a large number of I/O accesses can induce slow down on the file system for other jobs. To identify such jobs, we compute a metric that shows the average load during I/O-relevant phases.

The first step identifies I/O-intensive job segments (IOJS), i.e., JScore > 1, and counts occurrences $N = count(IOFS)$. Assume, the `max_score()` function returns the highest metric score of all metrics in a job segment. Then, the quotient of the `max_score()`'s sum and $N$ is I/O utilization for one particular file system. For handling several file systems, we compute a sum of the resulting values and obtain Job-I/O-Utilization (see Eq. (2)).

$$\text{Job-I/O-Utilization} = \sum_{FS} \frac{\sum_{j \in IOJS} \text{max\_score}(j)}{N} \tag{2}$$

Since, Job-I/O-Utilization considers only I/O intensive job segments, the condition `max_score()` $\geq 1$ is always true. Thus, Job-I/O-Utilization is defined for a job iff the job has at least some relevant I/O activity. Job-I/O-Utilization values are always $\geq 1$.

For a conventional mean-score computation, we would probably apply the `mean_score()` function to a job segment, instead of `max_score()`, to obtain a mean value of all metric scores in a job segment. This would provide a conventional mean value, as we would expect it. Although such a value might be more intuitive, the following considerations show that it is not robust enough for our purpose. Monitoring data (in particular historical data) may be incomplete or incompatible, e.g., when some metrics are not captured due a collector malfunction or when monitoring system changes after. As a consequence, conventional mean values for complete and incomplete job data may diverge quite substantially from one another, even for jobs with similar I/O performance. For illustration, consider a job segment with only one active metric segment, e.g., with score = 4, and others with scores = 0. The mean value would be smaller, if data for all 13 metrics are available as if only 8 metrics are present. This would adversely affect the result, assigning higher values to incomplete data. In this context of this work, this would be interpreted as higher I/O load. To prevent such a miss-calculation, we compute mean value of job segment max values. This method is independent of the number of metrics and fulfills our requirements. Even if one metric segment works with high performance, the whole job segment can be considered as loaded. This works as a perfect complement for the balance metrics.

*Job-I/O-Balance.* The balance metric indicates how I/O load is distributed between nodes during job runtime. Here again, we consider only I/O-intensive job segments ($IOJS$), i.e., JScore $> 1$ but divide them with the maximum score obtained on any single node. A perfect balance is 1.0 and a balance where 25% of nodes participate in I/O is 0.25.

For each job segment $j$, with $j \in IOJS$, we compute:

1. NScore for each node segment
2. Mean and max values of NScores
3. Job-I/O-Balance($j$) for a job segment, i.e., the quotient of mean and max values

The overall Job-I/O-Balance is the mean value of all Job-I/O-Balance(j) values, with $j \in IOJS$ (see Eq. (3)).

$$\text{Job-I/O-Balance} = \text{mean} \left( \left\{ \frac{\text{mean\_score (j)}}{\text{max\_score (j)}} \right\}_{j \in \text{IOJS}} \right) \tag{3}$$

### 3.5  Example

Assume a 4-node job with two I/O intensive job segments $s_{j_0}$ and $s_{j_5}$. Furthermore, assume, the job assesses two file systems $fs_1$ and $fs_2$. We compute Job-I/O-Utilization, Job-I/O-Problem-Time and Job-I/O-Balance metrics in Eqs. (4) to (6) for generic data illustrated in Fig. 2.

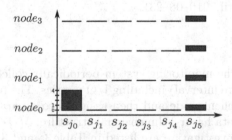

**Fig. 2.** Segment timeline. $s_{j_0}, s_{j_5} \in IOJS$ are I/O-intensive job segments.

$$\begin{aligned}
\text{max}_0 &= \text{max\_score}(s_{j_0}) & &= 4 \\
\text{max}_1 &= \text{max\_score}(s_{j_5}) & &= 1 \\
U_{fs1} &= \text{mean}(\{\text{max}_0, \text{max}_1\}) & &= 2.5 \\
U_{fs2} &= \text{mean}(\{\text{max}_0, \text{max}_1\}) & &= 2.5 \\
\text{Job-I/O-Utilization} &= U_{fs1} + U_{fs2} & &= 5 \tag{4}
\end{aligned}$$

$$N_{IOJS} = 2$$
$$N_{JS} = 6$$
$$\text{Job-I/O-Problem-Time} = \frac{N_{IOJS}}{N_{JS}} \qquad\qquad \approx 0.33 \qquad\qquad (5)$$

$$b_0 = \text{balance}(s_{j_0}) \qquad\qquad = 0.25$$
$$b_1 = \text{balance}(s_{j_5}) \qquad\qquad = 1$$
$$\text{Job-I/O-Balance} = \text{mean}(\{b_0, b_1\}) \qquad = 0,625 \qquad (6)$$

## 4    Data Exploration

DKRZ uses Slurm workload manager for scheduling jobs on Mistral on shared and non-shared partitions. The monitoring system of DKRZ [1] does not capture data on shared Slurm partitions, because it can not assign this data unambiguously to jobs. The problem hides in the (in-house) data collector, more precise, in the usage of proc files as its main data source. The point is that shared partitions can run two or more jobs on a compute node. Job activities can change the I/O counters in the proc files, but the changes can not be traced back to jobs. This kind of monitoring makes observation of individual jobs not feasible. In contrast, a non-shared partition, where only one job is allowed to run, does not suffer from this problem. Monitoring system assumes that all changes in proc files are a result of activities done by a currently running job.

This section deals with job data statistics of 1,000,000 job data downloaded from DKRZ's monitoring system. These data cover a time period of 99 days (from 2019–05–16 until 2019–08–23).

### 4.1    Job Data

In our experiments, the monitoring system periodically collects various metrics (according to a capture interval) including I/O metrics. The resulting time series is collected for each client node and then assigned to a parallel (SLURM) job. Ultimately, the job data has a 3-dimensional structure: $Metric \times Node \times Time$. Metrics used in our investigation are listed in Table 3a and 3b.

To reduce the overhead of the data acquisition and storage space, metadata and I/O metrics are selected in the following way: Similar metadata operations are combined into three different counters: read, modification and other accesses. Then, create and unlink counters are captured separately as these operations are performance critical. The exact group compositions and metric names are listed in Table 3a.

For I/O, we capture a set of counters: The read_* and write_* counters provide the basic information about file system access performed by the application. We also include the osc_read_*, osc_write_* that represent the actual data transfer between the node (Lustre client) and each server[3]. The metrics are listed in Table 3b.

## 4.2 Analysis Tool

The analysis tool is a product of our continuous research on monitoring data analysis. It requires an initial training, based on a relatively small job dataset, before it can be used for automatic job assessment. Therefore, in the first step, it downloads job data from a system-wide monitoring database and creates statistics about I/O performance on the HPC system. In the second step, these statistics are used for assessing individual jobs. The workflow is illustrated in Fig. 3.

**Table 3.** Data collectors run on all compute node and capture periodically thirteen I/O metrics (emphasized by **bold font**) and send them to a centralized database. These I/O metrics are computed from around thirty constantly growing proc counters in **/proc/fs/lustre/llite/lustre*-*/stats**. (Note: Lustre can reset counters at any time point.)

**md_read** = getattr + getxattr + readdir + statfs + listxattr + open + close

**md_mod** = setattr + setxattr + mkdir + link + rename + symlink + rmdir

**md_file_create** = create

**md_file_delete** = unlink

**md_other** = truncate + mmap + ioctl + fsync + mknod

*(a) Metadata metrics: data collector form groups of related metadata proc counters, compute sums, and assign the sums to corresponding metadata metrics.*

| | |
|---|---|
| **read_bytes** | **osc_read_bytes** |
| **read_calls** | **osc_read_calls** |
| **write_bytes** | **osc_write_bytes** |
| **write_calls** | **osc_write_calls** |
| *Application's I/O requests.* | *Lustre client I/O requests.* |

*(b) Data metrics: data collectors assign selected data related proc counter values directly to corresponding data metrics (proc counter names are omitted).*

## 4.3 Data Statistics

About 5.3% of data is empty. For these jobs neither data, nor metadata exist. We suppose these jobs are canceled, before Slurm is able to allocate nodes. After this filtering, 947445 job data are available.

---

[3] The Lustre client transforms the original file system accesses—made by the application—to Lustre specific accesses, for instance by utilizing the kernel cache. This can have a significant impact on I/O performance, when many small I/O accesses are created but coalesced.

1. Computing file system usage statistics

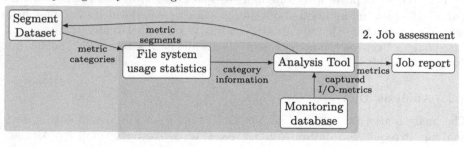

Fig. 3. Analysis tool workflow

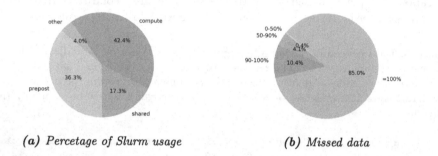

(a) Percetage of Slurm usage

(b) Missed data

Fig. 4. Statistics about Slurm jobs analysed.

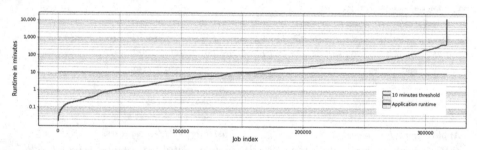

Fig. 5. Ordered job runtime (blue line) and 10 min threshold (red line). (Color figure online)

All nodes have access to two file systems; as both deliver similar performance values, a differentiation is not necessary. Therefore, in the course of the paper, we will summarize both partitions to one big partition, called "compute". The nodes of these partitions are reserved exclusively for a job. The monitoring system relies on the assumption that all I/O activities registered on these nodes refers to the running job. Conversely, other partitions can be shared by several jobs. Since the monitoring system captures node related data, monitoring data from these partitions can not be assigned unambiguously to a job. Thus, data from "shared", "prepost", and other small partitions is filtered out. A further filtering criteria is exit state of jobs. We analyze data only from successfully completed jobs. Statistics for completed jobs for Mistral's large partitions are shown in Fig. 4a. After filtering, 338,681 job data remain for analysis.

The next statistic describes the runtime of the successfully completed jobs. Below the red line are about 45% of jobs that are shorter than 10 min. As these jobs consume only 1.5% of available node hours, we do not expect to find significant I/O loads in there. Figure 5 illustrates the runtime of the remaining jobs, including the 10 min threshold (red line).

During our experiments, we encounter a problem with incomplete data. Sometimes, individual metrics, and occasionally, data from complete nodes are missing. The statistics are shown in Fig. 4b. The reasons can be, that some counters are not available during collector initialization, collectors can crash, or the database is overloaded and is not able to record data. For 4.5% of the jobs less than 90% of data is available, in 10.4% data is complete from 90% to 100%, and in the remaining 85.1% all data is available. It is not harmful for the training to lack some data as metric scores can be computed on partially available data. We believe the approach is sufficiently robust to process such data, but for assessment of individual jobs the results won't be perfectly accurate if they omitted some I/O phases.

## 5    Evaluation

This section uses our methodology to identify I/O-intensive applications on the Mistral supercomputer by doing a step-by-step evaluation of real data. Therewith, we validate that the strategy and metrics will allow us to identify I/O critical jobs and I/O segments within. The segment size used in the experiments is 10 min.

### 5.1    Limits

There is no perfect recipe for finding the best quantiles that meets everyone's needs, because file system usage and goals may be different. In our case, identification of outlier jobs requires quantiles in the upper range. We can see this in

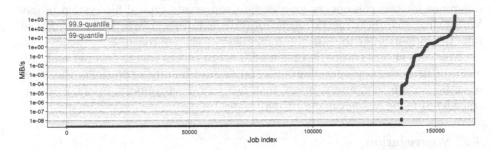

**Fig. 6.** Training data (subset) for read_bytes metric, and q99%- and q99.9%-quantiles (red lines). (Color figure online)

the example of `read_calls` segments in Fig. 6. The most blue dots are located close to 0 Op/s, which means that there is low or no I/O activity in most segments. We separated them by the 99-quantile (lower red line). The remaining high activity segments are significant for identification of high I/O load. The more of them are located in a job, the higher is the probability that this job causes a high I/O load. Additionally, the 99.9-quantile (the upper red line) separates high and critical activity segments. This separation defines segments with an exceptionally high I/O load. Generally speaking, the quantiles choice in this work is based on observations of file system usage on Mistral and rough ideas of what we want to achieve. We suspect it is transferable to other HPC systems, but this point was not investigated and requires a further study.

For limit calculation we use a 30 days training set consisting of 72,000 jobs. Their segmentation results in around 152,000,000 metrics segments. The resulting limits are listed in Table 5.

## 5.2   Categorization

In the next step, the limits are used for categorization of all job data (about 660 million metric segments) (Table 4). The result of categorization is shown in Table 5.

**Table 4.** Category scores for Mitral evaluation.

| Category name | MScore | Justification for Mscore value |
|---|---|---|
| LowIO | 0 | Ignore this category in mathematical expressions |
| HighIO | 1 | Consider this category in mathematical expressions |
| CriticalIO | 4 | CriticalIO is at least four times higher than HighIO |

The first observation is, that there are less `osc_read_*` and `osc_write_*` metrics reported than for other metrics. The reason for that is the file system changed from Lustre 2.7.14 to Lustre 2.11.0. Unfortunately, since Lustre 2.8, the proc files do not offer the `osc_read_*` and `osc_write_*` metrics anymore. We did not know that and captured incomplete data. (Fortunately, other sources provide this information and we can fix that in the future.) This trifle makes no difference for this concept, as long as data represents typical file system usage. We assume that 17M metric segments form a representative training set and take this opportunity to show the robustness of the approach.

The second observation is that modification of metadata, deleting and creation of files are rare operations. For delete and modify operations, the 99%-quantile is zero, i.e., any segment that has one delete/modify operation, it is considered to be in the category HighIO.

## 5.3   Aggregation

The conversion of metrics value to the score allows the aggregation of job data on job, node, and metric levels and of incompatible metrics, like `md_delete`

**Table 5.** Category statistics for training with segments size of 600 s.

| Metric | | Limits | | Number of occurrences | | |
|---|---|---|---|---|---|---|
| Name | Unit | q99 | q99.9 | LowIO | HighIO | CriticalIO |
| md_file_create | Op/s | 0.17 | 1.34 | 65,829 K | 622 K | 156 K |
| md_file_delete | Op/s | 0.00 | 0.41 | 65,824 K | 545 K | 172 K |
| md_mod | Op/s | 0.00 | 0.67 | 65,752 K | 642 K | 146 K |
| md_other | Op/s | 20.87 | 79.31 | 65,559K | 763K | 212 K |
| md_read | Op/s | 371.17 | 7084.16 | 65,281 K | 1,028 K | 225 K |
| osc_read_bytes | MiB/s | 1.98 | 93.58 | 17,317 K | 188 K | 30 K |
| osc_read_calls | Op/s | 5.65 | 32.23 | 17,215 K | 287 K | 33 K |
| osc_write_bytes | MiB/s | 8.17 | 64.64 | 16,935 K | 159 K | 26 K |
| osc_write_calls | Op/s | 2.77 | 17.37 | 16,926 K | 167K | 27K |
| read_bytes | MiB/s | 28.69 | 276.09 | 66,661 K | 865 K | 233 K |
| read_calls | Op/s | 348.91 | 1573.45 | 67,014 K | 360 K | 385K |
| write_bytes | MiB/s | 9.84 | 80.10 | 61,938 K | 619 K | 155 K |
| write_calls | Op/s | 198.56 | 6149.64 | 61,860 K | 662 K | 174 K |

and read_bytes. This is useful as it allows us to reduce the data for large jobs. Due to inability to aggregate, conventional dashboards contain many plots with detailed information, which, in turn, is hard to grasp and inconvenient to use. With uniform scoring aggregation it becomes an easy task. This is illustrated in Fig. 7. Data is aggregated from detailed view in Fig. 7a to reduced view in Fig. 7b, and finally to one single chart in Fig. 7c.

## 5.4  Metrics Calculation

Metrics calculation is the next logical step in our work. They describe specific I/O behavior by a meaningful number.

## 5.5  Job-I/O-Utilization (U)

The mean score metric filters non-I/O-intensive jobs out of the dataset. 41% jobs (151,777) have a Job-I/O-Utilization = 0. These jobs are of little interest to us, since they do not produce any noticeable load for our file system. The remaining 59% jobs (218,776) are selected for further investigations.

The distribution of Job-I/O-Utilization is shown in Fig. 8a. The utilization for one file system may be $U = 4$, if the file system is used to 100%. We can observe that for many jobs $U > 4$, which means these jobs are using two file systems at the same time. This may be a copy job that moves data from one file system to another.

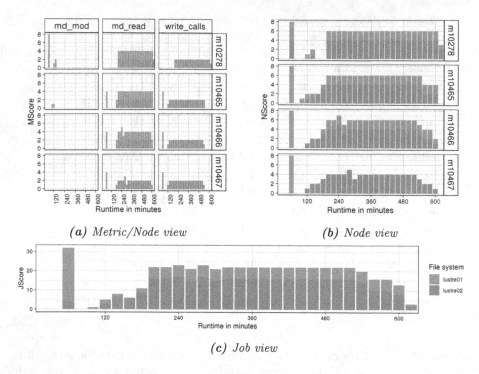

(a) Metric/Node view

(b) Node view

(c) Job view

**Fig. 7.** Segments visualization at different level of details.

## 5.6   Job-I/O-Balance (B)

Jobs that are running on 1 node are always balanced. There are about 66,049 (30%) jobs of this kind. Job-I/O-Balance for the remaining 152,727 (70%) jobs are visualized in Fig. 8b. The picture shows that a vast amount of jobs are not using parallel I/O or doing it insufficiently. 17,323 of the jobs are balanced to 50% or more. 4,122 of them are highly optimized and are running with almost 100% optimization.

We have to keep in mind that during categorization, all negligible I/O (i.e., if JScore = 0) is filtered out. That means, the balance metric focuses on significant I/O sizes.

List of jobs ordered by Job-I/O-Balance in increased order gives an overview of jobs with the lowest I/O balance. A closer look at the first entries reveals that Jobs with a fixed number of I/O nodes have also a small I/O balance value, but they are far behind in the list.

## 5.7   Job-I/O-Problem-Time (PT)

Surprisingly, we found that 142,329 (65%) jobs are pure I/O jobs, i.e., with Job-I/O-Problem-Time = 1. The other 76,447 (35%) jobs have a Job-I/O-Problem-Time < 1. The peaks in Fig. 8c at positions $1, 1/2, 1/3, 1/4, \ldots$

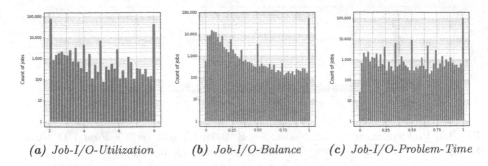

**(a)** *Job-I/O-Utilization*     **(b)** *Job-I/O-Balance*     **(c)** *Job-I/O-Problem-Time*

**Fig. 8.** Metric statistics

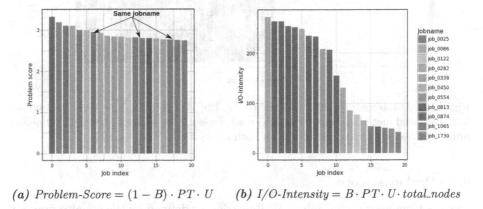

**(a)** $Problem\text{-}Score = (1 - B) \cdot PT \cdot U$     **(b)** $I/O\text{-}Intensity = B \cdot PT \cdot U \cdot total\_nodes$

**Fig. 9.** Penalty functions and the Top 20 jobs with a runtime >30 min. The color represents a unique job name. (Color figure online)

are mostly artifacts from short jobs. After filtering out jobs shorter than 2 h, they disappear, but peak at position 1 is still there.

## 6   Job Assessment

Job assessment is a semi-automated process. In the first step, penalty functions sort jobs according to user-defined requirements. Typically, a function is constructed such that each sub-optimal parameter increases its value. A job list can be sorted automatically by that value. The manual tasks in the second steps are visualization of top ranked jobs and actual assessment.

Based on our initial goals, we define two functions: (1) Problem-Score: for detection of potential inefficient file system usage and I/O-Intensity: for detection of high I/O loads. Both are defined and visualized in Fig. 9. The computation includes B, U, and PT metrics from the previous section and further parameters for computing a single value.

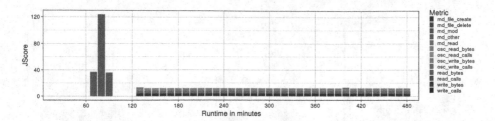

**Fig. 10.** Problem-Score ≈ 2.9: Nodes: 70; B: 0.05; PT:0.8; U: 7.5. First I/O phase: highly parallel metadata access; Second I/O phase: single node writes.

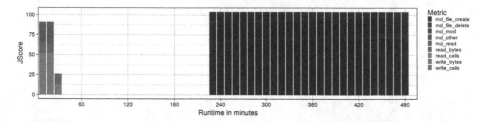

**Fig. 11.** I/O-Intensity ≈ 29.9; Nodes: 13; B: 1.0; PT: 0.6; U: 3.9.; First I/O phase: fully balanced metadata operations and reads on both file systems; Second I/O phase: fully balanced file create operations on both file systems.

## 6.1    Problem-Score

The Problem-Score is a product of all metrics, as defined by the penalty function in the Fig. 9a. For illustration, a 70-node job with Problem-Score ≈ 2.9 is visualized on node-level in Fig. 10. It represents a classic case of unoptimized single node I/O. In the picture, we see a short phase of metadata operations, and a 360 min long write phase. The node view (omitted, due to space restrictions) reveals also, that the short phase is fully balanced, and the long phase runs on a single node. The phases can be clearly identified by naked eye in the timeline.

When considering further jobs, we found other recurring and inefficient I/O patterns, e.g., partially or improperly balanced I/O. In all cases, different phases can be easily read from timelines, even if they are connected to each other or running in parallel.

## 6.2    I/O-Intensity

To identify applications that generate high I/O loads, we have also to consider the number of nodes. Here again, we use the same logic as before, i.e., when I/O load increases, I/O-Intensity must also increase. Now, high balance is a sign for load generation, and can be used directly in the function. All that is reflected in the penalty function in Fig. 9b.

A particularly interesting case is illustrated on job level in Fig. 11. This picture reveals that the job does I/O in two phases. Looking at the metric/node level (omitted, due to space restrictions), we see that the job (1) operates on both file systems, (2) reads data in the first phase and creates files in the second phase, and (3) both phases are fully balanced. The file creation phase takes longer than 240 min (>50% of job runtime). This extreme behavior can degrade the performance of Lustre metadata servers, affect the runtime of parallel running jobs, and slow down metadata operations for other users. We suppose that users and developers of this application are not aware of that, and store information in different files for reasons of convenience.

This job could be discovered even if all osc_* are missing. Obviously, the design of the approach is robust enough to handle missing data.

# 7 Conclusion

In this work, we developed and evaluated an approach for characterization of I/O phases utilizing monitoring infrastructure widely available and compute derived metrics for phases of application execution. In our experiments, these metrics support the detection of I/O-intensive and problematic jobs.

In the pre-processing part, we split monitoring data into fixed size time windows (segments). Then, data of several thousands of jobs are used for computing statistics representing typical file system usage. Based on statistics and average segment performance, we are able to assign a score value for each segment. These segment scores are the basis for the next processing.

Working with categories and scores significantly simplifies mapping of common I/O behavior to meaningful metrics. We derived the metrics Job-I/O-Balance, Job-I/O-Problem-Time, and Job-I/O-Utilization. These metrics can be used in any mathematical calculation, or in direct comparison of jobs, or for deriving new metrics.

Visualization of the derived metrics is easier to understand than visualization of raw data, e.g., because raw data can have a different semantics, an arbitrary value with high peaks. For the ordinary users, it is not always obvious, if the performance of such values is good or bad. The categorization hides all the details from users.

In our experiments, we could identify applications with high potential to degrade file system performance and applications with inefficient file system usage profile. By investigating raw data, we could verify that the presented approach supports the analysis. In our opinion, this approach is suitable for most current state-of-the-art cluster environments that are able to monitor suitable file system usage counters.

Ultimately, we work toward automatic analysis and reporting tools. Our next step is the data reduction, e.g., the grouping of similar profiles.

# References

1. Betke, E., Kunkel, J.: Footprinting parallel I/O – machine learning to classify application's I/O behavior. In: Weiland, M., Juckeland, G., Alam, S., Jagode, H. (eds.) ISC High Performance 2019. LNCS, vol. 11887, pp. 214–226. Springer, Cham (2019). https://doi.org/10.1007/978-3-030-34356-9_18
2. Carns, P.: Darshan. In: High performance parallel I/O. pp. 309–315. Computational Science Series, Chapman & Hall/CRC (2015)
3. Carns, P., et al.: Understanding and improving computational science storage access through continuous characterization. ACM Trans. Storage (TOS) **7**(3), 8 (2011)
4. Dayal, J., et al.: I/O containers: managing the data analytics and visualization pipelines of high end codes. In: 2013 IEEE International Symposium on Parallel Distributed Processing, Workshops and Ph.D. Forum, pp. 2015–2024, May 2013. https://doi.org/10.1109/IPDPSW.2013.198
5. Kunkel, J., Betke, E.: Tracking user-perceived I/O slowdown via probing. In: Weiland, M., Juckeland, G., Alam, S., Jagode, H. (eds.) ISC High Performance 2019. LNCS, vol. 11887, pp. 169–182. Springer, Cham (2019). https://doi.org/10.1007/978-3-030-34356-9_15
6. Kunkel, J.M., et al.: Tools for analyzing parallel I/O. In: Yokota, R., Weiland, M., Shalf, J., Alam, S. (eds.) ISC High Performance 2018. LNCS, vol. 11203, pp. 49–70. Springer, Cham (2018). https://doi.org/10.1007/978-3-030-02465-9_4
7. Sivalingam, K., Richardson, H., Tate, A., Lafferty, M.: Lassi: metric based I/O analytics for HPC. CoRR abs/1906.03884 (2019). http://arxiv.org/abs/1906.03884
8. Xie, B., et al.: Predicting output performance of a petascale supercomputer. In: Proceedings of the 26th International Symposium on High-Performance Parallel and Distributed Computing, HPDC 2017, pp. 181–192. ACM, New York (2017). https://doi.org/10.1145/3078597.3078614, https://doi.org/10.1145/3078597.3078614

# Emerging Technologies

# Embedding Algorithms for Quantum Annealers with Chimera and Pegasus Connection Topologies

Stefanie Zbinden[1,2], Andreas Bärtschi[2(✉)], Hristo Djidjev[2], and Stephan Eidenbenz[2]

[1] Department of Mathematics, ETH Zürich, 8092 Zürich, Switzerland
zbindens@student.ethz.ch
[2] CCS-3, Los Alamos National Laboratory, Los Alamos, NM 87545, USA
baertschi@lanl.gov

**Abstract.** We propose two new algorithms – Spring-Based MinorMiner (SPMM) and Clique-Based MinorMiner (CLMM) – which take as input the connectivity graph of a Quadratic Unconstrained Binary Optimization (QUBO) problem and produce as output an embedding of the input graph on a host graph that models the topology of a quantum computing device. As host graphs, we take the Chimera graph and the Pegasus graph, which are the topology graphs of D-Wave's 2000 qubit (first introduced in 2017) and 5000 qubit (expected 2020) quantum annealer devices, respectively. We evaluate our algorithms on a large set of random graph QUBO inputs (Erdős-Rényi $G_{n,p}$, Barabási-Albert and $d$-regular graphs) on both host topologies against other embedding algorithms. For the Pegasus topology, we find that CLMM outperforms all other algorithms at edge densities larger than 0.08, while SPMM wins at edge densities smaller than 0.08 for Erdős-Rényi graphs, with very similar transition densities for the other graph classes. Surprisingly, the standard D-Wave MinorMiner embedding algorithm – while also getting slightly outperformed by SPMM for sparse and very dense graphs on Chimera – does not manage to extend its overall good performance on Chimera to Pegasus as it fails to embed even medium-density graphs on 175–180 nodes which are known to have clique embeddings on Pegasus.

## 1 Introduction

Quantum annealers such as the D-Wave 2000Q offer high quality solutions to hard optimization problems, and have a relatively large number of (currently up to 2000) qubits, while the next-generation D-Wave Advantage (due in 2020) will have more than 5000 qubits. Because of the technological challenges in connecting qubits, existing qubit connectivity topologies are far from the desirable

Research presented in this article was supported by the Laboratory Directed Research and Development program of Los Alamos National Laboratory under project numbers 20180267ER / 20190065DR. Los Alamos report number LA-UR-20-22259.

© Springer Nature Switzerland AG 2020
P. Sadayappan et al. (Eds.): ISC High Performance 2020, LNCS 12151, pp. 187–206, 2020.
https://doi.org/10.1007/978-3-030-50743-5_10

**Table 1.** Study Parameters: we compare the performance of four embedding methods for three different QUBO graphs on the two main D-Wave host graph topologies.

| Embedding method | QUBO Class | Host Graph |
|---|---|---|
| MinorMiner (MM) [9,13] | Erdős-Rényi $G_{n,p}$ | Chimera C16 |
| Layout-Aware MinorMiner (LAMM) [28,29] | Barabási-Albert | Pegasus P16 |
| Spring-based MinorMiner (SPMM) | random $d$-regular | |
| Clique-based MinorMiner (CLMM) | | |

all-to-all topology, as a result limiting the sizes of the problems that can be solved on these devices. In fact, the currently used *Chimera* has degree 6 [7], while the *Pegasus* topology (available in 2020 with D-Wave Advantage) has degree 15 [5]. The programming model for the D-Wave quantum annealer consists of setting the coefficients of a quadratic optimization function on binary variables (called a Quadratic Unconstrained Binary Optimization (QUBO) problem) so that linear terms map to qubits and quadratic terms map to couplers between the corresponding qubits. In practical applications, we are given an input QUBO whose set of linear and quadratic weights does not directly map onto the physical topology of the D-Wave device, so we have to represent each variable by a set of qubits (chain) and decide how to map variables onto chains. This problem is usually modeled as a graph theoretic problem: Finding a *minor embedding* of the input QUBO graph into an input topology host graph, a classical algorithmic problem that is generally NP-hard [25]. The ability to embed practical QUBOs at larger and larger size directly correlates to the success and operational applicability of D-Wave devices when competing with classical devices.

In this paper, we propose and test two new embedding algorithms – Spring-based MinorMiner (SPMM) and Clique-based MinorMiner (CLMM). We study the performance of these algorithms as compared to two previously proposed methods: MinorMiner (MM) [9,13] and a recent adaptation, Layout-Aware MinorMiner (LAMM) [28,29]. All four algorithms are benchmarked on a large set of random input QUBO graphs that need to be embedded onto the Chimera and Pegasus topologies. As random graph classes, we study Erdős-Rényi $G_{n,p}$ graphs, Barabási-Albert graphs, and random $d$-regular graphs. Each of these graph classes has a density parameter and a graph order (size) that we vary in our experiments. We assess the performance of the four algorithms based on whether they are able to embed graphs. The parameters of our experimental study are given in Table 1. Our main findings are:

- On the Pegasus host graph, our Clique-based MinorMiner (CLMM) is a clear winner with our alternative Spring-Based MinorMiner (SPMM) algorithm edging out both CLMM and MM for very sparse graphs only. The relative ranking of the algorithms is the same across all three QUBO input classes with SPMM's advantage at sparse graphs most pronounced for $d$-regular graphs. Somewhat surprisingly, a threshold edge density exists that is very similar for all three random graph classes (at about $|E|/\binom{|V|}{2} \approx 0.08$) such that

CLMM and SPMM win at edge densities larger and smaller than the threshold, respectively ($E, V$ denote edges and nodes of the QUBO graph).
- On the Chimera host graph, SPMM wins over MM and LAMM at sparse and dense graphs, whereas MM and LAMM perform slightly better at medium density graphs. Again, SPMM's advantage at large sparse graphs is most pronounced for $d$-regular graphs.
- On the Chimera host graph, all algorithms easily manage to embed the previously largest known embeddable clique (at 65 vertices), whereas on Pegasus only CLMM finds embeddings of cliques with more than 180 nodes. In fact, using SPMM for Chimera and CLMM for Pegasus we find largest embeddable cliques at sizes 65 and 185 respectively.

The paper is organized as follows: We introduce the concepts of QUBOs, embeddings, host graphs and other background material including related work in more detail in Sect. 2. We describe the embedding algorithms in Sect. 3, and give details about the experimental design in Sect. 4. We present our results for the Pegasus host graph in Sect. 5 and for the Chimera host graph in Sect. 6, before concluding in Sect. 7.

## 2    Background

### 2.1    Quadratic Unconstrained Binary Optimization (QUBO)

Quadratic Unconstrained Binary Optimization (QUBO) is the problem of minimizing a quadratic function of binary variables, in one of the forms

$$\min_x \ \sum_{i=1}^{n} a_i x_i + \sum_{i<j} b_{ij} x_i x_j, \qquad x_i \in \{0,1\} \quad \text{(QUBO formulation)},$$

$$\text{or} \ \min_z \ \sum_{i=1}^{n} h_i z_i + \sum_{i<j} J_{ij} z_i z_j, \qquad z_i \in \{-1,+1\} \quad \text{(Ising formulation)}.$$

The two formulations are equivalent via bijective relations $h_i = \frac{1}{2}\left(a_i + \sum_j b_{ij}\right)$, $J_{ij} = \frac{b_{ij}}{4}$. Note that $J_{ij}$ is nonzero if and only if $b_{ij}$ is nonzero. Hence QUBO problems are naturally represented by a graph $P = (V_P, E_P)$, where in $V_P$ each variable $z_i$ is represented as a node $z_i$ with weight $h_i$, and in $E_P$ we have for every pair $i < j$ with nonzero $J_{ij}$ an edge $e = \{z_i, z_j\}$ with edge weight $J_{ij}$.

We remark that QUBOs are a class of NP-hard optimization problems; as we can use QUBOs to optimize the number of satisfied constraints in an instance of 0/1 Integer Programming – one of Karp's original 21 NP-complete problems [21].

### 2.2    Solving QUBOs on Quantum Annealers

Quantum Annealers such as D-Wave's 2000Q and the upcoming D-Wave Advantage [5] have quantum processors with a set of qubits $\mathcal{Q}$ and a set of couplers $\mathcal{C}$

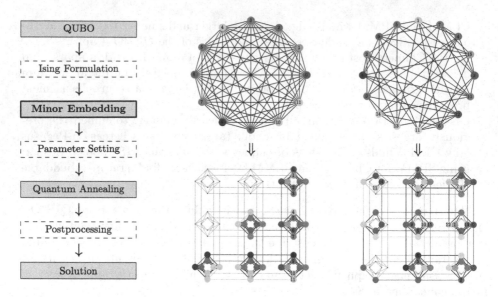

**Fig. 1.** Schematics of solving a QUBO instance with a Quantum Annealer (cf. [32]) **(left)** Full workflow **(center)** Clique minor embedding of a clique $K_{12}$ on a Chimera graph $C3$ **(right)** Heuristic minor embedding of a 16-node 7-regular graph on host $C3$.

between some pairs of qubits. If we identify the qubits with a node set $V_H$ and the couplers with an edge set $E_H$, the resulting connected structure is a graph $H = (V_H, E_H)$, called the host graph. The D-Wave programming model lets us set weights $h_i$ for every qubit $q_i \in \mathcal{Q}$ and weights $J_{ij}$ for every coupler $c_{ij} \in \mathcal{C}$. In an actual D-Wave calculation, the device uses quantum annealing to sample from low-energy eigenstates of the Hamiltonian

$$H = \sum_{i=1}^{n} h_i \sigma_z^{(i)} + \sum_{\{i,j\} \in E_H} J_{ij} \sigma_z^{(i)} \sigma_z^{(j)},$$

with Pauli-$Z$ operators $\sigma_z^{(i)}$ acting on qubit $q_i$.[1] As such, the spin configuration of a groundstate corresponds to an optimum solution of a QUBO in Ising formulation with the same weights $h_i, J_{ij}$.

However, most users will have QUBO problems from their application domains with corresponding QUBO graphs that are far from being subgraphs of the host graph. In order to be able to solve QUBOs using a quantum annealer, the standard approach (see Fig. 1) is to find a minor embedding of the QUBO graph into the host graph [11] and to set the $h_i, J_{ij}$ parameters accordingly [10]; i.e. one chains multiple qubits of the host graph with ferromagnetic couplings $J_{ij} \ll 0$ to represent a single variable of a QUBO (indicated by shared colors in Fig. 1 (center)/(right)). The better the embedding algorithm, the more QUBO

---

[1] We have $\sigma_z = \begin{pmatrix} 1 & 0 \\ 0 & -1 \end{pmatrix}$, $Id = \begin{pmatrix} 1 & 0 \\ 0 & 1 \end{pmatrix}$, and tensor product $\sigma_z^{(i)} = Id^{\otimes i-1} \otimes \sigma_z \otimes Id^{\otimes n-i}$.

problems can be solved by an annealer. Designing and testing capable embedding algorithms that are able to embed a large set of QUBO graphs is thus crucial to expand the set of applications for a quantum device such as D-Wave. The same holds true for CMOS annealers, such as those of Hitachi [33,36].

We note in passing that adiabatic quantum computing [15] – the theoretical inspiration for quantum annealer technology – is equivalent in power to standard gate-based quantum computing [2] that implements arbitrary unitary operations. However, the mapping challenge on gate-based quantum devices differs substantially from quantum annealers as logical variables are mapped only to single qubits and not to chains. To implement a gate between two non-neighboring qubits in a gate device, qubit states are swapped along paths of the host topology, giving a "time-dependent mapping", sometimes called routing. Depending on the application, this can be done heuristically [12], with exact solvers [35], or using a swap network [26]. Comparing state-of-the-art approaches to equality constraints implementation on a quantum annealer [34] and on a gate-based quantum computer [8] shows, on a concrete application, how different the mapping problem is for the two platforms.

## 2.3   Minor Embeddings

A *minor embedding* of a *pattern* graph $P = (V_P, E_P)$ into a *host* graph $H = (V_H, E_H)$ is a mapping $\varphi$ of each node in $V_P$ to a subset of nodes in $V_H$:

$$\varphi \colon V_P \to 2^{V_H},$$

where $2^{V_H}$ is the set of all subsets of $V_H$, such that

1. For each node $v$ in $V_P$, the set of nodes $\varphi(v)$ induces a connected subgraph in $H$, called the *chain* of $v$.
2. For every edge $e = \{u, v\}$ in $E_P$, there exist nodes $\tilde{u} \in \varphi(u)$ and $\tilde{v} \in \varphi(v)$ such that $\{\tilde{u}, \tilde{v}\} \in E_H$.
3. $\varphi(v) \cap \varphi(u) = \emptyset$ for all $u \neq v \in V_P$, i.e., each node $\tilde{v}$ of the host graph $H$ appears in the mapping of at most one node of the pattern graph $P$.

We call a mapping $\varphi$ a *chain mapping* if it satisfies Condition 1.. A chain mapping $\varphi$ is called a *semi-valid embedding* if it satisfies Condition 2. and is called a *chain placement* if it satisfies Condition 3.. Only if all three conditions are satisfied do we have a minor embedding. Colloquially, we abbreviate minor embedding with just embedding.

Finding a minor-embedding is NP-complete [25] except for (small) fixed pattern graphs [30], and the best known algorithms [1] are exponential in $|V_P|$ and the branch-width or tree-width of $H$ (which is $\Omega(\sqrt{|V_H|})$ for current annealers). Research on minor-embedding for annealers has therefore focused on finding fast and hiqh-quality heuristics. Existing approaches can best be described along one of two trajectories: (i) iteratively modify a semi-valid embedding to reduce the number of multiply used nodes $\tilde{v} \in V_H$ (the approach shared by the algorithms benchmarked in this paper), (ii) iteratively modify a chain placement

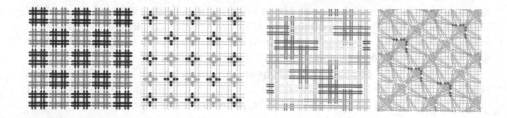

**Fig. 2. (left)** Chimera topology (D-Wave 2000Q): intersecting axis-parallel rectangles gives rise to a grid of $K_{4,4}$ tiles with vertical/horizontal connections. **(right)** Pegasus topology (D-Wave Advantage): non-bipartite graph & increased connectivity achieved through longer, shifted rectangles and couplers for pairs of neighboring parallel qubits. Rectangle drawings courtesy of Kelly Boothby (D-Wave Systems, Inc.).

to increase the number of represented edges $e \in E_P$ (recently proposed [32] for King's graphs, the topology of Hitachi CMOS annealers [33]).

Furthermore, good minor embeddings are known for highly structured pattern graphs such as cliques [6,24], cartesian products thereof [37], bicliques [19], cubic grids [20] and cylindrical lattices (square-octogonal and triangular) [23].

### 2.4 Chimera and Pegasus Topologies

The host graphs of current and upcoming D-Wave annealers can be understood starting from an intersection graph of axis-parallel rectangles (the qubits):

In Chimera [7], $4 \times 4$ intersecting orthogonal qubits with internal couplers give rise to biclique $K_{4,4}$ tiles. External couplers to adjacent horizontal respectively vertical qubits arrange these in a grid, where neighboring tiles are connected by 4 edges. All qubits (except those on the border) have degree 6, see Fig. 2 (left). The Chimera graph $C16$, such as in the D-Wave 2000Q, has $16 \times 16$ tiles for a total of 2048 qubits. We illustrate a smaller $C3$ in Fig. 1.

In Pegasus [5], qubit rectangles are longer and connect to 12 orthogonal qubits. Furthermore, horizontal and vertical qubits are shifted asymmetrically, and have additional odd couplers that connect pairs of neighboring parallel qubits, such that qubits have degree 15. This results in cells that are connected by 4, 8, or 16 edges, see Fig. 2 (right). The Pegasus graph $P16$, such as in the upcoming D-Wave Advantage, has $15 \times 15 \times 3$ cells, plus some partial cells on the border, for a total of 5640 qubits. We illustrate $P4$ in Fig. 3.

### 2.5 QUBO Random Graph Classes

To extend the range of embeddable QUBOs on current and next-generation devices, we benchmark embedding algorithms based on their performance in finding embeddings. Other metrics such as average or maximum chain lengths [29] are not a focus of this paper; hence the actual values of non-zero QUBO terms do not matter. Similarly, we only consider connected graphs (as one can always solve connected components independently) and do not consider any divide-and-conquer strategies [27]. We use three classes of random graphs as benchmarks:

(i) Erdős-Rényi graphs $G_{n,p}$ [18], where edges are included in the graph i.i.d with probability $p$, (ii) Barabási-Albert graphs $BA_{n,m}$ [3,4], in which, starting from $m$ isolated nodes, we insert $m - n$ nodes one by one, connecting each to $m$ existing nodes with preferential attachment proportional to the current degree distribution, (iii) random $d$-regular graphs, in which each node has degree $d$. By varying $p$, $d$ and $m$, respectively, we generate graphs of various densities.

We chose these three graph classes in order to test our algorithms on a diverse set of graphs: Erdős-Rényi graphs have a binomial (Poisson for small $p$) degree distribution, Barabási-Albert graphs have a power-law degree distribution (modeling networks), and $d$-regular graphs have a constant degree distribution.

In the following Section, we briefly present existing algorithms that we either compare to or use as a subroutine in our algorithms, which then follow next.

# 3    Minor Embedding Heuristics

## 3.1    Existing Embedding Algorithms

**MinorMiner.** The MinorMiner algorithm (MM), proposed in 2014 [9], is arguably the most prominent embedding algorithm, given its inclusion in D-Wave's Ocean software stack [13]. Given any QUBO graph $P$ and host graph $H$ as an input, it tries to find an embedding; and if not successful after a certain number of steps it returns an empty embedding. The MM algorithm starts from an *initial chain mapping* (with chains empty by default) and *repeatedly loops* over the nodes of $P$, to determine for each node $v \in V_P$ a (preliminary) chain as follows:

1. Remove the chain $\varphi(v) \subseteq E_H$ from the existing chain mapping.
2. Compute a node-weighted shortest paths tree in $H$ from each non-empty chain $\varphi(u)$, where $u$ is a neighbor of $v$ in $P$ ($\{u, v\} \in E_P$). The node weights in $H$ come with a high penalty term for using nodes in multiple chains.
3. Choose an optimal node $\tilde{v} \in V_H$ that minimizes the sum of distances according to the computed shortest paths trees. Extend $\tilde{v}$ to a chain $\varphi(v)$ by backtracking along the shortest paths trees, and re-add $\varphi(v)$ to the chain mapping.

This naturally splits MinorMiner into two phases: First, MM completes a single loop over the vertices $V_P$, after which the chain mapping $\varphi$ is in fact a *semi-valid embedding* (in which chains might still share qubits).

Secondly, MM enters a *fixing phase*, where consecutive loops over nodes in $V_P$ have the goal of fixing this semi-valid embedding. The algorithm restarts when there has been no progression for too many steps in a row[2], with limiting parameters on the total number of steps and number of restarts allowed. Thus,

---

[2] Even if the algorithm is already in a state with a valid embedding, progression is measured for example in having a smaller maximal chain size.

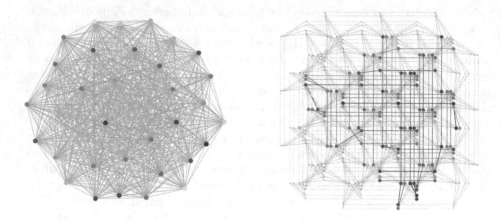

**Fig. 3.** Minor embedding of a $K_{36}$ on Pegasus $P4$. Horizontal/vertical edges are mainly used to connect chains internally; other edges act as couplers between different chains.

when the algorithm terminates, it might either return a valid embedding when it found one, or an empty embedding if it did not.

MM has a few other controls, such as the `initial_chain` parameter. This parameter can be used to feed the algorithm an initial chain mapping, which is then used in the first phase of finding a semi-valid embedding. However, the algorithm still iterates over all nodes. When it reaches a node which was assigned an initial non-empty chain, it still deletes and replaces that chain with the procedure outlined above.

**Layout-Aware MinorMiner.** A recent contribution to MinorMiner [29] has as its main focus QUBOs that come with a natural graph layout in the plane (think, e.g., of lattices in the simplest case). The implementation [28] takes a QUBO graph and its layout together with the host graph and a plane host graph layout as an input. The algorithm maps each variable node of the QUBO graph layout to the closest (in Euclidean metric) qubit node of the host graph layout. An additional diffusion phase shifts this mapping to achieve an even spreading of initial chains across tiles/cells of the topology, and then starts MinorMiner with the computed `initial_chain` mapping. However, not all QUBOs come with a natural layout; if the graph comes without a layout, their algorithm runs a Fruchterman-Reingold spring embedding algorithm to generate such a layout.

**Clique Embedding.** D-Wave has a host-specific clique embedding algorithm [6], which can quickly embed any clique up to a certain size $c_{host}$ into the Pegasus or the Chimera graph (this also implies an embedding algorithm for any graph with up to $c_{host}$ nodes). For Pegasus $P16$, the maximal clique size embeddable this way is $c_{host} = 180$, for Chimera $C16$ it is $c_{host} = 64$. Chains gained from this embedding have a very special shape: they are all paths which are "L-shaped" if drawn into the 2D-layout of the respective host graph, see Fig. 3.

## 3.2   Our Contribution

We propose, implement and compare two new algorithms: Clique-based MinorMiner (CLMM) and Spring-based MinorMiner (SPMM).

For CLMM, we construct an initial chain mapping for a subset of QUBO nodes, able to implement a coupling between any two chains of this node subset. For SPMM, we give an initial chain mapping for *all* QUBO nodes $V_P$, based on a force-directed graph drawing of $P$. In the second approach, there are no guarantees for existing couplings between chains. We then pass this initial chain mapping to MinorMiner with the `initial_chain` parameter.

**Clique-Based MinorMiner (CLMM).** For CLMM, we construct an initial chain mapping as follows: We run D-Waves clique embedding algorithm for a clique of size $k = \min(|V_P|, c_{\text{host}})$. The $k$ chains found this way are assigned to $k$ nodes of the QUBO graph, with the assignment depending on the density of $P$: If $|E_P|/\binom{|V_P|}{2} \geq 0.55$, they are assigned to the $k$ nodes of lowest degree, otherwise to $k$ random nodes. The remaining QUBO nodes are mapped to empty chains.

We also tested a wide variety of other density- and degree-based assignments, as well as a splitting or a multi-assignment of chains in exploratory runs. In contrast to these approaches, the presented (albeit simpler) settings performed significantly better and were thus used in the final experiments.

**Spring-Based MinorMiner (SPMM).** For SPMM, we construct an initial chain mapping as follows: (i) We use standard D-Wave layout functions to get a drawing of the Pegasus/Chimera host graph in the plane (cf. the host graphs in Fig. 2), and a tuned Fruchterman-Reingold algorithm (see below) to get a QUBO graph layout as well. (ii) We rescale both plane layouts to fit into a $[-1, 1] \times [-1, 1]$ square. (iii) We map each of the QUBO nodes $v$ to the closest qubit node in Euclidean metric.

Fruchterman-Reingold [16] is a force-directed graph drawing algorithm that computes a plane layout based on two principles: nodes pairwise repel each other, but nodes connected by an edge at the same time attract each other. The strength with which the latter takes place can be set for each edge individually; smaller weights implying a smaller attraction. For an edge $e = \{u, v\}$ we set weight$(e) = (2|E_P|/|V_P|)^2 \cdot (\deg(u) \deg(v))^{-1}$, where the weighting by node degrees ensures that neighboring nodes with high degrees are not too close to each other (as, intuitively, their chains need more space in the host graph) and where the first term is a normalization factor (normalizing weights in regular graphs to 1).

While SPMM and LAMM have some similarities, we find a significant performance difference on Pegasus graphs due to SPMM's improved use of edge weights for node attraction, substituting LAMM's consecutive diffusion phase.

## 4    Experimental Design

We present the results of a large factorial-design experiment to compare our two algorithms Clique-based MinorMiner (CLMM) and Spring-Based MinorMiner (SPMM) with the established MinorMiner (MM) and the recently proposed Layout-Aware MinorMiner (LAMM). We test the algorithms on the random QUBO graph classes $G_{n,p}$, Barabási-Albert, and $d$-regular. As host graphs, we use the D-Wave Pegasus host graph (used in the 5000 qubit model first out in 2020) as well as the previous Chimera topolgy (used until the 2000 qubit model).

For the Erdős-Rényi $G_{n,p}$ graph model, we generate five random graphs for each combination of values $n = \{1, \ldots, 425\}$ and $p = \{.01, .02, \ldots, 1.00\}$. While this would result in a total of $5 \cdot 450 \cdot 100 = 212,500$ graphs, we actually reduced this number to around $26,000$ graphs by carefully pruning the set of graphs for a specific algorithm once it has become clear – based on results for smaller/larger values of $n$ or $p$ – that the algorithm will always/never find an embedding. $G_{n,p}$ graphs have a sharp threshold of $n \cdot p > \ln n$ of being connected [14].

For the $d$-regular graph model (on Pegasus), we generate five graphs each for all combinations of $n = \{1, \ldots, 1200\}$ and $d = \{3, \ldots, 183\}$, employing again a pruning mechanism. On Chimera, we also use five graphs and cut off at 380 vertices and maximum $d = 64$ to account for the smaller host graph. Random $d$-regular graphs can be sampled quickly for $d \leq n/2$ [31] and uniformly at random for $d \in \mathcal{O}(n^{1/3-\varepsilon})$ [22]; we sample $(n-d)$-regular graphs as complements of $d$-regular graphs. $d$-regular graphs only exist for $2|E| = n \cdot d$ even and $d < n$.

For the Barabási-Albert graph model, we generate five graphs each for $n = \{1, \ldots, 1200\}$ and $m = \{1, \ldots, 110\}$ and employ pruning. The number of edges in $BA_{n,m}$ is $(n-m) \cdot m \leq (\frac{n-m+m}{2})^2 = n^2/4$ by AM-GM, with equality for $m = n/2$. Hence we get increasing graph density for $m$ up to $n/2$, and we restrict ourselves to this regime. All graphs are constructed with Python's `networkx`.

Our experiments were executed on LANL's Darwin Cluster [17] using a trivially parallel approach. Running times for individual graphs ranged from milliseconds to more than 10 min per graph, largely proportional to graph vertex and edge counts. Overall, the study consumed around $100,000$ core hours. We assess the different algorithms on whether they succeed in finding an embedding with the default parameters of MinorMiner, and not by running times, but overall we observed that running times were very comparable for all the tested algorithms.

## 5    Embeddings on the Pegasus Host Graph

**Embedding Erdős-Rényi Graphs on Pegasus.** Figure 4 shows our results for $G_{n,p}$ graphs on Pegasus for the four algorithms MM, LAMM, CLMM, and SPMM. The plot structure is as follows: The blue area on the bottom shows where $n \cdot p < \ln(n)$, the region of disconnected QUBOs excluded from this study. The red vertical line displays $c_{\text{host}} = 180$. Heatplot areas are colored using the green-to-white color scheme on the right of the plot. The color assigned to

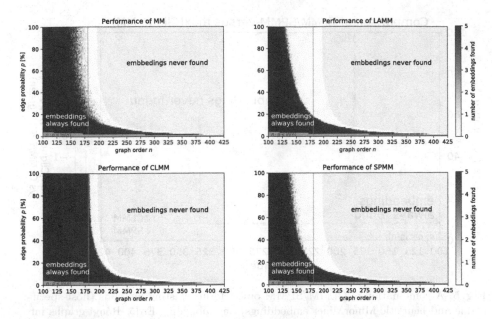

**Fig. 4.** Embedding performance of all algorithms for Erdős-Rényi graphs on Pegasus: **(top left)** MM, **(top right)** LAMM, **(bottom left)** CLMM, **(bottom right)** SPMM. (Color figure online)

a point $(n, p)$ corresponds to the number of times the algorithm succeeds at finding an embedding for the five $G_{n,p}$ graphs tested at point $(n, p)$. The large darker-green area on the left are pruned points, as we can be reasonably sure that the algorithm would always find an embedding since it does find embeddings reliably for larger graphs. Similarly, the light gray area on the right side of the plot represents pruned points, where we are reasonably sure that the algorithm would not find an embedding as it did not find embeddings on smaller and less dense graphs. More precisely, if an algorithm manages to embed a $G_{n,p}$ QUBO with high probability, it is even more likely that it will manage to embed a $G_{n-k,p}$ QUBO graph. Therefore, after testing for each $p$ where the transition from embeddable QUBO to non embeddable QUBO is, we tested a cone of width at least 10 on both sides around them as interesting points before pruning.

Contrasting the performance of the four algorithms, we note the following: The LAMM algorithm does not perform particularly well, perhaps unsurprisingly as $G_{n,p}$ graphs do not have a natural layout that would play to LAMM's core design element; LAMM does show a fairly quick transition from being able to embed all graphs (dark green) to no graphs (white). This transition is in fact more spread-out in the overall better performing SPMM algorithm. The standard MM algorithm sees an even farther spread-out transition when compared to both LAMM and SPMM and clearly outperforms LAMM and SPMM on dense graphs, while being outperformed by SPMM on very sparse graphs. However, MM is remarkably far off from being able to embed a clique of size 180 (the red vertical line). CLMM easily outperforms MM on dense graphs and interestingly shows a very cleanly defined transition from embeddable to non-embeddable.

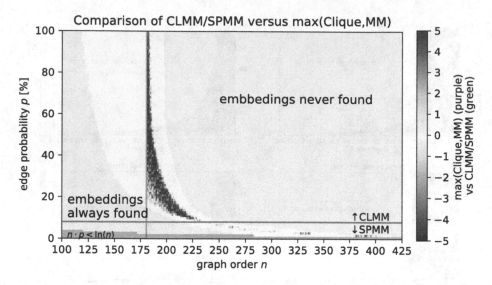

**Fig. 5.** A combination of CLMM/SPMM outperforms existing methods (host-specific clique and heuristic MinorMiner embeddings) on embedding Erdős-Rényi graphs into Pegasus at every value of $p$, with a sharp transition from CLMM to SPMM at $p = 0.08$. (Color figure online)

We get a more in-depth understanding of performance difference by looking at the difference plot in Fig. 5. Its structure is similar to the individual performance plots, except the color bar ranges from green (positive) to white (zero) to purple (negative). A point $(n, p)$ above (below) the blue line at $p = 0.08$ is assigned a color based on the number of embeddings found by CLMM (SPMM, respectively) *minus* the maximum of the number of embeddings found by the clique embedding algorithm or by MM. This way we capture the improvement SPMM gains for sparse graphs and the improvement CLMM gains on dense graphs in one plot. The transition between areas where CLMM and where SPMM are the respective best performing algorithms is sharp, around an edge density value of $|E_P|/\binom{|V_P|}{2} \approx p = 0.8$. In combination, our algorithms manage to outperform the already existing algorithms at every value of $p$, gaining the most around $p = 0.20$, and for $p = 0.02$ where the graphs get sparse enough such that SPMM's advantage over MM starts to get significant.

**Embedding Barabási-Albert and $d$-regular Graphs on Pegasus.** Figure 6 (top) shows a similar picture as Fig. 5, with CLMM outperforming MM on dense graphs and SPMM taking the lead on sparse graphs. However, as Barabási-Albert graphs for small $m$ are sparser than the sparsest Erdős-Rényi graphs we tested, the improvement of SPMM over MM is much more pronounced, being largest for $m = 2$. We again observe a sharp transition threshold between CLMM and SPMM at $m = 12$ around $n = 240$, corresponding to an edge density of $(n - m)m/\binom{n}{2} \approx 0.095$.

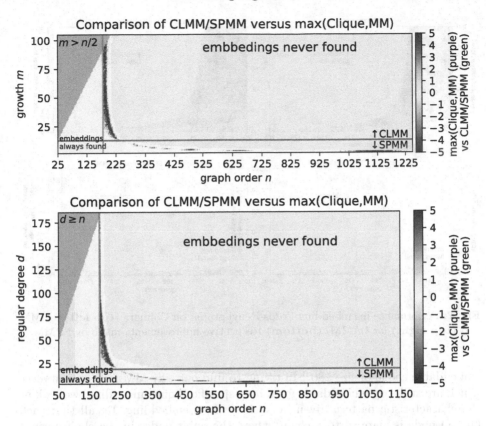

**Fig. 6. (top)** Performance comparison of CLMM/SPMM vs max(Clique, MM) for Barabási-Albert graphs on Pegasus, transitioning from CLMM to SPMM at $m = 12$. **(bottom)** Performance comparison of CLMM/SPMM vs max(Clique, MM) in embedding $d$-regular graphs into Pegasus, transitioning from CLMM to SPMM at $d = 18$. The plot omits odd columns to prevent distraction by empty data points for $n \cdot d$ odd.

Figure 6 (bottom) shows that on $d$-regular graphs, performance of CLMM, SPMM and MM mirrors their performance on Erdős-Rényi and Barabási-Albert graphs. Since $d$-regular graphs only exist for even $n \cdot d$, we omit odd $n$ columns from the plot (but not from the experiments, see the concluding data in Sect. 7). SPMM again gains the biggest advantage on the sparsest graphs, namely $d = 3$, while CLMM outperforms MM on dense graphs, with a transition threshold at $d = 18$, $n = 233$, corresponding to an edge density of $d/(n - 1) \approx 0.078$.

**Discussion.** We first discuss MM's poor performance on Pegasus, where the picture is quite bleak: Here, graphs have to be very sparse until MM manages to embed a graph of order 180 nodes, even though there exists a host-specific

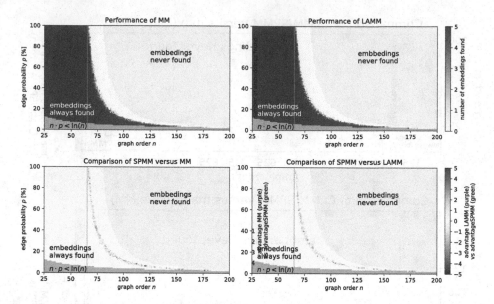

**Fig. 7.** Performance in embedding Erdős-Rényi graphs on Chimera (**top left**) for MM and (**top right**) for LAMM. (**bottom**) Respective improvements made by SPMM.

embeddable clique of size 180.[3] In trying to find out why MM fails on instances which are still easy embeddable via a host-specific clique embedding, we look at the characteristic pattern given by such a clique embedding. Recall that each QUBO node is mapped to a chain, where the qubit nodes in the chain form a path, linked mostly by edges that are horizontal or vertical in the graph (see Fig. 3). Looking at the layout of Pegasus, these are both the sparsest connections between neighboring cells as well as the edges which have the longest length. Therefore, the chains are able to "spread through the graph" using as few qubits as possible, leaving many unused edges suitable as couplers between different chains. However, MM does not distinguish between different types of cell-connecting edges when re-computing a chain of the chain mapping, possibly resulting in a worse solution at the end. In contrast, the edges between tiles of Chimera are all equivalent, so this kind of misstep cannot happen.

Secondly, we look at the link between CLMM and SPMM's performance and the sparsity of the graph. In embeddings for dense graphs, chains often form a path through a large part of the host graph, with few or no nodes of induced degree larger than two. We believe that providing initial "L-shaped" chains such as in CLMM may promote newly built chains to take on such shapes as well. On the other hand, for sparse graphs a well-chosen initial single-qubit chain such as in SPMM can enable short connections to neighboring chains, reducing the qubit footprint of a semi-valid embedding created after the first phase of MinorMiner.

---

[3] Especially compared to Chimera, where MM manages to find an embedding for $K_{65}$, the largest embeddable clique, given that $\mathrm{treewidth}(K_{65}) = 64 = \mathrm{treewidth}(C16)$.

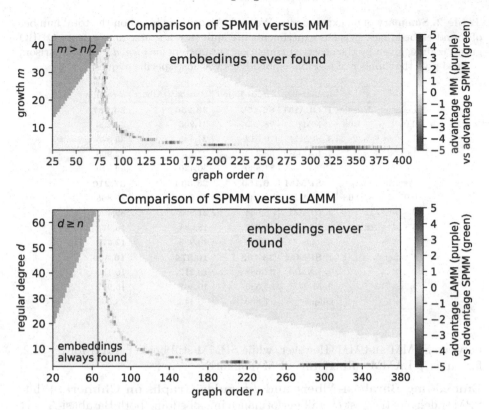

**Fig. 8.** Embedding performance of SPMM compared to its closest (QUBO graph type specific) competitor on Chimera: **(top)** SPMM vs MM for Barabási-Albert graphs, **(bottom)** SPMM vs LAMM for $d$-regular graphs, with odd $n$ columns omitted.

## 6    Embeddings on the Chimera Host Graph

On Chimera, we only compare the three algorithms MM, LAMM and SPMM. We did not test CLMM in great detail, as MM performs very similar, and since preliminary observations could not find any improvements of CLMM over MM.

**Embedding Erdős-Rényi Graphs on Chimera.** For each non-pruned parameter combination $(n, p)$, we generated five $G_{n,p}$ graphs which we tried to embed using MM, LAMM and SPMM. Figure 7 shows the performance of both MM (left) and LAMM (right) as well as the relative improvements made by SPMM (bottom). Perhaps a bit surprisingly, all algorithms manage to embed cliques of size 65, the largest embeddable clique and one node larger than the maximal clique found by the host-graph specific clique embedder.

SPMM performs better than MM on graphs with $p \geq 0.8$ and graphs with $p \leq 0.3$. However, for $0.3 < p < 0.8$, both algorithms perform comparably well. The performance difference between SPMM and LAMM is similar to the one

**Table 2.** Summary of all experiments: We rank Algorithms based on the total number of found embeddings. Pegasus experiments are split into a sparse and a dense QUBO graph regime, given by the observed transition parameters for $p, m, d$. For comparison, we also give the number of possible embeddings via host-specific cliques.

|                    | Ranking   | Erdős-Rényi | Barabási-Albert | $d$-regular |
|--------------------|-----------|-------------|-----------------|-------------|
| Pegasus (dense)    | 1. **CLMM** | **86,159**  | **38,256**      | **54,937**  |
| $0.08 < p \leq 1.00$ | 2. MM     | 78,230      | 31,206          | 44,229      |
| $12 < m \leq n/2$  | 3. SPMM   | 70,512      | 24,435          | 35,375      |
| $18 < d \leq n-1$  | 4. LAMM   | 68,349      | 23,248          | 32,998      |
|                    | Clique    | 81,530      | 30,420          | 49,410      |
| Pegasus (sparse)   | 1. **SPMM** | **6,150**   | **23,334**      | **37,210**  |
| $0.01 \leq p \leq 0.08$ | 2. MM   | 6,039       | 21,814          | 35,866      |
| $2 \leq m \leq 12$ | 3. CLMM   | 5,964       | 21,803          | 35,490      |
| $3 \leq d \leq 18$ | 4. LAMM   | 6,047       | 18,681          | 35,374      |
|                    | Clique    | 2,700       | 10,985          | 12,470      |
| Chimera            | 1. **SPMM** | **33,793**  | **10,874**      | **16,506**  |
|                    | 2. LAMM   | 33,688      | 10,217          | 16,132      |
|                    | 3. MM     | 33,530      | 10,367          | 15,972      |
|                    | Clique    | 27,860      | 5,445           | 8,060       |

between SPMM and MM. However, while SPMM still beats LAMM for $p \leq 0.2$, for larger $p$ LAMM outperforms SPMM slightly.

**Embedding Barabási-Albert and $d$-regular Graphs on Chimera.** While SPMM delivers the best overall performance in embedding both Barabási-Albert and $d$-regular graphs on Chimera, the second place depends on the graph class (MM for Barabási-Albert, LAMM for $d$-regular graphs). In Fig. 8 (top), we show the performance difference between SPMM and MM on Barabási-Albert graphs. While MM outperforms SPMM slightly on $m \geq 20$, the advantage of SPMM on small $m$ is much more apparent, especially at $m = 2$.

Figure 8 (bottom) shows the difference between embedding performances of SPMM and LAMM on $d$-regular graphs. For $15 \leq d \leq 64$, both algorithms perform comparably well, with a slight advantage to LAMM. For smaller degree, SPMM starts to clearly outperform LAMM (and MM), with the most significant improvement at $d = 3$. Again, we omit odd $n$ columns in the plot.

## 7  Conclusion

We studied the performance of two new embedding algorithms, Spring-based MinorMiner (SPMM) and Clique-based MinorMiner (CLMM), and contrasted these to existing embedding heuristics for the two different D-Wave host graph topologies Pegasus and Chimera. To the best of our knowledge, this is the first such study on the upcoming Pegasus topology. While we observed that the existing MinorMiner heuristic does not extend its overall good performance on Chimera to Pegasus, we show how to remedy the situation with our Clique-based and Spring-based MinorMiner variants, see Table 2.

We found that for certain values of the density parameters $p, m, d$ (used in Erdős-Rényi, Barabási-Albert and $d$-regular graphs, respectively) our algorithms significantly outperform the existing methods, increasing the number of embeddable QUBO graphs by double-digit percentages and enlarging the range of embeddable sparse graphs to graphs with over a hundred additional nodes. Detailed statistics are given in Fig. 9, where for each studied value of $p, m$ and $d$, we show the number of additionally embeddable graphs, both in absolute numbers (bar plots) as well as a percentage increase (line plot). We note that absolute numbers are normalized by the number of sampled graphs per data point (i.e. 5), and that for $d$-regular graphs, the bar plots show the expected factor 2 difference between odd and even values of $d$ (with the exception of 3-regular graphs, on which SPMM shows an exceptionally massive increase).

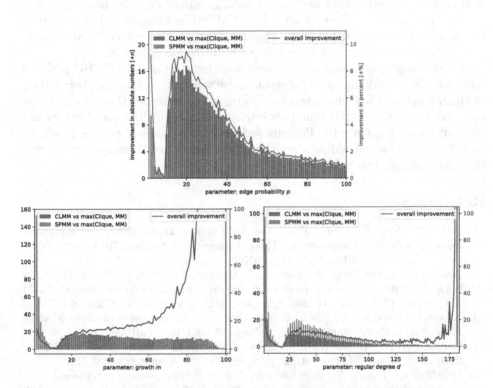

**Fig. 9.** Improvement of our two algorithms SPMM (orange) and CLMM (blue) compared to the maximal possible embeddability range with a host-specific clique or a heuristic MM embedding algorithm on Pegasus. Results for **(top)** Erdős-Rényi graphs, **(bottom left)** Barabási-Albert graphs, **(bottom right)** random $d$-regular graphs. (Color figure online)

In conclusion, we studied different random graphs to represent a wide variety of possible QUBO graphs and gave a detailed analysis of the performance of CLMM, SPMM, MM and the recent LAMM. A relative ranking of the algorithms based on the total number of found embeddings is given in Table 2. While SPMM and CLMM are the clear winners in their respective density domains, the order of the competitors can change depending on the graph class studied.

Though SPMM and CLMM outperform the standard algorithm MM, their simplicity is somewhat remarkable and of course they build upon the work of both the original MinorMiner paper [9] and its implementation [13] as a subroutine. We suggest that the MinorMiner parameter `initial_chain` be extended with 'clique' and 'spring' parameters to serve as calls to the respective CLMM and SPMM algorithms presented in this work.

*Future Work.* Future research directions are three-fold: First, we intend to add case studies of real-world QUBO instance graphs to include them in a full version of this paper, together with plots and results of all our experiments.

Secondly, we would like to study other (CMOS) host graphs [36] and compare our algorithms to simulated annealing-based approaches which were recently proposed in the literature [32] but not yet published as software.

Finally, applying various embedding algorithms to the same QUBO problem will result in embeddings with different characteristics, such as the distribution of chain lengths. These characteristics, in turn, will influence the chance of success and hence the overall time-to-solution of solving QUBO problems with a quantum annealer. Once the Pegasus architecture becomes available, it will be useful to compare embedding algorithms with respect to these metrics, as was done for Chimera before [29].

# References

1. Adler, I., Dorn, F., Fomin, F.V., Sau, I., Thilikos, D.M.: Faster parameterized algorithms for minor containment. Theor. Comput. Sci. **412**(50), 7018–7028 (2011). https://doi.org/10.1016/j.tcs.2011.09.015
2. Aharonov, D., van Dam, W., Kempe, J., Landau, Z., Lloyd, S., Regev, O.: Adiabatic quantum computation is equivalent to standard quantum computation. SIAM J. Comput. **37**(1), 166–194 (2007). https://doi.org/10.1137/S0097539705447323
3. Albert, R., Barabási, A.L.: Statistical mechanics of complex networks. Rev. Modern Phys. **74**(1), 47–97 (2002). https://doi.org/10.1103/RevModPhys.74.47
4. Barabási, A.L., Albert, R.: Emergence of scaling in random networks. Science **286**(5439), 509–512 (1999). https://doi.org/10.1126/science.286.5439.509
5. Boothby, K., Bunyk, P., Raymond, J., Roy, A.: Next-generation topology of d-wave quantum processors. Technical Report 14–1026A-C, D-Wave Systems (2019). https://www.dwavesys.com/resources/publications?type=white
6. Boothby, T., King, A.D., Roy, A.: Fast clique minor generation in Chimera qubit connectivity graphs. Quantum Inf. Process. **15**(1), 495–508 (2015). https://doi.org/10.1007/s11128-015-1150-6
7. Bunyk, P.I., et al.: Architectural considerations in the design of a superconducting quantum annealing processor. IEEE Trans. Appl. Superconductivity **24**(4), 1–10 (2014). https://doi.org/10.1109/TASC.2014.2318294
8. Bärtschi, A., Eidenbenz, S.: Deterministic preparation of dicke states. In: Fundamentals of Computation Theory, pp. 126–139. FCT 2019 (2019). https://doi.org/10.1007/978-3-030-25027-0_9

9. Cai, J., Macready, W.G., Roy, A.: A practical heuristic for finding graph minors. https://arxiv.org/abs/1406.2741 (2014)
10. Choi, V.: Minor-embedding in adiabatic quantum computation: I. The parameter setting problem. Quantum Inf. Process. **7**(5), 193–209 (2008). https://doi.org/10.1007/s11128-008-0082-9
11. Choi, V.: Minor-embedding in adiabatic quantum computation: II. Minor-universal graph design. Quantum Inf. Process. **10**(3), 343–353 (2011). https://doi.org/10.1007/s11128-010-0200-3
12. Cowtan, A., Dilkes, S., Duncan, R., Krajenbrink, A., Simmons, W., Sivarajah, S.: On the qubit routing problem. In: 14th Conference on the Theory of Quantum Computation, Communication and Cryptography, TQC 2019, pp. 5:1–5:32 (2019). https://doi.org/10.4230/LIPIcs.TQC.2019.5
13. D-Wave Systems: minorminer. https://github.com/dwavesystems/minorminer (2017), a heuristic tool for minor embedding
14. Erdős, P., Rényi, A.: On random graphs I. Publicationes Mathematicae **6**, 290–297 (1959). https://www.renyi.hu/~p_erdos/1959-11.pdf
15. Farhi, E., Goldstone, J., Gutmann, S., Sipser, M.: Quantum Computation by Adiabatic Evolution. https://arxiv.org/abs/quant-ph/0001106 (2000)
16. Fruchterman, T.M.J., Reingold, E.M.: Graph drawing by force-directed placement. Software: Practice and Experience 21(11), 1129–1164 (1991). https://doi.org/10.1002/spe.4380211102
17. Garrett, C.K.: The Darwin Cluster. Technical Report, LA-UR-18-25080, Los Alamos National Laboratory (2018). https://doi.org/10.2172/1441285
18. Gilbert, E.N.: Random graphs. Ann. Math. Stat. **30**(4), 1141–1144 (1959). https://doi.org/10.1214/aoms/1177706098
19. Goodrich, T.D., Sullivan, B.D., Humble, T.S.: Optimizing adiabatic quantum program compilation using a graph-theoretic framework. Quantum Inf. Process. **17**(5), 1–26 (2018). https://doi.org/10.1007/s11128-018-1863-4
20. Harris, R., et al.: Phase transitions in a programmable quantum spin glass simulator. Science **361**(6398), 162–165 (2018). https://doi.org/10.1126/science.aat2025
21. Karp, R.M.: Reducibility among Combinatorial Problems, pp. 85–103. Springer, US (1972). https://doi.org/10.1007/978-1-4684-2001-2_9
22. Kim, J.H., Vu, V.H.: Generating random regular graphs. In: 35th ACM Symposium on Theory of Computing, pp. 213–222. STOC 2003 (2003). https://doi.org/10.1145/780542.780576
23. King, A.D., et al.: Observation of topological phenomena in a programmable lattice of 1,800 qubits. Nature **560**(7719), 456–460 (2018). https://doi.org/10.1038/s41586-018-0410-x
24. Klymko, C., Sullivan, B.D., Humble, T.S.: Adiabatic quantum programming: minor embedding with hard faults. Quantum Inf. Process. **13**(3), 709–729 (2013). https://doi.org/10.1007/s11128-013-0683-9
25. Matoušek, J., Thomas, R.: On the complexity of finding iso- and other morphisms for partial k-trees. Dis. Math. **108**(1), 343–364 (1992). https://doi.org/10.1016/0012-365X(92)90687-B
26. O'Gorman, B., Huggins, W.J., Rieffel, E.G., Whaley, K.B.: Generalized swap networks for near-term quantum computing (2019). https://arxiv.org/abs/1905.05118
27. Pelofske, E., Hahn, G., Djidjev, H.: Solving large minimum vertex cover problems on a quantum annealer. In: 16th ACM International Conference on Computing Frontiers, pp. 76–84. CF 2019 (2019). https://doi.org/10.1145/3310273.3321562
28. Pinilla, J.P.: Embera (2019). https://github.com/joseppinilla/embera, a collection of minor-embedding methods and utilities

29. Pinilla, J.P., Wilton, S.J.E.: Layout-aware embedding for quantum annealing processors. In: High Performance Computing, pp. 121–139. ISC 2019 (2019). https://doi.org/10.1007/978-3-030-20656-7_7
30. Robertson, N., Seymour, P.: Graph. Minors. XIII the disjoint paths problem. J. Combinatorial Theory Ser. B **63**(1), 65–110 (1995). https://doi.org/10.1006/jctb.1995.1006
31. Steger, A., Wormald, N.C.: Generating random regular graphs quickly. Combinatorics Probability Comput. **8**(4), 377–396 (1999). https://doi.org/10.1017/S0963548399003867
32. Sugie, Y., et al.: Graph minors from simulated annealing for annealing machines with sparse connectivity. In: Theory and Practice of Natural Computing, pp. 111–123. TPNC 2018 (2018). https://doi.org/10.1007/978-3-030-04070-3_9
33. Takemoto, T., Hayashi, M., Yoshimura, C., Yamaoka, M.: A 2x30k-Spin multichip scalable annealing processor based on a processing-in-memory approach for solving large-scale combinatorial optimization problems. In: IEEE International Solid-State Circuits Conference, pp. 52–54. ISSCC 2019 (2019). https://doi.org/10.1109/ISSCC.2019.8662517
34. Vyskocil, T., Djidjev, H.: Embedding equality constraints of optimization problems into a quantum annealer. Algorithms **12**(4), 77 (2019). https://doi.org/10.3390/a12040077
35. Wille, R., Burgholzer, L., Zulehner, A.: Mapping quantum circuits to IBM QX architectures using the minimal number of SWAP and H Operations. In: 56th Annual Design Automation Conference 2019, DAC 2019, p. 142 (2019). https://doi.org/10.1145/3316781.3317859
36. Yamaoka, M., Yoshimura, C., Hayashi, M., Okuyama, T., Aoki, H., Mizuno, H.: A 20k-spin ising chip to solve combinatorial optimization problems with CMOS annealing. IEEE J. Solid-State Circ. **51**(1), 303–309 (2016). https://doi.org/10.1109/JSSC.2015.2498601
37. Zaribafiyan, A., Marchand, D.J.J., Changiz Rezaei, S.S.: Systematic and deterministic graph minor embedding for Cartesian products of graphs. Quantum Inf. Process. **16**(5), 1–26 (2017). https://doi.org/10.1007/s11128-017-1569-z

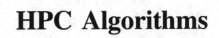

# HPC Algorithms

# Solving Acoustic Boundary Integral Equations Using High Performance Tile Low-Rank LU Factorization

Noha Al-Harthi, Rabab Alomairy$^{(\boxtimes)}$, Kadir Akbudak, Rui Chen, Hatem Ltaief, Hakan Bagci, and David Keyes

Extreme Computing Research Center, Computer, Electrical and Mathematical Sciences and Engineering Division, King Abdullah University of Science and Technology, Thuwal, Jeddah 23955, Saudi Arabia
{Noha.Harthi,Rabab.Omairy,Kadir.Akbudak,Rui.Chen,Hatem.Ltaief, Hakan.Bagci,David.Keyes}@kaust.edu.sa

**Abstract.** We design and develop a new high performance implementation of a fast direct LU-based solver using low-rank approximations on massively parallel systems. The LU factorization is the most time-consuming step in solving systems of linear equations in the context of analyzing acoustic scattering from large 3D objects. The matrix equation is obtained by discretizing the boundary integral of the exterior Helmholtz problem using a higher-order Nyström scheme. The main idea is to exploit the inherent data sparsity of the matrix operator by performing local tile-centric approximations while still capturing the most significant information. In particular, the proposed LU-based solver leverages the Tile Low-Rank (TLR) data compression format as implemented in the Hierarchical Computations on Manycore Architectures (HiCMA) library to decrease the complexity of "classical" dense direct solvers from cubic to quadratic order. We taskify the underlying boundary integral kernels to expose fine-grained computations. We then employ the dynamic runtime system StarPU to orchestrate the scheduling of computational tasks on shared and distributed-memory systems. The resulting asynchronous execution permits to compensate for the load imbalance due to the heterogeneous ranks, while mitigating the overhead of data motion. We assess the robustness of our TLR LU-based solver and study the qualitative impact when using different numerical accuracies. The new TLR LU factorization outperforms the state-of-the-art dense factorizations by up to an order of magnitude on various parallel systems, for analysis of scattering from large-scale 3D synthetic and real geometries.

**Keywords:** Tile low-rank LU-based solver · Boundary Integral Equations · Acoustic scattering · Task-based programming models · Dynamic runtime systems

© The Author(s) 2020
P. Sadayappan et al. (Eds.): ISC High Performance 2020, LNCS 12151, pp. 209–229, 2020.
https://doi.org/10.1007/978-3-030-50743-5_11

# 1    Introduction

Numerous science and engineering applications require solving large dense linear systems. In particular, the discretization of acoustic Boundary Integral Equations (BIE) using the Nyström method [22,43] leads to a linear system of equations, where the matrix is dense and non-symmetric. The direct method to solve such a non-symmetric system requires an LU decomposition (or factorization) [30]. LU factorization is an essential operation in linear algebra since it is used in many computational tasks: finding the matrix inverse, computing the matrix determinant, or even ranking the fastest supercomputers with the High Performance LINPACK (HPL) benchmark. As the problem dimensions increase, the cubic and quadratic complexities of the dense LU factorization for arithmetics and memory storage, respectively, make it prohibitively complex.

The matrix operator of the acoustic BIE contains the self-field, near-field, and far-field interactions and, therefore, inherently exhibits a data sparsity structure. Such structure may be exploited using low-rank approximations [31,37] to attain lower bounds for the arithmetic complexity and memory storage. The achieved accuracy is then controlled with an application-dependent threshold to ensure numerical correctness. The resulting approximated matrix system may then be solved using iterative methods that rely on fast algorithms. For instance, when combined with iterative solvers (e.g., GMRES [49]), the Fast Multipole Method (FMM) [32] may leverage the data sparsity structure and accelerate the matrix-vector multiplication by reducing its complexity from $O(N^2)$ to $O(N \log N)$ or even $O(N)$.

However, despite their enormous success, iterative methods may still encounter several major bottlenecks when compared to direct solvers. Indeed, iterative methods are often inadequate for ill-conditioned problems which arise when solving a scattering problem near resonant frequencies [2] or when the scatterer exhibits multi-scale geometric features. In contrast, direct methods are stable and are not as sensitive to ill-conditioning. It is only necessary to verify that they are sufficiently well-posed for the required level of accuracy with respect to floating point rounding error. Therefore, when the reliability and predictability of the solver and solution are crucial (e.g., production environments), direct solvers are often preferred. Moreover, iterative methods cannot directly exploit the structure of systems that are altered by a low-rank modification. Direct methods, on the other hand, are particularly effective at handling low-rank perturbations by incrementally updating the existing matrix factors. Last but not least, iterative methods cannot efficiently account for multiple right-hand sides. They often have to start from scratch for each right-hand side (e.g., calculation of monostatic radar cross section) except under certain circumstances (see [28,29] for economic reuse of Krylov spaces for *nearby* right-hand sides). Direct methods can efficiently work with multiple right-hand sides. As soon as the system matrix has been factorized, direct methods may apply the triangular solves to all right-hand sides at once, resulting in a much lower arithmetic complexity.

In this work, we propose a new high performance implementation of a direct LU-based solver for analyzing acoustic scattering from large 3D objects. The main idea is to exploit the data sparsity of the matrix operator by using the Tile Low-Rank (TLR) data compression format and approximate the off-diagonal tiles. The initial tile-centric compression phase permits to capture the most significant singular values up to an application-dependent accuracy threshold. The LU-based solver can then proceed to using the underlying TLR compressed data structure. We rely on task-based programming models to express the overall TLR LU-based solver into various fine-grained computational tasks operating on tiles. The TLR LU-based solver can actually be translated into a Directed Acyclic Graph (DAG), where nodes correspond to kernels and edges represent the data dependencies. We define an Array of Structure (AoS) of TLR data descriptors to effectively support the data distribution on shared as well as distributed-memory systems. We rely on the dynamic runtime system StarPU [13] to orchestrate the asynchronous executions of the tasks and track their respective data dependencies. We report accuracy results for scattering analysis of large-scale 3D synthetic and real geometries. We show then performance results on several shared-memory systems and compare against the-state-of-the-art dense linear algebra libraries. We further demonstrate the numerical robustness and performance scaling on 1024 nodes of a Cray XC40 dual-socket 16-core Intel Haswell system.

The remainder of the paper is organized as follows. Section 2 describes related work and summarizes our research contributions. Section 3 and 4 recall the background on the formulation and discretization of the acoustic BIE application and dense linear solvers, respectively. Section 5 introduces the task-based TLR LU-based solver algorithm and the corresponding computational kernels. Section 6 provides implementation details on the data distribution and the StarPU dynamic runtime systems. Section 7 highlights the numerical robustness of our TLR LU-based solver using 3D synthetic and real geometry testcases. Section 8 assesses the performance results on various systems and we conclude in Sect. 9.

## 2    Related Work

The application of direct solvers to matrix systems resulting from discretization of 3D problems has traditionally been considered expensive due to the high number of unknowns. However, the synergism between advanced matrix factorization methods, along with modern massively parallel hardware systems have created new opportunities to tackle such challenging problems. Indeed, direct methods have been used together with low-rank matrix representation schemes to reduce the arithmetic complexity. Introduced more than two decades ago, low-rank matrix approximations in the form of hierarchical matrices ($\mathcal{H}$-matrices) [31,36] represent a new compromise in the literature. Many state-of-the-art data compression formats for $\mathcal{H}$-matrix approximation (e.g., $\mathcal{H}^2$-matrix [16], Hierarchically Semi-Separable (HSS) [7,26,48], Block/Tile Low-Rank (BLR / TLR) [5,9],

Hierarchically Off-Diagonal Low-Rank (HODLR) [8,11]) have been developed to enable the use of finite element method (FEM) and boundary element method (BEM) in analysis of large-scale problems in a broad range of scientific applications. In particular, several $\mathcal{H}$-matrix arithmetics-accelerated schemes have been developed to solve surface integral equations discretized using the Method of Moments (MoM). For instance, direct solvers are coupled with nested and non-nested basis $\mathcal{H}$-matrix compression formats and deployed on shared [24,40,47,50,51] and distributed-memory systems [12,34,35] for large-scale electromagnetic scattering analysis.

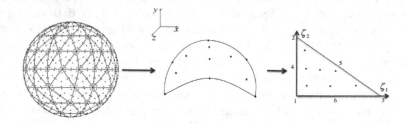

**Fig. 1.** Higher-order geometry modeling: the curvilinear triangular patch in the Cartesian domain and the parent triangle patch in the $(\xi_1, \xi_2)$ domain.

Compared to related work, we design and implement the Tile Low-Rank (TLR) LU-based solver for solving 3D acoustic Boundary Integral Equations (BIE) problems with the Nyström method. In this work, we prefer Nyström over MoM since it allows us to implement a higher-order discretization in a more straightforward way, without loosing generality. By adopting TLR, i.e., a flat tree data compression format, we trade off optimality with user productivity to reduce the deployment effort on massively parallel systems. Such approach has already demonstrated its effectiveness in solving large-scale scientific problems [6,23]. In fact, TLR may be considered as one step toward bridging the complexity gap (i.e., arithmetic and memory) between flat and hierarchical low-rank matrix formats [10]. Moreover, our systematic approach relies on asynchronous task scheduling using the dynamic runtime system StarPU to cope with the load imbalance issue. We apply our new solver to the analysis of scattering from 3D synthetic and real geometries, evaluate the numerical robustness and assess the performance results on various parallel systems.

## 3    The Acoustic Boundary Integral Equation Application

**Problem Definition.** For an acoustically rigid scatterer, the Helmholtz Boundary Integral Equation (BIE) in unknown pressure field $P(\mathbf{r})$ reads:

$$\frac{1}{2}P(\mathbf{r}) - \int_S P(\mathbf{r}')\partial_{n'}G(\mathbf{r},\mathbf{r}')dS' = P^{\text{inc}}(\mathbf{r}), \ \mathbf{r} \in S, \tag{1}$$

where $S$ is the surface of the scatterer, "$\partial_{n'}$" denotes the partial derivative in the direction of the surface normal unit vector $\hat{n}(r')$, $G(r, r') = e^{jk|r-r'|}/(4\pi|r-r'|)$ is the 3D scalar Green function of the unbounded domain where $S$ resides in, $P^{\text{inc}}(r)$ is the pressure field, and $r'$ and $r$ are source and observer points, respectively.

**Higher-Order Discretization Using Nyström Method.** To facilitate the numerical solution of Eq. (1), first, $S$ is divided into a mesh of $N$ curvilinear triangular patches, as seen in Fig. 1. A higher-order Nyström method [45] is then used on this mesh to discretize Eq. (1). To this end, the scalar version of the vector interpolation functions that have been introduced in [42] is used to expand the unknown $P(r)$. This function requires $M$ number of interpolation points to be defined on each patch. Inserting this expansion into Eq. (1) and testing the resulting equation at these interpolation points of each patch yield a linear system of equations $\bar{A}\bar{P} = \bar{P}^{\text{inc}}$, where $\bar{A}$ is a matrix of dimension $NM \times NM$, $\bar{P}^{\text{inc}}$ and $\bar{P}$ are vectors of dimension $NM$ storing samples of test incident field $P^{\text{inc}}(r)$, and (unknown) the pressure field $P(r)$ at the interpolation points. Their entries are given by:

$$\bar{A}_{ef,qj} = \frac{1}{2}\delta_{ef,qj} - \int_{S_q} \partial_{n'} G(r_{qj}, r') L_{qj}(r') ds',$$
$$\bar{P}_{ef}^{\text{inc}} = P^{\text{inc}}(r_{ef}),$$
$$\bar{P}_{qj} = P(r_{qj}), \tag{2}$$

for $e, q = 1, \ldots, N$, and $f, j = 1, \ldots, M$. Here, $\delta_{ef,qj} = 1$ for $ef = qj$ and zero otherwise, $r_{ef}$ is the testing (interpolation) point $e$ on patch $f$, $r_{qj}$ is the source (interpolation) point $q$ on patch $j$, $S_q$ is the surface of patch $q$, and $L_{qj}(r)$ is the interpolation function associated with point $r_{qj}$.

The surface integral in Eq. (2) is evaluated numerically after it is "mapped" onto a unit flat right-angle triangle (see Fig. 1). Furthermore, the computation of this integral calls for a singularity treatment scheme when $e = q$. Several approaches have been proposed in the literature (e.g., Duffy transformation [27], singularity subtraction technique (SST) [41], and polar coordinate transformation [33]). In this work, we use the polar coordinate transformation (PCT) based on the improved Guiggiani's method [18].

It should also be noted here that the acoustic BIE formulation used in this work suffers from the internal resonance problem, i.e., Eq. (1) has a null space at the frequencies that coincide with cavity modes/resonances of $S$ [15]. In other words, the pressure field solution on the surface of the scatterer does not generate any scattered/radiated fields. These resonance frequencies depend on the shape of the scatterer. The condition number of the matrix resulting from the discretization of the integral equation increases as the excitation frequency approaches any one of these resonance frequencies. Unless the two frequencies exactly coincide, the matrix system might still be solved but often iterative methods do not converge or require too many iterations to be considered efficient. For such cases, direct methods produce the solution more efficiently assuming the matrix is well-posed enough for the required level of accuracy with respect to floating point rounding error. Note that for the examples considered in the paper, the excitation frequency is sufficiently away from the resonance frequencies. The Burton-Miller formulation [20] can alleviate this problem of non-uniqueness. However, the discretization of this formulation requires the use of more complex singularity treatment techniques (particularly for higher-order discretizations) as the order of singularity increases. An accurate numerical result can still be achieved, even with the existence of the internal resonance problem, if the frequency does not coincide exactly with the resonance frequencies [25].

Once the linear system is built, the non-symmetric matrix $\bar{A}$ in double complex precision arithmetic is diagonally dominant due to the "self-patch interactions". The LU factorization may represent the adequate choice for direct solving the dense linear system, without the pivoting mechanism. Moreover, its off-diagonal blocks are usually data sparse and may be subject to low-rank approximations. Last but not least, the matrix $\bar{A}$ may need a proper row/column ordering of the patch indices [44] to decouple the "near-patch interactions" from "far-patch interactions" so that the compression phase may be further optimized.

## 4    The State-of-The-Art Dense LU-Based Solvers

LAPACK and ScaLAPACK are the *de facto* libraries for performing dense linear algebra operations. However, the algorithmic paradigm has shifted from block (i.e., coarse granularity) to tile (fine granularity) algorithms in response to manycore hardware evolution. Block algorithms emphasize efficient use of deep memory hierarchies, whereas tile algorithms focus on achieving a high level of concurrency.

**Block LU Algorithm.** The LU factorization provided in LAPACK and ScaLAPACK software packages is implemented as a high-level algorithm built on top of the Basic Linear Algebra Subprograms (BLAS) for LAPACK and the Basic Linear Algebra Communication Subprograms (BLACS) for ScaLAPACK. Conceptually, the matrix is divided into blocks of columns, commonly named panels, on which a partial pivoting scheme may be applied. The factorization then proceeds by an update of the trailing submatrix. This panel-update sequence continues until all panels are factorized. Block algorithms leverage the Level-3 BLAS matrix-matrix multiplication GEMM, resulting into a superior data reuse which is required to run efficiently on cache-based computer architectures. However, in-between synchronization points are required, due to the fork-join paradigm. The parallelism occurs only within each update phase and is expressed at the BLAS and BLACS levels, which eventually degrades the performance [3].

**Tile LU Algorithm.** To alleviate the synchronization bottleneck seen in block algorithms, the dense linear algebra community introduced a decade ago a redesign of matrix computation algorithms, named tile algorithms, using task-based programming models. The idea consists in splitting the matrix into tiles, on which elements are contiguous in memory for better cache usage. The panel factorization and the update of the trailing submatrix may now be represented into successive fine-grained computational

**Algorithm 1.** Dense Tile $LU$ factorization of a $N$-by-$N$ matrix $A$ composed of $nb \times nb$ tiles and solve.

```
1: p = N / nb                               ▷ number of tiles
2: for k = 1 to p do
3:     ZGETRF(A[k][k])
4:     for m = k+1 to p do
5:         ZTRSM('U', A[k][k], A[m][k])
6:     for n = k+1 to p do
7:         ZTRSM('L', A[k][k],A[k][n])
8:         for m = k+1 to p do
9:             ZGEMM(A[m][k],A[k][n],A[m][n])     ▷
                                    matrix-matrix multiplication
10: ZTRSM('L', A, RHS)        ▷ forward substitution
11: ZTRSM('U', A, RHS)        ▷ backward substitution
```

tasks operating on tiles. The fine granularity tasks weaken the synchronization points seen in block algorithms and create opportunities for asynchronous execution. The sequential tile algorithms can then be presented by a Directed Acyclic Graphs (DAG), where nodes and edges represent the computational tasks and the dependencies among the tasks, respectively. The key idea is to bring the parallelism to the fore by scheduling the DAG's sequential tasks using a dynamic runtime system. The runtime system is then in charge of orchestrating the tasks across the underlying shared and distributed-memory resources, while ensuring data dependencies are not violated. The performance advantages of tile over block algorithms have been discussed in the literature [4,17,21,46]. Algorithm 1 shows the pseudo-code of the dense tile LU-based solver in double complex precision arithmetic, involving three kernels, i.e., ZGETRF, ZTRSM, and ZGEMM, performing the LU factorization of the diagonal tile, the triangular matrix solve and the matrix-matrix multiplication, respectively. The corresponding DAG of the tile LU factorization for a 4-by-4 tile matrix is drawn in Fig. 2: the DAG width shows the critical path and the height exposes the concurrency.

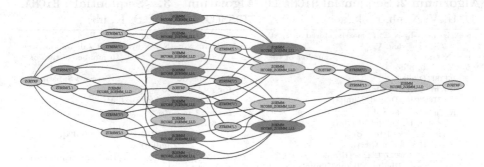

**Fig. 2.** Single DAG for the tile dense and tile low-rank LU factorization for a 4-by-4 matrix. Yellow nodes represent ZGETRF operations, blue and cyan nodes represent upper and lower ZTRSM operations, resp., and dark and light gray nodes represent ZGEMM and HCORE_ZGEMM_XXX operations, respectively. (Color figure online)

# 5  The Tile Low-Rank LU-Based Solver Algorithm

**The Tile Low-Rank Compression Format.** Following the principle of the dense tile algorithms, the Tile Low-Rank (TLR) algorithm exploits the data sparsity of the off-diagonal tiles [5,6]. The initial phase is to approximate each of the off-diagonal tiles of size $nb$ using the fast randomized singular value decomposition [39], while capturing only the most significant $k$ singular values and their associated singular vectors. The rank $k$ depends on the user-defined accuracy threshold. The diagonal tiles are typically full rank and may not be approximated. Then, each of the off-diagonal tiles $(i, j)$ can be represented by the product of two rectangular matrices $U_{ij}$ and $V_{ij}$ of size $nb \times k$. Once the tile-centric compression phase ends, the TLR LU-based solver phase can then carry on with the TLR matrix computation.

**Description of the Numerical Kernels.** The TLR LU-based solver algorithm requires new computational kernels. Compared to the sequential dense LU algorithm, the sequential TLR LU algorithm is quite similar, except that it necessitates a new matrix-matrix multiplication kernel that takes into account the data format (i.e., dense or TLR) of each operand A, B, and C. The new HCORE_ZGEMM_XXX has three variants to fully support the TLR LU-based solver algorithm: (1) HCORE_ZGEMM_LLL performing C = C+A*B, where A,B,C are TLR, (2) HCORE_ZGEMM_LLD performing C = C+A*B, where A, B are TLR; C is dense, and (3) HCORE_ZGEMM_LDD performing C = C+A*B, where A is TLR; B, C are dense (used in solve part). Algorithms 2 and 3 highlight the pseudo-codes of the sequential TLR LU factorization and its corresponding solver, respectively. The diagonal tiles need a special treatment for the matrix-matrix multiplication due to their dense data structure (i.e., HCORE_ZGEMM_LLD). The corresponding DAG of the TLR LU factorization for a 4-by-4 tile matrix is essentially the same as the tile dense LU, as shown in Fig. 2. However, the red circle tasks highlight the

---

**Algorithm 2. Sequential HiCMA_LU (D, U, V, N, nb, rank, acc)**

▷ A is an N-by-N TLR matrix stored in D, U, and V.
p = N / nb      ▷ number of tiles
**for** k = 1 to p **do**
  ZGETRF(D[k][k])
  **for** m = k+1 to p **do**
    ZTRSM('U', D[k][k], V[m][k])
  **for** n = k+1 to p **do**
    ZTRSM('L', D[k][k], U[k][n])
    **for** m = k+1 to p **do**
      **if** m == n **then**
        HCORE_ZGEMM_LLD(U[n][k],   V[n][k], U[k][n], V[k][n], D[n][n])
      **else**
        HCORE_ZGEMM_LLL(U[m][k],   V[m][k], U[k][n],   V[k][n],   U[m][n], V[m][n], rank, acc)
**return** D, U, V

---

**Algorithm 3. Sequential HiCMA_ZTRSM(D, U, V, N, B, K, nb)**

▷ Computes the solution of $AX = B$
▷ A / B are N-by-N / N-by-K TLR / dense matrices.
p = N / nb    q = K / nb    ▷ number of tiles of A and B
**for** k=1 to p **do**      ▷ Forward Substitution
  **for** n=1 to q **do**
    ZTRSM('L', D[k][k], B[k][n])
  **for** m=1 to p **do**
    **for** n=1 to q **do**
      HCORE_ZGEMM_LDD(U[m][k],   V[m][k],   B[k][n], B[m][n])
**for** k=1 to p **do**      ▷ Backward substitution
  **for** n=1 to q **do**
    ZTRSM('U', D[k][k], B[k][n])
  **for** m=1 to p **do**
    **for** n=1 to q **do**
      HCORE_ZGEMM_LDD(U[p-1-m][p-1-k],   V[p-1-m][p-1-k], B[p-1-k][n],B[p-1-m][n])
**return** B

difference when performing the matrix-matrix multiplication kernel with dense tile LU (i.e., ZGEMM) or TLR LU (i.e, the HCORE_ZGEMM_XXX variants).

The tile size $nb$ is a tunable parameter and has a significant effect on the overall performance as it trades off optimality and parallel performance [5,6,23]. The fixed accuracy allows for an application-dependent level of approximation for the off-diagonal tiles. However, this may engender variable ranks across off-diagonal tiles, which may cause load balancing issues. It is then paramount to rely on a dynamic runtime system to mitigate the load balancing issues, while maintaining high occupancy on the underlying hardware resources.

# 6   Implementation Details

**Array of TLR Structures.** We develop the new TLR LU factorization in the context of the Hierarchical Computations on Manycore Architectures (HiCMA [1] ) software library. We have extended HiCMA to support non-symmetric matrix computations, and given the BIE problems, we have also provided support for double complex precision arithmetic. HiCMA inherently provides a data descriptor for TLR using a 2D block cyclic data distributions, similar to the ScaLAPACK descriptor [5]. The TLR data descriptor specifies how the data should be distributed among processing units. To reduce the memory footprint, we have changed the existing Structure of TLR Arrays (SoA) for the data descriptor to an Array of TLR Structures (AoS). This allows us to allocate each logical tile using their respective sizes that depend on the rank $k$. This flexibility in handling the rank disparities is critical, especially when moving data in distributed-memory system environments. We also generate on-the-fly each dense tile individually using reusable buffers, before compressing them using the randomized SVD [39]. We initially allocate as many buffers as the number of processing units so that the matrix does not need to be wholly alive at any given time. Although TLR does not provide linear complexity, this format has enabled to solve challenging problems with a high number of unknowns on massively parallel distributed-memory system [6,23]. TLR adopts a flattened algorithmic design to further increase task parallelism in lieu of the plain recursive approach usually adopted in $\mathcal{H}$-matrix libraries [38]. TLR is actually a step toward reducing the complexity gap (i.e., arithmetic and memory) between flat and hierarchical low-rank matrix formats [10]. HiCMA relies on the dynamic runtime system StarPU to run in parallel, which is explained in the next section.

**The StarPU Task-Based Runtime Systems.** StarPU [13] is the standard dynamic runtime system for HiCMA. It handles the execution of generic task graphs, which results from the Sequential Task Flow (STF) programming model. Herein, the tasks are exposed to the runtime with hints on the data directions (i.e., StarPU_R, StarPU_W, and StarPU_RW). Then, the StarPU runtime system starts to dynamically schedule the given tasks asynchronously based on the given data directions. The StarPU runtime system abstracts the complexity of the underlying hardware and improve user productivity. StarPU supports shared

## Algorithm 4. Parallel HiCMA_LU (D, U, V, N, nb, rank, acc)

▷ A is an N-by-N TLR matrix stored in D, U, and V.
p = N / nb          ▷ number of tiles
**for** k = 1 to p **do**
   StarPU_Insert_Task(ZGETRF, StarPU_R,
      D[k][k],  StarPU_priority,
      5),
   **for** m = k+1 to p **do**
      StarPU_Insert_Task(ZTRSM,
         StarPU_R,  'U',  D[k][k],
         StarPU_RW,    V[m][k],
         StarPU_priority, 4)
   **for** n = k+1 to p **do**
      StarPU_Insert_Task(ZTRSM,
         StarPU_R,  'L',  D[k][k],
         StarPU_RW,    U[k][n],
         StarPU_priority, 4)
      **for** m = k+1 to p **do**
         **if** m == n **then**
            StarPU_Insert_Task(
            HCORE_ZGEMM_LLD,
            StarPU_R,        U[n][k],
            StarPU_R,        V[n][k],
            StarPU_R,        U[k][n],
            StarPU_R,        V[k][n],
            StarPU_RW,       D[n][n],
            StarPU_priority, 2)
         **else**
            StarPU_Insert_Task(
            HCORE_ZGEMM_LLL,
            StarPU_R,        U[m][k],
            StarPU_R,        V[m][k],
            StarPU_R,        U[k][n],
            StarPU_R,        V[k][n],
            StarPU_RW,       U[m][n],
            StarPU_RW,       V[m][b],
            StarPU_priority, 2, rank,
            acc)
**return** D, U, V

## Algorithm 5. Parallel HiCMA_ZTRSM(D, U, V, N, B, K, nb)

▷ Computes the solution of AX = B
▷ A / B are N-by-N / N-by-K TLR / dense matrices.
p = N / nb    q = K / nb    ▷ number of tiles of A and B
**for** k=1 to p **do**    ▷ Forward Substitution
   **for** n=1 to q **do**
      StarPU_Insert_Task(ZTRSM,
         StarPU_R,  'L',  D[k][k],
         StarPU_RW,      B[k][n],
         StarPU_priority, 5)
   **for** m=1 to p **do**
      **for** n=1 to q **do**
         StarPU_Insert_Task(
         HCORE_ZGEMM_LDD,
         StarPU_R,        U[m][k],
         StarPU_R,        V[m][k],
         StarPU_R,        B[k][n],
         StarPU_RW,       B[m][n],
         StarPU_priority, 4)
**for** k=1 to p **do** ▷ Backward substitution
   **for** n=1 to q **do**
      StarPU_Insert_Task(ZTRSM,
         StarPU_R,  'U',  D[p-1-k][p-1-k], StarPU_RW,
         B[k][n], StarPU_priority, 3)
   **for** m=1 to p **do**
      **for** n=1 to q **do**
         StarPU_Insert_Task(
         HCORE_ZGEMM_LDD,
         StarPU_R,   U[p-1-m][p-1-k], StarPU_R,
         V[p-1-m][p-1-k],
         StarPU_R,   B[p-1-k][n],
         StarPU_RW, B[p-1-m][n],
         StarPU_priority, 2)
**return** B

and distributed-memory systems (possibly equipped with GPUs). StarPU plays an even more major role when dealing with scattering analysis from 3D acoustic BIE problems than 2D Gaussian process, as seen in [5,6]. The large rank discrepancy between off-diagonal tiles is more severe in the herein studied applications. This creates load imbalance situations where resource may become idle. Thanks to the fine-grained computational tasks, StarPU can perform asynchronous executions by exploiting algorithmic lookahead to mitigate theses overheads and maximize hardware occupancy. Lookahead is achieved at runtime by using the task priority and the task window size features from StarPU. Basically, the task window size governs the number of queued tasks. The more tasks are queued, the more opportunities to create lookahead opportunities. Once the tasks shift to a ready state (i.e., tasks for which data dependencies are satisfied), they are executed following the order of their priorities. Algorithms 4 and 5 show the pseudo-codes of the parallel TLR LU factorization and its corresponding solver.

The API `StarPU_Insert_Task` queues the tasks with the data directions for each operand and eventually executes them, as soon as their data dependencies are satisfied. One of the interesting things to notice is the user productivity achieved when moving from sequential (i.e., Algorithms 2 and 3) to parallel TLR LU-based solver (i.e., Algorithms 4 and 5).

## 7    Numerical Accuracy

We assess the numerical accuracy and robustness of the `HiCMA` TLR LU-based solver. Figure 3 pictures the rank distribution of the initial matrix obtained after compression and presents the impact of using different accuracy thresholds on the matrix structure. The matrix size is 91368-by-91368 and tile size $nb = 3384$. There are 27 tiles in each dimension. The colors show the ranks of tiles, i.e., white tiles show the dense diagonal with full rank, red tones denote tiles with larger ranks, whereas blue tones denote tiles with smaller ranks. The highest ranks are located on tiles around the diagonal, which contains the near-field strong interactions. The smallest ranks are located on the off-diagonal tiles, which typically represent the far-field weak interactions. Furthermore, as the thresholds decrease, both average and maximum ranks become larger since the truncation step removes less singular values.

Singular value decay for specific tiles is depicted on Fig. 4. The tile location is chosen according to the distance from source point. We select tile on sub-diagonal which is close to self-interaction field, tile on the near field interaction, tile on the far interaction area, and last tile is on the farthest point. We can notice that when moving away from the source point the singular values decayed significantly compare to the near field interaction tile.

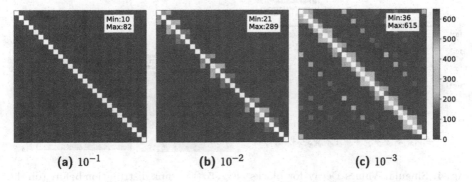

(a) $10^{-1}$          (b) $10^{-2}$          (c) $10^{-3}$

**Fig. 3.** The rank distribution of initial matrices obtained by compression for different accuracy thresholds. The matrix size is 91368-by-91368 and tile size $nb = 3384$. There are 27 tiles in each dimension. The colors show the ranks of tiles, i.e., red tones denote larger ranks, whereas blue tones denote smaller ranks. For smaller thresholds, both average and maximum ranks become larger. (Color figure online)

Figure 5 shows the rank distribution before and after HiCMA TLR LU factorization for the matrix size of 91368-by-91368. The tile size is 3384 where 27 tiles in each dimension, and the accuracy threshold is $10^{-3}$. It is interesting to see that the rank growth has been limited throughout the factorization.

To validate and demonstrate the accuracy of the solver, we consider scattering by a rigid sphere, so that the scattering fields can be easily verified and tested by comparing them with the analytical solutions (Mie Series Solution). Figure 6 compares the near scattered fields with the Mie scattered fields on a sphere with a radius $a = 1\,m$, and is discretized into $N = 15228$ high-order curvilinear iso-parametric quadrilateral elements and resulting in 91368 number of unknowns. The incident wave is a uniform plane wave with a frequency $f = 1978\,Hz$, and the propagation medium is air where the standard speed of sound in air is $c = 340.29m/s$. The solution is obtained using the HiCMA TLR LU-based solver for three different fixed accuracies, i.e., $1e-1$, $1e-2$ and $1e-3$. Then, as a post-processing step, we calculate the potential on a circle with a radius of 4m ($\theta \in [0°; 180°]; \phi = 0°$). Figures 6a and 6b plot the scattered potential amplitude and its difference from that computed using a Mie series code versus $\theta$ of this circle. We can see the error decreases as the accuracy increases, which demonstrates the correct implementation of the solver. While $1e-1$ degrades the numerical solution, an accuracy threshold of $1e - 2$ is typically satisfactory for the application requirement. With the accuracy threshold of $1e - 3$, the solver is in an "over-accurate" state, which results in an unnecessary computational load.

Next, to show the applicability of the solver, we consider scattering from a more complex realistic submarine geometry, as shown in Fig. 7. The submarine is contained within a box of dimensions $32.1 \times 3.6 \times 6.5$ meters, as shown in Fig. 7a.

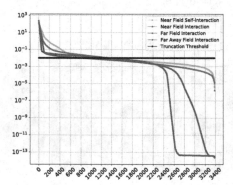
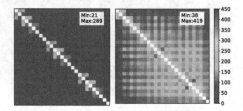

**Fig. 4.** Singular Values Decay for blocks (13,12), (15,11), (20,5) , and (27,1), respectively, of matrix size 91368-by-91368 and tile size is 3384

**Fig. 5.** The rank distribution before (on the left) and after (on the right) LU factorization. The matrix size is 91368-by-91368 and tile size is 3384, the accuracy threshold is $10^{-2}$. White color is used to represent dense tiles. The ranks become larger after factorization. (Color figure online)

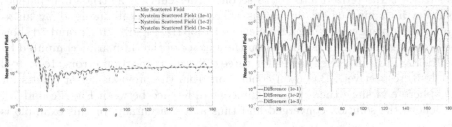

**(a)** Analytical near scattered potential vs Nyström near scattered potential

**(b)** Error difference

**Fig. 6.** Comparison of the near scattered potential computed on a circle with radius $a = 4\,$m for $\phi = 0°$ and $0° < \theta < 180°$ using the numerical solution (obtained by the HiCMA LU solver for accuracy $1e - 1$, $1e - 2$ and $1e - 3$) and the analytical solution, obtained using Mie series. The matrix size is 91368-by-91368 and tile size is 3384.

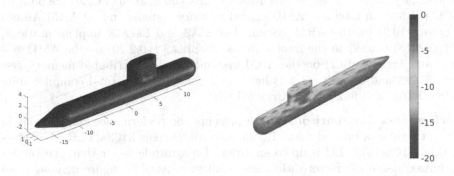

**(a)** Geometry (in terms of meters) of the structure.

**(b)** Potential on the surface with the truncation error of $1e - 1$.

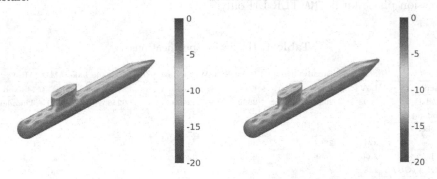

**(c)** Potential on the surface with the truncation error of $1e - 2$.

**(d)** Potential on the surface with the truncation error of $1e - 3$.

**Fig. 7.** Application of HiCMA TLR LU-based solver to the analysis of acoustic scattering from a submarine.

Its surface is discretized into 10818 second-order curvilinear triangular patches resulting in having 64908 unknowns. The submarine is illuminated by an x-propagating plane wave with a frequency of 1366 Hz. Figures 7b, 7c, and 7d show the pressure fields (in dB) induced on the surface of the submarine computed by the HiCMA TLR LU-based solver for three different truncation errors, 1e-1, 1e-2 and 1e-3, respectively. Based on conclusion from the previous set of results for the sphere and since there is no significant difference between Figs. 7c and 7d, we believe the solution converged and thus a 1e-2 accuracy for this example is enough.

## 8    Performance Results

**Environment Settings.** The experiments are carried on several shared and distributed-memory systems, as illustrated in Table 1. All computations are performed using double complex precision arithmetic and the presented results are an average of three consistent executions. HiCMA and StarPU (v1.2.6) are built by GCC (v5.5.0) on Intel and AMD shared-memory systems and by ARM Allinea Studio (v19.2) on the ARM system. For BLAS and LAPACK implementations, MKL (v2018) is used on the Intel systems, OpenBLAS (v0.2.20) on the AMD system, and ArmPL (v19.2) on the ARM system. On the distributed-memory system, HiCMA and StarPU (v1.2.6) have been compiled with Intel compiler suite (v18.0.1.163) and link against Cray MPICH.

**Performance Comparisons.** Fig. 8 presents the performance comparisons in time of vendor optimized dense LU factorization versus HiCMA TLR LU factorization. HiCMA TLR LU is up to an order of magnitude faster than the vendor optimized dense LU factorization across all systems. This figure demonstrates the portability of HiCMA TLR LU factorization. The times shown do not include the the matrix generation for both HiCMA TLR LU and dense LU, nor the compression phase for HiCMA TLR LU only.

**Table 1.** Hardware specifications.

| | Shaheen-2 | Broadwell(BDW) | Haswell(HSW) | Skylake (SKL) | Cascade Lake | AMD | ARM |
|---|---|---|---|---|---|---|---|
| Family | E5V3 | E5V4 | E5 | Scalable | Scalable | EPYC | Marvell |
| Model | 2698 | 2680 | 2699 | 2698 | 6248 | 7601 | ThunderX2 |
| Node(s) | 6144 | 1 | 1 | 1 | 1 | 1 | 1 |
| Socket(s) | 2 | 2 | 2 | 2 | 2 | 2 | 2 |
| Cores | 32 | 28 | 36 | 40 | 40 | 64 | 64 |
| GHz | 2.60 | 2.40 | 2.30 | 2.40 | 2.50 | 2.2 | 2.5 |
| DDR4 (GB) | 128 | 256 | 256 | 370 | 370 | 256 | 256 |
| L3 cache (MB) | 40 | 35 | 35 | 27.5 | 28 | 64 | 32 |

**Time Breakdown.** Fig. 9 shows the time spent in the generation and compression phases for the HiCMA TLR LU and dense LU on the Cascade Lake system for various matrix sizes. The time for the compression phase is negligible compared to the overall time to solution. The time for generation may be improved using Adaptive Cross Approximation technique [14] but this is beyond the scope of the paper.

**Accuracy Impact on the Performance.** Fig. 10 shows the accuracy impact on the overall performance. As we increase the accuracy threshold, the time to solution increases steadily due to larger ranks $k$ captured on each tile. The HiCMA TLR LU may actually becomes slower than the vendor optimized dense LU due to the expensive recompression step once $k > nb/2$.

**Performance on Distributed-Memory System.** Fig. 11a shows the performance of the dense LU factorization (i.e., the zgetrf_nopiv double complex LU routine without pivoting) from DPLASMA v2.0 [17] on up to 256 nodes and compares it against HiCMA LU factorization on 16 nodes only. Thanks to low-rank approximations, HiCMA TLR LU outperforms DPLASMA's dense LU across a range of matrix sizes, and up to an order of magnitude when using the same number of nodes. Figure 11b shows the performance scalability of HiCMA TLR LU on up to 1024 nodes with 2.5M unknowns.

**Traces.** Fig. 12 presents the execution trace of tile dense LU factorization as implemented in Chameleon and HiCMA TLR LU on four nodes with a matrix size of 74K. Each core of the four nodes has it timeline represented along the x axis. The blue colors corresponds to cores busy working, while the red colors show when the cores are idle. The gray area for the HiCMA trace does not record any activities since the code has already finished. While it is true that HiCMA TLR LU is much faster than tile dense LU factorization from Chameleon, we believe there is still room for improvement. Some of the off-diagonal tiles may have higher ranks, as seen in Fig. 5. Further runtime optimizations may be required to execute tasks along the critical path with higher priorities. Also, as seen in previous work [23], a hybrid data distribution combining 1D cyclic for the dense diagonal tiles and 2D cyclic for the off-diagonal tiles may result in a better load balancing.

# 9  Summary and Future Work

We present a new high performance implementation based on the Tile Low-Rank (TLR) LU factorization, which exploits the data sparsity of the matrix operator, in the context of scattering analysis from acoustic 3D boundary integral equations. Our high performance TLR LU factorization relies on task-based programming models associated with the StarPU dynamic runtime system. We extend and plan to integrate this new TLR LU into the existing HiCMA TLR software library. This synergistic software solution enables asynchronous executions of the TLR LU factorization, while mitigating the data motion overhead. We compare the obtained performance results of our TLR LU factorization against the state-of-the-art dense factorizations on several shared and distributed-memory systems. We achieve up to an order of magnitude performance speedup. We are

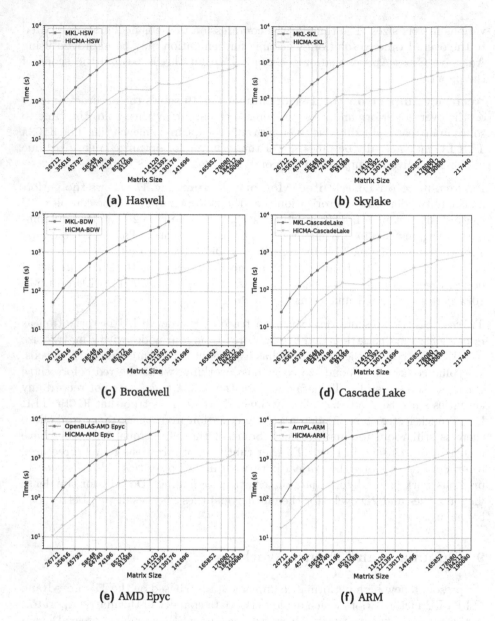

**Fig. 8.** Performance of HiCMA TLR LU versus vendor optimized dense LU on Intel systems (Haswell, Skylake, Broadwell, Cascade Lake), AMD Epyc, and ARM shared-memory systems.

able to solve the scattering analysis from 3D acoustic BIE problem with up to 2.5M unknowns in double complex precision arithmetics. Although our algorithmic and software solutions rely on StarPU, we would like to investigate the

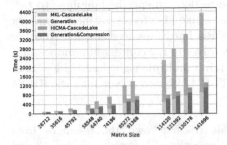
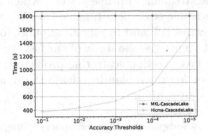

**Fig. 9.** Time breakdown comparing HiCMA Generation, Compression, and Computation with MKL Generation, and Computation on Cascade Lake shared-memory systems.

**Fig. 10.** Runtime HiCMA TLR LU factorization on Cascade Lake system for different accuracy thresholds. The matrix size is 114120-by-114120 and tile size $nb = 1902$.

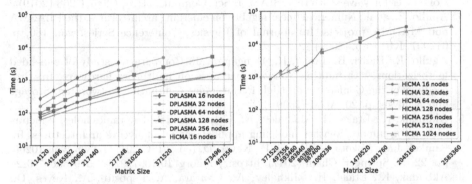

**(a)** Performance comparisons of DPLASMA's dense LU and HiCMA LU factorization.

**(b)** Performance scalability of HiCMA TLR LU.

**Fig. 11.** Performance assessment on distributed-memory environment.

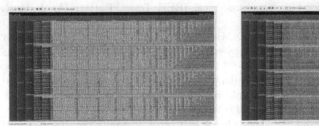

**(a)** Chameleon Dense ZGETRF time: 405.105s

**(b)** HiCMA TLR LU time: 116.809s

**Fig. 12.** Execution traces on four nodes with a matrix size of 74K. (Color figure online)

PaRSEC dynamic runtime system, which uses a domain specific language to target extreme scale performance [23]. We would like also to assess more complex geometries [19] and to provide support for GPU hardware accelerators. Another direction may be the study of our fast direct solver in the context of a monostatic radar cross-section scattering problem involving multiple right-hand sides. Last but not least, we plan to release the new TLR LU-based solver into the HiCMA open-source library.

**Acknowledgments.** For computer time, this research used the resources from KAUST Supercomputing Laboratory and the University of Bristol for *Shaheen-2* and *Isambard* core hours allocation, respectively.

# References

1. HiCMA (2017). https://github.com/ecrc/hicma
2. Abduljabbar, M., et al.: Extreme scale FMM-accelerated boundary integral equation solver for wave scattering. SIAM J. Sci. Comput. **41**(3), C245–C268 (2019)
3. Agullo, E., et al.: Numerical linear algebra on emerging architectures: the PLASMA and MAGMA projects. In: Journal of Physics: Conference Series. vol. 180, p. 012037. IOP Pub. (2009)
4. Agullo, E., Hadri, B., Ltaief, H., Dongarrra, J.: Comparative study of one-sided factorizations with multiple software packages on multi-core hardware. In: Proceedings of the Conference on High Performance Computing Networking, Storage and Analysis, p. 20. ACM (2009)
5. Akbudak, K., Ltaief, H., Mikhalev, A., Keyes, D.: Tile low rank cholesky factorization for climate/weather modeling applications on manycore architectures. In: Kunkel, J.M., Yokota, R., Balaji, P., Keyes, D. (eds.) ISC 2017. LNCS, vol. 10266, pp. 22–40. Springer, Cham (2017). https://doi.org/10.1007/978-3-319-58667-0_2
6. Akbudak, K., Ltaief, H., Mikhalev, A., Charara, A., Esposito, A., Keyes, D.: Exploiting data sparsity for large-scale matrix computations. In: Aldinucci, M., Padovani, L., Torquati, M. (eds.) Euro-Par 2018. LNCS, vol. 11014, pp. 721–734. Springer, Cham (2018). https://doi.org/10.1007/978-3-319-96983-1_51
7. Ambikasaran, S., Darve, E.: An $O(N\log N)$ fast direct solver for partial hierarchically semi-separable matrices. J. Sci. Comput. **57**(3), 477–501 (2013)
8. Ambikasaran, S., Foreman-Mackey, D., Greengard, L., Hogg, D.W., O'Neil, M.: Fast direct methods for Gaussian processes. IEEE Trans. Pattern Anal. Mach. Intell. **38**(2), 252–265 (2015)
9. Amestoy, P., Ashcraft, C., Boiteau, O., Buttari, A., L'Excellent, J.Y., Weisbecker, C.: Improving multifrontal methods by means of block low-rank representations. SIAM J. Sci. Comput. **37**(3), A1451–A1474 (2015)
10. Amestoy, P.R., Buttari, A., L'Excellent, J.Y., Mary, T.A.: Bridging the gap between flat and hierarchical low-rank matrix formats: the multilevel block low-rank format. SIAM J. Sci. Comput. **41**(3), A1414–A1442 (2019)
11. Aminfar, A., Ambikasaran, S., Darve, E.: A fast block low-rank dense solver with applications to Finite-Element matrices. J. Comput. Phys. **304**, 170–188 (2016)
12. Augonnet, C., Goudin, D., Kuhn, M., Lacoste, X., Namyst, R., Ramet, P.: A hierarchical fast direct solver for distributed memory machines with manycore nodes. Research report, CEA/DAM; Total E&P; Université de Bordeaux, October 2019. https://hal-cea.archives-ouvertes.fr/cea-02304706

13. Augonnet, C., Thibault, S., Namyst, R., Wacrenier, P.A.: StarPU: a unified plat-form for task scheduling on heterogeneous multicore architectures. Concurrency Comput. Practice Experience **23**(2), 187–198 (2011)
14. Bebendorf, M., Rjasanow, S.: Adaptive low-rank approximation of collocation matrices. Computing **70**, 1–24 (2003)
15. Bonnet, M.: Boundary integral equation methods for solids and fluids. Meccanica **34**(4), 301–302 (1999)
16. Börm, S.: Efficient numerical methods for non-local operators: H2-matrix compression, algorithms and analysis, vol. 14. European Mathematical Society (2010)
17. Bosilca, G., et al.: Flexible development of dense linear algebra algorithms on massively parallel architectures with DPLASMA. In: 2011 IEEE International Symposium on Parallel and Distributed Processing Workshops and Ph.d. Forum, pp. 1432–1441, May 2011
18. Bremer, J., Gimbutas, Z.: A Nyström method for weakly singular integral operators on surfaces. J. Comput. Phys. **231**(14), 4885–4903 (2012)
19. Bremer, J., Gillman, A., Martinsson, P.G.: A high-order accurate accelerated direct solver for acoustic scattering from surfaces. BIT Numerical Math. **55**(2), 367–397 (2015)
20. Burton, A.J., Miller, G.F.: The application of integral equation methods to the numerical solution of some exterior boundary-value problems. Proceedings of the Royal Society of London. A. Mathematical and Physical Sciences 323(1553), 201–210 (1971)
21. Buttari, A., Langou, J., Kurzak, J., Dongarra, J.: A class of parallel tiled linear algebra algorithms for multicore architectures. Parallel Comput. **35**(1), 38–53 (2009)
22. Canino, L.F., Ottusch, J.J., Stalzer, M.A., Visher, J.L., Wandzura, S.M.: Numerical solution of the Helmholtz equation in 2D and 3D using a high-order Nyström discretization. J. Comput. Phys. **146**(2), 627–663 (1998)
23. Cao, Q., et al.: Extreme-Scale Task-Based Cholesky Factorization Toward Climate and Weather Prediction Applications. Technical report (2019)
24. Chai, W., Jiao, D.: An LU decomposition based direct integral equation solver of linear complexity and higher-order accuracy for large-scale interconnect Extraction. IEEE Trans. Adv. Packag. **33**(4), 794–803 (2010)
25. Chandrasekhar, B., Rao, S.M.: Elimination of internal resonance problem associated with acoustic scattering by three-dimensional rigid body. J. Acous. Soc. Am. **115**(6), 2731–2737 (2004)
26. Corona, E., Martinsson, P.G., Zorin, D.: An $O(N)$ direct solver for integral equations on the plane. Appl. Comput. Harmonic Anal. **38**(2), 284–317 (2015)
27. Duffy, M.G.: Quadrature over a pyramid or cube of integrands with a singularity at a vertex. SIAM J. Numer. Anal. **19**(6), 1260–1262 (1982)
28. Farhat, C., Crivelli, L., Roux, F.X.: Extending substructure based iterative solvers to multiple load and repeated analyses. Comput. Methods Appl. Mech. Eng. **117**(1–2), 195–209 (1994)
29. Fischer, P.F.: Projection techniques for iterative solution of $Ax = b$ with successive right-hand sides. Comput. Methods Appl. Mech. Eng. **163**(1–4), 193–204 (1998)
30. Golub, G.H., Van, C.F.: Matrix computations, vol. 3. Third Edition, Johns Hopkins University Press (2012)
31. Goreinov, S., Tyrtyshnikov, E., Yeremin, A.Y.: Matrix-free iterative solution strategies for large dense linear systems. Numer. Linear Algebra Appl. **4**(4), 273–294 (1997)

32. Greengard, L., Rokhlin, V.: A fast algorithm for particle simulations. J. Comput. Phys. **73**(2), 325–348 (1987)
33. Guiggiani, M., Krishnasamy, G., Rudolphi, T.J., Rizzo, F.: A general algorithm for the numerical solution of hypersingular boundary integral equations. J. Appl. Mech. **59**(3), 604–614 (1992)
34. Guo, H., Liu, Y., Hu, J., Michielssen, E.: A butterfly-based direct integral-equation solver using hierarchical LU factorization for analyzing scattering from electrically large conducting objects. IEEE Trans. Antennas Propag. **65**(9), 4742–4750 (2017)
35. Guo, H., Hu, J., Nie, Z.: An MPI-OpenMP hybrid parallel -LU direct solver for electromagnetic integral equations. Int. J. Antennas Propag. **2015**, 1 (2015)
36. Hackbusch, W.: A sparse matrix arithmetic based on $\mathcal{H}$-matrices part I: Introduction to $\mathcal{H}$-matrices. Computing **62**(2), 89–108 (1999)
37. Hackbusch, W.: Hierarchical Matrices: Algorithms and Analysis, vol. 49. Springer, Heidelberg (2015). https://doi.org/10.1007/978-3-662-47324-5
38. Hackbusch, W., Börm, S.: Data-sparse approximation by adaptive $H^2$-matrices. Computing **69**(1), 1–35 (2002)
39. Halko, N., Martinsson, P.G., Tropp, J.A.: Finding structure with randomness: probabilistic algorithms for constructing approximate matrix decompositions. SIAM Rev. **53**(2), 217–288 (2011)
40. Heldring, A., Rius, J.M., Tamayo, J.M., Parrón, J., Ubeda, E.: Multiscale compressed block decomposition for fast direct solution of method of moments linear system. IEEE Trans. Antennas Propag. **59**(2), 526–536 (2011)
41. Järvenpää, S., Taskinen, M., Ylä-Oijala, P.: Singularity subtraction technique for high-order polynomial vector basis functions on planar triangles. IEEE Trans. Antennas Propag. **54**(1), 42–49 (2006)
42. Kang, G., Song, J., Chew, W.C., Donepudi, K.C., Jin, J.M.: A novel grid-robust higher order vector basis function for the method of moments. IEEE Trans. Antennas Propag. **49**(6), 908–915 (2001)
43. Kress, R.: Linear Integral Equations, 3rd edn. Springer, New York (2014). https://doi.org/10.1007/978-1-4614-9593-2
44. Morton, G.: A computer oriented geodetic data base and a new technique in file sequencing. International Business Machines Company, New York (1966)
45. Nyström, E.J.: Über die praktische auflösung von integralgleichungen mit anwendungen auf randwertaufgaben. Acta Mathematica **54**(1), 185–204 (1930)
46. Quintana-Ortí, G., Quintana-Ortí, E.S., Geijn, R.A., Zee, F.G.V., Chan, E.: Programming matrix algorithms-by-blocks for thread-level parallelism. ACM TOMS **36**(3), 14 (2009)
47. Rong, Z., et al.: Fast direct solution of integral equations with modified HODLR structure for analyzing electromagnetic scattering problems. IEEE Trans. Antennas Propag. **67**(5), 3288–3296 (2019)
48. Rouet, F.H., Li, X.S., Ghysels, P., Napov, A.: A distributed-memory package for dense hierarchically semi-separable matrix computations using randomization. ACM Trans. Math. Softw. (TOMS) **42**(4), 27 (2016)
49. Saad, Y., Schultz, M.H.: GMRES:a generalized minimal residual algorithm for solving nonsymmetric linear systems. SIAM J. Sci. Stat. Comp. **7**(3), 856–869 (1986)
50. Shaeffer, J.: Direct solve of electrically large integral equations for problem sizes to 1 M unknowns. IEEE Trans. Antennas Propag. **56**(8), 2306–2313 (2008)
51. Wei, J., Peng, Z., Lee, J.: A fast direct matrix solver for surface integral equation methods for electromagnetic wave scattering from non-penetrable targets. Radio Sci. **47**(05), 1–9 (2012)

# DGEMM Using Tensor Cores, and Its Accurate and Reproducible Versions

Daichi Mukunoki[1](✉), Katsuhisa Ozaki[2], Takeshi Ogita[3],
and Toshiyuki Imamura[1]

[1] RIKEN Center for Computational Science, Hyogo, Japan
{daichi.mukunoki,imamura.toshiyuki}@riken.jp
[2] Shibaura Institute of Technology, Saitama, Japan
ozaki@sic.shibaura-it.ac.jp
[3] Tokyo Woman's Christian University, Tokyo, Japan
ogita@lab.twcu.ac.jp

**Abstract.** This paper proposes a method for implementing dense matrix multiplication on FP64 (DGEMM) and FP32 (SGEMM) using Tensor Cores on NVIDIA's graphics processing units (GPUs). Tensor Cores are special processing units that perform $4 \times 4$ matrix multiplications on FP16 inputs with FP32 precision, and return the result on FP32. The proposed method adopts the Ozaki scheme, an accurate matrix multiplication algorithm based on error-free transformation for matrix multiplication. The proposed method has three prominent advantages: first, it can be built upon the cublasGemmEx routine using Tensor Core operations; second, it can achieve higher accuracy than standard DGEMM, including the correctly-rounded result; third, it ensures bit-level reproducibility even for different numbers of cores and threads. The achievable performance of the method depends on the absolute-value range of each element of the input matrices. For example, when the matrices were initialized with random numbers over a dynamic range of 1E+9, our DGEMM-equivalent implementation achieved up to approximately 980 GFlops of FP64 operation on the Titan RTX GPU (with 130 TFlops on Tensor Cores), although cublasDgemm can achieve only 539 GFlops on FP64 floating-point units. Our results reveal the possibility of utilizing hardware with limited FP32/FP64 resources and fast low-precision processing units (such as AI-oriented processors) for general-purpose workloads.

**Keywords:** Tensor cores · FP16 · Half-precision · Low-precision · Matrix multiplication · GEMM · Linear algebra · Accuracy · Reproducibility

## 1 Introduction

The increasing number of deep learning applications has triggered the development of special processing units such as Tensor Cores on NVIDIA's graphics processing units (GPUs) and Google's Tensor Processing Units (TPUs) in

© Springer Nature Switzerland AG 2020
P. Sadayappan et al. (Eds.): ISC High Performance 2020, LNCS 12151, pp. 230–248, 2020.
https://doi.org/10.1007/978-3-030-50743-5_12

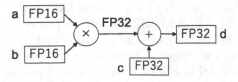

**Fig. 1.** Tensor Cores (FP16 computations with FP32 precision mode)

recent years. The kernel of such tasks is matrix multiplication, which does not require high-precision such as IEEE 754-2008 binary32 (known as single-precision or FP32, with an 8-bit exponent and a 23-bit fraction) and binary64 (known as double-precision or FP64, with an 11-bit exponent and a 52-bit fraction). The hardware instead supports fast, low-precision operations such as binary16 (known as half-precision or FP16, with a 5-bit exponent and a 10-bit fraction) and 8/16-bit integer operations.

One of the most widely used examples is Tensor Cores introduced in the Volta architecture, which computes a $4 \times 4$ matrix multiplication per clock with fused multiply-add operations. Although Tensor Cores support several data formats and computational precisions, the present paper focuses on FP16 computations with FP32 precision mode, which compute $d = a \times b + c$ with FP32 precision (Fig. 1). Here, $a$ and $b$ are FP16 values, and $c$ and $d$ are FP32. The Tensor Cores operate up to eight times faster than standard FP32 floating-point units (FPUs) on CUDA Cores. Many studies have exploited this tremendous performance of Tensor Cores in general tasks.

This paper presents a method for computing a general matrix multiply routine (GEMM) in level-3 basic linear algebra subprograms (BLAS) [4] on FP64 (DGEMM) and FP32 (SGEMM) using Tensor Cores. GEMM is one of the kernel operations of many scientific workloads, as well as high-performance Linpack. The proposed method is based on an accurate matrix multiplication algorithm based on error-free transformation for matrix multiplication, proposed by Ozaki et al. [13], also known as the Ozaki scheme. The advantages of this method are listed below.

- **Productive**: Being built upon the cublasGemmEx routine in cuBLAS[1] provided by NVIDIA, the method incurs a low development cost.
- **Accurate**: The method achieves higher accuracy than standard SGEMM and DGEMM even with correct-rounding.
- **Reproducible**: The method obtains the same (bitwise identical) result for the same input, even when the number of cores and threads differs in each execution.
- **Adaptable**: The concept is adaptable to other precisions.

Whereas some studies simply accelerate the computation not requiring high-precision by utilizing low-precision hardware, the present study attempts more

---

[1] http://developer.nvidia.com/cublas.

accurate computations by utilizing low-precision hardware. Our DGEMM implementations outperform cuBLAS DGEMM only on processors with limited FP64 support. However, the performance gain over FP64 FPUs is not necessarily important; rather, the intent is to increase the potential of low-precision hardware such as artificial intelligence (AI) oriented processors. Moreover, our method provides a new perspective on the efficient hardware design for both AI and traditional high-performance computing (HPC) workloads. For example, it may reduce the number of FP64 resources in exchange for massive low-precision support.

The remainder of this paper is organized as follows. Section 2 introduces related work, and Sect. 3 describes our methodology based on the Ozaki scheme. Section 4 implements the method, and Sect. 5 presents the accuracy and performance evaluations on Titan RTX and Tesla V100 GPUs. Section 6 discusses the perspective of future hardware design using our proposal. This paper concludes with Sect. 7.

## 2   Related Work

Several studies have attempted to utilize low-precision hardware designed for AI workloads for other purposes. For example, Haidar et al. [7] utilized standard FP16 and the Tensor Cores operation with FP32 precision in dense and sparse linear systems with iterative refinement. Energy improvement has also been studied [6]. Its error analysis was given by Carson and Higham [1]. Yang et al. [16] presented a Monte Carlo simulation of an Ising model using bfloat16 (BF16, with an 8-bit exponent and a 7-bit fraction) on Google's TPUs. These studies apply low-precision operations to the portions of code not requiring high accuracy, which can be computed at that precision level. Accordingly, their applicability is algorithm- or problem-dependent.

Similarly to the present study, several studies have attempted more accurate operations than those achieved by low-precision hardware. For example, Markidis et al. [11] proposed a method that improves the accuracy of matrix multiplication computed with Tensor Cores. Although their method is conceptually similar to ours, its capability is limited to the computation of matrices with dynamic ranges supported on FP16 with SGEMM-equivalent accuracy. Henry et al. [8] discussed the performance of high-precision operations with double-double arithmetic [2], a classic 2-fold precision arithmetic technique, on BF16 FPUs. Sorna et al. [15] proposed a method to improve the accuracy of 2D fast Fourier transform performed on Tensor Cores. We note that, in those studies, the performance gain over FP32 or FP64 FPUs was not necessarily important; rather, the intent was to increase the potential of low-precision hardware. Therefore, the hardware may need to be redesigned to balance the precisions supported on the FPUs. Our present discussion follows a similar direction.

The Ozaki scheme, which is the kernel of our proposed method, was originally proposed for accurate matrix multiplication by standard floating-point

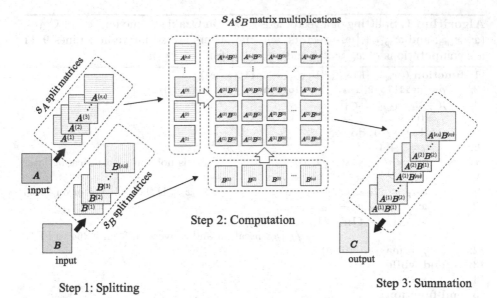

$s_A s_B$ matrix multiplications

Step 2: Computation

Step 1: Splitting

Step 3: Summation

**Fig. 2.** Schematic of matrix multiplication ($C = AB$) by Ozaki scheme (in this figure, scaling is omitted).

operations. OzBLAS [12]² implements accurate and reproducible BLAS routines on CPUs and GPUs based on the Ozaki scheme. Whereas OzBLAS was built on DGEMM performed on FP64 FPUs, the Ozaki scheme in the present study performs DGEMM/SGEMM operations using GEMM performed on Tensor Cores. Ichimura et al. [10] also reported a high-performance implementation of the Ozaki scheme based on FP64 operations on many-core CPUs.

## 3    Methodology

This section first describes the minimal scheme for computing DGEMM by the modified Ozaki scheme on Tensor Cores. Next, it presents additional techniques that accelerate the computations. In this paper, $\mathtt{fl}_{\mathrm{FP64}}(\cdots)$ and $\mathtt{fl}_{\mathrm{FP32}}(\cdots)$ denote the computations performed in FP64 and FP32 arithmetic, respectively, $\mathtt{u}_{\mathrm{FP64}}$ and $\mathtt{u}_{\mathrm{FP32}}$ denote the unit round-offs of FP64 ($\mathtt{u}_{\mathrm{FP64}} = 2^{-53}$) and FP32 ($\mathtt{u}_{\mathrm{FP32}} = 2^{-24}$), respectively, and $\mathbb{F}_{\mathrm{FP64}}$ and $\mathbb{F}_{\mathrm{FP16}}$ denote the sets of FP64 and FP16 floating-point numbers, respectively. $\mathbb{N}$ denotes the set of natural numbers including zero.

### 3.1    Ozaki Scheme for Tensor Cores

The Ozaki scheme performs an error-free transformation of matrix multiplication; specifically, the matrix multiplication is transformed into a summation of

---
² http://www.math.twcu.ac.jp/ogita/post-k/results.html.

**Algorithm 1.** Splitting of a vector $x \in \mathbb{F}_{\text{FP64}}{}^n$ in Ozaki scheme for Tensor Cores. ($x$, $x_{\text{tmp}}$, and $x_{\text{split}}[j]$ are vectors, and the others are scalar values. Lines 9–11 are computations of $x_i$, $x_{\text{tmp}_i}$, and $x_{\text{split}}[j]_i$ for $1 \leq i \leq n$)

```
 1: function (($x_split[1 : s_x], c[1 : s_x]) = Split(n, x))
 2:     ρ = ceil(log2(u_FP64^{-1}) - (log2(u_FP32^{-1}) - log2(n))/2)
 3:     μ = max_{1≤i≤n}(|x_i|)
 4:     j = 0
 5:     while (μ ≠ 0) do
 6:         j = j + 1
 7:         c[j] = τ = ceil(log2(μ))           // τ is hold on c for upscaling later
 8:         σ = 2^{ρ+τ}
 9:         x_tmp_i = fl_FP64((x_i + σ) - σ)    // x_tmp is the split vector on FP64
10:         x_i = fl_FP64(x_i - x_tmp_i)
11:         x_split[j]_i = fl_FP16(fl_FP64(2^{-τ} x_tmp_i))
                       // Downscaling and conversion from FP64 to FP16
12:         μ = max_{1≤i≤n}(|x_i|)
13:     end while
14:     s_x = j
15: end function
```

several matrix multiplications that can be performed on floating-point operations without rounding-errors. Figure 2 is a schematic of the whole Ozaki scheme. The method performs three major steps:

- **Step 1: Splitting** – element-wise splitting of the input matrices into several split matrices.
- **Step 2: Computation** – computation of all-to-all matrix products of the split matrices.
- **Step 3: Summation** – element-wise summation of the all-to-all matrix products.

We now describe each step in detail. For simplicity, we consider an inner product of two vectors $x, y \in \mathbb{F}_{\text{FP64}}{}^n$, but the approach is naturally extendible to matrix multiplication as it consists of inner products. Also, although we describe the case for DGEMM only, the same concept applies to SGEMM.

**Step 1: Splitting.** Algorithm 1 splits the input vectors on FP64 into several vectors on FP16 as follows.

$$x = 2^{c^{(x_1)}} x^{(1)} + 2^{c^{(x_2)}} x^{(2)} + \cdots + 2^{c^{(x_{s_x})}} x^{(s_x)}$$

$$y = 2^{c^{(y_1)}} y^{(1)} + 2^{c^{(y_2)}} y^{(2)} + \cdots + 2^{c^{(y_{s_y})}} y^{(s_y)}$$

$$x_p, y_q, s_x, s_y, c^{(p)}, c^{(q)} \in \mathbb{N}, x^{(p)}, y^{(q)} \in \mathbb{F}_{\text{FP16}}{}^n$$

A split vector is first obtained on FP64 and then converted (downscaled) to FP16. The conversion moves only the exponent and causes no significand-bit loss. Here, $2^{c^{(p)}}$ and $2^{c^{(q)}}$ are the downscaling factors (from FP64 to FP16) of the exponents of $\boldsymbol{x}^{(p)}$ and $\boldsymbol{y}^{(q)}$, respectively. At line 7 in Algorithm 1, $\tau$ reaches 1024 when $\mu =$DBL_MAX, meaning that $c^{(p)}$ and $c^{(q)}$ can be stored as 2-byte short integers. The splitting algorithm must satisfy the following properties:

1. If $\boldsymbol{x}^{(p)}{}_i$ and $\boldsymbol{y}^{(q)}{}_j$ are non-zero elements,

$$|\boldsymbol{x}^{(p)}{}_i| \geq |\boldsymbol{x}^{(p+1)}{}_i|, |\boldsymbol{y}^{(q)}{}_j| \geq |\boldsymbol{y}^{(q+1)}{}_j|$$

2. $(\boldsymbol{x}^{(p)})^T\boldsymbol{y}^{(q)}$ must be error-free in the FP32 computation:

$$(\boldsymbol{x}^{(p)})^T\boldsymbol{y}^{(q)} = \texttt{fl}_{\text{FP32}}((\boldsymbol{x}^{(p)})^T\boldsymbol{y}^{(q)}), 1 \leq p \leq s_x, 1 \leq q \leq s_y$$

Splitting can be understood as a translation from a floating-point representation to a fixed-point representation. The former of the above two properties means that the accuracy of the final result can be controlled (to lower accuracy) by omitting some split vectors from the lowest term. The accuracy of the final result obtainable with a certain number of split vectors depends on the length of the inner product and the range of the absolute values in each element of the input vectors. Note that to replace Tensor Cores by other FPUs with different precisions, we need to modify parameter $\rho$ in Algorithm 1, and the number of bits held in the split vectors ($\boldsymbol{x}^{(p)}$ and $\boldsymbol{y}^{(q)}$) depends on the precision of the FPUs.

**Step 2: Computation.** Next, the inner product $\boldsymbol{x}^T\boldsymbol{y}$ is computed as

$$\begin{aligned}
\boldsymbol{x}^T\boldsymbol{y} &= (2^{c^{(x_1)}}\boldsymbol{x}^{(1)} + 2^{c^{(x_2)}}\boldsymbol{x}^{(2)} + \cdots + 2^{c^{(x_{s_x})}}\boldsymbol{x}^{(s_x)})^T \\
&\quad (2^{c^{(y_1)}}\boldsymbol{y}^{(1)} + 2^{c^{(y_2)}}\boldsymbol{y}^{(2)} + \cdots + 2^{c^{(y_{s_y})}}\boldsymbol{y}^{(s_y)}) \\
&= 2^{c^{(x_1)}+c^{(y_1)}}\texttt{fl}_{\text{FP32}}((\boldsymbol{x}^{(1)})^T\boldsymbol{y}^{(1)}) + 2^{c^{(x_1)}+c^{(y_2)}}\texttt{fl}_{\text{FP32}}((\boldsymbol{x}^{(1)})^T\boldsymbol{y}^{(2)}) + \\
&\quad \cdots + 2^{c^{(x_1)}+c^{(y_{s_y})}}\texttt{fl}_{\text{FP32}}((\boldsymbol{x}^{(1)})^T\boldsymbol{y}^{(s_y)}) \\
&\quad + 2^{c^{(x_2)}+c^{(y_1)}}\texttt{fl}_{\text{FP32}}((\boldsymbol{x}^{(2)})^T\boldsymbol{y}^{(1)}) + 2^{c^{(x_2)}+c^{(y_2)}}\texttt{fl}_{\text{FP32}}((\boldsymbol{x}^{(2)})^T\boldsymbol{y}^{(2)}) + \\
&\quad \cdots + 2^{c^{(x_2)}+c^{(y_{s_y})}}\texttt{fl}_{\text{FP32}}((\boldsymbol{x}^{(2)})^T\boldsymbol{y}^{(s_y)}) \\
&\quad + \cdots \\
&\quad + 2^{c^{(x_{s_x})}+c^{(y_1)}}\texttt{fl}_{\text{FP32}}((\boldsymbol{x}^{(s_x)})^T\boldsymbol{y}^{(1)}) + 2^{c^{(x_{s_x})}+c^{(y_2)}}\texttt{fl}_{\text{FP32}}((\boldsymbol{x}^{(s_x)})^T\boldsymbol{y}^{(2)}) + \\
&\quad \cdots + 2^{c^{(x_{s_x})}+c^{(y_{s_y})}}\texttt{fl}_{\text{FP32}}((\boldsymbol{x}^{(s_x)})^T\boldsymbol{y}^{(s_y)})
\end{aligned}$$

Here, the computation of all-to-all inner products of the split vectors is performed: a total of $s_x s_y$ inner products are computed. $2^{c^{(x_p)}+c^{(y_q)}}$ is the upscaling factor that compensates the downscaling performed in the splitting process. By the second property of Algorithm 1, the inner products of the split vectors can be computed with Tensor Core operations because the inputs are stored in the FP16 format. When extending this example to matrix multiplication, the split matrices must be multiplied by the algorithm based on the standard inner product: divide-and-conquer approaches such as Strassen's algorithm are not permitted.

**Algorithm 2.** Matrix multiplication $C = AB$ ($A \in \mathbb{F}_{\text{FP64}}{}^{m \times k}$, $B \in \mathbb{F}_{\text{FP64}}{}^{k \times n}$, $C \in \mathbb{F}_{\text{FP64}}{}^{m \times n}$) with Ozaki scheme

---

1: **function** ($C = \text{DGEMM-TC}(m, n, k, A, B)$)
2:    $(A_{\text{split}}[1 : s_A], c_A[1 : s_A]) = \text{SplitA}(m, k, A)$    // $A_{\text{split}}$ is obtained on FP16
3:    $(B_{\text{split}}[1 : s_B], c_B[1 : s_B]) = \text{SplitB}(k, n, B)$    // $B_{\text{split}}$ is obtained on FP16
4:    $C_{ij} = 0$
5:    **for** $(q = 1 : s_B)$ **do**
6:       **for** $(p = 1 : s_A)$ **do**
7:          $C_{\text{tmp}} = \text{GEMM}_{\text{FP32}}(m, n, k, A_{\text{split}}[p], B_{\text{split}}[q])$
         // This can be performed using Tensor Cores as $A_{\text{split}}$ and $B_{\text{split}}$ are FP16
8:          $C_{ij} = C_{ij} + 2^{c_A[p]_i + c_B[q]_j} C_{\text{tmp}_{ij}}$
            // Computations for $1 \leq i \leq m$ and $1 \leq j \leq n$
9:       **end for**
10:   **end for**
11: **end function**

---

**Step 3: Summation.** Finally, the inner products of the split vectors are summed. The summation can be computed by FP64 arithmetic if the required accuracy is that of standard DGEMM. However, as $\text{fl}_{\text{FP32}}((x^{(p)})^T y^{(q)})$ in Step 2 has no rounding errors (being error-free), the correctly-rounded result of $x^T y$ can be obtained by summation with a correctly-rounded method such as Near-Sum [14]. The result is reproducible if the summation is performed by some reproducible method, even in FP64 arithmetic. As the summation is computed element-wise, the order of the computation is easily fixed.

**Whole Procedure on Matrix Multiplication.** Algorithm 2 computes the whole Ozaki scheme for matrix multiplication on Tensor Cores. Here, SplitA and SplitB perform the splitting in the inner product direction (along $k$-dimension) of matrices $A$ and $B$ respectively, using Algorithm 1. Note that as $A_{\text{split}}$ and $B_{\text{split}}$ can be stored on FP16, GEMM$_{\text{FP32}}$ can be performed by FP16 computations with FP32 precision on Tensor Cores through the cublasGemmEx routine in cuBLAS.

### 3.2   Fast Computation Techniques

To further improve the performance, the following methods modify Algorithm 1 or 2. Implementation-based speedup techniques that do not change the algorithm will be discussed in Sect. 4.

**Fast Mode.** As implemented in OzBLAS, we define a parameter $d \in \mathbb{N}, d \leq \max(s_x, s_y)$ that determines the number of split matrices in the computation. With $d$ specified, we can omit the computations $p + q > d + 1$ in $(x^{(p)})^T y^{(q)}$ in exchange for a small loss of accuracy. If the required accuracy is FP64 (equivalent to the standard DGEMM, as performed by the method that determines the

---

**Algorithm 3.** Determination of the number split matrices required to achieve the DGEMM equivalent accuracy with fast mode ($A \in \mathbb{F}_{\text{FP64}}{}^{m \times k}$, $B \in \mathbb{F}_{\text{FP64}}{}^{k \times n}$)

---

1: **function** ($d = \texttt{DetermineNumSplitMats}(m, n, k, A, B)$)
2:     ($A_{\text{split}}[1:s_A], c_A[1:s_A]) = \texttt{SplitA}(m, k, A)$     // from line 2 in Algorithm 2
3:     $e = (1, ..., 1)^T$
4:     $s = \texttt{fl}_{\text{FP64}}(2\sqrt{k}u_{\text{FP64}}(|A|(|B|e)))$
5:     $d = 2$
6:     **while** (1) **do**
7:         $t = \texttt{fl}_{\text{FP64}}((d+1)(|2^{c_A[d]_i}A_{\text{split}}[d]_{ij}|(|B|e)))$
8:         **if** ($s_i > t_i$ for $1 \leq i \leq m$) **then**
9:             **break**
10:         **end if**
11:         $d = d + 1$
12:     **end while**
13: **end function**

---

number of split matrices, described next), the accuracy loss is negligible. This technique reduces the number of matrix multiplications to $d(d+1)/2$ from $d^2$ at most.

**Estimating the Number of Split Matrices that Achieves FP64-equivalent Accuracy.** Splitting by Algorithm 1 automatically stops when $\mu = 0$; that is, when the accuracy of the final result is maximized. However, if the required accuracy is that of standard DGEMM performed on FP64 arithmetic (FP64-equivalent accuracy), we can estimate the minimum required number of splits by Algorithm 3 based on the probabilistic error bound [9] as

$$|\texttt{fl}_{\text{FP64}}(AB) - AB|e \lesssim 2\sqrt{k}u_{\text{FP64}}|A||B|e \tag{1}$$

where $e = (1, ..., 1)^T$ is introduced to avoid matrix multiplication in the estimation (note that at line 7 in Algorithm 3, $2^{c_A[d]_i}A_{\text{split}}[d]_{ij}$ is $d$-th non-downscaled split matrix stored on FP64. Hence, $\texttt{SplitA}$ at line 2 does not necessarily need to perform until $s_A$, and $\texttt{SplitA}$ and this algorithm can be integrated). This algorithm is designed to operate in fast mode. If the split number is determined such that Algorithm 1 executes until $\mu = 0$, the accuracy may be lower than that of standard DGEMM. In this case, we must disable the fast mode. Note that, a certain degree of difference between the desired (achieved by standard DGEMM) and obtained is expected in this method, because the number of split matrices is just estimated based on the probabilistic error bound, and will also be influenced by the vector $e$.

**Blocking Against Inner Product.** This step is not implemented in the present study. As $\rho$ in Algorithm 1 includes $n$, the dimension of the inner product, the number of splits required to achieve a certain accuracy depends on the inner-product-wise dimension of the matrix. Its increase can be avoided by employing a blocking strategy against the inner product-wise operations. The blocking size can be set to the minimum size that achieves the best performance. However, this strategy increases the summation cost; moreover, changing the block size may disturb the reproducibility except when the correctly-rounded computation is performed.

## 4  Implementation

### 4.1  Basic Design

Our DGEMM implementations, computing $C = \alpha AB + \beta C$, using Tensor Cores are referred to as DGEMM-TC, and two versions are implemented as described below.

- **DP-mode**: This mode achieves FP64-equivalent accuracy. The number of split matrices is determined automatically by Algorithm 3. Fast mode is automatically applied if possible. The summation is performed in FP64 arithmetic.
- **CR-mode**: This mode achieves the correctly-rounded result when $\alpha = 1$ and $\beta = 0$. The splitting iterates until all elements of the split matrices are zero. Fast mode is disabled. The summation is performed with NearSum when $\alpha = 1$ and $\beta = 0$ or in FP64 arithmetic in other cases.

We also implemented SGEMM-TC in SP-mode, which corresponds to the FP32 version of DGEMM-TC in DP-mode.

Our implementations are interface-compatible with the standard DGEMM and SGEMM routines, except for an argument for the pointer to a handler that holds some parameters including the address pointing to the working memory of the Ozaki scheme. The working memory is wholly allocated outside the BLAS routine to avoid the allocation time. The allocation is performed through a BLAS initialization function, which must be called in advance, similar to cublasInit in cuBLAS. In our implementation of Algorithm 1, max (at line 12) is obtained on the register through the shared memory, whereas $x$ is accessed at line 10. For downscaling (and upscaling in the summation), $2^n$ is computed by scalbn (double x, int n), a function that computes $2^n x$. In DP-mode, Algorithms 1 and 3 are performed simultaneously as the latter includes the former. The computation part is performed by cublasGemmEx, a matrix multiplication routine that uses Tensor Cores. This routine has several internal implementations[3], and can be selected as an argument. In this study, we used the default: CUBLAS_GEMM_DFALT_TENSOR_OP. $\alpha$ and $\beta$ are computed in the summation process.

### 4.2  Optimization

**Blocking to Reduce Memory Consumption.** Memory consumption is reduced by a blocking technique applied to the outer-product-wise direction

---

[3] The details are not presented.

(note that this blocking differs from the inner-product-wise blocking discussed in Subsect. 3.2). All procedures are blocked by dividing a matrix into a rectangle with block size $b_k$. In our implementation, the block size is determined as $b_k = \lceil n/\lceil n/b_{max} \rceil \rceil$. This blocking technique may reduce the performance, as the memory consumption shrinks towards $b_k = 1$, because each matrix multiplication more closely approaches the inner product.

**Further Performance Improvement.** Although not attempted in this study, the performance can be improved in several ways from an implementation technique perspective.

First, as implemented in OzBLAS, the computations of split matrices can be performed with batched BLAS (i.e., cublasGemmEx can be replaced with cublasGemmBatchedEx) because each matrix multiplication can be performed independently. We observed that the performance was improved when the matrix size was very small, or when the number of split matrices was relatively large, but was degraded in other cases.

Second, as discussed in the paper [13], a sufficiently sparse split matrix can be represented in sparse matrix form. Split matrices holding higher or lower bits of the input matrices may contain many zero elements. If a high-performance sparse matrix-matrix multiplication routine using Tensor Cores is provided, we might enhance the performance by switching the dense operation to a sparse operation.

### 4.3    Expected Performance and Memory Consumption

The most computationally complex part of matrix multiplication by this scheme is multiplying the split matrices using cublasGemmEx, which has $O(n^3)$ complexity. Ideally, the overall performance is thus determined by the number of GEMMs called in the computation and the GEMM throughput. For $d$ split matrices, the number of GEMM is $d^2$ in the standard method and $d(d+1)/2$ in fast mode. These values show how the performance overheads (in time) compare with that of a one-time execution of cublasGemmEx. However, our implementations contain several operations executed using FP64 FPUs. Whereas those portions have a computational complexity of $O(n^2)$ at most, they may affect the performance, if the hardware has limited FP64 support.

The memory consumption when $A \in \mathbb{F}_{FP64}{}^{m \times k}$ with $s_A$ split matrices and $B \in \mathbb{F}_{FP64}{}^{k \times n}$ with $s_B$ split matrices in the naive implementation (i.e., without the blocking technique) is $(s_A m + s_B n)k$ on FP16 for storing the split matrices. As shown in Algorithm 2, if the summation is performed immediately after each GEMM execution, $C_{tmp}$ requires $mn$ storage on FP32; however, in our implementation, owing to the convenience of implementing NearSum in CR-mode, all computation results are retained, requiring $s_A s_B mn$ of storage. After applying the blocking technique with block size $b_k$ in both the $m$ and $n$ dimensions, the memory consumption reduces to $(s_A + s_B)kb_k + s_A s_B b_k{}^2$ $(0 < b_k \leq m, n)$. On the other hand, as the $s_A$ and $s_B$ are unknown before execution and the working memory is allocated before execution to avoid the memory allocation time, a certain amount of memory must be allocated at initialization. We then determine the maximum possible block size under the memory constraint. In addition to the above, several working memory spaces are needed. The memory consumption of our implementation is not yet optimized and should be improved in future work.

## 5   Evaluation

### 5.1   Experimental Settings

The performance was mainly evaluated on NVIDIA Titan RTX, a Turing architecture GPU with a compute capability of 7.5. The theoretical peak performance (with a boost clock of 1.77 GHz[4]) is 509.76 GFlops on FP64, 16312.32 GFlops on FP32, and 130498.56 GFlops[5] on Tensor Cores with FP32 precision. This GPU has more limited FP64 support than the Tesla series targeting HPC workloads (1/32 of FP32 and 1/256 of Tensor Cores). The memory is 24 GB GDDR6 at 672.0 GB/s. The host machine was equipped with an Intel Core i7-5930K CPU running CentOS Linux release 8.1.1911 (4.18.0-147.3.1.el8_1.x86_64), CUDA 10.2, and CUDA driver version 440.44. The GPU codes were compiled by nvcc release 10.2, V10.2.89 with compiler options "-O3 -gencode arch=compute_60, code=sm_75".

Further evaluations were conducted on NVIDIA Tesla V100 (PCIe 32GB), which offers rich FP64 support (1/2 of FP32 and 1/16 of Tensor Cores). The Tesla V100 is a Volta architecture GPU with compute capability 7.0, and its theoretical peak performance (with a boost clock of 1.38 GHz) is 7065.6 GFlops on FP64, 14131.2 GFlops on FP32, and 113049.6 GFlops on Tensor Cores with FP32 precision. The memory is 32 GB HBM2 at 898.0 GB/s. The host machine was equipped with an Intel Xeon Gold 6126 CPU running Red Hat Enterprise Linux Server release 7.7 (3.10.0-1062.18.1.el7.x86_64), CUDA 10.2, and CUDA driver version 440.33.01. The codes for this GPU were compiled by nvcc release 10.2, V10.2.89 with "-O3 -gencode arch=compute_60, code=sm_70".

For accurate evaluation, we averaged the results of 10 executions after three warm-up executions. In our proposed method, the number of split matrices required to achieve a certain accuracy depends on the range of the absolute values in each element of the input matrices. To observe the performance degradation arising from this range, we initialized the input matrices with $(\text{rand} - 0.5) \times \exp(\phi \times \text{randn})$, where $\text{rand}$ is a uniform random number $[0, 1)$ and $\text{randn}$ is a random number selected from the standard normal distribution. The range of the absolute value of the input can be controlled by $\phi$, and is widened by increasing $\phi$. For example, fixing $m = n = k = 10240$ and varying $\phi = 0.1$, 1, and 2, the ranges were obtained as 9.8E−10 – 8.9E−01, 1.4E−09 – 1.6E+02,

---

[4] The actual clock can exceed the boost clock, depending on the individual product and the execution environment.

[5] 576 (Tensor Cores) × 1.77 (GHz) ×2 × $4^3$ (Flops) = 130498.56 (GFlops).

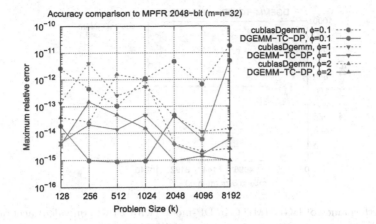

**Fig. 3.** Accuracy of cublasDgemm and DGEMM-TC in DP mode on Titan RTX. The maximum relative error is plotted against the results of MPFR 2048-bit. $\phi$ varies the range of the input values.

and 4.4E−10 − 4.8E+04, respectively. In all experiments, we allocated 20 GB to the working memory, and set the maximum block size to $b_k = 3584$. The scalar parameters were set as $\alpha = 1$ and $\beta = 0$.

## 5.2  DGEMM-TC

Figure 3 shows the accuracies of cublasDgemm and DGEMM-TC in DP-mode (DGEMM-TC-DP) for various input ranges (collected with different $\phi$ values) on Titan RTX. The maximum relative error is compared with the result of 2048-bit MPFR[6] [5] on FP64 (the results of MPFR are rounded to FP64). As the CR-mode with NearSum always obtained "zero," meaning that all the results were correctly-rounded, its results are omitted from Fig. 3. The accuracy of our implementation (solid lines) was equivalent to that of cublasDgemm (dotted lines), but some differences were observed, because our method (Algorithm 3) simply estimates the minimum number of split matrices that ensure similar accuracy to the classic DGEMM based on a probabilistic error bound of GEMM. The estimation further roughened by the $e = (1, ..., 1)^T$ term that avoids matrix multiplications in the estimation.

Figure 4 shows the performance of DGEMM-TC in DP-mode (with FP64-equivalent accuracy) for the $\phi$ values. "Flops (on DP)" is the number of floating-point operations on FP64 per second when viewed as the standard DGEMM (i.e., it is computed as $2mnk/t$, where $t$ denotes the execution time in seconds). Although the theoretical peak performance of the GPU on FP64 was only 510 GFlops (539 GFlops was observed on cublasDgemm with GPU boost), our implementation achieved up to approximately 980 GFlops (when $n = 7168$), outperforming cublasDgemm.

---

[6] http://www.mpfr.org.

242     D. Mukunoki et al.

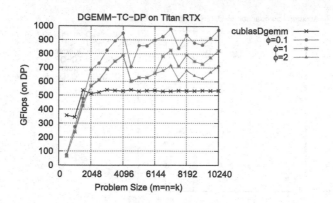

**Fig. 4.** Performance of DGEMM-TC in DP-mode (with FP64-equivalent accuracy) on Titan RTX. "Flops (on DP)" is the number of FP64 floating-point operations corresponding to the standard DGEMM. $\phi$ varies the range of the input values.

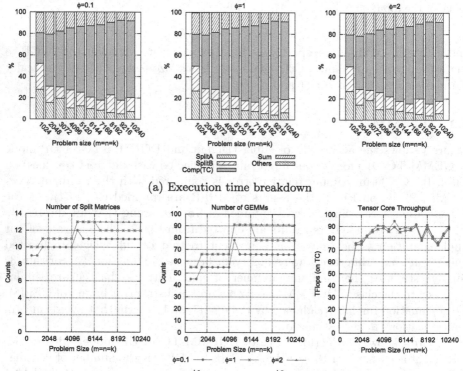

(a) Execution time breakdown

(b) The number of split matrices[†1] and GEMMs[†2] and Tensor Core throughput

**Fig. 5.** Details of DGEMM-TC in DP-mode (with FP64-equivalent accuracy) on Titan RTX. $\phi$ varies the range of the input values. †1: The same line plots the values of matrices $A$ and $B$. †1†2: Average over all blocks.

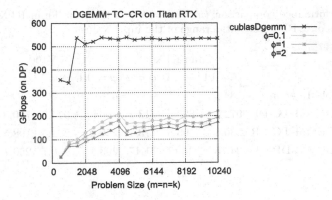

**Fig. 6.** Performance of DGEMM-TC in CR-mode (correctly-rounded) on Titan RTX. "Flops (on DP)" is the number of FP64 floating-point operations corresponding to the standard DGEMM. $\phi$ varies the range of the input values.

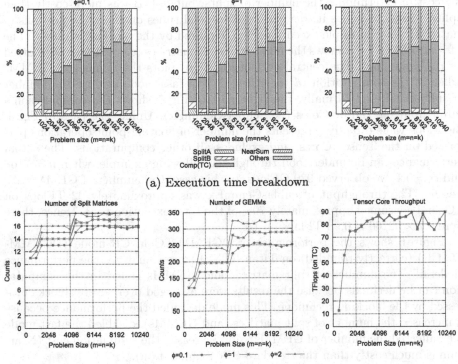

(a) Execution time breakdown

(b) The number of split matrices[†1] and GEMMs[†2] and Tensor Core throughput

**Fig. 7.** Details of DGEMM-TC in CR-mode (correctly-rounded) on Titan RTX. $\phi$ varies the range of the input values. †1: The same line plots the values of matrices $A$ and $B$. †1†2: Average over all blocks.

**Table 1.** Performance comparison ($m = n = k = 10240$) on Titan RTX and Tesla V100 (GFlops on DP). $\phi$ varies the range of the input values.

| | Titan RTX | | | Tesla V100 | | |
|---|---|---|---|---|---|---|
| | $\phi = 0.1$ | $\phi = 1$ | $\phi = 2$ | $\phi = 0.1$ | $\phi = 1$ | $\phi = 2$ |
| cublasDgemm | 534.1 | | | 6761 | | |
| DGEMM-TC-DP | 972.4 | 823.0 | 713.1 | 1064 | 914.3 | 790.8 |
| DGEMM-TC-CR | 220.4 | 193.5 | 173.1 | 255.0 | 222.5 | 198.5 |
| DGEMM-DP-CR | 24.75 | 21.17 | 21.17 | 293.1 | 250.7 | 250.7 |

Additional performance analyses are shown in Fig. 5. Panel (a) shows the execution time breakdown for $\phi = 0.1$–2, observed in the tenth (final) execution. The execution time was dominated by the Tensor Cores computations. The splitting execution SplitA was slightly slower than SplitB because it included the cost of determining the number of splits, but SplitB was more costly than SplitA overall, because it was performed several times on the same portions of matrix $B$. Such multiple executions were required by the blocking strategy. The left part of Fig. 5 (b) shows the number of split matrices ($d$) of $A$ and $B$ (plotted by the same line). The central part of Fig. 5 (b) plots the number of GEMMs called in the computation ($d^2$ or $d(d + 1)/2$ in fast mode against the number of split matrices $d$. Finally, the right part of Fig. 5 shows the computational throughput on Tensor Cores (i.e., cublasGemmEx). Unlike the case in Fig. 4, the Flops value directly represents the number of floating-point operations performed on the Tensor Cores, and excludes all other computations. The actual performance can be understood through the following example: when $n = 7168$ and $\phi = 0.1$, we observed 980 GFlops. In this case, the number of GEMM calls was 66. The throughput of cublasGemmEx was approximately 92 TFlops on TC, and consumed approximately 70% of the total execution time. Hence, there were $0.7 \times 92/66 \approx 0.98$ TFlops on DP.

Figure 6 shows the performance of DGEMM-TC in CR-mode (DGEMM-TC-CR) (correctly-rounded) on Titan RTX. Figure 7 analyzes the performance in detail. The number of split matrices and GEMMs called in the computation can be decimals because the results were averaged over several blocks processed by the blocking technique. This mode degraded the performance because it increased the number of split matrices (and GEMMs), disabled the fast mode (i.e., affected the number of GEMMs), and increased the summation cost (Near-Sum is much costly than the standard FP64 summation).

Finally, Table 1 summarizes the performances of DGEMM-TC with $m = n = k = 10240$ on Titan RTX and on Tesla V100, which has rich FP64 support. For comparison, we also show the performance of a correctly-rounded DGEMM implementation (DGEMM-DP-CR), which is based on the Ozaki scheme but uses cublasDgemm instead of cublasGemmEx (hence, the computation was performed using FP64 instead of Tensor Cores). On Tesla V100, DGEMM-TC in DP-mode could not accelerate cublasDgemm.

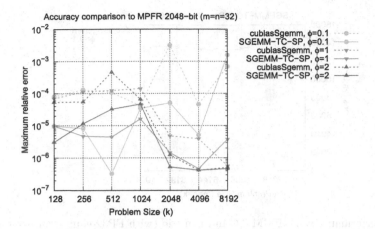

**Fig. 8.** Accuracy of cublasSgemm and SGEMM-TC in SP mode on Titan RTX. The maximum relative error is plotted against the results of MPFR 2048-bit. $\phi$ varies the range of the input values.

### 5.3    SGEMM-TC

Figure 8 shows the accuracy of cublasSgemm and SGEMM-TC in SP-mode for various input ranges (controlled by varying $\phi$) on Titan RTX. The results are compared on FP32 (the results of MPFR are rounded to FP32).

Figure 9 shows the performance of SGEMM-TC in SP-mode. Similarly to DGEMM-TC on Tesla V100, our proposed method was useless for accelerating SGEMM on this GPU with fast FP32 support, but outperformed DGEMM-TC. The reason for the superior performance is not discernible from Fig. 9; however, the number of split matrices decreased, and the execution time of the splitting and summation parts was reduced in SGEMM-TC.

## 6    Discussion

This section discusses perspectives for introducing our proposed approach into hardware design. Although our method is limited to inner product based computations, it extends the application range of hardware with limited (or no) FP32/FP64 resources and fast low-precision processing units for general purpose workloads. Consequently, we can consider reducing the number of FP64 (or even FP32) FPUs, as discussed by Domke et al. [3], by exchanging them with low-precision FPUs such as Tensor Cores. Our rationale is supported by the following situations.

- The demand for AI workloads not requiring FP64 is increasing, and such work is becoming a significant part of the total workloads of HPC systems.
- The performance of large-scale computations is becoming communication-bound as the degree of parallelism of HPC systems increases.

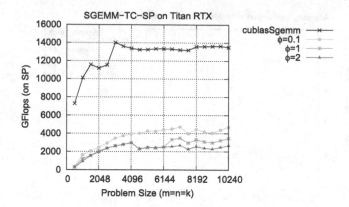

**Fig. 9.** Performance of SGEMM-TC in SP-mode (with FP32-equivalent accuracy) on Titan RTX. "Flops (on SP)" is the number of FP32 floating-point operations corresponding to the standard SGEMM. $\phi$ varies the range of the input values.

– The need for FP64 performance has reduced under the advance of mixed-precision techniques such as iterative refinement and precision-tuning.
– Low-precision hardware is easier to implement than high-precision hardware. In general, the complexity of $p$-bit precision hardware is $O(p^2)$. Currently, most processors only exploit the $O(p)$ benefit of instruction-level parallelism in single-instruction-multiple-data (SIMD) vectorization.
– Field-programmable gate arrays (FPGAs) are becoming a promising platform for HPC. Computations that do not fit into general processors can be accommodated by FPGAs. For instance, FPGAs can cover any "niche" demands for FP64 in future.

Accurate and high-precision computational methods, such as the proposed method and the other methods introduced in Sect. 2, may satisfy the "averaged" demand for the workloads requiring FP64 operations on an HPC system. Particularly in memory-bound operations, sufficient performance may be delivered by limited FP64 performance on hardware, or by software emulation of FP64 through multi-precision techniques; for example, "double-float" arithmetic as a float version of double-double arithmetic.

We now propose some hardware designs based on the Ozaki scheme. As described in Subsect. 3.1, the core concept of the Ozaki scheme is error-free transformation, which is similar to conversion from a matrix represented by floating-point numbers to matrices represented by fixed-point numbers. Accordingly, the length of the significand bit is important, and the exponent can be computed separately. Fast integer matrix multiplication (i.e., fast Arithmetic Logic Units) is desired for such a scheme because it requires fewer split matrices than the floating-point format for the same bit length. Moreover, this study effectively utilizes the Tensor Core design that computes FP16 data with FP32 precision and returns the result on FP32. Although the same idea can be implemented on standard FP16 FPUs, which adopt FP16 for both data format and computation, this implementation would increase the number of split matrices that achieve a given accuracy. This situation is worsened on BF16 FPUs, which have fewer significand bits. From this perspective, FPUs like the FP64 version of Tensor Cores are desired; as it computes $d = a \times b + c$ with FP64 accuracy, where $a$ and $b$ are FP32 and $c$ and $d$ are FP64. Such FPUs can adequately substitute full FP64 FPUs with the Ozaki scheme on DGEMM.

# 7  Conclusion

This paper presented an implementation technique for DGEMM and SGEMM using Tensor Cores that compute FP16 inputs with FP32 precision. Our method is based on the Ozaki scheme and is built upon cublasGemmEx, a GEMM implementation in cuBLAS performed on Tensor Cores. Besides providing a DGEMM and SGEMM compatible interface with equivalent accuracy, our technique can support accurate (correctly-rounded) and reproducible computations. The performance of our method depends on the range of the absolute values in each element of the input matrices. For instance, when matrices were initialized with random numbers over a dynamic range of 1E+9, and our DGEMM implementation with FP64-equivalent accuracy was run on Titan RTX with 130 TFlops on Tensor Cores, the highest achievement was approximately 980 GFlops of FP64 operation, although cublasDgemm can achieve only 539 GFlops on FP64 FPUs. The proposed method enhances the possibility of utilizing hardware with limited (or no) FP32/FP64 resources and fast low-precision processing units (such as AI-oriented processors) for general-purpose workloads. Furthermore, because the proposed method reduces the demand for FP64 FPUs in exchange for lower-precision FPUs, it will contribute to new perspectives of future hardware designs. Our code is available on our webpage[7].

**Acknowledgment.** This research was partially supported by the Japan Society for the Promotion of Science (JSPS) KAKENHI Grant Number 19K20286 and MEXT as "Exploratory Issue on Post-K computer" (Development of verified numerical computations and super high-performance computing environment for extreme researches). We thank Takeshi Terao (Shibaura Institute of Technology) for his helpful suggestion for the idea of the blocking toward inner product. This research used computational resources of Cygnus (for Tesla V100) provided by Multidisciplinary Cooperative Research Program in Center for Computational Sciences, University of Tsukuba.

# References

1. Carson, E., Higham, N.: Accelerating the solution of linear systems by iterative refinement in three precisions. SIAM J. Sci. Comput. **40**(2), A817–A847 (2018)
2. Dekker, T.J.: A floating-point technique for extending the available precision. Numerische Mathematik **18**, 224–242 (1971)

---

[7] http://www.math.twcu.ac.jp/ogita/post-k/results.html.

3. Domke, J., et al.: Double-precision FPUs in high-performance computing: an embarrassment of riches? In: Proceedings 33rd IEEE International Parallel and Distributed Processing Symposium (IPDPS 2019), pp. 78–88 (2019)
4. Dongarra, J.J., Du Croz, J., Hammarling, S., Duff, I.S.: A set of level 3 basic linear algebra subprograms. ACM Trans. Math. Softw. **16**(1), 1–17 (1990)
5. Fousse, L., Hanrot, G., Lefèvre, V., Pélissier, P., Zimmermann, P.: MPFR: a multiple-precision binary floating-point library with correct rounding. ACM Trans. Math. Softw. **33**(2), 13:1–13:15 (2007)
6. Haider, A., et al.: The design of fast and energy-efficient linear solvers: on the potential of half-precision arithmetic and iterative refinement techniques. In: Shi, Y., et al. (eds.) ICCS 2018. LNCS, vol. 10860, pp. 586–600. Springer, Cham (2018). https://doi.org/10.1007/978-3-319-93698-7_45
7. Haidar, A., Tomov, S., Dongarra, J., Higham, N.J.: Harnessing GPU tensor cores for fast FP16 arithmetic to speed up mixed-precision iterative refinement solvers. In: Proceedings International Conference for High Performance Computing, Networking, Storage, and Analysis (SC 2018), pp. 47:1–47:11 (2018)
8. Henry, G., Tang, P.T.P., Heinecke, A.: Leveraging the bfloat16 artificial intelligence datatype for higher-precision computations. In: Proceedings 26th IEEE Symposium on Computer Arithmetic (ARITH-26), pp. 69–76 (2019)
9. Higham, N.J., Mary, T.: A new approach to probabilistic rounding error analysis. SIAM J. Sci. Comput. **41**(5), A2815–A2835 (2019)
10. Ichimura, S., Katagiri, T., Ozaki, K., Ogita, T., Nagai, T.: Threaded accurate matrix-matrix multiplications with sparse matrix-vector multiplications. In: Proceedings 32nd IEEE International Parallel and Distributed Processing Symposium Workshops (IPDPSW). pp. 1093–1102 (2018)
11. Markidis, S., Chien, S.W.D., Laure, E., Peng, I.B., Vetter, J.S.: NVIDIA tensor core programmability, performance precision. In: Proceedings 32nd IEEE International Parallel and Distributed Processing Symposium Workshops (IPDPSW), pp. 522–531 (2018)
12. Mukunoki, D., Ogita, T., Ozaki, K.: Reproducible BLAS routines with tunable accuracy using ozaki scheme for many-core architectures. In: Proceedings 13th International Conference on Parallel Processing and Applied Mathematics (PPAM2019), Lecture Notes in Computer Science, vol. 12043, pp. 516–527 (2020)
13. Ozaki, K., Ogita, T., Oishi, S., Rump, S.M.: Error-free transformations of matrix multiplication by using fast routines of matrix multiplication and its applications. Numer. Algorithms **59**(1), 95–118 (2012)
14. Rump, S., Ogita, T., Oishi, S.: Accurate floating-point summation part ii: Sign, k-fold faithful and rounding to nearest. SIAM J. Sci. Comput. **31**(2), 1269–1302 (2009)
15. Sorna, A., Cheng, X., D'Azevedo, E., Won, K., Tomov, S.: Optimizing the fast fourier transform using mixed precision on tensor core hardware. In: Proceedings 25th IEEE International Conference on High Performance Computing Workshops (HiPCW), pp. 3–7 (2018)
16. Yang, K., Chen, Y.F., Roumpos, G., Colby, C., Anderson, J.: High performance monte carlo simulation of ising model on TPU clusters. In: Proceedings International Conference for High Performance Computing, Networking, Storage and Analysis (SC 2019), pp. 83:1–83:15 (2019)

# HPC Applications

# Using High-Level Synthesis to Implement the Matrix-Vector Multiplication on FPGA

Alessandro Marongiu and Paolo Palazzari[✉]

ENEA - Italian National Agency for New Technologies, Energy and Sustainable Economic Development, C.R ENEA Casaccia, Rome, Italy
paolo.palazzari@enea.it

**Abstract.** This work presents how to implement the Matrix-Vector Multiplication (MVM) onto FPGA through the QuickPlay High-Level Synthesis flow. The motivations arise from the Adaptive Optics field, where the MVM is the core of the real-time control algorithm which controls the mirrors of a telescope to compensate for the effects of the atmospheric turbulence. The proposed implementation of the MVM exploits four different levels of parallelism: spatial and pipeline parallelism are used both at the fine (scalar instructions) and at the coarse (vector instructions) levels. To characterize the architecture being developed, a performance model has been developed and validated through the actual results obtained from runs on a prototype board based on the Intel ARRIA10 FPGA. Some details are given to describe how the algorithm has been implemented using the QuickPlay HLS flow. Performance results are presented, in terms of sustained computational speed and resources used in the hardware implementation.

## 1 Introduction

In the framework of the research project Green Flash [1], we developed the work presented in this paper, aimed at efficiently implementing the Matrix-Vector Multiplication (MVM) on the FPGA technology. As discussed in [2–5], in Adaptive Optics (AO) the effect of the atmospheric turbulence is compensated using the mobile mirrors in the telescope, which are moved according to a given real-time control algorithm. The dominating part of such an algorithm, see technical annex of the project [1], is the execution of two MVMs, namely $s_k{}^* = Mv_k$ and $w_k = Rs_k^{pol}$.

In this paper we illustrate how we used QuickPlay [6], a High-Level Synthesis (HLS) design flow, to efficiently implement the MVM on FPGA. Representing one of the Level-2 BLAS functions [7], MVM is the basis for many algebraic computations and it is fundamental in many application domains. We underline that we see the presented work as a template of the methodology to be adopted when using HLS.

We start describing the problem to be solved, together with the constraints imposed by the challenges on the architecture to be implemented. Next, we present the formulation of the solution, explaining how parallelism should be exploited to obtain an efficient implementation. The implementation we propose in this paper uses four levels of parallelism: as the MVM is a collection of many independent scalar products, we introduce

© Springer Nature Switzerland AG 2020
P. Sadayappan et al. (Eds.): ISC High Performance 2020, LNCS 12151, pp. 251–269, 2020.
https://doi.org/10.1007/978-3-030-50743-5_13

pipeline and spatial parallelism both at the coarse level (parallelization among different scalar products) and at the fine level (parallelization within the computation of one scalar product). A performance model is derived to quantify the performance achievable through the proposed implementation: this phase is crucial to validate the performance of the HLS. When using HLS, it is crucial the preliminary determination of what can be achieved, checking after the synthesis that the results produced by the automated synthesis process comply with expectations: in lack of this modeling phase, we should rely only on comparisons with other implementations to (indirectly) evaluate the implementation produced by HLS. In this paper, the emphasis is put mainly on the evaluation of the quality of the implementation derived from the HLS flow, as we are not trying to assess the superiority of a given technology against another: discussing FPGA vs GPU is not the aim of this paper. For this reason, we put much effort into the modeling of the performance which can be theoretically achieved, to have an absolute criterion to evaluate the quality of the FPGA implementation: the closer is the performance to the theoretical forecast, the better it is.

The document is concluded with the presentation of the results, in terms of performance achieved in actual runs (GFlop/s) and resource used (LUT, memory blocks, DSP).

## 2 Related Work

Due to its relevance in many domains, the implementation of the MVM has been widely investigated; in particular, how to efficiently implement the operation on the FPGA technology has been investigated. In [8] the authors present a comparison of the implementation of the MVM, the gaxpy operation, on FPGA, GPU and CPU. They describe the FPGA implementation, organizing the internal dual-ported memories as V row banks which store the rows of the matrix; each of these banks is composed by B banks which store in an interleaved way the rows mapped into the row bank; thanks to this organization, at each clock cycle $V \times B$ elements can be read and written from and to the memory. These elements can feed $Q \leq V$ pipelined modules, each one computing a B-size scalar product. The work is further improved in [9], where the management of large external memory is added. In [10, 11] the FPGA implementation of the BLAS operations is discussed, with a special focus on the implementation of the reduction circuit needed in the accumulation involved in each BLAS operation. The authors in [12] report the FPGA implementation of the MVM and matrix-matrix product with a detailed analysis of the error propagation in the accumulation phase. Considering that the MVM problem is I/O bound and there is no benefit in increasing the parallelism beyond the I/O saturation, the authors propose to use some logic to implement the group-alignment based floating-point summation [13], which increases the numerical accuracy of the computation. The FPGA implementation of the BLAS is reported in [14]. In this work, while relying on the OpenCL framework [15] for the actual FPGA implementation, the authors give a detailed performance model to drive the selection of the parameters determining the tradeoff between speed and resource performance. Using the selected parameters, some code generators are activated to generate the OpenCL description of the optimized BLAS routine. The reader interested in the implementation of the MVM on GPU technology can refer to [16], which presents an analysis of the MVM implementation on GPU, together with a detailed performance model.

## 3    Problem Definition

The MVM is the basic operation to perform the Wavefront Reconstruction control algorithm; its usage is well known in the Adaptive Optics community and dates back to the late '80 s [17] and has been successively improved many times [2]. In our implementation, using single-precision floating-point arithmetic, we have to multiply two matrices $M[N_{means}, N_{rec}]$ and $R[N_{rec}, N_{means}]$ with the vectors $v_k[N_{rec}], s_k[N_{means}]$, being $N_{means} = 9232$ and $N_{rec} = 6316$.

Due to their size, $M$ and $R$ are stored in external memory. $M$ and $R$ do not change for a quite long time and must be multiplied many times by vectors $v_k$ and $s_k$; processing step $(k + 1)$ can start only when the $k^{th}$ step has finished.

Once the bandwidth BW to access the external memory is fixed, an upper bound for the speed of the computation is determined. To perform the MVM, the matrix must be read from the memory; when we refer to a generic matrix $M[n, m]$ and we indicate with D the floating-point data size expressed in bytes (in single-precision $D = 4$, in double-precision $D = 8$), the matrix size is $M_s = nmD$ [Bytes] and the time to read the matrix from external memory is

$$t_R = nmD/BW. \tag{1}$$

As the number of operations performed in the MVM is $n_{ops} = 2\ nm$ and the overall computing time cannot be smaller than $t_R$, the computing speed $S_C$ cannot be larger than $n_{ops}/t_R$ i.e.,

$$S_C \leq \frac{n_{ops}}{t_R} = \frac{2nm}{\frac{nmD}{BW}} = \frac{2BW}{D}. \tag{2}$$

Using single-precision floating-point, $D = 4$, the speed can never be greater than half of the available memory BW.

In the following sections, we will analyze how the MVM should be implemented to be as close as possible to the previous limit.

## 4    Guidelines for Implementation: Exploiting Coarse-Grained Parallelism

The MVM $b = M \times a$ $(M[n, m], a[m], b[n])$ is the collection of n independent scalar products between m-sized vectors i.e.,

$$b_i = m_i \cdot a\ i = 0, 1, \ldots, n - 1;\ b_i \in \mathbb{R};\ m_i \in \mathbb{R}^m;\ a \in \mathbb{R}^m. \tag{3}$$

Let's implement, in an optimized way, a kernel SP which performs a certain number of scalar products between one vector $a$ and several vectors read from the external memory; if we have $p$ external memory banks, we can partition[1] $\mathbf{M}$ in $p$ equal parts $\mathbf{M_p}$, each containing n/$p$ different matrix lines $\mathbf{m_{p,i}}$ with p = 0, 1, ..., $p - 1$ and i = 0, 1, ..., n/$p$ − 1 (each line is an m-sized vector), storing each $\mathbf{M_p}$ into a different memory bank. We instantiate $p$ replicas of the SP scalar product kernel and we distribute a copy of the $\mathbf{a}$ vector, to be read once, to all the SP kernels. Each SP kernel computes a portion $\mathbf{b_p}$ of the $\mathbf{b}$ result vector. The final vector is obtained properly merging (i.e., concatenating) all the $\mathbf{b_p}$ sub-vectors.

The degree of parallelism $p$ is selected to make (nearly) equal the BW requirement with the BW available toward the external memory (BW$_{\text{ExtMem}}$); let's indicate with BW$_{\text{req}}$ the memory bandwidth requested by the SP kernel (BW$_{\text{req}}$ will be quantified in the following).

The memory bandwidth required by the $p$ SP kernels is $p \times$ BW$_{\text{req}}$ and must be large enough to saturate BW$_{\text{ExtMem}}$ i.e., BW$_{\text{ExtMem}} \approx p \times$ BW$_{\text{req}}$ which gives

$$p \approx \text{BW}_{\text{ExtMem}}/\text{BW}_{\text{req}}. \qquad (4)$$

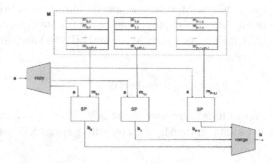

**Fig. 1.** Coarse-grained parallel architecture to implement the MVM

In the following, when giving numerical examples, we use the parameters characterizing the μXComp board, developed by MicroGate and equipped with an Intel ARRIA 10 GX1150 FPGA [18]. Referring to the previous example and to the four Hyper Memory Cube (HMC) banks present in the μXComp board (each HMC bank has a peak BW of 17 GB/s), BW$_{\text{ExtMem}}$ = 68 GB/s. In our implementation of the SP kernel BW$_{\text{req}}$ = 19.2 GB/s, so the degree of parallelism that can be efficiently supported is given by Eq. (4) which yields $p \approx 4$. Therefore, four SP kernels can be instantiated, each one accessing a different HMC bank.

## 5    The Scalar Product: Basic Pipelined Implementation

As a consequence of the discussion of the previous section, we recognize the scalar product as our coarse grain unit of parallelism. The scalar product can be implemented

---

[1] Let's assume n to be multiple of $p$; should this not being the case, (n%$p$) sets would have $\lfloor n/p \rfloor + 1$ lines and the remaining sets would contain $\lfloor n/p \rfloor$ lines.

with one pipelined MADD (one multiplier and one adder) which iteratively computes the recurrence

$$s_{i+1} = a_i \times b_i + s_i \quad i = 0, \ldots, n-1 \text{ with } s_0 = 0, a_i \in a, b_i \in b.$$

The computation of the next MADD operation is dependent on the completion of the previous operation, so a new MADD cannot start until the previous has finished, thus waiting for the latency L of the MADD.

To avoid paying this penalty, we can exploit the commutativity and associativity of the ADD operation (let us neglect the effects of the limited precision). Under the commutative and associative hypothesis for the ADD and assuming m to be an integer multiple of L, we can rewrite the scalar product as in the following

$$s = \sum_{i=0}^{m-1} (a_i \cdot b_i) = \sum_{i=0}^{L-1} \left( \sum_{j=0}^{\frac{m}{L}-1} a_{jL+i} \cdot b_{jL+i} \right) \tag{5}$$

where

- vectors **a** and **b** have been partitioned into L sub-vectors $a_i$ and $b_i$,
- L partial scalar products are computed (expression in brackets) and finally
- the result is derived by summing the L partial scalar products (external sum).

In the previous formulation, each partial scalar product has to be updated every L clock cycles; during its processing (requiring L cycles), the other L-1 partial scalar products will be processed, each one being at a different stage of the pipeline. Only the final (i.e., the external) sum requires the accumulation of values where the dependence cannot be completely hidden, thus imposing the payment of some pipeline penalty.

Following the previous approach, we can compute the scalar product in $N_{clk}$ clock cycles, as follows

$$N_{clk} = (m-1) + L + O(L_A * \log(L)) \tag{6}$$

where $(m-1) + L$, are the cycles needed to compute the m MADD operations and $O(L_A * \log(L))$ are the cycles needed to perform the final sum of the L partial scalar products ($L_A$ is the latency of the pipelined add operator) using L/2 adders; if $m \gg L$, $N_{clk} \approx m$. In our case $m \gg L$, so we compute the 2 m operations required by the scalar product in $N_{clk} \approx m$ clock cycles, thus sustaining 2 FP operations per cycle. The sustained speed of the computation is $S_C = 2f_{ck} = 300$ MFlop/s for $f_{ck} = 150$ MHz.

As seen in the previous section, to sustain the speed of the computation $S_C$ we must have a BW toward the memory which is at least twice the numerical value of $S_C$ (Eq. 2)). In this case, the memory BW required by the kernel would be $BW_{req} = 2 * S_C = 2 * 300 = 600$ MB/s. Referring to the BW of the HMC memory we are using ($\approx 6$ GB/s), to saturate the memory BW we should put $p = 68/0.6 = 112$ kernels in parallel, which would require 112 ports to access the external memory module: this huge number of ports is not realistic, so we have to find a way to increase the computational speed of the kernel which performs the basic scalar product, in order to use, with the $BW_{req}$ of a single kernel, a significant portion of the available memory BW.

# 6  The Scalar Product: Exploiting Spatial Parallelism

To increase the computational speed and the $BW_{req}$ of the kernel which computes the scalar product, we could further partition each of the L sub-vectors into P sub-vectors so that, at each cycle, we can start computing P independent partial scalar products.

Let's rewrite the Eq. (5) as in the following

$$s = \sum_{i=0}^{m-1} (a_i \cdot b_i) = \sum_{i=0}^{L-1} \sum_{j=0}^{P-1} \left( \sum_{k=0}^{\frac{m}{LP}-1} a_{iP+j+kLP} \cdot b_{iP+j+kLP} \right) \quad (7)$$

where vectors **a** and **b** have been partitioned into LP sub-vectors, each with m/(LP) elements; the generic sub-vector $\mathbf{v_{ij}}$ is defined as

$$\mathbf{v_{ij}} = \left\{ v_{iP+j+kLP} \mid k = 0, 1, \ldots, m/LP \right\} \quad i = 0, 1, \ldots, L-1 \quad j = 0, 1, \cdots, P-1.$$

Once partitioned **a** and **b** into the LP sub-vectors $\mathbf{a_{ij}}$ and $\mathbf{b_{ij}}$, we compute the LP partial scalar products $s_{ij}$ (expression in brackets in (7)), then we sum all the LP partial values to obtain the final result.

Using P MADDs, if we can read 2P floating-point values per cycle, the number of cycles to determine the LP partial scalar products is given by

$$N_{comp} = \left[ \left( \frac{m}{P} - 1 \right) + L \right]. \quad (8)$$

In fact, after L clock cycles, P MADD results are produced; the remaining (m – P) MADD results are produced in the following (m – P)/P cycles, as P new results are produced at every cycle.

Once generated the N = LP $s_{ij}$ values, they must be summed together to obtain the final scalar product.

As already discussed, we can use N/2 adders to perform the sum of N numbers in $[log_2(N)]L_A$ clock cycles. If we use $P_A < N$ adders, in each layer we can parallelize the sums among all the $P_A$ adders. It's easy to verify that the number of cycles to compute the sum of N = LP numbers using $P_A$ pipelined adders is given by

$$NCycles_{sum}(P_A) = \sum_{i=1}^{\lceil log_2(N) \rceil} \left( \left\lceil \frac{N}{2^i} \frac{1}{P_A} \right\rceil + L_A \right) \approx \frac{N}{P_A} + \lceil log_2(N) \rceil L_A. \quad (9)$$

The number of cycles $NCycles_{SP}$ necessary to compute the scalar product of two vectors of size $m$ using P pipelined MADD modules, with latency L, and $P_A$ pipelined adders, with latency $L_A$, is given by

$$NCycles_{SP} = N_{comp} + NCycles_{sum}(P_A). \quad (10)$$

From (8), (9) and (10) we get

$$NCycles_{SP} \approx \frac{m}{P} + L + \frac{LP}{P_A} + \lceil log_2(LP) \rceil L_A. \quad (11)$$

From the previous expression, we can compute the sustained speed of the computation (expressed in operations/cycle) as

$$\text{SustainedSpeed} = \frac{2m}{\frac{m}{P} + L + \frac{LP}{P_A} + \lceil \log_2(LP) \rceil L_A}. \tag{12}$$

In previous equation L and $L_A$ are fixed by the technology (for instance, with the current version of QuickCompiler and for the ARRIA10 FPGA, $L = 8$ and $L_A = 3$), m is fixed by the problem, P and $P_A$ are the parameters of the architecture that must be determined to maximize the sustained speed.

P must satisfy the following requirements:

– must be a power of 2, i.e. $P = 2^k$, because it determines the width of the internal memory used by the SP kernel (width of the memory must be a power of 2),
– must be large enough to nearly saturate the memory BW.

In our example, $f_{ck} = 150$ MHz and the BW to one bank of the HMC memory is 17 GB/s. Thus, the width W to saturate the BW is given by

$$W * f_{ck} = BW \, [\text{Byte/s}] => W = BW/f_{ck} [\text{Byte}]$$

which gives $W = 17000/150 = 113$ [Byte]. As W has to be a power of 2, we can set $W = 128$ [Byte] (the closest to 113), thus fixing the MADD parallelism to 32 (32 MADDs must read 64 floats/cycle; 32 floats come from the buffer memory connected to the HMC and storing a row of the matrix **M** and 32 floats come from the buffer memory connected to the input stream and storing the vector **a**, read only once at the very beginning).

When $P = 32$ and $m = 8K$ elements, the number of cycles necessary to compute the LP partial products $s_{ij}$ is (ref. to Eq. (8))

$$\text{NCycles}_{\text{comp}} = (m/P) - 1 + L = (8192/32) - 1 + 8 = 263.$$

If we set $P_A = 4$ (adder parallelism), the number of cycles to sum all the partial results is (ref. to Eq. (9))

$$\text{NCycles}_{\text{sum}}(P_A) \approx \frac{LP}{P_A} + \lceil \log_2(LP) \rceil L_A = \frac{8 \cdot 32}{4} + 8 \cdot 3 = 88.$$

With the previous values, the Eq. (9) gives a Sustained Speed of 46.7 operations/cycle; as $f_{ck} = 150$ MHz, the previous figure corresponds to

$$46.7 [\text{ops/cycle}] * 150 [\text{MHz}] = 7.0 [\text{GFlop/s}].$$

## 7  MVM: Coarse-Grained Pipelining

In the operation $\mathbf{b} = \mathbf{M} \times \mathbf{a}$, the result vector **b** can be computed through the following loop

```
for (1=0; 1<n;1++)
   b₁=m₁·a;   // m₁ is the l-th row of M
```

whose body can be decomposed in three basic operations:

```
for (1=0; 1<n; 1++){
   load m₁ from the external memory
   compute the LP partial scalar products sᵢⱼ
   compute the final result b₁ = Σᵢ,ⱼ (sᵢⱼ)
}
```

The loop can be repeated in different kernels when the matrix M is partitioned into $p$ submatrices, as depicted in Fig. 1.

Regarding the time complexity (expressed in number of clock cycles), we can write the following relations

– moving 4 m bytes from the external memory, accessible through a port with $W = 4P$ bytes, to the internal multi-ported memory requires the number of cycles

$$N_{mem} = \frac{m}{P} + L_m \qquad (13)$$

as the internal memory can accept 4P bytes/cycle; $L_m$ is the latency to access the external memory; if $Wf_{ck} = BW_{req} > BW_{ExtMem}$, the actual number of cycles will be larger than $N_{mem}$ because the required bandwidth $Wf_{ck}$ is larger than the available memory bandwidth;

– the number of cycles required to compute the LP partial scalar products is given by Eq. (8);

– the sum of LP values using $P_A$ floating-point adders (with latency $L_A$) requires the number of clock cycles $N_{Sum}(P_A)$ given by Eq. (9).

As the iterations of the loop are independent, the loop can be pipelined, at a coarse grain, with three pipeline stages:

– load vector $m_i$,
– compute the LP partial scalar products $s_{ij}$,
– sum the LP $s_{ij}$.

The duration of each stage of this "macro-pipeline" is given by

$$N_{PipeStage} = \max(N_{mem}, N_{comp}, N_{SUM}(P_A)). \qquad (14)$$

Being the loop fully pipelined, $n + 2$ "macro-pipeline" stages are required to process n matrix lines and to compute n scalar products. The number of cycles necessary to compute the whole MVM, using $p$ equal SP kernels, is given by

$$N_{Total} = \left(\frac{n}{p} + 2\right) N_{PipeStage}. \qquad (15)$$

The sustained speed (operations/cycle) is given by the ratio

$$S = \frac{N_{operations}}{N_{Total}} = \frac{2nm}{\left(\frac{n}{p} + 2\right)N_{PipeStage}}. \tag{16}$$

Let's consider the case characterized by the following parameters:

- $m = n = 8192$ (m: size of the vector, n: number of scalar products to be computed)
- $L_A = 3$, $L = 8$ and $L_m = 200$ cycles (latencies of FP adder, MADD and HMC)
- $P = 32$ (spatial parallelism, i.e., number of MADD operations performed in parallel)
- $P_A = 1$ (1 adder is used to sum the LP partial scalar products)
- $p = 2$ (kernel parallelism, i.e., number of equal kernels, each one performing the scalar product)

Previous values, when inserted in the expressions derived above, give the following values:

- $N_{mem} = m/P + L_m = 456$,
- $N_{comp} = m/P + L_{MADD} = 264$,
- 

$$N_{SUM}(P_A) \approx \frac{LP}{P_A} + \lceil log_2(LP) \rceil L_A = 280.$$

So $N_{PipeStage} = 456$ and the sustained speed, when $f_{ck} = 150$ MHz, is

$$S = \frac{N_{operations}}{N_{Total}} = \frac{2nm}{\left(\frac{n}{p} + 2\right)N_{PipeStage}} = 71.82\left[\frac{ops}{cycle}\right] = 10.8\left[\frac{GFlop}{s}\right].$$

It's worth to be underlined that, when we ran on the $\mu$XComp board the test developed using previous values, we measured an overall speed of 10.6 [GFlop/s], in perfect agreement with the performance foreseen by the model (see Table 1, reported in the section related to performance).

## 8 FPGA Implementation of the MVM Through the QuickPlay HLS

In this section, we analyze the actual FPGA implementation of the MVM algorithm, based on the considerations illustrated in the previous sections.

To achieve the FPGA implementation, we use the Accelize HLS framework (QuickPlay with its embedded QuickCompiler HLS engine [6], formerly produced by Accelize and to be shortly released as Open Source SW).

We refer to the architecture depicted in Fig. 1 and, in the following Fig. 2, we report the QuickPlay schematic representing that architecture, in the case of $p = 4$ SP kernels.

In the previous design, we can recognize the four VectorMatrixProduct kernels, each performing n/4 scalar products: they are connected to four different HMC memory banks. The first mySplit kernel is used to divide the input data coming from the input port in

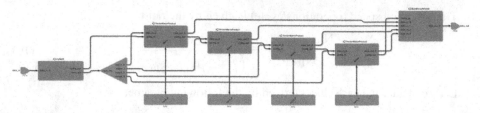

**Fig. 2.** Top level of the design with p = 4 SP kernels, as shown in the QuickPlay VisualEditor

a) the configuration part (8 bytes sent to the config_in - config_out chain to distribute the Id of the computing kernels) and
b) the data part (data are the values of the matrix **M** to be stored in the memory and the vector **a** to be multiplied with the matrix) which is sent to the 4 computing kernels through a streamCopy kernel.

The last BuildResultVector kernel is used to concatenate the results produced by the four VectorMatrixProduct kernels, generating the result vector.

## 8.1 The Scalar Product

As seen in the Sect. 6, the basic step to compute the scalar product between the $l^{th}$ row of the matrix ($\mathbf{m}_l$) and the input vector **a** is the following

```
compute the LP values
```

$$s_{ij} = \mathbf{m}_{l:ij} \cdot \mathbf{a}_{ij} = \sum_{k=0}^{\frac{m}{LP}-1} \left( m_{l:ip+j+kLP} \cdot a_{ip+j+kLP} \right) \begin{matrix} i = 0, 1, \dots, L-1 \\ j = 0, 1, \dots, P-1 \end{matrix}$$

which requires the computation of LP partial scalar products. The basic operation to implement these scalar products is the vector multiply-and-add pipelined function which takes as input P pairs of single-precision floating-point variables and produces P floating-point values (in our implementation P = 32), performing the computation

$$c_i \mathrel{+}= a_i \times b_i; \quad i = 1, 2, \dots, P.$$

The sketch of the QuickPlay C code to implement the vector pipelined MADD is the following

```
/*#qp pipeline */
Void MADD(float a1,…a32, float b1,… b32,float &c1,… &c32)
{
    c1 += a1*b1;
    …
    c32 += a32*b32;
}
```

Thanks to the /*#qp pipeline*/ directive the previous function is synthesized as a pipelined function which performs $2P = 64$ floating-point operations per cycle (P add and P mul).

From the synthesis reports of QuickCompiler we know that previous function requires 7 cycles to produce the output results, so $L_{MADD} = 7$ cycles; we use $L = 8$ to include the cycle needed to read the data from the memory. The MADD is implemented through the instantiation of 32 fp adders and 32 fp multipliers.

The MADD() function computes the LP scalar products $s_{ij}$ $i = 0, .., L - 1$ and $j = 0, 1, ..., P - 1$ through the following code:

```
count=0; count1=1; ...,count31=31; //init the 32 count vars
/*#qp unroll 32*/
for (i=0; i<(m)/(L*P); i++){
  a1 = a[count];
  ...
  a32 = a[count31];
  b1 = b[count];
  ...
  b32 = b[count31];
//1st group of 32 MADD scalar operations
  MADD(a1, ...,a32,b1,...,b32,s0_0,...,s0_31);
  Inc(count,...,count31);//each count var is incremented by 32
  ...
  a1 = a[count];
  ...
  a32 = a[count31];
  b1 = b[count];
  ...
  b32 = b[count31];
//8th group of 32 MADD scalar operations
  MADD(a1,...,a32,b1,...,b32,s7_0,...,s7_31);
  Inc(count,...,count31); //each count var is incremented by 32
}
```

In our example the size of the vector m assumes the value $m = 8192$ and $L \times P = 256$. The loop is executed $m/(LP) = 8192/256 = 32$ times, so the directive /*#qp unroll 32*/ unrolls completely the loop.

The scalar variables a1, ..., b32 are read from the FastMemory a[] and the FastMemory b[] in one clock cycle.

## 8.2  FastMemory

The FastMemory modules are the memories used by QuickCompiler to map internal arrays. They are implemented on embedded ram and are described by the tuple

$$FastMemory = <W, G, N, DType, Size>$$

262    A. Marongiu and P. Palazzari

- W is the width of the wide "external" port.
- G is the number of independent groups, each group being formed by N ports; usually G = 2 (as the embedded Ram modules are dual-ported)
- N is the number of typed ports in each of the G groups. Each port presents a data which has size DType;
- DType is the size (in bytes) of the data type stored in the FastMemory. In QuickCompiler, each array is stored in a different FastMemory.
- Size is the size of the memory, expressed in Bytes.

FastMemory has $G \times N + 1$ ports.

The large external port, whose width is W = N * DType, is used to transfer data to/from streams or to/from external memories through the qpReadStream(), qpWriteStream() and memcpy() functions. The bandwidth of read/write through this port is given by BW = W * $f_{ck}$ [Byte/s]; typical value is W = 128 [B], $f_{ck}$ = 150 MHz and BW = 19.2 GB/s. The latency to access external memories depends on the available memory controller; the HMC controller in the $\mu$XComp board is characterized by a latency $L_m$ = 200 cycles.

The $G \times N$ "internal" ports, whose size is DType, are accessed by the kernel. The internal BW, between the FastMemory and the computing kernel, is G times the BW of the external port. The latency to read a data from the FastMemory to the kernel is one cycle while writing a data from the kernel to the fast memory is accomplished in the same cycle.

Since W ≥ Dtype, each group of ports allows accessing N = W/DType elements of an array at the same clock cycle. As the memory is organized in word of W bytes, when the first port of a group is used it selects the memory word being accessed and it allows the other ports of its group to access the other array elements of the word.

The FastMemories a[m] and b[m] have been declared with the directive /*#qp ports 2 32*/ which specifies that the array, composed by m = 8K float elements, is stored in a memory which has G = 2 groups of N = 32 ports accessible in parallel, every port being four bytes wide (as they are float data type). Both a and b FastMemories are characterized by the tuple

<W = 128, G = 2, N = 32, DType = 4, Size = 32768>.

This means that up to 64 floats can be read/written in parallel in one clock cycle.

In one iteration of the loop, the LP $s_{ij}$ values are updated; values $s_{ij}$ are mapped onto the variables si_j (i = 0, .., 7 and j = 0, .., 31).

The previous loop-code is scheduled by the QuickCompiler HLS engine as described in Sect. 6, with the performance given by Eq. (8).

Looking in the QuickCompiler timing report, we see that the execution of the module implementing the previous code requires 264 clock cycles, in perfect agreement with the formula derived from the analysis $N_{comp} = m/P + L_{MADD}$.

After having computed the LP $s_{ij}$ values, we must sum them together to obtain the result i.e., we must implement the expression

$$b_l = \sum_{i=0}^{L-1} \sum_{j=0}^{P-1} (s_{ij}).$$

The previous formula is very simply computed through the following (not pipelined) function

```
float Sum(float s0_0,..., float s7_31)
{
    float result;
    result =s0_0+s0_1+...+s0_31+s1_0+...+s7_31; //256 operands
    return result;
}
```

which is scheduled by QuickCompiler on one fp adder and requires 263 clock cycles to be executed, slightly better than the simplified model presented in the Sect. 6, Eq. (9), which was foreseeing 280 clock cycles (in our simplified model we are neglecting the possibility to start the computation of a new layer of sums in the tree adding scheme before terminating the previous layer).

Putting the things together, the number of cycles requested to compute the scalar product of two vectors **a** and **b**, each containing $m = 8192$ floating-point values and stored in two dedicated FastMemory modules, each module having $G = 2$ groups of $N = 32$ ports 4 bytes wide, requires $264 + 263 = 527$ clock cycles. This figure corresponds to (nearly) 31 [flop/cycle] which, for a clock frequency $f_{ck} = 150$ [MHz], gives the sustained speed $S = 31 * 150 = 4650$ [MFlop/s].

### 8.3  MVM with a Coarse-Grained Pipeline

We use the just described scalar product module as a basic block to perform the MVM; the pseudo-code for the MVM is the following:

```
load vector a;
for (i=0; i<n; i++)
{
    load m_i, the i^th row of M;
    Compute the LP s_ij values as partial scalar products
    Sum all the s_ij
}
```

While the loading of the **a** vector is negligible, as it is performed only once, before starting the actual computation loop, the load of the $\mathbf{m_i}$ vector is relevant because it lasts for $N_{mem} = L_{mem} + m * D/W$ cycles, being

- $L_{mem}$ the latency to access the external memory (in our case $L_{mem} \approx 200$)
- W the width of the "external" port of the FastMemory (W = 128 [Byte])

In our case ($n = m = 8192$, $W = 128$, $L_{MADD} = 8$, $L_A = 3$, $P_A = 1$)

- $N_{mem} = 456$
- $N_{comp} = 264$
- $N_{sum} = 263$

and the global number of cycles necessary to compute $\mathbf{b} = \mathbf{M} \times \mathbf{a}$ is given by

$$N_{seq} = n * (N_{mem} + N_{comp} + N_{sum}). \tag{17}$$

As the number of floating-point operations to compute the MVM is $N_{flop} = 2\ nm$, the speed expressed in number of operations per cycle is given by

$$S_{ops/cycle} = \frac{2nm}{n(N_{mem} + N_{comp} + N_{sum})} \approx 16.7 \left[ \frac{ops}{cycle} \right].$$

Considering that each iteration of the computing loop is independent on the others, it is immediate to think to a pipelined scheme to overlap the three operations (Fig. 3):

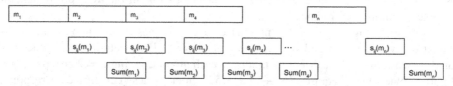

**Fig. 3.** Gantt for the pipelined execution of the MVM

The computation, arranged according to previous scheduling, can be executed in $N_{pipe}$ cycles

$$N_{pipe} = n * N_{mem} + N_{comp} + N_{sum}. \tag{18}$$

The speed-up of the pipelined implementation, with respect to the not-pipelined implementation, is given by

$$S = \frac{N_{seq}}{N_{pipe}} = \frac{8.1 \times 10^6}{3.7 \times 10^6} = 2.2$$

from which we can derive the expected speed for the pipelined implementation, in ops/cycle, through the following expression

$$S_{ops/cycle}(pipe) = S_{ops/cycle}(seq) * S = 16.7 * 2.16 = 36.01 \left[ \frac{ops}{cycle} \right].$$

The speed, in flop/s, is obtained as in the following

$$S_{flops/s} = S_{ops/cycle} * f_{ck} = 36.01 * 150 = 5411 \left[ \frac{MFlops}{s} \right].$$

The scheduling described in Fig. 3 is enforced by the QuickPlay HLS when compiling the following code:

```
...
qpReadStream(d_in_0,a1,NbElem*sizeof(float));//read vect a ⎫
ReadVector(b1, Matrix,row); row++; // read a row of M       ⎪
ComputePartialScalarProducts(a1, b1, cr0_0,..., cr0_31);    ⎪
sum1 = Sum(cr0_0,..., cr0_31);                              ⎬ preamble
ReadVector(b2, Matrix, row); row++;                         ⎪
ComputePartialScalarProducts(a1, b2, cr0_0,..., cr0_31);    ⎪
ReadVector(b3, Matrix, row);  row++;                        ⎭
for (i=0; i<myNbProducts-6; i+=3)
{
  Write(dout,sum1,false); //send an element of the result
                                     //vector
  sum2 = Sum(cr0_0,..., cr0_31);
  Write(dout,sum2,false);
  ComputePartialScalarProducts(a1, b3, cr0_0,..., cr0_31);
  sum3 = Sum(cr0_0,..., cr0_31);
  Write(dout,sum3,false);
  ReadVector(b1, Matrix, row); row++;
  ComputePartialScalarProducts(a1, b1, cr0_0,..., cr0_31);
       sum1 = Sum(cr0_0,..., cr0_31);
  ReadVector(b2, Matrix, row);    row++;
  ComputePartialScalarProducts(a1, b2, cr0_0,..., cr0_31);
  ReadVector(b3, Matrix, row); row++;
}
Write(dout,sum1,false);                                     ⎫
i++;   //i is the number of written values                  ⎪
sum2 = Sum(cr0_0,..., cr0_31);                              ⎪
Write(dout,sum2,false);                                     ⎬ postamble
       i++;   //i is the number of written values           ⎪
ComputePartialScalarProducts(a1, b3, cr0_0,..., cr0_31);    ⎪
sum3 = Sum(cr0_0,..., cr0_31);                              ⎪
Write(dout,sum3,i==NbProducts-1);                           ⎭
...
```

In previous code we can recognize three sections:

- the preamble, to fill the pipeline modules; in this section, we find the read (once for all) of the a vector, the read of the first three rows of M, two computations of the partial scalar results and one sum operation.
- the loop, which implements the steady-state of the pipelined behavior; in this section we find three reads of rows of M, three computations of partial scalar result, three sum operations and the write to the output of three results i.e., the manual unroll of three complete processing of three rows of M;
- the postamble, which empties the pipeline (no more matrix rows are read). In this phase it is finished the processing of the last three rows. It is the dual of the preamble; we have no read, one computation of the partial scalar products, two sum operations and three write of the results.

To ensure the parallel execution of the different functions accessing the same array, we used three different buffers to store the rows of matrix M.

The QuickPlay project which instantiates all the available 4 HMC memory modules, each connected to one Compute MatrixVectorProduct, is reported in Fig. 2.

Both the input and output ports have been mapped onto a PCIe interface.

The PCIe IP, HMC controller IP, clock and reset generator IP, as well as the copy IP and the FIFO IP are all part of the QuickPlay distribution and are instantiated by the tool in a transparent way (clock & reset generator, FIFO) or based on the configuration derived from the Visual Editor. The computing kernels are generated by QuickCompiler, the HLS engine of QuickPlay.

## 9   Performance Results

To show the performance achieved, in terms of both speed and resource usage, we report for the different designs developed (with 1, 2, 3 and 4 kernels, each performing the MVM on a portion of the matrix M)

- the sustained speed [GFlop/s] measured on actual runs on the MicroGate board (equipped with one ARRIA 10 FPGA and 4 HMC memory banks),
- the resource used (ALM - Arithmetic Logic Modules, memory modules M20K).

**Table 1.** Results when implementing the MVM with 1, 2, 3 and 4 SP kernels

|              | 1 Kernel | 2 Kernels | 3 Kernels | 4 Kernels |
|--------------|----------|-----------|-----------|-----------|
| Speed [GFlop/s] | 5.3   | 10.6      | 15.9      | 21.0      |
| ALM          | 88547    | 190648    | 264600    | 282473    |
| M20K         | 500      | 959       | 1378      | 2045      |

The design presents nearly linear scaling for computational performance.

To understand how resources are used, we report, for the largest design using four equal MatrixVectorProduct kernels, the percentage of the resources (ALM, M20K) used to implement

- the PCIe interfacing IP: ALM 2.7%, M2K 0.7%
- the MatrixVectorProduct kernels: ALM 5.3%, M2K 8.1% each kernel
- the HMC memory controllers: ALM 7.0%, M2K 5.7% each controller
- the other auxiliary modules (reset and clock generators, FIFOs, mySplit and BuildResultVector modules, …): ALM 18.6%, M2K 22.9%

When the FPGA board was configured with the design using four SP kernels, the power consumption of the board was 40 W, resulting in the energy efficiency of 0.53 GFlop/s/W.

Even if we think that comparison with other implementations is a weak way to evaluate an implementation, we report an alternative realization of the MVM to verify that the proposed solution is aligned with what is allowed by the current technology.

The work presented in [14] reports the implementation of several BLAS routines, including the MVM. The performance of this routine is reported in the case of a 1024 ×

1024 matrix stored within the internal RAM, thus not requiring any communication with the DDR banks; in the case of vectorization width set to 64 (i.e., performing in parallel 64 multiply operations) it is reported a computing speed greater than 20 GFlop/s (both in single and in double precision). While giving an idea of the performance achievable by the hardware in the FPGA, such a figure would require a significantly large I/O BW to be sustained for larger matrices (as the 8Kx8k matrices used in our case): the proper buffering and macro-pipelining of the computation to sustain the traffic with the DDR memory is not addressed in [14], not being this the core of the FBLAS implementation.

## 10   Future Developments

Looking at the Gantt reported in Fig. 3, we see that the transfer of one line of matrix M from memory lasts longer (456 cycles) than the computation of the partial scalar products (264 cycles) and the final sum (263 cycles). This happens because QuickPlay HLS does not support outstanding read operations, which would allow overlapping different memory transfers. Could we use outstanding memory reads, the latency of the next transfer could be overlapped with the actual data transfer of the current, as in the following:

In the previous figure, we decomposed the time to transfer data from HMC to the kernel into the latency $L(m_i)$ and the actual data transfer. It's easy to verify that the number of cycles needed to perform the computation shown in Fig. 4 is given by

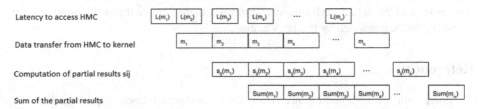

**Fig. 4.** Pipelined implementation with support to outstanding read operations

$$N_{pipe} = n * \max(L(m), N_{mem}, N_{comp}, N_{sum}) + L(m) + N_{mem} + N_{comp} + N_{sum}.$$

In our case ($n = m = 8192$) the values are $L(m) = 200$, $N_{mem} = 256$, $N_{comp} = 256$ and $N_{sum} = 263$ which yield

$$N_{pipe} = n * 264 + 983$$

Previous value corresponds to

$$S_{ops/cycle}(pipe) = \frac{2nm}{264n + 983} \approx 62 \left[ \frac{ops}{cycle} \right]$$

i.e., 9.3 GFlop/s when $f_{ck} = 150$ MHz, very close to the limit imposed by the memory BW.

## 11  Conclusions

The activities performed to implement on FPGA the MVM through the QuickPlay HLS flow have been described.

We started formalizing the problem, describing how parallelism is a key factor to achieve the expected performance and we showed how parallelism could be introduced at 4 different levels:

- (spatial) parallelization over the different rows of the matrix, computing in parallel the scalar products between the input vector and p different rows of the matrix M
- parallelization (pipelining) of the basic scalar product, achieved thanks to the introduction of L different independent partial scalar products to break the data dependence characterizing the classical accumulation scheme (L is the latency of the basic Multiply and Add pipelined operation)
- parallelization derived from the iteration of the previous decomposition, dividing each of the L sub-vectors into P smaller sub-vectors, thus performing in parallel P pipelined partial scalar products
- coarse-grained pipelining, overlapping different phases of successive scalar products when multiplying the input vector by different rows of the matrix M (read from external memory, computation of the partial scalar products, sum of the partial results).

Some models to compute the expected performance of the algorithm we have implemented have been presented and discussed. We found a good agreement between the forecasted and the actual performance. This agreement demonstrates the good quality of the hardware generated by the HLS engine.

## References

1. Energy efficient high performance computing for real-time science. http://greenflash-h2020.eu/
2. Piatrou, P., Gilles, L.: Robustness study of the pseudo open-loop controller for multiconjugate adaptive optics. Appl. Opt. **44**(6), 1003–1010 (2005)
3. Gendron, E., et al.: A novel fast and accurate pseudo-analytical simulation approach for MOAO. In: Proceedings of the SPIE 9148, Adaptive Optics Systems IV (2014)
4. Gendron, E., et al.: High performance pseudo-analytical simulation of multi-object adaptive optics. In: Euro-Par (2014)
5. Guyon, O., et al.: The compute and control for adaptive optics (CACAO) real-time control software package. In: Proceedings of the SPIE 10703, Adaptive Optics Systems VI (2018)
6. Monboisset, S.: A novel approach to software-defined FPGA computing. XCell Software J. (2), 38–45 (2015)
7. BLAS (Basic Linear Algebra Subprograms). http://www.netlib.org/blas/
8. Kestur, S., et al.: BLAS Comparison on FPGA, CPU and GPU. In: ISVLSI (2010)
9. Kestur, S., et al.: Towards a universal FPGA matrix-vector multiplication architecture. In: IEEE 20th International Symposium on Field-Programmable Custom Computing Machines (2012)
10. Zhuo, L., Prasanna, V.: High performance linear algebra operations on reconfigurable systems. In: SuperComputing SC 2005 (2005)

11. Zhuo, L., Morris, G., Prasanna, V.: Designing scalable FPGA-based reduction circuits using pipelined floating-point cores. In: 19th IEEE International Parallel and Distributed Processing Symposium (2005)
12. He, C., Qin, G., Ewing, R.: High-precision BLAS on FPGA-enhanced computers. In: International Conference on Engineering of Reconfigurable Systems & Algorithms, ERSA 2007 (2007)
13. He, C., Qin, G., Lu, M., Zhao, W.: Accurate floating-point summation with group-alignment technioque on FPGA. In: The International Conference on Engineering and Reconfigurable Systems and Algorithms (2006)
14. De Matteis, T., de Fine Licht, J., Hoefler, T.: FBLAS: streaming linear algebra on FPGA. http://arXiv.org/abs/1907.07929(2019)
15. Intel: Intel FPGA SDK for OpenCL (2018). https://www.intel.com/content/www/us/en/pro grammable/products/design-software/embedded-software-developers/opencl/support.html
16. Abdelfattah, A., Keyes, D., Ltaief, H.: KBLAS: an optimized library for dense matrix-vector multiplication on GPU accelerators. ACM Trans. Math. Softw. **42**(3), 1–31 (2016)
17. Boyer, C., Michau, V., Rousset, G.: Adaptive optics: interaction matrix measurements and real-time control algorithms for the COME-ON project. In: SPIE Astronomical Telescopes and Instrumentation for the 21st Century, Tucson, AZ, United States (1990)
18. Patauner, C., et al.: FPGA based microserver for high performance real-time computing in Adaptive Optics. In: Proceedings of the "Adaptive Optics for Extremely Large Telescopes" (AO4ELT5) (2017)

# Enabling Execution of a Legacy CFD Mini Application on Accelerators Using OpenMP

Ioannis Nompelis[1], Gabriele Jost[2], Alice Koniges[3(✉)], Christopher Daley[4], David Eder[5], and Christopher Stone[6]

[1] University of Minnesota, Minneapolis, MN, USA
nompelis@umn.edu
[2] NASA Ames Research Center, Mountain View, CA, USA
Gabriele.Jost@nasa.gov
[3] University of Hawai'i at Mānoa, Honolulu, HI, USA
koniges@hawaii.edu
[4] NERSC/LBL, Berkeley, CA, USA
csdaley@lbl.gov
[5] MHPCC, University of Hawai'i, Kihei, HI, USA
dceder@hawaii.edu
[6] PACE/Georgia Tech, Atlanta, GA, USA
chris.stone@gatech.edu

**Abstract.** We describe the process and outcome of our efforts to port a legacy Fortran benchmark code to heterogeneous GPU-accelerated computing architectures using OpenMP. The benchmark code is one of the multi-zone NAS Parallel Benchmarks (NPB-MZ) called SP-MZ. This "mini-app" mimics the computation and data movement that is found in popular legacy and modern implicit computational fluid dynamics (CFD) solvers. Our objective was to examine how efficiently legacy Fortran codes can be ported to accelerators by leveraging OpenMP directives. We describe the development and optimization process and demonstrate the performance impact of various code modifications. We show select profiling results from the NVIDIA Visual Profiler (nvpp) to help others diagnose and overcome performance issues in their own applications. We present results for two compute systems endowed with NVIDIA V100 accelerators.

**Keywords:** Accelerator · Fortran · GPU · OpenMP · Implicit CFD

## 1 Introduction

The latest computing architectures that are deployed in existing supercomputing installations have very closely followed hardware trends that were propelled by emergent fields of computational science, such as machine learning, data mining and artificial intelligence. These emergent fields use methodologies that can take

© Springer Nature Switzerland AG 2020
P. Sadayappan et al. (Eds.): ISC High Performance 2020, LNCS 12151, pp. 270–287, 2020.
https://doi.org/10.1007/978-3-030-50743-5_14

advantage of large numbers of low-power processors, as they require simple linear algebra operations to be performed on compactly sized chunks of independent data. As a result, high levels of parallelism are possible because concurrency is relatively easy to realize when processing data without the need of frequent exchanges of information. The pipelining that is possible by means of forming and executing small kernels on streams of data can be done very efficiently on large numbers of co-processors, similar to how graphics processing units (GPU) operate to form graphics pipelines. This hardware model was adopted as a means to provide a large number of theoretical floating point operations for the cost incurred; here we note that cost implies powering, packaging, and cooling the processing units.

While these GPU architectures are generally optimal in data-science fields, they are more difficult to exploit for the traditional algorithms of physical problems, which involve the solution to partial-differential equations that have inherent strong coupling of the data structures. However, this shift in hardware is also inevitable due to the exhaustion of raw computational power achievable by increasing processor clock-speeds and physically compacting the processor footprints. As a result, researchers in the physical sciences that require more computational power and performance have to undergo a paradigm shift, where the methods must take advantage of the new architectures. Legacy codes generally have a history of testing, user bases, I/O, and other aspects that make them staples of the HPC landscape. Thus refactoring and porting them to GPU accelerated nodes is critically important. Our work specifically explores a path forward for porting codes written in Fortran that are already OpenMP enabled on the CPU. For reasons of portability, the OpenMP API [3] is an appropriate direction. Alternative APIs such as OpenACC [2] will require similar modifications, with similar syntax, and can benefit from the work presented here.

Other avenues for porting methodologies exist, for example frameworks that act as "middle-writers" for executing code such that porting, data movement and portability are entirely opaque to the programmer. Kokkos [15] and Raja [17] are two such frameworks that have been demonstrated to make simulation software portable. However, this is not a viable option for porting legacy codes, and especially codes written in legacy Fortran.

This manuscript is organized as follows. First, we discuss the OpenMP framework, and in particular the "Target" constructs that are used for programming co-processor accelerators. We then describe our general porting strategy and discuss some related work. Section 2 discusses the parallel benchmark mini-app that we have chosen for this study. Section 3 describes the evaluation systems, compiler directives and run-time execution environment for our experiments. Results are presented alongside the code modifications that were made and are found in Sects. 4 and 5. We provide some concluding remarks in the final section.

## 1.1 Programming with OpenMP Target Offload

There are various methods of programming co-processor accelerators. Vendor specific libraries, for example, such as NVIDIA$^{TM}$ cuBLAS [4] or cuFFT [1] usually provide good performance with a small programming effort. However, they limit portability and require that the application kernels match the pattern of the library routines. Low level frameworks such as CUDA™ [5] or OpenCL [16] are suitable for general kernel patterns but require higher programming effort. The use of CUDA also limits portability.

Compiler directive based APIs, such as OpenMP, require only moderate programming effort with acceptable performance for multi-core nodes. OpenMP is a well established programming API for shared memory systems that was first standardized in 1997. It has since been augmented such that it includes directives for support of accelerators. It provides compiler directives, runtime library routines and environment variables. Accelerator programming support has been available since OpenMP 4.0 and the functionality was greatly extended in OpenMP 4.5. Support is provided to

- Identify kernels for offloading to the accelerator device
- Semi-explicitly specify parallelism
- Manage data transfer between the host and accelerator device.

The new OpenMP 4.5 functionality seamlessly integrates into existing OpenMP code and is supported by many compilers such as GNU Fortran (gfortran) [12], Cray™ ftn, and IBM™ xlf.

## 1.2    Porting Strategy

As alluded to earlier, there are three high-level aspects of porting solvers to heterogeneous accelerated systems that must be evaluated in advance of committing to a given approach:

- performance: the amount of performance that is desirable and is realizable when using accelerators
- portability: what level of abstraction can be maintained to allow for a desired level of portability across systems
- intrusiveness: the amount of alteration to the baseline code and to the data structures that is necessary or is tolerated.

The focus of this work is high performance for the accelerator. We aimed towards portability by employing the OpenMP standard for accessing accelerators. In terms of code alteration, minimal modification to the baseline code was desired and we tried to limit re-factoring of code and changes in data structures. During the development process we documented the code changes and their impact on GPU and CPU performance. In essence, our effort consisted of an assessment of performance gains as a function of the level of alteration made to the mini-app.

## 1.3    Related Work

Previously, the C implementations of the single zone NAS Parallel Benchmarks FT, LU and BT [10]. Were ported to accelerators using OpenMP 4.5, which was presented at OpenMPCon 2018 [14]. The focus of the current work differs from the previous work in that we targeted multi-zone codes, and chose SP-MZ implemented in Fortran as an example. Use of OpenACC to parallelize CFD algorithms is described in [22]. Various other work has been done using OpenACC for CFD codes [19]. The focus of the current work differs from previous efforts in that we targeted multi-zone CFD codes implemented in Fortran and we are using OpenMP 4.5 as the API.

The basis of our work was established during a Hackathon event sponsored by the Department of Energy [7].

## 2    NAS Parallel Benchmark SP-MZ

This effort centered on legacy computational fluid dynamics solvers written in Fortran and their potential for porting to and acceleration with heterogeneous computing systems. In order to avoid the complexity of porting a production solver, we restricted this effort to a mini application that retains the character of the Navier-Stokes equations and employs a common numerical method. While modern CFD solvers employ a mix of structured and unstructured grids, we restricted this work to a structured discretization, which is typical of legacy codes, to avoid the complexity of building kernels out of unstructured data.

We used the multi-zone NAS parallel benchmark suite in this work. The NPB-MZ [23] suite consists of three mini applications. These are multi-zone versions of the well known NAS Parallel Benchmarks BT, SP and LU [10, 21]. SP-MZ supports distributed and shared-memory parallelism with MPI and OpenMP. Zone-level parallelism is exploited using MPI and parallelism within each zone is exploited using OpenMP. Version 3.4 of the SP-MZ mini-app has 3,515 total lines of code (LoC). The mini-app contains only 1809 LoC associated with the implicit integration (i.e. the core arithmetic computation of the CFD solver), which includes MPI function calls and OpenMP directives. The small size of the mini-app allows an end-to-end refactoring and several iterations on offloading strategies. The general execution flow of the original SP-MZ hybrid code is depicted in Fig. 1.

### 2.1    The Underlying Numerical Method

The mini application is intended to mimic the performance characteristics of CFD applications that use the diagonalized Beam-Warming [11] alternating direction implicit (ADI) algorithm (i.e. the Pulliam-Chaussee algorithm). Major CFD software packages use this algorithm to simulate a wide variety of compressible flows for external aerodynamics applications. SP-MZ uses this implicit integration algorithm and it is designed to model the key performance characteristics of larger CFD applications.

Key features include the formation of the explicit right-hand-side (RHS) vector with finite differences and the factorization of the scalar pentadiagonal (SP) matrices along each grid line in all three directional sweeps. For a mesh

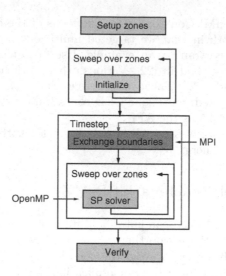

**Fig. 1.** Execution flow of the SP-MZ Benchmark

with $N^3$ points, the ADI scheme requires that $N^2$ SP line matrices (with N rows) be factored and equations solved in each of the sweeps. Fast assembly and factorization of the SP matrices is key to achieving high performance in the mini-app (and similar real CFD applications). In any refactoring effort of similar algorithms, efficient linear solvers on GPUs are needed for scalar and block tri- and penta-diagonal matrices.

Briefly, the SP-MZ benchmark solves a set of discretized nonlinear partial differential equations (PDEs) based on the Navier-Stokes equations. When discretized on a structured grid using 1st or 2nd-order (central) finite-differences for spatial derivatives and an implicit backwards Euler time differencing method, the three-dimensional equations result in a banded, block-matrix with three, non-adjacent sub- and super-diagonal bands. The block-matrix elements are $5 \times 5$ submatrices. This block-matrix system is considered too large to solve with either direct or iterative methods. Instead, the discretized PDE system is *approximately factorized* (AF) spatially such that each spatial direction can be solved independently. That is, if the original discretized system is written as:

$$[I - h\{A_x + B_y + C_z\}](U^{n+1} - U^n) = R(U^n) \qquad (1)$$

the approximate factorization, following Beam and Warming [11], is:

$$[I - h \, A_x][I - h \, B_y][I - h \, C_z](U^{n+1} - U^n) = R(U^n) \qquad (2)$$

Here, $A_x$, $B_y$, $C_z$ contain the implicit spatial difference operators, $U^{n+1}$ is the state vector solution at the next (future) time-step, $h$ is the step size, and $R$ contains all forcing terms and explicit terms at the $n^{\text{th}}$ time level. Equation 2 can be solved in three sequential steps representing directional solution sweeps:

$$[I - h \, A_x]\delta U^x = R(U^n) \qquad (3)$$

$$[I - h \ B_y]\delta U^y = \delta U^x \tag{4}$$

$$[I - h \ C_z]\delta U \ = \delta U^y \tag{5}$$

with $\delta U = U^{n+1} - U^n$. In this form, which resembles an *alternating direction implicit* (ADI) algorithm, only block *tridiagonal* matrices must be factored. Note that in the spatial decoupling in each directional sweep, multiple block tridiagonal systems must be solved. That is, if the mesh has $N_x \times N_y \times N_z$ points, then $N_y \times N_z$ block-tridiagonal *line* matrix equations must be solved in the $x$ solution direction sweep.

The approximate factorization form requires less storage and less computational time to solve than the nonfactorized Eq. 1. The computational cost and storage can be reduced further by solving the diagonalized form [10,20] of Eq. 5. The block-matrix elements have all real eigenvalues and a complete set of eigenvectors. As such, the coupled systems are cast into a decoupled, diagonal form with some loss of accuracy. The diagonalization recasts the problem from one of solving block-tridiagonal systems (with five unknowns per block) to one of solving five decoupled scalar-pentadiagonal systems. Furthermore, three of the SP systems have the same matrix and can be solved together. The diagonalization requires some additional vector-matrix operations compared to the coupled form, but uses less storage and requires fewer computations. Further details on the diagonalization can be found in [20].

The multi-zone aspect of the SP-MZ relates to the domain decomposition approach. The global three-dimensional mesh is partitioned into the $x$ and $y$ directions. The 2$^{nd}$-order spatial scheme requires an overlap of $\pm 1$ *ghost* (or *rind*) points. The implicit AF scheme is applied independently within each mesh zone and each MPI process is assigned one or more zones. That is, within each time-step, each zone is integrated independently.

The major computational costs of the SP-MZ benchmark are the evaluation of the right-hand-side terms $R(U^n)$ in Eq. 5, the assembly of the three SP matrices, and solution of the five decoupled equations in the three spatial directions. The SP systems are solved using a variant of the *Thomas algorithm* (TA) for scalar matrices. The TA is inherently sequential, however, many independent mesh-line matrices can be solved concurrently.

## 3   Testing Architectures

Two types of systems were used in this work: the IBM-built "Ascent" system, which is similar to the "Summit" supercomputer [9] and the Cray-built "Cori" [6] system.

### 3.1   The Ascent/Summit Compute Node

The Ascent system [8] is located at the Oak Ridge Leadership Computing Facility (OLCF). Ascent is a system that is identical to the Summit supercomputer in terms of compute node hardware, and it serves as a training system. Each compute node has two banks of 256 GB DDR4 memory, and each bank is connected via a 170 GB/s bus to an IBM Power9 CPU with 21 physical cores. Each core can support up to 4 hardware threads for a total of 84 threads per CPU. The CPUs are connected to each other with a 64 GB/s bus. Each CPU has access to 3 Volta V100 GPUs, and each of the GPU accelerators accesses 16 GB HBM2 memory via a 900 GB/s bus. The 3 GPU accelerators on each bank are connected to the CPU and to each other via a 50 GB/s NVLink2 bus.

One Fortran compiler available on Ascent and the one used in this work is the Fortran compiler "xlf" that is part of the IBM$^{TM}$XL compiler suite. The message passing interface for Ascent is provided by IBM Spectrum MPI. Interactive job submission and run-time support is provided through the IBM Spectrum Load Sharing Facility (LSF).

For our study we used cuda/10.1 and the IBM xlf v16.1 compiler with the following flags:

```
xlf −qfixed −qpreprocess −O3 −g −q64 −qsmp=omp −qoffload
```

## 3.2  The Cori Compute Node

The Cori system is located at NERSC. Cori is a Cray XC40 supercomputer that comprises of a mix of Intel Xeon "Haswell" nodes and Intel Xeon Phi "Knights Landing" nodes. A small set of "Skylake" nodes (18 in total) with GPU accelerators are accessible via Cori. This will henceforth be referred to as Cori GPU. There are 2 Skylake CPU sockets on each Cori GPU node, each containing 20 cores, and sharing 384 GB DDR4 memory. Each Cori GPU node contains 8 Volta V100 GPUs, each with 16 GB HBM2 memory, and connected to each other in a "hybrid cube-mesh" topology via a NVLink2 interconnect. The Cori GPU nodes are intended to help users prepare for the GPU-accelerated nodes in the Perlmutter supercomputer to be deployed at NERSC in 2020.

The Fortran compilers available on the Cori GPU nodes include GNU-8.1.1, PGI-19.7, Intel-18.0.1.163, Cray-9.0.0 and LLVM/Flang-7.0. Neither PGI nor Intel compilers currently provide OpenMP GPU offload support. We also found that the OpenMP GPU offload support in the GNU and LLVM/Flang compilers failed even in simple benchmark programs. Therefore, we used the Cray compiler in this study. The Cray compiler is accessed using the Cray$^{TM}$ "ftn" MPI and math library wrapper script. A major limitation of the Cray compiler on Cori GPU is that the Cray MPI stack is not supported and so Cray compiler experiments were limited to single process tests only.

For our study we used Cray-9.0.0 with the following flags:

```
ftn −O3 −h omp −h noacc −haccel=nvidia70
                              −h cpu=haswell −h fp3
```

The reason we optimized for the Haswell processor architecture is that Cray-9.0.0 does not provide optimizations for the Skylake processor architecture.

# 4    From OpenMP 3.1 to OpenMP 4.5

In this section we describe our porting strategy and discuss code transformations that enabled performance gains.

## 4.1    Identifying Kernels and Describing the Parallelism

In our current implementation we focused on exploiting GPU parallelism within the zones. We demonstrate our approach with the example in the code snippets shown in Fig. 2, part of one of the most time-consuming routines in the module that solves the factored system in the x-direction (running index "i"). This segment implements forward and backward substitution, and portions of the code have been removed to ease presentation. The OpenMP directives indicate how the loops are to be parallelized to perform forward and backward substitution along the i-direction of the data structures.

The refactored code in Fig. 2 uses the `TARGET` construct to offload the code region to the accelerator. The `TEAMS DISTRIBUTE` constructs create a league of teams and distributes the loop iterations across teams. The code transformations of our initial implementation are as follows:

- We manually inlined routines called within OpenMP target regions. An example is routine `lhsinit` in the code listing.
- We transposed some of the arrays to allow for stride one memory access. This is essential for good performance on the GPU because it enables coalesced memory accesses. An example is the array `rhst` in the code listing.
- We used the OpenMP `COLLAPSE` clause to collapse as many loops as possible. The code in the listing permits only 2 loop collapses; collapsing 3 loops was possible in some other routines.
- The original code contains two-dimensional arrays which are declared as `THREADPRIVATE`. However, the effect of an access to a `THREADPRIVATE` variable in a `TARGET` region is unspecified according to the OpenMP Standard. We found that OpenMP `PRIVATE` arrays per thread gave poor performance because of the large size of the arrays. Therefore, we made the array shared. This was accomplished by adding two extra dimensions. An example is the array `lhs4` in the code listing.
- To exploit some of the available zone-level parallelism within the code, we enabled asynchronous kernel execution using deferred OpenMP target tasks with dependencies. This is why the directive in the code listing contains the `NOWAIT` and `DEPEND` clauses. The execution flow of SP-MZ with potential kernel overlap is depicted in the pseudo-code in Fig. 3.

In what follows, we will refer to the implementation described above as our *initial port*. We refer to the original code as the *baseline* version.

## 4.2    Further Optimizing Parallelism and Data Movement

Details on the performance analysis of our initial implementation are provided in the next section. After profiling, we implemented some additional optimizations.

Implementation optimized for CPUs

```
!$OMP  PARALLEL DO DEFAULT(SHARED)
!$OMP&   PRIVATE(fac2,m,fac1,i2,i1,ru1,i,j,k)
!$OMP&   SCHEDULE(STATIC) COLLAPSE(2)
 do k = 1, nz-2
   do j = 1, ny-2

       call lhsinit(lhs, lhsp, lhsm, nx-1)
       ....    !--- operations localized at "i"

       do i = 0, nx-3     !---- Thomas alg. forward elim.
         i1 = i + 1
         i2 = i + 2
         fac1       = 1.d0/lhs(3,i)
         lhs(4,i)   = fac1*lhs(4,i)
         lhs(5,i)   = fac1*lhs(5,i)
         do m = 1, 3
            rhs(m,i,j,k) = fac1*rhs(m,i,j,k)
         end do
         lhs(3,i1) = lhs(3,i1) -
                            lhs(2,i1)*lhs(4,i)
         lhs(4,i1) = lhs(4,i1) -
                            lhs(2,i1)*lhs(5,i)

         do m = 1, 3
            rhs(m,i1,j,k) = rhs(m,i1,j,k) -
                            lhs(2,i1)*rhs(m,i,j,k)
         end do
         ....
         lhsm(4,i1) = lhsm(4,i1) -
                            lhsm(2,i1)*lhsm(5,i)
         ....
       end do
       ....
   end do
 end do
```

Implementation optimized for GPUs

```
!$OMP   TARGET TEAMS DISTRIBUTE
!$OMP&   PARALLEL DO SIMD COLLAPSE(2)
!$OMP&   NOWAIT DEPEND( inout: rhs )
!$OMP&      MAP( ALLOC: lhs4, lhsp4, lhsm4, rhst )
!$OMP&      PRIVATE(fac2,m,fac1,i2,i1,ru1,i)
!$OMP&      PRIVATE( cv_im1, cv_ip1 )
!$OMP&      PRIVATE( rhon_ip1, rhon_im1, rhon_i )
 do k = 1, nz-2
   do j = 1, ny-2

     lhs4 (j,1:5,    0,k) = 0.0d0
     lhs4 (j,1:5,nx-1,k) = 0.0d0
     ....    !--- operations localized at "i"

     do i = 0, nx-3     !---- Thomas alg. forward elim.
       i1 = i  + 1
       i2 = i  + 2
       fac1          = 1.d0/lhs4(j,3,i,k)
       lhs4(j,4,i,k) = fac1*lhs4(j,4,i,k)
       lhs4(j,5,i,k) = fac1*lhs4(j,5,i,k)
       do m = 1, 3
            rhst(j,m,i,k) = fac1*rhst(j,m,i,k)
       end do
       lhs4(j,3,i1,k) = lhs4(j,3,i1,k) -
                        lhs4(j,2,i1,k)*lhs4(j,4,i,k)
       ....
     end do
     ....
   end do
 end do
```

**Fig. 2.** Code fragments showing base language code and OpenMP directives to execute efficiently on CPUs and GPUs

- We eliminated some small host-to-device ("HtoD") data transfers by using the **DECLARE TARGET** construct to declare some of the constants on the device. Furthermore, we declared some subroutine arguments to have the **VALUE** attribute. We found that the xlf compiler did not transfer the associated data as part of the kernel launch if they were passed by reference. However, passing the data by value circumvented the issue.

```
Partition domain into zones
For all zones:
        initialize zone
For all time-steps:
        Communication rind data
                For all zones:
                        Pack zone's face points into buffer.
                Call MPI Send/Recv to exchange buffers with neighbors.
                For all zones:
                        Unpack buffer and update zone ghost points.
                For all zones:
                        Enqueue SP/ADI solver for zone. Async execution on device.
                Wait for all zones to complete async execution.
Verify results
```

**Fig. 3.** Pseudo-code for asynchronous execution in SP-MZ

- We improved the parallelism in the small loop over the two-dimensional slabs of all zones to accelerate the copy in/out kernels. Instead of a kernel for each rind copy in/out in "exch-bc" for each zone, we created a target region over the zone loop so all the copy in/out operations run within the same kernel. The drawback is that the number of zones shrinks since we end up with just a few or even one gang/team/threadblock.
- Using preallocated lhs scratch memory for all zones improved performance. The original implementation used dynamic allocation for each zone inside of the x, y, and z solvers. This required frequent device allocations with global barriers. We pre-allocated a large temporary array for all the lhs structures on all zones and passed them to the x, y and z solver routines.
- We merged asynchronous kernels with communication optimizations. This removed some unnecessary HtoD and DtoH transfers. We also combined the PARALLEL DO directives with TARGET TEAMS DISTRIBUTE since this enables the compiler to generate simpler code where all GPU threads execute the same computation on different data. It allows the compiler to generate code that maps better to GPU hardware [18].

In what follows, we refer to the implementation containing these optimizations as the *optimized version*.

We monitored the incremental performance changes during the development process on the Ascent system, which is shown in Fig. 4. The host configuration used 21 OpenMP threads bound to 1 CPU socket and the device configuration used 1 process bound to 1 CPU socket, which offloaded work to 1 GPU. The intention of this graph is to show the performance in the absence of MPI.

The Roman numerals correspond to the following code changes.

(I) Baseline
(II) Transposed arrays to support coalesced memory operations; replaced dependencies on one-dimensional, thread-private (host) scratch arrays with four-dimensional scratch arrays.
(III) Changed index ordering in x-solve to improve memory coalescing.
(IV) Reduced or eliminated unnecessary host-to-device transfers.
(V) Merged target, teams distribute, and parallel do directives into one combined directive and additionally used loop collapsing.

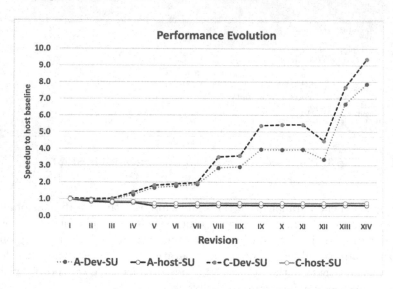

**Fig. 4.** Incremental performance change during the development process on the Ascent system: Dev-SU and host-SU stands for speed-up on device and host respectively. A and C indicate the Benchmark Class. Note the Dev-SU increases but host-SU decreases during the development process

(VI) Enabled kernel task dependencies to allow asynchronous execution.

(VII) Improved efficiency of ghost/rind data buffer fill kernels.

(VIII) Enabled asynchronous rind fill kernels.

(IX) Added loop scalars to private clauses to avoid unnecessary host-to-device transfers before kernel execution.

(X) Added CUDA-aware MPI option to bypass host transfers during MPI communication.

(XI) Improved parallelism and occupancy of rind fill in/out routines.

(XII) Added `SIMD` to the `PARALLEL DO` directive to improve performance when using the Cray compiler.

(XIII) Change argument passing from by-reference to by-value to allow the IBM OpenMP v4.5 compiler to avoid unnecessary host-to-device transfers.

(XIV) Combined all rind/ghost cell fill in/out routines to execute in one kernel instead of one per zone. That is, changed parallelism from within each zone to all zones at once.

The chart also shows that code changes that improved GPU performance, at times decreased CPU performance. There are several reasons for this. Most important is the fact that there is poorer cache locality. Furthermore, the IV change introduced additional arrays, which hurt host performance. The XII change modified the IBM compiler code generation in a negative way. Figure 4 shows IBM performance, although the XII change describes an optimization for the Cray compiler.

# 5    Performance Studies

In this section we show timings on our different evaluation systems and discuss performance analysis results. We collected performance results for 3 different benchmark classes.

- Class A: 4 × 4 zones, 128 × 128 × 16 grid points
- Class C: 16 × 16 zones, 480 × 320 × 28 grid points
- Class D: 32 × 32 zones, 1632 × 1216 × 34 grid points.

A characteristic of SP-MZ is that all zones are of equal size. Provided that a high performance MPI library is available and that there are no memory constraints imposed by the problem size, it is best to exploit zone level parallelism via MPI rather than using hybrid MPI+OpenMP. The baseline measurements on Ascent were thus obtained in MPI-only configuration. We could not do this on Cori GPU with the Cray compiler because of the lack of MPI support. Thus we used the nested OpenMP implementation of SP-MZ that is part of the NPB 3.4 distribution for the CPU-only measurements. We ran this version with OpenMP threads on the outer level parallel region to exploit zone parallelism only, making it more of a fair comparison against the Ascent MPI-only experiment on CPUs. We ran the MPI+OpenMP target offload implementation of SP-MZ on Cori GPU by using a single process and a "dummy" MPI library.

The CPU-only configuration on the Ascent system used in Fig. 5 is different from the one used in Fig. 4. The purpose of Fig. 4 is to show the performance in the absence of MPI. In Fig. 5, on the other hand, we want to show the best possible result that can be obtained on the CPU, which is using 42 MPI ranks on zone level. This is the reason why speed-up on CPU versus GPU is not as high in Fig. 5 as in Fig. 4. Using 84 ranks/threads and 168 ranks/threads on the IBM Power9 did not yield a performance gain since the code is memory bandwidth limited.

Figures 5 and 6 show the performance in GFLOP/s that we obtained on Ascent and Cori GPU for different benchmark classes. The Class D problem on a single Ascent GPU failed and thus we only have results for the smaller problem sizes for this case. The results show that the performance is generally highest for Class D, which is the largest problem size. The CPU-only results are approximately a factor of 2 higher on Ascent than Cori-GPU. This is most likely because of NUMA penalties affecting the OpenMP version of SP-MZ. The best single GPU performance we obtained was approximately a factor of 2 slower than the best CPU-only performance. The benefit of GPUs is only really seen when running the Class D problem on all 6 GPUs of an Ascent compute node. Here, performance is approximately 4x higher than the corresponding MPI-only configuration on CPUs.

We used the nvprof profiler to collect performance statistics. We noticed that in the optimized code, the CUDA API overhead decreased significantly in comparison to the initial port. The biggest impact was observed on the `cuMemcpyHtoDAsync` call, which we attribute to the excess HtoD transfers of

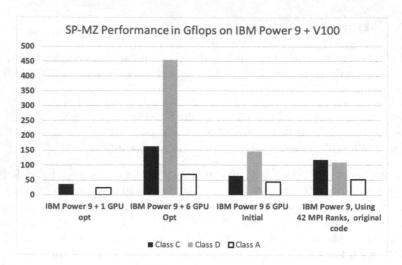

**Fig. 5.** Single node performance for different classes of the SP-MZ Benchmark on Ascent, using 1 GPU and 6 GPUs on the node. Class D for a single GPU failed.

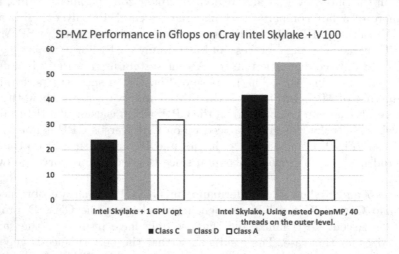

**Fig. 6.** Performance for different classes of the SP-MZ Benchmark on Cori GPU

the small constants. Those issues were fixed with the OpenMP "declare target" directive to make variables available on the device across target regions. As noted previously, we also declared some subroutine arguments to be passed by value rather than being passed by reference. An example for this are the array dimensions in the calls to the solver routines. Another good performance boost came from using the pre-allocated lhs scratch memory for all zones.

As described in Sect. 4 we used the OpenMP tasking mechanism to allow for kernel execution overlap. In principle, this allows one to "implicitly" compute SP-MZ zones in parallel because the work per zone is independent. We used

OpenMP dependencies for each zone to enable computation for different zones to execute concurrently. Figures 7 and 8 display the execution timeline generated by the NVIDIA nvvp visual profiler on Ascent and Cori-GPU, respectively. The results were obtained by running 10 iterations of the Class C benchmark. The "Compute" part of the timeline, shows that there was not much overlap of the kernel execution. We observed that only 2 streams were used for the execution of the kernels. On the Cori system, on the other hand, kernel execution overlapped. This can be clearly seen in the nvvp execution timeline in Fig. 8. Here we observed that 7 streams were used for the kernel execution. Another observation is, that the IBM compiler introduces additional Memcpy (HtoD) because variables are not passed by value as part of the kernel launch.

The lines in the "Compute" part of the timeline, show whether kernels were running concurrently. The results show that on Ascent we did not get the amount of overlap we were hoping for, while we could clearly observe overlapping kernels on the Cori system. It is unclear why there was not more overlap with the IBM compiler on the Ascent system. We could work around this manually by adding explicit zone-level parallelism. This would be achieved by lifting the "target teams" region to the sweep over the zones. All ADI functions will need to be target functions that could then be called at the team level. We consider such an implementation as an item for future work.

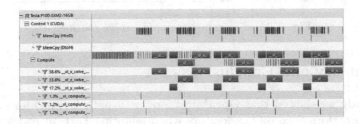

**Fig. 7.** Execution timeline of SP-MZ Class C on Ascent as seen on the profiler

We mentioned in Sect. 4 that the CPU performance degraded during the development process. While the code is functionally portable between different hardware platforms, its performance is clearly not. We introduced code patterns that improve GPU performance, but degrade performance on the CPU. We noticed, for example, that the solver in z dimension suffered most during the development process. In the refactored code, the stride on the inner, non-vectorized loop is very large. So this is an issue of terrible cache reuse, as it will thrash the L1 cache considerably. A code snippet of the loop in question is displayed in Fig. 9.

While performance portability is very important, this was not the focus of our effort. We plan to address this in future work. The question of performance portability for directive-based programming is addressed in [13], for example.

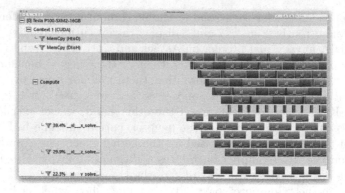

**Fig. 8.** Execution timeline of SP-MZ Class C on Cori GPU as seen on the profiler

```
! sequential loop
          do   k =   1, nz-2
              ...
              ru1  = c3c4*rho_i(i,j,k-1)
              cv_km1 = ws(i,j,k-1)
              rhos_km1 = dmax1(dz4 + con43 * ru1,
  >                            dz5 + c1c5 * ru1,
  >                            dzmax + ru1,
  >                            dz1)
              ...
              lhs4(i,2,j,k) = -dttz2 * cv_km1 - dttz1 * rhos_km1
              lhs4(i,4,j,k) =  dttz2 * cv_kp1 - dttz1 * rhos_kp1
              ...
          end do
```

**Fig. 9.** Inner loop in refactored z solve routine

# 6   Summary and Conclusions

In this study we showed that OpenMP 4.5 offers a path forward for achieving reasonable performance on accelerators when adapting Fortran codes that are over 10 years old. We described our experience using the OpenMP 4.5 support for heterogeneous compute nodes. We found that the compiler directives permitted us to port the legacy Fortran CFD mini-application for execution on compute nodes endowed with NVIDIA V100 GPU accelerators. We collected results on two different evaluation systems and conducted performance studies.

As a positive observation, we note that using OpenMP compiler directives permitted us to port the code within one week of programming effort. We also note that significant code changes were required to obtain acceptable performance. What is important to emphasize is that our approach was one-sided, in the sense that we targeted code execution and performance gains only on GPUs; no effort was made to retain performance for execution on CPUs. During the development process, we noticed that code changes that improved the performance on the GPU accelerators actually decreased performance on CPUs. This implies that when porting legacy codes (i.e. codes not originally designed to use co-processors), different aspects of the numerical method at hand may have to be handled differently and distributed across co-processors and the CPUs. An approach that is designed systematically to leverage GPUs/co-processors and CPUs in a manner tailored to the numerical method can potentially yield much higher performance gains. We envision that such an approach is a suitable path forward.

Another positive aspect was, that we did not find a lack of functionality in OpenMP when comparing it to OpenACC. The lack of a *present* clause did not present a hurdle. Using OpenMP tasking allowed us to implement asynchronous execution expressing the dependences more explicitly than using the OpenACC *async* construct.

The flip side of using the convenience of OpenMP is that we depend very much on compiler support. We have mentioned a number of system specific issues we encountered. Performance optimization is also difficult, as it is often not clear if poor performance is due to poorly chosen directives or bad code generated by the compiler. We plan further studies to investigate such issues.

A number of paths to portability (e.g. Kokkos, Raja, and Thrust), can work well for C++ codes, but are not appropriate for codes entirely written in Fortran. OpenMP can play an important role here. In our work we focused on exclusively porting code to GPUs, where we also observed minor degraded CPU-only performance. However, we expect that porting of Fortran codes without such performance decreases will be possible in the future. There are a number of research projects on the way addressing specifically performance portability of Fortran codes as discussed in [13]. The porting process will greatly improve as 5.0 features become available, where one will be able to use different functions and directives for specific vendor hardware, and in that sense OpenMP can undertake the middleware role (like Kokkos, for example), performing appropriate changes based on hardware. Our future work will include enabling explicit zone-level parallelism, compute kernel optimization and multi-node scaling studies.

**Acknowledgments.** The authors would like to thank all those who helped with valuable advice during the NERSC/OLCF Oakland Hackathon, especially, Kevin Gott and Jack Deslippe from NERSC and Tom Papatheodore from OLCF for facilitation of an excellent hackathon experience, Max Katz and Angela Chen from NVIDIA who taught us a lot about profiling, and Fazlay Rabbi from NERSC who helped us with compiling and benchmarking on the Ascent and Cori systems. Thanks to Joel Bretheim from the Naval Research Lab, who contributed to the code optimizations. Special thanks go to Kelvin Li from IBM for advising on the changes of Fortran value versus by-reference arguments. I. Nompelis would like to thank Prof. G. V. Candler's group from the Department of Aerospace Engineering and Mechanics, Univ. of Minnesota for their support. This research used resources of the National Energy Research Scientific Computing Center (NERSC), a U.S. Department of Energy Office of Science User Facility operated under Contract No. DE-AC02-05CH11231. This research also used resources of the Oak Ridge Leadership Computing Facility (OLCF), which is a DOE Office of Science User Facility supported under Contract No. DE-AC05-00OR22725. We thank OLCF and NERSC for their support during our study. This work was partially funded by NASA Contract No: 80ARC018D001. Work at the hackathon included funding from the Department of Defense High Performance Computing Modernization

Program (HPCMP) under User Productivity, Technology Transfer and Training (PETTT) Contract No. GS04T09DBC0017 and for the University of Hawai'i under Maui High Performance Computing Center (MHPCC) Contract No. N00024-19-D-6400.

# References

1. CUDA CuFFT Library (2017). http://developer.download.nvidia.com/compute/cuda/1.0/CUFFT_Library_1.0.pdf
2. The OpenACC application programming interface (2018). https://www.openacc.org/sites/default/files/inline-files/OpenACC.2.7.pdf
3. The OpenMP API specification for parallel programming (2018). https://www.openmp.org
4. cuBLAS Library (2019). https://docs.nvidia.com/pdf/CUBLAS_Library.pdf
5. CUDA toolkit documentation (2019). https://docs.nvidia.com/cuda/
6. NERSC development system documentation (2019). https://docs-dev.nersc.gov/cgpu/
7. *NERSC OLCF GPU Hackathon* (2019). https://sites.google.com/lbl.gov/july2019-gpu-hackathon
8. Summit training system (ascent) (2019). https://www.olcf.ornl.gov/for-users/system-user-guides/summit/summit-user-guide/#training-system-(ascent)
9. Summit user guide (2019). https://www.olcf.ornl.gov/for-users/system-user-guides/summit/
10. Bailey, D., et al.: The NAS parallel benchmarks. Tech. rep. NRN Technical report NRN-94-007, NASA Ames Research Center (March 1994)
11. Beam, R.M., Warming, R.F.: An implicit factored scheme for the compressible Navier-stokes equations. AIAA J. **16**, 393–401 (1978)
12. Brook, P., et al.: GNU Fortran (2019). https://gcc.gnu.org/fortran/
13. Clement, V., et al.: The CLAW DSL: abstractions for performance portable weather and climate models. In: Proceedings of the Platform for Advanced Scientific Computing Conference. PASC 2018. ACM, New York (2018). https://doi.org/10.1145/3218176.3218226
14. Diaz, J.M.M., Jost, G., Chandrasekaran, S., Pino, S.: Is OpenMP 4.5 target off-load ready for real life? - a case study of three benchmark kernels. https://openmpcon.org/wp-content/uploads/2018_Session1_Diaz.pdf
15. Edwards, H.C., Trott, C.R., Sunderland, D.: Kokkos: enabling manycore performance portability through polymorphic memory access patterns. J. Parallel Distrib. Comput. **74**(12), 3202–3216 (2014). https://doi.org/10.1016/j.jpdc.2014.07.003. http://www.sciencedirect.com/science/article/pii/S0743731514001257. Domain-Specific Languages and High-Level Frameworks for High-Performance Computing
16. Group, K.O.W.: The OpenCL specification v2.2-11 (2019). https://www.khronos.org/registry/OpenCL/specs/2.2/pdf/OpenCL_API.pdf
17. Hornung, R., et al.: ASC tri-lab co-design level 2 milestone report. Tech. rep., Lawrence-Livermore National Laboratories (September 2015)
18. Jacob, A.C., et al.: Efficient fork-join on GPUs through warp specialization. In: 2017 IEEE 24th International Conference on High Performance Computing (HiPC), pp. 358–367 (December 2017). https://doi.org/10.1109/HiPC.2017.00048
19. McCall, A.J.: Multi-level parallelism with MPI and OpenACC for CFD applications. Ph.D. thesis, Virginia Tech (2017)

20. Pulliam, T., Chaussee, D.: A diagonal form of an implicit approximate-factorization algorithm. J. Comput. Phys. **39**, 347–363 (1981)
21. Shan, H., et al.: A programming model performance study using the NAS parallel benchmarks. Sci. Program. **18**(3–4), 153–167 (2010). https://doi.org/10.1155/2010/715637
22. Stone, C.P., Elton, B.H.: Accelerating the multi-zone scalar pentadiagonal CFD algorithm with OpenACC. In: Proceedings of the Second Workshop on Accelerator Programming Using Directives, WACCPD 2015, pp. 2:1–2:7. ACM, New York (2015). https://doi.org/10.1145/2832105.2832110
23. Van der Wijngaart, R.F., Jin, H.: NAS parallel benchmarks, multi-zone versions. Tech. rep., NASA Ames Research Center (July 2003)

# Load-Balancing Parallel Relational Algebra

Sidharth Kumar$^{(\boxtimes)}$ and Thomas Gilray

University of Alabama at Birmingham, Birmingham, USA
{sid14,gilray}@uab.edu

**Abstract.** Relational algebra (RA) comprises a basis of important operations, sufficient to power state-of-the-art reasoning engines for Datalog and related logic-programming languages. Parallel RA implementations can thus play a significant role in extracting parallelism inherent in a wide variety of analytic problems. In general, bottom-up logical inference can be implemented as fixed-point iteration over RA kernels; relations dynamically accumulate new tuples of information according to a set of rules until no new tuples can be discovered from previously inferred tuples and relevant rules (RA kernels). While this strategy has been quite successful in single-node contexts, it poses unique challenges when distributed over many-node, networked clusters—especially regarding how the work-load is balanced across available compute resources.

In this paper, we identify two fundamental kinds of load imbalance and present a strategy to address each. We investigate both spatial load imbalance—imbalance across each relation (across compute nodes)—and temporal load imbalance–imbalance in tuples produced across fixed-point iterations. For spatial balancing, we implement refinement and consolidation procedures. For temporal balancing, we implement a technique that permits the residual workload from a busy iteration to roll over to a new iteration. In sum, these techniques permit fully dynamic load-balancing of relational algebra that is robust to changes across time.

**Keywords:** Parallel relational algebra · Load balancing · Logic programming · Message passing interface · All-to-all communication

## 1 Introduction

Relational algebra (RA) comprises an important basis of operations. It can be used to implement a variety of algorithms in satisfiability and constraint solving [21], graph analytics [24], program analysis and verification [19], deductive databases [16], and machine learning [22]. Many of these applications are, at their heart, cases of logical inference; a basis of performant relational algebra is sufficient to power state-of-the-art forward-reasoning engines for Datalog and related logic-programming languages.

Quite recently, some efforts [5,14] have explored methods for exploiting the massive parallelism available on modern clusters in a single relational-algebra

© Springer Nature Switzerland AG 2020
P. Sadayappan et al. (Eds.): ISC High Performance 2020, LNCS 12151, pp. 288–308, 2020.
https://doi.org/10.1007/978-3-030-50743-5_15

operation, making it possible to extract data-parallelism across individual operations for relations at scale. Instead of only decomposing tasks in a broader logical inference problem, such approaches could permit extreme scaling for problems involving only a small number of distinct tasks in a principled manner. A fundamental problem such approaches must contend with is that of inherent imbalance possible among the relation data. For example, a *join* of two relations (an operation that generalizes both Cartesian product and intersection by matching only specified columns) may most naturally be decomposed across many processes or threads by grouping like keys on like processes, permitting most of the join to be parallelized completely. If a relation is imbalanced among its keys (exhibits *"key skew"*), this imbalance will also be represented in the decomposition of the join operation, which is highly undesirable for performance.

In this paper, we discuss both the problem of dynamic changes in spatial imbalance, where operations on relations become imbalanced due to key skew in the relation itself, and the problem of temporal imbalance, where operations on relations may vary significantly in their output when repeated. While past work has given mention of replication-based strategies for remediating spatial imbalance [5] and has implemented *static* replication strategies [14], no existing approach offers a solution that is robust to arbitrary changes in relation balance across time, or to sudden explosions in operation output.

*We make three novel contributions* to the literature on effectively parallelizing relational algebra:

- We explore spatial load imbalance in relational algebra and present two techniques for dynamically balancing relations across MPI processes at scale.
- We explore temporal load imbalance in relational algebra and present an iteration-buffering technique for mitigating against the effects of explosions in workload and guarding against resultant failures.
- We present an evaluation of our two approaches, together and in isolation, using random, real world, and corner-case relation topologies, illuminating a space of tunings and demonstrating effectiveness using 256–32,768 processes.

In Sect. 2, we describe background and related work on relational algebra. In Sect. 3, we discuss our implementation using MPI, describe two kinds of load imbalance, and present three techniques for mitigating such load imbalance. In Sect. 4, we present an evaluation of our approaches using the Theta supercomputer and discuss tuning the framework and our observations.

## 2    Parallel Relational Algebra

This section reviews some standard relational operations such as union, product, intersection, natural join, selection, renaming, and projection, along with their use in implementing algorithms for bottom-up logical inference engines. We discuss existing approaches to parallelizing relational algebra (RA) on single-node systems, and then on many-node systems.

We make a few typical assumptions about relational algebra that diverge from those of traditional set operations. Specifically, we assume that all relations are sets of flat (first-order) tuples of integers with a fixed, homogeneous arity. Although our approach may extend naturally to relations over any enumerable domains (e.g., booleans, symbols/strings, etc), we also assume that such values are interned and assigned a unique enumerated identity. Several RA operations are especially standard and form a simple basis for computation. *Cartesian product* is defined as for sets except it only yields flat first-order tuples and never nested tuples. The *Union* and *Intersection* of two relations are defined as for sets except that these operations require both relations to have the same arity.

*Projection* is a unary operation that removes a column or columns from a relation—and thus any duplicate tuples that result from removing these columns. Projection of relation $R$ restricts $R$ to a particular set of columns $\alpha_0, \ldots, \alpha_j$, where $\alpha_0 < \ldots < \alpha_j$, and is written $\Pi_{\alpha_0,\ldots,\alpha_j}(R)$. For each tuple, projection retains only the specified columns. *Renaming* is a unary operation that renames columns (i.e., reorders columns, as column names are just their index). Renaming columns can be defined in different ways, including renaming all columns at once. We define a renaming operator, $\rho_{\alpha_i/\alpha_j}(R)$, to swap two columns, $\alpha_i$ and $\alpha_j$ where $\alpha_i < \alpha_j$—an operation that may be repeated to rename/reorder any number of columns. In practice, our implementation offers a combined projection and reordering operation that generalizes these two operations more efficiently.

$$\Pi_{\alpha_0,\ldots,\alpha_j}(R) \triangleq \{(r_{\alpha_0},\ldots,r_{\alpha_j}) \mid (r_0,\ldots,r_k) \in R\}$$

$$\rho_{\alpha_i/\alpha_j}(R) \triangleq \{(\ldots,r_{\alpha_j},\ldots,r_{\alpha_i},\ldots) \mid (\ldots,r_{\alpha_i},\ldots,r_{\alpha_j},\ldots) \in R\}$$

Two relations can also be *joined* into one on a subset of columns they have in common. *Natural Join* combines two relations into one, where a subset of columns are required to have matching values, and generalizes both intersection and Cartesian product operations.

Consider a relation $G$, shown in Fig. 1, as a table, and at the top of Fig. 2, as a graph.

| G | |
|---|---|
| 0 | 1 |
| A | B |
| A | C |
| B | D |
| C | D |
| D | E |

| G joined with G | | |
|---|---|---|
| 0 | 1 | 2 |
| A | B | D |
| A | C | D |
| B | D | E |
| C | D | E |

$\rho_{0/1}(\rho_{0/1}(G) \bowtie_1 G)$

**Fig. 1.** Graph $G$ and the result of $G$-join-$G$.

Joining $G$ on its second column with $G$ on its first column yields a new relation, with three columns, encoding all paths of length 2 through the graph $G$, where each path is made of three nodes in order.

To formalize natural join as an operation on such a relation, we parameterize it by the number of columns that must match, assumed to be the first $j$ of each relation (if they are not, a renaming operation must come first). The join of relations $R$ and $S$ on the first $j$ columns is written $R \bowtie_j S$ and defined:

$$R \bowtie_j S \triangleq \{ (r_0,\ldots,r_k,s_j,\ldots,s_m) \\ \mid (\ldots,r_k) \in R \wedge (\ldots,s_m) \in S \wedge \bigwedge_{i=0..j-1} r_i = s_i \}$$

Note that to compute the join of $G$ on its second column with $G$ on its first column, we first have to reverse $G$'s columns, computing $\rho_{0/1}(G)$, so we may then compute a join on one column: $\rho_{0/1}(G) \bowtie_1 G$. To present the resulting paths of length two in order again, we may use renaming to swap the join column back to the middle position, as shown in Fig. 1. Our implementation (detailed in Sect. 3) provides more general operations that make this administrative renaming occur only implicitly, on the fly.

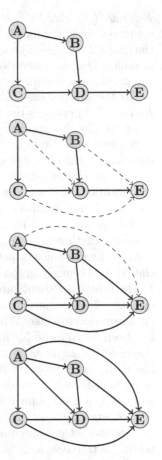

### 2.1 Motivation: Logical Inference

One of the simplest common algorithms that may be implemented efficiently as a loop over high-performance relational algebra primitives, is computing the *transitive closure* (TC) of a relation or graph. For example, consider our example graph $G \subset \mathbb{N}^2$ where each symbol $\mathbf{A}$ through $\mathbf{E}$ has been encoded or interned as an integer: $G = \{(0_\mathbf{A}, 1_\mathbf{B}), (1_\mathbf{B}, 3_\mathbf{D}), (0_\mathbf{A}, 2_\mathbf{C}), (2_\mathbf{C}, 3_\mathbf{D}), (3_\mathbf{D}, 4_\mathbf{E})\}$ (a subscript shows each integer's interpretation as a symbol or vertex name). Renaming to swap the columns of $G$, results in a graph, $\rho_{0/1}(G)$, where all arrows are reversed in direction. If this graph is joined with $G$ on only the first column (meaning $G$ is joined on its second columns with $G$ on its first column), via $\rho_{0/1}(G) \bowtie_1 G$, we get a set of triples $(b, a, c)$—specifically $\{(1_\mathbf{B}, 0_\mathbf{A}, 3_\mathbf{D}), (2_\mathbf{C}, 0_\mathbf{A}, 3_\mathbf{D}), (3_\mathbf{D}, 1_\mathbf{B}, 4_\mathbf{E}), (3_\mathbf{D}, 2_\mathbf{C}, 4_\mathbf{E})\}$—that encode paths of length two in the original graph where $a$ leads to $b$ which leads to $c$. Projecting out the initial column, $b$, with $\Pi_{1,2}(\rho_{0/1}(G) \bowtie_1 G)$ yields pairs $(a, c)$ encoding paths

**Fig. 2.** Each iteration of computing transitive closure for a small example relation $G$.

of length two from $a$ to $c$ in the original graph $G$. (Note that this projection step not only removes a column but a row as well, as $(1_\mathbf{B}, 0_\mathbf{A}, 3_\mathbf{D})$ and $(2_\mathbf{C}, 0_\mathbf{A}, 3_\mathbf{D})$ are duplicates if not differentiated by their middle, $b$, node). If we compute the union of this graph with the original $G$, we obtain a relation encoding paths of length one or two in $G$. This graph, $G \cup \Pi_{1,2}(\rho_{0/1}(G) \bowtie_1 G)$, is second from the top in Fig. 4 with new edges styled as dashed lines.

We can encapsulate this step in a function $Extend_G$ which takes a graph $T$, and returns $T$'s edges extended with $G$'s edges, unioned with $G$.

$$Extend_G(T) \triangleq G \cup \Pi_{1,2}(\rho_{0/1}(T) \bowtie_1 G)$$

The original graph $G$, at the top of Fig. 4, is yielded for $Extend_G(\bot)$, the graph below it is returned for $Extend_G^2(\bot)$, the graph below that is returned for

$Extend_G{}^3(\bot)$, etc. As $Extend_G$ is repeatedly applied from an empty input, each result encodes ever longer paths through $G$, as shown. In this case for example, the graph $Extend_G{}^3(\bot)$ encodes the transitive closure of $G$—all paths in $G$ reified as edges. One final iteration, computing $Extend_G{}^4(\bot)$, is required to check that the process successfully reached a fixed point for $Extend_G$.

In the general case, for any graph $G$, there exists some $n \in \mathbb{N}$ such that $Extend_G{}^n(\bot)$ encodes the transitive closure of $G$. The transitive closure may be computed by repeatedly applying $Extend_G$ in a loop until reaching an $n$ where $Extend_G{}^n(\bot) = Extend_G{}^{n-1}(\bot)$ in a process of *fixed-point iteration*. In the first iteration, paths of length one are computed; in the second, paths of length one or two are computed, and so forth. After the longest path in $G$ is found, just one additional iteration is necessary as a fixed-point check to confirm that the final graph has stabilized in this process of path inference.

Computing transitive closure is a simple example of logical inference. From paths of length zero (an empty graph) and the existence of edges in graph $G$, we deduce the existence of paths of length $0 \dots 1$. From paths of length $0 \dots n$ and the original edges in graph $G$, we deduce the existence of paths of length $0 \dots n+1$. The function $Extend_G$ above performs a single round of inference, finding paths one edge longer than any found previously and exposing new deductions for a next iteration to make. When the computation reaches a fixed point, the solution has been found as no further paths may be deduced from available facts. In fact, the function $Extend_G$ is a quite-immediate encoding, in relational algebra, of the transitivity property itself, $T(a,c) \Longleftarrow G(a,c) \vee T(a,b) \wedge G(b,c)$, a logical constraint for which we desire a least solution. $T$ satisfies this property *exactly* when $T$ is a fixed-point for $Extend_G$ and the transitive closure of $G$.

Solving logical and constraint problems in this way is precisely the strategy of *bottom-up logic programming*. Bottom-up logic programming begins with a set of facts (such as $T(a,b)$—the existence of an edge in a graph $T$) and a set of inference rules and performs a least-fixed-point calculation, accumulating new facts that are immediately derivable, until reaching a minimal set of facts consistent with all rules.

This kind of logical inference forms the semantics of *Datalog*, a bottom-up logic-programming language supporting a restricted logic corresponding roughly to first-order HornSAT—the SAT problem for conjunctions of Horn clauses [3]. A *Horn clause* is a disjunction of atoms where all but one is negated: $a_0 \vee \neg a_1 \vee \dots \vee \neg a_j$. By DeMorgan's laws we may rewrite this as $a_0 \vee \neg(a_1 \wedge \dots \wedge a_j)$ and note that this is an implication: $a_0 \leftarrow a_1 \wedge \dots \wedge a_j$. In first-order logic, atoms are predicates (in this case, with universally quantified variables). A Datalog program is a set of such rules,

$$P(x_0, \dots, x_k) \leftarrow Q(y_0, \dots, y_j) \wedge \dots \wedge S(z_0, \dots, z_m),$$

and its input is a database of initial facts called the *extensional database* (EDB). Running the datalog program makes explicit the *intensional database* (IDB) which extends facts in the EDB with all facts transitively derivable via the program's rules. In the usual Datalog notation, computing transitive closure of a graph is accomplished with two rules:

```
    T(x,y) <- G(x,y).                    T(x,z) <- T(x,y), G(y,z).
```

The first rule says that any edge, in G, implies a path, in T (taking the role of the left operand of union in $Extend_G$ or the left disjunct in our implication); the second rule says that any path $(x, y)$ and edge $(y, z)$ imply a path $(x, z)$ (adding edges for the right operand of union in $Extend_G$). Other kinds of graph mining problems, such as computing triangles or $k$-cliques, can also be naturally implemented as Datalog programs [23]. Our primary motivation for developing distributed RA is as a back-end for an Datalog-like logic-programming language.

Each Datalog rule may be encoded as a function $Extend$ (between databases) where a fixed point for the function is guaranteed to be a database that satisfies the particular rule. Atoms in the body (premise) of the implication, where two columns are required to match, are refined using a selection operation; e.g., atom $S(a, b, b)$ is computed by RA $\sigma_{\alpha_1 = \alpha_2}(S)$. Conjunction of atoms in the body of the implication is computed with a join operation: e.g., in the second rule above, this is the second column of path joined with the first of edge, or $\rho_{0/1}(\text{path}) \bowtie_1 \text{edge}$. These steps are followed by projection to only the columns needed in the head of the rule and any necessary column reordering. Finally, the resulting relation is unioned with the existing relation in the head of the implication to produce $F$'s output, an updated database (e.g., with an updated path relation in the examples above).

Each Datalog rule may be encoded as a monotonic function $F$ (between databases) where a fixed point for the function is guaranteed to be a database that satisfies the particular rule. Once a set of functions $F_0 \ldots F_m$, one for each rule, are constructed, Datalog evaluation operates by iterating the IDB to a mutual fixed point for $F_0 \ldots F_m$.

## 2.2 Implementing Parallel Relational Algebra

In our discussion of both TC computation and Datalog generally, we have elided important optimizations and implementation details in favor of formality regarding the main ideas of both. In practice, it is inefficient to perform multiple granular RA operations separately to perform a selection, reorder columns, join relations, project out unneeded columns, reorder columns again, etc, when iteration overhead can be eliminated and cache coherence improved by fusing these operations. In practice, high-performance Datalog solvers perform all necessary steps at once, supporting a generalization of the operations we have discussed that can join, select, reorder variables, project, and union, all at once.

In addition, both transitive closure and Datalog generally, as presented above, are using naïve fixed-point iteration, recomputing all previously discovered edges (i.e., facts) at every iteration. Efficient implementations are *incrementalized* and only consider facts that can be extended to produce so-far undiscovered facts. For example, when computing transitive closure, another relation $T_\Delta$ is used which only stores the longest paths in $T$—those discovered in the previous iteration. When computing paths of length $n$, in fixed-point iteration $n$, only new paths discovered in the previous iteration, paths of length $n - 1$, need to be considered, as shorter paths extended with edges from $G$ necessarily yield paths which have been discovered already. This optimization is known as *semi-naïve evaluation* [3]. Each non-static relation (such as $T$) is effectively partitioned into three relations: $T_{\text{full}}$, $T_\Delta$, and $T_{\text{new}}$. $T_{\text{full}}$ stores all facts discovered more than 1 iteration ago; $T_\Delta$ stores all facts that were newly discovered in the previous iteration, and is joined with $G$ each iteration to discover new facts; and $T_{\text{new}}$ stores all these facts, newly discovered in the current iteration. At the end of each iteration, $T_\Delta$'s tuples are added to $T_{\text{full}}$, $T_\Delta$'s pointer is swapped with the pointer to $T_{\text{new}}$, and $T_{\text{new}}$ is emptied to prepare for the next iteration.

The state of the art evaluating Datalog is perhaps best embodied in the Soufflé engine [9–11,19]. Soufflé systematically optimizes the RA kernels obtained from an input Datalog program, partially evaluating and staging the resulting RA for the task at hand. Soufflé also performs a strongly-connected-component analysis to extract separate inference tasks connected in a dependency (directed, acyclic) graph—stratifying SCC evaluation. RA itself is performed using a series of nested loops that utilize efficient data-structures to iterate over the tuples of a relation, iterate over tuples that match a subset of column-values, and insert new tuples. Figure 3 shows a portion of the exact C++ code produced by Soufflé (v1.5.1) for the two-rule TC program shown above (indentation and code comments have been added by the authors to improve clarity).

To compute $\rho_{0/1}(T_\Delta) \bowtie_1 G$, first the outer relation (the left-hand relation—in this case $T_\Delta$) is partitioned so that Soufflé may process each on a separate thread via OpenMP (line 1 in Fig. 3). For each partition, a loop iterates over each tuple in the current partition of $T_\Delta$ (line 2) and computes a selection tuple, key, representing all tuples in $G$ that match the present tuple from $T_\Delta$ in its join-columns (in this case the second column value, env0[1]). This selection tuple is then used to produce an iterator selecting only tuples in $G$ whose column-0 value matches the particular tuple env0's column-1 value. Soufflé thus iterates over each $(x, y) \in T_\Delta$ and creates an iterator that selects all corresponding $(y, z) \in G$. Soufflé iterates over all matching tuples in $G$ (line 5), and then constructs a tuple $(x, z)$, produced by pairing the column-0 value of the tuple from $T_\Delta$, env0[0], with the column-1 value of the tuple from $G$, env1[1], which is inserted into $T_{\text{new}}$ (line 8) only if it is not already in $T_{\text{full}}$ (line 6).

Given this architecture, Soufflé achieves good performance by using fast thread-safe data-structures, template specialized for common use cases, that represent each relation extensionally—explicitly storing each tuple in the relation, organized to be amenable to fast iteration, selection, and insertion. Soufflé includes a concurrent B-tree implementation [10] and a concurrent blocked prefix-tree implementation [11] as underlying representations for relations along with a global symbol table storing intern values. Soufflé does not support MPI or distributed computation of Datalog programs.

## 2.3   Related Work on Distributed Relational Algebra

The double-hashing approach, with local hash-based joins and hash-based distribution of relations, is the most commonly used method to distribute join

```
    // Partition T_delta for a pool of OpenMP threads; iterate over parts
1   pfor(auto it = part.begin(); it<part.end();++it){
      // Iterate over each tuple, env0, of T_delta (in each partition)
2     try{for(const auto& env0 : *it) {
        // Construct an iterator selecting tuples in G that match env0
3       const Tuple<RamDomain,2> key({{env0[1],0}});
4       auto range = rel_1_edge->equalRange_1(key,
                              READ_OP_CONTEXT(rel_1_edge_op_ctxt));
        // Iterate over matching tuples in G
5       for(const auto& env1 : range) {
          // Has this output tuple already been discovered (is in T_full)?
6         if(!(rel_2_path->contains(Tuple<RamDomain,2>({{env0[0],env1[1]}}),
                              READ_OP_CONTEXT(rel_2_path_op_ctxt)))) {
            // Construct the output tuple and insert it into T_new
7           Tuple<RamDomain,2> tuple({{static_cast<RamDomain>(env0[0]),
                              static_cast<RamDomain>(env1[1])}});
8           rel_4_new_path->insert(tuple,
                              READ_OP_CONTEXT(rel_4_new_path_op_ctxt));
9         }
10      }
11    }} catch(std::exception &e){SignalHandler::instance()->error(e.what());}
12  }
```

**Fig. 3.** The join of a TC computation, as implemented by Soufflé.

operations over many nodes in a networked cluster computer. This algorithm involves partitioning relations by their join-column values so that they can be efficiently distributed to participating processes [6,7]. The main insight behind this approach is that for each tuple in the outer relation, all relevant tuples in the inner relation must be hashed to the same MPI process or node, permitting joins to be performed locally on each process.

Recently, radix-hash join and merge-sort join algorithms have been evaluated using this approach [5]. Both these algorithms partition data so that they may be efficiently distributed to participating processes and are designed to minimize inter-process communication. One-sided RMA operations remotely coordinate distributed joins and parallelize communication and computation phases. Experiments for this work scaled join operations to 4,096 nodes, and reached extremely high peak tuples/second throughput, but this work does not address materializing and reorganizing relations for subsequent iterations—challenges required to implement fixed-point algorithms over RA. In addition, this work only considers uniform (perfectly balanced) relations, citing balancing of relations as future work and does not represent realistic workloads because each key has exactly one matching tuple in each relation being joined. A key advantage of this approach is that radix-hash join and merge-sort join, used on each process, support acceleration via AVX/SIMD instructions and exhibit good cache behavior [4,12].

Our recent approach proposes adapting the representation of imbalanced relations by using a two-layered distributed hash-table to partition tuples over a fixed set of *buckets*, and, within each bucket, to a dynamic set of *subbuckets* which may vary across buckets [14]. Each tuple is assigned to a bucket based on a hash of its join-column values, but within each bucket, tuples are hashed on non-join-column values, assigning them to a local subbucket, then mapped to an

MPI process. This permits buckets that have more tuples to be split across multiple processes, but requires some additional communication among subbuckets for any particular bucket. Our previous work presents a static refinement strategy that is used before fixed-point iteration to decide how many subbuckets to allocate per bucket, and compares two approaches for mapping subbuckets to processes. This implementation does not address dynamic refinement across fixed-point iterations; as relations accumulate new tuples, the difference between the largest subbucket and the smallest subbucket can grow or diminish.

Our implementation heavily relies on all-to-all communication. We use the `MPI_Alltoallv` function to transmit data from every process to every other process. Our use is related to distributed hash tables more generally [17], which make effective use of all-to-all communication, except that we co-locate multiple distributed hash tables for the purposes of performing efficient joins. `MPI_Alltoallv` is one of the most communication-intensive collective operations used across parallel applications such as CPMD [1], NAMD [18], LU factorization, parallel sorting, fast fourier transform (FFT) and matrix transpose. Much research [13,20] has gone into developing scalable implementations of collective operations; most of the existing HPC platforms therefore have a scalable implementation of all-to-all operations.

# 3    Balancing Distributed Relational Algebra

In this section, we extend previous approaches to efficiently distributing relational algebra by developing strategies that mitigate load-imbalance in a fully dynamic manner. First, we describe the architecture of our join operation in detail to ground this discussion. Following [14], we distribute each relation across a fixed number of logical *buckets* (chosen to match the number of MPI processes in our experiments). Each bucket has a variable number of *subbuckets*, that can increase as needed for buckets containing disproportionately large numbers of tuples. Each subbucket belongs to just one bucket and is hosted by a single MPI process, but a single MPI process may host any number of subbuckets.

To distribute subbuckets to managing processes, we use a round-robin mapping scheme. The example in Fig. 4 shows the round-robin mapping of subbuckets to processes where there are 5 buckets with 2 subbuckets each and 5 MPI processes. This process requires a very small amount of added communication, but ensures that no process manages more than one subbucket more than any other.

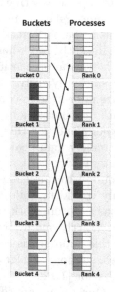

**Fig. 4.**    Round-robin mapping of subbuckets to processes.

Locally, subbuckets store tuples using B-trees (an approach used by Soufflé), which carries several advantages over the double-hashing approach's use of hash tables. Crucially, hash-tables can lead to a resizing operation that delays synchronization.

Figure 5 shows a schematic diagram of our join algorithm in the context of an incrementalized TC computation. A join operation can only be performed for two *co-located relations*: two relations each keyed on their respective join columns that share a bucket decomposition (but not necessarily a subbucket decomposition for each bucket). This ensures that the join operation may be performed separately on each bucket as all matching tuples will share a logical bucket; it does not, however, ensure that all pairs of matching tuples will share the same subbucket as tuples are assigned to subbuckets (within a bucket) based on the values of non-join columns, separately for each relation.

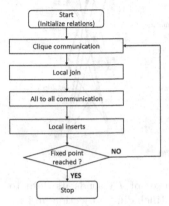

**Fig. 5.** Major steps in our join algorithm, in the context of TC.

The first step in a join operation is therefore an *intra-bucket communication* phase within each bucket so that every subbucket receives all tuples for the outer relation across all subbuckets (while the inner relation only needs tuples belonging to the local subbucket). Following this, a *local join* operation (with any necessary projection and renaming) can be performed in every subbucket, and, as output tuples may each belong to an arbitrary bucket in the output relation, an MPI *all-to-all* communication phase shuffles the output of all joins to their managing processes (preparing them for any subsequent iteration). Finally, upon receiving these output tuples from the previous join, each process inserts them into the local B-tree for $T_{\text{new}}$, propagates $T_\Delta$ into $T_{\text{full}}$ and $T_{\text{new}}$ becomes $T_\Delta$ for the next iteration along with a empty $T_{\text{new}}$. If no new tuples have been discovered, globally, a fixed point has been reached and iteration may halt.

Intra-bucket communication (shown on the left of Fig. 6) uses MPI point-to-point communication to shuffle all tuples from each subbucket of the outer relation (in the case of T-join-G in TC, $T_\Delta$) to all subbuckets of the inner-relation (in the case of TC, $G$), which will subsequently perform local, per-subbucket joins. It may seem appealing to fuse the final all-to-all communication phase among buckets with the intra-bucket communication of the next iteration, sending new tuples (for $T_\Delta$ in the next iteration) directly to all subbuckets of $G$; however, doing this fusion forgoes an opportunity for per-subbucket deduplication and yields meaningful slowdowns in practice.

The local join phase proceeds in a fully parallel and unsynchronized fashion. Each process iterates over its subbuckets, performing a single join operation for each. Our join is implemented as a straightforward tree-based join as shown in the center of Fig. 6. In this diagram, colors are used to indicate the hash value of each tuple as determined by its join-column value. The outer relation's local tuples are iterated over, grouped by key values. For each key value, a lookup is

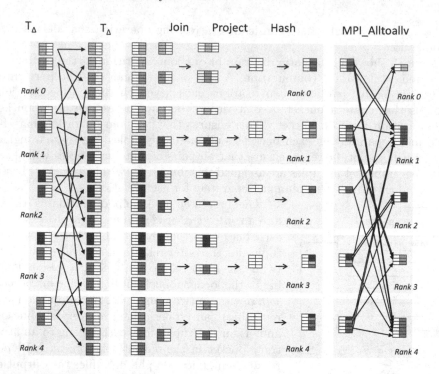

**Fig. 6.** (Left) Intra-bucket communication; each subbucket of $T_\Delta$ sends its data to all subbuckets of $G$. (Center) Local, per-subbucket joins (including projection and re-hashing). (Right) All to all communication.

performed to select a portion of the tree storing the inner relation's local tuples where all tuples have a matching key value (in this case on the first column of $G$). For two sets of tuples with matching join-column values, we effectively perform a Cartesian product computation, producing one tuple for all output pairs. Each output tuple has any needed projection and renaming of columns performed on-the-fly; in this case, the prior join columns that matched are projected away. These output tuples are temporarily stored in a tree, to perform local dedu-plication, and are then staged for transmission to new managing subbuckets in their receiving relation. After the join, each output tuple belongs to $T_{\text{new}}$ ($T_\Delta$ in the next iteration) and must be hashed on the final column to determine which bucket it belongs to, and on all other columns to determine which subbucket within that bucket. While we follow Soufflé in implementing B-tree-based joins on each process, other approaches may be able to take better advantage of AVX instructions and on-chip caching [4,12]. We plan to investigate alternatives in the future and believe them to be largely orthogonal to our paradigm for decom-position, communication, and balancing of relations. Other future work includes taking advantage of thread-level parallelism offered by multi-core nodes. In par-ticular, we plan to parallelize sub-bucket joins across concurrent threads.

Next, an all-to-all communication phase (shown on the right side of Fig. 6) transmits materialized joins to their new bucket-subbucket decomposition in $T_{new}$. After being hashed on their new join column value to assign each to a bucket, and on all non-join-column values to assign each to a subbucket, the managing process for this subbucket is looked up in a local map and tuples are organized into buffers for MPI's `All_to_allv` synchronous communication operation. When this is invoked, all tuples are shuffled to their destination processes.

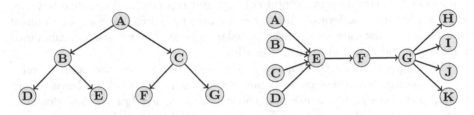

**Fig. 7.** A complete binary tree with height 2 and down-directed edges (left); a bowtie graph with width 4 and length 3 (right).

Finally, after the synchronous communication phase, $T_\Delta$ is locally propagated into $T_{full}$, which stores all tuples discovered more than 1 iteration ago. New tuples are checked against this $T_{full}$ to ensure they are genuinely new facts (paths in $G$), and are inserted into a B-tree for $T_{new}$ on each receiving process to perform remote deduplication. At this point, the iteration ends, $T_{new}$ becomes $T_\Delta$ for the subsequent iteration, and an empty $T_{new}$ is allocated. If no new tuples were actually discovered in the previous iteration, a fixed-point has been reached and no further iterations are needed as the database as stabilized.

## 3.1   Two Kinds of Load-Imbalance

We consider two kinds of load-imbalance and how they might occur and change across iterations of a transitive closure computation: *spatial load imbalance*, when a relation's stored tuples are mapped unevenly to processes, and *temporal load imbalance*, when the number of output tuples produced varies across iterations.

Consider the class of relations that encode complete binary trees of height $H$, where directed edges face either strictly downward or upward. The left side of Fig. 7 shows an example of a downward-facing complete binary tree with height 2. If a downward-facing relation in this class is keyed on its first column, there is no load imbalance as each key has exactly two tuples (two children per parent); if it is keyed on its second column, there is likewise no load imbalance as each key has exactly one tuple (one parent

| Direction | $T$ | $G$ |
|---|---|---|
| **Up** | $O(2^{H-D})$ | $O(1)$ |
| **Down** | $O(D)$ | $O(1)$ |

**Fig. 8.** Worst-case imbalance for $T$ and $G$ in TC computation (for complete binary tree topology).

per child). If we use an up-directed binary tree instead, these are reversed; either way, the relation is initially balanced. Now what happens when we compute its TC?

The TC of a down-directed complete binary tree of height $H$ (keyed on column 0) has significant spatial imbalance. The root node has $O(2^H)$ tuples (edges) hosted on its process, while nodes at depth $H - 1$ have only 2. If the relation is keyed on the second column (or if we use an up-directed tree), then there is a natural imbalance that increases linearly with depth. In a TC computation, as relation $T$ is keyed on its second column, not the first, a down-directed tree exhibits the more moderate imbalance; for an upward-facing complete binary tree, $T$ has a worst-case exponential imbalance ratio. The worst-case imbalance ratios for $T$ and $G$ are summarized in Fig. 8.

The complete binary tree topology graphs are perhaps corner cases for relation imbalance, however such relations can occur in the wild, and even more moderate degrees of imbalance can cause relational algebra to slow down or crash in practice. Relational algebra that is suitable for arbitrary workloads must handle arbitrary degrees of spatial imbalance gracefully, and if used within a fixed-point loop (as is the case for general logical inference applications), relations must support dynamic spatial refinement that is efficient enough to handle arbitrary changes in imbalance across time—both increases and decreases.

Now consider the bowtie topology shown on the right side of Fig. 7. Each bowtie-topology graph has a width $W$ and length $L$, and is formed by connecting $W$ nodes each to the starting node of a string of $L$ nodes, connected on the far side to another $W$ nodes each. What happens when computing the TC of an arbitrary bowtie relation? The first iteration, a join between a bowtie relation and itself, yields $2W + L - 1$ new edges; in fact, at every iteration until the last, the worst-case join output is in $O(W + L)$. At the final iteration, however, the number of output tuples suddenly becomes quadratic in the width of the bowtie, $O(W^2)$, as each of the leftmost nodes are paired with each of the rightmost nodes. This illustrates a case of temporal imbalance—a large bowtie can produce fewer than $100K$ tuples one iteration and more than $1B$ tuples the next.

A general-purpose system for relational algebra should also be robust to unexpected surges in the per-iteration workload, adapting itself to dynamic changes in the overall workload across time. While bowtie graphs represent corner cases, it is common to see join output change significantly from iteration to iteration when computing TC of real-world graphs as well (see Table 1).

## 3.2   Three Techniques for Adaptive Load-Balancing

Now we describe three techniques that, used in conjunction, can remediate both kinds of imbalance illustrated in the previous section: bucket refinement, bucket consolidation, and iteration roll-over. *Bucket refinement* is a dynamic check for each bucket to see if its subbuckets are significantly heavier than average, triggering a refinement in which new subbuckets are allocated to support this larger number of tuples. *Bucket consolidation* occurs only if there are a significant number of refined buckets, and consolidates buckets into fewer subbuckets when spatial imbalance has lessened. Finally, *iteration roll-over* allows particularly busy iterations to be interrupted part-way, with completed work being processed immediately and with the residual workload from the iteration "rolling over".

Bucket refinement is one of two techniques we use to address natural spatial imbalance among the keys of a relation. Refinement is used to check for disproportionately *heavy* subbuckets (those with more than the average number of tuples), and to spread this load across an increased number of subbuckets. Checking for needed refinement is a lightweight, but non-trivial step, so we only perform this imbalance check every $N$ iterations (where $N$ is an adjustable parameter). In our experiments, we use both $N = 2$ and $N = 10$ but observed only a small difference in performance. To check for refinement, the heaviest subbucket in each bucket is compared with the average subbucket size across all buckets; when the ratio is greater than 3-to-1, we refine this bucket, quadrupling its subbucket count from 1 to 4, from 4 to 16, from 16 to 64, etc; the subbucket count in each bucket is always maintained as a power of 4. This additional allocation of subbuckets extends the round-robin mapping maintained in lock-step on all processes by transmitting a small amount of meta-data during the global all-to-all phase. An immediate point-to-point communication is triggered especially to distribute three-quarters of the tuples from each subbucket in a refined bucket to processes hosting newly allocated subbuckets.

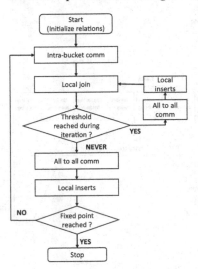

**Fig. 9.** The major steps in our join algorithm with iteration roll-over added.

Bucket consolidation is a complementary technique for combining previously split subbuckets when spatial load imbalance has again lessened. The imbalance check for bucket consolidation is guarded by a global check to see if greater than 60% of buckets have been refined to 4 or more subbuckets. When this is the case, all buckets containing subbuckets with a below-average tuple-count are consolidated into $\frac{1}{4}$ as many subbuckets. This process uses the same communication machinery as bucket refinement; a special point-to-point communication is used to redistribute tuples into a smaller number of buckets, all of which are freshly allocated using our round-robin allocation scheme to prevent pathological cases.

Iteration roll-over guards against severe cases of temporal imbalance which can slow evaluation, through thrashing of memory, or crash a process. As in the case of our bowtie topology, the shape of a graph can cause a sudden explosion of work in a single iteration. This requires our algorithm to be on-guard for temporal imbalance at every iteration, as opposed to spatial imbalance where we may avoid some overhead by checking for imbalance intermittently. As each local join is processed, grouped by key-column values, a count of output tuples is maintained and at each new key-column value we check to see if it has passed some fixed *threshold value* (a tunable parameter—we experiment with several threshold values). When the threshold has been exceeded, we stop computing the join and transmit the partial join output to destination processes for remote deduplication early.

This step is shown in Fig. 9. When a threshold value is reached during the local-join phase, an all-to-all communication is triggered, followed by local inserts in each destination subbucket. Then, instead of the iteration ending (with propagation from each $R_\Delta$ to $R_{\text{full}}$ and from each $R_{\text{new}}$ to $R_\Delta$), the previous iteration continues exactly where it left off. We may also think of this an *inner iteration* as opposed to the normal *outer iterations* of semi-naïve evaluation. Each inner iteration batches the threshold value in output tuples to promote cache coherence and prevent overflow.

# 4   Evaluation

We begin by studying the impact of spatial and temporal load balancing in isolation. Following this, we analyze the impact of both forms of load balancing, jointly, on real-world graphs and at scale.

We performed our experiments for this work on the Theta Supercomputer [2] at the Argonne Leadership Computing Facility (ALCF). Theta is a Cray machine with a peak performance of 11.69 petaflops, 281,088 compute cores, 843.264 TiB of DDR4 RAM, 70.272 TiB of MCDRAM and 10 PiB of online disk storage. We performed our experiments using the SuiteSparse Matrix Collection [8].

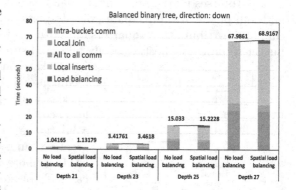

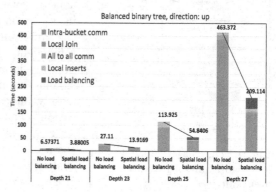

## 4.1   Spatial Load Balancing

We evaluate the performance of spatial load-balancing, in Fig. 10, by computing the transitive closure of eight balanced binary-tree graphs (depths: 21, 23, 25, 27, for each

**Fig. 10.** TC computation for complete binary trees (depths 21, 23, 25 and 27) for up (top) and down (bottom) pointing edges with and without load balancing.

edge direction: *up* and *down*). We run all these experiments at 512 cores, both with and without spatial load balancing turned on. The transitive closure for the graphs (in order of increasing tree depth) generated 39,845,890, 176,160,770, 771,751,938 and 3,355,443,202 edges, respectively (taking 21, 23, 25 and 27 iterations to converge). Note that both up-directed (UP) and down-directed (DOWN) graphs (of equal depth) produce the same number of edges.

We observed dynamic load balancing lead to a roughly 2× improvement for UP graphs. As an example, for the graph with depth 27, load balancing led the total runtime to go down from 463 s to 209 s. In our experiments, we set the load-imbalance check to be performed every other iteration, as this is the sole feature under consideration; for all four graphs, however, actual re-balancing (refinement of buckets) occurred only five times each, with the cumulative number of sub-buckets increasing dynamically from 512 to 1088 in every case.

On the other hand, load balancing does not yield any improvement for DOWN graphs. This is despite the fact that computing the TC UP and DOWN graphs produces the same number of edges and takes the same number of iterations to converge in both cases. What differs is how tuples are distributed among keys (values for the join column); with linear imbalance in the DOWN case and exponential imbalance in the UP case. We note that TC for UP graphs can be computed as efficiently as DOWN graphs if we change our iterated join from T-join-G to G-join-T, but this optimization requires a priori knowledge of the final graph's topology, which is likely unavailable. Our approach aims to be as relation agnostic as is possible, so that arbitrary logical inference tasks may be scaled effectively.

It may be surprising that DOWN graphs do not show some lesser need for dynamic re-balancing as they evolve from being perfectly balanced to being linearly imbalanced. This would be the case if each key were mapped to a unique bucket. Since keys are hashed to a smaller number of buckets, however, we only observe a 1.001 imbalance ratio for height-25 DOWN trees and we observe a 204.8 inter-bucket imbalance ratio for height-25 UP trees. This means hashing keys to buckets has a modest ameliorating effect on imbalance that can be sufficient, but not in cases of severe imbalance.

## 4.2 Temporal Load Balancing

Temporal load balancing is a key safety feature, without which it can become impossible to make meaningful progress due to continuous page faults. We demonstrate this particular use case for an extreme scenario, where thresholding acts as a critical component. We use a very large graph Hardesty3 [8] (40,451,631 edges) that generates an overwhelming number of edges at an accelerating pace. Without thresholding, a process gets overwhelmed by the computational workload and runs out of memory. We applied a modified version of the transitive closure problem where, instead of trying to reach the fixed point, we restricted our computation to run only 20 iterations. (At the end of iteration 20, we have computed all paths of up to length 20.) We ran our experiments at 32,768 cores, both with and without temporal load balancing. Without load balancing, we

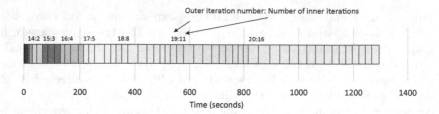

**Fig. 11.** Breakdown of time taken to finish 20 iterations (paths of length 20) using temporal load balancing.

were only able to complete iteration 16, whereas with load balancing we were able to finish all 20 iterations. The number of edges generated at the end of 20 iterations was 913,419,562,086 (13.3 Terabytes). We have plotted a breakdown of time taken during every iteration in Fig. 11. We observed temporal load balancing was used for all iterations after the 14th iteration, the 19$^{th}$ and 20$^{th}$ iterations, for example, were broken into 11 and 16 inner iterations respectively. Also, it can be seen that the aggregate time taken increases significantly with every iteration. For these experiments, we used a threshold of 8,000,000. It took 1,256 s to finish running 20 iterations.

Temporal balancing can also be used as an optimization technique for extreme topology graphs such as the bowtie (see Fig. 7). To demonstrate this, we used a bow-tie graph with a width of 10,000 vertices and length of 10 vertices. This graph generates 10,000 × 10,000 edges in the 10$^{th}$ iteration, when all vertices on the left side of the bowtie each discover paths to all vertices on the right side of the bowtie. For the first 10 iterations, the number of edges pro-

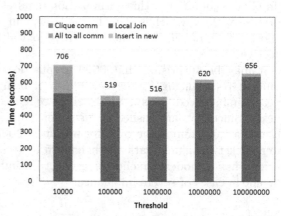

**Fig. 12.** Time to compute TC for bow-tie topology graph with varying thresholds.

duced every iteration is roughly 20,000 whereas the number of edges generated in the 10$^{th}$ iteration is 100,000,000, leading to a temporal imbalance ratio of about 5,000. We run our experiments at 256 cores with 5 different threshold values: 10,000, 100,000, 1,000,000, 10,000,000, and 100,000,000. The transitive closure of the graph generated 400,440,055 edges. While the number of outer iterations is 10 for all thresholds, the number of inner iterations varied as 20,020, 3,343, 402, 49 and 13. Note that small threshold values lead to an unnecessarily increased number of inner iterations and hence an increased number of all to all communication epochs. Smaller threshold values also lead to more-optimized local join phases, as the nested B-tree data structures holding relations do not grow very large, leading to better cache coherence while performing lookups and inserts.

We plot our results in Fig. 12. We observe a best timing of 516 s for a threshold of 1,000,000 tuples. At this threshold, we achieve a good balance between the extra time taken for all-to-all communication phases versus the time saved during each local join phase. Lower thresholds make the problem bounded by communication (all-to-all phase) whereas higher thresholds make the problem bounded by computation (local join phase). At larger process counts, we observed better performance for larger threshold values. For example, at 8,192 cores the transitive closure of graph sgpf5y6 with edge count 831,976 took 384, 559 and 590 s for threshold values 100,000,000, 10,000,000 and 1,000,000 respectively. We use temporal load balancing primarily as a safety check, although it is also a practical optimization for corner-case topology graphs. We believe that our design is flexible enough to be tuned to different scales and different degrees in imbalance in the input graph.

## 4.3 Transitive Closure at Scale

We also performed experiments to study the impact of load balancing on real-world and random graphs. We compute the transitive closure of six real world graphs [8] and two random graphs generated via RMAT [15]. All our experiments were performed at 8,192 processes with both temporal and spatial load-balancing enabled. In these experiments we check for spatial imbalance every tenth iteration and temporal imbalance at every iteration—the roll-over threshold is set at 8,000,000 tuples. Our results are shown in Table 1. All graphs except TSC_OPF_300 make use of spatial load balancing. We also note that graphs sgpf5y6, RMAT_1, and RMAT_2 make use of temporal load balancing, as the number of edges generated for these graphs grow at a rapidly increasing rate (respectively, 76, 2, and 9 billion edges in the first 20 iterations).

**Table 1.** List of eight (6 real world + 2 random) graphs used in our evaluation.

| Name | Edges | Time (seconds) | Spatial balancing | Temporal balancing | Iterations | TC Edges |
|------|-------|----------------|-------------------|--------------------|------------|----------|
| lhr34 | 764,014 | 64.3391 | ✓ | | 30 | 1,233,554,044 |
| nemeth13 | 241,989 | 28.8445 | ✓ | | 310 | 45,186,771 |
| sgpf5y6 | 831,976 | 578.641 | ✓ | ✓ | 20 | 76,382,533,943 |
| rim | 1,014,951 | 46.7834 | ✓ | | 30 | 508,931,041 |
| TSC_OPF_300 | 415,288 | 2.11 | | | 30 | 1,876,367 |
| RMAT_1 | 200000 | 68.8143 | ✓ | ✓ | 20 | 2,502,341,599 |
| RMAT_2 | 400000 | 220.993 | ✓ | ✓ | 20 | 9,481,998,719 |

We also performed strong scaling studies for the graphs in Table 1, we report the performance numbers for four graphs lhr34, sgpf5y6, TSC_OPF_300, and rim in Fig. 13. For graph lhr34 we observe 7× improvement in performance while going from 512 processes to 8,192 processes. Further breakdown shows that we achieve a scaling efficiency of 74% while going from 512 processes to 2048 processes and an efficiency of 60%

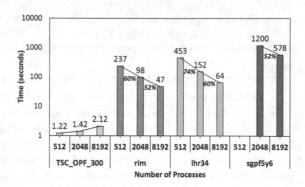

**Fig. 13.** Strong-scaling plots for lhr34, sgpf5y6, TSC_OPF_300, and rim graphs. Numbers in red shows scaling efficiency. (Color figure online)

while going from 2048 to 8192 processes. For graph rim we observe an overall improvement of 5× (scaling efficiency shown in figure). Graph TSC_OPF_300 demonstrates a trend reversal, with performance worsening with increased process count. Our observation shows that the degree of extractable parallelism varies across graphs, depending on the connectivity, topology and the size of the graph. For example, TSC_OPF_300 is sparsely connected (as seen from the small TC size), requires very few iterations to converge and thus, is not suitable for a large process run.

We also make the observation that for a given workload, there is a range of processes that exhibits good scaling and beyond which performance starts to suffer due to workload scarcity and increased communication costs.

## 5   Conclusion

In this paper, we have explored the issue of inherent imbalance in relations, and across iterations of fixed-point computations. We have described three techniques for mitigating these issues dynamically in parallel relational algebra, distributed in a data-parallel manner across many cores, and have evaluated our approach by computing the transitive closures of real world, random, and corner-case graphs.

**Acknowledgement.** We are thankful to the Argonne Leadership Computing Facility's Director's Discretionary (DD) program for providing us with compute hours to run our experiments on the Theta Supercomputer.

## References

1. CPMD Home Page. http://www.cpmd.org/
2. Theta ALCF Home Page. https://www.alcf.anl.gov/theta
3. Abiteboul, S., Hull, R., Vianu, V.: Foundations of Databases: The Logical Level. Addison-Wesley Longman Publishing Co. Inc., Boston (1995)

4. Balkesen, C., Alonso, G., Teubner, J., Özsu, M.T.: Multi-core, main-memory joins: sort vs. hash revisited. Proc. VLDB Endow. **7**(1), 85–96 (2013)
5. Barthels, C., Müller, I., Schneider, T., Alonso, G., Hoefler, T.: Distributed join algorithms on thousands of cores. Proc. VLDB Endow. **10**(5), 517–528 (2017)
6. Cacace, F., Ceri, S., Houtsma, M.A.W.: An overview of parallel strategies for transitive closure on algebraic machines. In: America, P. (ed.) PDS 1990. LNCS, vol. 503, pp. 44–62. Springer, Heidelberg (1991). https://doi.org/10.1007/3-540-54132-2_49
7. Cheiney, J.P., de Maindreville, C.: A parallel strategy for transitive closure using double hash-based clustering. In: Proceedings of the Sixteenth International Conference on Very Large Databases, pp. 347–358. Morgan Kaufmann Publishers Inc., San Francisco (1990)
8. Davis, T.A., Hu, Y.: The University of Florida sparse matrix collection. ACM Trans. Math. Softw. **38**(1), 1:1–1:25 (2011)
9. Jordan, H., Scholz, B., Subotić, P.: SOUFFLÉ: on synthesis of program analyzers. In: Chaudhuri, S., Farzan, A. (eds.) CAV 2016. LNCS, vol. 9780, pp. 422–430. Springer, Cham (2016). https://doi.org/10.1007/978-3-319-41540-6_23
10. Jordan, H., Subotić, P., Zhao, D., Scholz, B.: A specialized B-tree for concurrent datalog evaluation. In: Principles and Practice of Parallel Programming, PPoPP 2019, pp. 327–339. ACM, New York (2019)
11. Jordan, H., Subotić, P., Zhao, D., Scholz, B.: Brie: a specialized trie for concurrent datalog. In: Proceedings of the 10th International Workshop on Programming Models and Applications for Multicores and Manycores, PMAM 2019, pp. 31–40. ACM, New York (2019)
12. Kim, C., et al.: Sort vs. hash revisited: fast join implementation on modern multi-core CPUs. Proc. VLDB Endow. **2**(2), 1378–1389 (2009)
13. Kumar, R., Mamidala, A., Panda, D.K.: Scaling alltoall collective on multi-core systems. In: 2008 IEEE International Symposium on Parallel and Distributed Processing, pp. 1–8 (April 2008)
14. Kumar, S., Gilray, T.: Distributed relational algebra at scale. In: International Conference on High Performance Computing, Data, and Analytics (HiPC). IEEE (2019)
15. Leskovec, J., Chakrabarti, D., Kleinberg, J., Faloutsos, C.: Realistic, mathematically tractable graph generation and evolution, using kronecker multiplication. In: Jorge, A.M., Torgo, L., Brazdil, P., Camacho, R., Gama, J. (eds.) PKDD 2005. LNCS (LNAI), vol. 3721, pp. 133–145. Springer, Heidelberg (2005). https://doi.org/10.1007/11564126_17
16. Liu, M., Dobbie, G., Ling, T.W.: A logical foundation for deductive object-oriented databases. ACM Trans. Database Syst. (TODS) **27**(1), 117–151 (2002)
17. Pan, T.C., Misra, S., Aluru, S.: Optimizing high performance distributed memory parallel hash tables for DNA k-mer counting. In: SC18: International Conference for High Performance Computing, Networking, Storage and Analysis, pp. 135–147. IEEE (2018)
18. Phillips, J.C., Kumar, S., Kale, L.V.: NAMD: biomolecular simulation on thousands of processors. In: Proceedings of the 2002 ACM/IEEE Conference on Supercomputing, SC 2002, pp. 36–36 (November 2002)
19. Scholz, B., Jordan, H., Subotić, P., Westmann, T.: On fast large-scale program analysis in datalog. In: Proceedings of the 25th International Conference on Compiler Construction, CC 2016, pp. 196–206. ACM, New York (2016)
20. Thakur, R., Rabenseifner, R., Gropp, W.: Optimization of collective communication operations in MPICH. High Perform. Comput. Appl. **19**(1), 49–66 (2005)

21. Torlak, E., Jackson, D.: Kodkod: a relational model finder. In: Grumberg, O., Huth, M. (eds.) TACAS 2007. LNCS, vol. 4424, pp. 632–647. Springer, Heidelberg (2007). https://doi.org/10.1007/978-3-540-71209-1_49
22. Van Gael, J.A.F.M., Herbrich, R., Graepel, T.: Machine learning using relational databases (29 January 2013). uS Patent 8,364,612
23. Wang, K., Zuo, Z., Thorpe, J., Nguyen, T.Q., Xu, G.H.: RStream: marrying relational algebra with streaming for efficient graph mining on a single machine. In: 13th {USENIX} Symposium on Operating Systems Design and Implementation ({OSDI} 18), pp. 763–782 (2018)
24. Zinn, D., Wu, H., Wang, J., Aref, M., Yalamanchili, S.: General-purpose join algorithms for large graph triangle listing on heterogeneous systems. In: Proceedings of the 9th Annual Workshop on General Purpose Processing Using Graphics Processing Unit, GPGPU 2016, pp. 12–21. ACM, New York (2016)

# Sparse Linear Algebra on AMD and NVIDIA GPUs – The Race Is On

Yuhsiang M. Tsai[1] , Terry Cojean[1] , and Hartwig Anzt[1,2](✉)

[1] Karlsruhe Institute of Technology, 76131 Karlsruhe, Germany
hartwig.anzt@kit.edu
[2] University of Tennessee, Knoxville, TN 37996, USA

**Abstract.** Efficiently processing sparse matrices is a central and performance-critical part of many scientific simulation codes. Recognizing the adoption of manycore accelerators in HPC, we evaluate in this paper the performance of the currently best sparse matrix-vector product (SPMV) implementations on high-end GPUs from AMD and NVIDIA. Specifically, we optimize SPMV kernels for the CSR, COO, ELL, and HYB format taking the hardware characteristics of the latest GPU technologies into account. We compare for 2,800 test matrices the performance of our kernels against AMD's hipSPARSE library and NVIDIA's cuSPARSE library, and ultimately assess how the GPU technologies from AMD and NVIDIA compare in terms of SPMV performance.

**Keywords:** Sparse matrix vector product (SpMV) · GPUs · AMD · NVIDIA

## 1 Introduction

The sparse matrix vector product (SPMV) is a heavily-used and performance-critical operation in many scientific and industrial applications such as fluid flow simulations, electrochemical analysis, or Google's PageRank algorithm [11]. Operations including sparse matrices are typically memory bound on virtually all modern processor technology. With an increasing number of high performance computing (HPC) systems featuring GPU accelerators, there are significant resources spent on finding the best way to store a sparse matrix and optimize the SPMV kernel for different problems.

In this paper, we present and compare four SPMV strategies (COO, CSR, ELL, and HYB) and their realization on AMD and NVIDIA GPUs. We furthermore assess the performance of each format for 2,800 test matrices on high-end GPUs from AMD and NVIDIA. We also derive performance profiles to investigate how well the distinct kernels generalize. All considered SPMV kernels are integrated into the GINKGO open-source library[1], a modern C++ library designed for the iterative solution of sparse linear systems, and we demonstrate

---

[1] https://ginkgo-project.github.io.

© Springer Nature Switzerland AG 2020
P. Sadayappan et al. (Eds.): ISC High Performance 2020, LNCS 12151, pp. 309–327, 2020.
https://doi.org/10.1007/978-3-030-50743-5_16

that these kernels often outperform their counterparts available in the AMD hipSPARSE and the NVIDIA cuSPARSE vendor libraries.

Given the long list of efforts covering the design and evaluation of SpMV kernels on manycore processors, see [2,7] for a recent and comprehensive overview of SpMV research, we highlight that this work contains the following novel contributions:

- We develop new SpMV kernels for COO, CSR, ELL and HYB that are optimized for AMD and NVIDIA GPUs and outperform existing implementations. In particular, we propose algorithmic improvements and tuning parameters to enable performance portability.
- We evaluate the performance of the new kernels against SpMV kernels available in AMD's hipSPARSE library and NVIDIA's cuSPARSE library.
- Using the 2,800 test matrices from the Suite Sparse Matrix Collection, we derive performance profiles to assess how well the distinct kernels generalize.
- We compare the SpMV performance limits of high-end GPUs from AMD and NVIDIA.
- Up to our knowledge, GINKGO is the first open-source sparse linear algebra library based on C++ that features multiple SpMV kernels suitable for irregular matrices with back ends for both, AMD's and NVIDIA's GPUs.
- We ensure full result reproducibility by making all kernels publicly available as part of the GINKGO library, and archiving the performance results in a public repository[2].

Before providing more details about the sparse matrix formats and the processing strategy of the related SpMV routines in Sect. 3, we recall some basics about sparse matrix formats in Sect. 2. In Sect. 3.4, we combine several basic matrix storage formats into the so-called "hybrid" format (HYB) that splits the matrix into parts to exploit the performance niches of various basic formats. In a comprehensive evaluation in Sect. 4, we first compare the performance of GINKGO's SpMV functionality with the SpMV kernels available in NVIDIA's cuSPARSE library and AMD's hipSPARSE library, then derive performance profiles to characterize all kernels with respect to specialization and generalization, and finally compare the SpMV performance of AMD's RadeonVII GPU with NVIDIA's V100 GPU. We conclude in Sect. 5 with a summary of the observations.

## 2    Review of Sparse Matrix Formats

For matrices where most elements are zero, which is typical for, e.g., finite element discretizations or network representations, storing all values explicitly is expensive in terms of memory and computational effort. In response, sparse matrix formats reduce the memory footprint and the computational effort by focusing on the nonzero matrix values [3]. In some cases, additionally storing some zero elements can improve memory access and data-parallel processing [4].

---

[2] https://github.com/ginkgo-project/ginkgo-data/tree/2020_isc.

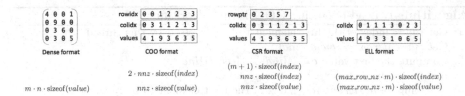

**Fig. 1.** Different storage formats for a sparse matrix of dimension $m \times n$ containing $n_z$ nonzeros along with the memory consumption [6].

While there exists a long and still expanding list of sparse matrix formats (some of them tailored towards specific problems), we illustrate some of the most common basic formats (DENSE, COO, CSR, ELL) in Fig. 1.

The optimization of the SpMV kernel for manycore GPUs remains a topic of major interest [5,9,12]. Many of the most recent algorithm developments increase the efficiency by using prefix-sum computations [13] and intra-warp communication [10] on modern manycore hardware.

## 3  Sparse Matrix Vector Kernel Designs

We realize all SpMV kernels in the vendors' native languages: CUDA for NVIDIA GPUs and HIP for AMD GPUs. Given the different hardware characteristics, see Table 1, we optimize kernel parameters like group size for the distinct architectures. More relevant, for the CSR, ELL, and HYB kernels, we modify the SpMV execution strategy for the AMD architecture from the strategy that was previously realized for NVIDIA architectures [2].

### 3.1  Balancing COO SpMV Kernel

Flegar et al. [6] introduced a load-balancing COO SpMV based on the idea of parallelizing across the nonzeros of a sparse matrix. This way, all threads have the same workload, and coalesced access to the column indexes and the values of the sparse matrix is enabled. At the same time, parallelizing across nonzeros requires the use of atomicAdd operations to avoid race conditions, see Algorithm 1.

Flegar et al. [6] also introduced an "oversubscribing" parameter $\omega$ that controls the number of threads allocated to each physical core. When increasing the oversubscribing, we have more active threads to hide the latency of data access and atomicAdds [1]. At the same time, it increases the number of atomicAdds invocations and the overhead of context switching. Using an experimental assessment on all of the 2,800 matrices from the Suite Sparse Matrix Collection, Flegar et al. [6] identifies oversubscribing parameters $\omega_{\text{NVIDIA}}$ that draw a good balance between these aspects. Similarly to Flegar et al. [6], we use experiments to identify good choices $\omega_{\text{AMD}}$ for AMD architectures by considering oversubscribing

---

**Algorithm 1.** Load-balancing COO kernel algorithm.

---

1: Get $ind$ = index of the first element to be processed by this thread
2: Get $current\_row = rowidx[ind]$.
3: Compute the first value $c = A[ind] \times x[colidx[ind]]$
4: **for** i = 0 .. $nz\_per\_warp$; i+ = $warpsize$ **do**
5:     Compute $next\_row$, row index of the next element to be processed
6:     **if** any thread in the warp's $next\_row$ != $current\_row$ or it is the final iteration **then**
7:         Compute the segmented scan according to $current\_row$.
8:         **if** first thread in segment **then**
9:             atomicAdd $c$ on output vector by the first entry of each segment
10:        **end if**
11:        Reinitialize $c = 0$
12:    **end if**
13:    Get the next index $ind$
14:    Compute $c+ = A[ind] \times x[colidx[ind]]$
15:    Update $current\_row$ to $next\_row$
16: **end for**

---

parameters $\omega = 2^k (0 \le k \le 7)$. In the GINKGO library and our experiments, we use the setting

$$\omega_{\text{NVIDIA}} = \begin{cases} 8 & (n_z < 2 \cdot 10^5), \\ 32 & (2 \cdot 10^5 \le n_z < 2 \cdot 10^6), \\ 128 & (2 \cdot 10^6 \le n_z) \end{cases} \quad \omega_{\text{AMD}} = \begin{cases} 2 & (n_z < 10^5), \\ 8 & (10^5 \le n_z < 10^7). \\ 32 & (10^7 \le n_z) \end{cases}$$

### 3.2 CSR SpMV Kernel

The most basic CSR SpMV kernel (*basic* CSR) assigns only one thread to each row, which results in notoriously low occupancy of GPU. In Algorithm 2, we assign a "subwarp" (multiple threads) to each row, and use warp reduction mechanisms to accumulate the partial results before writing to the output vector. This *classical* CSR assigning multiple threads to each row is inspired by the performance improvement of the ELL SpMV in [2]. We adjust the number of threads assigned to each row to the maximum number of nonzeros in a row. We select

$$\text{subwarp size} = 2^k (0 \le k \le 5 \text{ (NVIDIA) or 6 (AMD)})$$

as the closest number smaller or equal to the maximum number of nonzeros in a row, i.e.

$$\text{subwarp size} = \max \left\{ 2^t \le max\_row\_nnz | t \in \mathbb{Z}, 0 \le t \le \log_2(\text{device warpsize}) \right\}$$

In Fig. 5 in Sect. 4, we visualize the performance improvements obtained from assigning multiple threads to each row and observe that the *basic* CSR SpMV is not always slower. In particular for very unbalanced matrices, assigning the same parallel resources to each row turns out to be inefficient. In response, we

---

**Algorithm 2.** GINKGO'S classical CSR kernel.

---

1:  Get $row$ = the row index
2:  Compute $subrow$ = the step size to next row
3:  Get $step\_size$ = the step size to next element of value.
4:  Initialize value $c = 0$
5:  **for** $row = row$ .. #$rows$, $row+ = subrow$ **do**
6:      **for** $idx = row\_ptr[row]$ .. $row\_ptr[row + 1]$, $idx+ = step\_size$ **do**
7:          Compute $c = val[idx] * b[col[idx]]$
8:      **end for**
9:      Perform warp reduction of $c$ on the warp
10:     **if** thread 0 in subwarp **then**
11:         Write $c$ to the output vector
12:     **end if**
13: **end for**

---

design a *load-balancing* CSRI which follows the strategy of the COO SPMV described in Sect. 3.1 to balance the workload across the compute resources. For an automatic strategy selection in Algorithm 3, we define two variables $nnz\_limit$ and $row\_len\_limit$ to control the kernel selection on NVIDIA and AMD GPUs. $nnz\_limit$ reflects the limit of total nonzero count, and $row\_len\_limit$ reflects the limit of the maximum number of stored elements in a row. For AMD GPUs, $nnz\_limit$ is $10^8$ and $row\_len\_limit$ is 768. For NVIDIA GPUs, $nnz\_limit$ is $10^6$ and $row\_len\_limit$ is 1024.

---

**Algorithm 3.** GINKGO'S CSR strategy.

---

1:  Compute $max\_row\_nnz$ = the maximal number of stored element per rows.
2:  **if** #$nnz > nnz\_limit$ or $max\_row\_nnz > row\_len\_limit$ **then**
3:      Use load-balance CSR Kernel
4:  **else**
5:      Use classical CSR Kernel
6:  **end if**

---

### 3.3   ELL SpMV Kernel

In [2], the authors demonstrated that the ELL SPMV kernel can be accelerated by assigning multiple threads to each row, and using an "early stopping" strategy to terminate thread blocks early if they reach the padding part of the ELL format. Porting this strategy to AMD architectures, we discovered that the non-coalesced global memory access possible when assigning multiple threads to the rows of the ELL matrix stored in column-major format can result in low performance. The reason behind this is that the strategy in [2] uses threads of the same group to handle one row, which results in adjacent threads always reading matrix elements that are $m$ (matrix size or stride) memory locations apart. To overcome this problem, we rearrange the memory access by assigning the threads of the same group to handle one column like the classical ELL kernel, but assigning several groups to each row to increase GPU usage. Because the threads handling the elements of a row may be of the same thread block but are no longer part of the same warp, we can not use warp reduction for the partial sums but need to invoke atomicAdds on shared memory. Figure 2 visualizes the different memory access strategies.

In our experiments, we set the "group_size" to multiple of 32 for both AMD and NVIDIA architectures. The group_size is the number of contiguous element read by thread block, and the num_group is the number of thread in the thread block accessing the same row. We use block size = 512 in ELL kernel. To make the "group_size" is the multiple of 32, we set the max of $num\_group = block\_size/min\_group\_size = 512/32 = 16$. We visualize in Fig. 8 the improvement of the new ELL SpMV kernel over the kernel previously employed [2].

---

**Algorithm 4.** Ginkgo's ELL SpMV kernel.

---
1: Initialize Value $c = 0$
2: Compute $row$ = the row idx
3: Compute $y$ = the start index of row
4: Compute $step\_size$ = the step size to next element
5: Initialize shared memory $data$
6: **for** $idx = y \mathinner{.\,.} max\_row\_nnz, idx+ = step\_size$ **do**
7:     Compute $ind$ = index of this element in the ELL format
8:     **if** $A(row, colidx[ind])$ is padding **then**
9:         break
10:     **end if**
11:     Perform local operation $c+ = A(row, colidx[ind]) * x[colidx[ind]]$
12: **end for**
13: Perform atomicAdd $c$ to $data[threadIdx.x]$
14: **if** thread 0 in group **then**
15:     atomicAdd $data[threadIdx.x]$ on the output vector
16: **end if**

---

In Algorithm 4, we present the ELL SpMV kernel implemented in Ginkgo for SIMD architectures like GPUs. The number of groups assigned to a row is computed via Algorithm 5. Generally, the number of the group is increased with the number of nonzero elements accumulated in a single row. However, if $num\_group = 16$, multiple thread block may be assigned to the same row, see line 8 in Algorithm 5. This strategy aims at increasing the occupancy of the GPU multiprocessors when targeting short-and-wide matrices that accumulate many elements in few rows. After the group is determined, the start index for a specific thread is computed in lines 2 in Algorithm 4 with the step size which is same as the total number of threads accessing the same row. The threads process the data with the loop in lines 6–12. This kernel still uses the early stopping in lines 8–10 introduced in [2]. After completion of the matrix vector

**Algorithm 5.** GINKGO's automatic ELL kernel configuration.

1: Initialize num_group = 1
2: Initialize nblock_per_row = 1
3: Compute ell_ncols = maximum number of non zero elements per row
4: Get nwarps = total number of warps available on the GPU
5: **if** ell_ncols / nrows > $1e - 2$ **then**
6:     Compute num_group = $min(16, 2^{ceil(log_2(ell\_ncols))})$
7:     **if** num_group == 16 **then**
8:         Compute nblock_per_row = $max(min(ell\_ncols/16, nwarps/nrows), 1)$
9:     **end if**
10: **end if**

multiplication step, the partial sums accumulated in thread-local variables are reduced (line 13) and added to the output vector in global memory, see line 15. Even though this operation requires an atomic operation as multiple groups (part of distinct thread blocks) may operate on the same row, the chance of atomic collisions is small due to the previous reduction in line 13.

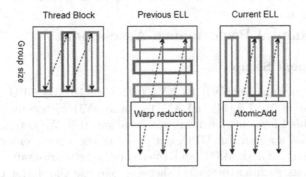

**Fig. 2.** Comparison of the memory access for different ELL SPMV kernels.

### 3.4 Hybrid Matrix Formats and Optimal Matrix Splitting

GINKGO's hybrid ("HYB") format splits the matrix into two parts and stores the regular part in the ELL format and the irregular part in the COO format. Flegar et al. [6] demonstrated that GINKGO'S COO SPMV achieves good performance for irregular matrices on NVIDIA architectures, and the results in Sect. 4 confirm that GINKGO'S COO SPMV performs well also on AMD architectures. How the HYB format partitions a matrix into the ELL and the COO part impacts the memory requirements and performance. Anzt et al. [2] derived strategies basing the partitioning on the nonzeros-per-row distribution of the matrix. We modify this strategy by adding a condition based on the ratio between the maximum nonzeros-per-row and the number of rows. For $R$ being the set of the nonzeros-per-row values, we define the function $Q_R$ and $F_R$:

$$Q_R(x) := \min\{t \in \mathbb{N} \mid x < F_R(t)\}, \qquad F_R(t) := \frac{|\{r \in R \mid r \le t\}|}{|R|}.$$

We recall that Anzt et al. [2] introduced hybrid$\{n\}$ which takes the nonzeros of the row at the $n\%$-quantile in the ascending ordering of the nonzero-per-row values, $Q_R(n\%)$. A variant denoted with "hybridminstorage" selects

$$n\% = \left\lfloor \frac{\#rows \times sizeof(index)}{sizeof(value) + 2 \times sizeof(index)} + 1 \right\rfloor$$

according to the (bit-)size of the value and index arrays, i.e. hybridminstorage is hybrid25 when storing the values in 64-bit doubles and the indexes in 32-bit integers [2]. In this paper, we enhance the hybrid$\{n\}$ partitioning from Anzt et al. [2] by enforcing the limitation that the maximum nonzero-per-row of the ELL part can at most be $\#rows * 0.0001$. We consider the resulting strategy "hybridlimit$\{n\}$" and select hybridlimit33 (label "HYB") as our default strategy according to the performance evaluation in Fig. 11 in Sect. 4.

# 4    Experimental Performance Assessment

## 4.1    Experiment Setup

In this paper, we consider NVIDIA's V100 (SXM2 16 GB) GPU with support for compute capability 7.0 [14] and AMD's RadeonVII with compute capability gfx906. See Table 1 for some hardware specifications [16]. We note that the AMD RadeonVII is not a server-line GPU, but provides the same memory bandwidth as the AMD HPC GPU MI50, and thus should be comparable for memory bound operations such as the SpMV kernels. We use the major programming ecosystems for the distinct architectures - CUDA for NVIDIA GPUs and HIP for AMD GPUs. CUDA GPU kernels were compiled using CUDA version 9.2, and HIP GPU kernels were compiled using HIP version 2.8.19361.

**Table 1.** Specifications of the V100 SXM2 16 GB and the RadeonVII [16].

|  | Warpsize | Bandwidth | FP64 performance | L1 cache | L2 cache |
|---|---|---|---|---|---|
| V100 | 32 | 897 GB/s | 7.834 TFLOPS | 128 KB | 6 MB |
| RadeonVII | 64 | 1024 GB/s | 3.360 TFLOPS | 16 KB | 4 MB |

The performance evaluation covers more than 2,800 test matrices of the Suite Sparse Matrix Collection [15]. Some matrices contain dense rows, which makes the conversion to the ELL format virtually impossible. We ignore those matrices in the performance evaluation of the ELL SpMV kernel.

All experiments are performed in IEEE double precision arithmetic, and the GFLOP/s rates are computed under the assumption that the number of flops is always $2n_z$, where $n_z$ is the number of nonzeros of the test matrix (ignoring padding).

## 4.2  COO SpMV Performance Analysis

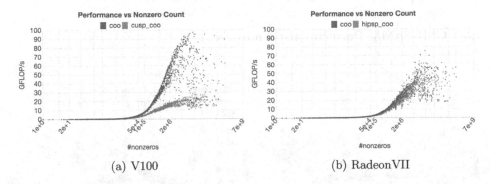

(a) V100                    (b) RadeonVII

**Fig. 3.** Performance of GINKGO'S and vendors' COO SpMV

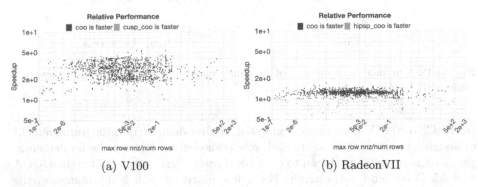

(a) V100                    (b) RadeonVII

**Fig. 4.** Releative performance of GINKGO'S and vendors' COO SpMV (Color figure online)

We first evaluate the performance of the load-balancing COO SpMV kernel. In Fig. 3a, we compare against cuSPARSE's COO kernel (cusparseD-hybmv with `CUSPARSE_HYB_PARTITION_USER` and threshold of 0), in Fig. 3b, we compare against hipSPARSE's COO kernel (hipsparseDhybmv with `HIPSPARSE_HYB_PARTITION_USER` and threshold of 0). Each dot reflects one test matrix from the Suite Sparse collection. The x-axis is the nonzero count of the matrix, and the y-axis is the performance in GFLOP/s. In Fig. 4, we present the speedup of GINKGO'S SpMV over cuSPARSE's COO implementation and hipSPARSE's COO implementation, respectively. Red dots reflect test matrices where GINKGO outperforms the vendor library, green dots reflect cases where the vendor library is faster. Despite the fact that the irregularity of a matrix heavily impacts the SpMV kernels' efficiency, we can observe that GINKGO's COO SpMV achieves much higher performance than both NVIDIA's and AMD's COO kernels in most cases. Overall, GINKGO achieves an average speedup of about 2.5x over cuSPARSE's COO SpMV and an average speedup of about 1.5x over hipSPARSE COO SpMV.

### 4.3  CSR SpMV Performance Analysis

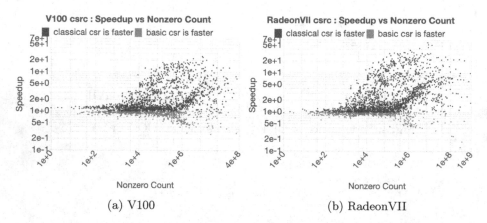

(a) V100                    (b) RadeonVII

**Fig. 5.** Performance improvement of (current) classical CSR SpMV and (previous) basic CSR SpMV.

In the CSR SpMV performance analysis, we first demonstrate the improvement of assigning multiple threads to each row (*classical* CSR) over the implementation assigning only one thread to each row (*basic* CSR) see Fig. 5 for the CUDA and AMD backend, respectively. For a few matrices with many nonzeros, the *basic* CSR is 5x–10x faster than the *classical* CSR. To overcome this problem, we use Algorithm 3 in GINKGO that chooses the load-balancing CSRI algorithm for problems with large nonzero counts.

Next, we compare the performance of the GINKGO CSR SpMV (that automatically interfaces to either the load-balancing CSRI kernel or the classical CSR, see Sect. 3.2) with the vendors' CSR SpMV. Anzt et al. [2] identified the cusp_csr kernel (cusparseDcsrmv) as the overall performance winner among the different NVIDIA CSR implementations. For the AMD CSR SpMV kernel, we use the CSR kernel (hipsparseDcsrmv) provided in hipSPARSE. For completeness, we mention that the rocSPARSE library (outside the HIP ecosystem) contains a CSR kernel that renders better SpMV performance for irregular matrices on AMD GPUs. We refrain from considering it as we want to stay within the

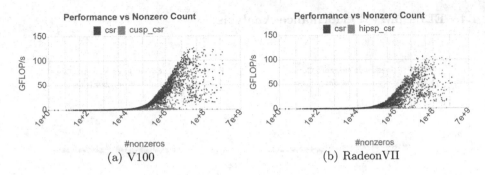

**Fig. 6.** Performance of GINKGO'S and vendors' CSR SPMV

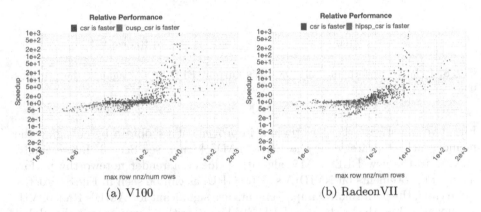

**Fig. 7.** Relative performance of GINKGO'S and vendors' CSR SPMV

HIP ecosystem, which is anticipated to serve as primary dissemination tool for AMD's sparse linear algebra technology.

In Fig. 6, we compare the GINKGO CSR SPMV with the `cusparseDcsrmv` CSR kernel available in NVIDIA's cuSPARSE library and the `hipsparseDcsrmv` CSR kernel available in AMD's hipSPARSE library, respectively. In the relative performance analysis, Fig. 7, we use the ratio $\frac{max(row\_n_z)}{num\_rows}$ for the x-axis as this is the parameter used in GINKGO'S CSR SPMV to decide which CSR algorithm is selected. GINKGO CSR achieves significant speedups for large x-values (up to 900x speedup on V100 and 700x speedup on RadeonVII). At the same time, there are a few cases where the GINKGO CSR SPMV is slower than the library implementations (up to 20x slowdown on V100 and 5x slowdown on RadeonVII).

## 4.4  ELL SpMV Performance Analysis

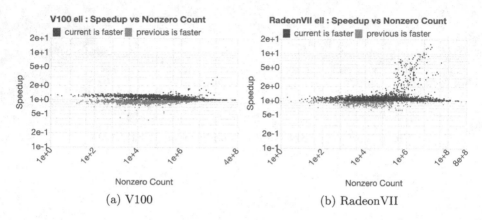

(a) V100                                   (b) RadeonVII

**Fig. 8.** Relative performance of GINKGO'S current ELL SpMV against the previous one

First, we investigate the performance improvement we obtain by changing the memory access strategy for the ELL SpMV kernel, see Sect. 3. Interestingly, moving to the new ELL SpMV algorithm does not render noteworthy performance improvements on NVIDIA's V100 GPU, as can be seen in Fig. 8a. At the same time, the performance improvements are significant for AMD's RadeonVII, as shown in Fig. 8b. In the new ELL SpMV algorithm, we improve the global memory access at the cost of atomicAdd operations on shared memory (which are more expensive than warp reductions). In consequence, the current ELL SpMV is not always faster than the previous ELL SpMV.

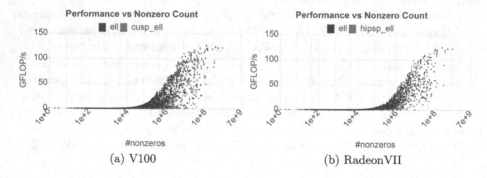

(a) V100                                   (b) RadeonVII

**Fig. 9.** Performance of GINKGO'S and vendors' ELL SpMV (Color figure online)

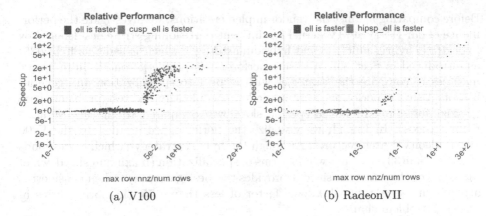

Fig. 10. Relative performance of GINKGO'S and vendors' ELL SPMV

In Fig. 9, we compare GINKGO'S ELL SPMV kernel against cuSPARSE cusparseDhybmv with CUSPARSE_HYB_PARTITION_MAX ELL kernel and hipSPARSE hipsparseDhybmv with HIPSPARSE_HYB_PARTITION_MAX ELL kernel, respectively. hipSPARSE ELL employs a limitation not to process matrices that have more than $\frac{\#nnz-1}{\#rows} + 1$ elements in a row. Thus, we have much fewer data points for the hipSPARSE ELL SPMV (the blue points in Fig. 9b). In Fig. 10, GINKGO'S ELL is faster than their counterparts available in the vendors libraries if the ratio $\frac{max(row\_n_z)}{num\_rows} > 10^{-2}$. For the other cases, GINKGO and the vendor libraries are comparable in their ELL SPMV performance.

## 4.5   HYB SpMV Performance Analysis

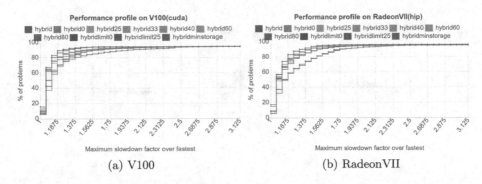

Fig. 11. Performance profile comparing the different GINKGO HYB splitting strategies

Before comparing against the vendor implementations, we investigate the performance of our HYB SpMV kernel for different partitioning strategies denoted by hybrid$\{n\}$, hybridlimit$\{n\}$, and hybridminstorage (which is same as hybrid25) as introduced in Sect. 3.4. We use a performance profile [8] on all Suite Sparse matrices to compare the strategies with respect to specialization and generalization. Using a performance profile allows to identify the test problem share (y-axis) for a maximum acceptable slowdown compared to the fastest algorithm (x-axis). In Fig. 11, we visualize the performance profiles for the V100 and RadeonVII architectures. Although the hybrid strategy (which corresponds to hybridlimit33) does not win in terms of specialization (maximum slowdown of 1), we favor this strategy since it provides the best generality: when considering a maximum acceptable slowdown factor of less than 1.75, this format wins in terms of problem share.

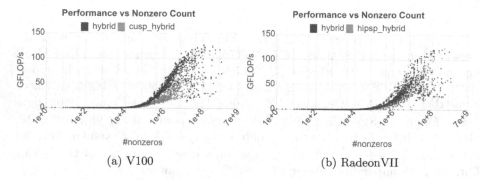

(a) V100                                  (b) RadeonVII

**Fig. 12.** Performance of GINKGO'S and vendors' HYB SpMV

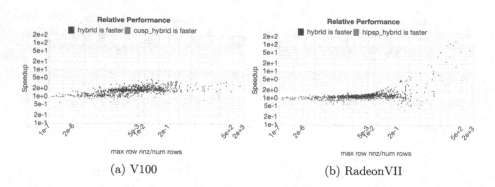

(a) V100                                  (b) RadeonVII

**Fig. 13.** Relative performance of GINKGO'S and vendors' HYB SpMV

In Fig. 12, we see that GINKGO'S HYB SpMV achieves similar peak performances like cuSPARSE's cusparseDhybmv HYB SpMV and hipSPARSE's hipsparseDhybmv HYB SPMV, but GINKGO has much higher performance averages than cuSPARSE or hipSPARSE. Figure 13a and Fig. 13b visualize the HYB SPMV performance relative to the vendor libraries, and we identify significant speedups for most problems and moderate slowdowns for a few cases.

## 4.6   All SpMV Performance Profile Analysis

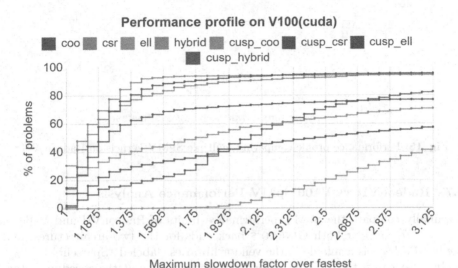

**Fig. 14.** Performance profile comparing multiple SPMV kernels on V100.

In Fig. 14, we use the performance profile to assess the specialization and generalization of all matrix formats we consider. In Fig. 14, GINKGO's CSR is the fastest for about 30% of the test cases, and GINKGO's HYB is the winner in terms of generality (if the acceptable slowdown factor is larger than 1.0625). Very similarly, in Fig. 15, GINKGO's CSR is the fastest kernel for roughly 30% of the test cases, and GINKGO's HYB is the generalization-winner if the acceptable slowdown factor is larger than 1.375. We note that the hipSPARSE ELL stays at a low problem ratio as it employs a limitation to not process matrices that have more than $\frac{\#nnz-1}{\#rows} + 1$ elements in a row.

We already noticed in the analysis comparing GINKGO's different SPMV kernels to the vendor libraries that AMD's hipSPARSE library generally features much better-engineered kernels than NVIDIA's cuSPARSE library. In consequence, also the performance profiles of AMD's SPMV kernels are much closer to GINKGO's SPMV kernel profiles than NVIDIA's SPMV kernel profiles.

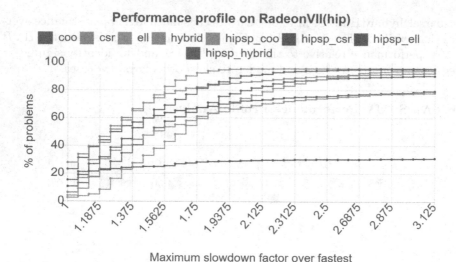

**Fig. 15.** Performance profile comparing multiple SPMV kernels on Radeon VII.

## 4.7  RadeonVII vs V100 SpMV Performance Analysis

We finally compare the SPMV performance limits of RadeonVII and V100 in Fig. 16. We consider both GINKGO'S back ends for the two architectures, and the SPMV kernels available in the vendor libraries (labeled "Sparselib").

In most cases, the V100 is faster than RadeonVII, but the speedup factors are moderate, with an average around 2x. RadeonVII shows better performance for matrices that contain many nonzeros. The higher memory bandwidth of the RadeonVII might be a reason for these performance advantages, but as there are typically many factors (such as context switch, warp size, the number of multiprocessors, etc.) affecting the performance of SPMV kernels, identifying the origin of the performance results is difficult.

While NVIDIA's V100 outperforms AMD's RadeonVII in most tests, we acknowledge that the price for a V100 (16 GB SXM2) is currently more than an order of magnitude higher than for a RadeonVII[3]

---

[3] In December 2019, the list price for NVIDIA's V100 (16 GB SXM2) is US$ 10,664.-, the list price for AMD's RadeonVII is US$ 699.-.

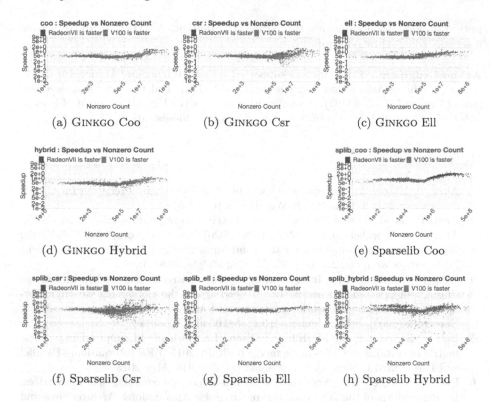

(a) GINKGO Coo          (b) GINKGO Csr          (c) GINKGO Ell

(d) GINKGO Hybrid                    (e) Sparselib Coo

(f) Sparselib Csr       (g) Sparselib Ell       (h) Sparselib Hybrid

**Fig. 16.** Comparison of the SPMV kernel implementations of hipSPARSE on Radeon-VII and cuSPARSE on V100

## 5    Summary and Outlook

In this paper, we have presented a comprehensive evaluation of SPMV kernels for AMD and NVIDIA GPUs, including routines for the CSR, COO, ELL, and HYB format. We have optimized all kernels for the latest GPU architectures from both vendors, including new algorithmic developments and parameter tuning. All kernels are part of the GINKGO open source library, and typically outperform their counterparts available in the vendor libraries NVIDIA cuSPARSE and AMD hipSPARSE. We accompany te kernel release with a performance database and a web tool that allows investigating the performance characteristics interactively. We also conducted an extensive SPMV performance comparison on both AMD RadeonVII and NVIDIA V100 hardware. We show that despite NVIDIA's V100 providing better performance for many cases, AMD's RadeonVII with the hipSPARSE library is able to compete against NVIDIA's V100 in particular for matrices with a high number of non zero elements. In addition, we note that due to the price discrepancy between the two hardware (AMD's RadeonVII is roughly 6.6% of the price of an NVIDIA's V100), the AMD hardware provides a much better performance-per-dollar ratio. This may indicate that after a long period of NVIDIA dominating the HPC GPU market, AMD steps up to recover a serious competitor position.

**Acknowledgment.** This work was supported by the "Impuls und Vernetzungsfond" of the Helmholtz Association under grant VH-NG-1241, and the US Exascale Computing Project (17-SC-20-SC), a collaborative effort of the U.S. Department of Energy Office of Science and the National Nuclear Security Administration.

# References

1. Anzt, H., Chow, E., Dongarra, J.: On block-asynchronous execution on GPUs. Technical report 291, LAPACK Working Note (2016)
2. Anzt, H., et al.: Load-balancing sparse matrix vector product kernels on GPUs. ACM Trans. Parallel Comput. **7**(1), 1–26 (2020). https://doi.org/10.1145/3380930
3. Barrett, R., et al.: Templates for the Solution of Linear Systems: Building Blocks for Iterative Methods, 2nd edn. SIAM, Philadelphia (1994)
4. Bell, N., Garland, M.: Implementing sparse matrix-vector multiplication on throughput-oriented processors. In: Proceedings of the Conference on High Performance Computing Networking, Storage and Analysis, SC 2009, pp. 1–11. ACM, New York (2009). https://doi.org/10.1145/1654059.1654078
5. Dalton, S., Baxter, S., Merrill, D., Olson, L., Garland, M.: Optimizing sparse matrix operations on GPUs using merge path. In: 2015 IEEE International Parallel and Distributed Processing Symposium, pp. 407–416, May 2015
6. Flegar, G., Anzt, H.: Overcoming load imbalance for irregular sparse matrices. In: Proceedings of the 7th Workshop on Irregular Applications: Architectures and Algorithms, IA3 2017, pp. 1–8. ACM, New York (2017). https://doi.org/10.1145/3149704.3149767
7. Grossman, M., Thiele, C., Araya-Polo, M., Frank, F., Alpak, F.O., Sarkar, V.: A survey of sparse matrix-vector multiplication performance on large matrices. CoRR (2016). http://arxiv.org/abs/1608.00636
8. Higham, D., Higham, N.: Matlab Guide. Society for Industrial and Applied Mathematics (2005). https://doi.org/10.1137/1.9780898717891
9. Hong, C., Sukumaran-Rajam, A., Nisa, I., Singh, K., Sadayappan, P.: Adaptive sparse tiling for sparse matrix multiplication. In: Proceedings of the 24th ACM SIGPLAN Symposium on Principles and Practice of Parallel Programming, PPoPP 2019, Washington, DC, USA, 16–20 February 2019, pp. 300–314 (2019). https://doi.org/10.1145/3293883.3295712
10. Hong, S., Kim, S.K., Oguntebi, T., Olukotun, K.: Accelerating CUDA graph algorithms at maximum warp. In: Proceedings of the 16th ACM SIGPLAN Symposium on Principles and Practice of Parallel Programming, PPOPP 2011, San Antonio, TX, USA, 12–16 February 2011, pp. 267–276 (2011). https://doi.org/10.1145/1941553.1941590
11. Langville, A.N., Meyer, C.D.: Google's PageRank and Beyond: The Science of Search Engine Rankings. Princeton University Press, Princeton (2012)
12. Merrill, D., Garland, M.: Merge-based parallel sparse matrix-vector multiplication. In: Proceedings of the International Conference for High Performance Computing, Networking, Storage and Analysis, SC 2016, pp. 1–12. IEEE Press, Piscataway (2016). http://dl.acm.org/citation.cfm?id=3014904.3014982

13. Merrill, D., Garland, M., Grimshaw, A.S.: High-performance and scalable GPU graph traversal. ACM Trans. Parallel Comput. (TOPC) **1**(2), 1–30 (2015). https://doi.org/10.1145/2717511
14. NVIDIA Corp.: Whitepaper: NVIDIA Tesla V100 GPU Architecture (2017)
15. SuiteSparse: Matrix Collection (2018). https://sparse.tamu.edu. Accessed Apr 2018
16. TechPowerUp: GPU database (2019). https://www.techpowerup.com/gpu-specs/

# Scaling Genomics Data Processing with Memory-Driven Computing to Accelerate Computational Biology

Matthias Becker[1]([✉]), Umesh Worlikar[1], Shobhit Agrawal[2], Hartmut Schultze[4], Thomas Ulas[3], Sharad Singhal[5], and Joachim L. Schultze[1,3]

[1] PRECISE, Platform for Single Cell Genomics and Epigenomics at the German Center for Neurodegenerative Diseases (DZNE) and the University of Bonn, Bonn, Germany
Matthias.Becker@dzne.de
[2] West German Genome Center (WGGC), Bonn, Germany
[3] Genomics and Immunoregulation, LIMES Institute, University of Bonn, Bonn, Germany
[4] Hewlett Packard Enterprise, Ratingen, Germany
[5] Hewlett Packard Labs, Palo Alto, USA

**Abstract.** Research is increasingly becoming data-driven, and natural sciences are not an exception. In both biology and medicine, we are observing an exponential growth of structured data collections from experiments and population studies, enabling us to gain novel insights that would otherwise not be possible. However, these growing data sets pose a challenge for existing compute infrastructures since data is outgrowing limits within compute. In this work, we present the application of a novel approach, Memory-Driven Computing (MDC), in the life sciences. MDC proposes a data-centric approach that has been designed for growing data sizes and provides a composable infrastructure for changing workloads. In particular, we show how a typical pipeline for genomics data processing can be accelerated, and application modifications required to exploit this novel architecture. Furthermore, we demonstrate how the isolated evaluation of individual tasks misses significant overheads of typical pipelines in genomics data processing.

**Keywords:** Computational biology · Memory-Driven Computing · Genomics

## 1 Introduction

Life and medical sciences are evolving towards a data-driven research model. The leading biological institutions face a new challenge in dealing with data. Interdisciplinary collaborations are aimed at accelerating this digitalization of research. The use of compute clusters and cloud services has become more common with growing data sets. High-performance computing (HPC) is relevant for

---

The original version of this chapter was revised: The chapter was made open access. The correction to this chapter is available at https://doi.org/10.1007/978-3-030-50743-5_28

P. Sadayappan et al. (Eds.): ISC High Performance 2020, LNCS 12151, pp. 328–344, 2020.
https://doi.org/10.1007/978-3-030-50743-5_17

many modeling and simulation aspects in the life sciences, as indicated by the study of genome-scale biochemical reaction networks [12].

This trend towards data-driven research challenges a community that is witnessing an explosion in accumulated data sizes. The European Bioinformatics Institute (EBI) has reported [10] a growth of data stored from 120 PB to 160PB from 2016 to 2018. The number of deposited high-throughput sequencing data sets at the US National Center for Bioinformatics (NCBI) shows exponential growth in the last years, as depicted in Fig. 1. This can be explained by the decline in sequencing costs, reduction in sequencing times, and availability of diverse sequencing platforms.

Another source of increasing data sets is comprehensive collections like population studies. These studies follow a large number of participants for a long time and acquire different modalities, like image data and multi-omics data. Storing and processing such data collections is challenging not only because of their sizes but also because the data needs to be available without delays for the researchers. While researching health-related questions, large time-series data sets can be helpful but pose a challenge for storage systems.

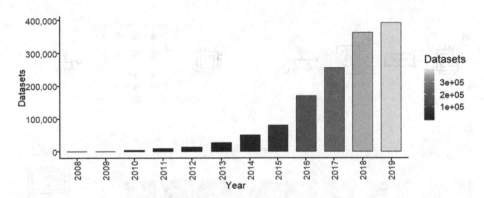

**Fig. 1.** Number of high throughput sequencing (HTS) data sets uploaded to NCBI per year. The 2019 data is still incomplete, since most studies are only uploaded to NCBI once they are published.

In this work, we want to demonstrate how a novel architecture, named Memory-Driven Computing (MDC), can be used for processing genomics sequencing data.

## 2   Memory-Driven Computing

While the data sets used in research are continually growing, the computing power is not keeping up. The end of Moore's law [31] seems to have finally been reached. Current approaches to scaling focus on distributing workloads among processing nodes in large clusters. However, these clusters come with growing costs, in particular from energy consumption that limits similar future scaling. Also, genomics tasks often cannot be easily distributed among many nodes, e.g., gene regulation network processing deals with densely connected graphs.

## 2.1 Novel Architecture Tailored for Data Science

To overcome these shortcomings, Hewlett Packard Enterprise (HPE) has proposed a novel architecture: Memory-Driven Computing. Unlike traditional, processor-centric systems, it puts the memory (and therefore the user data) at the center of the architecture [7]. This is realized by going from the traditional von Neumann architecture, as shown in Fig. 2a, established since 1953, towards a more memory-centric approach (Fig. 2b). To eliminate overheads, remote data access no longer has to traverse the host processor, but is handled by the memory fabric. Traditional local storage and memory are bundled into a persistent memory pool that can be realized through technologies such as the memristor [9]. Finally, the underlying fabric between all components, including processors, will be switching from electrical to optical connections. This is necessary to overcome the required energy for moving growing data sets.

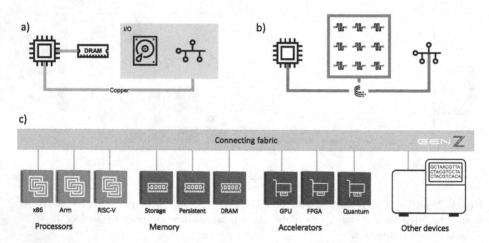

**Fig. 2.** (a) The traditional von Neumann architecture defines the processor as the central component. (b) MDC puts persistent memory at the center of the system. Components are linked through an optical fabric. (c) The connecting fabric, e.g., Gen-Z, puts different components from the processor-, memory- and accelerator class in a single shared address space. Other specialized devices like sequencers for data generation could also be integrated.

## 2.2 Composable Infrastructure

In this composable infrastructure, compute power can be attached to the memory as required to allow scaling. All components share the address space and are connected through a fabric like Gen-Z [13] that also controls data access and security, which are essential properties when working with sensitive medical data. Besides CPUs and memory, other components like accelerators and GPUs can be integrated. Since the fabric is well-specified[1], it is also possible to incorporate more specialized data sources, e.g., sequencing machines, to avoid data transfer to the fabric attached memory. Traditional HPC architectures typically offer large numbers of standardized nodes, grouped into different classes, like high-memory or GPU-nodes. Often these systems are specially tailored for simulation applications but do not fit well to other tasks like genomics data processing. With MDC, it is possible to group the fabric-connected components dynamically into task-tailored systems.

### 2.3   Transition Path Towards MDC

The idea behind MDC touches all components in computer systems. A hardware transition to MDC cannot realistically happen in a single step, but rather is a process. The first components like Gen-Z enabled devices, are expected in 2020, and other techniques like memristor-based storage for persistent fabric attached memory are still a few years out. Nonetheless, it is already possible to apply MDC principles. Existing large-memory machines can exploit an abundance of memory. Systems like the HPE Superdome Flex offer a shared address space between multiple nodes for applications. Software development can also use smaller servers or even laptops to emulate fabric attached memory using the Fabric Attached Memory Emulation (FAME)[2].

Software adapted for MDC has provided large performance gains [8] and allows us to think in new paradigms as memory pools enable new programming models [19]. The transition to MDC follows an iterative process of preparing and modifying an application. The preparation starts with the definition of goals and metrics, defining the optimization target, e.g., doubling the number of tasks per time. This is followed by a baseline performance measurement. The results are used to perform a cost/benefit analysis to identify the MDC modifications, e.g., modifications to exploit the abundance of memory through different data structures or the elimination of I/O. During the modification phase, the developers need to apply MDC principles and modify the application. Finally, the fine-tuning based on the initially defined metrics and goals can be performed. More details can be found in Sect. 5.

## 3   Related Work

Genomics data processing is a challenging task and, therefore, an excellent use case to evaluate MDC. In this section, we discuss prior work, beginning with in-memory genomics data processing approaches. Schapranow et al. [29] have

---

[1] The full specification is available in [13].
[2] http://github.com/FabricAttachedMemory/Emulation.

employed an in-memory database to accelerate the alignment tool BWA on a cluster, a method similar to MapReduce. They have reported an improvement of 89% for a cluster of 25 machines. Firnkorn et al. [11] have followed a similar path and compare the use of in-memory databases (SAP HANA) to a traditional RDBMS (MySQL) for alignment focussed on direct matches. While they have observed an acceleration factor of 27, the comparison was made against a highly unusual tool that is not specialized in alignment. Finally, Li et al. [25] have improved the processing of genomic data using the SPARK framework by introducing improved compression of genomic data to optimize data transfer between the nodes. Hajj et al. [15] have demonstrated new address space concepts using samtools.

Other approaches use specialized hardware. Luo et al. [26] have used GPUs for alignment. Lavenier et al. [23] and Kim et al. [21] have explored the use of completely new hardware for genomics data processing. They propose to use processing within the memory to minimize data access time and maximize bandwidth. The pre-alignment steps of Kim et al. lead to an end-to-end improvement between $2\times$ and $3.5\times$. Alser et al. [5] propose another FPGA based tool for pre-alignment; they achieve a $10\times$ acceleration for this task using a Virtex-7 FPGA using Xilinx VC709 board running at 250 MHz. Kaplan et al. [18] propose a novel resistive approximate similarity search accelerator (RASSA) that exploits charge distribution and parallel in-memory processing to reflect a mismatch count between DNA sequences. Their pre-alignment software achieves $16$–$77\times$ improvements in long reads.

Finally, different programming languages have been explored to accelerate the preprocessing of genomics data. Herzeel et al. [16] have proposed a multithreaded framework for sequence analysis to leverage the concurrency features of the Go programming language. Tarasow et al. [30] have investigated the parallel processing features of the programming language D to improve genomics processing speed.

## 4    Application in Bioinformatics

From an HPC perspective, bioinformatics applications often fall in either of two categories: I/O-bound and compute-bound. I/O-bound applications typically transform or annotate data. They operate on significant inputs and produce large outputs while the actual transformation task takes little to no computational effort. Compute-bound tasks are not limited by I/O, their primary work, e.g., assembly or modeling or cellular interaction, is the limiting factor. While many compute-bound applications operate on large data sets, the I/O part can often be neglected in comparison to the main functionality. In previous work, it has been shown that compute-bound applications still can benefit from the abundance of memory available in MDC [6].

## 4.1    Typical Preprocessing Tasks and Pipeline Structures

In this work, we will focus on optimizing an I/O-bound application since there is a lot of overhead that can be eliminated with MDC, and such applications are common in the typical structures of bioinformatic preprocessing tasks. The preprocessing of next-generation sequencing (NGS) genomics data consists of initial quality controls, demultiplexing of data from multiple experiments (which have been multiplexed to reduce costs), alignment to a reference genome and further quality controls as shown in Fig. 3. These steps can be performed through several competing tools that often specialize in certain types of experiments. Considering single-cell genomics, the number of involved tools increases, and the pipelines become more complex. This has lead to the development of specialized bioinformatics pipelines and dedicated workflow managers like Snakemake [22].

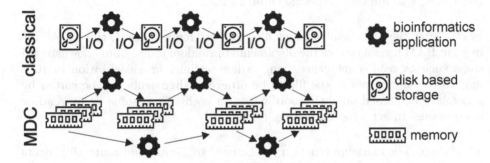

**Fig. 3.** Classical bioinformatics pipelines are a series of tools that exchange data through large files on disk-based storage. With MDC, the data is kept in memory, and I/O can be avoided. Parallel processing with different tools does not impose a penalty for random data access that is known from existing storage systems that often are optimized for serial or streaming data access.

These pipelines deal with large input files, and many tools transform the data, annotate information, or change the order of the content. They take an input and produce an output of a similar size. This leads to a large number of intermediate files, and therefore these tools are often I/O-bound. The last step in the preprocessing typically performs a data reduction, going from alignments to gene expression information. Here, we will demonstrate the use case for the I/O-bound application samtools, which is a common tool for processing aligned reads or alignments.

## 4.2    Application: Samtools

Samtools [24] is a standard tool for processing alignments in Structured Alignment Map (SAM) and binary SAM (BAM) files [2]. These files contain tens to hundreds of millions of alignments in a single file and must be efficient to deal with growing data sets. An alignment consists of core information like genomic position, the actual sequence, the associated quality values, and auxiliary information, including tags to store key-value pairs of different data types.

We have evaluated the broad functionality of samtools (version 1.9) to select commands that are used most frequently in the community as well as those that could benefit most from eliminating I/O. In the following, we list these commands, briefly describe their functionality, and classify the output that they produce. A comprehensive overview of samtools and the details for each command can be found in the documentation [3].

**View.** Samtools provides the view command to convert between SAM and BAM format. Often tools only support one of these formats, or conversion to BAM is needed to reduce file sizes in storage. SAM files can be useful for visual inspection of the data since SAM is human readable. It is also possible to specify filter criteria, e.g., to filter for a specific chromosome.

**Sort.** After the alignment of input files to a reference genome, the output file (e.g., in BAM format) stores the alignments in random order. Many downstream steps such as read-count generation, variant calling, or visualization in IGV require the alignments in the file to be ordered. Alignments can be sorted by genomic order based on their coordinates on each chromosome or by read or query names to get a technical ordering.

**Markdup.** The markdup function can be used to identify duplicate alignments from a coordinate/position sorted file. The duplicate reads are referred to as the primary reads whose coordinates are matching. The highest quality of a duplicate is kept, and others are marked with the duplicate flag. Removal of duplicate reads, generated due to PCR amplification or sequencing, is an indispensable step for the processing of alignment data as it affects the overall quality and downstream steps of NGS analysis.

**Fixmate.** To prepare a file for the markdup command, it has to be modified with the fixmate command to add MS (mate score) and MC (CIGAR string for mate/next segment) tags. The MS tag is used by the markdup function to select the best reads to keep.

**Combined Commands.** Often, the functionality of samtools is not used independently, but multiple commands interact. An example is the marking of duplicate reads in a data set. This task consists of four consecutive steps: sorting by query name, the fixmate command, sorting by genomic position, and finally, actual marking of the duplicates. Often these steps are connected through files (see Fig. 4). It is also possible to connect the tools with a pipe; this avoids I/O but still requires serialization and deserialisation of the data between the individual steps. The serialization and deserialization steps convert between in-memory and on-disk representation of SAM records.

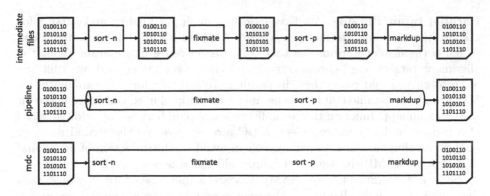

**Fig. 4.** Samtools commands can be concatenated with multiple approaches: Data exchange through files (top) or a pipeline (middle). We propose to share data in memory (bottom) to remove unnecessary overhead.

# 5  Modifications to Exploit Memory-Driven Computing

Running an unmodified application in an MDC environment already yields the benefit of accelerated data access, since no storage systems and drivers are involved. However, to fully exploit this environment, memory-mapping the data is recommended and can often be easily added. Besides this, two significant areas for benefiting from MDC exist: First, we can eliminate all I/O operations for data input and output. This also applies to temporary data and data exchange between applications. Existing storage systems often are optimized for serial or streaming data access. Random access from a single application or multiple applications reduces data throughput significantly. Since the central memory pool does not require traditional access patterns for performance reasons (e.g., linear reading), parallel processing of data becomes feasible. This speeds up quality control tools and preprocessing in parallel or similar use cases, where I/O bottlenecks are common. In a second step, the internal data structures of an application can be modified to benefit from the abundance of memory in MDC environments. This could be, for example, extensive pre-calculation of intermediate results to replace standard computations with a simple look-up.

We have applied these principles to samtools to benefit from I/O elimination and improved data passing between different functionalities of the application.

## 5.1  Samtools

Samtools stores data in the Sequence Alignment Map (SAM)-format [2], which is text-based. A binary version of this format (BAM) exists as well. Finally, a text-based column-oriented version (CRAM) exists but is of no practical relevance. In this work, we present four contributions to the main functionality of samtools in the areas of I/O reduction that include input and output parsing, removal of intermediate files, and the better integration of multiple commands. Samtools is available as open source and written in C.

**Parallel Input Parsing.** We have modified the input loading and parsing for the two most common formats, SAM and BAM. In both formats, we first need to parse the header information that contains reference information about the alignment targets (e.g., chromosomes) and their sizes. Afterward, we split the file into chunks and parse them in parallel. To fully exploit the capabilities of MDC, we have modified all I/O to use memory-mapped files, which are based on the posix mmap() function that establishes a mapping between an address space of a process and a memory object. MDC already gives us the shared memory pool for storing our data, therefore, we can avoid the introduction of additional frameworks like MPI-IO which introduce additional layers.

Sequence Alignment Map (SAM) files are a line-based format where each line contains a single alignment. Alignments require header information, and it needs to be loaded first. Next, we split the file into byte-regions and process them in parallel. Through MDC, the data is already in memory, and random access bears no extra costs. The start of the regions does not necessarily coincide with the beginning of a line, hence parsing only starts after the next newline. Correspondingly, the last line is parsed beyond the end of the region to capture the full alignment information.

Binary SAM (BAM) files consist of a series of gzip-compressed blocks that contain the header and alignment information. Again, the header needs to be parsed first, just like for SAM files. Next, the compressed blocks containing the alignments can be processed. A single block can hold up to 64 KB of alignment information. Since there is no reliable indicator for the beginning of a compressed block, it is not possible to simply split the file into equally sized regions. Therefore, we first create an index of all blocks. This task takes very little time since the file is already in memory. The index is then used to distribute the contents for parallel decompression and alignment parsing, as shown in Fig. 5a.

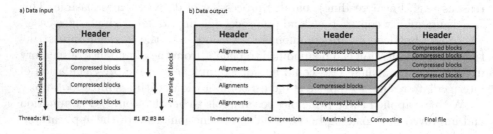

**Fig. 5.** Parallel input and output. The BAM file is initially scanned for blocks and then parsed in parallel. The output works by writing into sufficiently large regions of the file, followed by a later removal intermediate unused spaces.

**Parallel Output Writing.** The process of writing alignment data starts with storing the header information. Afterward, we estimate the average size of an alignment to assess the overall file size. This allows us to allocate sufficient space in a memory-mapped file for the output. We split the output into parts that are saved into different regions of the output file. Unused space remains in each region because the estimation of the expected size is designed to overestimate so that all alignments will fit. In the last step, we move the file parts to eliminate the unused space, and finally, we truncate the file to the actual size. These steps are shown in Fig. 5b. For BAM files, we estimate the required size for uncompressed data. However, usually, good compression can be achieved, and therefore the final file size is much smaller.

**Intermediate Data Storage.** The data processing commands of samtools often require some temporary storage. The sorting command pre-sorts data in blocks and finally merges them into the final file. For smaller files, these temporary blocks are held in memory, but this no longer applies to growing data sets. Similarly, the markdup and fixmate commands use temporary storage for intermediate data. In our approach, we load the full data set into memory to avoid additional I/O. We have modified samtools to remove temporary files. With all data in memory, sorting can be easily performed without temporary files using the C++ extensions for parallelism [17]. The temporary data storage of the fixmate and markdup commands can be resolved by instead keeping a list of references to the alignments that otherwise would have been written to disk.

**Pipelining Commands.** We have found that certain samtools commands are often run together. We have chosen the marking of duplicates pipeline for investigation and optimization. Since data parsing and I/O consume a large part of the runtime, we have modified the commands to take a list of alignments in memory and to work on that data. Therefore, we have modified the sorting, fixmate, and markdup commands to work with a list of alignments that we obtain from the input parsing. Although fixmate and markdup are sequential tasks, we still can remove the input parsing or deserialisation.

**Memory-Management.** A growing number of processing threads, in particular during the input parsing, allocate many small memory parts. With massive input files, tens to hundreds of million allocations are required during input parsing. With the default allocator (from glibc), the central lock for the memory-list is a bottleneck that significantly slows down the input parsing. The core information for an alignment is of fixed size, and it is accompanied by a variable-length string for storing sequence and auxiliary information. This results in two allocations per alignment. For the core information, the memory can be pre-allocated in larger batches due to its known size, the sequence and auxiliary information requires custom allocations. We have considered specialized allocators like jemalloc [1] and tcmalloc [14] that use per-thread pools as well as a non-freeing custom allocation solution, that acquires large portions of memory per thread and uses them for allocations. This custom allocator is experimental only to understand the difficulties of many small allocations from a large number of threads and should not be used in outside of experiments, since it does not track the allocated memory, and therefore, is not able to free memory again.

These modifications are designed to be reusable and are available on Github: https://github.com/schultzelab/samtools-mdc. This includes the parallel reading and writing functions for SAM and BAM files. Samtools-mdc is designed to be a drop-in replacement for samtools. SAM/BAM reading and writing has been separated from the data modification (e.g. sorting) to allow re-use of components.

## 6 Evaluation and Results

We have used two systems to evaluate our MDC-modifications. We took a typical Dell blade server, as it is common among bioinformatics groups, with two sockets, 32 cores, 64 threads, and a total of 768 GB memory. As a second system, we have used an HPE Superdome Flex, with two nodes, 16 sockets, 144 cores, and 288 threads and a total of 6 TB memory. The abundance of memory in this system is close to our expectation in an MDC environment, although larger systems (up to 48 TB) exist. The Superdome Flex implements MDC principles and provides a single address space across the nodes through a custom interconnect and firmware. Future systems are expected to include Gen-Z hardware. We have collected data points for different numbers of threads, with 1, 16, 32 and 64 collected on the smaller blade system and 144 and 288 gathered on the Superdome Flex system.

We have selected a range of samples[3] from the National Institutes of Health Sequence Read Archive [4] to get coverage of typical input files sizes. These ten samples cover different studies and multiple diseases. An overview of the samples is shown in Table 1. We have grouped the samples by size into three categories: small, medium, and large.

### 6.1  Memory Allocation

Our initial experiments show that memory allocation is a crucial factor in processing SAM and BAM files. The loading process requires multiple allocations per read, and this becomes an increasing challenge with a growing number of parallel reading threads.

To test the allocations strategies, we read the three sample groups with different allocators and multiple thread numbers, ranging from 1 to 288, and report the cumulated time per group. The results, differentiated between bam and sam files, are shown in Fig. 6. It can be seen immediately that the default allocator consistently shows the worst performance, both with just a single thread as well as with large numbers of threads (144, 288). In most cases, tcmalloc performs equal or worse in comparison to jemalloc. Our custom allocator shows the best performance for most cases; however, we discarded it since it is not a full implementation but rather a proof-of-principle.

---

[3] We have used hisat 2.0.4 [20] to perform the alignment and to produce the BAM files.

**Table 1.** Ten selected samples from NCBI presented corresponding to the number of reads contained. They are grouped by size into three categories (1, 2, 3; small, medium, large).

| Sample | Number of reads | Study | Group | Disease |
|---|---|---|---|---|
| GSM1641335 | 397748 | GSE67184 | Small | Malaria |
| GSM1540592 | 950441 | GSE63085 | Small | Control |
| GSM1113415 | 9004143 | GSE45735 | Small | Influenza vaccination |
| GSM1273616 | 11215264 | GSE52656 | Small | AML |
| GSM2309852 | 20339057 | GSE86884 | Medium | Kidney transplant |
| GSM1576441 | 21396334 | GSE64655 | Medium | Influenza vaccination |
| GSM1521568 | 22655944 | GSE62190 | Medium | AML |
| GSM1554600 | 34059694 | GSE63646 | Large | AML |
| GSM2324152 | 44470876 | GSE87186 | Large | BCG vaccination |
| GSM1540488 | 54561415 | GSE63085 | Large | Lyme disease |

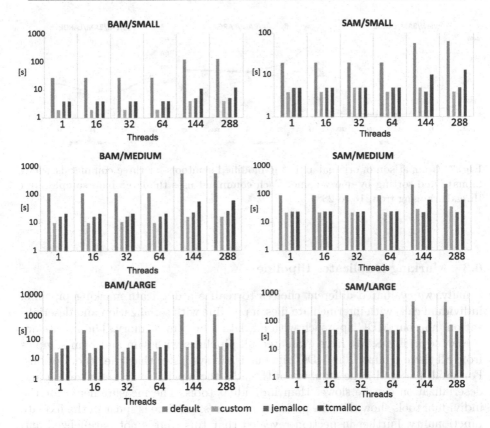

**Fig. 6.** Cumulative times to fully load the small, medium and large samples in SAM and BAM format into memory using different allocators (see Sect. 5.1, Memory-Management) and number of threads.

## 6.2   Samtools Commands

Next, we evaluated different samtools commands. The results present a broad range of behavior, and we show examples in Fig. 7. All examples use the large bam sample group. The view command shows consistently better performance for the MDC-optimised version of samtools (mdc) when compared to the original (unmodified) samtools (orig). The fixmate use case contains program logic that is not parallelized, and the streaming architecture of the original samtools shows better performance than the modified version. Samtools (mdc) loads the complete data set first, performs the fixmate operation, and then writes the complete data set; samtools (orig) uses a streaming approach that is more suited for this specific task. Finally, sorting by query name shows slightly better results of the MDC-optimised version for smaller numbers of threads and similar performance for larger thread numbers (64, 144, 288). With growing thread numbers, samtools (orig) is configured to retain growing parts of the data set in memory, similar to our approach.

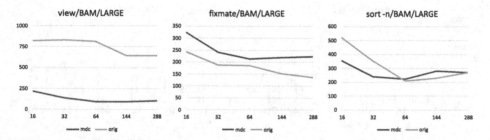

**Fig. 7.** Comparison of original and mdc-modified samtools for three commands: view, fixmate and sorting by query name. Each command uses the large bam samples and threads ranging from 16 to 288.

## 6.3   Marking Duplicates Pipeline

Finally, we evaluated different choices to realize a duplicate marking pipeline: individual calls with intermediate files, a pipeline with serialization and deserialization, and our MDC approach with all data stored in memory. The results are presented in Fig. 8. We have evaluated all pipelines with sam and bam samples from all three groups. The MDC pipeline is always faster than the other options. For small files and large numbers of threads, the pipeline with serialization and deserialization can be slower than individual tools. The measurements for the individual tools show that the majority of processing time is spent in the fixmate functionality. Further inspection revealed that this step is not parallelized and it would be an opportunity for future work.

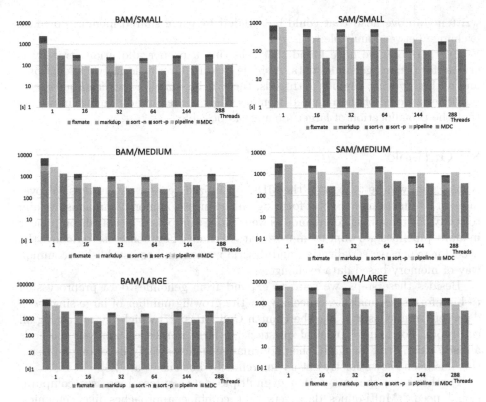

**Fig. 8.** Evaluation of duplicate marking using individual commands (stacked results), a pipeline, and our MDC approach. We have tested the bam (left) and sam (right) files of different sizes and report cumulative results per size group. Single-threaded MDC results for sam files had to be omitted to technical problems. Sort/sort -n denotes sorting by query name, sort -p is sorting by genomic position.

## 7  Discussion

Samtools is already optimized for single commands; the streaming approach of samtools shows satisfactory performance. Some commands are not parallelized, and the streaming might prevent this. Especially the fixmate functionality consumes a significant amount of time. If we analyze not just single commands but rather pipelines that combine multiple commands, we can see that data exchange between the individual commands limits the throughput. Using a pipe instead of intermediate files shows an acceleration but still comes with overhead from serialization and deserialization.

With MDC, we can remove I/O from intermediate files, and we can share data in native data types. This gives an additional acceleration over the pipeline approach, and we believe this to be true of other pipelines. However, the input and output of the current MDC version are still files and need to be parsed and written - an overhead that could be avoided by using shared memory for data exchange between multiple tools.

Furthermore, we have found that selecting a proper allocation strategy is crucial for parsing genomics data. A single read requires at least two allocations, and with a growing number of threads, the synchronization overhead becomes a bottleneck. Some of the required memory objects are already known in size so that the pre-allocation of larger amounts is possible.

## 8 Outlook

A next step will be to expand the MDC optimized version of samtools to cover more of its functionality. After focusing on the most common commands, we aim to study the remaining commands as well. Since samtools is a central component in many pipelines, we want to improve data exchange between tools to remove the need for expensive serialization and deserialization and to establish a common way of memory-based data exchange.

Besides these steps, we want to expand from genomics data preprocessing to bioinformatics analysis, especially for the growing number of large single-cell data sets from consortia like the Human Cell Atlas [27] which try to catalog all cell types. For many biological questions, a large number of analysis methods already exist. Still, for many, the performance is increasingly becoming an issue, this has been shown for trajectory inference by Saelens et al. [28].

Furthermore, the integration of multiple data sources increases computational needs. Multi-omics data sets that combine approaches like genomics, lipidomics, and proteomics allow gaining novel insights into biological processes. Another domain that produces growing data sets for analysis is spatial approaches that combine the capture of omics data with spatial and image information. This also provides a link to population studies whose growing data production poses an increasing challenge.

**Acknowledgment.** This work was funded in part by the HGF grant sparse2big, the FASTGenomics grant of the German Federal Ministry for Economic Affairs and Energy, and by the Deutsche Forschungsgemeinschaft (DFG, German Research Foundation) under Germany's Excellence Strategy—EXC2151/1—390873048. We want to thank Milind Chabbi, Bill Hayes, Keith Packard, Patrick Demichel, Binoy Arnold, Robert Peter Haddad, Eric Wu, Chris Kirby, Rocky Craig from Hewlett Packard Enterprise and Hewlett Packard Labs and the bioinformatics group at the AG Schultze at the Life and Medical Sciences Institute at the University of Bonn.

## References

1. jeMalloc. http://jemalloc.net
2. SAM specification (2019). http://samtools.github.io/hts-specs/SAMv1.pdf
3. SAMtools 1.9 documentation (2019)
4. The National Institutes of Health (NIH) Sequence Read Archive (SRA) (2019). https://www.ncbi.nlm.nih.gov/sra/

5. Alser, M., Hassan, H., Xin, H., Ergin, O., Mutlu, O., Alkan, C.: GateKeeper: a new hardware architecture for accelerating pre-alignment in DNA short read mapping. Bioinform. **33**(21), 3355–3363 (2017). https://doi.org/10.1093/bioinformatics/btx342. (Oxford England)
6. Becker, M., et al.: Accelerated genomics data processing using memory-driven computing (accepted). In: Proceedings of the 6th International Workshop on High Performance Computing on Bioinformatics (HPCB 2019) in conjunction with the IEEE International Conference on Bioinformatics and Biomedicine (BIBM 2019), San Diego, USA (2019)
7. Bresniker, K.M., Singhal, S., Williams, R.S.: Adapting to thrive in a new economy of memory abundance. Computer **48**(12), 44–53 (2015). https://doi.org/10.1109/JSTQE.2012.2236080
8. Chen, F., et al.: Billion node graph inference: iterative processing on the machine. Tech. rep. (2016). https://www.labs.hpe.com/publications/HPE-2016-101
9. Chua, L.: Memristor-the missing circuit element. IEEE Trans. Circuit Theory **18**(5), 507–519 (1971). https://doi.org/10.1109/TCT.1971.1083337
10. Cook, C.E., et al.: The European Bioinformatics Institute in 2018: tools, infrastructure and training. Nucl. Acids Res. (2019). https://doi.org/10.1093/nar/gky1124
11. Firnkorn, D., Knaup-Gregori, P., Lorenzo Bermejo, J., Ganzinger, M.: Alignment of high-throughput sequencing data inside in-memory databases. Stud. Health Technol. Inform. **205**, 476–480 (2014). https://doi.org/10.3233/978-1-61499-432-9-476
12. Fröhlich, F., Kaltenbacher, B., Theis, F.J., Hasenauer, J.: Scalable parameter estimation for genome-scale biochemical reaction networks. PLoS Comput. Biol. (2017). https://doi.org/10.1371/journal.pcbi.1005331
13. Gen-Z Consortium: Gen-Z core specification 1.0 (2018). https://genzconsortium.org/specification/core-specification-1-0/
14. Ghemawat, S., Menage, P.: Tcmalloc: thread-caching malloc (2007). http://goog-perftools.sourceforge.net/doc/tcmalloc.html
15. Hajj, I.E., et al.: SpaceJMP : programming with multiple virtual address spaces. In: ASPLOS, pp. 353–368, No. Section 3 (2016). https://doi.org/10.1145/2872362.2872366
16. Herzeel, C., Costanza, P., Decap, D., Fostier, J., Verachtert, W.: elPrep 4: a multi-threaded framework for sequence analysis. PLoS ONE **14**(2), 1–16 (2019). https://doi.org/10.1371/journal.pone.0209523
17. Programming Languages – Technical Specification for C++ Extensions for Parallelism. ISO/IEC TS 19570:2018. Standard (November 2018)
18. Kaplan, R., Yavits, L., Ginosar, R.: RASSA: resistive pre-alignment accelerator for approximate DNA long read mapping. IEEE Micro **39**, 44–54 (2018). https://doi.org/10.1109/MM.2018.2890253
19. Keeton, K.: The machine : an architecture for memory-centric computing. In: Workshop on Runtime and Operating Systems for Supercomputers (ROSS), p. 2768406 (June 2015)
20. Kim, D., Paggi, J.M., Park, C., Bennett, C., Salzberg, S.L.: Graph-based genome alignment and genotyping with HISAT2 and HISAT-genotype. Nat. Biotechnol. (2019). https://doi.org/10.1038/s41587-019-0201-4
21. Kim, J.S., et al.: GRIM-filter: fast seed location filtering in DNA read mapping using processing-in-memory technologies. BMC Genomics **19**(Suppl 2) (2018). https://doi.org/10.1186/s12864-018-4460-0
22. Köster, J., Rahmann, S.: Snakemake-a scalable bioinformatics workflow engine. Bioinformatics (2012). https://doi.org/10.1093/bioinformatics/bts480

23. Lavenier, D., Roy, J.F., Furodet, D.: DNA mapping using processor-in-memory architecture. In: Proceedings - 2016 IEEE International Conference on Bioinformatics and Biomedicine, BIBM 2016, pp. 1429–1435 (2017). https://doi.org/10.1109/BIBM.2016.7822732

24. Li, H., et al.: The sequence alignment/map format and SAMtools. Bioinformatics **25**(16), 2078–2079 (2009). https://doi.org/10.1093/bioinformatics/btp352

25. Li, X., Tan, G., Wang, B., Sun, N.: High-performance genomic analysis framework with in-memory computing. ACM SIGPLAN Not. **53**(1), 317–328 (2018). https://doi.org/10.1145/3200691.3178511

26. Luo, R., et al.: SOAP3-dp: fast, accurate and sensitive GPU-based short read aligner. PLoS ONE **8**(5) (2013). https://doi.org/10.1371/journal.pone.0065632

27. Regev, A., et al.: The Human Cell Atlas White Paper (October 2018). http://arxiv.org/abs/1810.05192

28. Saelens, W., Cannoodt, R., Todorov, H., Saeys, Y.: A comparison of single-cell trajectory inference methods. Nat. Biotechnol. **37**(5), 547–554 (2019). https://doi.org/10.1038/s41587-019-0071-9

29. Schapranow, M.P., Plattner, H.: HIG - an in-memory database platform enabling real-time analyses of genome data. In: Proceedings - 2013 IEEE International Conference on Big Data, Big Data 2013, pp. 691–696 (2013). https://doi.org/10.1109/BigData.2013.6691638

30. Tarasov, A., Vilella, A.J., Cuppen, E., Nijman, I.J., Prins, P.: Genome analysis Sambamba : fast processing of NGS alignment formats. Bioinformatics **31**(November), 2032–2034 (2017). https://doi.org/10.5281/zenodo.13200.Contact

31. Theis, T.N., Philip Wong, H.S.: The end of Moore's Law: a new beginning for information technology. Comput. Sci. Eng. **19**(2), 41–50 (2017). https://doi.org/10.1109/MCSE.2017.29

# Performance Modeling
# and Measurement

# Footprint-Aware Power Capping for Hybrid Memory Based Systems

Eishi Arima[1,2]([✉]), Toshihiro Hanawa[1], Carsten Trinitis[2], and Martin Schulz[2]

[1] The University of Tokyo, Tokyo, Japan
{arima,hanawa}@cc.u-tokyo.ac.jp
[2] Technical University of Munich, Munich, Germany
{Carsten.Trinits,schulzm}@in.tum.de

**Abstract.** High Performance Computing (HPC) systems are facing severe limitations in both power and memory bandwidth/capacity. By now, these limitations have been addressed individually: to improve performance under a strict power constraint, power capping, which sets power limits to components/nodes/jobs, is an indispensable feature; and for memory bandwidth/capacity increase, the industry has begun to support hybrid main memory designs that comprise multiple different technologies including emerging memories (e.g., 3D stacked DRAM or Non-Volatile RAM) in one compute node. However, few works look at the combination of both trends.

This paper explicitly targets power managements on hybrid memory based HPC systems and is based on the following observation: in spite of the system software's efforts to optimize data allocations on such a system, the effective memory bandwidth can decrease considerably when we scale the problem size of applications. As a result, the performance bottleneck component changes in accordance with the footprint (or data) size, which then also changes the optimal power cap settings in a node. Motivated by this observation, we propose a power management concept called *footprint-aware power capping (FPCAP)* and a profile-driven software framework to realize it. Our experimental result on a real system using HPC benchmarks shows that our approach is successful in correctly setting power caps depending on the footprint size while keeping around 93/96% of performance/power-efficiency compared to the best settings.

## 1  Introduction

Power consumption has become the major design constraint when building supercomputers or High Performance Computing (HPC) systems. For instance, the US DOE once had set a power constraint of 20 MW per future exascale system to ensure their economical feasibility. To achieve orders of magnitude performance improvement under such a strict power constraint, we must develop sophisticated power management schemes. To this end, *power capping* (setting a power constraint to each job/node/component) and *power shifting* (shifting power among components depending on their needs under a given power budget) are promising and the most common approaches [5, 9, 20, 27, 28, 31, 33].

P. Sadayappan et al. (Eds.): ISC High Performance 2020, LNCS 12151, pp. 347–369, 2020.
https://doi.org/10.1007/978-3-030-50743-5_18

At the same time, we continue to face limited memory bandwidths and capacities in HPC systems. On the one hand, to improve bandwidth, architecting main memories with 3D stacked DRAM technologies, such as HBM [36] and HMC [6], is an attractive approach. However, these technologies have limited capacity-scalability compared to conventional DDR-based DRAM [16]. On the other hand, using emerging scalable NVRAMs (Non-Volatile RAMs, e.g., PRAM [8,19,26,30], ReRAM [2], STT-MRAM [3,18,23] and 3D Xpoint memory [14]) are promising in terms of capacity, but these technologies are generally much slower than conventional DRAM. As a consequence, the industry has been shifting toward hybrid memory designs: main memories with multiple different technologies (e.g., 3D stacked DRAM + DDR-based DRAM [16] or DRAM + NVRAM [14]), which are usually heterogeneous in bandwidth and capacity.

Driven by these trends, this paper focuses on a power management technique explicitly tailored for such hybrid memory based systems. Our approach is based on the following observation: when we scale the problem size (e.g., by using finer-grained and/or larger-scaled mesh models for scientific applications), the performance bottleneck can change among components. As a result, the optimal power budget settings also change due to this *bottleneck shifting* phenomenon. Thus, to exploit higher performance under a power constraint, we should also *shift power* between CPU and memory system in accordance with the *footprint (or data) size* of applications, which we call *footprint-aware power capping (or FPCAP)* in this paper. As we often use various problem settings for each scientific application, this footprint awareness is critically important.

To realize the concept of FPCAP, we first formulate the power allocation problem and provide a regression-based performance model to solve it. Then, based on the formulations, we present a profile-based software framework that optimizes the power allocation to each component based on an efficient offline model-fitting methodology as well as an online heuristic algorithm. Our experimental results measured on a real system shows that our approach achieves near optimal allocations under various power caps.

The followings are the major contributions of this study:

- We demonstrate the bottleneck shifting phenomenon by scaling the problem size on a hybrid memory based system and propose a power management concept called FPCAP.
- We quantify its potential benefit using various mini HPC applications chosen from the CORAL benchmark suite.
- We formulate the power allocation problem and present an empirical performance model to solve it.
- Based on this formulation, we provide a profile-based software framework consisting of an efficient calibration method as well as an algorithm based on a hill climbing based heuristic.
- We evaluate our approach on a hybrid memory based system. The experimental result shows that our framework is successful in setting power caps to components in accordance with the footprint size.

## 2   Background and Related Work

Various power management schemes for large-scaled systems have been proposed so far, and such schemes generally assume hierarchical power controls and can be classified into global or local parts. Figure 1 illustrates a typical power control hierarchy for them. In the figure, the power scheduler distributes power budgets or sets power constraints to nodes/jobs (*global control*). Then, in each node/job the allocated power is distributed to the components with the goal of maximizing performance by shifting power from non-bottleneck components to the bottleneck one (*local control*). Our paper belongs to the latter part and is the first work that (1) *focuses on the bottleneck shifting phenomenon when scaling the problem size on the hybrid memory based nodes* and (2) *provides a power allocation scheme based on the observation.*

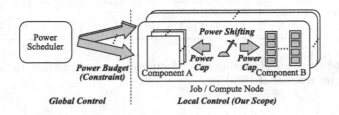

**Fig. 1.** Assuming hierarchical power management

The followings summarize the related work to ours.

**Global Power Controls:**  Since the power consumption of large-scaled systems have become a significant problem, various power scheduling schemes and implementations for them have been proposed so far [5,9,28,31,33]. These studies are usually based on the concept of overprovisioning: installing more hardware than the system can afford in terms of power, and intelligently controlling power supply to each job/node while keeping the total system power constraint [27]. Although these studies are very useful to improve the total throughput under the system power constraint, they focus on how to distribute power budgets across nodes/jobs and thus are orthogonal to ours.

**Local Power Controls:**  The concept of power shifting firstly appeared in [10], and power capping was proposed to enable power shifting [20]. Since then, various other local power management techniques have been proposed. However, ours is the first work in providing a way to optimize the power allocations to *CPU* and *hybrid memory system* in accordance with the *footprint size.* Several studies focused on power shifting between processors (CPU or GPU) and memories [7,10,12,24,29,32], but they did not target hybrid memory systems. Others propose various approaches based on different concepts: power shifting in a NUMA node [11], CPU-GPU power optimizations [4,17], power shifting between CPUs and networks [21,22], and I/O-aware power shifting [35], which do not consider memories.

**Power Management for Hybrid Memory Systems:** As DRAM scaling is at risk, many studies have focused on hybrid memory architectures, and some of them proposed power control schemes for them. H. Park et al. [26] uses DRAM as a cache in a DRAM-PRAM hybrid memory system and applies cache-decay, a power reduction technique that turns-off unused cachelines, to save the refresh power of DRAM. Other studies aim at optimizing data allocations on DRAM-PRAM hybrid memories to reduce the impact of the write access energy of PRAM [30,39]. Although these approaches are promising, they still focus only on hybrid main memory systems—ours covers both memories and processors and optimizes power allocations to them. Moreover, these studies are based on architectural simulations, and thus most of them require hardware modifications, while ours works on real systems.

```
#pragma omp parallel for simd
for (i = 0; i < N; i ++) { A[i] = A[i] * B[i] ... * B[i]; }
```

**Fig. 2.** Tested synthetic streaming code (footprint size ∝ N, arithmetic intensity or simply AI ∝ the number of *B[i])

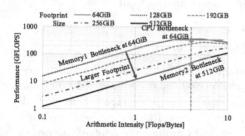

**Fig. 3.** Measured rooflines [38]

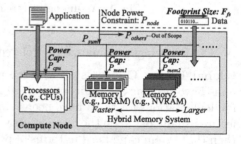

**Fig. 4.** Concept of our proposal

## 3   Motivation and Approach

The goal of this research is to provide a power management scheme suitable for emerging HPC nodes composed of *hybrid main memories* under a given node power constraint. When we execute scientific applications on HPC systems, we usually utilize various problem inputs, which can considerably change the *footprint size* (the memory consumption of the running application). For instance, we change the granularity/scale of mesh models and/or the number of time steps for scientific applications. Under such scenarios, *footprint-awareness* is essential to optimize the power settings of the components, which will be described in the following subsections.

## 3.1   Motivation: Roofline Observation

We execute the synthetic streaming code shown in Fig. 2 on our hybrid memory based system whose configurations are provided in Sect. 6. In this experiment, we change the footprint size and the arithmetic intensity (or simply *AI*) of this application by scaling the array size ($N$) and the number of arithmetic operations ($*B[i]$). Figure 3 describes the results. The horizontal axis indicates the arithmetic intensity (Flops/Bytes), while the vertical axis shows the performance (GFLOPS). The shapes of the curves can be well-explained by the roofline model [38]: (1) for smaller arithmetic intensity, the performance is capped by the memory system bandwidth (the slope lines), which means *the memory system is the performance bottleneck*; (2) but for higher arithmetic intensity, it is limited by the CPU throughput (the horizontal lines)—in other words *the CPU is the performance bottleneck*.

In this evaluation, we observe the phenomenon of *bottleneck shifting*: although the system software attempts to optimize the data mapping on the hybrid main memory, the effective bandwidth decreases as the footprint size scales due to more frequent accesses to the large (but slow) memory, and as a result, the slope line in Fig. 3 moves toward the downside[1]. Because of this effect, *the performance bottleneck can shift from the CPU to the memory system* even for CPU intensive workloads when we increase the footprint size. As the fundamental principle of the power management for power constrained systems is *allocating more power budget on the bottleneck component*, thus focusing on this phenomenon is a pivotal approach.

## 3.2   Concept: Footprint-Aware Power Capping

Driven by the above observation, we propose a power management concept called *footprint-aware power capping (or FPCAP)* that optimizes power allocations to CPUs/memories in a node depending on the **footprint size ($F_{fs}$)** as well as the application features under a given node power constraint ($P_{node}$) that is assigned by the power scheduler of the system. The concept is illustrated in Fig. 4. In this figure, we optimize the power budget allocations (or power caps) to the CPUs ($P_{cpu}$) and the Memory $i$ ($P_{memi})_{i=1,2,...}$ in accordance with these inputs. In the figure, $P_{others}$ shows the total power limits of the other components that are out of the scope of this paper, which we follow the prior node-level power management studies [7,12,32]. More specifically, we assume $P_{others}$ is reserved accordingly, and we focus on distributing the rest of the allocated node power budget $P_{sum}(= P_{node} - P_{others})$ to the CPUs and the memories under the constraint of $P_{cpu} + P_{mem1} + \cdots \leq P_{sum}$.

---

[1] This phenomenon could happen on traditional systems using monolithic main memories when the footprint size were in the neighborhood of *the on-chip cache capacity* (at most few 10 MB), which is not the case for HPC applications in general.

### 3.3 Performance Impact

Next, we demonstrate the potential performance benefit of FPCAP using our hybrid memory based system. More specifically, we observe how the optimal combination of $\{P_{cpu}, P_{mem1}, P_{mem2}\}$ changes depending on the footprint sizes using Small or Large problems while keeping the total power cap at a constant value (here, we set $\sum P_x = P_{sum} = 260[W]$). At the same time, we also confirm the performance impacts of naive power allocations that do not consider the footprint size of applications. The details of the system settings as well as the workload specifications including the definitions of Small/Large problems will be provided later in Sect. 6.

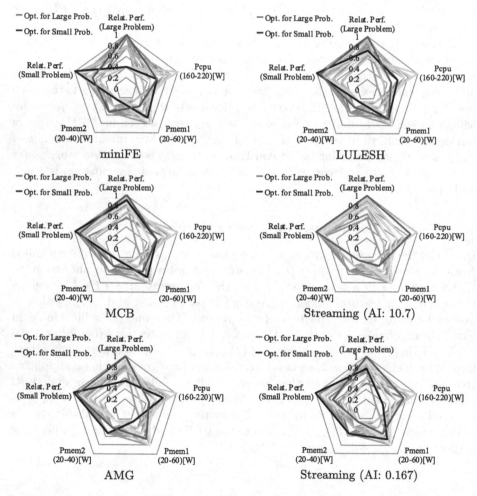

**Fig. 5.** Performance comparison of various power allocation settings (constraint: $P_{sum} = 260[W]$) for two different problem settings (Small/Large problems) (Color figure online)

Figure 5 illustrates the evaluation results for different applications. Each spider graph indicates the relative performance of two different problems along with the power cap settings for all the possible power combinations under the given total power constraint. Here, the performance is normalized to that of the optimal combination for each problem/application. In the figures, the optimal settings for Small/Large problems are highlighted with black/red lines.

Overall, the impact of power cap settings on performance is quite significant, and some cases also a slowdown can happen when the power allocations are not set accordingly. In addition, the optimal power allocations changes when we scale the problem sizes for most of the applications, thus FPCAP is effective.

For miniFE, LULESH and MCB allocating more power budgets on Memory 2 is effective when we scale the footprint sizes, which matches our roofline analysis provided in the last subsection. Also, the footprint size does not affect the performance bottleneck for very CPU intensive codes such as our synthetic code (Streaming (AI: 10.7)) described in Sect. 3.1, thus the optimal settings do not change for it when we change the problem size. For AMG and Streaming (AI: 0.167), reducing $P_{mem2}$ is effective when the footprint size is scaled. One major reason of this phenomenon is that the software-based data management adopted on our system—CPU also consumes power to handle the data transfers between Memory 1 and Memory 2, which can also change the performance bottleneck among the components.

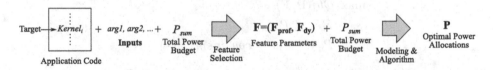

**Fig. 6.** Overall parameters transformation

**Table 1.** Definitions of parameters/functions

| Application related parameters | |
|---|---|
| *Kernel* | Target kernel in an application |
| **Inputs** | Inputs for the application: $\mathbf{Inputs} = (arg1, arg2, \cdots)$ |
| **F** | Feature parameters that represent the kernel + inputs ($\mathbf{F} = (\mathbf{F_{prof}}, \mathbf{F_{dy}})$) |
| $\mathbf{F_{prof}}$ | Parameters obtained after a profile run (e.g., FP operations per instruction) |
| $\mathbf{F_{dy}}$ | Parameters dynamically collected at runtime (e.g., **footprint size** $F_{fs}$) |
| Power related parameters | |
| **P** | Vector of power allocations to components: $\mathbf{P} = (P_{cpu}, P_{mem1}, P_{mem2}, \cdots)$ |
| $P_x$ | Allocated power budget to a component $x$ ($x = cpu, mem1, mem2, \cdots$) |
| $S_{P_x}$ | Set of power cap values for a component $x$: $P_x \in S_{P_x}(x = cpu, mem1, mem2, \cdots)$ |
| $P_{sum}$ | Given total power constraint |
| Objective functions | |
| Obj($\mathbf{P}, \mathbf{F}$) | Objective function to be maximized (e.g., Obj($\mathbf{P}, \mathbf{F}$) = Perf($\mathbf{P}, \mathbf{F}$)) |
| Perf($\mathbf{P}, \mathbf{F}$) | Performance as a function of $\mathbf{P}$ and $\mathbf{F}$ |
| PowEff($\mathbf{P}, \mathbf{F}$) | Power efficiency: Perf($\mathbf{P}, \mathbf{F}$)$/\sum P_x$ |

# 4    Formulation and Modeling

Motivated by the observation in the last section, we optimize the power allocations to components while taking the footprint size and other aspects into
considerations (FPCAP). In this section, we firstly formulate the problem definition. Then, we provide a simple model to solve it.

## 4.1    Problem Formulation

Figure 6 summarizes how parameters are transformed through our optimization.
Our approach receives a kernel code region ($Kernel$), inputs for the applications
such as arguments (**Inputs**) that determine the footprint size ($F_{fs}$), and the
total power constraint or budget ($P_{sum}$) set to the power capping targets within
a node ($cpu, mem1, \cdots$). We then convert two of them ($Kernel$ & **Inputs**) into
feature parameters (**F**) that represent the behavior of the kernel executed with
the inputs. The feature parameter vector is divided into profile-based statistic
($\mathbf{F_{prof}}$) and dynamically collected information ($\mathbf{F_{dy}}$), of which the latter includes
the footprint size ($F_{fs}$). Finally, based on our modeling/algorithm provided later,
we optimize the power caps to different components (**P**).

This can be formulated as the following optimization problem:

$$given \ Kernel, \textbf{Inputs}, P_{sum}(\Rightarrow \mathbf{F}, P_{sum})$$
$$\max \ Obj(\mathbf{P}, \mathbf{F})$$
$$s.t. \ \Sigma P_x \leq P_{sum}$$
$$P_x \in S_{p_x}(x = cpu, mem1, \cdots)$$

Here, we consider maximizing the objective function $Obj(\mathbf{P}, \mathbf{F})$ under the power
constraint $P_{sum}$. This objective function can be performance ($Pref(\mathbf{P}, \mathbf{F})$),
power efficiency ($PowEff(\mathbf{P}, \mathbf{F})$), or others. The power cap allocated to a component $x$ is taken from a set of pre-determined power cap values $S_{P_x}$. Note that
the functions and parameters used here are summarized in Table 1.

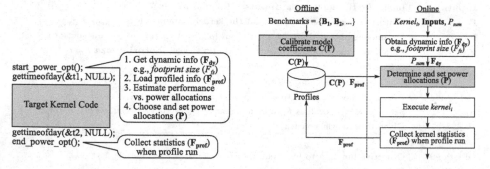

**Fig. 7.** Kernel-level optimization          **Fig. 8.** Framework overview

## 4.2   Performance Model

In this study, we utilize a widely-used linear regression model for our performance estimation. More specifically, we estimate performance as follows:

$$Perf(\mathbf{P}, \mathbf{F}) = C_1(\mathbf{P})H_1(\mathbf{F}) + C_2(\mathbf{P})H_2(\mathbf{F}) + \cdots = \mathbf{C}(\mathbf{P}) \cdot \mathbf{H}(\mathbf{F}) \qquad (1)$$

$\mathbf{C}(\mathbf{P})$ is a vector of coefficients that are functions of the power allocations ($\mathbf{P}$). Further, $\mathbf{H}(\mathbf{F})$ is a vector of basis functions that depend on the feature parameters ($\mathbf{F}$). We can determine $\mathbf{C}(\mathbf{P})$ by applying the method of least squares (or regression analysis), while using the pairs of measured $Perf(\mathbf{P}, \mathbf{F})$ and $\mathbf{H}(\mathbf{F})$— the details of this are explained in the next section. In addition, the definitions of $\mathbf{H}(\mathbf{F})$ used in our evaluation, which cover footprint awareness, are provided in Sect. 6.

## 5   System Design

Based on the formulation/modeling provided in the last section, we introduce a system design to realize our approach. More specifically, we first explain the overview of our optimization framework and then describe our efficient calibration methodology to set the model coefficients. Finally, we provide our power allocation algorithm.

### 5.1   Framework Overview

Figure 7 demonstrates our optimization methodology. Following the prior node-level power management studies [4,34], we consider an application kernel-level power optimization. The library call start_power_opt() in the figure first collects the needed feature values ($\mathbf{F}$) and then distributes the allocated power budget to the components based on the obtained statistics. Here, we assume the library interacts with the system resource manager and receives the total power budget ($P_{sum}$), which is given as an environment variable and manually set in our evaluation. The library call end_power_opt() indicates the end point of the kernel, and thus the optimization finishes here. In addition, we acquire $\mathbf{F_{prof}}$ at this point during a profile run, which can be initiated by the user or is conducted when there is no profile for the application. On the other hand, scale/inputs dependent features ($\mathbf{F_{dy}}$), such as the footprint size ($F_{fs}$), need to be obtained at every execution.

Figure 8 illustrates the workflow of our framework. Before using our power optimization approach, the offline calibration process is needed to determine the coefficients ($\mathbf{C}(\mathbf{P})$) in our model. This is conducted *only once for a system* by using a set of benchmarks, each of which consists of a kernel and inputs. Then, we optimize the power cap settings ($\mathbf{P}$) by using $\mathbf{C}(\mathbf{P})$ as well as $\mathbf{F}$ and $P_{sum}$ at runtime.

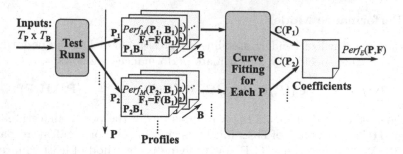

**Fig. 9.** Model calibration overview

## 5.2   Efficient Coefficients Calibration

Figure 9 illustrates how we set the model coefficients appropriately through the calibration process. The inputs here are a set of power cap combinations ($T_{\mathbf{P}}$) and a set of benchmarks ($T_{\mathbf{B}}$). Then, we measure the performance ($Perf_M(\mathbf{P}, \mathbf{B})$) as well as the feature parameters ($\mathbf{F}$) for each power cap combination and each benchmark. By using these measured statistics, we identify the coefficients vector ($\mathbf{C(P)}$) for each power budget setting through the least-square curve fitting method. Then, we store the obtained coefficients in a file which is utilized at runtime to estimate the performance ($Perf_E(\mathbf{P}, \mathbf{F})$). Note that the definitions of functions/parameters used here are summarized in Table 2.

We determine all coefficients by only exploring a limited area of the entire space of all power cap combinations ($U_{\mathbf{P}}$) as examining all possible combinations for the calibration would be practically infeasible, especially for larger numbers of power caps and components. More specifically, we just scale the power cap value of one of the components turn-by-turn, obtain the coefficients for these power cap settings, and then estimate all coefficients for the entire power combination space by applying the following simple linear interpolation:

$$C_i(\mathbf{P}) = C_i(\mathbf{P^{max}}) + \{C_i(P_{cpu}, P_{mem1}^{max}, P_{mem2}^{max}, \cdots) - C_i(\mathbf{P^{max}})\}$$
$$+ \{C_i(P_{cpu}^{max}, P_{mem1}, P_{mem2}^{max}, \cdots) - C_i(\mathbf{P^{max}})\} + \cdots \quad (2)$$

Figure 10 illustrates how our approach improves the calibration efficiency in terms of the exploration space reduction. Although the brute force based naive

**Table 2.** Parameters/functions used in our calibration

| Symbols | Remarks |
|---|---|
| $Perf_M(\mathbf{P}, \mathbf{B})$ | Measured performance as a function of $\mathbf{P}$ and $\mathbf{B}$ (benchmark) |
| $Perf_E(\mathbf{P}, \mathbf{F})$ | Estimated performance using our model: $Perf_E(\mathbf{P}, \mathbf{F}) = \mathbf{C(P)} \cdot \mathbf{H(F)}$ |
| $T_{\mathbf{P}}(\subseteq U_{\mathbf{P}})$ | Set of tested power combinations: $T_{\mathbf{P}} = \{\mathbf{P_1}, \mathbf{P_2}, \cdots\}$, $\mathbf{P_j} = (P_{cpu}^j, P_{mem1}^j, \cdots)$ |
| $T_{\mathbf{B}}$ | Set of tested benchmarks: $T_{\mathbf{B}} = \{\mathbf{B_1}, \mathbf{B_2}, \cdots\}$, $\mathbf{B_k} = (Kernel_k, \mathbf{Inputs_k})$ |
| $U_{\mathbf{P}}$ | Set of all the power budget combinations: $U_{\mathbf{P}} = \{(P_{cpu}, P_{mem1}, \cdots) \mid \forall P_x \in S_{P_x}\}$ |
| $\mathbf{P^{max}}$ | Maximum power cap settings: $\mathbf{P^{max}} = (P_{cpu}^{max}, P_{mem1}^{max}, \cdots)$, $P_x^{max} = \max(S_{P_x})$ |

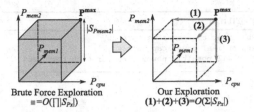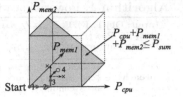

**Fig. 10.** Efficient exploration in our calibration    **Fig. 11.** Hill climbing algorithm

exploration examines all the power cap combinations ($T_\mathbf{P} = U_\mathbf{P}$), ours just moves the space linearly. As a consequence, the number of tested power combinations is reduced significantly from $O(\prod |S_{P_x}|)$ to $O(\sum |S_{P_x}|)$.

## 5.3 Power Allocation Algorithm

Next, based on the calibrated performance model, we optimize the power allocations for the running job under the given power constraint. As the brut-force approach searches for the best in the large number of combinations represented as $O(\prod |S_{P_x}|)$, which is practically infeasible, especially for larger numbers of power cap values and components, we alternatively consider an algorithm based on a hill climbing heuristic. The overview of the algorithm is illustrated in Fig. 11. We firstly set the power cap of each component at its minimum, and then we choose one and increase its power cap step-by-step while the total power cap meets the constraint. In each step, we select the component that improves the objective function the most with the one-step power cap increment. Although, the algorithm can finish at a locally optimal point, it does work well for monotonically increasing functions, such as performance, which increases with higher power cap allocations ($P_x$).

The precise form of our approach is described in Algorithm 1. The algorithm returns an estimated optimal power allocations vector ($\mathbf{P}$) for the given objective function, job features, and power constraint ($Obj$, $\mathbf{F}$, $P_{sum}$). The Lines 1 to 4 represent the initialization process: setting all power caps to minimums and sorting the set of power caps of each component in the ascending order. Then, the main loop follows after this—here, we increase the power caps of components step-by-step. In the inner-most loop (Line 7 to 13), we increase the power cap of each component by one step in each turn and register both its ID and the value of the objective function, if it meets all of the following conditions (Line 10): (1) the power cap did not reach the maximum in this previous; (2) the objective function returns the temporal optimum; and (3) the sum of the power caps is less than or equal to the power constraint. When this inner-most loop finishes, we decide whether we need to update the power cap combinations (Line 14 to 18). If the objective function value is improved in the above inner-most loop, we select the registered component and update its power cap by popping the front one from the associated power cap set; otherwise we just abort here. Finally, at the Line 20, we return the chosen power cap combinations.

---

**Algorithm 1:** Power allocation algorithm

---

**Input:** $\text{Obj}(\mathbf{P}, \mathbf{F}), \mathbf{F}, P_{sum}$ // Maximize Obj under the power constraint
**Output:** $\mathbf{P} = (P_{cpu}, P_{mem1}, \cdots)$ // Return optimal power cap values
**Preset parameters:** $S_{P_{cpu}}, S_{P_{mem1}}, \cdots$ // All possible power caps for each component

```
   /* Set each element of P to the minimum                                    */
1  foreach c ∈ {cpu, mem1, ...} do
2      S'_Pc ← SortAscending(S_Pc);
3      Pc ← PopFront(S'_Pc); // Take out the minimum power cap
4  end
   /* Main loop (go to the best direction step-by-step)                       */
5  while S'_Pcpu ∪ S'_Pmem1 ∪ ... ≠ φ do
6      bestv ← Obj(P, F); bestc ← Null;
7      foreach c ∈ {cpu, mem1, ...} do
          /* Increase the power cap of c by one step                          */
8          P' ← P; // Set P' (= temporal next point) as P (= current)
9          P'_c ← Front(S'_Pc); // Update P' by increasing the power cap of c
          /* Existence/improvement/constraint checks                          */
10         if (P'_c ≠ Null) ∧ (Obj(P', F) > bestv) ∧ (∑ P'_x ≤ P_sum) then
11             | bestv ← Obj(P', F); bestc ← c; // Update the temporal best
12         end
13     end
14     if bestc ≠ Null then
15         | P_bestc ← PopFront(S'_P_bestc);// Take out the front element from the power cap
                  set of bestc and update P
16     else
17         | break; // Already reached at an optimal point
18     end
19 end
20 return P;
```

---

# 6  Evaluation Setup

**Environment:** Our approach is applicable to any system that meets the following conditions: (1) the main memory is heterogeneous in terms of capacity and performance; and (2) component-wise power/performance controls are possible. In this evaluation, we use the platform summarized in Table 3, which follows the above conditions. As shown in the table, our main memory consists of DDR4

**Table 3.** System configurations

| Name | Remarks |
|---|---|
| CPU Package | Xeon Gold 6154 Processor (Skylake) x2 sockets, 36 cores |
| Memory System | **DRAM (Memory 1):** DDR4-2666 x12 DIMMs, 12ch, 192 GB, 256 GB/s(max), **NVRAM (Memory 2):** Intel Optane SSD P4800X x2 cards, 750 GB, 4.8 GB/s (read max), 4.0 GB/s (write max), **Data management:** IMDT [14] |
| OS | Cent OS 7.4 |
| Compiler | Intel C++/Fortran Compiler 17.0.4, **Options:** -O3 -qopenmp -xCORE-AVX512 |
| Power caps[W] | $S_{p_{cpu}} = \{160, 170, \cdots, 280\}$, $S_{p_{mem1}} = \{20, 30, \cdots, 60\}$, $S_{p_{mem2}} = \{20, 30, 40\}$ |

DRAM and PCIe attached NVRAM (Intel 3D Xpoint Optane [14]). By using Intel Memory Drive Technology (IMDT) [14], we can use the NVRAM as a part of the main memory[2]. More specifically, it works as a virtual machine monitor dedicated to the data management among the different kinds of memories, and these memories are used in a hierarchical manner: the DRAM is accessed first, and if it turns out to be a miss, then data swap happens (at page-level granularity). Note that our approach is applicable/extensible to any other emerging platforms with hybrid main memories such as 3D stacked DRAM + DIMM-based DRAM like Knights Landing [16] or DRAM + DIMM-based NVRAM like DCPMM [15], if they accept component-wise power managements. Only one thing we need to do to apply our method to them is just calibrating the model coefficients beforehand (or for finer tuning, adding/optimizing the basis functions for the target system is one option).

**Power Controls:** For the power management, we set various power cap values to the CPU and the DRAM through an interface based on RAPL (Running Average Power Limit) [13], which are listed in Table 3. Since power capping is not supported on our NVRAM, we emulate it by limiting the PCIe link speed (Gen1/2/3). More specifically, the link speed (Genx, $x = 1, 2, 3$) is selected so that the NVRAM power cap ($P_{mem2}$) fits the following:

$$P_{mem2} = P_{dynamic}(x) + P_{static} + P_{margin}(x) \qquad (3)$$
$$P_{dynamic}(x) = B_{link}(x)/B_{link}(3) * P_{dynamic}(3) \qquad (4)$$

The first equation ensures that the power cap value ($P_{mem2}$) is dividable into the dynamic power part ($P_{dynamic}$), the static power ($P_{static}$) and the accordingly set margin to round up ($P_{margin} < 10[\text{W}]$). The second equation ensures that the dynamic power limit is proportional to its link bandwidth ($B_{link}$). We use this because (1) the link speed limits the memory access frequency, and (2) the dynamic power consumption is, in principle, equal to the product of the energy consumption per access and the access frequency. We take $B_{link}(x)$, $P_{static}$ and $P_{dynamic}(3) + P_{static}$ from the official specs and determine the link speed for a given $P_{mem2}$. More specifically, we set the link as Gen1/2/3 for $P_{mem2} = 20/30/40$ [W], respectively.

**Methodology:** To evaluate our approach, we use the synthetic code (Streaming) shown in Fig. 2 (Sect. 3.1) as well as several mini applications chosen from the CORAL benchmark suite [25]: AMG, LULESH, MCB and miniFE. For each application, we regard the main loop as a target kernel. The benchmark set ($T_B$) used for our calibration process is listed in Table 4; we test various inputs for each application kernel. Then, by using the obtained coefficients, we optimize the power allocations for the workloads listed in Table 5. Here, the data footprint fits within the fast memory (192[GB]) for Small problems, but it does not for Large problems.

---

[2] Persistent Memory Development Kit (PMDK) also supports an automatic data management feature and can be used for this purpose [1].

**Table 4.** Benchmarks ($T_{\mathbf{B}}$) used for our calibration

| (Kernel, Inputs) |
|---|
| (miniFE, I1 = "-nx 512 -ny 512 -nz 512"), (miniFE, I2 = " -nx 896 -ny 896 -nz 640"), |
| (miniFE, I3 = "-nx 1024 -ny 512 -nz 512"), (miniFE, I4 = "-nx 1024 -ny 768 -nz 640"), |
| (miniFE, I5 = "-nx 1024 -ny 1024 -nz 512"), (miniFE, I6 = "-nx 1024 -ny 1024 -nz 640"), |
| (LULESH, I1 = "-s 400"), (LULESH, I2 = "-s 450"), (LULESH, I3 = "-s 500"), |
| (LULESH, I4 = "-s 550"), (LULESH, I5 = "-s 600"), (LULESH, I6 = "-s 645"), |
| (MCB, I1 = "–nZonesX=2048 –nZonesY = 2048"), (MCB, I2 = "–nZonesX=4096 –nZonesY = 2048"), |
| (MCB, I3 = "–nZonesX=4096 –nZonesY = 3072"), (MCB, I4 = "–nZonesX=4096 –nZonesY = 4096"), |
| (MCB, I5 = "–nZonesX=5120 –nZonesY = 4096"), (MCB, I6 = "–nZonesX=6144 –nZonesY = 4096"), |
| (Streaming(AI: 10.7), I1 = "$N = 16G$"), (Streaming(AI: 10.7), I2 = "$N = 24G$"), |
| (Streaming(AI: 10.7), I3 = "$N = 32G$"), (Streaming(AI: 10.7), I4 = "$N = 48G$"), |
| (Streaming(AI: 10.7), I5 = "$N = 64G$"), (Streaming(AI: 10.7), I6 = "$N = 80G$"), |
| (AMG, I1 = "-n 512 512 256"), (AMG, I2 = " -n 512 521 512"), (AMG, I3 = "-n 640 512 640"), |
| (AMG, I4 = "-n768 768 512"), (AMG, I5 = "-n 640 640 640"), (AMG, I6 = "-n 1024 640 512"), |
| (Streaming(AI: 0.167), I1 = "$N = 16G$"), (Streaming(AI: 0.167), I2 = "$N = 24G$"), |
| (Streaming(AI: 0.167), I3 = "$N = 32G$"), (Streaming(AI: 0.167), I4 = "$N = 48G$"), |
| (Streaming(AI: 0.167), I5 = "$N = 64G$"), (Streaming(AI: 0.167), I6 = "$N = 80G$") |

**Table 5.** Problem settings for our power allocation evaluation

| Application | [Problem]: (Inputs, Footprint Size[GB]) |
|---|---|
| miniFE | [Small]: ("-nx 1024 -ny 512 -nz 512", 129), [Large]: ("-nx 1024 -ny 1024 -nz 640", 321) |
| LULESH | [Small]: ("-s 400", 62), [Large]: ("-s 645", 258) |
| MCB | [Small]: ("–nZonesX = 2048 –nZonesY = 2048", 57), [Large]: ("–nZonesX = 5120 –nZonesY = 4096", 279) |
| AMG | [Small]: ("-n 512 512 512", 141), [Large]: ("-n 1024 640 512", 354) |
| Stream(AI:*) | [Small]: ("$N = 8G$", 64), [Large]: ("$N = 32G$", 256) |

Next, Table 6 describes the feature parameters ($\mathbf{F}$) utilized in our evaluation. On one hand, we measure $\mathbf{F_{dy}}$ at every run, while on the other hand, we collect $\mathbf{F_{prof}}$ only once for an application, especially with the Small problems shown in Table 5. By using PAPI [37], we collected these feature parameters[3]. Note that, through our preliminary evaluation, we confirmed that all of $\mathbf{F_{prof}}$, including the LLC (Last Level Cache) access statistics ($F_{p3}$ and $F_{p4}$), are almost constant when we scale the problem sizes from few GiB to few 100 GiB for these applications, thus we consider them as scale-independent, yet application-specific parameters in this work.

---

[3] We disable IMDT when collecting $\mathbf{F_{prof}}$ as it prevents us from accessing hardware counters. But, this is not the case when we use PMDK for the data management.

**Table 6.** Feature parameter selections ($\mathbf{F} = (\mathbf{F_{prof}}, \mathbf{F_{dy}})$)

| Types | Parameter remarks |
|---|---|
| $\mathbf{F_{prof}}$ | $F_{p1} = (\text{\# of FP operations})/(\text{\# of instructions})$, <br> $F_{p2} = (\text{\# of non FP arithmetic instructions})/(\text{\# of instructions})$, <br> $F_{p3} = (\text{\# of LLC misses})/(\text{\# of instructions})$, <br> $F_{p4} = (\text{\# of LLC misses})/(\text{\# of LLC accesses})$, |
| $\mathbf{F_{dy}}$ | $F_{d1} = (\text{footprint Feature parameter selections size } F_{fs})/(\text{capacity of Memory1})$ |

**Table 7.** Basis function setups ($\mathbf{H(F)} = (H_1(\mathbf{F}), H_2(\mathbf{F}), \cdots)$)

| Function Definitions |
|---|
| $H_1 = F_{p1}$, $H_2 = F_{p2}$, $H_3 = F_{p3}$, $H_4 = F_{p3} * F_{d1}$ $H_5 = F_{p3} * F_{p4}$, $H_6 = F_{p3} * F_{p4} * F_{d1}$, <br> $H_7 = 1$ (constant) |

Table 7 shows the list of the basis functions ($\mathbf{H(F)}$) utilized in our evaluation. By using $H_1$ and $H_2$, we detect the CPU load and how much it affects the power capping settings. In addition to them, we also consider the traffic on the overall hybrid memory system and how each of them are accessed by using the functions $H_3$, $H_4$, $H_5$, and $H_6$. Because $F_{p3}$ is equal to the frequency of accesses to the memory system, $H_3$ indicates how heavily it is used. In addition, we utilize $F_{p4}$ and/or $F_{d1}$ for $H_4$, $H_5$ and $H_6$ due to the following reasons: (1) because the LLC hit rate $F_{p4}$ is sensitive to the memory access pattern, we can use it to cover this aspect; (2) to take problem scale into account, we further utilize $F_{d1}$ here as well. These parameters are multiplied by $F_{p3}$ as the impacts of access-pattern/problem-scale on performance depend on the access frequency, and we thus take the correlation of these parameters into consideration.

Although this selection of parameters and the function settings are effective, as shown in the next section, it may be possible to further improve the accuracy by consider additional aspects. For instance, adding other memory-access related parameters, such as working-set size, could be a good option for workloads with more complicated inputs. We can provide such an extensibility in a straightforward manner by making the model parameters/terms modifiable by users and then making them available to the other parts of the framework, like calibration and power allocation.

## 7  Experimental Results

In Figs. 12 and 13, we compare performance/power-efficiency across methods using different problem sizes. Here, we set $P_{sum}$ to 300[W] and utilize $Perf()/PowEff()$ as the objective function in our approach through the measurements of Figs. 12 and 13. The vertical axis indicates relative performance or power-efficiency, normalized to the optimal power cap combinations that maximize the given objective function. The *Worst* combination is chosen from the

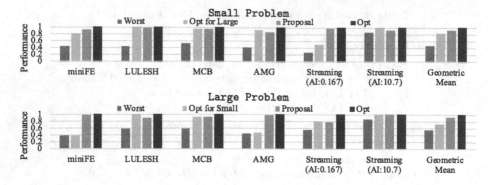

**Fig. 12.** Performance comparisons at $P_{sum} = 300[\text{W}]$ for different problem sizes (U: Small, D: Large)—the objective function for our approach is $Perf()$

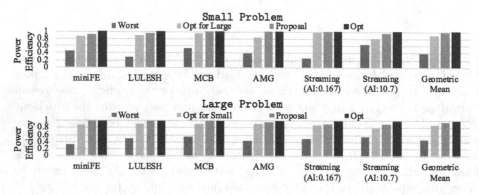

**Fig. 13.** Power-efficiency comparisons at $P_{sum} = 300[\text{W}]$ for different problem sizes (U: Small, D: Large)—the objective function for our approach is $PowEff()$

settings that meet $\sum P_x = P_{sum}$ or $\sum P_x \leq P_{sum}$ in Fig. 12 or Fig. 13 so that the objective function is minimized[4]. GeometricMean indicates the geometric mean of performance or power efficiency across all workloads for each method. Overall, our approach achieves near optimal performance/power-efficiency: on average, our approach keeps 93.7%/96.2% or 92.3%/95.4% of performance/power-efficiency compared to the optimal for Small or Large problems. Note that these numbers are quite important as we consider the situation where the power scheduler distributes power budgets to the nodes, and each node needs to optimize the power allocations to the components while keeping the given power constraint, which is regarded as common in future power-constrained supercomputers.

Then, we scale the total power budget ($P_{sum}$) and observe performance and power efficiency for all the above methods. In Fig. 14, we summarize the

---

[4] If we choose the worst of $\{\forall \mathbf{P} | \sum P_x \leq P_{sum}\}$ for the performance evaluation, it will always mean setting all power caps to the minimum. Therefore, we set the constraint as $\sum P_x = P_{sum}$ for Worst in the performance evaluation.

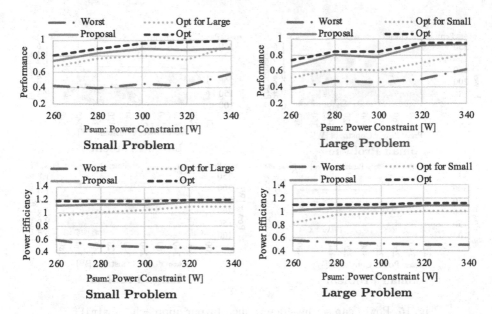

**Fig. 14.** Performance (U) and Power efficiency (D) as functions of the node power constraint for different problem sizes

experimental result using the geometric mean of performance/power-efficiency across all workloads. In the graphs, the X-axis indicates the node power constraint ($P_{sum}$), while the Y-axis shows relative performance or power efficiency normalized to the maximum power cap setting ($\mathbf{P} = \mathbf{P^{max}}$). As shown in the figures, our approach is very close to the optimal regardless of the problem size, the objective function, or the total power budget.

Next, we demonstrate how our approach distributes the given power budget ($P_{sum}$) depending on several aspects by using miniFE as an example. Figure 15 illustrates the breakdowns of power allocations in accordance to the given power constraint ($P_{sum}$) as well as the objective function for different problem sizes (Small/Large). The horizontal axis represents the power constraint ($P_{sum}$), while the vertical axis indicates the breakdown or relative performance/power-efficiency normalized to $\mathbf{P} = \mathbf{P^{max}}$. Note that the performance or power-efficiency curves in the figures are the estimated values provided by our model, and the allocations are based on them.

According to the figures, even for the same application, the power allocation decisions can change considerably depending on the objective function as well as the problem settings. For Small, our method initially allocates power to the memory system side and then shifts to the CPU side until reaching 340[W] to maximize performance (upper left figure). However, when the problem size is scaled, the CPU and the first memory need less power. This is because the second memory becomes the significant bottleneck, and allocating more power to the others does not help with improving performance (upper right figure).

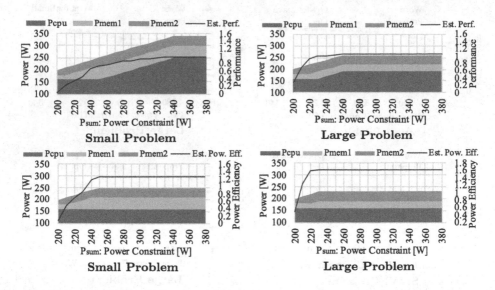

**Fig. 15.** Power cap settings determined by our approach for `miniFE`

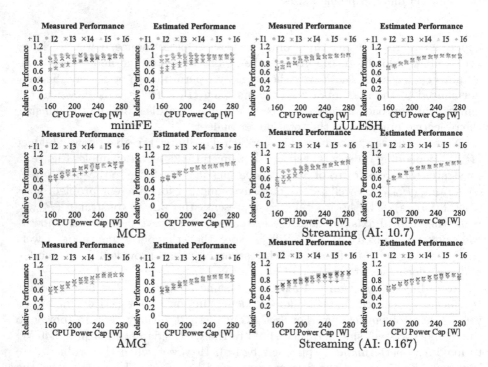

**Fig. 16.** Comparison of measured (left) and estimated (right) performance for different $P_{cpu}$ ($P_{mem1} = P_{mem1}^{max} = 60[W]$, $P_{mem2} = P_{mem2}^{max} = 40[W]$)

As for the power efficiency (lower figures), our approach stops the power allocations earlier because it requires large enough performance gain that is worthwhile putting additional power. For most of the evaluated workloads, we also observe the exact same situation: the given power budget cannot be fully used, especially when the problem size is scaled. We regard this as an opportunity to improve the whole system efficiency (e.g., by returning such extra power budget to the system manager and allocating it to other jobs).

Further, in Fig. 16, 17, and 18, we demonstrate the model calibration result using the workloads described in Table 4. For each graph, the horizontal axis indicates the power capping value set at each component, while the vertical axis represents relative performance which is normalized to that at best—namely, setting $\mathbf{P}$ at $\mathbf{P^{max}}$. Each legend is associated with the problem (or inputs) settings shown in Table 4. Here, we applied the method of least squares using sets of relative performance and feature parameters brought by the workloads. Overall, our approach successfully captures the characteristics of these applications including the footprint size dependency, and the estimated result is close to the measured performance for almost all the cases (the average error is only 6.00%).

Finally, we measured the time overhead of our approach, which turned out to be negligible. More specifically, it took only around 200 μs, 1 μs, and 80 μs for

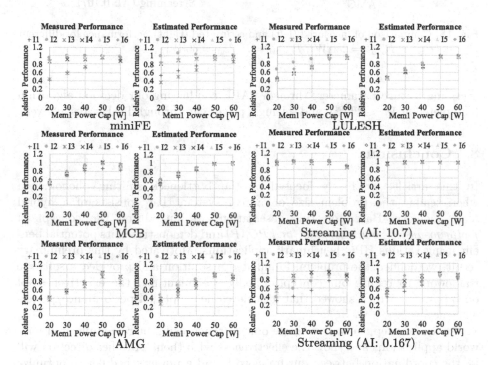

**Fig. 17.** Comparison of measured (left) and estimated (right) performance for different $P_{mem1}$ ($P_{cpu} = P_{cpu}^{max} = 280[W]$, $P_{mem2} = P_{mem2}^{max} = 40[W]$)

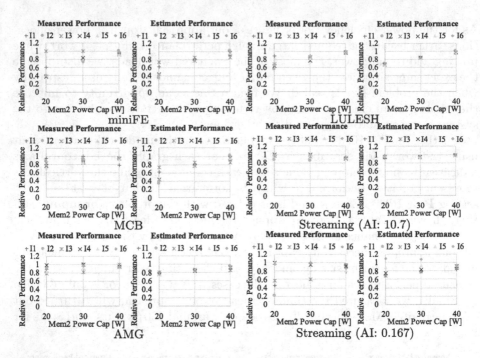

**Fig. 18.** Comparison of measured (left) and estimated (right) performance for different $P_{mem2}$ ($P_{cpu} = P_{cpu}^{max} = 280[W]$, $P_{mem1} = P_{mem1}^{max} = 60[W]$)

accessing feature parameters through PAPI, conducting our decision algorithm (completed at $\mathbf{P} = \mathbf{P^{max}}$), and setting a power cap through RAPL, respectively.

# 8    Conclusions

In this article, we firstly focused on the bottleneck shifting phenomenon when scaling the problem size on a real system that consists of a hybrid main memory. Based on this observation, we introduced the concept of *footprint-aware power capping (or FPCAP)* and demonstrated its potential benefit using various HPC benchmark applications. Motivated by this preliminary result, we defined the problem, formulated a solution and provided a software framework to realize our concept. Finally, we quantified the effectiveness of our approach, which showed that it achieves near optimal performance/power-efficiency.

As a next-step, we will evaluate our approach using more complicated real-world applications and show the effectiveness with them. Another direction will be the coordination between our framework and a power scheduler to optimize both intra- and inter-node power budget settings at the same time. We expect that this will have a significant impact on full system energy efficiency, as the power budget to a node is prone to be under-utilized when the footprint size is large. Consequently, sending this as feedback to the power scheduler will help whole system performance/energy-efficiency under the total power constraint. Another promising direction is an extension of our work to cover other kinds of systems (e.g., CPU + GPU/FPGA + hybrid memory) or other application areas, such as data analytics or machine learning using various types of hybrid memories. Although we may have to update the parameters/terms of the regression model, the concept of FPCAP and the approaches used in our framework will carry forward and improve system efficiency.

**Acknowledgments.** We would like to express our gratitude to the anonymous reviewers for their valuable suggestions. We also thank all the members of CAPS at TU Munich and the folks in ITC, U Tokyo for discussions. This work is partly supported by the following grants: Research on Processor Architecture, Power Management, System Software and Numerical Libraries for the Post K Computer System of RIKEN; JSPS Grant-in-Aid for Research Activity Start-up (JP16H06677); and JSPS Grant-in-Aid for Early-Career Scientists (JP18K18021).

# References

1. PMDK: Persistent Memory Development Kit. http://www.pmem.io
2. Akinaga, H., et al.: Resistive random access memory (ReRAM) based on metal oxides. Proc. IEEE **98**(12), 2237–2251 (2010)
3. Arima, E., et al.: Immediate sleep: reducing energy impact of peripheral circuits in STT-MRAM Caches. In: ICCD, pp. 149–156 (2015)
4. Bailey, P.E., et al.: Adaptive configuration selection for power-constrained heterogeneous systems. In: ICPP, pp. 371–380 (2014)
5. Cao, T., et al.: Demand-aware power management for power-constrained HPC systems. In: CCGrid, pp. 21–31 (2016)
6. Consortium, H.M.C.: Hybrid memory cube specification 2.1. Last Revision (January 2015)
7. Deng, Q., et al.: CoScale: coordinating CPU and memory system DVFS in server systems. In: MICRO, pp. 143–154 (2012)
8. Dhiman, G., et al.: PDRAM: a hybrid PRAM and DRAM main memory system. In: DAC, pp. 664–669 (2009)
9. Ellsworth, D.A., et al.: Dynamic power sharing for higher job throughput. In: SC, pp. 80:1–80:11 (2015)
10. Felter, W., et al.: A performance-conserving approach for reducing peak power consumption in server systems. In: ICS, pp. 293–302 (2005)
11. Ge, R., et al.: Application-aware power coordination on power bounded NUMA multicore systems. In: ICPP, pp. 591–600 (2017)
12. Hanson, H., et al.: Processor-memory power shifting for multi-core systems. In.: 4th Workshop on Energy Efficient Design (2012). http://research.ihost.com/weed2012/pdfs/paper%20A.pdf. Accessed 4 June 2020
13. Imes, C., et al.: CoPPer: soft real-time application performance using hardware power capping. In: ICAC, pp. 31–41 (2019)
14. Intel: Intel® Memory Drive Technology, Set Up and Configuration Guide (2017)
15. Izraelevitz, J., et al.: Basic Performance Measurements of the Intel Optane DC Persistent Memory Module. arXiv preprint arXiv:1903.05714 (2019)

16. Jeffers, J., et al.: Intel Xeon Phi Processor High Performance Programming: Knights, Landing edn. Morgan Kaufmann Publishers Inc., San Francisco (2016)
17. Komoda, T., et al.: Power capping of CPU-GPU heterogeneous systems through coordinating DVFS and task mapping. In: ICCD, pp. 349–356 (2013)
18. Kültürsay, E., et al.: Evaluating STT-RAM as an energy-efficient main memory alternative. In: ISPASS, pp. 256–267 (2013)
19. Lee, B.C., et al.: Architecting phase change memory as a scalable dram alternative. In: ISCA, pp. 2–13 (2009)
20. Lefurgy, C., et al.: Power capping: a prelude to power shifting. Clust. Comput. **11**(2), 183–195 (2008)
21. Li, J., et al.: Power shifting in thrifty interconnection network. In: HPCA, pp. 156–167 (2011)
22. Miwa, S., et al.: Profile-based power shifting in interconnection networks with on/off links. In: SC, pp. 37:1–37:11 (2015)
23. Noguchi, H., et al.: 7.2 4Mb STT-MRAM-based cache with memory-access-aware power optimization and write-verify-write/read-modify-write scheme. In: ISSCC, pp. 132–133 (2016)
24. Nugteren, C., et al.: Roofline-aware DVFS for GPUs. In: ADAPT, pp. 8:8–8:10 (2014)
25. ORNL, ANL, LLNL: CORAL Benchmark Codes (2013). https://asc.llnl.gov/CORAL-benchmarks/
26. Park, H., et al.: Power management of hybrid DRAM/PRAM-based main memory. In: DAC, pp. 59–64 (2011)
27. Patki, T., et al.: Exploring hardware overprovisioning in power-constrained, high performance computing. In: ICS, pp. 173–182 (2013)
28. Patki, T., et al.: Practical resource management in power-constrained, high performance computing. In: HPDC, pp. 121–132 (2015)
29. Paul, I., et al.: Harmonia: balancing compute and memory power in high-performance GPUs. In: ISCA, pp. 54–65 (2015)
30. Ramos, L.E., et al.: Page placement in hybrid memory systems. In: ICS, pp. 85–95 (2011)
31. Sakamoto, R., et al.: Production hardware overprovisioning: real-world performance optimization using an extensible power-aware resource management framework. In: IPDPS, pp. 957–966 (2017)
32. Sarood, O., et al.: Optimizing power allocation to CPU and memory subsystems in overprovisioned HPC systems. In: CLUSTER, pp. 1–8 (2013)
33. Sarood, O., et al.: Maximizing throughput of overprovisioned HPC data centers under a strict power budget. In: SC, pp. 807–818 (2014)
34. Sasaki, H., et al.: An intra-task DVFS technique based on statistical analysis of hardware events. In: CF, pp. 123–130 (2007)
35. Savoie, L., et al.: I/O aware power shifting. In: IPDPS, pp. 740–749 (2016)
36. Standard, J.: High Bandwidth Memory (HBM) DRAM. JESD235 (2013)
37. Terpstra, D., et al.: Collecting performance data with PAPI-C. In: Müller, M., Resch, M., Schulz, A., Nagel, W. (eds.) Tools for High Performance Computing 2009, pp. 157–173. Springer, Heidelberg (2010). https://doi.org/10.1007/978-3-642-11261-4_11
38. Williams, S., et al.: Roofline: an insightful visual performance model for multicore architectures. Commun. ACM **52**(4), 65–76 (2009)
39. Wu, K., et al.: Unimem: runtime data managementon non-volatile memory-based heterogeneous main memory. In: SC, pp. 58:1–58:14 (2017)

# Offsite Autotuning Approach

## Performance Model Driven Autotuning Applied to Parallel Explicit ODE Methods

Johannes Seiferth$^{(\boxtimes)}$, Matthias Korch, and Thomas Rauber

Department of Computer Science, University of Bayreuth, Bayreuth, Germany
{johannes.seiferth,korch,rauber}@uni-bayreuth.de

**Abstract.** Autotuning (AT) is a promising concept to minimize the often tedious manual effort of optimizing scientific applications for a specific target platform. Ideally, an AT approach can reliably identify the most efficient implementation variant(s) for a new platform or new characteristics of the input by applying suitable program transformations and analytic models. In this work, we introduce Offsite, an offline AT approach that automates this selection process at installation time by rating implementation variants based on an analytic performance model without requiring time-consuming runtime tests. From abstract multilevel description languages, Offsite automatically derives optimized, platform-specific and problem-specific code of possible variants and applies the performance model to these variants.

We apply Offsite to parallel numerical methods for ordinary differential equations (ODEs). In particular, we investigate tuning a specific class of explicit ODE solvers, PIRK methods, for four different initial value problems (IVPs) on three different shared-memory systems. Our experiments demonstrate that Offsite can reliably identify the set of most efficient implementation variants for different given test configurations (ODE solver, IVP, platform) and effectively handle important AT scenarios.

**Keywords:** Autotuning · Performance modeling · Description language · ODE methods · ECM performance model · Shared-memory

## 1 Introduction

The performance of scientific applications strongly depends on the characteristics of the targeted computing platform, such as, e.g., the processor design, the core topology, the cache architectures, the memory latency or the memory bandwidth. Facing the growing diversity and complexity of today's computing landscape, the task of writing and maintaining highly efficient application code is getting more and more cumbersome for software developers. A highly optimized implementation variant on one target platform, might, however, perform poorly on another platform. That particular poorly performant implementation variant, though, could again potentially outperform all other variants on the

The original version of this chapter was revised: The chapter was reverted to a regular, non-Open Access chapter. The correction to this chapter is available at https://doi.org/10.1007/978-3-030-50743-5_28

P. Sadayappan et al. (Eds.): ISC High Performance 2020, LNCS 12151, pp. 370–390, 2020.
https://doi.org/10.1007/978-3-030-50743-5_19

next platform. Hence, in order to achieve a high efficiency and obtain optimal performance when migrating an existing scientific application, developers need to tune and adapt the application code for each specific platform anew.

## 1.1 Related Work

A promising concept to avoid this time-consuming, manual effort is **autotuning** (AT), and many different approaches have been proposed to automatically tune software [2]. AT is based on two core concepts: *(i)* the generation of optimized implementation variants based on program transformation and optimization techniques and *(ii)* the selection of the most efficient variant(s) on the target platform from the set of generated variants. In general, there are *(i)* **offline** and *(ii)* **online** AT techniques. Offline AT tries to select the supposedly most efficient variant at installation time without actual knowledge of the input data. Such approaches are applicable for use-cases, whose execution behavior does not depend on the input data. This is the case, e.g., for dense linear algebra problems, which can, i.a., be tuned offline with *ATLAS* [23], *PATUS* [6] and *PhiPAC* [4]. In other fields, such as sparse linear algebra or particle codes, characteristics of the input data heavily influence the execution behavior. By choosing the best variant at runtime—when all input is known—, online AT approaches such as *Active Harmony* [22], *ATF* [17] and *Periscope* [9] incorporate these influences.

Selecting a suitable implementation variant from a potentially large set of available variants in a time-efficient manner is a big challenge in AT. Various techniques and search strategies have been proposed in previous works to meet this challenge [2]. A straightforward approach is the time-consuming comparison of variants by runtime tests, possibly steered by a single search strategy, such as an exhaustive search or more sophisticated mathematical optimization methods like *differential evolution* [7] or *genetic algorithms* [25] or a combination of multiple search strategies [1]. [16] proposes a hierarchical approach that allows the use of individual search algorithms for dependent subspaces of the search space.

As an alternative to runtime tests, analytic performance models can be applied to either select the most efficient variant or to reduce the number of tests required by filtering out inefficient variants beforehand. In general, two categories of performance models are distinguished: (i) **black box models** applying statistical methods and machine learning techniques to observed performance data like hardware metrics or measured runtimes in order to learn to predict performance behavior [15,20], and (ii) **white box models** such as the *Roofline model* [8,24] or the *ECM performance model* [12,21] that describe the interaction of hardware and code using simplified machine models. For loop kernels, the *Roofline* and the *ECM model* can be constructed with the *Kerncraft* tool [11]. Kerncraft is based on static code analysis and determines ECM contributions from application (assembly; data transfers) and machine information (in-core port model; instruction throughput).

## 1.2  Main Contributions

In this work, we propose **Offsite**, an offline AT approach that automatically identifies the most efficient implementation variant(s) during installation time based on performance predictions. These predictions stem from an analytic performance prediction methodology for explicit ODE methods proposed by [19] that uses a combined white and black box model approach based on the ECM model. The main contributions of this paper are:

*(i)* We develop a novel offline AT approach for shared-memory systems based on performance modelling. This approach automates the task of generating the pool of possible implementation variants using abstract description languages. For all these variants, our approach can automatically predict their performance and identify the best variant(s). Further, we integrated a database interface for collected performance data which enables the reusability of data and which allows to include feedback from possible online AT or actual program runs.
*(ii)* We show how to apply Offsite to an algorithm from numerical analysis with complex runtime behavior: the parallel solution of IVPs of ODEs.
*(iii)* We validate the accuracy and efficiency of Offsite for different test configurations and discuss its applicability to four different AT scenarios.

## 1.3  Outline

Section 2 details the selected example use-case (PIRK methods) and the corresponding testbed. Based on this use-case, Offsite is described in Sect. 3. In Sect. 4, we experimentally evaluate Offsite in four different AT scenarios and on three different target platforms. Section 5 discusses possible future extensions of Offsite and Sect. 6 concludes the paper.

## 2  Use-Case and Experimental Test Bed

### Use-Case: PIRK Methods

As example use-case, we study **parallel iterated Runge–Kutta (PIRK) methods** [13], which are part of the general class of explicit ODE methods, and solve an ODE system $\mathbf{y}'(t) = \mathbf{r}(t, \mathbf{y}(t))$, $\mathbf{y}(t_0) = \mathbf{y}_0$, $\mathbf{y} \in \mathbb{R}^n$ by performing a series of time steps until the end of the integration interval is reached. In each time step, a new numerical approximation $\mathbf{y}_{\kappa+1}$ for the unknown solution $\mathbf{y}$ is determined by an explicit predictor–corrector process in a fixed number of sub steps.

PIRK methods are an excellent candidate class for AT. Their complex four-dimensional loop structure (Listing 1) can be modified by loop transformations resulting in a large pool of possible implementation variants whose performance behavior potentially varies highly depending on: *(i)* the composition of computations and memory accesses, *(ii)* the number of stages of the base ODE method, *(iii)* the characteristics of the ODE system solved, *(iv)* the target hardware, *(v)* the compiler and the compiler flags, and *(vi)* the number of threads started.

```
1   for l ← 1,...,s do Y_l^(0) ← y_κ
2   for k ← 1,...,m do
3     for l ← 1,...,s do
4       Y_l^(k) ← y_κ + h_κ ∑_{i=1}^s a_li F_i^(k-1)  with  F_i^(k-1) ← r(t_κ + c_i h_κ, Y_i^(k-1))
5   y_{κ+1} ← y_κ + h_κ ∑_{i=1}^s b_i F_i^(m)
```

**Listing 1.** Time step function of a PIRK method.

**Table 1.** Characteristics of the test set of IVPs.

| IVP | Cusp | IC | Medakzo | Wave1D |
|---|---|---|---|---|
| Acces distance[a] | Unlimited | Limited | Unlimited | Limited |
| Computational behavior | Mixed | Compute-bound | Mixed | Memory-bound |

[a] In practice, many IVPs are sparse, i.e. only access few components of $\mathbf{Y}$ when evaluating function $\mathbf{r}$ (line 4, Listing 1). A special case of sparse is *limited access distance* $d(\mathbf{r})$, where $r_j$ only accesses components $y_{j-d(\mathbf{r})}$ to $y_{j+d(\mathbf{r})}$.

## Test Set of Initial Value Problems

In our experiments, we consider a broad set of IVPs (Table 1) that exhibit different characteristics: *(i) Cusp* combines Zeeman's cusp catastrophe model for a threshold-nerve-impulse mechanism with the van der Pol oscillator [10], *(ii) IC* describes a traversing signal through a chain of $N$ concatenated inverters [3], *(iii) Medakzo* describes the penetration of radio-labeled antibodies into a tissue infected by a tumor [14], and *(iv) Wave1D* describes the propagation of disturbances at a fixed speed in one direction [5].

## Test Set of Target Platforms

We conducted our experiments on three different shared-memory systems (Table 2). For all experiments, the CPU clock was fixed, hyper-threading disabled and thread binding set with *KMP_AFFINITY=granularity=fine,compact*. All codes were compiled with the Intel C compiler and flags *-O3*, *-xAVX* and *-fno-alias* set.

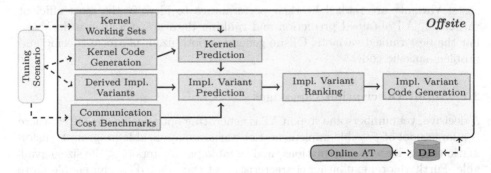

**Fig. 1.** Workflow of the Offsite autotuning approach.

**Table 2.** Characteristics of the test set of target platforms.

| Name | HSW | IVB | SKY |
|---|---|---|---|
| Micro-architecture | Haswell EP | Ivy-Bridge EP | Skylake SP |
| CPU | Xeon E5-2630 v3 | Xeon E5-2660 v2 | Xeon Gold 6148 |
| De-facto frequency | 2.3 GHz | 2.2 GHz | 1.76 GHz |
| Cores | 8 | 10 | 20 |
| L1 cache (data) | 32 kB | 32 kB | 32 kB |
| L2 cache | 256 kB | 256 kB | 1 MB |
| L3 cache (shared) | 20 MB | 25 MB | 27.5 MB |
| Cache line size | 64 B | 64 B | 64 B |
| *Measured memory bandwidth* | | | |
| Load only | 50 GB/s | 47 GB/s | 118 GB/s |
| *FLOPs per cycle (double precision)* | | | |
| ADD/FMA/MUL | 4/8/4 | 4/-/4 | 16/32/16 |
| Compiler | icc 19.0.5 | icc 19.0.4 | icc 19.0.2 |

## 3  Offsite Autotuning Approach

In this work, we introduce the **Offsite** offline AT approach on the example of explicit ODE methods. Before starting a new Offsite run, the *tuning scenario* desired, which consists of: *(i)* the pool of possible implementations and program transformations, *(ii)* the ODE base method(s), *(iii)* the IVP(s), and *(iv)* the target platform, is defined using description languages in the YAML standard[1].

From its input data, Offsite automatically handles the whole tuning workflow (Fig. 1). First, Offsite generates optimized, platform-specific and problem-specific code for all kernels and derives all possible implementation variants. Applying an analytic performance prediction methodology, the performance of each kernel is predicted for either *(i)* a fixed ODE system size $n$—if specified by the user or prescribed by the ODE[2]—or *(ii)* a set of relevant ODE system sizes determined by a working set model. The performance of a variant is derived by combining the predictions of its kernels and adding an estimate of its synchronization costs. Variants are ranked by their performance to identify the most efficient variant(s). All obtained prediction and ranking data are stored in a database. For the best ranked variants, Offsite generates optimized, platform-specific and problem-specific code.

### 3.1  Input Description Languages

A decisive, yet cumbersome step in AT is generating optimized code. Often, there is a large pool of possible implementation variants, applicable program transformations (e.g. loop transformations) and tunable parameters (e.g. tile sizes) available. Furthermore, exploiting characteristics of the input data can enable more

---

[1] YAML is a data serialization language; https://yaml.org.
[2] There are scalable ODE systems but also ODEs with a fixed size [10].

optimizations (e.g. constant propagation). Writing all variants by hand, however, would be tedious and error-prone and there is demand for automation. In this work, we introduce multilevel description languages to describe implementations, ODE methods, IVPs and target platforms in an abstract way. Offsite can interpret these languages and automatically derives optimized code.

```
1 stages: 4
2 order: 7
3 corrector_steps: 6
4 A: [["0.1130", "-0.0403", "0.0258",
       "-0.0099"], ..., [...]]
5 b: ["0.2205", ...]
6 c: ["0.1130 - 0.0403 + 0.0258 -
       0.0099", ...]
```

**Listing 2.** ODE method description format on the example of *Radau II A (7)*.

```
1 components:
2   first: 1
3   size: n-1
4   code: |
5     (((U_op - %in[j]) * R - (eta * ((%in[j-1] -
           U_th) * (%in[j-1] - U_th) - (%in[j
           -1] - %in[j] - U_th) * (%in[j-1] - %
           in[j] - U_th)))) / C);
6 constants:
7   - double R = 1.0
8   - ...
```

**Listing 3.** IVP description format on the example of *InverterChain*.

**The Base ODE Method** of a PIRK method is characterized by its Butcher table—i.e., coefficient matrix $A$, weight vector $b$, node vector $c$—and a small set of properties: *(i)* number of stages $s$, *(ii)* order $o$, *(iii)* number of corrector steps $m$. Exploiting these properties, however, can have a large impact on the efficiency of an implementation variant and should be included into the code generation in order to obtain the most efficient code. The $i$-loop in Listing 4, e.g., might be replaceable by a single vector operation for specific $s$, or zero entries in the Butcher table might allow to save computations.

Listing 2 shows the ODE method description format on the example of *Radau II A (7)* which is a four-stage method with order seven applying six corrector steps per time step. To save space, only an excerpt of the Butcher table is shown with a reduced number of digits.

**IVPs** are described in the IVP description format shown by *IC* (Listing 3):

*(i)* **components** describes the $n$ components of the IVP. Each component contains a **code** YAML block that describes how function evaluation $\mathbf{r}(t_\kappa + c_i h_\kappa, \mathbf{Y}_i^{(k-1)})$ (l. 4, Listing 1) will be substituted during code generation whereby **%in** is a placeholder for the used input vector $\mathbf{Y}_i^{(k-1)}$. Adjacent components that execute the same computation can be described by a single block whereby **first** denotes the first component and **size** specifies the total number of adjacent components handled by that particular block.

*(ii)* **constants** defines IVP-specific parameters replaced with their actual values during code generation and might possibly enable further code optimizations. In IVP *IC*, e.g., a multiplication could be saved if electrical resistance $R$ equals 1.0.

**Target Platform and Compiler** are described using the machine description format introduced by Kerncraft[3]. Its general structure is tripartite: *(i)* the execution architecture description, *(ii)* the cache and memory hierarchy description, and *(iii)* benchmark results of typical streaming kernels.

**Implementation Variants** of numerical algorithms are abstracted by description languages as (i) **kernel templates** and (ii) **implementation skeletons**.

*Kernel Templates* define basic computation kernels and possible variations of this kernel enabled by program transformations that preserve semantic correctness. Listing 4 shows the kernel template description format on the example of *APRX*, which covers computation $\sum_{i=1}^{s} b_i \mathbf{F}_i^{(m)}$ (1. 5, Listing 1):

*(i)* <u>datastructs</u> defines required data structures.
*(ii)* <u>computations</u> describes the computations covered by a kernel template. Each computation corresponds to a single line of code and has an unique identifier (e.g. *C1* in Listing 4). Computations can contain IVP evaluations which are marked by keyword <u>%RHS</u> and are replaced by an IVP component during code generation (e.g. for *IC* by line 5 of Listing 3). Hence, if a kernel template contains <u>%RHS</u>, a separate, specialized kernel version has to be generated for each IVP component.
*(iii)* <u>variants</u> contains possible kernels of a kernel template enabled by program transformations. For each kernel, its workings sets (<u>working sets</u>) and its program code (<u>code</u>) are specified. The <u>code</u> block defines the order of computations and the program transformations applied using four different keywords. Computations are specified by keyword <u>%COMP</u> whose parameter must correspond to one of the identifiers defined in the <u>computations</u> block (e.g. *C1* in Listing 4). For-loop statements are defined by keywords <u>%LOOP_START</u> and <u>%LOOP_END</u>. The first parameter of <u>%LOOP_START</u> specifies the loop variable name, the second parameter defines the number of loop iterations, and an optional third parameter <u>unroll</u> indicates that the loop will be unrolled during code generation. In addition, loop-specific pragmas can be added using keyword <u>%PRAGMA</u>.

*Implementation Skeletons* define processing orders of kernel templates and required communication points. From skeletons, concrete implementation variants are derived by replacing its templates with concrete kernel code. Listing 6 shows the implementation skeleton description format on the example of skeleton *A* which is a realization of a PIRK method (Listing 1) that focuses on parallelism across the ODE system, i.e its *n* equations are distributed blockwise among the threads. *A* contains a loop *k* over the *m* corrector steps dividing each corrector step into two templates: *RHS* computes the IVP function evaluations (1. 5, Listing 1) which are then used to compute the linear combinations (1. 4, Listing 1) in *LC*. Per corrector step, two synchronizations are needed as *RHS*—depending

---

[3] For example files, we refer to https://github.com/RRZE-HPC/kerncraft.

on the IVP solved—can potentially require all components of the linear combinations from the last iteration of $k$. After all corrector steps are computed, the next approximation $y_{\kappa+1}$ is calculated by templates *APRX* and *UPD* (l. 6, Listing 1). Four keywords suffice to specify skeletons:

*(i)* %LOOP_START and %LOOP_END define for-loops.

*(ii)* %COM states communication operations of an implementation skeleton. Skeleton $A$, e.g., requires $2m + 2$ barrier synchronizations.

*(iii)* %KERNEL specifies an executed kernel template. Its parameter must correspond to the name of an available kernel template. During code generation %KERNEL will be replaced by actual kernel code (e.g. *APRX* in Listing 7).

```
1  datastructs:
2  - double b[s]
3  - double F[s][n]
4  - double dy[n]
5  computations:
6    C1: dy[j]=dy[j]+b[i]*F[i][j]
7  variants:
8  - name: APRX_ij
9    code: |
10      %PRAGMA nounroll_and_jam
11      %LOOP_START i s
12      %LOOP_START j n
13        %COMP C1
14      %LOOP_END j
15      %LOOP_END i
16    working sets: {"(s+1)*n+s","2*n"}
17  - name: APRX_ji
18    code: |
19      %LOOP_START j n
20      %LOOP_START i s unroll
21        %COMP C1
22      %LOOP_END i
23      %LOOP_END j
24    working sets: {"(s+1)*n+s"}
```

**Listing 4.** Kernel template description YAML on the example of *APRX*.

```
1  code: |
2    %COM omp_barrier
3    %LOOP_START k m
4      %KERNEL RHS
5      %COM omp_barrier
6      %KERNEL LC
7      %COM omp_barrier
8    %LOOP_END k
9    %KERNEL RHS
10   %COM omp_barrier
11   %KERNEL APRX
12   %KERNEL UPD
```

**Listing 6.** Implementation skeleton description format on the example of $A$.

```
1  double F[4][161]; // s=4; n=161
2  double dy[161]; // n=161
3  for(int j=0; j<161; ++j) { // unrolled i
        ; replaced b[i]; n=161
4    dy[0] += 0.2205 * F[0][j];
5    dy[1] += 0.3882 * F[1][j];
6    dy[2] += 0.3288 * F[2][j];
7    dy[3] += 0.0625 * F[3][j];
8  }
```

**Listing 5.** Code generated for kernel *APRX_ji* of kernel template *APRX* when specialized in *Radau II A(7)* and $n = 161$.

```
1  void timestep(...) {
2  #omp barrier
3    for(k=0; k<6; ++k) { // m=6
4      // Code for template RHS
5  #omp barrier
6      // Code for template LC
7  #omp barrier
8    }
9  #omp barrier
10   // Code for template RHS
11   // Kernel APRX
12   for(int j=0; j<161; ++j) { //
                unrolled i; replaced b[i]; n=161
13     dy[0] += 0.2205 * F[0][j];
14     dy[1] += 0.3882 * F[1][j];
15     dy[2] += 0.3288 * F[2][j];
16     dy[3] += 0.0625 * F[3][j];
17   }
18   // Code for template UPD
19 }
```

**Listing 7.** Code generated for a variant of impl. skeleton $A$ using kernel *APRX_ji* specialized in *Radau II A(7)*, $n = 161$.

## 3.2 Rating Implementation Variant Performance

Offsite can automatically identify the most efficient implementation variant(s) from a pool of available variants using analytic performance modelling (Fig. 1):

*(i)* In a first step, Offsite automatically generates code for all kernels in a special code format processable by kerncraft[4]. Kernel code generation (*Kernel Code Generation* in Fig. 1) includes specializations of the code on the target platform, IVP, ODE method and (if fixed) ODE system size $n$. Listing 5 exemplary shows the code generated for kernel *APRX_ji* of kernel template *APRX* (Listing 4) when specialized in ODE method *Radau II A(7)* and $n = 161$. As specified in the template description, the $j$ loop is unrolled completely. Further, Butcher table coefficients (**b**) and known constants ($s = 4$, $n = 161$) are substituted.

*(ii)* In some tuning scenarios, the ODE system size $n$ is not yet known during installation time. Giving predictions for all valid $n$ values, however, is in general not feasible. By applying a working set model (Sect. 3.4), Offsite automatically determines for each kernel a set of relevant $n$ (*Kernel Working Sets*, Fig. 1) for which predictions are then obtained in the next step.

*(iii)* Offsite automatically computes node-level runtime predictions (Sect. 3.3) for each implementation variant (*Impl. Variant Prediction*, Fig. 1) by adding up the kernel predictions of its kernels and adding an estimate of its communication costs (*Communication Cost Benchmarks*, Fig. 1), which Offsite derives from benchmark data. For each of the kernel codes generated in step *(i)*, its kernel prediction is automatically derived by Offsite (*Kernel Prediction*, Fig. 1) whereby Kerncraft is used to construct the ECM model.

*(iv)* Using these node-level runtime predictions, Offsite ranks implementation variants by their performance (*Impl. Variant Ranking*, Fig. 1).

*(v)* From the ranking of implementation variants, Offsite automatically derives the subset $\Lambda$ of the best rated variant(s) which contains all variants $\lambda$ whose performance is within a user-provided maximum deviation from the best rated variant. For each variant of $\lambda$, Offsite generates optimized, platform-specific and problem-specific code (*Impl. Variant Code Generation*, Fig. 1). Listing 7 shows an excerpt of the code generated for a variant of implementation skeleton $A$ which substitutes kernel template *APRX* with kernel *APRX_ji* and was specialized in ODE method *Radau II A(7)*, IVP *IC* and $n = 161$.

### 3.3 Performance Prediction Methodology

The performance prediction methodology applied by Offsite expands [19] and comprises: *(i)* a node-level runtime prediction of an implementation variant and *(ii)* an estimate of its intra-node communication costs.

**Node-Level Runtime Prediction.** Base of the node-level prediction is the analytic *ECM (Execution-Cache-Memory) performance model*. For an in-depth explanation, we refer to [12,21]. The ECM model gives an estimation of the number of CPU cycles per cache line (CL) required to execute a particular loop kernel on a multi- or many-core chip which includes contributions from the in-

---

[4] In this work, version *0.8.3* of the Kerncraft tool was used.

core execution time $T_{\text{core}}$ and the data transfer time $T_{\text{data}}$:

$$T_{\text{core}} = \max(T_{\text{OL}}, \ T_{\text{nOL}}) , \tag{1}$$

$$T_{\text{data}}^{\text{L3}} = T_{\text{L1L2}}^{\text{data}} + T_{\text{L2L3}}^{\text{data}} + T_{\text{L2L3}}^{\text{p}} . \tag{2}$$

$T_{\text{core}}$ is defined as the time required to retire the instructions of a single loop iteration under the assumptions that (i) there are no loop-carried dependencies, (ii) all data are in the L1 data cache, (iii) all instructions are scheduled independently to the ports of the units, and (iv) the time to retire arithmetic instructions and load/store operations can overlap due to speculative execution depending on the target platform. Hence, the unit that takes the longest to retire its instructions determines $T_{\text{core}}$. $T_{\text{data}}^{\text{level}}$ factors in the time required to transfer all data from its current location in the memory hierarchy to the L1 data cache and back. The single contributions of transfers between levels $i$ and $j$ of the memory hierarchy $T_{ij}^{\text{data}}$ are determined depending on the amount of transferred CLs. Depending on the platform used, an optional latency penalty $T_{ij}^{p}$ might be added. In (2) $T_{\text{data}}^{\text{level}}$ is exemplarily shown for data coming from the L3 cache under the assumption that a latency penalty between L2 and L3 cache has to be factored in on the platform used. Combining all contributions, a single-core prediction

$$T_{\text{ECM}}^{\text{level}} = \max(T_{\text{OL}}, \ T_{\text{nOL}} + T_{\text{data}}^{\text{level}}) \tag{3}$$

can be derived, whereby the overlapping capabilities of the target platform determine whether a contribution is considered overlapping or non-overlapping. Offsite obtains ECM model predictions (3) for all kernels $\lambda$ using Kerncraft. For each kernel, *kernel runtime prediction*

$$\phi_\lambda = \alpha_\lambda \cdot \beta_\lambda \cdot \delta^{-1} \cdot f^{-1} \tag{4}$$

yields the runtime in seconds of kernel $\lambda$, where $\alpha_\lambda$ is (3) computed for a specific number of running cores $\tau$, $\beta_\lambda$ is the number of loop iterations executed, $\delta$ is the number of data elements fitting into one CL and $f$ is the CPU frequency. By summing up the individual kernel runtime predictions $\phi_\lambda$ of its basic kernels $\lambda$ and adding an estimate of its communication costs $t_{\text{com}}$ (in seconds), the *node-level runtime prediction* $\theta_\epsilon$ of an implementation variant $\epsilon$ is given by:

$$\theta_\epsilon = \sum_\lambda \phi_\lambda + t_{\text{com}} . \tag{5}$$

*Remark:* [19] used an older *Kerncraft* version that could not yet return ECM predictions for multiple core counts $\tau$ with a single run, but further returned the kernel's saturation point $\sigma_\lambda$. Hence, [19] used an extra factor $\min(\tau, \sigma_\lambda)^{-1}$ in (4).

**Estimate of Intra-node Communication Costs.** The costs of the occurring intra-node communication ($t_{\text{com}}$) depend on the number of communication operations executed. The implementation variants considered in this work, solely use

OpenMP barrier operations to synchronize threads. Offsite automatically benchmarks the costs of the OpenMP barrier operations depending on the number of
threads and stores the obtained data in its database for future runs.

*Remark:* Since this works serves as an introduction to Offsite, we focus on
OpenMP-only implementations. The general workflow, however, is also applicable to other communication schemes (e.g. MPI-only or hybrid OpenMP-
MPI)—granted suitable benchmarks exist for all communication operations—as
$t_{com}$ only influences (5). The applicability of the performance prediction methodology to hybrid OpenMP-MPI implementations on cluster systems was shown
in [18].

**Reusability of Performance Predictions.** Its database enables Offsite to
reuse prediction and ranking data in future Offsite runs. Prediction data (e.g.
kernel runtime predictions) collected for a specific implementation variant can
be reused to estimate other variants (if they share the kernel) or to estimate
other IVPs (if the kernel contains no IVP evaluations). In the context of AT,
this is a decisive advantage compared to runtime testing which would require
to also run each further added variant or (when switching the IVP) to run all
variants anew.

### 3.4  Working Set Model

If the ODE system size $n$ is not fixed—either by the user or restrictions of the
IVP—selecting the most efficient implementation variant(s) at installation time
leads to an exhaustive search over the possibly vast space of values for $n$. To
minimize the number of predictions required per kernel, the set of estimated $n$
values is reduced by a model-based restriction, the **working set** of the kernel,
which corresponds to the amount of data referenced by a kernel.

We use the working sets to identify for each kernel the maximum $n$ that still
fit into the single cache levels. Using these maximums, ranges of consecutive $n$
values for which the ECM prediction (3) stays constant[5] can be derived. The
medium values of these ranges form the working set of the kernel.

## 4  Experimental Evaluation

We validate Offsite using the experimental test bed introduced in Sect. 2. In
particular, we study the efficiency of Offsite in four AT scenarios when tuning
four different IVPs on three different target platforms and compare the ideal
case and four AT strategies:

---

[5] The ECM prediction factors in the location of data in the memory hierarchy. As a
simplified assumption—neglecting overlapping effects at cache borders—, this means
that as long as data locations do not change, the ECM model yields the same value
for a kernel independent from the actual $n$.

(i) *BestVariant* covers the case that the most efficient implementation variant is already known (e.g. from previous execution) and no AT is required.

(ii) *RunAll* runs all variants in order to identify the most efficient variant.

(iii) *OffsitePreselect5* (*OffPre5*) runs an Offsite determined subset of all variants, which contains all variants withing a 5% deviation of the best ranked variant, to identify the most efficient variant of that subset.

(iv) *OffsitePreselect10* (*OffPre10*) allows a bigger deviation (10%) than *OffPre5* and, thus, potentially also runs more variants[6]. While potentially leading to more tuning overhead, *OffPre10* might be able to identify the best variant for applications for which predictions are inaccurate and *OffPre5* fails.

(v) *RandomSelect* randomly runs 20 of the total 56 variants.

## 4.1   Derived Implementation Variants

Table 3 summarizes the implementation skeletons and kernel templates used in this work. In total, we consider eight skeletons from which 56 implementation variants can be derived. Each table row shows the templates required by a particular skeleton. E.g., skeleton *A* (Listing 6) uses templates *LC*, *RHS*, *APRX* and *UPD*. Twelve different variants can be derived from *A* as there are six different kernels of *LC* (enabled by loop interchanges, unrolls, pragmas) and two of *APRX*.

**Table 3.** Overview of the implementation variants considered.

| Kernel Template[a] (#Kernels) | | Implementation Skeleton | | | | | | | |
|---|---|---|---|---|---|---|---|---|---|
| | | A (12) | B (12) | C (2) | D (2) | E (2) | F (2) | G (12) | H (12) |
| LC | (6) | × | × | | | | | × | × |
| RHS* | (1) | × | × | | | | | × | × |
| RHSLC* | (1) | | | × | × | × | × | | |
| APRX | (2) | × | × | | | | | | |
| RHSAPRX* | (2) | | | | | × | | × | |
| UPD | (1) | × | | × | | × | | × | |
| APRXUPD | (2) | | × | | × | | | | |
| RHSAPRXUPD* | (2) | | | | | | × | | × |

[a] A kernel template marked with * contains evaluations of the IVP.

In total, 17 different kernels can be derived from the eight kernel templates available. To predict the performance of all 56 variants, only these 17 kernels have to be estimated. Further, when obtaining predictions off all 56 variants for a different IVP, only those four templates that contain IVP evaluations—and thus their six corresponding kernels—need to be re-evaluated, while prediction data of the remaining kernels can be retrieved from database.

---

[6] Step-up time is the same for *OffPre5* and *OffPre10* as determining their set of considered variants is carried out by the same single database operation.

## 4.2  At Scenario – All Input Known

As first test scenario, we consider the case that all input is known at installation time, in particular the ODE system size $n$. In such cases, Offsite is applied without the working set model. Performance predictions, however, are only obtained for that particular $n$ and a new Offsite run would be required if $n$ changes.

Table 4 compares the accuracy and efficiency of the single AT strategies when tuning four different IVPs on three different target platforms for $n = 36,000,000$ and ODE method *Radau II A(7)*. For Offsite strategies *OffPre5* and *OffPre10*, $t_{step}$ yields the time in seconds it takes to execute a time step using the measured best implementation variant from the subset $\Lambda$ of variants $\lambda$ tested by that strategy. *Performance loss* denotes the percent runtime deviation of that particular measured best variant from the variant selected by *BestVariant* ($t_{best}$). Ideally, an AT strategy correctly identifies the measured best variant and, thus, would suffer no performance loss. For an AT strategy, $|\Lambda|$ yields the cardinality of subset $\Lambda$ and the percent *tuning overhead* of applying that strategy is defined as $\frac{t_{tune}-|\Lambda|t_{best}}{|\Lambda|t_{best}} \cdot 100$ where $t_{tune} = \sum_{\lambda \in \Lambda} t_\lambda$ is the time required to test all variants and $|\Lambda|t_{best}$ is the time needed to execute the measured best variant instead.

**Haswell.** AT strategy *RunAll* causes a significant tuning overhead for all IVPs, while *OffPre5* and *OffPre10* only lead to marginal overhead as the subset of tested variants is considerably smaller, while still being able to select the measured best variant for all IVPs but *Wave1D*.

**IvyBridge.** Again, *RunAll* leads to decisive overhead compared to either of the two Offsite strategies and the measured best variant is correctly identified for all IVPs. However, for IVP *IC* only *OffPre10* finds the best variant. As *IC* is compute-bound (Table 1), the IVP evaluation dominates the computation time while the order of the remaining computations has only minor impact. Hence, already minor jitter can lead to a different variant being selected.

**Skylake.** Similar observations as on the two previous systems can be made on Skylake. The overhead of both Offsite strategies is marginal compared to *RunAll*. For all IVPs, the measured best variant is successfully identified.

**Table 4.** Comparison of different AT strategies applied to four different IVPs with $n = 36,000,000$ and *Radau II A(7)*.

| | IVP | Cusp | IC | Medakzo | Wave1D |
|---|---|---|---|---|---|
| Haswell | **BestVariant** | F_-*ji | F_-*ij | F_-*ji | H_LCjli_-*ij |
| (8 cores) | **BestVariant** $t_{step}$[s] | 1.28 | 0.80 | 1.29 | 1.04 |
| | **AT strategy – OffPre5** | | | | |
| | $\|A\|$ (tuning overhead) | 3 (1%) | 3 (3%) | 2 (2%) | 3 (5%) |
| | $t_{step}$[s] selected variant (perf. loss) | 1.28 (–) | 0.80 (–) | 1.29 (–) | 1.08 (4%) |
| | **AT strategy – OffPre10** | | | | |
| | $\|A\|$ (tuning overhead) | 3 (1%) | 3 (3%) | 3 (1%) | 4 (5%) |
| | $t_{step}$[s] selected variant (perf. loss) | 1.28 (–) | 0.80 (–) | 1.29 (–) | 1.08 (4%) |
| | **AT strategy – RunAll** | | | | |
| | $\|A\|$ (tuning overhead) | 56 (42%) | 56 (44%) | 56 (20%) | 56 (16%) |
| IvyBridge | **BestVariant** | E_-*ji | F_-*ij | F_-*ji | F_-*ji |
| (10 cores) | **BestVariant** $t_{step}$[s] | 1.16 | 0.725 | 1.20 | 1.04 |
| | **AT strategy – OffPre5** | | | | |
| | $\|A\|$ (tuning overhead) | 3 (3%) | 1 (1%) | 3 (1%) | 3 (0.4%) |
| | $t_{step}$[s] selected variant (perf. loss) | 1.16 (–) | 0.734 (1%) | 1.20 (–) | 1.04 (–) |
| | **AT strategy – OffPre10** | | | | |
| | $\|A\|$ (tuning overhead) | 3 (3%) | 3 (3%) | 3 (1%) | 3 (0.4%) |
| | $t_{step}$[s] selected variant (perf. loss) | 1.16 (–) | 0.725 (–) | 1.20 (–) | 1.04 (–) |
| | **AT strategy – RunAll** | | | | |
| | $\|A\|$ (tuning overhead) | 56 (54%) | 56 (59%) | 56 (41%) | 56 (44%) |
| Skylake | **BestVariant** | E_-*ji | F_-*ji | F_-*ji | F_-*ji |
| (20 cores) | **BestVariant** $t_{step}$[s] | 0.43 | 0.24 | 0.45 | 0.40 |
| | **AT strategy – OffPre5** | | | | |
| | $\|A\|$ (tuning overhead) | 3 (1%) | 3 (2%) | 3 (1%) | 3 (%) |
| | $t_{step}$[s] selected variant (perf. loss) | 0.43 (–) | 0.24 (–) | 0.45 (–) | 0.40 (–) |
| | **AT strategy – OffPre10** | | | | |
| | $\|A\|$ (tuning overhead) | 3 (1%) | 3 (2%) | 3 (1%) | 3 (1%) |
| | $t_{step}$[s] selected variant (perf. loss) | 0.43 (–) | 0.24 (–) | 0.45 (–) | 0.40 (–) |
| | **AT strategy – RunAll** | | | | |
| | $\|A\|$ (tuning overhead) | 56 (69%) | 56 (65%) | 56 (41%) | 56 (44%) |

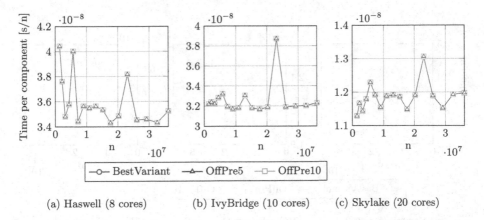

(a) Haswell (8 cores)          (b) IvyBridge (10 cores)          (c) Skylake (20 cores)

**Fig. 2.** Comparison of AT strategies applied to *Cusp* with varying $n$ and *Radau II A(7)*.

### 4.3    At Scenario – Unknown ODE System Size

The next scenario considered is that of a still unknown ODE system size $n$ at installation time. In these cases, the working set model is applied to determine a set of sample $n$ values for which Offsite computes predictions and from which predictions for the whole range of possible $n$ are derived. As this requires computing multiple performance predictions, a single Offsite run takes longer than in the previous scenario. This particular Offsite run, however, already covers all possible $n$ and no further run will be required when switching $n$ at a later point.

Figures 2 and 3 show for the single implementation variants selected as best variant by the AT strategies considered, the time per time step of *IC* and *Cusp* on three platforms (each using their max. number of cores). On the x-axis, $n$ is plotted up to $n = 60,000,000$. The y-axis shows the time per component of $n$ in seconds needed by a specific variant to solve a time step for *Radau II A(7)*.

**Tuning Cusp (Fig. 2).** On *Haswell* (Fig. 2a), *OffPre5* and *OffPre10* select the same subset of three variants independent of $n$. Both strategies always correctly identify the measured best variant. The same observations can be made on *Ivy-Bridge* (Fig. 2b) and on *Skylake* (Fig. 2c) where also the same subset of three variants is selected and the measured best variant is always found.

**Tuning IC (Fig. 3).** On *Haswell* (Fig. 3a), the same subset of one (for *OffPre5*) respectively of two variants (for *OffPre10*) is picked for $n$ up to 8,500,000. For bigger $n$, both strategies select the same three variants. Except for $n = 5,760,000$, *OffPre10* always correctly finds the measured best variant. The single variant selected by *OffPre5* is slightly off for $n = 1,440,000$ and $n = 2,560,000$. In both cases, however, the absolute time difference is only marginal. *IC* is compute-bound (Table 1) and, thus, the IVP evaluation dominates the computation time. Hence, in particular for small $n$, the order of the remaining computations has only minor impact on the time and already minor jitter can lead to a different variant being selected.

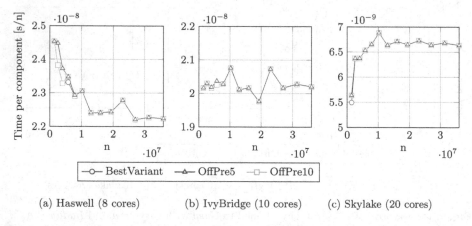

(a) Haswell (8 cores)        (b) IvyBridge (10 cores)        (c) Skylake (20 cores)

**Fig. 3.** Comparison of AT strategies applied to *IC* with varying $n$ and *Radau II A(7)*.

Strategy *OffPre5* selects on *IvyBridge* (Fig. 3b) the same variant for all $n$ while *OffPre10* adds two additional variants for $n \geq 2{,}560{,}000$. While *OffPre10* always finds the measured best variant, *OffPre5* is slightly off for $n = 4{,}000{,}000$ and $n = 5{,}760{,}000$ but the absolute time difference is only marginal.

On *Skylake* (Fig. 3c), the same variant is selected for $n$ up to 1,440,000 by both Offsite strategies while for larger $n$ two additional variants are considered. Except for $n = 1{,}440{,}000$ both strategies manage to always correctly identify the measured best variant. As on the two previous systems, the absolute time difference is again only marginal.

### 4.4   At Scenario – Variable Number of Cores

Offsite is capable of predicting the performance of an implementation variant for different core counts $\tau$ with a single AT run. In this AT scenario, we consider tuning an IVP for a fixed ODE system size $n$ and multiple core counts.

Figure 4 shows the effectiveness of different AT strategies compared to strategy *RunAll* when tuning IVP *IC* on three target platforms for $n = 9{,}000{,}000$ and *Radau II A(7)*. On the $x$-axis, we plot the number of cores $\tau$. The $y$-axis plots for different AT strategies the percent *performance gain* $\Pi$ achieved by applying that particular strategy instead of *RunAll* which tests all 56 variants ($t_{\text{RA}}$). The performance gain is defined as $\frac{t_{\text{RA}} - t_{\text{AT}}}{t_{\text{RA}}} * 100$ where $t_{\text{AT}}$ includes the time to run the variants $\Lambda$ tested by that strategy and the time to run the measured best variant from $\Lambda$ an additional $56 - |\Lambda|$ times. Ideally, the bar of an AT strategy would be close to the horizontal line of *BestVariant*.

**Haswell (Fig. 4a).** Depending on the number of cores $\tau$, *OffPre5* selects different subsets $\Lambda$. For $\tau < 8$, the same variant is selected, while for $\tau = 8$ two additional variants are selected. Using *OffPre10*, these two variants are also included for $\tau = 4$. For all $\tau$, a significant performance gain close to *BestImplVariant* can be observed with either Offsite strategy. The total performance gain grows with $\tau$ as the performance gap between best and worst variant also increases. While outperforming *RunAll*, *RandomSelect* is far off from the maximum gain.

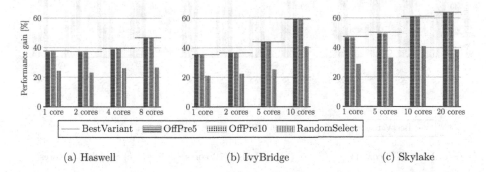

(a) Haswell            (b) IvyBridge            (c) Skylake

**Fig. 4.** Percent performance gain achieved by different AT strategies when tuning IVP *IC* for different core counts, *Radau II A(7)* and $n = 9{,}000{,}000$.

**IvyBridge (Fig. 4b).** *OffPre5* selects the same variant for all core counts $\tau$. Using *OffPre10*, two further variants are selected for $\tau = 20$. Again, a considerable performance gain close to *BestImplVariant*, can be observed for all $\tau$ when using either Offsite strategy while *RandomSelect* is far off from that ideal gain.

**Skylake (Fig. 4c).** Both Offsite strategies select the same three variants for $\tau = 20$, while the same single variant is selected for smaller core counts. As on the two previous target platforms, both Offsite strategies are close to *BestImplVariant* while *RandomSelect* is again further off.

### 4.5   At Scenario – Variable ODE Method

In the last AT scenario, we consider tuning an IVP for a fixed ODE system size $n$ for four different ODE methods. Depending on the characteristics of the ODE method, different optimizations might be applicable—for specific number of stages $s$, e.g., loops over $s$ can be replaced by a vector operation—which potentially results in varying efficiency of the same implementation variant for different ODE methods.

Figure 5 shows the effectiveness of different AT strategies when tuning IVP *IC* on three target platforms for $n = 9,000,000$ and four different ODE methods: *(i) Radau I A(5)* ($s = 3$, $m = 4$), *(ii) Radau II A(7)* ($s = 4$, $m = 6$), *(iii) Lobatto III C(6)* ($s = 4$, $m = 5$), and *(iv) Lobatto III C(8)* ($s = 5$, $m = 7$). On the $x$-axis the ODE method used is shown. The $y$-axis plots for each AT strategy the percent performance gain $\Pi$ achieved by applying that particular strategy instead of *RunAll* which tests all 56 variants. The bar of an AT strategy is ideally close to the horizontal line of *BestVariant*.

**Haswell (Fig. 5a).** *OffPre5* selects the same subset of two variants for *Lobatto III C(6)* and *Radau I A(5)*. For *Lobatto III C(8)* and *Radau II A(7)*, an additional variant is selected. Using *OffPre10*, these three variants are selected for all ODE

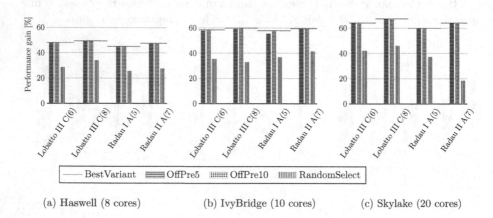

(a) Haswell (8 cores)         (b) IvyBridge (10 cores)         (c) Skylake (20 cores)

**Fig. 5.** Percent performance gain achieved by different AT strategies when tuning IVP *IC* for different ODE methods and $n = 9,000,000$.

methods. For all ODE methods, a significant performance gain close to *BestImplVariant* can be observed when using one of the two Offsite strategies. Further, both strategies decisively outperform *RandomSelect*.

**IvyBridge (Fig. 5b).** For all ODE methods, the same single variant is chosen when using *OffPre5*, while *OffPre10* selects two variants for *Lobatto III C(6)* and the same three variants for *Lobatto III C(8)* and *Radau II A(7)*. As on *Haswell*, the performance gain of both Offsite strategies for all ODE methods is close to the maximum gain, while the achieved gain of *RandomSelect* is far off from *BestImplVariant*.

**Skylake (Fig. 5c).** Both Offsite strategies select the same subset of three variants for all ODE methods but for *Radau I A(5)* which only selects two variants when using *OffPre5*. Again, the performance gain achieved by both strategies is close to *BestVariant* while *RandomSearch* is further off.

## 5   Future Extensions

Our future work includes expanding Offsite to cluster systems as well as AMD and ARM platforms. Further, we plan to extend Offsite to a combined offline-online AT approach that incorporates feedback data from previous online AT (or program runs) and to study whether these data can be used to predict the performance in scenarios with unknown input data (e.g. new IVP).

### Expansion to Cluster Systems

We expect that extending the approach to cluster systems will raise additional challenges (design-wise and implementation-wise) which could be neglected in the current shared-memory setting:

*(i)* To integrate the costs of inter-node communication operations, additional benchmarks are needed and database tables might have to be adjusted. Furthermore, this requires extending the YAML specifications and implementation variant code generator to support inter-node communication operations.
*(ii)* Similar to [18], the performance prediction methodology needs to be adapted to incorporate inter-node communication costs.
*(iii)* For more complex ODEs systems, e.g. ones with many different types of components and differing computation costs, the workflow has to be adjusted slightly. In particular, the load distribution needs to be taken into account.

### Extension to a Combined Offline-Online AT Approach

The database plays a vital role in the extension to a combined offline-online AT approach as it is supposed to serve as an interface between both AT phases. Currently, the database stores prediction and ranking data for reuse in future offline runs. For a combined approach, additions and modifications to the database will be necessary to incorporate feedback data from program runs/online AT to verify or improve predictions.

**Applicability to Other Programs**

The kernel templates used to describe PIRK methods correspond to basic linear algebra functions (e.g. LC is a matrix multiplication). This makes Offsite applicable to more complex applications that can be broken down into linear algebra functions (e.g. PCG solver [12]). In most cases, this is possible without any or only minor extensions to the current YAML specifications. Minor extensions might include supporting additional communication operations or keywords for special operations (e.g. MIN). Major extensions might be needed for applications where the equations themselves or even the number of equations change for different time intervals (e.g. grid resolution). The general approach will not be applicable to highly dynamic and irregular systems like particle simulations (tree codes).

## 6   Conclusion

In this work, we have introduced the Offsite AT approach which automates the process of identifying the most efficient implementation variant(s) from a pool of possible variants at installation time. Offsite ranks variants by their performance using analytic performance predictions. To facilitate specifying tuning scenarios, multilevel YAML description languages allow to describe these scenarios abstractly and enable Offsite to automatically generate optimized codes. Moreover, we have demonstrated that Offsite can reliably tune a representative class of parallel explicit ODE methods, PIRK methods, by investigating different AT scenarios and AT strategies on three different shared-memory platforms.

**Acknowledgments.** This work is supported by the German Ministry of Science and Education (BMBF) under project number 01IH16012A. Furthermore, we thank the Erlangen Regional Computing Center for granting access to their IvyBridge and Skylake systems.

## References

1. Ansel, J., et al.: OpenTuner: an extensible framework for program autotuning. In: Proceedings of the 23rd International Conference on Parallel Architecture and Compilation Techniques, PACT 2014, pp. 303–316. ACM, August 2014. https://doi.org/10.1145/2628071.2628092
2. Balaprakash, P., et al.: Autotuning in high-performance computing applications. Proc. IEEE **106**(11), 2068–2083 (2018). https://doi.org/10.1109/JPROC.2018.2841200
3. Barthel, A., Günther, M., Pulch, R., Rentrop, P.: Numerical techniques for different time scales in electric circuit simulation. In: Breuer, M., Durst, F., Zenger, C. (eds.) High Performance Scientific and Engineering Computing, pp. 343–360. Springer, Heidelberg (2002). https://doi.org/10.1007/978-3-642-55919-8_38
4. Bilmes, J., Asanovic, K., Chin, C.W., Demmel, J.: Optimizing matrix multiply using PHiPAC: a portable, high-performance, ANSI C coding methodology. In: Proceedings 11th International Conference on Supercomputing, ICS 1997, pp. 340–347. ACM, July 1997. https://doi.org/10.1145/263580.263662

5. Calvo, M., Franco, J.M., Randez, L.: A new minimum storage runge-kutta scheme for computational acoustics. J. Comput. Phys. **201**(1), 1–12 (2004). https://doi.org/10.1016/j.jcp.2004.05.012
6. Christen, M., Schenk, O., Burkhard, L.: PATUS: a code generation and autotuning framework for parallel iterative stencil computations on modern microarchitectures. In: 2011 IEEE International Parallel Distributed Processing Symposium, pp. 676–687, May 2015. https://doi.org/10.1109/IPDPS.2011.70
7. Das, S., Mullick, S.S., Suganthan, P.N.: Recent advances in differential evolution - an updated survey. Swarm Evol. Comput. **27**, 1–30 (2016). https://doi.org/10.1016/j.swevo.2016.01.004
8. Denoyelle, N., Goglin, B., Ilic, A., Jeannot, E., Soussa, L.: Modeling non-uniform memory access on large compute nodes with the cache-aware roofline model. IEEE T. Parall. Distr. **30**(6), 1374–1389 (2019). https://doi.org/10.1109/TPDS.2018.2883056
9. Gerndt, M., César, E., Benkner, S. (eds.): Automatic Tuning of HPC Applications - The Periscope Tuning Framework. Shaker Verlag (2015)
10. Hairer, E., Wanner, G.: Solving Ordinary Differential Equations II: Stiff and Differential-Algebraic Problems. Springer, Heidelberg (2002). 2nd rev. edn
11. Hammer, J., Eitzinger, J., Hager, G., Wellein, G.: Kerncraft: a tool for analytic performance modeling of loop kernels. In: Niethammer, C., Gracia, J., Hilbrich, T., Knüpfer, A., Resch, M.M., Nagel, W.E. (eds.) Tools for High Performance Computing 2016, pp. 1–22. Springer, Cham (2017). https://doi.org/10.1007/978-3-319-56702-0_1
12. Hofmann, J., Alappat, C., Hager, G., Fey, D., Wellein, G.: Bridging the Architecture Gap: Abstracting Performance-Relevant Properties of Modern Server Processors (2019). https://arxiv.org/abs/1907.00048, Preprint
13. van der Houwen, P.J., Sommeijer, B.P.: Parallel iteration of high-order runge-kutta methods with stepsize control. J. Comput. Appl. Math. **29**(1), 111–127 (1990). https://doi.org/10.1016/0377-0427(90)90200-J
14. Mazzia, F., Magherini, C.: Test Set for Initial Value Problem Solvers, Release 2.4, February 2008. https://archimede.dm.uniba.it/~testset/
15. Mendis, C., Renda, A., Amarasinghe, S., Carbin, M.: Ithemal: accurate, portable and fast basic block throughput estimation using deep neural networks. In: Proceedings of the 36th International Conference on Machine Learning. Proceedings of the Machine Learning Research, vol. 97, pp. 4505–4515. PMLR, June 2019
16. Pfaffe, P., Grosser, T., Tillmann, M.: Efficient hierarchical online-autotuning: a case study on polyhedral accelerator mapping. In: Proceedings of the ACM International Conference on Supercomputing, ICS 2019, pp. 354–366. ACM, New York (2019). https://doi.org/10.1145/3330345.3330377
17. Rasch, A., Gorlatch, S.: ATF: a generic directive-based auto-tuning framework. Concurr. Comput. Pract. Exper. **31**(5), e4423 (2019). https://doi.org/10.1002/cpe.4423
18. Scherg, M., Seiferth, J., Korch, M., Rauber, T.: Performance prediction of explicit ODE methods on multi-core cluster systems. In: Proceedings of the 2019 ACM/SPEC International Conference on Performance Engineering, ICPE 2019, pp. 139–150. ACM (2019). https://doi.org/10.1145/3297663.3310306
19. Seiferth, J., Alappat, C., Korch, M., Rauber, T.: Applicability of the ECM performance model to explicit ode methods on current multi-core processors. In: Yokota, R., Weiland, M., Keyes, D., Trinitis, C. (eds.) ISC High Performance 2018. LNCS, vol. 10876, pp. 163–183. Springer, Cham (2018). https://doi.org/10.1007/978-3-319-92040-5_9

20. Shudler, S., Vrabec, J., Wolf, F.: Understanding the scalability of molecular simulation using empirical performance modeling. In: Bhatele, A., Boehme, D., Levine, J.A., Malony, A.D., Schulz, M. (eds.) ESPT/VPA 2017-2018. LNCS, vol. 11027, pp. 125–143. Springer, Cham (2019). https://doi.org/10.1007/978-3-030-17872-7_8
21. Stengel, H., Treibig, J., Hager, G., Wellein, G.: Quantifying performance bottlenecks of stencil computations using the execution-cache-memory model. In: Proceedings of the 29th ACM International Conference on Supercomputing, pp. 207–216. ICS 2015. ACM (2015). https://doi.org/10.1145/2751205.2751240
22. Tiwari, A., Hollingsworth, J.K.: Online adaptive code generation and tuning. In: Proceedings of the 2011 IEEE International Parallel Distributed Processing Symposium, IPDPS 2011, pp. 879–892. IEEE, May 2011. https://doi.org/10.1109/IPDPS.2011.86
23. Whaley, R.C., Petitet, A., Dongarra, J.: Automated empirical optimizations of software and the ATLAS project. Parallel Comput. **27**(1), 3–35 (2001). https://doi.org/10.1016/S0167-8191(00)00087-9
24. Williams, S., Waterman, A., Patterson, D.: Roofline: an insightful visual performance model for multicore architectures. Commun. ACM **52**(4), 65–76 (2009). https://doi.org/10.1145/1498765.1498785
25. Yount, C., Tobin, J., Breuer, A., Duran, A.: YASK - yet another stencil kernel: a framework for HPC stencil code-generation and tuning. In: 2016 6th International Workshop on Domain-Specific Languages and High-Level Frameworks for High Performance Computing, WOLFHPC, pp. 30–39. IEEE, November 2016. https://doi.org/10.1109/WOLFHPC.2016.08

# Desynchronization and Wave Pattern Formation in MPI-Parallel and Hybrid Memory-Bound Programs

Ayesha Afzal[1], Georg Hager[1(✉)], and Gerhard Wellein[1,2]

[1] Erlangen Regional Computing Center (RRZE), 91058 Erlangen, Germany
{ayesha.afzal,georg.hager,gerhard.wellein}@fau.de
[2] Department of Computer Science, University of Erlangen-Nürnberg,
91058 Erlangen, Germany

**Abstract.** Analytic, first-principles performance modeling of distributed-memory parallel codes is notoriously imprecise. Even for applications with extremely regular and homogeneous compute-communicate phases, simply adding communication time to computation time does often not yield a satisfactory prediction of parallel runtime due to deviations from the expected simple lockstep pattern caused by system noise, variations in communication time, and inherent load imbalance. In this paper, we highlight the specific cases of provoked and spontaneous desynchronization of memory-bound, bulk-synchronous pure MPI and hybrid MPI+OpenMP programs. Using simple microbenchmarks we observe that although desynchronization can introduce increased waiting time per process, it does not necessarily cause lower resource utilization but can lead to an increase in available bandwidth per core. In case of significant communication overhead, even natural noise can shove the system into a state of automatic overlap of communication and computation, improving the overall time to solution. The saturation point, i.e., the number of processes per memory domain required to achieve full memory bandwidth, is pivotal in the dynamics of this process and the emerging stable wave pattern. We also demonstrate how hybrid MPI-OpenMP programming can prevent desirable desynchronization by eliminating the bandwidth bottleneck among processes. A Chebyshev filter diagonalization application is used to demonstrate some of the observed effects in a realistic setting.

## 1 Introduction

In principle, a parallel computer should be a deterministic system. Given some code and hardware specifications, it should be possible to predict the runtime of the program and measure it consistently in repeated experiments. Analytic, first-principles performance models such as Roofline [21] or ECM [10,19] approximate this goal on the core and socket level. Although residual deviations and statistical variations remain, these models can yield valuable insights into the hardware bottlenecks of computation despite the simplifications that go into

© The Author(s) 2020
P. Sadayappan et al. (Eds.): ISC High Performance 2020, LNCS 12151, pp. 391–411, 2020.
https://doi.org/10.1007/978-3-030-50743-5_20

the model assumptions. One of these is the notion that all cores or hardware threads execute the same code on different data, which is often true for programs exploiting thread-level loop parallelism. With message passing, however, the dependencies among instruction streams (processes) are less tight, and communication overhead complicates the picture. Ideally, one would like to add communication models such as the Hockney model [7] or its refinements on top of Roofline or ECM, but this is too simplistic: System noise, variations in network bandwidth and latency, load imbalance, and strong one-off delays can cause global effects such as desynchronization and traveling idle waves [2,15]. Using threaded MPI processes changes the phenomenology and dynamics of the system, because socket-level bottlenecks (i.e., memory bound vs. core bound) play a decisive role. It is therefore necessary to shed light on the dynamic processes that lead to desynchronization and global structure formation in pure MPI and threaded MPI programs.

An *idle wave* is a period of idleness caused by a strong delay in computation or communication on one process of an MPI program. It travels across the MPI processes with a speed that is governed by the particular communication characteristics (distance of communication, eager vs. rendezvous mode, etc.) and interacts with other idle waves, computational noise, and system noise in a nonlinear way. In this paper, we extend a previous study on the dynamics of idle waves with core-bound pure-MPI programs [2] towards the memory-bound case, i.e., codes with a low computational intensity. These exhibit saturation characteristics when running on multiple cores connected to a single memory interface (the *contention domain*[1]). The basic mechanisms are investigated using parallel microbenchmarks that are amenable to straightforward node-level performance modeling and can be easily altered to mimic different application characteristics.

We start by comparing the dynamics of traveling idle waves generated by injected one-off delays between core-bound and memory-bound MPI programs with negligible communication overhead and perfect load balance. More complex dynamics can be observed in the memory-bound case within the memory domain and when crossing domain boundaries (sockets, nodes). Even after the idle wave is gone, a distinctive "computational wave" pattern prevails that is governed by the topological properties of the MPI program (inter-process communication dependencies, boundary conditions) and the location of the memory bandwidth saturation point, i.e., the number of processes required for full memory bandwidth utilization. In case of significant communication overhead, a massive one-off delay is not required to provoke the wave pattern; the natural system noise or a single, small disturbance of regularity in computation or communication time is sufficient. Based on these observations, we study the impact of using threaded MPI processes. Multithreading has an influence on the bandwidth saturation point, and filling the contention domain with a multi-threaded MPI process effectively generates a bandwidth-scalable code. This answers the long-standing question why a nonreflective introduction of OpenMP threading into

---

[1] This is usually identical to a ccNUMA domain and often, but not always, a full CPU socket.

an MPI-only code can in some cases cause a slowdown even if OpenMP-specific overheads are negligible [5,22]. Finally, we employ an application code implementing Chebyshev Filter Diagonalization (ChebFD) for a topological insulator problem to show the relevance of our findings in a real-world scenario.

The configuration parameter space of MPI and hybrid MPI-OpenMP parallel programs is huge. Here we restrict ourselves to simple, bidirectional point-to-point communication using eager or rendezvous protocols (depending on the message size).

This paper is organized as follows: Sect. 2 details our experimental environment and methodology. In Sect. 3 we study the propagation of an injected, one-off delays, contrasting memory-bound with core-bound scenarios. Computational wavefronts in memory-bound programs emerging from idle waves are covered in Sect. 4. Section 5 deals with the spontaneous formation of wavefronts and its consequences on program performance, and in Sect. 6 we showcase some of the observed effects using an application code. Section 7 covers related work and Sect. 8 concludes the paper and gives an outlook to future work.

*Contributions.* This work makes the following novel contributions:

- We show the characteristics of idle waves traveling through memory-bound MPI applications on multicore clusters, and how they differ from the core-bound case studied in prior work [2].
- We show that the forced emergence of computational wave patterns via desynchronization by one-off delays only occurs with memory-bound code.
- We show that the average available memory bandwidth per core in an established computational wave (desynchronized state) is larger than in the synchronous state while the core is executing application code. The wave settles in a state where the number of active processes per contention domain is near the memory bandwidth saturation point.
- We show how natural system noise leads to spontaneous desynchronization and computational wave formation if there is significant communication overhead.
- We show that desynchronization can lead to automatic overlap of communication and computation, reducing overall time to solution. Significant intra-node communication overhead can reduce this gain.
- We show that the introduction of threaded MPI processes can prevent the formation of computational waves and automatic communication overlap if one process is used per contention domain, effectively recovering the characteristics of a scalable pure MPI code.

## 2 Experimental Environment and Methodology

### 2.1 Cluster Test Bed and External Tools

In order to ensure that our observed phenomenology is not specific to a singular hardware or software setup, four different clusters were used to conduct various experiments:

- Emmy[2], a QDR-InfiniBand cluster with dual-socket nodes comprising ten-core Intel Xeon "Ivy Bridge" CPUs ans Hyper-Threading (SMT) enabled,
- Meggie[3], an Omni-Path cluster with dual-socket nodes comprising ten-core Intel Xeon "Broadwell" CPUs and Hyper-Threading (SMT) disabled,
- Hazel Hen[4], a Cray XC40 with Aries interconnect and 12-core Intel Xeon "Haswell" CPUs,
- SuperMUC-NG[5], an Omni-Path cluster with dual-socket nodes comprising 24-core Intel Xeon "Skylake SP" CPUs.

Details of the hardware and software environments on these systems can be found in Table 1.

**Table 1.** Key hardware and software specifications of systems

| Systems | Emmy | Meggie | Hazel Hen (CRAY XC40) | SuperMUC-NG |
|---|---|---|---|---|
| Intel Xeon Processor | Ivy Bridge EP | Broadwell EP | Haswell EP | Skylake SP |
| Processor model | E5-2660 v2 | E5-2630 v4 | E5-2680 v3 | Platinum 8174 |
| Base clock speed | 2.2 GHz | 2.2 GHz | 2.5 GHz | 3.10 GHz(2.3 GHz used*) |
| Physical cores per Dual socket node | 20 | 20 | 24 | 48 |
| LLC size | 25 MB | 25 MB | 30 MB | 33 MB |
| Memory per node (type) | 64 GB (DDR3) | 64 GB (DDR4) | 128 GB (DDR4) | 96 GB (DDR4) |
| Theor. memory bandwidth | 51.2 GB/s | 68.3 GB/s | 68.3 GB/s | 128 GB/s |
| Node interconnect | QDR InfiniBand | Omni-Path | Cray Aries | Omni-Path |
| Interconnect topology | Fat-tree | Fat-tree | Dragonfly | Fat-tree |
| Raw bandwidth per Link and direction | 40 Gbit s$^{-1}$ | 100 Gbit s$^{-1}$ | 126 Gbit s$^{-1}$ | 100 Gbit s$^{-1}$ |
| Software | | | | |
| Compiler | Intel C++ v2019.4.243 | Intel C++ v2019.4.243 | Cray C++ v8.7.10 | Intel C++ v2019.4.243 |
| Message passing library | Intel MPI v2019u4 | Intel MPI v2019u4 | Cray MPICH v7.7.6 | Intel MPI v2019u4 |
| Operating system | CentOS Linux v7.7.1908 | CentOS Linux v7.7.1908 | SESU Linux ENT. Server 12 SP3 | SESU Linux ENT. Server 12 SP3 |
| Tools | | | | |
| ITAC | v2019u4 | v2019u4 | § | v2019 |
| LIKWID | 5.0.0 | 5.0.0 | § | 4.3.3 |

* A power cap is applied on SuperMUC-NG, i.e., the CPUs run by default on a lower than maximum clock speed (2.3 GHz instead of 3.10 GHz).
§ C++ high-resolution Chrono clock for timing measurement.

[2] https://anleitungen.rrze.fau.de/hpc/emmy-cluster.
[3] https://anleitungen.rrze.fau.de/hpc/meggie-cluster.
[4] https://hlrs.de/systems/cray-xc40-hazel-hen.
[5] https://doku.lrz.de/display/PUBLIC/SuperMUC-NG.

We used Intel trace analyzer and collector (ITAC)[6] for timeline visualization (except on `Hazel Hen`, where traces were recorded by explicit timing measurements), the C++ high-resolution `Chrono` clock for timing, and `likwid-perfctr` from the `LIKWID` tool suite[7] for memory bandwidth measurements.

## 2.2 Experimental Parameters and Methodology

We took a number of measures to create a reproducible experimental environment and minimize any noise from system sources. On the `Emmy` and `Meggie` systems, we ran all multi-node experiments on nodes connected to a single leaf switch. Core-thread affinity was enforced. The computational workload for the core-bound case was a number of back-to-back divide instructions (`vdivpd`), which have a low but constant throughput on Intel architectures if "simple" denominators are avoided. Except for the application case study, the memory-bound workload comprised simple kernels like STREAM triad. One-off idle periods were generated by massively extending one computational phase via doing extra work.

Most microbenchmark experiments were performed on two nodes only, since the basic phenomenology is visible even on this scale. Bidirectional point-to-point communication between MPI processes employed a standard `MPI_Isend/MPI_IRecv/MPI_Waitall` sequence. Before actual measurements were taken, at least two warm-up time steps with barrier synchronization were performed to allow the MPI and OpenMP runtimes to settle and eliminate first-call overhead. We only report statistical variation in measurements where the relative spread was larger than 5%. Unless otherwise stated, the clock speed of processors was fixed. On `SuperMUC-NG` the active power capping feature leads to an effective clock speed of 2.3 GHz, which was validated by the `likwid-perfctr` tool.

## 3 Idle Wave Mechanisms for Memory-Bound Code

In [2], idle waves were shown to have *nonlinear* characteristics, i.e., colliding waves interact and partially cancel each other. Noise, i.e., short delays from different sources such as load imbalance, varying communication characteristics, or system noise, causes the decay of traveling idle waves. In this section, we compare the known dynamics of idle waves between core-bound code and memory-bound code. For brevity and to avoid confusion, we will call the two phenomena *core-bound* and *memory-bound idle wave*, respectively. We also restrict ourselves to the case of negligible communication overhead, i.e., a small communication-to-computation ratio.

---

[6] https://software.intel.com/en-us/trace-analyzer.
[7] http://tiny.cc/LIKWID.

## 3.1  Idle Wave Propagation Speed

Figure 1a shows a traveling idle wave on the `SuperMUC-NG` system with core-bound code. The leading and the trailing edges of the wave are parallel, and due to the communication characteristics (bidirectional next-neighbor, eager mode, closed ring) the waves emanating from the idle injection cancel each other after one half round trip. The memory-bound code in Fig. 1b shows a very different pattern: Since the available memory bandwidth per core declines after the saturation point, the length of any particular execution phase on any particular MPI process depends on how many other processes are executing user code at the same time on the same contention domain. If $b(N)$ is the STREAM memory bandwidth with $N$ processes, transferring a data volume of $V$ bytes with a single process takes a time of

$$T_{\text{exec}} = \frac{NV}{b(N)}. \tag{1}$$

In the saturation phase, where $N > N_{\text{sc}}$, $b(N) \sim \text{const.}$ and thus $T_{\text{exec}} \sim NV$, i.e., as the front (back) of the idle wave progresses through the cores of a socket and more (fewer) cores participate in code execution, the time per iteration goes up (down). Hence, the forward and backward edges of the idle wave ripple through the system at *variable* propagation speeds.

The expression for the silent-system idle wave propagation speed from [2] still holds, but with modifications. Instead of the whole idle wave velocity, we can only draw conclusions for either of its two edges at a single moment in time since the execution time obeys the relation (1). The *local* velocity is

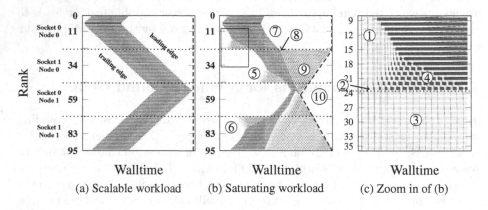

(a) Scalable workload    (b) Saturating workload    (c) Zoom in of (b)

**Fig. 1.** Timelines of idle waves through MPI code (one process per core) with different workload characteristics, negligible communication overhead, and bidirectional next-neighbor communication in a closed ring topology on `SuperMUC-NG`. The $y$ axis is the MPI rank and the $x$ axis is wall-clock time. Red indicates waiting time (within the MPI library) while white or light blue denote user code (50 iterations). The injected delay of about 25 execution phases is shown in dark blue. (a) Core-bound code with execution phase of 10 ms, (b) memory-bound STREAM triad code (overall data transfer volume of 4.8 GB, evenly distributed across all cores for a computation phase of 11.5 ms), (c) zoom-in of marked area in (b). (Color figure online)

$$v_{\text{silent}}(N) = \frac{\sigma \cdot d}{NV/b(N) + T_{\text{comm}}} \quad \left[\frac{\text{ranks}}{\text{s}}\right],$$ (2)

where $N$ is the number of processes executing code. This means that $v_{\text{silent}}$ can be different for processes on the same contention domain, which will be investigated further in the next section. $T_{\text{comm}}$ is the communication time, $d$ parameterizes the distance of communicating processes, and $\sigma \in \{1, 2\}$ is a correction factor that depends on communication characteristics, e.g., communication patterns (uni- vs. bidirectional), flavors (multiple split-waits vs. one wait-for-all), and protocols (eager vs. rendezvous) [2].

Note that (2) even holds for hybrid MPI/OpenMP programs that communicate only outside parallel regions. In this case, $N$ is the number of active multi-threaded MPI processes on a socket. If the process spans the full socket, $N = 1$ and the propagation speed does not vary. This setting will be analyzed in Sect. 5.3.

## 3.2  Idle Wave Decay

In [2] it was shown that noise, i.e., small statistical disturbances of the pure lock-step pattern, cause the decay of traveling idle waves, possibly to the point where a one-off injection does not even impact the time to solution of the program. In a noise-free system, a core-bound idle wave does not decay, but eventually interacts with itself or with the boundaries of an open process topology.

The propagation and decay mechanisms of memory-bound idle waves are much different since the propagation speed of the trailing and leading edges is strongly influenced by topological domain boundaries, specifically those between adjacent contention domains. Together with the contention effect, decay occurs even on a silent system. Figure 1(b, c) shows the basic phenomenology: As the idle wave progresses through the contention domain (from core 5 to 23 as shown in the upper section of Fig. 1b and in the upper half of Fig. 1c), the trailing edge is gradually getting steeper as fewer cores participate in the computation (cores 6–16 ①) because more bandwidth becomes available per core. On the other hand, idle phases are emanating from the end of the domain (core 23 ②) because the next contention domain (core 24 and up, ③) is still executing with all cores and is thus slower per core. These small idle waves propagate up and interact with the main idle wave on cores 17–23 ④, effectively causing its partial decay. The same occurs on the second contention domain at cores 39–47 ⑤ and, in reverse direction due to the wrapping around of the wave, on the fourth domain on cores 72–80 ⑥.

Domain boundaries and the memory bottleneck are just as important for the leading edge dynamics. Within the domain where the one-off delay was injected (cores 6–23 ⑦), the leading edge of the idle wave is not straight but shows a slowdown as time progresses. This is because the number of active cores on the contention domain increases as the wave propagates, and the available memory bandwidth per core goes down as soon as contention sets in. Eventually, the leading edge hits the boundary to the next contention domain. Right after this point ⑧ the first domain is free of any delay and the bulk-synchronous execution is restored there. The idle wave is now progressing entirely through the second domain. Since the first domain is in synchronous state and there is idleness on the second domain, more bandwidth is available per core on the latter, so the computation phases are shorter and there is waiting time (small red boxes in the timeline graph ⑨). The key observation here is that the second domain does not go back to a synchronized state; computation alternates with waiting times on every process, but enough cores are active concurrently to saturate the memory bandwidth. Hence, the overall throughput of the second domain is the same as on the first but the processes are out of sync. Finally, after the preset number of time steps has passed, the computation terminates. Processes that have collected less idle time because of the decay of the injected idle wave (on the second to fourth domain) finish early, as shown by the dashed blue line in Fig. 1b ⑩. A distinctive wave-like pattern emerges across all contention domains but the one in which the idle wave was injected. We call this pattern a "computational wavefront."

## 4    Induced Computational Wavefronts

In this section, we will further analyze the generating mechanisms of computational wavefronts with memory-bound MPI code that emerge from singular one-off delays. We restrict ourselves to the case of negligible communication overhead. *Spontaneous* wavefront formation and significant communication overhead are linked and will be covered in Sect. 5.

### 4.1    Wavefront Amplitude vs. Processes per Contention Domain

A computational wavefront is a stable structure that can be visualized by marking the wallclock time of a specific time step on each MPI process in a bulk-synchronous iterative application. In a fully synchronized state, the pattern is a straight line perpendicular to the time axis. Desynchronization causes wave-like patterns like the one shown in Fig. 1b. We have shown above that the memory-bound nature of the code is crucial for desynchronization, so we start with a series of experiments with progressively more severe memory bottlenecks. Figure 2 shows six timelines of memory-bound MPI programs on the Emmy system (parameters as in Fig. 1) after injecting a one-off delay. The difference among the six cases is the number of MPI processes per contention domain (socket). In the scalable regime (up to $N = 3$ cores per socket) the idle wave causes no visible computational wave. As soon as the bandwidth bottleneck becomes relevant, i.e., when using more cores leads to less bandwidth available per core, (here at $N \gtrsim 4$), the damping effect on the idle wave sets in although it is weak at first (Fig. 2c,d). Our experiments show, however, that even in this regime a stable computational wave persists, albeit with a low amplitude ①. At strong saturation ($N \gtrsim 7$) the fully developed wave is clearly visible. In all cases, the desynchronization prevails even after the idle wave has died out, and even on

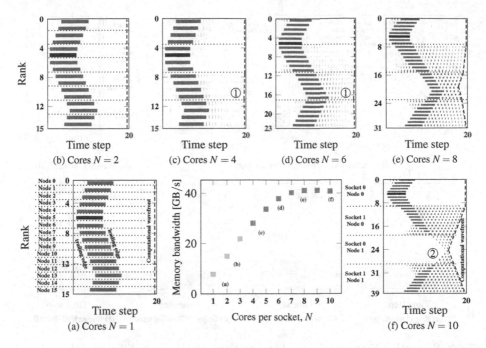

**Fig. 2.** Idle wave-induced computational wavefront pattern formation with memory-bound (STREAM triad with nontemporal stores) workload on the Emmy system with varying number of MPI processes per contention domain (socket). Overall triad data volume was 9.6 GB, other parameters as in Fig. 1. Middle panel: memory bandwidth versus number of cores for the STREAM triad benchmark on one socket. (a)–(f) Idle wave propagation with 1,...,10 cores per contention domain over 20 time steps. Horizontal dashed lines denote socket boundaries except in (a), where one process per node was run on the first core of the first socket. Computational wavefronts are shown with blue dashed lines. (Color figure online)

contention domains that were never traversed by it (cores 20–29 in Fig. 2f ②). Note also that the socket on which the idle wave was originally injected is still synchronized.

This shows that strong computational wave patterns require a strong memory bandwidth saturation. Note that wave patterns will also form without initial one-off idle injection, but this is a very slow process so we provoked it by "kicking" the system. This "kick" will not be required when there is significant communication overhead. See Sect. 5 for details.

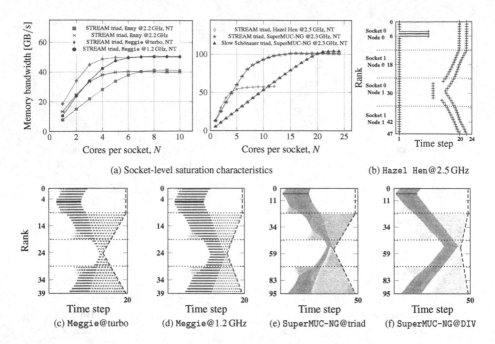

**Fig. 3.** Saturation characteristics of benchmark platforms with different code and frequency settings and their influence on computational wave formation. (a) Bandwidth saturation of microbenchmarks on a contention domain (MPI strong scaling) on four systems: STREAM triad on `Emmy` with vs. without NT stores and on `Meggie` using Turbo Mode vs. lowest core frequency. On `SuperMUC-NG`, using STREAM triad and a "slow" Schönauer triad, and standard STREAM triad on `Hazel Hen`. (b)–(f) Timeline visualization of idle wave-induced computational wave emergence under different saturation conditions. On `Hazel Hen`, ITAC was not available so the trace was taken via explicit timing measurements.

## 4.2    Saturation Point and Wavefront Amplitude

There is still the question whether the saturation point, i.e., how many processes are needed to attain maximum memory bandwidth, plays any role. Our benchmark platforms exhibit different characteristics in this respect, as shown in Fig. 3a: The Broadwell CPUs on `Meggie` have the convenient property that the saturated memory bandwidth depends only weakly on the clock speed, so we set the core frequency to a constant 1.2 GHz or activated "Turbo Mode." The latter led to clock frequency varying from 3.0 GHz (1 core) to 2.4 GHz (full socket) along the scaling curve. On `SuperMUC-NG` with its 24 cores per contention domain and fixed 2.3 GHz clock speed, we employed a modified variant of the Schönauer vector triad that has a higher computational cost $(A(:)=B(:)+\cos(C(:)/D(:)))$ in order to increase $N_{sc}$ from about 14 to 20 cores. As a side effect, the saturation point becomes more sharply defined. On `Emmy`, using nontemporal (NT) stores for the STREAM triad the single-core bandwidth is about a factor of two lower than with standard stores, shifting the saturation point further out.

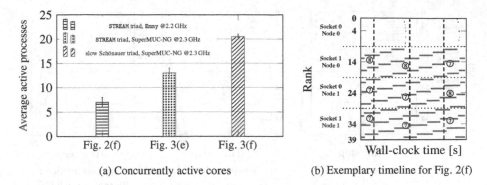

(a) Concurrently active cores        (b) Exemplary timeline for Fig. 2(f)

**Fig. 4.** (a) Average number of MPI processes executing user code concurrently for the fully developed steady state computational waves (wavelength MPI_COMM_SIZE) in Figs. 2(f), 3(e), and 3(f). Minimum and maximum values among 60 samples along the timeline are indicated as whiskers. Data points were taken from the timeline data as shown in (b). Numbers in circles denote number of active processes at this point in time on this contention domain.

In Fig. 3b–f these variants are tested for their reaction to injected idle waves when using all cores on the contention domain. The data shows that the more data hungry the serial code (i.e., the earlier the saturation point), the stronger the damping. This was expected from the analysis in Fig. 1. In addition, an early saturation point causes a large amplitude of the generated computational wavefront (compare Fig. 3c and d, and Fig. 3e and f). Thus, the saturation point impacts the amplitude of the computational wavefront. Since the wavefront is defined by a constant time step ID across processes, a large wave amplitude indicates a larger inter-process skew, i.e., stronger desynchronization, which causes longer waiting times within MPI calls despite negligible communication volume. Since the computational wave survives even long after the idle wave has died out, it is impossible for these waiting times to cause reduced memory bandwidth utilization (else the still-synchronized contention domain would eventually catch up). It thus seems that there are is always a sufficient number of computing processes within the computational wave to still reach bandwidth saturation. Figure 4a shows the average number of computing processes within the fully developed wave for the three cases in Figs. 2(f), 3(e), and 3(f). Comparing with Fig. 3a it is evident that this number is very close to the bandwidth saturation point (at 7, 13, and 20 cores, respectively). Hence, the computational wave settles at an amplitude that allows for just enough active processes to saturate the memory bandwidth, but not more. The inevitable waiting times caused by desynchronization are perfectly overlapped with user code execution.

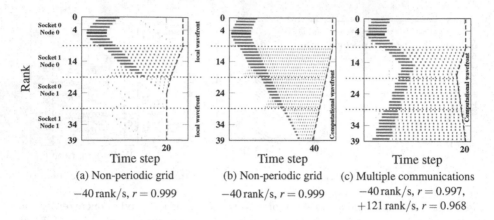

(a) Non-periodic grid
$-40\,\text{rank/s}, r = 0.999$

(b) Non-periodic grid
$-40\,\text{rank/s}, r = 0.999$

(c) Multiple communications
$-40\,\text{rank/s}, r = 0.997,$
$+121\,\text{rank/s}, r = 0.968$

**Fig. 5.** Shape and slope of memory-bound computational wavefront with different communication topologies and patterns on the Emmy system. The measured slope(s) of the computational wave(s) in ranks per second is/are indicated together with correlation coefficients of linear fits. Code properties are the same as in Fig. 2. The $x$ axis shows walltime but the time step at which the computation was terminated is indicated. (a) Open boundary conditions, next-neighbor communication, short one-off idle injection, (b) open boundary conditions, next-neighbor communication, long one-off idle injection, (c) periodic boundary conditions, next-neighbor communication along rising ranks, next- and next-to-next neighbor communication along falling ranks, short one-off idle injection.

## 4.3   Influence of Communication Patterns and Injection Length

In Fig. 5 we investigate how the shape and slope of an induced computational wave depends on the communication pattern (distance of point-to-point communication) and topology (open vs. periodic boundary conditions). In Fig. 5a we injected a short idle period into a code with open boundary conditions and next-neighbor bidirectional communication. The corresponding idle wave in negative rank direction dies at rank 0, as expected [2]. The idle wave in the positive rank direction hardly travels beyond the next contention domain (node 0, socket 1) before dying out, but a computational wave prevails on that domain in the form of a single ramp with a slope of $-40\,\text{rank/s}$. Doubling the duration of the injection (Fig. 5) leads to a longer idle wave that extends across three sockets in positive rank direction, and so does the generated computational wave. Its slope, however, is the same as in the previous case. The strength of the initial idle wave thus has no influence on the local slope of the computational wave.

The experiment in Fig. 5c shows the influence of communication patterns. Each MPI process communicates with its next neighbor in positive rank direction and with its next- and next-to-next neighbors in negative rank direction; moreover, the topology was changed to periodic boundary conditions. The idle wave can now roll over the system boundary and eventually annihilates itself. Its leading edges are governed by the known mechanisms investigated in [2]: The idle wave in negative rank direction is three times faster than the one in positive rank direction. The resulting computational wave is continuous (because of the boundary condition) and shows two distinct slopes, which are different from the slopes of the idle wave but have the same 3:1 ratio. Hence, the slopes involved in the computational wave are influenced by the same communication parameters that govern the slopes of the idle wave, but the absolute slopes are different, which translates into different wave amplitudes. As shown in the previous sections, they depend on the saturation characteristics of the memory-bound code.

## 5   Spontaneous Computational Wavefronts

With negligible communication overhead, the desynchronization phenomena described above can be observed when provoked by a rather strong one-off delay injection. They only occur spontaneously, i.e., via the normal system noise, over very long time scales. Moreover, although the available memory bandwidth per process is larger in the desynchronized state, the runtime of the whole program, i.e., the wall-clock time required for the slowest process to reach the last time step, cannot be reduced in this scenario since no significant overhead is overlapped with code execution.

In this section we show how computational wavefronts and desynchronization can occur *spontaneously* via natural system noise if there is significant communication overhead, which paves the way towards automatic communication-computation overlap.

### 5.1   Pure MPI

In Fig. 6 we show four phases of a timeline of a memory-bound STREAM triad code on four sockets of Emmy and an initial communication overhead of ≈25%. One MPI process was run per core with bidirectional next-neighbor communication, open boundary conditions, and a message size of 5 MB. The synchronized state from the beginning soon dissolves. After 100 time steps (second phase), local wavefronts have emerged, but no global state is reached yet. Within 500 time steps (third phase), a global wave has formed, and it persists till the end of the program (50 000 time steps). Interestingly, although the wavelength and amplitude of the computational wave are rather constant, the pattern can shift across the MPI ranks over time: After 26 s of walltime the slowest process is on socket 1, while after 2000 s it is on socket 0. The cause for such shifts are small perturbations (natural noise), whose close investigation is left for future work.

The overall MPI time per process goes up when entering the wave state as expected because waiting time is added on top of actual communication time. However, since communication can be overlapped with execution, performance increases. In our particular case, the total average (computation plus communication/waiting) time per iteration goes down from $30\,\mathrm{ms} + 10\,\mathrm{ms} = 40\,\mathrm{ms}$ to $20\,\mathrm{ms} + 17.5\,\mathrm{ms} = 37.5\,\mathrm{ms}$, i.e., by about 6%.

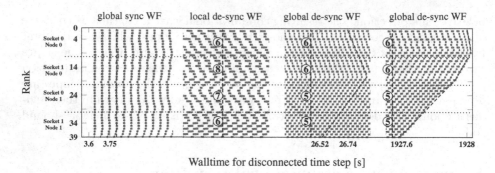

**Fig. 6.** 50 000 iterations run of an MPI-parallel STREAM triad code (non-periodic grid, bidirectional next-neighbor communication, 4.8 GB overall data volume) on the Emmy system (normal stores, saturation at 5–6 cores). The four phases show different cutouts of the complete timeline near the indicated walltimes. Synchronized state (phase 1): 30 + 10 ms average compute + communication intervals. Fully developed wavefront (phase 3, 4): 20 + 17.5 ms average compute + communication. Numbers of concurrent working processes per domain are indicated in circles.

## 5.2  Latency- vs Bandwidth-Dominated Overhead

There are two potential benefits from desynchronization: Better memory bandwidth utilization by the application code and better network interface utilization (not discussed here). These advantages are partially offset by the memory bandwidth drawn by MPI communication of large messages. For example, in the experiment in Fig. 6, each message had a size of 5 MB. In particular the intra-node point-to-point communication can aggregate to a significant data volume (at least 20 MB per process and time step in this case, and probably more depending on the implementation of intra-node MPI), reducing the bandwidth available to the application code. This is why the theoretical speedup of 25% could not be obtained.

## 5.3  Threaded MPI Processes

All phenomenology discussed so far can also be observed with hybrid MPI+OpenMP codes that communicate only outside OpenMP-parallel regions. However, spanning an MPI process across several cores on a contention domain is equivalent to reducing the number of cores, which makes for weaker saturation characteristics as discussed in Sects. 4.1 and 4.2. If the number of threads per process is large enough to show linear bandwidth scaling across processes, spontaneous wave formation and automatic overlap will not occur.

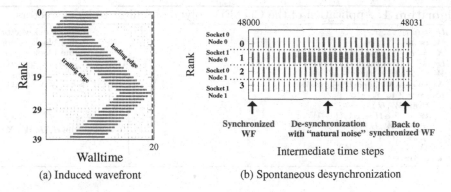

**Fig. 7.** MPI+OpenMP hybrid execution of parallel STREAM triad on Emmy with bidirectional next-neighbor communication, periodic boundary conditions, and the same overall data volume as in Fig. 6 but with 10 threads per process and one process per contention domain. (a) 40 processes on 20 nodes with negligible communication overhead and an idle injection on process 5 for first 20 iterations, (b) four processes on two nodes with 5 MB MPI message size for intermediate 31 iterations over a complete run of 50 000 timesteps.

Figure 7a shows an injected idle wave on Emmy with 40 MPI processes by ten threads each, running the STREAM triad with one process per contention domain, bidirectional next-neighbor communication (negligible overhead), and periodic boundary conditions. Since there is no bandwidth contention among processes, the situation is very similar to Fig. 1 and Fig. 2a: The idle wave is hardly damped and eventually cancels itself, with no discernible desynchronization prevailing and no computational wave following up. The memory-bound nature of the code is of no significance.

The property of scalable code to automatically eliminate idle waves by the interaction of the trailing edge with system noise (which was thoroughly studied in [2]) leads to the important and general conclusion that spontaneous desynchronization does not occur in this case. Figure 7b shows a timeline of four MPI processes with ten threads each, running on four contention domains of Emmy. System noise causes a delay with subsequent desynchronization, which is quickly dissolved and the system returns to the synchronized state. One can argue that there is more to hybrid MPI+OpenMP programming than optimizing communication overhead; "full hybrid" codes, in which one MPI process spans a full contention domain (or more), do not profit from desynchronization and automatic overlap since they enforce a lock-step across threads.

We have to add that we have deliberately chosen a simplified scenario where the number and size of point-to-point messages sent between processes does not depend on the number of threads per process. In real-world codes, many effects complicate matters, especially when comparing pure MPI with MPI+OpenMP code for the same problem since the number of messages and (probably) the communication volume changes [18]. A thorough study of this problem area is left for future work.

---

**Algorithm 1.** Application of the ChebFD polynomial filter to block vectors.

```
 1: U := u_1, ..., u_{n_s}                              ▷ define block vector
 2: W := w_1, ..., w_{n_s}                              ▷ define block vector
 3: X := x_1, ..., x_{n_s}                              ▷ define block vector
 4: U ← (αH + β1)X                                               ▷ spmmv()
 5: W ← 2(αH + β1)U − X                                          ▷ spmmv()
 6: X ← g_0 c_0 X + g_1 c_1 U + g_2 c_2 W             ▷ baxpy()+bscal()
 7: for p = 3 to n_p do
 8:     swap(W, U)
 9:     W ← 2(αH + β1)U − W
10:     η_p ← ⟨W, U⟩                                 ▷ CHEBFD_OP(H, U, W, X)
11:     μ_p ← ⟨U, U⟩
12:     X ← X + g_p c_p W
13: end for
```

---

# 6  Chebychev Filter Diagonalization

Chebyshev filter diagonalization (ChebFD) [17] is a popular technique for calculating inner or extremal eigenvalues of large sparse matrices. It is based on subspace projection via polynomial filters constructed from Chebyshev polynomials. ChebFD is applied in many problems in quantum physics and chemistry, such as the study of topological materials (e.g., graphene) or electronic structure calculations based on density functional theory. Although the basic algorithm is just a sequence of simple vector operations and sparse matrix-vector multiplications (SpMV), it is amenable to loop fusion and blocking optimizations [12].

We use the scalable ChebFD implementation, specifically the application of the polynomial filter to a block of vectors. The compute kernels and implementation alternatives are available with the open-source GHOST[8] library for download. This is the dominant part of the full ChebFD algorithm, which still requires an orthogonalization procedure that is omitted here without loss of generality. The code supports MPI+OpenMP parallelism.

Algorithm 1 shows the basic algorithm. $H$ is the Hamiltonian matrix describing the physical system, while $U$, $W$, and $X$ are blocks of $n_s$ vectors, with $n_s$ being the dimension of the search space. The loop from line 7 to 13 iterates up to the polynomial degree $n_p$, which determines how selective the polynomial filter will be. The goal of the algorithm is the computation of the polynomial filter coefficients $\{\eta_p\}$ and $\{\mu_p\}$, which requires global scalar products (lines 10 and 11). However, since these coefficients are not needed until after the end of the calculation, the global reduction can be postponed and leads to an algorithm without synchronization points or global operations. The body of the $p$ loop can then be fused completely into a single kernel CHEBFD_OP for better cache reuse. Our implementation uses a blocking optimization that processes blocks of $n_b$ vectors at a time for improved cache efficiency. Details can be found in [12].

Our specific application case is a topological insulator of size $128 \times 64 \times 64$ with periodic boundary conditions. This leads to a Hamiltonian of dimension $2^{21}$ and $2.71 \times 10^6$ nonzeros. The full working set is about 6.7 GB (double precision matrix, 4-byte indices, plus all block vectors) when using $n_s = 128$ search vectors

---

[8] https://bitbucket.org/essex/ghost.

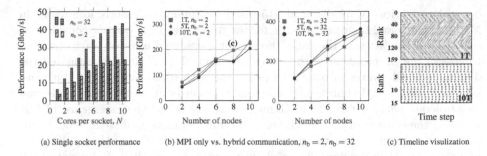

(a) Single socket performance     (b) MPI only vs. hybrid communication, $n_b = 2, n_b = 32$     (c) Timeline visulization

**Fig. 8.** ChebFD application for the topological insulator matrix `Topi-128-64-64` (`static OpenMP` scheduling, AVX vectorized and aligned execution, $n_{iter} = 5$) running on (single leaf switch connected) homogeneous `Emmy` nodes. (a) Performance scaling with OpenMP on a contention domain for $n_b = 2$ and $n_b = 32$, (b) scaling up to 10 nodes for $n_b = 2$ and $n_b = 32$, and different numbers of threads per process, (c) timeline for a specific number of iterations of pure MPI vs. full hybrid execution for $n_b = 2$ and 8 `Emmy` nodes.

and a polynomial filter degree $n_p = 500$, which are realistic values. The optimistic code balance assuming perfect cache reuse on the block vectors is [12]

$$B_c = \frac{260/n_b + 80}{146} \frac{\text{byte}}{\text{flop}}, \tag{3}$$

which is well beyond the machine balance of all current CPUs even for large $n_b$, rendering the code memory bound according to a naive Roofline model. In reality, the $n_b = 32$ case is already close to core bound since intra-cache data transfers begin to limit the performance of the code on some platforms, such as `Emmy` [13]: Fig. 8a shows performance vs. cores per socket for $n_b = 2$ and $n_b = 32$, and indeed the latter cannot fully saturate the bandwidth and achieves only 41 Gflop/s out of the bandwidth-bound Roofline limit of 66 Gflop/s. Figure 8b shows strong scaling from 2–10 nodes for both cases with 2 (10 threads each) to 20 (single-threaded) MPI processes on each `Emmy` node. At $n_b = 2$, fewer threads have a clear advantage while the situation is reversed at $n_b = 32$. The more saturating code ($n_b = 2$) has ample opportunity for desynchronization without threading (which is shown in the timeline comparison in Fig. 8c). In Fig. 8c, the upper panel shows MPI only while the lower panel shows hybrid with 10 threads (1 process) per socket, both on eight `Emmy` nodes. The more scalable code ($n_b = 32$) shows no spontaneous desynchronization without threading, and the fully hybrid code can benefit from the reduced number of MPI messages.

## 7 Related Work

There is very little research on idle wave propagation and pattern formation in parallel code, especially in the context of memory-bound programs. Hence, none of the existing prior work addressed spontaneous pattern formation and desynchronization. Markidis et al. [15] used a simulator to study idle waves in MPI programs and their propagation for the first time. They did not consider the socket-level character of the code, though, and assumed a linear wave equation to govern the propagation of the waves. Afzal et al. [1,2] have investigated the dynamics of idle waves in pure MPI programs with core-bound code. Our work builds on theirs and significantly extends it towards memory-bound code and spontaneous pattern formation. Gamell et al. [6] noted the emergence of idle waves in the context of failure recovery and failure masking of stencil codes, but the speed of propagation, the memory-bound characteristics of the application, and the corresponding damping mechanisms were not studied. Böhme et al. [4] presented a tool-based approach to attribute propagating wait states in MPI programs to their original sources, helping to identify and correct the root issues. Global properties of such waves like damping and velocity, or the interaction with memory-bound code, were ignored, however.

There is a vast body of research that targets the characterization of noise as well as its mitigation via explicit techniques, such as dynamic load balancing, MPI process placement, synchronization of OS influence, and lightweight OS kernels [3,14,16,20]. In contrast, the present paper investigates the *favorable* consequences of noise as an enabling factor for desynchronization and – in case of memory-bound code – automatic partial overlap of communication and computation.

## 8   Conclusion and Outlook

We have shown how the memory-bound nature of load-balanced MPI programs without explicit synchronization or global operations and homogeneous communication characteristics is directly linked to the damping of idle waves and to desynchronization effects. The key concept is the *computational wave*, a stable pattern marked by different processes reaching a given step within an application run at different times. Such patterns can be provoked by injected one-off delays or emerge spontaneously; rapid, spontaneous pattern formation caused by natural system noise is only possible with significant communication overhead. In a desynchronized state, the time spent in MPI routines is larger but the available memory bandwidth per process is higher. There is evidence that a computational wave settles in a state where the number of processes concurrently running user code within a contention domain is very close to the bandwidth saturation point. Desynchronization also enables automatic hiding of communication overhead, which can in some cases improve the performance of a program. This overlap may not be perfect due to the MPI communication requiring part of the memory bandwidth.

From the viewpoint of memory bandwidth, using a single, multi-threaded MPI process per contention domain effectively recovers a scalable code. In this case, automatic overlap does not occur and (induced or spontaneous) delays die out automatically. Multi-threaded MPI processes pay off mainly at larger core counts, where applications become more communication-intensive in strong scaling scenarios [5]. One main benefit from using threaded processes is a reduction in the number of messages. Thus, fewer threads per process can improve performance if process desynchronization can be leveraged for communication overlap without too much impact on the communication efficiency.

We consider studying microbenchmarks and simple applications as a necessary prerequisite to understand basic mechanisms. While our results were first obtained using simple microbenchmark codes on four different cluster systems, we have demonstrated the emergence of computational waves and the detrimental effect of full hybrid mode using a Chebyshev Filter application from quantum physics. Our coverage of the topic is certainly limited to the "barrier-free bulk-synchonous" pattern, i.e., regular communication-computation phases without explicit or implicit synchronization.

*Future Work.* Although we could uncover some of the mechanisms behind the computational wave formation in a qualitative way, a detailed quantitative understanding of these effects is still out of reach. For example, the length of computation and communication phases influences the idle wave velocity according to Eq. (2). A higher idle wave velocity will cause a smaller computational wave amplitude. Currently this is just an observation and we lack a quantitative model. Additionally, there is no actual mathematical *proof* of stability for computational waves, or a proof of instability for the bulk-synchronous state. We have also just scratched the surface of how threaded MPI processes, natural system noise, and network contention change the underlying mechanisms. For example, even with core-bound code there may be a strong bottleneck on the network interface if parallel program is strongly communication bound, and desynchronization does occur in this case as well. It will be helpful to have a controlled, noise-free experimental environment in which all relevant aspects, from code characteristics to communication parameters and contention effects, can be influenced at will. Well-known networking simulation tools [11], e.g., SST[9] or CODES[10], cannot accurately take resource sharing beyond network aspects into account since that would require a separate performance model on the node, such as the ECM model [9]. We are currently working on a high-performance simulation tool that goes far beyond existing simulators such as LogGOPSim [8].

**Acknowledgments.** This work was supported by KONWIHR, the Bavarian Competence Network for Scientific High Performance Computing in Bavaria, under project name "OMI4papps." We are indebted to LRZ Garching for granting CPU hours on SuperMUC-NG.

# References

1. Afzal, A., Hager, G., Wellein, G.: Delay flow mechanisms on clusters. In: Poster at EuroMPI: 10–13 September 2019, Zurich, Switzerland (2019). https://hpc.fau.de/files/2019/09/EuroMPI2019_AHW-Poster.pdf

---

[9] http://sst-simulator.org/.
[10] https://press3.mcs.anl.gov/codes/.

2. Afzal, A., Hager, G., Wellein, G.: Propagation and decay of injected one-off delays on clusters: a case study. In: 2019 IEEE International Conference on Cluster Computing, CLUSTER 2019, Albuquerque, NM, USA, 23–26 September 2019, pp. 1–10 (2019). https://doi.org/10.1109/CLUSTER.2019.8890995

3. Bhatele, A., Mohror, K., Langer, S.H., Isaacs, K.E.: There goes the neighborhood: performance degradation due to nearby jobs. In: Proceedings of the International Conference on High Performance Computing, Networking, Storage and Analysis SC 2013, pp. 1–12 (2013). https://doi.org/10.1145/2503210.2503247

4. Böhme, D., et al.: Identifying the root causes of wait states in large-scale parallel applications. ACM Trans. Parallel Comput. **3**(2), 11:1–11:24 (2016). https://doi.org/10.1145/2934661. ISSN: 2329–4949

5. Chorley, M.J., Walker, D.W.: Performance analysis of a hybrid MPI/OpenMP application on multi-core clusters. J. Comput. Sci. **1**(3), 168–174 (2010). https://doi.org/10.1016/j.jocs.2010.05.001

6. Gamell, M., et al.: Local recovery and failure masking for stencil-based applications at extreme scales. In: Proceedings of the International Conference for High Performance Computing, Networking, Storage and Analysis SC 2015, pp. 1–12, November 2015. https://doi.org/10.1145/2807591.2807672

7. Hockney, R.W.: The communication challenge for MPP: Intel Paragon and Meiko CS-2. Parallel Comput. **20**(3), 389–398 (1994). https://doi.org/10.1016/S0167-8191(06)80021-9. ISSN: 0167–8191

8. Hoefler, T., Schneider, T., Lumsdaine, A.: LogGOPSim - simulating large-scale applications in the LogGOPS model. In: Proceedings of the 19th ACM International Symposium on High Performance Distributed Computing, pp. 597–604. ACM, Chicago, June 2010. https://doi.org/10.1145/1851476.1851564. ISBN: 978-1-60558-942-8

9. Hofmann, J., Hager, G., Fey, D.: On the accuracy and usefulness of analytic energy models for contemporary multicore processors. In: Yokota, R., Weiland, M., Keyes, D., Trinitis, C. (eds.) ISC High Performance 2018. LNCS, vol. 10876, pp. 22–43. Springer, Cham (2018). https://doi.org/10.1007/978-3-319-92040-5_2

10. Hofmann, J., et al.: Bridging the architecture gap: abstracting performance-relevant properties of modern server processors. arXiv (2019, Submitted). arXiv:1907.00048 [cs.DC]

11. Kenny, J.P., Sargsyan, K., Knight, S., Michelogiannakis, G., Wilke, J.J.: The pitfalls of provisioning exascale networks: a trace replay analysis for understanding communication performance. In: Yokota, R., Weiland, M., Keyes, D., Trinitis, C. (eds.) ISC High Performance 2018. LNCS, vol. 10876, pp. 269–288. Springer, Cham (2018). https://doi.org/10.1007/978-3-319-92040-5_14

12. Kreutzer, M., et al.: Chebyshev filter diagonalization on modern manycore processors and GPGPUs. In: Yokota, R., Weiland, M., Keyes, D., Trinitis, C. (eds.) ISC High Performance 2018. LNCS, vol. 10876, pp. 329–349. Springer, Cham (2018). https://doi.org/10.1007/978-3-319-92040-5_17

13. Kreutzer, M., et al.: Performance engineering of the Kernel Polynomial Method on large-scale CPU-GPU systems. In: 2015 IEEE International Parallel and Distributed Processing Symposium, pp. 417–426, May 2015. https://doi.org/10.1109/IPDPS.2015.76

14. León, E.A., Karlin, I., Moody, A.T.: System noise revisited: enabling application scalability and reproducibility with SMT. In: 2016 IEEE International Parallel and Distributed Processing Symposium (IPDPS), pp. 596–607 (2016). https://doi.org/10.1109/IPDPS.2016.48

15. Markidis, S., et al.: Idle waves in high-performance computing. Phys. Rev. E **91**(1), 013306 (2015). https://doi.org/10.1103/PhysRevE.91.013306
16. Petrini, F., Kerbyson, D.J., Pakin, S.: The case of the missing supercomputer performance: achieving optimal performance on the 8,192 processors of ASCI Q. In: 2003 ACM/IEEE Conference on Supercomputing, pp. 55–55. IEEE (2003). https://doi.org/10.1145/1048935.1050204
17. Pieper, A., et al.: High-performance implementation of Chebyshev filter diagonalization for interior eigenvalue computations. J. Comput. Phys. **325**, 226–243 (2016). https://doi.org/10.1016/j.jcp.2016.08.027
18. Rabenseifner, R., Hager, G., Jost, G.: Hybrid MPI/OpenMP parallel programming on clusters of multi-core SMP nodes. In: 2009 17th Euromicro International Conference on Parallel, Distributed and Network-based Processing, Los Alamitos, CA, USA, pp. 427–436. IEEE Computer Society, Feburary 2009. https://doi.org/10.1109/PDP.2009.43
19. Stengel, H., Treibig, J., Hager, G., Wellein, G.: Quantifying performance bottlenecks of stencil computations using the execution-cache-memory model. In: Proceedings of the 29th ACM International Conference on Supercomputing, ICS 2015, Newport Beach, CA. ACM (2015). https://doi.org/10.1145/2751205.2751240
20. Weisbach, H., Gerofi, B., Kocoloski, B., Härtig, H., Ishikawa, Y.: Hardware performance variation: a comparative study using lightweight kernels. In: Yokota, R., Weiland, M., Keyes, D., Trinitis, C. (eds.) ISC High Performance 2018. LNCS, vol. 10876, pp. 246–265. Springer, Cham (2018). https://doi.org/10.1007/978-3-319-92040-5_13
21. Williams, S., Waterman, A., Patterson, D.: Roofline: an insightful visual performance model for multicore architectures. Commun. ACM **52**(4), 65–76 (2009). https://doi.org/10.1145/1498765.1498785. ISSN: 0001-0782
22. Wu, X., Taylor, V.: Using processor partitioning to evaluate the performance of MPI, OpenMP and hybrid parallel applications on dual-and quad-core Cray XT4 systems. In: The 51st Cray User Group Conference (CUG2009), pp. 4–7 (2009). http://faculty.cse.tamu.edu/wuxf/papers/cug09.pdf

# Understanding HPC Benchmark Performance on Intel Broadwell and Cascade Lake Processors

Christie L. Alappat[1], Johannes Hofmann[2], Georg Hager[1(✉)], Holger Fehske[3], Alan R. Bishop[4], and Gerhard Wellein[1,2]

[1] Erlangen Regional Computing Center (RRZE), 91058 Erlangen, Germany
georg.hager@fau.de
[2] Department of Computer Science, University of Erlangen-Nuremberg,
91058 Erlangen, Germany
[3] Institute of Physics, University of Greifswald, 17489 Greifswald, Germany
[4] Science, Technology and Engineering Directorate,
Los Alamos National Laboratory, Los Alamos, USA

**Abstract.** Hardware platforms in high performance computing are constantly getting more complex to handle even when considering multicore CPUs alone. Numerous features and configuration options in the hardware and the software environment that are relevant for performance are not even known to most application users or developers. Microbenchmarks, i.e., simple codes that fathom a particular aspect of the hardware, can help to shed light on such issues, but only if they are well understood and if the results can be reconciled with known facts or performance models. The insight gained from microbenchmarks may then be applied to real applications for performance analysis or optimization. In this paper we investigate two modern Intel x86 server CPU architectures in depth: Broadwell EP and Cascade Lake SP. We highlight relevant hardware configuration settings that can have a decisive impact on code performance and show how to properly measure on-chip and off-chip data transfer bandwidths. The new victim L3 cache of Cascade Lake and its advanced replacement policy receive due attention. Finally we use DGEMM, sparse matrix-vector multiplication, and the HPCG benchmark to make a connection to relevant application scenarios.

**Keywords:** Benchmarking · Microbenchmarking · x86 · Intel

## 1 Introduction

Over the past few years the field of high performance computing (HPC) has received attention from different vendors, which led to a steep rise in the number of chip architectures. All of these chips have different performance-power-price points, and thus different performance characteristics. This trend is believed to continue in the future with more vendors such as Marvell, Huawei, and Arm

© The Author(s) 2020
P. Sadayappan et al. (Eds.): ISC High Performance 2020, LNCS 12151, pp. 412–433, 2020.
https://doi.org/10.1007/978-3-030-50743-5_21

entering HPC and related fields with new designs. Benchmarking the architectures to understand their characteristics is pivotal for informed decision making and targeted code optimization. However, with hardware becoming more diverse, proper benchmarking is challenging and error-prone due to wide variety of available but often badly documented tuning knobs and settings.

In this paper we explore two modern Intel server processors, Cascade Lake SP and Broadwell EP, using carefully developed micro-architectural benchmarks, then show how these simple microbenchmark codes become relevant in application scenarios. During the process we demonstrate the different aspects of proper benchmarking like the importance of appropriate tools, the danger of black-box benchmark code, and the influence of different hardware and system settings. We also show how simple performance models can help to draw correct conclusions from the data.

Our microbenchmarking results highlight the changes from the Broadwell to the Cascade Lake architecture and their impact on the performance of HPC applications. Probably the biggest modification in this respect was the introduction of a new L3 cache design.

This paper makes the following relevant contributions:

- We show how proper microarchitectural benchmarking can be used to reveal the cache performance characteristics of modern Intel processors. We compare the performance features of two recent Intel processor generations and resolve inconsistencies in published data.
- We analyze the performance impact of the change in the L3 cache design from Broadwell EP to Skylake/Cascade Lake SP and investigate potential implications for HPC applications (effective L3 size, scalability).
- For DGEMM we show the impact of varying core and Uncore clock speed, problem size, and sub-NUMA clustering on Cascade Lake SP.
- For a series of sparse matrix-vector multiplications we show the consequence of the nonscalable L3 cache and the benefit of the enhanced effective L3 size on Cascade Lake SP.
- To understand the performance characteristics of the HPCG benchmark, we construct and validate the roofline model for all its components and the full solver for the first time. Using the model we identify an MPI desynchronization mechanism in the implementation that causes erratic performance of one solver component.

This paper is organized as follows. After describing the benchmark systems setup in Sect. 2, microarchitectural analysis using microbenchmarks (e.g., load and copy kernels and STREAM) is performed in Sect. 3 to 5. In Sect. 6 we then revisit the findings and see how they affect code from realistic applications. Section 7 concludes the paper.

**Related Work.** There is a vast body of research on benchmarking of HPC systems. The following papers present and analyze microbenchmark and application performance data in order to fathom the capabilities of the hardware.

Molka et al. [17] used their BenchIT microbenchmarking framework to thoroughly analyze latency and bandwidth across the full memory hierarchy of Intel Sandy Bridge and AMD Bulldozer processors, but no application analysis or performance modeling was done. Hofmann et al. [9,11] presented microbenchmark results for several Intel server CPUs. We extend their methodology towards Cascade Lake SP and also focus on application-near scenarios. Saini et al. [20,21] compared a range of Intel server processors using diverse microbenchmarks, proxy apps, and application codes. They did not, however, provide a thorough interpretation of the data in terms of the hardware architectures. McIntosh-Smith et al. [15] compared the Marvell ThunderX2 CPU with Intel Broadwell and Skylake using STREAM, proxy apps, and full applications, but without mapping architectural features to microbenchmark experiments. Recently, Hammond et al. [6,7] performed a benchmark analysis of the Intel Skylake and Marvell ThunderX2 CPUs, presenting results partly in contradiction to known hardware features: Cache bandwidths obtained with standard benchmark tools were too low compared to theoretical limits, the observed memory bandwidth with vectorized vs. scalar STREAM was not interpreted correctly, and matrix-matrix-multiplication performance showed erratic behavior. A deeper investigation of these issues formed the seed for the present paper. Finally, Marjanović et al. [13] attempted a performance model for the HPCG benchmark; we refine and extend their node-level model and validate it with hardware counter data.

## 2    Testbed and Environment

All experiments were carried out on one socket each of Intel's Broadwell-EP (BDW) and Cascade Lake-SP (CLX) CPUs. These represent previous- and current-generation models in the Intel line of architectures, which encompass more than 85% of the November 2019 TOP500 list. Table 1 summarizes key specifications of the testbed. Measurements conducted on a Skylake-SP Gold-6148 (SKX) machine are not presented as the results were identical to CLX (successor) in all the cases.

The Broadwell-EP architecture has a three-level inclusive cache hierarchy. The L1 and L2 caches are private to each core and the L3 is shared. BDW supports the AVX2 instruction set, which is capable of 256-bit wide SIMD. The Cascade Lake-SP architecture has a shared non-inclusive victim L3 cache. The particular model in our testbed supports the AVX-512 instruction set and has 512-bit wide SIMD. Both chips support the "Cluster on Die [CoD]" (BDW) or "Sub-NUMA Clustering [SNC]" (CLX) feature, by which the chip can be logically split in two ccNUMA domains.

Unless otherwise specified, hardware prefetchers were enabled. For all microbenchmarks the clock frequency was set to the guaranteed attainable frequency of the processor when all the cores are active, i.e., 1.6 GHz for CLX and 2.0 GHz for BDW. For real application runs, Turbo mode was activated. The Uncore clock speed was always set to the maximum possible frequency of 2.4 GHz on CLX and 2.8 GHz on BDW.

Both systems ran Ubuntu version 18.04.3 (Kernel 4.15.0). The Intel compiler version 19.0 update 2 with the highest optimization flag (-O3) was used throughout. Unless otherwise stated, we added architecture-specific flags -xAVX (-xCORE-AVX512 -qopt-zmm-usage=high) for BDW (CLX). For experiments that use MKL and MPI libraries we used the version that comes bundled with the Intel compiler. The LIKWID tool suite in version 4.3 was used for performance counter measurements and benchmarking (likwid-perfctr and likwid-bench). Note that likwid-bench generates assembly kernels automatically, providing full control over the executed code.

**Table 1.** Key specification of test bed machines.

| Microarchitecture | Broadwell-EP (BDW) | Cascade Lake-SP (CLX) |
|---|---|---|
| Chip Model | Xeon E5-2697 v4 | Xeon Gold 6248 |
| Supported core freqs | 1.2–3.6 GHz | 1.2–3.9 GHz |
| Supported Uncore freqs | 1.2–2.8 GHz | 1.0–2.4 GHz |
| Cores/Threads | 18/36 | 20/40 |
| Latest SIMD extension | AVX2/FMA | AVX-512 |
| L1 cache capacity | 18 × 32 KiB | 20 × 32 KiB |
| L2 cache capacity | 18 × 256 KiB | 20 × 1 MiB |
| L3 cache capacity | 45 MiB (18 × 2.5 MiB) | 27.5 MiB (20 × 1.375 MiB) |
| Memory Configuration | 4 ch. DDR4-2400 | 6 ch. DDR4-2933 |
| LD/ST throughput | 2 LD, 1 ST (AVX) | 2 LD, 1 ST (AVX512) |
| L1 - L2 bandwidth | 64 B/cy | 64 B/cy |
| L2 - L3 bandwidth | 32 B/cy | 16 B/cy + 16 B/cy |
| Theor. Mem. Bandwidth | 76.8 GB/s | 140.8 GB/s |
| Operating system | Ubuntu 18.04.3 | Ubuntu 18.04.3 |
| Compiler | Intel 19.0 update 2 | Intel 19.0 update 2 |

**Influence of Machine and Environment Settings.** The machine and environment settings are a commonly neglected aspect of benchmarking. Since they can have a decisive impact on performance, all available settings must be documented. Figure 1(a) shows the influence of different operating system (OS) settings on a serial load-only benchmark running at 1.6 GHz on CLX for different data-set sizes in L3 and memory. With the default OS setting (NUMA balancing on and transparent huge pages (THP) set to "madvise"), we can see a 2× hit in performance for big data sets. The influence of these settings can be seen for multi-core runs (see Fig. 1(a) right) where a difference of 12% is observed between the best and default setting on a full socket. This behavior also strongly depends on the OS version. We observed it with Ubuntu 18.04.3 (see Table 1). Consequently, we use the setting that gives highest performance, i.e., NUMA balancing off and THP set to "always," for all subsequent experiments.

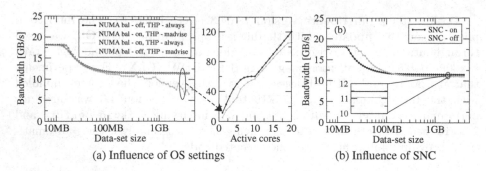

**Fig. 1.** (a) Performance impact of NUMA balancing and transparent huge pages (THP) on a load-only streaming benchmark on CLX. The left figure in (a) shows the single core performance over different data set sizes for various OS settings. The right figure in (a) shows the performance influence of the best and worst setting for different number of cores with a data-set size of 3 GB per core. (b) Performance effect of sub-NUMA clustering (SNC) on single core for the same load-only benchmark. For the experiment in (a) SNC was enabled and in (b) NUMA balancing was disabled and THP set to "always."

Modern systems have an increasing number of knobs to tune on system startup. Figure 1(b) shows the consequences of the sub-NUMA clustering (SNC) feature on CLX for the load-only benchmark. With SNC active the single core has local access to only one sub-NUMA domain causing the shared L3 size to be halved. For accesses from main memory, disabling SNC slightly reduces the single core performance by 4% as seen in the inset of Fig. 1(b).

## 3    Single-Core Bandwidth Analysis

Single-core bandwidth analysis is critical to understand the machine characteristics and capability for a wide range of applications, but it requires great care especially when measuring cache bandwidths since any extra cycle will directly change the result. To show this we choose the popular bandwidth measurement tool `lmbench` [16]. Figure 2 shows the load-only (full-read or frd) bandwidth obtained by `lmbench` as a function of data set size on CLX at 1.6 GHz. Ten runs per size are presented in a box-and-whisker plot.

Theoretically, one core is capable of two AVX-512 loads per cycle for an L1 bandwidth of 128 byte/cy (204.8 Gbyte/s @ 1.6 GHz). However, with the compiler option -O2 (default setting) it deviates by a huge factor of eight (25.5 Gbyte/s) from the theoretical limit. The characteristic strong performance gap between L1 and L2 is also missing. Therefore, we tested different compiler flags and compilers to see the effect (see Fig. 2) and observed a large span of performance values. Oddly, increasing the level of optimization (-O2 vs -O3) dramatically decreases the performance. The highest bandwidth was attained for -O2 with the architecture-specific flags mentioned in Sect. 2. A deeper investigation reveals

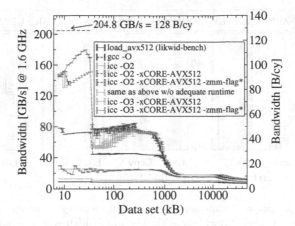

**Fig. 2.** Load-only bandwidth as a function of data set size on CLX. The plot compares the bandwidth obtained from `likwid-bench` with that of `lmbench`. `likwid-bench` is able to achieve 88% of the theoretical L1 bandwidth limit (128 byte/cy). The extreme sensitivity of `lmbench` benchmark results to compilers and compiler flags is also shown. The "zmm-flag*" refers to the compiler flag `-qopt-zmm-usage=high`.

that this problem is due to compiler inefficiency and the nature of the benchmark. The frd benchmark performs a sum reduction on an integer array; in the source code, the inner loop is manually unrolled 128 times. With `-O2` optimization, the compiler performs exactly 128 ADD operations using eight AVX-512[1] integer ADD instructions (`vpaddd`) on eight independent registers. After the loop, a reduction is carried out among these eight registers to accumulate the scalar result. However, with `-O3` the compiler performs an additional 16-way unrolling on top of the 128-way manual unrolling and generates sub-optimal code with a long dependency chain and additional instructions (blends, permutations) inside the inner loop, degrading the performance. The run-to-run variability of the highest-performing `lmbench` variant is also high in the default setting (cyan line). This is due to an inadequate number of warmup runs and repetitions in the default benchmark setting; increasing the default values (to ten warmup runs and 100 repetitions) yields stable measurements (blue line).

We are forced to conclude that the frd benchmark does not allow any profound conclusions about the machine characteristics without a deeper investigation. Thus, `lmbench` results for frd (e.g., [6,7,20,21]) should be interpreted with due care. However, employing proper tools one can attain bandwidths close to the limits. This is demonstrated by the AVX-512 load-only bandwidth results obtained using `likwid-bench` [24]. As seen in Fig. 2, with `likwid-bench` we get 88% of the theoretical limit in L1, the expected drops at the respective cache sizes, and much less run-to-run variations.

---

[1] 16 integer elements in an AVX512 register.

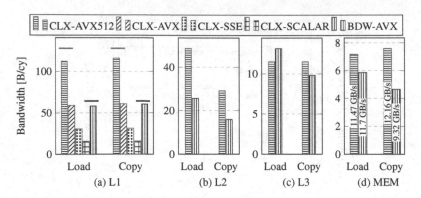

**Fig. 3.** Single-core bandwidth measurements in all memory hierarchy levels for load-only and copy benchmarks (`likwid-bench`). The bandwidth is shown in byte/cy, which is a frequency-agnostic unit for L1 and L2 cache. For main memory, the bandwidth in Gbyte/s at the base AVX512/AVX clock frequency of 1.6 GHz/2 GHz for CLX/BDW is also indicated. Different SIMD widths are shown for CLX in L1. Horizontal lines denote theoretical upper bandwidth limits.

Figure 3 shows application bandwidths[2] from different memory hierarchy levels of BDW and CLX (load-only and copy kernels). The core clock frequency was fixed at 1.6 and 2 GHz for CLX and BDW, respectively, with SNC/CoD switched on. The bandwidth is shown in byte/cy, which makes it independent of core clock speed for L1 and L2 caches. Conversion to Gbyte/s is done by multiplying the byte/cy value with the clock frequency in GHz. The effect of single-core L1 bandwidth for scalar and different SIMD width is also shown in Fig. 3(a) for CLX. It can be seen that the bandwidth reduces by 2× as expected when the SIMD width is halved each time.

## 4   Intel's New Shared L3 Victim Cache

From BDW to CLX there are no major observable changes to the behavior of L1 and L2 caches, except that the L2 cache size has been significantly extended in CLX. However, starting from Skylake (SKX) the L3 cache has been redesigned. In the following we study the effects of this newly designed non-inclusive victim L3 cache.

### 4.1   L3 Cache Replacement Policy

A significant change with respect to the L3 cache concerns its replacement policy. Since SNB, which used a pseudo-LRU replacement strategy [1], new Intel microarchitectures have implemented dynamic replacement policies [8] which

---

[2] Application bandwidth refers to the bandwidth as seen by the application without the inclusion of hidden data traffic like write-allocate transfers.

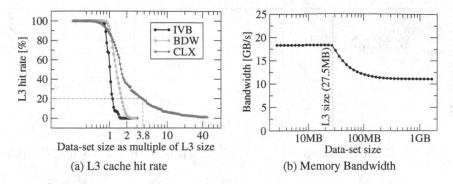

(a) L3 cache hit rate                    (b) Memory Bandwidth

**Fig. 4.** (a) Demonstration of the implications of the change in cache-replacement policy across processor generations using the L3-cache hit rate. (b) Bandwidth for a load-only data-access pattern on CLX (using `likwid-bench`). In (a), data for the older Intel Ivy Bridge Xeon E5-2690 v2 (IVB) is included for reference.

continuously improved the cache hit rate for streaming workloads from generation to generation. Instead of applying the same pseudo-LRU policy to all workloads, post-SNB processors make use of a small amount of dedicated leader sets, each of which implements a different replacement policy. During execution, the processor constantly monitors which of the leader sets delivers the highest hit rate, and instructs all remaining sets (also called follower sets) to use the best-performing leader set's replacement strategy [19].

Experimental analysis suggests that the replacement policy selected by the processor for streaming access patterns involves placing new cache lines only in one of the ways of each cache set; the same strategy is used when prefetching data using the `prefetchnta` instruction (cf. Section 7.6.2.1 in [1]). Consequently, data in the remaining ten ways of the sets will not be preempted and can later be reused.

Figure 4(a) demonstrates the benefit of this replacement policy by comparing it to previous generations' L3 caches. The figure shows the L3-cache hit rate[3] for different data-set sizes on different processors for a load-only data access pattern. To put the focus on the impact of the replacement policies on the cache hit rate, hardware prefetchers were disabled during these measurements. Moreover, data-set sizes are normalized to compensate the processors' different L3-cache capacities. The data indicates that older generations' L3 caches offer no data reuse for data set sizes of two times the cache capacity, whereas CLX's L3 delivers hit rates of 20% even for data sets almost four times its capacity. Reuse can by detected even for data sizes more than ten times the L3 cache size on CLX.

The fact that this improvement can also be observed in practice is demonstrated in Fig. 4(b), which shows measured bandwidth for the same load-only

---

[3] Based on performance-counter data for the `MEM_LOAD_RETIRED.L3_HIT` and `MISS` events.

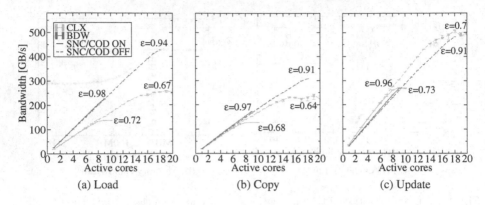

**Fig. 5.** L3 bandwidth of load, copy, and update benchmarks measured on CLX and BDW. The saturation of L3 bandwidth on CLX architecture can be clearly seen. The parallel efficiency of each NUMA domain is further labeled in the plot.

data-access pattern on CLX. For this measurement, all hardware prefetchers were enabled. The data indicates that the L3-cache hit-rate improvements directly translate into higher-than-memory bandwidths for data sets well exceeding the L3 cache's capacity.

### 4.2    L3 Scalability

Starting from Intel's Sandy Bridge architecture (created in 2011) the shared L3 cache of all the Intel architectures up to Broadwell is known to scale very well with the number of cores [11]. However, with SKX onwards the L3 cache architecture has changed from the usual ring bus architecture to a mesh architecture. Therefore in this section we test the scalability of this new L3 cache.

In order to test the L3 scalability we use again the `likwid-bench` tool and run the benchmark with increasing number of cores. The data-set size was carefully chosen to be 2 MB per core to ensure that the size is sufficiently bigger than the L2 cache however small enough such that no significant data traffic is incurred from the main memory.

The application bandwidths of the three basic kernels load-only, copy and update are shown in Fig. 5 for CLX and BDW. As the update kernel has equal number of loads and stores it shows the maximum attainable performance on both architectures. Note that also within cache hierarchies write-allocate transfers occur leading to lower copy application bandwidth. The striking difference between CLX and BDW for load-only bandwidth can finally be explained by the bi-directional L2-L3 link on CLX which only has half the load-only bandwidth of BDW (see Table 1).

In terms of scalability we find that the BDW scales almost linearly and attains an efficiency within 90%, proving that the BDW has an almost perfectly scalable L3 cache. However, with CLX this behavior has changed drastically and the L3 cache saturates at higher core counts both with and without SNC enabled, yielding an efficiency of about 70%. Consequently, for applications that employ L3 cache blocking it might be worthwhile to consider L2 blocking instead on SKX and CLX. Applications that use the shared property of L3 cache like some of the temporal blocking schemes [12, 25] might exhibit a similar saturation effect as in Fig. 5.

The effect of SNC/COD mode is also shown in Fig. 5, with dotted lines corresponding to SNC off mode and solid to SNC on mode. For CLX with SNC off mode the bandwidth attained at half of the socket (ten threads) is higher than SNC on mode. This is due to the availability of $2\times$ more L3 tiles and controllers with SNC off mode.

# 5   Multi-core Scaling with STREAM

The STREAM benchmark [14] measures the achievable memory bandwidth of a processor. Although the code comprises four different loops, their performance is generally similar and usually only the triad ($A(:)=B(:)+s*C(:)$) is reported. The benchmark output is a bandwidth number in Mbyte/s, assuming 24 byte of data traffic per iteration. The rules state that the working set size should be at least four times the LLC size of the CPU. In the light of the new LLC replacement policies (see Sect. 4.1), this appears too small and we chose a 2 GB working set for our experiments.

Since the target array A causes write misses, the assumption of the benchmark about the code balance is wrong if write-back caches are used and write-allocate transfers cannot be avoided. X86 processors feature *nontemporal store* instructions (also known as *streaming stores*), which bypass the normal cache hierarchy and store into separate write-combine buffers. If a full cache line is to be written, the write-allocate transfer can thus be avoided. Nontemporal stores are only available in SIMD variants on Intel processors, so if the compiler chooses not to use them (or is forced to by a directive or a command line option), write-allocates will occur and the memory bandwidth available to the application is reduced. This is why vectorization *appears* to be linked with better STREAM bandwidth, while it is actually the nontemporal store that cannot be applied for scalar code. Note that a careful investigation of the impact of write-allocate policies is also required on other modern processors such as AMD- or ARM-based systems.[4]

Figure 6 shows the bandwidth reported by the STREAM triad benchmark on BDW and CLX with (a,b) and without (c) CoD/SNC enabled. There are three data sets in each graph: full vectorization with the widest supported SIMD instruction set and standard stores (ST), scalar code, and full vectorization with nontemporal stores (NT). Note that the scalar and "ST" variants have very similar bandwidth, which is not surprising since they both cause write-allocate transfers for an overall code balance of 32 byte/it. The reported saturated bandwidth of the "NT" variant is higher because the memory interface delivers roughly the

---

[4] For example, on the Marvell ThunderX2 and many other ARM-based architectures, an automatic detection of streaming patterns can be activated that allows to avoid the write-allocate by claiming cache lines directly at the L2 cache [4].

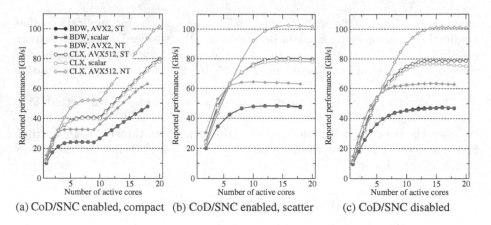

(a) CoD/SNC enabled, compact  (b) CoD/SNC enabled, scatter    (c) CoD/SNC disabled

**Fig. 6.** STREAM TRIAD scaling on BDW (closed symbols) and CLX (open symbols) with (a) CoD/SNC enabled and compact pinning of threads to cores, (b) CoD/SNC enabled and scattered pinning of threads to cores, and (c) CoD/SNC disabled. "NT" denotes the use of nontemporal stores (enforced by the -qopt-streaming-stores always), with "ST" the compiler was instructed to avoid them (via -qopt-streaming-stores never), and the "scalar" variant used non-SIMD code (via -no-vec). The working set was 2 GB. Core/Uncore clock speeds were set to 1.6 GHz/2.4 GHz on CLX and 2.0 GHz/2.8 GHz on BDW to make sure that no automatic clock speed reduction can occur. Note that the "scattered" graphs start at two cores.

same bandwidth but the code balance is only 24 byte/it. This means that the actual bandwidth is the same as the reported bandwidth; with standard stores, it is a factor of 4/3 higher. In case of BDW, the NT store variant thus achieves about the same memory bandwidth as the ST and scalar versions, while on CLX there is a small penalty. Note that earlier Intel processors like Ivy Bridge and Sandy Bridge also cannot attain the same memory bandwidth with NT stores as without. The difference is small enough, however, to still warrant the use of NT stores in performance optimization whenever the store stream(s) require a significant amount of bandwidth.

The peculiar shape of the scaling curve with CoD or SNC enabled and "compact" pinning (filling the physical cores of the socket from left to right, see Fig. 6(a)) is a consequence of the static loop schedule employed by the OpenMP runtime. If only part of the second ccNUMA domain is utilized (i.e., between 10 and 17 cores on BDW and between 11 and 19 cores on CLX), all active cores will have the same workload, but the cores on the first, fully occupied domain have less bandwidth available per core. Due to the implicit barrier at the end of the parallel region, these "slow" cores take longer to do their work than the cores on the other domain. Hence, over the whole runtime of the loop, i.e., including the waiting time at the barrier, each core on the second domain runs at the average performance of a core on the first domain, leading to linear scaling. A "scattered" pinning strategy as shown in Fig. 6(b) has only one saturation curve,

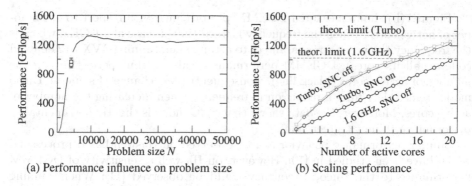

(a) Performance influence on problem size      (b) Scaling performance

**Fig. 7.** DGEMM performance subject to (a) problem size $N$ and (b) number of active cores for $N = 40,000$. (Color figure online)

of course. Note that the available saturated memory bandwidth is independent of the CoD/SNC setting for both CPUs.

# 6  Implications for Real-World Applications

In the previous sections we discussed microbenchmark analysis of the two Intel architectures. In the following we demonstrate how these results reflect in real applications by investigating important kernels such as DGEMM, sparse matrix-power-vector multiplication, and HPCG. According to settings used in production-level HPC runs, we use Turbo mode and switch off SNC unless specified otherwise. Statistical variations for ten runs are shown whenever the fluctuations are bigger than 5%.

## 6.1  DGEMM—Double-Precision General Matrix-Matrix Multiplication

If implemented correctly, DGEMM is compute-bound on Intel processors. Each CLX core is capable of executing 32 floating-point operations (flops) per cycle (8 DP numbers per AVX-512 register, 16 flops per fused multiply-add (FMA) instruction, 32 flops using both AVX-512 FMA units). Running DGEMM on all twenty cores, the processor specimen from the testbed managed to sustain a frequency of 2.09 GHz. The upper limit to DGEMM performance is thus 1337.6 Gflop/s.

Figure 7(a) compares measured full-chip performance of Intel MKL's DGEMM implementation on CLX in Turbo mode (black line) to theoretical peak performance (dashed red line). The data indicates that small values of $N$ are not suited to produce meaningful results. In addition to resulting in sub-optimal performance, values of $N$ below 10,000 lead to significant variance in measurements, as demonstrated for $N = 4096$ using a box-plot representation (and reproducing the results from [7]).

Figure 7(b) shows measured DGEMM performance with respect to the number of active cores. When the frequency is fixed (in this case at 1.6 GHz, which is the frequency the processor guarantees to attain when running AVX-512 enabled code on all its cores), DGEMM performance scales all but perfectly with the number of active cores (black line). Consequently, the change of slope in Turbo mode stems solely from a reduction in frequency when increasing the number of active cores. Moreover, the data shows that SNC mode is slightly detrimental to performance (blue vs. green line).

Similar performance behavior can be observed on Haswell-based processors, which have been studied in [10]. However, on Haswell a sensitivity of DGEMM performance to the Uncore frequency could be observed [11]: When running cores in Turbo mode, increasing the Uncore frequency resulted in a decrease of the share of the processor's TDP available to the cores, which caused them to lower their frequency. On CLX this is no longer the case. Running DGEMM on all cores in Turbo mode results in a clock frequency of 2.09 GHz independent of the Uncore clock. Analysis using hardware events suggests that the Uncore clock is subordinated to the core clock: Using the appropriate MSR (0x620), the Uncore clock can only be increased up to 2.4 GHz. There are, however, no negative consequences of this limitation. Traffic analysis in the memory hierarchy indicates that DGEMM is blocked for the L2 cache, so the Uncore clock (which influences L3 and memory bandwidth) plays no significant role for DGEMM.

## 6.2 SpMPV – Sparse Matrix-Power-Vector Multiplication

The SpMPV benchmark (see Algorithm 1) computes $y = A^p x$, where $A$ is a sparse matrix, as a sequence of sparse matrix-vector products. The SpMPV kernel is used in a wide range of numerical algorithms like Chebyshev filter diagonalization for eigenvalue solvers [18], stochastic matrix-function estimators used in big data applications [22], and numerical time propagation [23].

The sparse matrix is stored in the compressed row storage (CRS) format using double precision, and we choose $p = 4$ in our experiments. For the basic sparse matrix vector (SpMV) kernel we use the implementation in Intel MKL 19.0.2. The benchmark is repeated multiple times to ensure that it runs for at least one second, so we report the average performance over many runs.

We selected five matrices from the publicly available SuiteSparse Matrix Collection [5]. The choice of matrices was motivated by some of the hardware properties (in particular L3 features) as investigated in previous sections via microbenchmarks. The details of the chosen matrices are listed in Table 2. The matrices were pre-processed with reverse Cuthill-McKee (RCM) to attain better data locality; however, all performance measurements use the pure SpMPV execution time, ignoring the time taken for reordering.

**L3 Scalability.** Figure 8a shows the performance scaling of the ct20stif matrix on CLX and BDW. This matrix is just 32 MB in size and fits easily into the caches of both processors. Note that even though CLX has just 27.5 MiB of L3, it is

**Algorithm 1.** SpMPV algorithm: $y = A^p x$

1: $double :: A[nnz]$
2: $double :: y[p+1][nrows], x[nrows]$
3: $y[0][*] = x[*]$
4: **for** $i = 1 : p$ **do**
5: $\quad y[i][*] = A * y[i-1][*]$

a non-inclusive victim cache. The applicable cache size using all cores is thus the aggregate L2/L3 cache size, 47.5 MiB. The L3 bandwidth saturation of CLX as shown in Sect. 4.2 is reflected by the performance saturation in the SpMPV benchmark. For this matrix, BDW performs better than CLX since the sparse matrix kernel is predominantly load bound and limited by the bandwidth of the load-only microbenchmark (see Fig. 5a).

Despite this advantage, the in-cache SpMPV scaling on BDW is not linear (parallel efficiency $\varepsilon = 67.5\%$ at all cores), which differs from the microbenchmark results in Fig. 5a. The main reason is the active Turbo mode, causing the clock speed to drop by 25% when using all cores (BDW: 3.6 GHz at single core to 2.7 GHz at full socket; CLX: 3.8 GHz at single core to 2.8 GHz at full socket).

**L3 Cache Replacement Policy.** We have seen in Sect. 4.1 that CLX has a more sophisticated adaptive L3 cache replacement policy, which allows it to extend the caching effect for working sets as big as ten times the cache size. Here we show that SpMPV can profit from this as well. We choose three matrices that are within five times the L3 cache size (index 2, 3, and 4 in Table 2) and a moderately large matrix that is 37 times bigger than the L3 cache (index 5 in Table 2).

Figure 8b shows the full-socket performance and memory transfer volume for the four matrices. Theoretically, with a least-recently used (LRU) policy the benchmark requires a minimum memory data transfer volume of $12 + 28/N_{nzr}$ bytes per non-zero entry of the matrix [3]. This lower limit is shown in Fig. 8b (right panel) with dashed lines. We can observe that in some cases the

**Table 2.** Details of the benchmark matrices. $N_r$ is the number of matrix rows, $N_{nz}$ is the number of nonzeros, and $N_{nzr} = N_{nz}/N_r$. The last column shows the total memory footprint of the matrix (in CRS storage format).

| Index | Matrix name | $N_r$ | $N_{nz}$ | $N_{nzr}$ | Size (MB) |
|-------|-------------|-------|----------|-----------|-----------|
| 1 | ct20stif | 52,329 | 2,698,463 | 52 | 32 |
| 2 | boneS01 | 127,224 | 6,715,152 | 53 | 81 |
| 3 | ship_003 | 121,728 | 8,086,034 | 66 | 97 |
| 4 | pwtk | 217,918 | 11,634,424 | 53 | 140 |
| 5 | dielFilterV3real | 1,102,824 | 89,306,020 | 81 | 1072 |

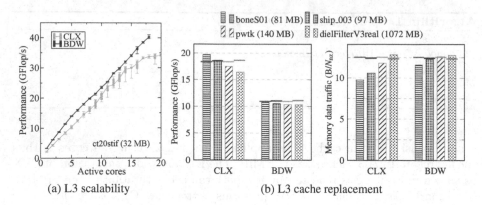

**Fig. 8.** SpMPV benchmark results on CLX and BDW (CoD/SNC off, Turbo mode). (a) Performance for the `ct20stif` matrix, which fits in the L3 cache. (b) Performance and memory data transfer volume for four different matrices. Dashed lines mark upper limits from a roofline model using the saturated load-only memory bandwidth.

actual memory traffic is lower than the theoretical minimum, because the L3 cache can satisfy some of the cacheline requests. Even though CLX and BDW have almost the same amount of cache, the effect is more prominent on CLX. On BDW it is visible only for the `boneS01` matrix, which is 1.7× bigger than its L3 cache, while on CLX it can be observed even for larger matrices. This is compatible with the microbenchmark results in Sect. 4.1. For some matrices the transfer volume is well below 12 bytes per entry, which indicates that not just the vectors but also some fraction of the matrix stays in cache.

As shown in the left panel of Fig. 8b, the decrease in memory traffic directly leads to higher performance. For two matrices on CLX the performance is higher than the maximum predicted by the roofline model (dashed line) even when using the highest attainable memory bandwidth (load-only). This is in line with data presented in [3].

## 6.3  HPCG – High Performance Conjugate Gradient

HPCG[5] (High Performance Conjugate Gradient) is a popular memory-bound proxy application which mimics the behavior of many realistic *sparse* iterative algorithms. However, there has been little work to date on analytic performance modeling of this benchmark. In this section we analyze HPCG using the roofline approach.

The HPCG benchmark implements a preconditioned conjugate gradient (CG) algorithm with a multi-grid (MG) preconditioner. The linear system is derived from a 27-point stencil discretization, but the corresponding sparse matrix is explicitly stored. The benchmark uses the two BLAS-1 kernels DOT and WAXPBY and two kernels (SpMV and MG) involving the sparse matrix.

---

[5] http://www.hpcg-benchmark.org/.

---

**Algorithm 2.** HPCG

---

1: **while** $k \leq iter$ & $r_{norm}/r_0 > tol$ **do**
2:     $z = MG(A,r)$                            $- >$ MG sweep
3:     $oldrtz = rtz$
4:     $rtz = \langle r,z \rangle$                      $- >$ DOT
5:     $\beta = rtz/oldrtz$
6:     $p = \beta * p + z$                        $- >$ WAXPBY
7:     $Ap = A * p$                              $- >$ SpMPV
8:     $pAp = \langle p,Ap \rangle$                    $- >$ DOT
9:     $\alpha = rtz/pAp$
10:    $x = x + \alpha * p$                       $- >$ WAXPBY
11:    $r = r - \alpha * Ap$                      $- >$ WAXPBY
12:    $r_{norm} = \langle r,r \rangle$                  $- >$ DOT
13:    $r_{norm} = sqrt(r_{norm})$
14:    $k + +$

---

The chip-level performance of HPCG should thus be governed by the memory bandwidth of the processor. Since the benchmark prints the Gflop/s performance of all kernels after a run, this should be straightforward to corroborate. However, the bandwidth varies a lot across different kernels in HPCG (see Table 3): For the WAXPBY kernel (`w[i]=a*x[i]+y[i]`), which has a code balance of 12 byte/flop[6], the reported performance is 5.14 Gflop/s on a full socket of BDW. On the other hand, for the DOT kernel with a reported code balance of 8 byte/flop the benchmark reports a performance of 10.16 Gflop/s. According to the roofline model this translates into memory bandwidths of 61.7 Gbyte/s and 81.3 Gbyte/s, respectively. The latter value is substantially higher than any STREAM value presented for BDW in Fig. 6. In the following, we use performance analysis and measurements to explore the cause of this discrepancy, and to check whether the HPCG kernel bandwidths are in line with the microbenchmark analysis.

*Setup.* For this analysis we use the recent reference variant of HPCG (version 3.1), which is a straightforward implementation using hybrid MPI+OpenMP parallelization. However, the local symmetric Gauss-Seidel (symGS) smoother used in MG has a distance-1 dependency and is not shared-memory parallel. The main loop of the benchmark is shown in Algorithm 2, where $A$ is the sparse matrix stored in CRS format.

As the symGS kernel consumes more than 80% of the entire runtime, the benchmark is run with pure MPI using one process per core. The code implements weak scaling across MPI processes; we choose a local problem size of $160^3$ for a working set of about 1.3 GB per process. The maximum number of CG iteration was set at 25, the highest compiler optimization flag was used

---

[6] The plain WAXPBY kernel has a code balance of 16 byte/flop if a write-allocate transfer must be accounted for; however, in HPCG it is called with `w[]` and `x[]` being the same array, so no write-allocate applies.

(see Table 1), and the contiguous storage of sparse matrix data structures was enabled (-DHPCG_CONTIGUOUS_ARRAYS).

*Performance Analysis of Kernels.* We use the roofline model to model each of the four kernels separately. Due to their strongly memory-bound characteristics, an upper performance limit is given by $P_x = b_s/C_x$, where $b_s$ is the full-socket (saturated) memory bandwidth and $C_x$ is the code balance of the kernel $x$. As we have a mixture of BLAS-1 ($N_r$ iterations) and sparse ($N_{nz}$ iterations) kernels, $C_x$ is computed in terms of bytes required and work done per row of the matrix.

The reference implementation has three DOT kernels (see Algorithm 2). Two of them need two input vectors (lines 4 and 8 in Algorithm 2) and the other requires just one (norm computation in line 12), resulting in a total average code balance of $C_{DOT} = ((2 \cdot 16 + 8)/3)$ byte/row $= 13.3$ byte/row. All three WAXPBY kernels need one input vector and one vector to be both loaded and stored, resulting in $C_{WAXPBY} = 24$ byte/row. For sparse kernels, the total data transferred for the inner $N_{nzr}$ iterations has to be considered. As shown in Sect. 6.2, the optimal code balance for SpMV is $12 + 28/N_{nzr}$ bytes per non-zero matrix entry, i.e., $C_{SpMV} = (12N_{nzr} + 28)$ byte/row. Note that this is substantially different from the model derived in [13]: We assume that the RHS vector is loaded only once, which makes the model strictly optimistic but is a good approximation for well-structured matrices like the one in HPCG. For the MG preconditioner we consider only the finest grid since the coarse grids do not substantially contribute to the overall runtime. Therefore the MG consists mainly of one symGS pre-smoothing step followed by one SpMV and one symGS post-smoothing step. The symGS comprises a forward sweep (0:nrows) followed by a backward sweep (nrows:0). Both have the same optimal code balance as SpMV, which means that the entire MG operation has a code balance of five times that of SpMV: $C_{MG} = 5C_{SpMV}$.

The correctness of the predicted code balance can be verified using performance counters. We use the likwid-perfctr tool to count the number of main memory data transfers for each of the kernels.[7] Table 3 summarizes the predicted and measured code balance values for full-socket execution along with the reported performance and number of flops per row for the four kernels in HPCG. Except for DDOT, the deviation between predicted and measured code balance is less than 10%.

*MPI Desynchronization.* Surprisingly, DDOT has a measured code balance that is lower than the model, pointing towards caching effects. However, a single input vector for DDOT has a size of 560 MB, which is more than ten times the available cache size. As shown in Sect. 4.1, even CLX is not able to show any significant caching effect with such working sets. Closer investigation revealed *desynchronization* of MPI processes to be the reason for the low code balance: In Algorithm 2 we can see that the DOT kernels can reuse data from previous

---

[7] See https://github.com/RRZE-HPC/likwid/wiki/TestAccuracy for validation of the data groups.

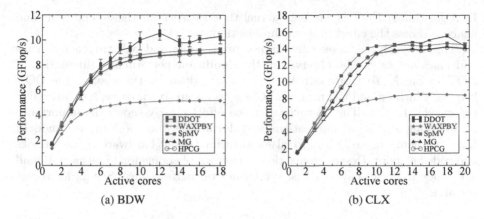

**Fig. 9.** Performance of different kernels in the HPCG benchmark (reference implementation) as a function of active cores.

**Table 3.** Summary of the roofline performance model parameters and measurements for HPCG kernels. Predicted and measured values for code balance and performance are shown in columns three to six. The last two columns compare the predicted and measured performance of the entire solver.

| Arch | Kernels | Code balance ($C_x$) | | Performance ($P_x$) | | Flops ($F_x$) | Calls ($I_x$) | HPCG perf. | |
|------|---------|------|------|------|------|------|------|------|------|
| | | Pred. | Measured | Pred. | Measured | | | Pred. | Measured |
| | | byte/row | byte/row | Gflop/s | Gflop/s | flops/row | | Gflop/s | Gflop/s |
| BDW | DDOT | 13.30 | 11.13 | 10.23 | 10.16 | 2 | 3 | 10.27 | 8.98 |
| | WAXPBY | 24.00 | 24.11 | 5.67 | 5.14 | 2 | 3 | | |
| | SpMV | 352.00 | 385.61 | 10.43 | 9.28 | 54 | 1 | | |
| | MG | 1760.00 | 1952.09 | 10.43 | 9.04 | 270 | 1 | | |
| CLX | DDOT | 13.30 | 12.68 | 17.29 | 14.34 | 2 | 3 | 17.37 | 13.95 |
| | WAXPBY | 24.00 | 24.02 | 9.58 | 8.39 | 2 | 3 | | |
| | SpMV | 352.00 | 382.68 | 17.64 | 14.46 | 54 | 1 | | |
| | MG | 1760.00 | 1944.31 | 17.64 | 14.05 | 270 | 1 | | |

kernels. For example, the last DOT (line 12) reuses the $r$ vector from the preceding WAXPBY. Therefore, if MPI processes desynchronize such that only some of them are already in DOT while the others are still in preceding kernels (like WAXPBY), then the processes in DOT can reuse the data, while the others just need to stream data as there is no reuse. To have a measurable performance impact of the desynchronization phenomenon, a kernel $x$ should satisfy the following criteria:

– no global synchronization point between $x$ and its preceding kernel(s),
– some of the data used by $x$ and its predecessor(s) are the same,
– the common data used by the kernels should have a significant contribution
  in the code balance ($C_x$) of the kernel.

In Algorithm 2, DOT is the only kernel that satisfies all these conditions and hence it shows the effect of desynchronization.

This desynchronization effect is not predictable and will vary across runs and machines as can be observed in the significant performance fluctuation of DOT in Fig. 9. To verify our assumption we added barriers before the DOT kernels, which caused the measured $C_{\mathrm{DOT}}$ to go up to 13.3 byte/row, matching the expected value. The desynchronization effect clearly shows the importance of analyzing statistical fluctuations and deviations from performance models. Ignoring them can easily lead to false conclusions about hardware characteristics and code behavior. Desynchronization is a known phenomenon in memory-bound MPI code that can have a decisive influence on performance. See [2] for recent research.

*Combining Kernel Predictions.* Once the performance predictions for individual kernels are in place, we can combine them to get a prediction of the entire HPCG. This is done by using a time-based formulation of the roofline model and linearly combining the predicted kernel runtimes based on their call counts. If $F_{\mathrm{x}}$ is the number of flops per row and $I_{\mathrm{x}}$ the number of times the kernel $x$ is invoked, the final prediction is

$$T_{\mathrm{HPCG}} = \sum_x I_{\mathrm{x}} T_{\mathrm{x}} \quad \forall x \in \{\mathrm{DOT}, \mathrm{WAXPBY}, \mathrm{SpMV}, \mathrm{MG}\}, \tag{1}$$

$$\text{where } T_{\mathrm{x}} = F_{\mathrm{x}} N_{\mathrm{r}} / P_{\mathrm{x}}. \tag{2}$$

Table 3 gives an overview of $F_{\mathrm{x}}$, $I_{\mathrm{x}}$, and $C_{\mathrm{x}}$ for different kernels and compares the predicted and measured performance on a full socket. The prediction is consistently higher than the model because we used the highest attainable bandwidth for the roofline model prediction. For Intel processors this is the load-only bandwidth $b_{\mathrm{S}} = 115\,\mathrm{Gbyte/s}\,(68\,\mathrm{Gbyte/s})$ for CLX (BDW), which is approximately 10% higher than the STREAM values (see Sect. 5). Figure 9 shows the scaling performance of the different kernels in HPCG. The typical saturation pattern of memory-bound code can be observed on both architectures.

## 7    Conclusions and Outlook

Two recent, state-of-the-art generations of Intel architectures have been analyzed: Broadwell EP and Cascade Lake SP. We started with a basic microarchitectural study concentrating on data access. The analysis showed that our benchmarks were able to obtain 85% of the theoretical bandwidth limits. For the first time, the performance effect of Intel's newly designed shared L3 victim cache was demonstrated. During the process of microbenchmarking we also identified the importance of selecting proper benchmark tools and the impact of various hardware, software, and OS settings, thereby proving the need for detailed documentation. We further demonstrated that the observations made in microbenchmark analysis are well reflected in real-world application scenarios.

To this end we investigated the performance characteristics of DGEMM, sparse matrix-vector multiplication, and HPCG. For the first time, a roofline model of HPCG and its components was established and successfully validated for both architectures. Performance modeling was used as a guiding tool throughout this work to get deeper insight and explain anomalies.

Future work will include investigation of benchmarks for random and latency-bound codes along with the development of suitable performance models. The existing and further upcoming wide range of architectures will bring more parameters and benchmarking challenges, which will be very interesting and worthwhile to investigate.

**Acknowledgments.** We are indebted to Thomas Zeiser and Michael Meier (RRZE) for providing a reliable benchmarking environment. This work was partially funded via the ESSEX project in the DFG priority programme 1648 (SPPEXA) and by the German Ministry of Science and Education (BMBF) under project number 01IH16012C (SeASiTe).

# References

1. Intel 64 and IA-32 Architectures Optimization Reference Manual. Intel Press, 2016 June 2016. http://www.intel.com/content/dam/www/public/us/en/documents/manuals/64-ia-32-architectures-optimization-manual.pdf
2. Afzal, A., Hager, G., Wellein, G.: Desynchronization and wave pattern formation in MPI-parallel and hybrid memory-bound programs (2020). https://arxiv.org/abs/2002.02989. Accepted for ISC High Performance 2020
3. Alappat, C.L., et al.: A recursive algebraic coloring technique for hardware-efficient symmetric sparse matrix-vector multiplication (2020). Accepted for publication in ACM Transactions on Parallel Computing.https://doi.org/10.1145/3399732
4. ARM: ARM Cortex-A75 Core Technical Reference Manual - Write streaming mode. http://infocenter.arm.com/help/index.jsp?topic=/com.arm.doc.100403_0200_00_en/lto1473834732563.html. Accessed 26 Mar 2020
5. Davis, T.A., Hu, Y.: The University of Florida sparse matrix collection. ACM Trans. Math. Softw. **38**(1), 1:1–1:25 (2011). http://doi.acm.org/10.1145/2049662.2049663
6. Hammond, S., et al.: Evaluating the Marvell ThunderX2 server processor for HPC workloads. In: The 6th Special Session on High-Performance Computing Benchmarking and Optimization (HPBench 2019) (2019)
7. Hammond, S., Vaughan, C., Hughes, C.: Evaluating the Intel Skylake Xeon processor for HPC workloads. In: 2018 International Conference on High Performance Computing Simulation (HPCS), pp. 342–349, July 2018. https://doi.org/10.1109/HPCS.2018.00064
8. Wong, H.: Intel Ivy Bridge Cache replacement policy. http://blog.stuffedcow.net/2013/01/ivb-cache-replacement/
9. Hofmann, J., Fey, D., Eitzinger, J., Hager, G., Wellein, G.: Analysis of Intel's haswell microarchitecture using the ECM model and microbenchmarks. In: Hannig, F., Cardoso, J.M.P., Pionteck, T., Fey, D., Schröder-Preikschat, W., Teich, J. (eds.) ARCS 2016. LNCS, vol. 9637, pp. 210–222. Springer, Cham (2016). https://doi.org/10.1007/978-3-319-30695-7_16

10. Hofmann, J., Hager, G., Fey, D.: On the accuracy and usefulness of analytic energy models for contemporary multicore processors. In: Yokota, R., Weiland, M., Keyes, D., Trinitis, C. (eds.) ISC High Performance 2018. LNCS, vol. 10876, pp. 22–43. Springer, Cham (2018). https://doi.org/10.1007/978-3-319-92040-5_2

11. Hofmann, J., Hager, G., Wellein, G., Fey, D.: An analysis of core- and chip-level architectural features in four generations of intel server processors. In: Kunkel, J.M., Yokota, R., Balaji, P., Keyes, D. (eds.) ISC 2017. LNCS, vol. 10266, pp. 294–314. Springer, Cham (2017). https://doi.org/10.1007/978-3-319-58667-0_16

12. Malas, T.M., Hager, G., Ltaief, H., Keyes, D.E.: Multidimensional intratile parallelization for memory-starved stencil computations. ACM Trans. Parallel Comput. **4**(3), 12:1–12:32 (2017). http://doi.acm.org/10.1145/3155290

13. Marjanović, V., Gracia, J., Glass, C.W.: Performance modeling of the HPCG benchmark. In: Jarvis, S.A., Wright, S.A., Hammond, S.D. (eds.) PMBS 2014. LNCS, vol. 8966, pp. 172–192. Springer, Cham (2015). https://doi.org/10.1007/978-3-319-17248-4_9

14. McCalpin, J.D.: Memory bandwidth and machine balance in current high performance computers. IEEE Comput. Soc. Tech. Comm. Comput. Archit. (TCCA) Newsl. **2**, 19–25 (1995)

15. McIntosh-Smith, S., Price, J., Deakin, T., Poenaru, A.: A performance analysis of the first generation of HPC-optimized arm processors. Concurr. Comput.: Pract. Exp. **31**(16), e5110 (2019). https://onlinelibrary.wiley.com/doi/abs/10.1002/cpe.5110. e5110 cpe.5110

16. McVoy, L., Staelin, C.: Lmbench: portable tools for performance analysis. In: Proceedings of the 1996 Annual Conference on USENIX Annual Technical Conference ATEC 1996, pp. 23–23. USENIX Association, Berkeley (1996). http://dl.acm.org/citation.cfm?id=1268299.1268322

17. Molka, D., Hackenberg, D., Schöne, R.: Main memory and cache performance of Intel Sandy Bridge and AMD Bulldozer. In: Proceedings of the Workshop on Memory Systems Performance and Correctness MSPC 2014, pp. 4:1–4:10. ACM, New York (2014). http://doi.acm.org/10.1145/2618128.2618129

18. Pieper, A., et al.: High-performance implementation of Chebyshev filter diagonalization for interior eigenvalue computations. J. Comput. Phys. **325**, 226–243 (2016). http://www.sciencedirect.com/science/article/pii/S0021999116303837

19. Qureshi, M.K., Jaleel, A., Patt, Y.N., Steely, S.C., Emer, J.: Adaptive insertion policies for high performance caching. In: Proceedings of the 34th Annual International Symposium on Computer Architecture ISCA 2007, pp. 381–391. ACM, New York (2007). http://doi.acm.org/10.1145/1250662.1250709

20. Saini, S., Hood, R.: Performance evaluation of Intel Broadwell nodes based supercomputer using computational fluid dynamics and climate applications. In: 2017 IEEE 19th International Conference on High Performance Computing and Communications Workshops (HPCCWS), pp. 58–65, December 2017. https://doi.org/10.1109/HPCCWS.2017.00015

21. Saini, S., Hood, R., Chang, J., Baron, J.: Performance evaluation of an Intel Haswell- and Ivy Bridge-based supercomputer using scientific and engineering applications. In: 2016 IEEE 18th International Conference on High Performance Computing and Communications; IEEE 14th International Conference on Smart City; IEEE 2nd International Conference on Data Science and Systems (HPCC/SmartCity/DSS), pp. 1196–1203, December 2016. https://doi.org/10.1109/HPCC-SmartCity-DSS.2016.0167

22. Staar, P.W.J., et al.: Stochastic matrix-function estimators: scalable big-data kernels with high performance. In: 2016 IEEE International Parallel and Distributed Processing Symposium (IPDPS), pp. 812–821, May 2016. https://doi.org/10.1109/IPDPS.2016.34

23. Suhov, A.Y.: An accurate polynomial approximation of exponential integrators. J. Sci. Comput. **60**(3), 684–698 (2014). https://doi.org/10.1007/s10915-013-9813-x

24. Treibig, J., Hager, G., Wellein, G.: likwid-bench: an extensible microbenchmarking platform for x86 multicore compute nodes. In: Brunst, H., Müller, M., Nagel, W., Resch, M. (eds.) Parallel Tools Workshop, pp. 27–36. Springer, Heidelberg (2011). https://doi.org/10.1007/978-3-642-31476-6_3

25. Wellein, G., Hager, G., Zeiser, T., Wittmann, M., Fehske, H.: Efficient temporal blocking for stencil computations by multicore-aware wavefront parallelization. In: 2009 33rd Annual IEEE International Computer Software and Applications Conference, vol. 1, pp. 579–586, July 2009. https://doi.org/10.1109/COMPSAC.2009.82

# Timemory: Modular Performance Analysis for HPC

Jonathan R. Madsen[1]([✉]), Muaaz G. Awan[1], Hugo Brunie[1], Jack Deslippe[1],
Rahul Gayatri[1], Leonid Oliker[2], Yunsong Wang[1], Charlene Yang[1],
and Samuel Williams[2]

[1] NERSC, Lawrence Berkeley National Laboratory, Berkeley, CA, USA
jrmadsen@lbl.gov
[2] CRD, Lawrence Berkeley National Laboratory, Berkeley, CA, USA

**Abstract.** HPC has undergone a significant transition toward heterogeneous architectures. This transition has introduced several issues in
code migration to support multiple frameworks for targeting the various architectures. In order to cope with these challenges, projects such
as Kokkos and LLVM create abstractions which map a generic front-
end API to the backend that supports the targeted architecture. This
paper presents a complementary framework for performance measurement and analysis. Several performance measurement and analysis tools
in existence provide their capabilities through various methods but the
common theme among these tools are prohibitive limitations in terms
of user-level extensions. For this reason, software developers commonly
have to learn multiple tools and valuable analysis methods, such as
the roofline model, are frequently required to be generated manually.
The timemory framework provides complete modularity for performance
measurement and analysis and eliminates all restrictions on user-level
extensions. The timemory framework also provides a highly-efficient and
intuitive method for handling multiple tools/measurements (*i.e.,* "components") concurrently. The intersection of these characteristics provide
ample evidence that timemory can serve as the common interface for
existing performance measurement and analysis tools. Timemory components are developed in C++ but includes multi-language support for
C, Fortran, and Python codes. Numerous components are provided by
the library itself – including, but not limited to, timers, memory usage,
hardware counters, and FLOP and instruction roofline models. Additionally, analysis of the intrinsic overhead demonstrates superior performance
in comparison with popular tools.

**Keywords:** C · C++ · Python · CUDA · Fortran · Instrumentation ·
Timing · Memory · Performance · Cross-platform · Measurement ·
Cross-language · Analysis · Hardware-counters · Roofline · MPI ·
CUPTI · PAPI · Gotcha · UPC++ · gperftools · TAU · Caliper ·
LIKWID · Score-P · VTune · NVTX · ERT · Timemory

P. Sadayappan et al. (Eds.): ISC High Performance 2020, LNCS 12151, pp. 434–452, 2020.
https://doi.org/10.1007/978-3-030-50743-5_22

# 1   Introduction

A straightforward modular system for user-defined performance measurements and analysis is notably absent from the vast ecosystem of specialized and generic tools for sophisticated performance measurements and reflective analysis. The modular compiler infrastructure provided by LLVM [18] is an excellent example of the benefits of modularity and has resulted in the development of a number of tools filling various generic and specialized needs [19]. The programming model abstractions provided by Kokkos [7] is an excellent example of using C++ templates to provide a generic and flexible front-end that adapts to the targeted architecture at compile-time. Timemory attempts to provide the analogue to the LLVM infrastructure and Kokkos model in the realm of performance measurement and analysis. The framework provides a viable solution to a common instrumentation interface [5] for multiplexing performance measurement and analysis tools. As a common instrumentation interface, timemory would provide a straightforward method for projects with existing instrumentation APIs to locally[1] wrap their existing API and introduce a significant number of new capabilities to the existing tool[2] while requiring no significant changes to the tool itself. Projects that adopt the timemory framework gain the capability to arbitrarily define multiple bundles of performance measurement and analysis tools to the need of the project and can customize the activation or deactivation of these tools in any manner desired. This paper will outline the current state of performance tools, highlight several key innovations developed in timemory, and then provide examples which demonstrate how these innovations have enabled an extensive suite of tools and capabilities.

The timemory library is written in C++14 using template metaprogramming, is presently available for codes written in C, C++, Python, and Fortran, and supports interoperability with CUDA, MPI, UPC++, and various forms of multi-threading. Overall, the contributions through timemory include:

- Common performance measurement and analysis framework with full support for user-level extensions
- Common framework for: generation of custom event-based, statistical, and/or instrumentation profilers, custom preload libraries, and tool multiplexing
- Type-safe method for arbitrarily wrapping existing tools which can store data in any valid C++ data type
- Highly-efficient instrumentation API with almost negligible overhead when disabled at runtime
- Static and dynamic generation of arbitrary component bundles
- Intermixed call-stack tracing, timeline tracing, and flat-profiling
- Intermixed usage of different tool bundles[3].

---

[1] *i.e.,* within the existing project's code and without any required changes upstream to timemory.

[2] Cross-language support, JSON/XML/text output, call-graphs, statistical analysis, plotting, sampling, MPI support, UPC++ support, multi-threading support.

[3] *e.g.,* Bundle of A, B, and C can be used alongside bundle of A, C, and D and/or bundle of E, F, and G.

# 2    Motivation

## 2.1    Need for Composite Components

A variety of performance measurement and analysis tools co-exist in the HPC ecosystem. Well known examples include TAU [26], Caliper [6], HPCToolkit [1], and LIKWID [28]. Each one of these tools provide their capabilities via design abstractions around the lower-level interfaces for the hardware and generally build upon the work of more specialized libraries such as PAPI [27], CUPTI [9], and Linux perf [11]. However, each tool tends to have a special set of features in order to provide a unique draw and use case scenario. The special set of feature(s) provided by the tools form a complementary set of capabilities with other tools which make them worthwhile to use in combination, however in order to provide these features, there is commonly a redundancy in basic functionality[4] [17]. The most disparate properties among these tools is the data storage model, control methods, and input/output schema. The data storage model is influenced heavily by the design of the library and very few libraries directly expose methods for accessing the raw data handled by the library. The plausible culprit for the commonality of obscuring the data storage model is the type-obfuscation that arises from either the common C-style generic design patterns, which commonly restrict supported data types to those listed in an enumeration, and the C++-style generic design pattern of dynamic polymorphism, which requires non-templated types for virtual functions. Thus, providing access to the data model is not only prone to complexity and lack of type-safety but it may also have to be completely re-factored to support new features which necessitate adding explicit support for new data types.

The timemory library presents an unique solution to these challenges. Through the use of C++ template meta-programming, a package can expose any number of unique C++ classes that encapsulate a performance measurement or analysis pattern. The C++ classes have only one core requirement: a public type declaration of the `value_type` used by the component, which can be any valid C++ data type, including `void`. In timemory, only the names for the functions are required to be consistent and there are no restrictions on the data types that non-void functions return. Thus, one component can implement the data access member function `get()` to return a floating-point value and another component can implement this member function to return an array of integers. Once this minimal set of requirements is provided, the component can be bundled alongside any number of other components into a single handle. Various other capabilities/features can be activated within a component simply through implementing the corresponding member function inside the component. These member functions are optional due to extensive use of SFINAE and empty base-class implementations of these functions. Additionally, components

---

[4] Support for various parallelization models, data acquisition techniques (instrumentation, sampling, etc.), and injection techniques (symbol overloading, binary modification, etc.).

can be designed as composites of other components. This building-block characteristic is unique to the framework and strengthens the argument for timemory
as the universal interface for performance measurement and analysis.

## 2.2  Need for Common Instrumentation Interface

Numerous tools provide instrumentation APIs that are directly inserted into the
application source code. The instrumentation APIs for many tools provide the
capability to enable/disable a tool when connected, provide context labels for
code regions, and track simple event metrics. Common examples include the
ittnotify [8] API for Intel's VTune Amplifier and Advisor, NVTX for NVIDIA's
Nsight and NVprof, gperftools, LIKWID, TAU, and Score-P [17]. Some of these
tools center their usage around a command-line tool while other tools, such as
the Caliper package, focus their usage around instrumentation markers.

The potential for performance degradation via instrumentation APIs, even
when dormant at runtime, is supported by the results of applying an edge-case
scenario of injecting 500,000 runtime-disabled instrumentation points within a
matrix multiplication benchmark (Fig. 1) to Caliper, TAU, and timemory [5].
Unlike statistical profilers which take measurements at a given rate, the overhead of deterministic instrumentation cannot be fully negated and the overhead
associated with the instrumentation is subject to high variability: Caliper markers increased run time by ~397% while TAU markers increased run time by
~262%. These overheads stand in stark contrast to the methods provided by
timemory, which increased the runtime by a minimum of ~42% and a maximum
of ~82%. The primary objective of timemory is not to serve as a replacement for
Caliper, TAU, etc. but, instead, provide a common, easily extendable interface

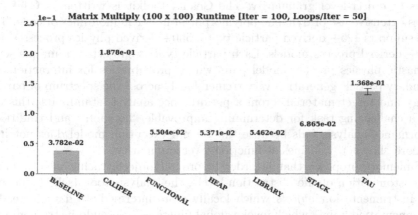

**Fig. 1.** Average (samples = 100) runtime of 500,000 dormant instrumentations for
100 × 100 Matrix-Multiply Calculation. BASELINE is without instrumentation, CALIPER
is with Caliper instrumentation, TAU is with TAU instrumentation, and remaining
data points (FUNCTIONAL, HEAP, LIBRARY, STACK) use different models of timemory
instrumentation, where each model has different compile-time and runtime capabilities.

for the deployment of performance analysis tools which is optimized for minimal overhead when not being utilized. With concerns about unintentional overhead minimized, HPC developers can safely provide built-in performance monitoring which can deploy whichever performance tool(s) are available for a given architecture. Significant progress towards this objective has been achieved: at present, timemory provides one or more components for ARM-MAP, Caliper, TAU, LIK-WID, CrayPAT, Intel VTune, Intel Advisor, gperftools, CUDA, NVTX, CUPTI, and PAPI.

### 2.3   Need for Object-Level Analysis Granularity

Profiling tools generally support one or more granularities for reporting performance measurements: functions, addresses, lines, and files, in descending order of commonality. However, object-oriented programming is a widely utilized paradigm in HPC and is supported by C++, Fortran, and Python. The tasking and object-oriented model presents a challenge for performance measurements frameworks using a procedural design. Since the lifetime of objects typically overlap, these designs struggle to distinguish measurements from different objects when only the function, file, and line metadata is available. In other words, object-oriented codes violate the LIFO model of function call-stacks that these frameworks might rely upon. Furthermore, providing measurements and analysis for an object introduces a configuration issue for the tool when objects derive from abstract objects because the tool (ideally) should support the user coalescing the data at an arbitrary abstraction granularity of their choosing.

The Geant4 toolkit [2] – a Monte Carlo particle transport toolkit for the simulation of the passage of particles through matter[5] – provides an excellent example of the need for a new performance analysis model that tracks measurements at object-level granularity. The Geant4 toolkit is written in C++ and makes extensive use of dynamic polymorphism in ∼1 million lines of code. This code supports 125+ derived particle types, 550+ derived physics processes, and 1000+ derived process models. Each particle type is subject to a unique set of stochastic physics process model pairs whose probabilities for interaction and secondary particle generation vary tremendously across the spectrum of particle energy and target material. From a performance analysis standpoint, this creates a challenging task for determining improvable "hotspots" and traditional performance analysis fails because the Geant4 execution model does not have any core "hotspot" routines at function-level granularity.

Timemory proposes that in order to provide object tracing measurements and customization of the abstraction-level[6], the analysis tool itself should provide instrumentation *objects* which locally store intermediate data instead of instrumentation points which invoke global functions or pseudo-instrumentation objects which couple the global function invocations to RAII. With this intermediate storage design, these instrumentation objects can be inserted into the

---

[5] *i.e.,* Radiation shielding, particle accelerator simulations, nuclear reactor design.
[6] *i.e.,* Ability to associate measurements with either the derived or abstract object.

target object itself at the desired abstraction-level, be treated by the application as just another member variable, increase data locality for measurements, and support asynchronous paradigms. Timemory also proposes that a well-designed framework adhering to these principles should provide multiple variants of these instrumentation objects which (A) utilize RAII to easily couple of the measurement scope to the scope of the target object and (B) permit the insertion or activation of different analysis types during compilation and/or runtime.

## 3  Library Design

The timemory library is implemented in C++14 with the curiously recurring template pattern (CRTP) style and was designed from the outset to:

- Allow for user-level implementations of tools (also called "components")
- Allow for components to store measurements in an arbitrary data type
- Allow for arbitrary bundling of tools into a single handle
- Fully support modularity
- Utilize thread-local memory to minimize synchronization bottlenecks
- Strictly avoid spawning background work in library core
- Minimize any runtime logic which can be evaluated at compile-time
- Minimize overhead when enabled at compile-time but disabled at runtime
- Provide an easy-to-use interface.

A sample of the basic design of timemory in C++ is demonstrated in Listing 1.1.

**Listing 1.1.** Sample Usage in C++ of bundle of tools combining: wall-clock timer, peak memory measurement, and various markers for external tools which are removed at compile-time when not available.

```
1   #include <timemory/timemory.hpp>
2   using namespace tim::component;
3   using markers_t = type_list<nvtx_marker, likwid_marker, tau_marker>;
4   using tools_t = tim::component_tuple<wall_clock, peak_rss, markers_t>;
5
6   void foo() {
7       tools_t obj("foo");      // create marker
8       obj.start();             // start all components
9       sleep(1);                // sleep for 1 second
10      obj.stop();              // stop all components
11      // access specific component
12      wall_clock* wc      = obj.get<wall_clock>();
13      double      elapsed = wc->get();      // computed value
14      std::string unit    = wall_clock::display_unit();
15      // Output: "Wall time: 1.000 sec"
16      printf("Wall time: %f %s\n", elapsed, unit.c_str());
17  }
```

## 3.1  Components

Timemory uses the term "component" to refer to a single structure that provides a certain functionality in the form of a "caliper" (*i.e.*, a region enclosed by a `start` and `stop`). The definition of a component is straightforward and a sample is provided in Listing 1.2. In general, a component inherits from a templated base class and specifies itself as the first template parameter and the data type that the component will be using to store the metric (if any). The data type can be any valid C++ data type, *e.g.*, `int`, `double`, `vector<MyClass>`, etc. Components that accumulate no internal data, such as a component that just forwards the marker labels to another tool, can designate the data type as `void`.

**Listing 1.2.** Sample component in timemory. The macros `TIMEMORY_<XYZ>` are used for type declarations and setting type-traits which activate various features for the type, *e.g.*, statistics, unit conversion support, category-specific formatting, etc.

```
1  TIMEMORY_DECLARE_COMPONENT(wall_clock)
2  TIMEMORY_CONCRETE_TRAIT(uses_timing_units, wall_clock, true_type)
3  TIMEMORY_CONCRETE_TRAIT(is_timing_category, wall_clock, true_type)
4  TIMEMORY_STATISTICS_TYPE(wall_clock, double)
5
6  struct wall_clock : public base<wall_clock, int64_t>
7  {
8      static string     label()       { return "wall"; }
9      static string     description() { return "wall-clock timer"; }
10     static value_type record()      { return get_time_now(); }
11     // 'value' and 'accum' are inherited int64_t
12     void   start() { value = record(); }
13     void   stop()  { value = (record() - value); accum += value; }
14     // 'get_units()' is base-class func controlled via type-traits
15     double get() const            { return accum * get_units(); }
16  };
```

Several type-traits are provided to customize functionality, provide default output formatting, unit support and conversions, etc. The details of the various type-traits are beyond the scope of this paper with the exception of the most important type-trait with respect to portability: `is_available`. This type-trait creates a template meta-programming system through which a type can be forward declared, and thus be portably declared as a component in a bundle, but filtered out entirely from the template specification before the type is instantiated when `is_available` evaluates to false. Thus, `tuple<A, B, C>` will be implicitly implemented as `tuple<A, B>` if component `C` is not available. The timemory-provided components which rely on external packages use the absence of the package-specific pre-processor definition (*e.g.*, `TIMEMORY_USE_PAPI`) to set the `is_available` type-trait to false. In addition to the portability benefits, this feature also allows timemory to minimally function as a header-only library for C++ codes.

## 3.2  Data Storage

The data storage for each component type is handled dynamically via storage class singletons that are templated on the component type. Each storage class singleton maintains a unique call-graph per-thread (see Fig. 2) for components which store data. This call-graph handles the accumulation of data throughout the application and supports arbitrarily mixing hierarchical, timeline, and flat node insertion modes. This approach also enables an arbitrary number of components to operate independently by eliminating the need for fixed array limits on the number of tools that can concurrently allocate storage space. Furthermore, since the component-specific storage is templated on the component type, the data storage model ensures complete type-safety.

## 3.3  Parallelism Support

The timemory framework supports both MPI and UPC++ for distributed memory parallelism and neither backend imposes any communication overhead during the application execution outside of the one-time communication to the zeroth rank during finalization and output. Within a process, timemory makes careful use of static and thread-local static storage singletons to provide an efficient model for multi-threading which is highly scalable for HPC. The data storage model is entirely free from the use of synchronization primitives (*i.e.*, locks) outside of the construction and destruction of the storage singleton on a worker

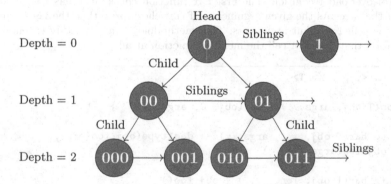

**Fig. 2.** Call-graph per component. Each node is keyed to a label (*e.g.*, function name, file, and line number) and contains an instance of the component. The component instance within the call-graph provides data-storage only. When a new component instance is created and assigned a label, the component searches the children of the current node for a matching key. If no matching key is found, the component creates a new node. The address of the node is stored internally in the component and when the component instance is stopped, the instances adds its data to the component at that node address and resets it's internal data to zero. Thus, temporary component instances are fully responsible for finding and creating new nodes for persistent storage and updating those nodes.

thread. During the construction of the storage singleton on a worker thread, the master instance is locked to ensure the worker-thread can safely bookmark (perform a copy) the current instrumentation stack location. Beyond this point, no synchronization is performed until the worker thread terminates and cleans up the thread-local memory. At this point, the manager thread is locked and the instrumentation stack from the worker thread is inserted as a child of the bookmarked location on the master thread.

## 3.4 Bundling Components

Timemory provides variadic template wrappers that allow multiple components to be bundled together into a single handle whose member functions correspond to the invocation of the similarly named member function for each component. The variadic template wrappers rely on the temporary construction of operation classes which are templated per-component (see Listing 1.3). These operation classes are the key to the flexibility of timemory. These classes provide both the ability to specialize the behavior of a component in a multiplexing scenario (see Listing 1.4) and provide a generic interface for calling similarly named member functions with different signatures per component through the use of SFINAE (see Listing 1.3). The instantiation and translation of these concepts for a generic variadic wrapper (Listing 1.5) is demonstrated in Listing 1.6.

**Listing 1.3.** Sample `foo` operation struct that is templated on a component. SFINAE is used to determine desired call signature at compile-time and `int` and `long` are used to control overload resolution. The first `bar` function checks if T has `foo()` member function that accepts the given arguments. If this check fails, then the `foo()` member function is called without arguments. This methodology can be easily extended to a third option that does not call the member function at all.

```
template <typename T>
struct foo {
    foo(T obj, args...) { bar(obj, 0, args...);  }

    auto bar(T obj, int, args...) -> decltype(obj.foo(args...), void())
    { obj.foo(args...);  }

    void bar(T obj, long, ...) { obj.foo();  }
};
```

**Listing 1.4.** Sample specialization of `foo` operation struct from Listing 1.3 for component **A** where it is known that **A** does not accept arguments and has `foo()` member function

```
template <> struct foo<A> { foo(T obj, ...) { obj.foo(); } };
```

**Listing 1.5.** Sample of internals from generic variadic component wrapper (`template <typename... T> struct` **`component_tuple`**) combining concepts from Listing 1.2 and Listing 1.3. Template parameters are omitted for readability.

```
// generic data type held by component_tuple<T...>
tuple<T...> m_data;
// generic foo member function for component_tuple<T...>
void foo(args...) { apply<operation::foo<T>...>(m_data, args...); }
    };
```

**Listing 1.6.** Sample of internals from generic variadic component wrapper `component_tuple<A, B>` when Listing 1.5 is instantiated with types A and B. Template parameters are omitted for readability.

```
// data type held by component_tuple<A, B>
tuple<A, B> m_data;
// foo member function for component_tuple<A, B> after instantiation
void foo(args...) {
    operation::foo<A>(get<0>(m_data), args...);
    operation::foo<B>(get<1>(m_data), args...); }
};
```

The variadic wrappers are provided in numerous flavors for compile-time and runtime configuration via various type-traits, configuration bundles, callbacks, and custom environment variables. These various methods are provided to empower projects to build in custom schemes for utilizing their bundles which conform to the standard configuration methods of the project itself. Thus, the timemory framework facilitates the generation of easy-to-use built-in performance diagnostic tools that can be quickly switched on by developers and users when performance analysis is either desired or required.

## 4   Profiling Capabilities

Profilers generally fall into two broad categories: statistical profilers which operate via sampling and instrumentation profilers. Instrumentation profilers effectively inject additional instructions into the binary and are implemented through several methods: manually, automatic source-level (tool that modifies source-code), compiler-assisted, binary translation (tool that modifies compiled binary), runtime instrumentation (tool that supervises and controls execution after temporarily injecting instrumentation), and runtime injection (a lightweight form of runtime instrumentation that instruments jumps to helpers functions). At present, timemory supports manual instrumentation, runtime instrumentation for dynamically-linked binaries via Gotcha [23], binary translation, runtime instrumentation, and a simple command-line execution wrapper similar to the UNIX command-line tool `time` except with extensions to include memory and I/O values and rates and hardware counters. Additionally, timemory distributes a number of "instrumentation libraries" which provide simple function interfaces for activating instrumentation around performance monitoring APIs exposed by several commonly-used APIs, *e.g.,* Kokkos, MPI, and OpenMP. These instrumentation libraries can be directly inserted into the application codes or injected externally via binary translation or runtime instrumentation. For Python codes, the timemory package supports context-managers and decorators for instrumenting specific functions and regions of code and can also leverage the built-in debugging and profiling capabilities of the interpreter.

**Dynamic Instrumentation.** Timemory provides a command-line tool, `timemory-run`, for runtime instrumentation and binary translation of dynamically- and statically-linked binaries via the Dyninst [4] toolkit. The command-line tool combines a number of features derived from various positive experiences with existing profiling tools. These features include: using regular expressions (regex) and/or text files for precise selection of which modules and functions to instrument (inclusive, exclusive, and inclusive/exclusive unions), lightweight stub instrumentation during binary translation for `LD_PRELOAD`, loop instrumentation, defining the default set of components during binary translation, insertion of user-defined functions from custom instrumentation libraries, and two different modes which offer a choice between whether the dynamic instrumentation is affected by manual timemory instrumentation with the C/C++/Fortran library interface. With respect to these two different "modes" of instrumentation, an application using manual timemory instrumentation may be precisely configured at a high-level to collect different components in different regions of the code and dynamic instrumentation may be deployed for fine-grained analysis. In one scenario, a user may want to keep these precise configurations intact as a reference point for the overhead of the fine-grained analysis. In another scenario, the user may want to propagate these precise configurations to the dynamic instrumentation. The aforementioned "modes" of instrumentation address these two scenarios. In one mode, the set of components collected by the dynamic instrumentation points are configurable via its own distinct environment variable and unaffected by changes to the component collection set via the library interface. In the second mode, instrumentation is synchronized with the manual instrumentation: both the manual and dynamic instrumentation are configurable with the same environment variable and modifications to the instrumentation component set via the library interface are applied to the dynamic instrumentation.

**Statistical Profiling.** At present, timemory does not provide an API for the generation of performance measurements via sampling on par with the facilities for instrumentation. However, the need for this capability was factored into the design of the library and is currently being deployed in the `timem` execution wrapper. This command-line tool is similar to the UNIX `time` command except it extends the measurement set beyond timers to include resource usage and hardware counter measurements. This command-line tool uses a fork + execv model and thus, in order to post-process and produce output, only the parent process can invoke start and stop on the component bundle since the child process never returns. Although this model does not present issues for numerous components that either inherently include or are configurable to include activity within child processes, certain components such as those which read from Linux process ID files (*e.g.,* /proc/<PID>/statm) or hardware counters must record measurements at or very near the end of the child process but before the child process exits and execution on the parent process resumes (where stop on the component bundle in the parent process is called). Thus, when building this command-line tool, the components with this criteria must be customized to sample their value(s) during an interrupt and measurements during the stop operation must be either be discarded or the operation itself should not be invoked. Through the use of a local specialization on the corresponding operation classes introduced in Sect. 3.4, this is easily accomplished: operation::start<T> and operation::stop< T> for any component T requiring sampling is locally specialized so that the start and stop member functions of an instance of T are never invoked when start or stop is invoked on the component bundle and operation::sample<T> is specialized for these components to update their values accordingly. The success of this model for the timem executable will likely serve as a template for the creation of independent sampling libraries which can be inserted into applications directly and/or through the dynamic instrumentation command-line tool.

**Gotcha Support.** The timemory library simplifies using Gotcha for re-writing the Global Offset Table on the Linux operating system that links inter-library call-sites and variable references to their targets. In general, a set of components for performance measurement or analysis can be injected around any externally linked function in as little as 2–3 lines of code plus one line for each function to be wrapped.

Listing 1.7 demonstrates a hypothetical timemory Gotcha implementation which wraps a wall-clock timer around the C exp(double) function and a C++ function, sum_exp, which takes an array of floating-point values and accumulates the result of calling exp in each value. Thus, invocation of the sum_exp function with two floating-point values results in a nested hierarchy of one wall-clock measurement around sum_exp at depth 0 and two wall-clock measurements around exp as children of sum_exp in the call-graph (see Listing 1.8).

**Listing 1.7.** Sample Gotcha specification around two external dynamically-linked functions: exp and sum_exp

```
1  using wc_t  = component_tuple<wall_clock>;
2  using got_t = gotcha<2, wc_t>;
3
4  extern "C" double exp(double);
5  double sum_exp(vector<double>);
6
7  int main() {
```

```
 8 │  got_t::get_initializer() = [](){
 9 │  { TIMEMORY_C_GOTCHA   (got_t, 0, exp);
10 │    TIMEMORY_CXX_GOTCHA(got_t, 1, sum_exp); };
11 │
12 │    auto_tuple<got_t> obj("example");
13 │    auto ret = sum_exp({ 1.0, 2.0});
14 │ }
```

**Listing 1.8.** Abbreviated output for Listing 1.7

| LABEL        | COUNT | DEPTH | METRIC | UNITS | SUM   |
|--------------|-------|-------|--------|-------|-------|
| >>> sum_exp  | 1     | 0     | wall   | msec  | 0.072 |
| >>> \|_exp    | 2     | 1     | wall   | msec  | 0.043 |

In addition to instrumenting functions, the timemory Gotcha component can be used to provide wholesale function replacement of the Gotcha wrappee when (1) a third template parameter is provided, (2) the third template parameter is a timemory component, and (3) the timemory component provided as the third template parameter has an overloaded function operator (operator()) whose return type and arguments match the function being wrapped, e.g., to replace double exp(double), the timemory component provided as the third template parameter must provide double operator()(double). Thus, not only can the timemory Gotcha component be utilized to instrument external function calls but it can also be utilized to provide wholesale replacement of external function calls for optimization, as illustrated in Sect. 5.2. Finally, similar to the operator() overloading scheme, components which are instrumenting functions instead of replacing them can provide void audit(Args...) member functions where Args... matches the function parameter types of the original function and/or the return type of the original function to gain access to the values of the input parameters before the original function is invoked and the return value of the original function before it returns.[7]

**Instrumentation Libraries.** Timemory distributes several stand-alone libraries which can be utilized to activate instrumentation around APIs which provide their own performance monitoring framework, e.g., Kokkos, MPI, and OpenMP. With respect to Kokkos, timemory generates one traditional profiling library whose selection of components is configurable via environment variables at runtime and then over a dozen of pre-configured profiling libraries with dedicated functionality, e.g., kp_timemory_trip_count.so is explicitly configured to collect trip-counts, kp_timemory_cpu_flops.so is explicitly configured to count floating-point operations, etc. Concerning OpenMP, timemory distributes a library that provides instrumentation via the OMPT [13] call-back system.

---

[7] Users can also alternatively provide void audit(string, Args...) if the (demangled) name of the function is required.

For MPI, timemory distributes a library which leverages it's Gotcha capabilities to wrap the equivalent of the PMPI [22] interface without breaking any existing user-defined MPI functions using the PMPI interface. Additionally, both the OpenMP and MPI instrumentation libraries provide reference counting modes to enable scoped instrumentation. Although these libraries will satisfy the needs of the vast majority of use cases, we would like to note that the implementation of these instrumentation libraries is straight-forward and the MPI and OpenMP instrumentation libraries require less than 100 lines of code – with minimal effort these libraries can be customized to include user-defined components which, when paired with the Gotcha method to wrap the targeted function call, can produce instrumentation libraries which are capable of replacing the original function call or analyzing the input parameters and return values of the function call and then inserted into the binary via the dynamic instrumentation tool.

# 5   Novel Use Cases

## 5.1   Performance Measurements and Analysis in Geant4

Section 3.4 introduced the concept of using timemory to build an extensible, built-in performance measurement and analysis framework that conforms to the design of the project. This concept was put into practice within the Geant4 toolkit, whose description was provided in Sect. 2.3.

The Geant4 source code implements a G4TiMemory header file which provides empty macro replacements when Geant4 is configured without timemory support. When Geant4 is configured with timemory support, Geant4 takes advantage of the pre-defined `tim::auto_timer` bundle to instrument always-on high-level measurements around approximately two dozen core routines. To provide user-customizable performance analysis in low-level functions invoked at a high frequencies, Geant4 defines a `G4Profiler` class templated on the value of the profiler type enumeration and a variadic list of types that form an instrumentation context (see Listing 1.9). Using this scheme, each instrumentation instance can arbitrarily adapt to the runtime data analyzed in the callbacks and selectively: enable/disable the instrumentation, customize the label, and add/remove components.

**Listing 1.9.** Geant4 Profiler Definitions for timemory. The `query`, `label`, and `tweak` functions apply their arguments to call-backs provided by the user-application. `G4ProfilerBundle` is an alias to the timemory `user_bundle` component which provides an interface for manipulating an array of components during runtime.

```
template <size_t Category, typename... Types>
class G4Profiler {
    using type     = tim::auto_tuple<G4ProfilerBundle<Category>>;
    static bool    query(Types...);
    static string  label(Types...);
    static type&   tweak(type&, Types...);
};
```

**Listing 1.10.** Hypothetical User Configuration of G4TrackProfiler which only instruments Electrons, customizes the label to reflect the physical volume of track, and defaults to wall-clock and thread-specific cpu-clock timers for instrumentation unless the electron energy is below 100 keV, at which point the API supplements the instrumentation to include data collection for the classical roofline plot on the CPU. Data types abbreviated for readability, assume all code is specifically applied to the G4TrackProfiler.

```
get_query()   = [](G4Track* t) { return t->GetType() == Electron; };
get_labeler() = [](G4Track* t) { return t->GetVolumeName(); };
get_tweak()   = [](auto& p, G4Track* t) {
    if(t->GetEnergy() < 100.*keV) { p.insert<cpu_roofline_flops>(); }
    return p;
configure<wall_clock, thread_cpu_clock>();
};
```

## 5.2   Mixed-Precision Analysis

Floating-point arithmetic [15,16] is ubiquitous in High Performance Computing applications and it is the source of numerical bugs [10]. Due to the complexity of understanding the impact of floating-point arithmetic on result accuracy, many applications are written entirely with double precision despite the growing gap between half, single, and double precision performance [21].

The precision required in different phases of an application to achieve the desired precision in the result remains an open question. One of the projects at NERSC consists of developing a systematic approach to optimize scientific applications using multiple precisions for calls to mathematical library functions (exp, log, sin, cos, etc.). The basic idea is to intercept these function calls and to execute some of them in lower precision, searching the space by using existing heuristics [25].

Section 4 introduced the timemory Gotcha capability for providing wholesale function replacement for optimization purposes and Listing 1.11 demonstrates the simplicity of this feature: the struct `mixed_prec_exp_t` shown there is a fully-defined timemory component. Additionally, as a by-product of the object-based design of and reference counting within the Gotcha component, timemory introduces the concept of a "scoped Gotcha", which deactivates the Gotcha wrapper when no object of that Gotcha component is within a start/stop region. Thus, in the mixed-precision analysis scenario, the developer can perform piece-wise analysis by simply changing the scope(s) of one or more instances of this component within a variadic wrapper, executing the application, and validating the result(s) until all regions which permit mixed-precision have been identified.

**Listing 1.11.** Using the Gotcha framework through timemory component

```
struct mixed_prec_exp : tim::component::base<mixed_prec_exp, void>
{
  double operator()(double v) { return PrecisionTuner(expf, exp, v); }
};
// pair the operator of mixed_prec_exp with a Gotcha
using mixed_prec_exp_t = gotcha<1, tuple<>, mixed_prec_exp>;
```

## 5.3  Roofline

The roofline model [29] is a visually intuitive performance model used to bound the performance of various numerical methods and operations running on multi-core, many-core, or accelerator processor architectures. It is a valuable tool in HPC to determine inherent performance limitations related to locality, band-width, and different parallelization paradigms.

The roofline model is an excellent example of the benefits of the timemory design. The generation of a roofline plot requires 3 capabilities: (1) a method for measuring the wall-clock run-time for all the desired regions, (2) a method for collecting the desired hardware-counter values for the all the desired regions, and (3) an empirical method for approximating the peak performance charac-teristics (*i.e.*, the "roof" part of the roofline). Although numerous existing tools undoubtedly included the capabilities #1 and #2 and capability #3 could be provided by the user's runtime, these tools do not expose enough modularity for this calculation to be fully integrated into the tool itself with respect to input and output. In other words, the lack of modularity in these tools necessitates the user engage in post-processing of the data outside of the application execution in order to generate the final result. Within the timemory framework, combining these three capabilities into a stand-alone output is arbitrary to provide since (1) there are no restrictions with respect to components using other components, (2) components are designed to be fully-functional when used explicitly instead of through a variadic wrapper, and (3) explicitly used component instances without variadic wrappers do not interact with the global call-graph storage unless the insert_node() and pop_node() member functions are invoked[8].

At present, timemory is the only existing tool, to the knowledge of the authors, that is capable of generating the roofline for both the CPU and GPU. Furthermore, timemory contains a built-in extension of the Roofline Model Toolkit [20] that is capable of stand-alone execution and provides a level of cus-tomization unavailable in any existing Roofline tools. The design of the roofline toolkit is such that the traditional algorithms for calculating the various peak-performance metrics of the roofline, *e.g.*, fused-multiply-add operations, can be customized within user applications in order to better emulate the operations of the target application.

---

[8] Thus, this eliminates the potential for data-corruption in the call-graph storage.

## 5.4   Instruction Roofline

Timemory provides support for instructions roofline plot generation on the GPU for applications which are integer heavy and do not make use of floating-point instructions. In [12] authors have used a GPU Kernel of Smith-Waterman algorithm [3] (GPU-BSW) as a case-study. Here, we use the Diagonal-Major memory indexing version of the same kernel to validate the timemory generated instruction roofline against the manually generated one in [12].

We used timemory's built-in features to auto-generate the instruction roofline shown in Fig. 3. It can be observed that the timemory generated roofline is similar to the manually created roofline in [12] for the same kernel on the same GPU (NVIDIA V100).

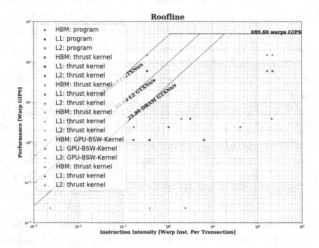

**Fig. 3.** Timemory generated instruction roofline for the diagonal major indexing GPU-BSW kernel

## 6   Future Work

In the near future, planned support includes MPI performance variables (MPI-T) [24] and extensions to the Python interface for post-processing context-trees and Jupyter notebooks. In the long-term, there are two goals for timemory which have not been prioritized. The first goal is to add support for compiler-assisted instrumentation in the form of compiler-flags and pragmas. The second goal is support for ClangJIT [14] which could theoretically add limited support for the injection of new components from C, Python, and Fortran.

## 7   Conclusion

This paper presents a unified framework for performance measurement and analysis, timemory. It provides an easy-to-use interface, supports multiple programming languages, object-level measurement granularity, and superior performance in runtime overhead. The most significant contributions of timemory lie in its modular design, straightforward implementation of complex analysis methods such as the Roofline analysis, flexibility and extensibility for user-defined analysis, simplifications to the Gotcha model, and wide applicability to modern architectures such as CPUs and GPUs. With these favorable features, HPC users and performance engineers are expected to be able to perform profiling and analysis of large scale HPC applications in an easier, faster, and more flexible way.

**Acknowledgment.** Authors from Lawrence Berkeley National Laboratory were supported by the U.S. Department of Energy's Advanced Scientific Computing Research Program under contract DE-AC02-05CH11231.

This research used resources of the National Energy Research Scientific Computing Center, which is supported by the Office of Science of the U.S. Department of Energy under contract DE-AC02-05CH11231.

# References

1. Adhianto, L., et al.: HPCToolkit: tools for performance analysis of optimized parallel programs. Concurr. Comput.: Pract. Exp. **22**(6), 685–701 (2010). https://doi.org/10.1002/cpe.v22:6. http://hpctoolkit.org
2. Agostinelli, S., et al.: Geant4 simulation toolkit, **506**(3), 250–303 (2003). https://doi.org/10.1016/S0168-9002(03)01368-8. http://www.sciencedirect.com/science/article/pii/S0168900203013688
3. Awan, M.G.: GPU accelerated smith-waterman for performing batch alignments (GPU-BSW) (2019). https://github.com/m-gul/GPU-BSW
4. Bernat, A.R., et al.: Anywhere, any-time binary instrumentation. In: PASTE 2011, pp. 9–16. ACM, New York (2011). https://doi.org/10.1145/2024569.2024572
5. Boehme, D., et al.: The case for a common instrumentation interface for HPC codes. In: Workshop on Programming and Performance Visualization Tools (ProTools 19) (October 2019)
6. Boehme, D., et al.: Caliper: performance introspection for HPC software stacks. In: SC 2016, pp. 47:1–47:11. IEEE Computer Society (November 2016). http://dl.acm.org/citation.cfm?id=3014904.3014967. lLNL-CONF-699263
7. Carter Edwards, H., et al.: Kokkos. J. Parallel Distrib. Comput. **74**(12), 3202–3216 (2014). https://doi.org/10.1016/j.jpdc.2014.07.003
8. Corp., I.: Intel VTune profiler user guide - instrumenting your application (2019)
9. Corp., N.: CUPTI documentation (2019). https://docs.nvidia.com/cupti/Cupti/index.html
10. Di Franco, A., et al.: A comprehensive study of real-world numerical bug characteristics, pp. 509–519 (October 2017). https://doi.org/10.1109/ASE.2017.8115662
11. Dimakopoulou, M., et al.: Reliable and efficient performance monitoring in Linux. In: SC 2016, pp. 34:1–34:13. IEEE Press, Piscataway (2016). http://dl.acm.org/citation.cfm?id=3014904.3014950
12. Ding, N., et al.: An instruction roofline model for GPUs. In: Performance Modeling, Benchmarking and Simulation (PMBS19) (2019)
13. Eichenberger, A.E., et al.: OMPT: an OpenMP tools application programming interface for performance analysis. In: Rendell, A.P., Chapman, B.M., Müller, M.S. (eds.) IWOMP 2013. LNCS, vol. 8122, pp. 171–185. Springer, Heidelberg (2013). https://doi.org/10.1007/978-3-642-40698-0_13

14. Finkel, H., et al.: ClangJIT: enhancing C++ with just-in-time compilation. CoRR (2019). http://arxiv.org/abs/1904.08555
15. Goldberg, D.: What every computer scientist should know about floating-point arithmetic. ACM Comput. Surv. **23**(1), 5–48 (1991). https://doi.org/10.1145/103162.103163. http://portal.acm.org/citation.cfm?doid=103162.103163
16. Kahan, W.: Personal website (2008). http://people.eecs.berkeley.edu/~wkahan/. Accessed 16 Dec 2019
17. Knüpfer, A., et al.: Score-p: a joint performance measurement run-time infrastructure for periscope, scalasca, tau, and vampir. In: Tools for High Performance Computing 2011, pp. 79–91. Springer, Heidelberg (2012). https://doi.org/10.1007/978-3-642-31476-6_7
18. Lattner, C., Adve, V.: LLVM: a compilation framework for lifelong program analysis & transformation. In: Proceedings of the International Symposium on Code Generation and Optimization: Feedback-directed and Runtime Optimization, CGO 2004, pp. 75–86. IEEE Computer Society, Washington (2004). http://dl.acm.org/citation.cfm?id=977395.977673
19. LLVM: LLVM (2019). https://llvm.org/
20. Lo, Y.J., et al.: Roofline model toolkit: a practical tool for architectural and program analysis. In: Jarvis, S.A., Wright, S.A., Hammond, S.D. (eds.) PMBS 2014. LNCS, vol. 8966, pp. 129–148. Springer, Cham (2015). https://doi.org/10.1007/978-3-319-17248-4_7
21. Markidis, S., et al.: NVIDIA tensor core programmability, performance & precision, pp. 522–531 (May 2018). https://doi.org/10.1109/IPDPSW.2018.00091. arXiv: 1803.04014
22. Mintchev, S., Getov, V.: PMPI: high-level message passing in Fortran77 and C. In: Hertzberger, B., Sloot, P. (eds.) HPCN-Europe 1997. LNCS, vol. 1225, pp. 601–614. Springer, Heidelberg (1997). https://doi.org/10.1007/BFb0031632
23. Poliakoff, D., LeGendre, M.: Gotcha: an function-wrapping interface for HPC tools. In: Bhatele, A., Boehme, D., Levine, J.A., Malony, A.D., Schulz, M. (eds.) ESPT/VPA 2017-2018. LNCS, vol. 11027, pp. 185–197. Springer, Cham (2019). https://doi.org/10.1007/978-3-030-17872-7_11
24. Ramesh, S., et al.: MPI performance engineering with the MPI tool interface: The integration of mvapich and tau, EuroMPI 2017, pp. 16:1–16:11. ACM, New York (2017). https://doi.org/10.1145/3127024.3127036
25. Rubio-González, C., et al.: Precimonious: tuning assistant for floating-point precision, pp. 1–12 (November 2013). https://doi.org/10.1145/2503210.2503296
26. Shende, S.S., Malony, A.D.: The tau parallel performance system. Int. J. High Perform. Comput. Appl. **20**(2), 287–311 (2006). https://doi.org/10.1177/1094342006064482
27. Terpstra, D., et al.: Collecting performance data with PAPI-C. In: Müller, M., Resch, M., Schulz, A., Nagel, W. (eds.)Tools for High Performance Computing 2009, pp. 157–173. Springer, Heidelberg (2010). https://doi.org/10.1007/978-3-642-11261-4_11
28. Treibig, J., et al.: LIKWID: a lightweight performance-oriented tool suite for x86 multicore environments. In: ICPPW 2010, pp. 207–216. IEEE Computer Society, Washington (2010). https://doi.org/10.1109/ICPPW.2010.38
29. Williams, S., et al.: Roofline: an insightful visual performance model for multicore architectures. Commun. ACM **52**(4), 65–76 (2009). https://doi.org/10.1145/1498765.1498785

# Programming Models and Systems Software

# TeaMPI—Replication-Based Resilience Without the (Performance) Pain

Philipp Samfass[1]($\boxtimes$), Tobias Weinzierl[2], Benjamin Hazelwood[2],
and Michael Bader[1]

[1] Technische Universität München, 85748 Garching, Germany
{samfass,bader}@in.tum.de
[2] Computer Science, Institute for Data Science, Durham University,
DH13LE Durham, Great Britain
tobias.weinzierl@durham.ac.uk, ben.hazelwood@featurespace.co.uk

**Abstract.** In an era where we can not afford to checkpoint frequently, replication is a generic way forward to construct numerical simulations that can continue to run even if hardware parts fail. Yet, replication often is not employed on larger scales, as naïvely mirroring a computation once effectively halves the machine size, and as keeping replicated simulations consistent with each other is not trivial. We demonstrate for the ExaHyPE engine—a task-based solver for hyperbolic equation systems— that it is possible to realise resiliency without major code changes on the user side, while we introduce a novel algorithmic idea where replication reduces the time-to-solution. The redundant CPU cycles are not burned "for nothing". Our work employs a weakly consistent data model where replicas run independently yet inform each other through heartbeat messages whether they are still up and running. Our key performance idea is to let the tasks of the replicated simulations share some of their outcomes, while we shuffle the actual task execution order per replica. This way, replicated ranks can skip some local computations and automatically start to synchronise with each other. Our experiments with a production-level seismic wave-equation solver provide evidence that this novel concept has the potential to make replication affordable for large-scale simulations in high-performance computing.

## 1 Introduction

Supercomputing roadmaps predict that machines soon will suffer from hardware unreliability [11]. A linear correlation between system size and the number of failures has already been observed [27], as effects alike bias temperature instabilities or hot carrier injection diminish the mean time between failures (MTBF) for the individual components. For the next generation of machine sizes, a preserved or reduced MTBF however implies that codes have to be prepared for parts of the machine going down unexpectedly, either through hard errors or soft errors corrupting the code's state. Alternatively, parts might become unacceptably slow as hardware or software error correction [22] step in. We thus need

© Springer Nature Switzerland AG 2020
P. Sadayappan et al. (Eds.): ISC High Performance 2020, LNCS 12151, pp. 455–473, 2020.
https://doi.org/10.1007/978-3-030-50743-5_23

resilient codes. Numerical simulations will have to be at the forefront here. With their massive concurrency going full speed and their strong causal dependencies between intermediate results they are vulnerable to hardware failures.

For numerical simulations, we distinguish three strategies to inject resilience: (i) Codes can be prepared algorithmically to recover from drop-outs of compute nodes. (ii) Codes can checkpoint and restart if hardware fails. (iii) Codes can run computations redundantly.

The first variant works only if the underlying problem allows us to recover information even if data is "lost". Elliptic equations fall into this category: If we know the solution around a region that has dropped out, we can reconstruct the solution within the domain [1,17]. Another example for algorithmic recovery is the combination technique, where a drop-out of some data might (slightly) reduce the solution accuracy but the overall algorithm can cope with it [18]. In both cases, the numerical scheme itself has to be resiliency-ready.

Checkpointing works more in a black-box fashion, but the time to write a checkpoint has to be significantly smaller than the MTBF. We also have to be willing to spend CPU cycles and energy on I/O, which typically is costly [15]. For in-memory checkpointing which mitigates the speed and energy penalty, we need "spare" storage. As checkpoints are costly one way or the other, partial checkpoint-restart is a must. Containment domains [9] for example ask the programmer to decompose the application into task-similar constructs with manual state preservation, error detection and recovery. Some tasking runtime systems such as ParSEC [4] provide a framework for the "automatic" re-execution of task sub-graphs in combination with checkpointing. A sophisticated example for checkpointing is to run the recalculation with a different numerical scheme [22]. This realises a hybrid between an algorithmic approach and checkpoints.

If algorithmic resiliency is not at hand and checkpointing cannot be afforded, replication of work, i.e., data redundancy, is the prime solution. If a node or memory drops out, we simply swap in the replicated data. Cloud computing, sensor networks, desktop grids, peer-to-peer networks, and almost every other field that requires resilient computations [5] base their fault tolerance upon the idea of replicating resources. Capability high-performance computing (HPC) in contrast tends not to use replication. If we duplicate a computation, we effectively half the machine—which renders the prime character of capability computing absurd. Since supercomputers however tend to become so ill-balanced w.r.t. I/O capabilities vs. compute resources that we cannot afford to checkpoint frequently, we will eventually be forced to employ replication nevertheless [12,13,24]. We therefore need to reduce its pain.

Our paper introduces a novel idea to do so, together with a prototypical implementation of team-based MPI replication, called teaMPI. We demonstrate its potential for a high-order discontinuous Galerkin code for hyperbolic equation systems, i.e., a solver for which we are not aware of any straightforward algorithmic resiliency strategy. Our approach relies on replication on the MPI rank level. Each rank is replicated $K$ times, while the simulation per rank is phrased in tasks. A task is an atomic unit, i.e., it has a well-defined input and output and, once it becomes ready, can be executed without any further dependencies. To benefit from our techniques, codes need not be task-based only, but the heavy workload should be phrased as tasks. Furthermore, we require that tasks allow us to send their outcome via MPI, and they should have some slack, i.e., should not be part of the critical path. That is, there is some freedom to move their startup time around, without immediately penalising the overall time-to-solution.

With such tasks, we can replicate each rank $K$ times without a $K\times$ overhead in compute time: We shuffle the task execution order per replication, i.e., we make each rank process sets of ready tasks in a slightly different order. Furthermore, we let each rank offer its task outcomes to other replicas. Whenever a task is about to be executed on a rank, this rank now can first check whether the task outcome is already available from a replica. If so, it skips the execution. All techniques affect the task runtime, i.e., can be invisible to the simulation [29]. To the best of our knowledge, this is the first approach offering full simulation replication without a full multiplication of compute workload. It is thus a fundamental contribution towards affordable replication-based resiliency in HPC.

While our paper focuses on speed of execution, we can detect certain hard failures as well, using a concept called *heartbeats*. Since we keep redundant copies of data, we could, similar to RAID systems, replace corrupt ranks. However, a discussion and presentation of such a swapping strategy is beyond the scope of this paper. Furthermore, we do not yet link our work to MPI-based run-through-stabilisation techniques [3,8,14], which inject further technical and implementation difficulties. Finally, replication in HPC remains a double-edged sword: While it offers fault-tolerance, it also requires to use more memory, network bandwidth and compute units, i.e., CPU hours, per simulation run. Our approach reduces the compute cost compared to naïve replication. We however neglect the increased memory [2] and network stress. For many applications, users will have to balance the replication-based resilience against these facets of increased cost.

The remainder of the text is organised as follows: We establish our terminology in Sect. 2 and sketch the replication mechanisms. Our core contribution is the introduction of the task-based result sharing (Sect. 3) which eventually reduces the workload per rank whenever results from a replica drop in on time. The realisation and encapsulation of the whole idea is subject of discussion in Sect. 4, before we study the method's runtime implications (Sect. 5). A brief conclusion and outlook in Sect. 6 wrap up the discussion.

## 2    Team-Based Resiliency with Heartbeats

We first introduce the terminology which underlies our algorithmic contributions. The terminology is also adopted by our software teaMPI which realises the proposed ideas. teaMPI plugs into the MPI standard profiling interface (PMPI). By mapping physical ranks onto logical numbers and altering the MPI communicator size (number of ranks) exposed to SPMD user code, it transparently reorganises and replicates MPI ranks in multiple teams:

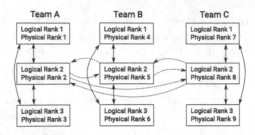

**Fig. 1.** Illustration of a replication-based run with three teams, each hosting three ranks. In the baseline code, ranks communicate only with their team members (solid arrows), but they send heartbeats in regular time intervals to their replicas (dotted arrows, only illustrated for the logical ranks 2).

**Definition 1 (Team).** *All the ranks of an application (without any redundancy) form a team. If we run a code with K-fold redundancy, the global set of ranks is split into K teams. Each team consists of the same number of ranks, sees only the ranks of its own team, and runs asynchronously from all the other teams. Each team consequently hosts one application instance of its own.*

With this definition, each rank belongs uniquely to one team. If there are $K$ teams, each rank has $K-1$ replicas belonging to other teams. The teams are completely autonomous, i.e., independent of the other teams, and therefore consistent only in themselves: We run the code $K$ times and each run completes all computations and has all data. There is neither some kind of lockstepping nor any data sharing in this baseline version of teaMPI.

With teaMPI, our team-based replication for SPMD is totally transparent: An application neither does need to replicate data structures nor does it need to be aware of the replication. Teams are formed from subsets of MPI ranks at the simulation start-up. All subsequent communication calls to both point-to-point and collective MPI routines are mapped by teaMPI to communication within the teams. We work with both data and computation redundancy: Each team is a complete application instance, and, due to SPMD, a send within team A from rank $r_1^{(A)}$ to rank $r_2^{(A)}$ will have a matching send in team B from $r_1^{(B)}$ to $r_2^{(B)}$.

Running an application with teaMPI logically means the same as using a communicator decomposition and making each communicator run the whole simulation. Teams do not have to be consistent all the time. They are *weakly consistent* and fully asynchronous without added overhead for message consistency checking. Instead of an in-built sanity check for MPI messages, we rely on low-frequency consistency checks:

**Definition 2 (Heartbeat).** *Each rank in each team issues a heartbeat after every $\Delta t_{HB}$ seconds. Heartbeats are sent to all replica of a rank (replication multicast) and only carry the elapsed wall time since the last heartbeat. They are sent out in a fire-and-forget fashion.*

While all other MPI communication is restricted to intra-team only and transfers data from the user space, heartbeats are simple non-blocking messages exchanged between the replicas which do not carry any user data. We clearly distinguish *intra-team* from *inter-replica* communication (Fig. 1). The latter is hidden from the user code and is no arbitrary inter-team data exchange. It only "couples" replicas. As mainstream HPC machines lack support for hard real-time scheduling, we weaken the $\Delta t_{HB}$ property: We launch a task which reschedules itself all the time with a low priority and issues a heartbeat as soon as at least $\Delta t_{HB}$ seconds have expired since the last heartbeat task.

**Definition 3 (Team divergence).** *A rank of a team diverges if the time in-between two heartbeats increases compared to this in-between time in other teams. A team diverges if at least one rank of this team diverges.*

Divergence is a *relative* quantity. It results from a comparison of local in-between times to the time stamps carried by arriving messages. If a rank is overbooked with tasks and its heartbeat task thus is issued with $\Delta t \gg \Delta t_{HB}$, it is reasonable to assume that any replica faces a similar delay of heartbeats as it "suffers" from high workload, too. Divergence is also an *observable* property: A rank can identify a slowing down replica, and a slow rank can identify itself as diverging by receiving faster heartbeats from other ranks. Finally, divergence is an *asynchronous* property, as we use the timestamps written into the heartbeats to compute in-between times. Local clocks do not have to be synchronised and we try to eliminate MPI message delivery/progression effects.

Divergence nevertheless remains a *statistic* quantity: As we work in a multi-tasking MPI+X environment, a single late heartbeat is not a reliable indicator that a rank is suffering from errors or overheating and thus is going down. If we observe divergence over a longer time span or define well-suited timeouts $\Delta t_{HB} \geq \Delta t_{\text{timeout}}$, we can however spot failing ranks.

Each team does exactly the same calculations and thus eventually reaches the same state, but the heartbeats run asynchronously on-top and do not impose any synchronisation. They can identify that a rank is going down as it becomes slower, or they can identify complete drop-outs. They are ill-suited to spot data inconsistency. However, we hypothesize that data inconsistencies eventually manifest in corrupted data and thus in the drop-out of a complete team; which we can detect again.

Our transparent replication is similar to the one used in RedMPI, e.g. [16]. RedMPI and other replication models however enforce a strong consistency model among replicated ranks, i.e., make all replicas have exactly the same state subject to temporal shifts. Individual MPI messages are double-checked against replicas for soft errors. This adds synchronisation. Strong consistency on the message level furthermore becomes particularly challenging when wildcard MPI receive operations are used. We avoid this cliff.

To constrain overhead, many approaches do not replicate data and compu-tations automatically and persistently, but enable replication on-demand. The ARRIA distributed runtime system, e.g. [28] schedules and replicates tasks based

**Algorithm 1.** Wrap around the task scheduler with task sharing: We plug into the transition from a ready task into a running task and skip the execution if a task is already available from another team. In return, we send out our task results whenever we have processed a task locally. This is done through a special teaMPI routine, since teaMPI's user interface does not support inter-team communication. We assume the application has equipped the task with MPI serialisation/deserialisation routines.

```
1: function RUNTASKIFNOTRECEIVED(task t)
2:     id ← COMPUTEUNIQUEID(t)
3:     if database.contains(id) then      ▷ id computed by other team, reuse outcome
4:         copy received outcome into task's output buffers
5:         free task outcome
6:         database.delete(id)
7:     else                                         ▷ id not yet in database
8:         RUNTASK(t)
9:         send (id) plus task outcome to all replicas
10:    end if
11: end function
```

on predictions about their probability of failure, while the work in [23] allows to spawn resilient tasks that use either replicated execution or checkpointing for resilience depending on the programmer's choice. Our replication is persistent.

# 3   Task Sharing

teaMPI makes both data as well as all computations redundant. In order to save compute time, we however propose an algorithm where teams exchange outcomes of tasks.

**Definition 4 (Shareable task).** *The tasks of interest for this paper have four important properties: (i) They are compute-heavy, i.e., exhibit a high arithmetic intensity. (ii) They are not a member of the critical path. We can delay their execution once they are spawned by some time without slowing down the application immediately. (iii) They have an outcome with a relatively small footprint relative to their compute cost, and the outcome is serialisable. We can send it around through MPI. (iv) They have a globally unique id.*

Uniqueness incorporates both the data the task is working on plus its action. As we work with a time stepping solver, each task also is unique by the time step it belongs to. Two tasks $t^{(A)}$ and $t^{(B)}$ from two different teams $A$ and $B$ thus have the same id if and only if they perform the same action on the same data of their respective application and are issued by the same time step.

From a user's point of view, teaMPI allows ranks only to exchange data within their team, while teaMPI itself exchanges heartbeats between teams. To reduce the total cost despite the replication, we introduce further inter-team

---

**Algorithm 2.** Event handler that is invoked every time a task drops in from another team's rank.

```
1: function HANDLETASKRECEIVE(task t)
2:     id ← COMPUTEUNIQUEID(t)
3:     if database.contains(id) then        ▷ id already in database, do nothing
4:         deallocate t    ▷ happens if two teams compute id around the same time
5:     else                                        ▷ id not yet in database
6:         database.insert(id,t)
7:     end if
8: end function
```

---

data flow from hereon. Both this further flow and the heartbeats however do not introduce arbitrary point-to-point connections. They solely remain inter-replica.

Our extension is a straightforward augmentation of the task runtime (Algorithm 1): The runtime on a rank sends the outcome of any shareable task that it has completed to all replicas, i.e., all the corresponding ranks in the other teams. They receive and store them in a database. For every ready shareable task that is to be launched, we hence validate first that its outcome has not yet been received. If this is not the case, we execute the actual task (and eventually distribute its result). If a task outcome is already in our database, we do not have to compute the task any more. It is sufficient to roll over the received task result and to skip the actual computation. To make this work, the scheduling is complemented by a receive handler listening for task results (Algorithm 2).

The database is a map from task ids onto task outcomes. An entry in the database indicates that a task outcome has been received. A database of received tasks as sketched so far would grow monotonically, since tasks might drop in while they are computed. We thus equip each database entry with a timeout and run a garbage collection regularly. It removes all entries and cleans up buffers for tasks which are considered to be too old. Such a timeout could rely on heartbeat counts ("received more than x heartbeats before"). For explicit timestepping, it is however more convenient to use the time step counter. Entries older than the most recent time step won't be used anymore and can safely be discarded.

The algorithmic blueprint so far saves compute cost whenever a team lags behind. The team running ahead completes its tasks and sends out the results. The team behind picks up the results and skips its own computations. If two teams are roughly running in-sync, we have to modify the scheduling slightly to benefit from the exchange between replicas:

**Definition 5 (Task shuffling).** *Let $\{t_1, t_2, t_3, \ldots\}$ be a set of tasks that are issued as ready or released as ready in one rush by our application. The first team A schedules $\{t_1^{(A)}, t_{K+1}^{(A)}, t_{2K+1}^{(A)}, \ldots\}$ prior to $\{t_2^{(A)}, t_{K+2}^{(A)}, t_{2K+2}^{(A)}, \ldots\}$ and so forth. The second team B schedules $\{t_2^{(B)}, t_{K+2}^{(B)}, t_{2K+2}^{(B)}, \ldots\}$ prior to $\{t_3^{(B)}, t_{K+3}^{(B)}, t_{2K+3}^{(B)}, \ldots\}$ and eventually $\{t_1^{(B)}, t_{K+1}^{(B)}, t_{2K+1}^{(B)}, \ldots\}$. This pattern continues for all teams.*

Each team permutes its shareable tasks modulo the number of teams. In practice, it is convenient to realise this through task priorities where high priority tasks are scheduled prior to low priority tasks. We start from the application's task priorities but then add subpriorities with a modulo counter which realise the shuffling. Such shuffling even works for applications which do not issue tasks in a batch but fire them one by one. Shuffling weakens the task scheduling consistency, and effectively the data consistency between the teams. The only situation where it might not ensure a differing task execution ordering is when ranks issue tasks non-deterministically. In this case, the randomness plus the shuffling might yield similar task execution orders for different teams. Yet, this is unlikely.

# 4    Implementation

teaMPI is implemented as a C++ library. Using the PMPI interface, teaMPI intercepts the relevant MPI calls and redirects them onto communicators or different physical ranks, respectively. We mainly wrap blocking and nonblocking point-to-point routines as well as collectives. Relying on PMPI makes teaMPI portable. For a replication factor $K$, an application with $R$ ranks is started with a total of $K \cdot R$ ranks. This yields $K$ teams with $R$ ranks each. Within MPI's initialisation, teaMPI creates subcommunicators for all intra-team communication. Each subsequent user MPI call is hijacked by teaMPI and internally mapped onto an MPI call on the appropriate subcommunicator.

## 4.1    Implementation Decisions

*Heartbeats Without a Hard Real-Time Environment.* Issuing heartbeats during the simulation requires particular care. If we make heartbeats dependent on the progression of the numerical simulation (for example by posting a heartbeat after every time step), a single slow rank would delay the heartbeats of other ranks in its team: In classical domain-decomposition approaches (as in our example application), point-to-point messages to "neighbour" ranks are required before a new simulation time step can be started. A single slow rank will therefore delay its neighbours, too. With a heartbeat after each time step, it would thus not be possible to isolate an individual slow or failing rank. We could only identify *teams* hosting a slow or dropped-out rank.

teaMPI's heartbeats are issued by a special heartbeat task on each rank. The heartbeat reschedules itself until program termination. It stores the time stamp of the most recent heartbeat. Whenever invoked, the heartbeat task checks whether at least $\Delta t_{HB}$ seconds have elapsed since the last heartbeat. If so, a new heartbeat message is issued and the stored time stamp is updated. We rely on two assumptions: (i) Tasks run agnostic of MPI synchronization and the progression of the numerical algorithm. That is, even if some ranks cannot proceed with their next time step due to missing MPI messages, they will nevertheless process the heartbeat task. (ii)  If a rank crashes, it stops issuing heartbeats. If it slows down significantly, also its heartbeat task will be triggered less often, resulting in increased time intervals between two heartbeats. This allows us to single out a failing rank. The $\Delta t_{HB}$ ensures that the system is not flooded with heartbeat messages and is not overly sensitive to small performance fluctuations [6].

In our implementation, we use Intel's Threading Building Blocks (TBB), an abstraction from the actual hardware threading. TBB lacks support for real-time tasking. This introduces uncertainty. We do not know when exactly heartbeats are triggered. We can not ensure that the time in-between two heartbeat sends equals the prescribed $\Delta t_{HB}$. We might even end up with situations where a rank $r^{(A)}$ sends more heartbeats to its replica $r^{(B)}$ than the other way around.

This challenge seems to be amplified when ranks deploy their results to replicas. Any deployment moves computational load between replicas and thus, on purpose, unbalances ranks belonging to different teams. Real-time heartbeats would be agnostic of this. However, their usage would contradict our assumption that hardware failures announce themselves often through a performance degradation. We launch heartbeats with a fixed, reasonably high priority and rely on the runtime to schedule the heartbeats fairly and, more importantly, roughly with the same time intervals $\Delta t_{HB}$ on all teams. It is obvious that a more mature solution would use a burn-in phase without any replication data sharing to determine a proper priority. The important implementation remark is that we use a comparison of local heartbeat in-between times to the in-between times of received heartbeats to identify slow downs.

On the receiver side, we rely on MPI polling for the heartbeats: Whenever a heartbeat task becomes active, we both send out our heartbeat (multicast) and probe on available incoming ones. If there are heartbeats in the MPI queue, we dump them into a local array. Unexpected message arrivals should be avoided in MPI. Yet, heartbeats do not induce a major runtime penalty. With only the timestamp, their message footprint is small.

*Task Sharing.* For the inter-team data exchange, teaMPI does not hijack standardised MPI, but offers dedicated routines. These routines expose additional inter-team communicators and teaMPI's knowledge about the number of teams to the application. This way, the application can circumvent native MPI communication which is wrapped by teaMPI and only designed for intra-team exchange. Task outcome sharing is multicasts sending one piece of data to all replicas. To use these routines, we make use of a previously developed communication infrastructure that relaxes the binding of tasks to their spawning rank [26]: tasks and their outcomes can migrate dynamically at runtime to other processes. For this, we add meta data (the unique ids) to the tasks and MPI sending/receiving wrappers around both the meta data, input arguments and output. All the wrapping is not for free: Task outcome sharing in the resiliency context pays off if the tasks are of reasonable workload. We hence solely wrap compute-heavy tasks [7].

*Runtime Wrapper Realisation.* Whenever a task outcome has been computed, it is buffered first before we distribute it among the replicas. This is because we use non-blocking communication and the teams run asynchronously. A team progresses its computation irrespectively of teaMPI's communication. Without task outcome buffering, outgoing data may become inconsistent, as the application might already overwrite the send buffer with new data. To avoid some of the overhead of the buffering, we wrap the sends into another condition clause: We check before line 9 in Algorithm 1 once more whether the task outcome has been received already. If so, we know that at least one replica is ahead and has multicasted the task outcomes to the other teams while we computed locally. There is no need to distribute the local outcome once more.

Buffering is also required on the receiver side. A zero-copy approach is impossible, as the receiving rank might be slightly ahead of the sender and compute the task already itself while it receives data. Alternatively, it might lag behind and might not even have created the task including its output data fields.

## 4.2   Implementation Pitfalls

An efficient implementation of task migration between teams is technically delicate, as we are confronted with a highly dynamic communication pattern. We cannot predict which team will be fast or how many tasks the teams exchange. Instead, we receive unexpected MPI messages, as task outcomes arrive unexpectedly, while it is essential to fully overlap task sharing-related communication with the application and to receive shared task outcomes as quickly as possible.

*MPI Progression.* Even though launched through non-blocking MPI, messages may actually not be progressed internally by the MPI implementation [19]. Instead, communication request handles need to be checked for completion repeatedly through MPI_Test for example. Furthermore, standard MPI neither triggers an interrupt if messages arrive unexpectedly nor supports a mechanism to tell the runtime when investments into MPI progression calls actually pay off.

Too little investment into MPI progression would be lethal for our task sharing approach. We are dealing with unexpected messages which might use a rendez-vous protocol. If they are not detected in a timely manner, they are useless for the replicas and even might delay the baseline application. We therefore need frequent MPI_Iprobes. Probes detect (unexpected) incoming messages and thus issue MPI_Irecvs for pending incoming tasks which consequently are progressed through MPI_Test. Shared task outcomes consequently arrive timely.

Different to our previous work where we did interweave MPI progression with the standard tasking [26], we found it vital for teaMPI to dedicate one core to an asynchronously running communication thread [19], similar to our previous work [20,25]. It is responsible for both the progression of MPI messages (using MPI testing), MPI_Iprobes for detecting messages, as well as the progression of the task sharing algorithm (e.g., buffering received task outcomes and inserting them into the task outcome database). It ensures that task sharing actually overlaps and is hidden from the user code.

*Memory and Communication Overhead.* Task sharing runs risk to result in an excessive memory footprint and to yield many outstanding MPI receive and send handles. Due to the buffering, open communication requests do not allow us to

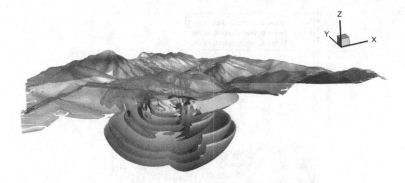

**Fig. 2.** Visualization of an example setup simulated with our code by  courtesy of Maurizio Tavelli [30].

free allocated buffers and handles. We therefore limit the number of open send requests per process. This effectively constrains the memory overhead and also the number of open data exchange handles.

For explicit time stepping, this artificial limitation makes it convenient to drop incoming tasks immediately if they belong to a past time step. In our algorithmic blueprint, it is rare that this happens: If a rank is significantly ahead of a replica, it has fed the replica's team with task outcomes which in turn makes the replica skip all task outcome sharing. Once we limit the number of tasks, we however might run into situations where ranks receive outdated task outcomes. While the garbage collection would remove these as well, it is reasonable to pipe the incoming data into a temporary buffer right away.

## 5   Results

Our tests are conducted on the SuperMUC-NG supercomputer operated by the Leibniz Supercomputing Centre. SuperMUC-NG consists of Intel Skylake Xeon Platinum 8174 nodes, where each node hosts $2 \times 24$ cores, running at a nominal clock frequency of 2.3 GHz. Intel Omnipath serves as interconnect. We use Intel MPI, Intel Compiler 2019, and Intel's TBB for the multithreading.

We benchmark performance and functionality against a seismology simulation for the LOH.1 setup [10]. The simulation relies on an engine for solving systems of hyperbolic partial differential equations (PDEs) and employs an explicit, high order Discontinuous Galerkin scheme in space and time (ADER-DG). Its spatial discretisation stems from dynamically adaptive Cartesian meshes, while the code phrases its execution in tasks relying on TBB. Although we study a benchmark, i.e., strip the code off many features such as the integration of real geometries and subsurface data or extensive postprocessing and I/O, these core features already make up a challenging setup characterising production runs. An example visualization obtained with our framework is shown in Fig. 2.

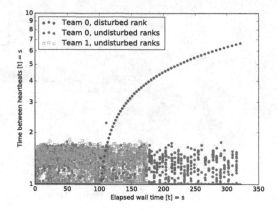

**Fig. 3.** Time between heartbeats on 56 nodes on SuperMUC-NG if a single node is increasingly delayed.

ADER-DG is a numerical scheme splitting up each time step into a space-time prediction, a Riemann solve and a correction phase. We found the prediction to be responsible for the majority of the runtime [6] and thus make only prediction tasks migration-ready.

One core is sacrificed to a communication thread with task sharing. If not stated differently, we do not take this additional core into account when we compare the performance of teaMPI with task sharing to a baseline code without task sharing: both the baseline as well as the task sharing versions use the same number of cores for computations. We, however, also provide data for one setup where both the baseline and the task sharing variant use the same number of cores per process: i.e., the task sharing variant uses one core less for computation than the baseline due to the core dedicated to the communication thread. Readers may recalibrate all other data accordingly or agree that the progression thread is a workaround for an MPI weakness.

## 5.1    Heartbeats

We first demonstrate how teaMPI can be used to identify failing or slow ranks with ExaHyPE. Let 56 nodes of SuperMUC-NG host two teams, each consisting of 28 MPI ranks. Each rank is responsible for one part of the three-dimensional grid. It is evenly distributed, i.e., the setup is load-balanced. We configure each rank to send a heartbeat every $\Delta t_{HB} = 1\,s$, but artificially delay one rank in the first team in order to simulate a failing node. This is achieved by repeatedly pausing and resuming its process. A delay of 0.1 s kicks in after 100 s. From here, the delays increase by 0.1 s every time. This resembles an anticipated scenario where a failing node gradually decreases its clock frequency before it finally goes down completely. teaMPI's goal has to be to identify this situation on time.

A plot of the time in-between heartbeats over the first 20 timesteps (Fig. 3) unmasks the failing rank. This rank delays its whole team 0. As a result,

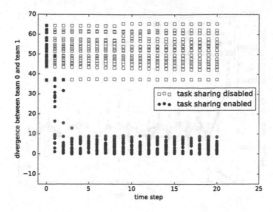

**Fig. 4.** Team divergence for two teams for different initial delays.

team 0 finishes later and posts more heartbeats compared to the ranks in team 1. Although one heartbeat per second is chosen, the task-based heartbeat implementation makes the actual task timings become fuzzy and consistently exceed 1s, resulting in scheduling effects.

Every rank observes its replicas through the heartbeats. We cannot directly, i.e., in an unfiltered way, use the in-between time between heartbeats to identify failures. Instead, time averages have to be used to assess the healthiness of a replica. Although a slow rank affects all members of its team (and it is thus difficult to identify a failing rank by measuring time per time step of a team), our heartbeats are well-suited to identify which rank is to blame for a delay.

## 5.2   Robustness Against Temporary Delays

If a single rank and, hence, team is temporarily delayed through I/O or non-persistent hardware deteriorations (overheating) for example, task sharing should enable the delayed team to "catch up" with the faster teams. To validate this hypothesis, we rerun the two-team setup but artificially delay the startup of one rank of the first team: We pause the rank for a certain time $t$ directly at startup. To exclude stochastic effects, we make $t \in [45\,\text{s}, 65\,\text{s}]$ uniformly distributed and run the code with and without task outcome sharing.

Let $t_i^{(A)}$ be the timestamp of the start of the $i$-th timestep of team $A$. For teams $A$ and $B$, we can then quantify the divergence at the $i$th timestep as $d_i^{(A,B)} = |(t_i^{(A)} - t_i^{(B)})|$. Without task sharing, an initial start offset between both teams persists throughout the simulation (Fig. 4), while task outcome sharing makes the divergence decrease rather quickly: the fast team "drags along" the slow team, as it feeds it with task results.

We investigate this effect further by plotting the accumulated number of reused tasks with task sharing for the two teams (Fig. 5). Initially, the undisturbed team reuses little to no task results from the replica team, as the disturbed

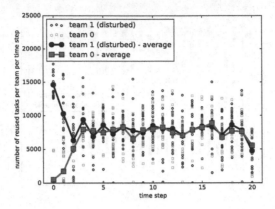

**Fig. 5.** Number of reused tasks per team per time step for different initial random delays (with task sharing).

team cannot provide its results in a timely manner. At the same time, the disturbed team reuses tasks starting from the first timestep. It catches up. For the delayed team, the number of reused tasks per time step *decreases* over time as it catches up. Accordingly, the number of reused tasks per time step increases for the undisturbed team. Once the delayed team has caught up, the teams share tasks evenly as a result of our shuffling approach.

## 5.3 Upscaling

We next study two strong scaling setups with two teams, where we gradually increase the number of cores per rank or team, respectively (Fig. 6). We compare the task sharing measurements to both a baseline that uses the same number of cores for computation (Fig. 6a) and to a baseline that uses one additional core for computation (the core that is sacrificed to a communication thread in the task sharing variant, Fig. 6b). We start with a domain decomposition of the computational grid that is well-balanced, using 28 partitions for example. These 28 partitions are mapped onto 28 ranks which are all deployed to one node. Then we grant each rank more and more cores until the experiment eventually spreads all 28 nodes. We do a similar experiment with 731 ranks or partitions, respectively. This setup eventually employs 731 nodes and 35088 cores. Each experiment is conducted for three polynomial orders of the underlying Discontinuous Galerkin scheme. The polynomial order determines how expensive the compute-heavy tasks for which we enable task sharing are relative to the total runtime. The higher the order the more dominant these tasks.

Task sharing yields a speedup of up to 1.5× for most measurements. In fact, task sharing can even compete with a baseline that uses an additional core for computation in some cases, although at reduced speedups (compare Fig. 6a and Fig. 6b). However, both experiments run into strong scaling effects at higher core counts: If the number of cores per rank exceeds a certain threshold, the

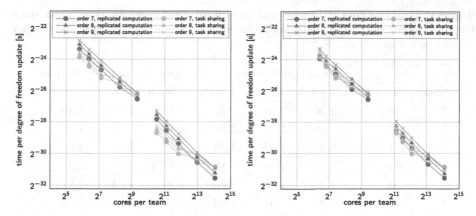

(a) Same number of computation cores for baseline and task sharing.   (b) Baseline uses one additional core for computation compared to task sharing.

**Fig. 6.** Up-scaling of two teams to up to 731 nodes and 35088 cores for varying polynomial orders: Green lines show the normalized times per degree of freedom update if task sharing is enabled, while the red lines illustrate the vanilla variant where computation is done redundantly. (Color figure online)

speedup induced by teaMPI's replication breaks down. This breakdown occurs the earlier the smaller the polynomial order, i.e., the smaller the relative cost of the shared compute tasks is relative to the total compute time. In the breakdown regime, the rate of reused task outcomes decreases significantly up to the point where hardly any computed result can be picked up by another team and all computations are effectively replicated. We invest twice the compute resources, but obtain the time-to-solution of a run without any replication.

For most setups, our task outcome sharing however pays off. Our two teams double the number of cores and thus compute cost, but we get replication plus a significant speedup by means of walltime. The advantageous property is lost if the balancing of cores per rank to compute cost of the shared tasks becomes disadvantageous—which is a direct implication of "too many cores per rank": With too many, the pressure on the communication system increases as tasks are processed and sent at a higher speed. The single communication thread and the interconnect can no longer sustain a fast enough transfer rate of task results. It just becomes cheaper to run all computations locally even though they are done somewhere else, too.

We continue our experimental section with further experiments where we use more than two teams (Table 1). The speedup behaviour persists, yet, we need an even higher relative compute load per task to benefit from yet another team. More than three teams does not lead to any significant improvement of the time to solution anymore. As three teams are sufficient to implement resiliency where two "valid" ranks overrule the outcome of a corrupted one, we conclude that any usage of more than three teams is likely esoteric. To confirm this hypothesis, experiments with validation routines however are required. This is out of scope here.

**Table 1.** Total cost (in CPU hours) and speedup (in time-to-solution) with task sharing, each normalized to a single-team baseline at varying polynomial orders and number of cores per team.

| | | Total cost (CPUh) | | | Speedup (time-to-solution) | | |
|---|---|---|---|---|---|---|---|
| Order | Cores/team | 2 teams | 3 teams | 4 teams | 2 teams | 3 teams | 4 teams |
| 7 | 56 | 1.39 | 1.69 | 2.22 | 1.43 | 1.77 | 1.80 |
| 7 | 112 | 1.38 | 1.73 | 2.04 | 1.45 | 1.74 | 1.96 |
| 7 | 224 | 1.35 | 1.66 | 1.93 | 1.48 | 1.81 | 2.07 |
| 7 | 448 | 1.36 | 1.60 | 1.85 | 1.47 | 1.88 | 2.17 |
| 8 | 56 | 1.35 | 1.63 | 2.05 | 1.49 | 1.84 | 1.96 |
| 8 | 112 | 1.34 | 1.61 | 1.92 | 1.50 | 1.86 | 2.08 |
| 8 | 224 | 1.30 | 1.57 | 1.84 | 1.54 | 1.92 | 2.18 |
| 8 | 448 | 1.30 | 1.53 | 1.71 | 1.54 | 1.96 | 2.34 |
| 9 | 56 | 1.30 | 1.61 | 1.94 | 1.54 | 1.86 | 2.06 |
| 9 | 112 | 1.25 | 1.47 | 1.81 | 1.61 | 2.04 | 2.21 |
| 9 | 224 | 1.24 | 1.44 | 1.68 | 1.62 | 2.09 | 2.38 |
| 9 | 448 | 1.21 | 1.47 | 1.57 | 1.65 | 2.03 | 2.54 |

$k$-fold replication comes at the expense of $k$-times increased total memory consumption plus increased communication needs. On top of this, the bookkeeping of task outcomes requires further resources. We quantified the memory overhead of task sharing by repeatedly sampling each rank's memory consumption during program execution (Fig. 7) after the computational grid has been allocated. In conjunction with system noise, task sharing yields a variable memory consumption pattern as task outcomes are allocated and freed dynamically. Yet, the typical additional memory overhead of task sharing remains under control at around 20% additionally used memory.

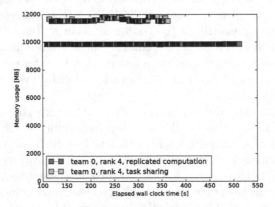

**Fig. 7.** Memory consumption of task sharing vs the baseline variant without task sharing for a selected representative rank.

# 6 Conclusion and Outlook

Our paper introduces teaMPI, an MPI wrapper/plugin which replicates a simulation multiple times. We call the replicas teams. The teams run completely asynchronously. They do however exchange heartbeats. If the time in-between the heartbeats received vs. the local heartbeats diverges, we consider this to be a reliable indicator for faults. While any rank can spot any performance degradation of a replica rank, it is important to note that the heartbeats do not synchronise the replicas at all and, thus, do not introduce any performance penalty. The actual compute cost of replicas is reduced as we make each rank share its task outcomes with the replicas which, whenever these task outcomes drop in on time, skip their local computations and instead use the results from another rank from another team. This technique reduces the total CPUh cost, as long as the computation is phrased in tasks, and as long as we do not work in the strong scaling regime: Enough ready tasks have to be available, so we can shuffle their order and do not make threads idle.

Our paper introduces an elegant, minimalist and powerful new idea rendering replication in HPC economically feasible. It is however a conceptional piece of work. To translate it into a production environment, we need, on the one hand, the integration with modern MPI versions which support resiliency. On the other hand, we have to solve four further fundamental challenges: First, our code lacks a mature communication performance model for task sharing. Specifically, it would never share too many task outcomes such that the overall performance suffers. Second, the task outcome sharing makes the whole simulation more sensitive to soft faults (bit flips, e.g.) [22]: If a task yields an invalid outcome, this outcome might corrupt all other teams. There is a need to develop checksums or hash techniques that can spot such cases and veto the pollution of a run with invalid data. The heartbeat messages might be canonical candidates to carry such crossvalidation records. Third, we have to generalise our notion of shareable tasks. Our strategy relies on the fact that a code yields many shareable tasks, and that these tasks make up a significant part of the runtime. To make the concept applicable to a wider range of code characteristics, we have to develop mechanisms that can migrate and share whole task subgraphs such that more fine granular tasking benefits from our ideas, too. Finally, our approach increases the pressure on the MPI interconnects. It will be subject of future work to analyse how this pressure can be reduced. To this end, we plan to investigate whether emerging technologies such as SmartNICs can be exploited to offload the task sharing fully to the network hardware and to guarantee sufficient MPI progress.

**Acknowledgements.** This work received funding from the European Union's Horizon 2020 research and innovation programme under grant agreement No 671698 (ExaHyPE), and from EPSRC's Excalibur programme under grant number EP/V00154X/1 (ExaClaw). It used the facilities of the Hamilton HPC Service of Durham University. We particularly acknowledge the support of the Gauss Centre for Supercomputing e.V. (www.gauss-centre.eu) for providing computing time on the GCS

Supercomputer SuperMUC at Leibniz Supercomputing Centre (www.lrz.de). Thanks are due to all members of the ExaHyPE consortium who made this research possible, particularly to Dominic E. Charrier for writing most of the engine code and to Leonhard Rannabauer for development of the seismic models on top of the engine. The underlying software, i.e. both ExaHyPE [21] and teaMPI, are open source (www.exahype.org and www.peano-framework.org/index.php/teampi).

# References

1. Altenbernd, M., Göddeke, D.: Soft fault detection and correction for multigrid. Int. J. High Perform. Comput. Appl. **32**(6), 897–912 (2018)
2. Biswas, S., de Supinski, B.R., Schulz, M., Franklin, D., Sherwood, T., Chong, F.T.: Exploiting data similarity to reduce memory footprints. In: 2011 IEEE International Parallel and Distributed Processing Symposium, pp. 152–163 (2011)
3. Bland, W., Bouteiller, A., Herault, T., Bosilca, G., Dongarra, J.: Post-failure recovery of MPI communication capability: design and rationale. Int. J. High Perform. Comput. Appl. **27**(3), 244–254 (2013)
4. Cao, C., Herault, T., Bosilca, G., Dongarra, J.: Design for a soft error resilient dynamic task-based runtime. In: 2015 IEEE International Parallel and Distributed Processing Symposium, pp. 765–774 (2015)
5. Cappello, F.: Fault tolerance in petascale/ exascale systems: current knowledge, challenges and research opportunities. Int. J. High Perform. Comput. Appl. **23**(3), 212–226 (2009)
6. Charrier, D.E., et al.: Studies on the energy and deep memory behaviour of a cache-oblivious, task-based hyperbolic PDE solver. Int. J. High Perform. Comp. Appl. **33**(5), 973–986 (2019)
7. Charrier, D., Hazelwood, B., Weinzierl, T.: Enclave tasking for discontinuous Galerkin methods on dynamically adaptive meshes. SIAM J. Sci. Comput. **42**(3), C69–C96 (2020)
8. Chen, Z., et al: Fault tolerant high performance computing by a coding approach. In: Proceedings of 10th ACM SIGPLAN Symposium on Principles and Practice of Parallel Programming, pp. 213–223. ACM (2005)
9. Chung, J., et al.: Containment domains: a scalable, efficient, and flexible resilience scheme for exascale systems. In: SC 2012: Proceedings of the International Conference for HPC, Networking, Storage and Analysis, pp. 1–11 (2012)
10. Day, S.M., et al.: Tests of 3D elastodynamics codes: final report for lifelines program task 1A02. Technical report (2003)
11. Dongarra, J., et al.: Applied mathematics research for exascale computing. Technical report, Lawrence Livermore National Lab (2014)
12. Engelmann, C., Ong, H.H., Scott, S.L.: The case for modular redundancy in large-scale high performance computing systems. In: Proceedings of 8th IASTED International Conference on Parallel and Distributed Computing and Networks, vol. 1, pp. 189–194 (2009)
13. Engelmann, C.: Scaling to a million cores and beyond: using light-weight simulation to understand the challenges ahead on the road to exascale. Future Gener. Comput. Syst. **30**, 59–65 (2014)
14. Fagg, G.E., et al.: Process fault tolerance: semantics, design and applications for high performance computing. Int. J. High Perform. Comput. Appl. **19**(4), 465–477 (2005)

15. Ferreira, K., et al.: Evaluating the viability of process replication reliability for exascale systems. In: 2011 International Conference for HPC, Networking, Storage and Analysis (SC), pp. 1–12 (2011)
16. Fiala, D., Mueller, F., Engelmann, C., Ferreira, K., Brightwell, R., Riesen, R.: Detection and correction of silent data corruption for large-scale high-performance computing. In: Proceedings of 25th IEEE/ACM International Conference on HPC, Networking, Storage and Analysis, pp. 78:1–78:12. ACM, November 2012
17. Göddeke, D., Altenbernd, M., Ribbrock, D.: Fault-tolerant finite-element multigrid algorithms with hierarchically compressed asynchronous checkpointing. Parallel Comput. **49**(C), 117–135 (2015)
18. Heene, M., Hinojosa, A.P., Bungartz, H.-J., Pflüger, D.: A massively-parallel, fault-tolerant solver for high-dimensional PDEs. In: Desprez, F., et al. (eds.) Euro-Par 2016. LNCS, vol. 10104, pp. 635–647. Springer, Cham (2017). https://doi.org/10.1007/978-3-319-58943-5_51
19. Hoefler, T., Lumsdaine, A.: Message progression in parallel computing - to thread or not to thread? In: IEEE International Conference on Cluster Computing, pp. 213–222 (2008)
20. Klinkenberg, J., Samfass, P., Bader, M., Terboven, C., Müller, M.S.: Chameleon: reactive load balancing for hybrid MPI+OpenMP task-parallel applications. J. Parallel Distr. Comput. **138**, 55–64 (2020)
21. Reinarz, A., et al.: ExaHyPE: an engine for parallel dynamically adaptive simulations of wave problems. Comput. Phys. Commun., 107251 (2020)
22. Reinarz, A., Gallard, J.M., Bader, M.: Influence of a-posteriori subcell limiting on fault frequency in higher-order DG schemes. In: IEEE/ACM 8th Workshop on Fault Tolerance for HPC at eXtreme Scale, FTXS@SC 2018, pp. 79–86 (2018)
23. Rezaei, A., Khetawat, H., Patil, O., Mueller, F., Hargrove, P., Roman, E.: End-to-end resilience for HPC applications. In: Weiland, M., Juckeland, G., Trinitis, C., Sadayappan, P. (eds.) ISC High Performance 2019. LNCS, vol. 11501, pp. 271–290. Springer, Cham (2019). https://doi.org/10.1007/978-3-030-20656-7_14
24. Riesen, R., Ferreira, K., Stearley, J.: See applications run and throughput jump: the case for redundant computing in HPC. In: Proceedings of International Conference on Dependable Systems and Networks, pp. 29–34 (2010)
25. Samfass, P., Klinkenberg, J., Bader, M.: Hybrid MPI+OpenMP reactive work stealing in distributed memory in the PDE framework sam(oa)$^2$. In: IEEE International Conference on Cluster Computing, pp. 337–347, September 2018
26. Samfass, P., Weinzierl, T., Charrier, D.E., Bader, M.: Lightweight task offloading exploiting MPI wait times for parallel adaptive mesh refinement. In: Concurrency and Computation: Practice and Experience (2020, to appear)
27. Schroeder, B., Gibson, G.A.: A large-scale study of failures in high-performance computing systems. IEEE Trans. Depend. Secur. Comput. **7**(04), 337–350 (2010)
28. Simon, T., Dorband, J.: Improving application resilience through probabilistic task replication. In: ACM Workshop on Algorithmic and Application Error Resilience, June 2013
29. Subasi, O., Yalcin, G., Zyulkyarov, F., Unsal, O., Labarta, J.: Designing and modelling selective replication for fault-tolerant HPC applications. In: 17th IEEE/ACM International Symposium on Cluster, Cloud and Grid Computing (CCGRID), pp. 452–457 (2017)
30. Tavelli, M., Dumbser, M., Charrier, D.E., Rannabauer, L., Weinzierl, T., Bader, M.: A simple diffuse interface approach on adaptive Cartesian grids for the linear elastic wave equations with complex topography. J. Comput. Phys. **386**, 158–189 (2019)

# Pattern-Aware Staging for Hybrid Memory Systems

Eishi Arima[1,2]([✉]) and Martin Schulz[2]

[1] The University of Tokyo, Tokyo, Japan
`arima@cc.u-tokyo.ac.jp`
[2] Technical University of Munich, Munich, Germany
`schulzm@in.tum.de`

**Abstract.** The ever increasing demand for higher memory performance and—at the same time—larger memory capacity is leading the industry towards hybrid main memory designs, i.e., memory systems that consist of multiple different memory technologies. This trend, however, naturally leads to one important question: how can we efficiently utilize such hybrid memories? Our paper proposes a software-based approach to solve this challenge by deploying a *pattern-aware* staging technique. Our work is based on the following observations: (a) the high-bandwidth fast memory outperforms the large memory for memory intensive tasks; (b) but those tasks can run for much longer than a bulk data copy to/from the fast memory, especially when the access pattern is more *irregular/sparse*. We exploit these observations by applying the following staging technique *if the accesses are irregular and sparse*: (1) copying a chunk (few GB of sequential data) from large to fast memory; (2) performing a memory intensive task on the chunk; and (3) writing it back to the large memory. To check the *regularity/sparseness* of the accesses *at runtime* with negligible performance impact, we develop a lightweight pattern detection mechanism using a *helper threading* inspired approach with two different **Bloom filters**. Our case study using various scientific codes on a real system shows that our approach achieves significant speed-ups compared to executions with using only the large memory or hardware caching: 3× or 41% speedups in the best, respectively.

## 1 Introduction

The performance of future computing systems relies less and less on computational power, but directly depends on both memory performance and capacity [26,29]. At the same time, classical DRAM technologies are at risk in scaling bandwidth/capacity, and thus systems built solely on them will face severe limitations [29]. In order to counteract these trends, new and promising technologies, such as 3D stacking, HMC [9] or HBM [18,23], have been developed, but face limitations in terms of capacity and scalability [23]. Therefore, to increase the memory capacity, DIMM-based off-package memories including NVRAM, such as Intel's 3D XPoint memory [16], are still needed, but also face limitations, this

---

ⓒ The Author(s) 2020, corrected publication 2020
P. Sadayappan et al. (Eds.): ISC High Performance 2020, LNCS 12151, pp. 474–495, 2020.
https://doi.org/10.1007/978-3-030-50743-5_24

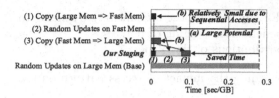

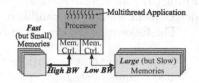

**Fig. 1.** Concept of our staging technique    **Fig. 2.** Target architecture

time in terms of bandwidth-scalability due to power constraints on the memory bus/modules [8] and the number of off-package pins [32]. Driven by these diverging observations, adopting hybrid memory architectures, which combine different memory technologies on a single node, is an important design option for next generation computing systems from supercomputers to main stream systems [15,17,18,34,35].

While such hybrid memory systems have the potential to improve the performance of memory intensive applications, it is still unclear how to exploit—at the same time—both the available performance and the capacity on such hybrid memory systems. As an answer to this open question, we propose a software-based *pattern-aware staging* technique. Our core concept follows the fundamental observations[1] demonstrated in Fig. 1: (a) the high-bandwidth fast memory outperforms the large memory for the memory intensive *random* updates task, but (b) it takes a much longer time than the *sequential* copy tasks.

We exploit these observations to accelerate memory intensive tasks by using the staging technique shown in the figure *if the accesses are irregular and sparse*: (1) copying a large chunk of data from large to fast memory, (2) performing accesses on the chunk, and (3) writing it back to the large memory. We apply this technique when the data footprint is larger than the fast memory. In this technique, the data is divided into chunks of a few GB, and the staged access is, in turn, applied to each of them. Several recent studies also focus on the data managements for hybrid memory systems [3,6,11,21,27,36,38], but none of them *exploits this large performance impact of the access pattern to improve software-based data placement decisions at runtime*.

To successfully enable our pattern-aware staging technique, we need to detect when it is profitable to apply. For this, we propose a lightweight software-based mechanism that dynamically samples small parts of the access sequence, analyzes the access pattern in terms of regularity/sparseness, and then decides—at runtime—whether to apply staging or not. More specifically, we sample addresses using our new mechanism inspired by *helper threading* [19,25], and then we efficiently characterize the pattern based on two different detectors implemented using *Bloom filters*: a Page Address Filter (PAF) for sparseness and a Stride

---

[1] This experiment was performed on a real system described in Sect. 6. The same number/size of memory references are issued for both the random/copy tasks (details are provided in Sect. 2.3).

Filter (SF) for regularity analysis. Finally, we propose a quantitative scheme to detect if an application can likely benefit from staging or not.

The followings are the major contributions of this paper:

- We focus on the observations regarding the impact of access pattern on the effectiveness of staging.
- Based on the above observations, we propose a software-based data management scheme called *pattern-aware staging*.
- We propose a simple dynamic address sampling mechanism inspired by software-based helper threading [19,25].
- We realize a lightweight pattern characterization scheme using two different small Bloom filters: PAF and SF.
- We propose a quantitative approach to make a decision based on the outputs of the above access pattern analysis.
- Finally, we evaluate our pattern-aware staging approach on a real system using scientific kernels.

## 2   Staging Accesses in Hybrid Memory

Figure 2 illustrates the target architecture of this study: the processor has multiple separated memory controllers, each of which is connected to a set of memories: one consists of fast but small memories; while the other one consists of large but slow memories. Looking forward, this kind of architecture is not only considered indispensable for any next generation high performance computing systems, covering exascale supercomputers and beyond [34,35], but is also poised to find its way into mainstream systems [18]. One example of this is installing both high-bandwidth 3D-stacked DRAMs (e.g., HBM [18,23] or HMC [9]) and conventional DDR modules in one compute board, which is supported in recent products such as Intel Knights Landing (KNL) processors [17] and Intel Agilex SoCs [15], and will be so in the future systems [18,35]. Another example is integrating both DRAM and NVRAM modules into DIMM slots, which is supported in Intel Cascade Lake processors [16]. In general, they are *heterogeneous in terms of bandwidth* as the 3D-stacked DRAMs can offer higher bandwidth scalability [9,17,18,23], and the bandwidth of NVRAM is limited [16] due to the significant memory access overheads [11,38].

### 2.1   Concept of Memory Staging

The goal of this research is to provide an easy to use way for *memory consuming/intensive applications* to exploit the performance of the fast memory, while also being able to utilize the capacity of the large memory in hybrid memory systems. In particular, to enjoy the bandwidth heterogeneity, we target memory-intensive multi-threaded applications with high instruction/data/thread-level parallelisms, which thus can become *bandwidth-limited*.

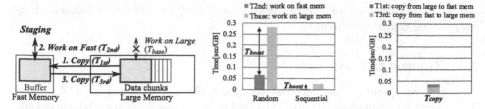

Fig. 3. Overview of staging    Fig. 4. Performance boost    Fig. 5. Copy overhead

To achieve this goal, we aim at utilizing corse-grained data transfers/copies (data chunks in the order of GBs). This is because (1) over GBs of memory space is already available even in the fast memory, (2) accessing a large enough chunk is essential to exploit the bandwidth in the fast memory, and (3) we can allocate larger pages for larger chunks to mitigate the virtual/physical address translation overhead. As few applications naturally expose such coarse-grained accesses, we revisit the concept of *access staging* and adapt and extend it for managing data in hybrid memory systems.

Figure 3 illustrates an overview. First, we reserve a buffer (up to a few GB) in the fast memory and divide the large data, still stored in the slow memory, into the several data chunks matching the buffer size in the fast memory. For each data chunk, we then apply data staging as follows: (1) copy the data from the large memory to the fast memory, (2) perform bandwidth-critical tasks in the fast memory, and (3) return the data to the large memory by copying it back. We then iterate this process across all data chunks, until all chunks are processed.

In this work, we purposely do not consider overlapping or pipelining between the different stages of processing consecutive data chunks. *The detailed reasons behind this will be discussed in* Sect. 8.

## 2.2 Balancing Performance Boost and Overhead

To achieve performance improvements, we must apply our staging technique only when the performance boost gained in the second stage ($T_{boost}$) is larger than the copy overhead caused by the first and third stages ($T_{copy}$). These overheads can be formulated by using the parameters shown in Fig. 3. Here, $T_{base}$ represents the execution time without staging, while $T_{1st}$, $T_{2nd}$ and $T_{3rd}$ represent the execution time of the first, second, and third stages in the staging technique, respectively. We can obtain a performance improvement when these times meet the following condition: $T_{base} > T_{1st} + T_{2nd} + T_{3rd} \Leftrightarrow T_{boost}(= T_{base} - T_{2nd}) > T_{copy}(= T_{1st} + T_{3rd})$. These times, however, depend on the characteristics of the *memory access patterns* in the targeted code or algorithm, which we need to carefully consider when determining wether we apply the staging or not. Further, to reduce the copy overhead, in certain cases we can *remove* the first stage or third stage in our approach. More specifically, we remove the third stage (writing back a chunk to the large memory) for read only tasks. Likewise, we remove the first stage (reading a chunk from the large memory) for write only tasks such as overwriting temporary arrays.

### 2.3 Tradeoff Observations

In Fig. 4, we quantify the performance boost ($T_{boost}$) by comparing $T_{2nd}$ and $T_{base}$. For this evaluation, we utilized a real hybrid memory system whose details are shown in Sect. 6. The vertical axis shows the execution time that is divided by the data size, i.e., the inverse of bandwidth. In this evaluation we analyze the performance boost for two different access patterns. For *random* we performed one billion random memory accesses on an 8 GB data array whose data element size is eight bytes; for *sequential* we examined sequential memory references on the same 8 GB data array, also by issuing one billion memory references.

As shown in the figure, the fast memory outperforms the large memory for both tasks. This is because the former has significantly more parallelism in ranks/banks/channels than the latter, and thus can provide data much faster regardless of access patterns if the accesses are intensive.

On the other hand, the random access pattern takes much longer to complete than the sequential one, which is a well-known phenomenon [14] happens also in NVRAMs [16,38], and hence $T_{boost}$ has to become much longer for the former. This is caused by the fundamental fact that memory systems are optimized in a way that they can exploit the bandwidth for sequential accesses by interleaving data across banks/ranks/channels [5], while utilizing open page policies [20]. Therefore, more *irregular* patterns cause more bank/rank/channel level conflicts [33]. Further, such accesses are very *sparse* (and hence come with very low locality) and thus these contentions can occur very frequently as, under such conditions, on-chip caches cannot help with reducing the number of accesses to memory.

Figure 5 represents the copy overhead ($T_{copy}$) between the two different memories. By comparing Fig. 4 and Fig. 5, we find that the significance of the copy overhead depends on the access types of the codes. As shown in the figures, it is better to move data for the random access pattern ($T_{boost} > T_{copy}$), but we should not do so for the sequential accesses ($T_{boost} < T_{copy}$). *Note that this pattern-aware comparison is universally valid for any hybrid memories—the application to other systems will be discussed in* Sect. 8.

## 3  Pattern-Aware Staging

Following the insights in the last section, we developed a lightweight software mechanism called ***pattern-aware staging*** that dynamically detects access patterns and decides on the fly whether to apply data staging or not. Figure 6 shows the overview with block diagrams. By a statical source-to-source transformation, the following functionalities are augmented into the original code as well as the staging: sampling the access sequence for a chunk just before executing the task, characterizing the pattern, and then using this information to make a decision

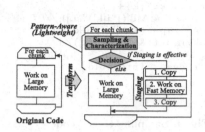

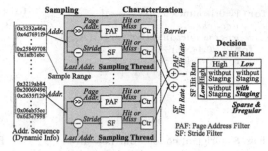

**Fig. 6.** Block diagram for Pattern-Aware Staging

**Fig. 7.** Overall strategy of pattern analysis

on whether we use the staging or not, i.e., we make a pattern-aware decision. The time and memory overhead of this analysis part has to be small enough in order for this scheme to be effective. We achieve this by (1) limiting the number of samples obtained, (2) parallelizing the sampling across multiple threads, and (3) using a filter-based efficient pattern-analysis, as described below. We perform this analysis *at runtime* as it is both more convenient for the user and more flexible to adapt to varying application behavior such as *input dependencies* than performing a static, offline based pattern-analysis. Consequently, *no profile from a previous run is needed for the application of our method.*

Figure 7 describes the concepts behind our pattern analysis component, which consists of three parts: sampling, characterization and decision. Each *Sampling Thread* in the figure acquires a part of the address sequence and analyzes the pattern *at runtime*. For this we use two separate detectors in the form of (Bloom) filters—a Page Address Filter (PAF) and a Stride Filter (SF)—as indicators. These filters keep the recent history of inputs (page-addresses/access-strides) and can thereby provide an answer on whether an input page-address/access-stride exists in the recent access history or not. *A* **low hit rate in the PAF** *indicates low data locality, and thus a* **sparse** *access pattern. Additionally, a* **low hit rate in the SF** *indicates that accesses are* **irregular**. More specifically, when accesses are more regular, the number of different access strides detected in the SF decreases and hence hits in the SF increase. For example, for an access pattern with only one constant stride, the SF only has one entry and shows a hit for all access except for the initial one.

After completing the sampling, we collect the hit/miss records of these two filters using a reduction operation and with that complete the characterization part. Based on the obtained statistics, we then make a decision based on the following observation: if the accesses are *sparse* and *irregular*, the task is likely to take much longer time than the copy and thus the performance boost brought by data staging will be larger and hence worthwhile.

```
for(i=0;i<num_chunks;i++){
  //processing ith chunk
  #pragma our_directive target(A[][])
  for(j=0;j<M;j++){
    for(k=0;k<N;k++){
      A[i][(j*I[k])%L]+=1;
    }
  }
}
```

```
for(j=0;j<M;j++){
  for(k=0;k<N;k++){
    // Load(&A[i][(j*I[k])%L]);//HT
    PAF.input(&A[i][(j*I[k])%L]);
    SF.input(&A[i][(j*I[k])%L]);
    [Abort when # of sampling
       exceeds threshold]
  }
}
```

Fig. 8. Original code + our new directive

Fig. 9. Sampling thread code

```
for(i=0;i<num_chunks;i++){
  //processing ith chunk
  [Put the sampling thread code here (inline)]
  if(decision_making(args)){
    [code with staging]
  }else{
    [code without staging]
  }
}
```

Fig. 10. Pattern-aware staging code

## 4  Sampling and Characterization

### 4.1  Sampling Threads

Figure 8 represents a sample pseudo code to apply our pattern-aware staging technique[2]. In this figure, the two-dimensional array (A[num_chunks][L]) can be divided into chunks, and the outermost for loop then selects one of them turn by turn. The 3rd line in the figure shows our newly introduced directive to specify the target array to apply our technique to. Here, we assume the following scenario: when a compiler comes across this directive, it automatically attempts to transform this original code into the pattern-aware staging code in Fig. 9 and 10 for the target array. Although the transformation is performed by hand in this paper, as in previous studies on compiler-based pre-execution or helper thread prefetching [19, 25], this can be automated using, e.g., a source-to-source compiler [24, 30], similar to previous software-based data management studies [22, 28, 31].

Next, we describe the sampling thread code[3] in Fig. 9. This code can be considered a modified version of the inner two loops of Fig. 8. The 6th line, commented-out in Fig. 9, shows the original helper threading approach.

---

[2] Here, to simplify the explanation, we utilize the sequential code. But, our codes are actually parallelized with OpenMP in our evaluation.

[3] In our evaluation, we parallelize the code as follows: (1) to abort OpenMP *parallel for* loops on the way, we utilize *cancel for* statement; (2) to minimize the communications among threads, we set the statistics of the filters as private variables and collect them using *atomic* statement just after the end of the samplings.

Instead of calculating A[i][(j*I[k])%L] += 1, it prefetches data using the address (&A[i][(j*I[k])%L]), which is achieved by distilling the codes to execute only the address generation paths [19,22,25,31]. Similar to this, our sampling mechanism just obtains the same address and utilizes it as an input for the filters (PAF and SF). Note that, if the array is accessed multiple times in the loop (e.g., unrolled loop), we add the filter input and increment the sample count accordingly. When the total number of sampled addresses exceeds a given threshold, we abort the loops and collect the statistics. Putting it all together, this sampling code is inlined at the 3rd line in Fig. 10, just before the decision making function *decision_making(args)*. While this direct inlining of the code could be optimized by spawning separate sampling threads and overlapping them with the main threads, we decided to avoid this extra complexity due to the negligible sampling and characterization overhead shown in Fig. 13 (Sect. 4.3).

## 4.2   Access Characterization

We characterize the sampled address sequence in terms of *sparseness* and *regularity* using the PAF/SF as described in Sect. 3. To realize this, these filters have to be *efficient in memory and time overheads*. For this reason we turn to Bloom filters, as they fulfill the requirements, as laid out below.

**The Filter Mechanism.** We assume each filter has three functionalities: *Test()*, *Set()*, and *Clear* as shown in Fig. 11. First, the *Clear* function is used to initialize/reset the contents of the filter. For each access, we use the *Test()* function to examine whether an incoming element $x$ (page-address/stride for PAF/SF, respectively) is recorded in the filter or not. If it returns a hit, then the corresponding hit counter is incremented, otherwise the miss counter is incremented and *Set()* is called to register $x$ in the filter to detect future accesses.

**Bloom Filter Based Implementation.** To implement PAF and SF, we utilize Bloom filter, which is a probabilistic data structure that can record a large set of elements with a small memory footprint [4]. Figure 12 shows their principle structure: it consists of a bit array, which stores the elements in the filter, and multiple hash functions, each of which returns an index to the bit array. At first, all of the bits are set to zero. Then, to register input elements (e.g., in our case page-addresses/strides for PAF/SF), we can use the *Set()* function to identify the bits associated with the input using the hash functions and then set them to one. We use the *Test()* function to extract the bits associated with an input element using an AND operation on the bits pointed to by the hash functions: it should return a hit (1) if an element was recorded before, otherwise a miss (0).

In the figure, $Test(x)$ returns a hit because $x$ was already registered (*True Positive*). The output of $Test(z)$ is a miss, as $z$ has not appeared, yet, at this point (*True Negative*). However, due to the hash collisions, $Test(w)$ can return also a wrong answer: a hit for a non-registered element $w$ (*False Positive*). Small numbers of false positives do not have a significant impact, but to avoid too frequent false positives, the size of the bit array must be chosen large enough. Thus, the memory overhead and the false positive probability are an important trade-off, which is further influenced by picking the right hash functions. Further,

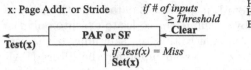

**Fig. 11.** Filter operations

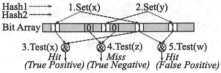

**Fig. 12.** Bloom filter mechanism

after recording a certain amount of records, the *Clear* function must be used to re-initialize the filter contents; otherwise the filter can be filled with positive values and always return hits.

### 4.3    Quantitative Analysis

We evaluate the overhead/effectiveness of our sampling and characterization approach using access patterns for various sparse matrices. The matrices are collected from the Florida sparse matrix collection [10] and are listed in Table 2. Assuming SpMV with CRS format [2], we use the column indices of each matrix as an index array to a vector and analyze the access patterns with using our sampling and characterization approach. For this evaluation, we use our hybrid memory system whose detailed configuration is shown in Sect. 6. The configurations for our sampling phase and the filters are summarized in Table 1.

Figure 13 compares the time overhead between 1 or 8 GB copy operations $(T_{1st} + T_{3rd})$ and our sampling and characterization approach. The X-axis indicates the sampled addresses for both PAF and SF in each thread, while the Y-axis represents the time overhead. For the sampling and characterization overhead, each value shows the average time with the standard deviation across workloads.

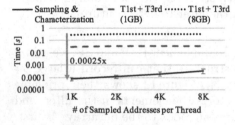

**Fig. 13.** Time overhead comparison

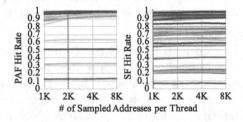

**Fig. 14.** Hit rates v.s. # of sampling

**Table 1.** Sampling and filter settings

| Sampling | |
|---|---|
| # of samples/thread | 2 K (1 K → 8 K in Fig. 13/14) |
| # of threads | 64 |
| Filters (PAF/SF) | |
| Size [B] ($=2^N/8$) | 256 (64 → 512 in Fig. 15) |
| Trigger for *Clear* | 256 unique inputs |
| # of hashes | 2 |
| $hash_k(x)$ $(k = 0, 1)$ | $(x >> (N * k)) \& (2^N - 1)$ |

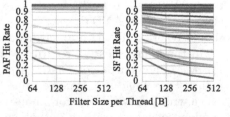

**Fig. 15.** Hit rates v.s. filter size

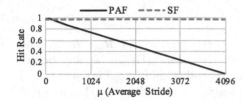
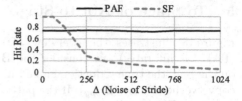

**Fig. 16.** Hit rates vs. $\mu$ ($\Delta = 0$—fixed)    **Fig. 17.** Hit rates vs. $\Delta$ ($\mu = 1K$—fixed)

As shown in the figure, when we limit the number of sampled addresses to less than 8 K per thread, the overhead of our approach becomes quite small (less than 1%) compared with the few GB of round-trip copy operations. In particular, it takes just *0.025%* of time compared with a 8 GB copy at 1K samples.

Figure 14 shows how many sampled addresses are needed to obtain accurate enough PAF/SF hit rates. The X-axis shows the number of sampled addresses per thread, while the Y-axis represents the PAF/SF hit rates. Each line in the figure is associated with one of the matrices listed in Table 2. As the graph shows, the PAF/SF hit rates are almost constant when we sample more than 2 K/1 K addresses per thread. Based on this result, we limit ourselves to 2 K/1 K addresses per thread for the PAF/SF. The time overhead of this is less than *0.040%* compared to the 8 GB copy operations, as shown in Fig. 13.

Figure 15 presents the PAF/SF hit rates as a function of the filter size. We scale the filter size from 64 B to 512 B (512 bit to 4096 bit) per thread while fixing the maximum number of filter inputs as 256. As shown in the figure, as the filter size scales, the PAF/SF hit rates become smaller, i.e., fewer false positive happen. However, they are almost constant when the size is larger than 256 B. Based on this result, we choose 256 B for both PAF and SF.

Finally, Fig. 16 and 17 demonstrate how well our Bloom filter based detectors can represent the *sparseness/regularity* of memory accesses. In this evaluation, we examine a synthetic memory access code, in which the address of $i$th memory reference ($Addr_i$) is defined as follows: $Addr_i = Addr_{i-1} + \mu + URAND(-\Delta, \Delta)$ ($i > 0$). Namely, $\mu$ is the *average stride* of the accesses, which determines the *sparseness*, while $URAND(-\Delta, \Delta)$ is a *random noise* following a uniform distribution ranging from $-\Delta$ to $\Delta$, thus affects the *regularity*. As shown in those figures, each filter is effective to sense the associated access feature.

**Table 2.** Selected matrices

| Matrix name |
| --- |
| 2cubes_sphere, audikw_1, eu-2005, europe_osm, F1, FullChip, G_n_pin_pout, GL7d20, Hamrle3, hugebubbles-00020, HV15R, offshore, pkustk14, poisson3Db, pre2, rajat29, road_usa, scircuit, soc-sign-epinions, thermomech_dK, thermomech_dM, tmt_unsym, torso3, tx2010, wiki-Talk, wikipedia-20061104 |

## 5   To Stage or Not to Stage?

Figure 18 illustrates the overview of our strategy: on the $R_{paf}$-$R_{sf}$ plane (PAF/SF hit rates), we consider the Break Even Line (BEL)—at any points on the line, the time reduction gained in the second stage ($T_{boost}$) is equal to the copy overhead time ($T_{copy}$). If the pattern feature vector ($R_{paf}, R_{sf}$) is mapped below the BEL on the plane, we can achieve speed-up with the staging, otherwise not. The BEL is formulated as follows: $T_{boost}(R_{paf}, R_{sf}, P) - T_{copy}(P) = 0$.

In addition to the pattern features, this function also utilizes additional input parameters (denoted through the set $P = \{R_{write}, R_{util}, P_{else}\}$), which help fine tune the shape of the BEL. The definitions of these parameters are listed in Table 3. $T_{boost}()$ (the performance gain) will be shorter if the chunk is less utilized ($R_{util}$ is smaller), and it will also depend on the read/write access rate as read/write bandwidths are different in various memory systems. Furthermore, $T_{1st}/T_{3rd}$ in $T_{copy}()$ can be skipped if the chunk is read- or write-only ($R_{write}=0$ or 1) as described in Sect. 2.2. These parameters can be collected at such as the code transformation time[4].

### 5.1   Decision Criterium

First, we formulate $T_{copy}()$ [s/GB] as follows:

$$T_{copy}(P) = \alpha \cdot 1/B_{1st} + \beta \cdot 1/B_{3rd} = \alpha T_{1st} + \beta T_{3rd} \tag{1}$$

In the equation, $B_{1st}/B_{3rd}$ and $T_{1st}/T_{3rd}$ represent the copy bandwidth and the time per GB of the first/third stages, respectively (see also Sect. 2.2). Here, $\alpha = 0/\beta = 0$ stands when the write-/read-only case (namely, $R_{write} = 1/0$), otherwise we set $\alpha = 1/\beta = 1$, respectively. Note that $T_{copy}()$ does not depend on $R_{paf}$, $R_{sf}$, $R_{util}$, or others as it has nothing to do with how the chunk is accessed during the task except for $R_{write}$.

Second, we define $T_{boost}()$ [s/GB] (time per chunk size) as follows:

$$T_{boost}(R_{paf}, R_{sf}, P) = S(R_{util}, P_{else}) \cdot T'_{boost}(R_{paf}, R_{sf}, R_{write}) \tag{2}$$

Here, we divide $T_{boost}()$ into memory access pattern (or types) dependent/independent parts. $T'_{boost}()$ is a pattern dependent function, which can be regarded as the special case of $T_{boost}()$, namely when $S() = 1$ stands. $S()$ is a scaling factor, which is independent of the access pattern/types. In this paper, we utilize $S(R_{util}, P_{else}) = R_{util}$ assuming that a task takes N times longer when the access sequence also becomes N times longer with the same access pattern/types, which is generally the case. Further extensions of $S()$ will be discussed in Sect. 8.

---

[4] When we convert memory references into filter inputs in a target loop (see Sect. 4.1), we can also count the number of loads/stores in the loop and thus can estimate the write rate ($R_{write}$). As for $R_{util}$, we assume the chunk size is designated by the programmers, but we need to know the number of iterations of the target loop to obtain the number of references. One option for doing this is, like the parallel for statement in OpenMP, limiting the applicable targets to the canonical form loops. Another option is providing a mechanism to predict it.

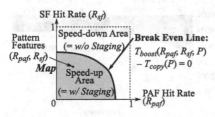

**Fig. 18.** Overview of decision making strategy

**Table 3.** Functions and parameters

| Time Functions/Parameter [s/GB] | |
|---|---|
| $T_{boost}()$ | Speed-up gained in the second stage |
| $T_{copy}()$ | Time overhead of the copy operations |
| $T_{th}$ | Threshold to set the decision aggressiveness |
| Pattern Features | |
| $R_{paf}$ | Page Address Filter (PAF) hit rate [0:1] |
| $R_{sf}$ | Stride Filter (SF) hit rate [0:1] |
| Additional parameters for fine tuning ($P$) | |
| $R_{write}$ | # of writes per reference on the chunk [0:1] |
| $R_{util}$ | # of references per element on the chunk |
| $P_{else}$ | Empty set, reserved for further tuning |

Then, we utilize the following linear approximation:

$$T'_{boost}(R_{psf}, R_{sf}, R_{write}) = R_{paf}C_0(R_{write}) + R_{sf}C_1(R_{write}) + C_2(R_{write}) \qquad (3)$$

We determine the coefficients ($C_i$) by testing the following three patterns on each memory (fast/large) for a fixed $R_{write}$: (1) random accesses on a large enough array ($R_{paf} \simeq 0, R_{sf} \simeq 0$), (2) accesses with a long enough stride ($R_{paf} \simeq 0, R_{sf} \simeq 1$), and (3) sequential streaming accesses ($R_{paf} \simeq 1, R_{sf} \simeq 1$). By acquiring $T'_{boost}()$ with measurements for these patterns (here put as $T_{rand}, T_{strd}$, and $T_{seq}$) and solving the given linear equations, we can gain $C_i$ for a fixed $R_{write}$.

We decide on whether to stage or not, based on these functions, combined with a threshold $T_{th}$. More specifically, we apply the staging if the following condition holds:

$$T_{boost}(R_{paf}, R_{sf}, P) - T_{copy}(P) > T_{th} \qquad (4)$$

When $T_{th}$ is set lower/higher, the staging is applied more aggressively/conservatively, respectively. We assume the parameter is predetermined, but as an option, this should also be controllable by users depending on their confidence.

## 5.2  Accuracy Analysis

We evaluate the accuracy of our staging criteria using synthetic workloads. The system/coefficients setups will be described in Sect. 6, and the sampling thread settings are based on the evaluation in Sect. 4.3. We apply our staging technique to the source vectors in SpMV operations (CRS format) whose matrices are listed in Table 2 in Sect. 4.3. In this evaluation, we utilize multiple vectors and organize a chunk by using consecutive vectors. The number of vectors is set so that the total data size becomes around 90 GB. Also, we scale the number of rows of the matrices from 1 to 1/32 to change the chunk utilization ($R_{util}$).

Figure 19 demonstrates the performance impact of false decisions. The horizontal axis represents workload number, while the vertical axis indicates relative performance, which is normalized to that of *Large Mem Only* (the pure large memory only solution). The workloads appear in the left side of the figure have smaller $R_{util}$ but higher $R_{sf}$ and $R_{paf}$—chunks are less utilized and more regularly accessed with higher locality. In this graph, the threshold parameter $T_{th}$

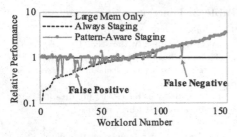

**Fig. 19.** Impact of false decisions

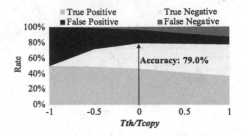

**Fig. 20.** Correctness of decisions

is set to 0. In the figure, *Always Staging* means the staging is always applied regardless of the access features.

According to the figure, the false decisions (*False Positive/Negative* in the figure) occur more often when the performance impact of decision makings is less significant (*Always Staging* and *Large Mem Only* are closer), which is a preferable feature for our approach. This is because (1) our approach basically compares $T_{boost}$ and $T_{copy}$, which is equal to comparing the performance of *Always Staging* and *Large Mem Only* as $|T_{boost} - T_{copy}| = |(T_{1st} + T_{2nd} + T_{3rd}) - T_{base}|$ (see also Sect. 2.2); and thus (2) this comparison becomes more error tolerant when the performance difference of the two approaches becomes larger.

Figure 20 shows the breakdown of decision types as a function of $T_{th}/T_{copy}$ ($T_{th}$: the threshold parameter used in decisions). In the figure, "True" means the decision is correct, and "Positive" represents the staging is conducted—the equation $T_{boost}() - T_{copy}() > T_{th}$ is expected to stand. As shown in the figure, 79% of the decisions are correct ("True Positive/Negative") at $T_{th}/T_{copy} = 0$. We can trade-off "False Positive" and "False Negative" by changing the threshold $T_{th}$. According to the figure, scaling $T_{th}/T_{copy}$ from 0 to 1 has no significant impact on the decision accuracy, allowing users to freely choose the right tradeoff. To balance false positives/negatives, we choose 0.5 in Sect. 6 and 7.

## 6   Evaluation Setup

Table 4 summarizes the environment for our experiments. We utilize a KNL-based system whose nodes provide a hybrid memory system [17]. The fast memory in the system supports both software-based scratch pad mode (*Flat*) and hardware-based data management (*Cache*), and we choose the former for our approach. The operating system used for the evaluation is Cent OS 7 and we use Intel C/C++ compiler (ICC) with the listed options. The sampling thread settings are based on the evaluation in Sect. 4.3, and the threshold parameter $T_{th}/T_{copy}$ is set to 0.5. Through this evaluation we set the number of threads to 256 for all of the applications. In our implementation, a 16 GB buffer is allocated to the fast memory using the memkind library [7], which is designed to use different kinds of memories in a node.

## 6.1 Coefficients Calibration

Before applying our approach, we have to correctly set the coefficients described in Sect. 5.1: $T_{1st}$, $T_{3rd}$, $T_{rand}$, $T_{strd}$ and $T_{seq}$. Here, we summarize how to acquire them. First, to obtain $T_{rand}$, $T_{strd}$ and $T_{seq}$ for a given $R_{write}$, we measure the bandwidth of the following tasks on both fast and large memories: (1) 1G times random accesses on an 8 GB array, (2) 2 M times stride accesses on 8 GB array (4 K + B stride) and (3) a streaming task on 8 GB array. In this paper, the measurements are performed for $R_{write} = \{0, 0.5, 1\}$ by changing the rate of load/store operations in the main loop of the test tasks. Second, to determine $T_{1st}$ and $T_{3rd}$, we just measure the copy bandwidth between the memories.

## 6.2 Implementation and Workloads

Our proposal is implemented manually in each application, following the example of various published studies of software-based data management [19,25]. In this evaluation, to represent widely used kernels for a range of applications especially in scientific computing, we choose various benchmarks from HPC Challenge (HPCC), NAS Parallel Benchmarks (NPB), and also use stencil codes (Jacobi2D/3D). The followings are the details:

*RandomAccess (HPCC)*: This application randomly updates a big table. We repeat the main update loop multiple times, and, in the loop, we filter the update accesses: only the accesses to a target area (chunk) pass the filter [14]. By doing so, we can restrain the accesses within the buffer in the fast memory and, at the same time, can conduct all the update accesses. Note that we apply this to all methods that we compare. In this evaluation, the total table size and the chunk size are set to 64 GB and 16 GB, respectively.

*PTRANS (HPCC)*: This application transposes a matrix and adds it to another $(T+ = A^T)$. These matrices are dividable into sub-matrices (chunks), and we apply our technique to the source matrix $A$, which is accessed with a long stride. In this evaluation, the total size of the matrices, and the chunk size are 96 GB (=48 GB × 2) and 16 GB, respectively

Table 4. Evaluation environment

| Name | Remarks |
|---|---|
| CPU | XeonPhi 7210, 64cores, 1.3 GHz, quadrant mode |
| Memory | **Fast Memory:** MCDRAM, 8ch, **450 GB/s**, 100 + ns, 16 GB, flat/cache mode<br>**Large Memory:** DDR4 DRAM, 2ch, 90 GB/s, 100 + ns, **96 GB**<br>**Measured Copy Bandwidth:** 79.7 [GB/s] (1st stage), 42.1 [GB/s] (3rd stage) |
| OS | CentOS 7 |
| Compiler | ICC 19.0, options: -O3, -qopenmp, -lmemkind, -xMIC-AVX512 |

***FFT (HPCC)***: This workload calculates one dimensional FFT using two 32 GB arrays: input and output array. We apply our staging technique to the output array by dividing it into 4 GB × 8 chunks. Through the evaluation, a temporal array is located at the fast memory.

***STREAM (HPCC)***: In this workload, a simple vector operation $dst = src$ is performed, and we applied our method to the destination vector $dst$. In the evaluation, the total data size is around 96 GB, and the chunk size is 16 GB.

***Jacobi2D/3D***: We utilize 5/7-point 2D/3D Jacobi stencil codes. In these codes, we keep the results of all time steps to different arrays (= chunks). We apply our technique to the source array, which is heavily loaded in the stencil operations. In this evaluation, the chunk size is set to 8 GB (the array size for one time step), and the total data size is 80 GB.

***IntegerSort (NPB)***: This workload sorts an integer array by counting the distribution of the elements (bucket sort). Our approach is applied to the array of the distribution (16 GB = the chunk size). The total data size is around 64 GB.

***ConjugateGradient(NPB)***: In this kernel, we focus on the iterative SpMV operations, as it is the major performance bottleneck. We apply our technique to the source vector for the SpMV operations whose size is 2 GB (= the chunk size). The total data size is 90 GB, which includes multiple different vectors.

### 6.3   Compared Methods

For the above workloads, we compare the performance of the following methods:
***LO:*** The execution with the ***L***arge memory ***O***nly (baseline).
***NP:*** The execution with a ***N***umactl command with ***P***referred option, which preferentially stores data on the fast memory [17].
***HC:*** The fast memory works as a direct mapped ***H***ardware ***C***ache [17].
***PS:*** The execution with our ***P***attern-aware ***S***taging.

## 7   Experimental Result

Figure 21 compares the performance among the methods across all applications. The vertical axis indicates relative performance that is normalized to *LO* for each application. `GeometricMean` in the figure shows the geometric mean of performance across all the workloads for each method. Our method (*PS*) achieves a factor of three performance improvement over *LO* at the best case and on average, it improves performance by a factor of 1.9. As the data management policy of *NP* is naive, it does not improve performance except for `STREAM`. Compared to hardware cache (*HC*), our approach has the following benefits: (1) ours purposely puts the useful chunk of data on the fast memory based on the pattern-analysis thus can avoid unnecessary allocations/conflicts on it; (2) ours can fully utilize the hardware resources of the fast memory, but the hardware cache wastes the available bandwidth/storage due to the hardware overheads such as tags. Thanks

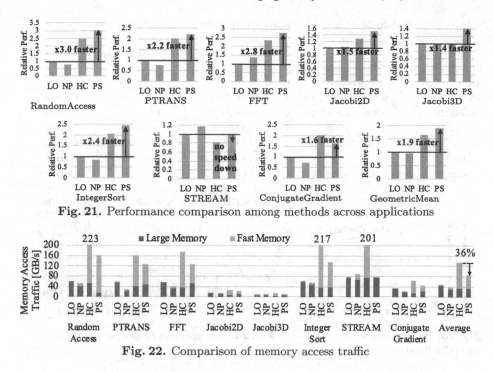

**Fig. 21.** Performance comparison among methods across applications

**Fig. 22.** Comparison of memory access traffic

to these characteristics, our *PS* outperforms *HC* for almost all workloads in this evaluation (up to 41%).

Figure 22 demonstrates the memory access traffic (or bandwidth consumption) on the two different memories. The measurement was accomplished through Intel PCM, a well-known performance monitoring tool. Although our approach increases the data traffic compared with *LO/NP* due to the additional data transfer between the memories, it reduces 36% of the traffic compared with *HC* on average. This is because *HC* induces unnecessary data conflicts on the fast memory, while ours not as described later. This traffic reduction will lead to a considerable power reduction on the memory system as a consequence.

One exception in Fig. 21 is `ConjugateGradient` (the hardware cache works better than ours), and we can see the reason in Fig. 23: in the figure, the X-axis represents the total data size, while the Y-axis indicates the relative performance normalized to *LO* at 16 GB. When the data footprint size is small enough, the hardware cache approach can keep almost all the useful data on the fast memory, thus it works well. However, as we scale the data size, more conflicts happen on the fast memory, which degrades performance significantly. In contrast to this, ours can explicitly hold the useful data without conflicts on the fast memory no matter how much we scale the total footprint. Therefore, if we would scale the data size more (over 96 GB, the capacity limitation in our system), ours would work better than the hardware cache for this workload.

Finally, we summarize the statistics of our approach in Table 5. The pattern features ($R_{paf}$, $R_{sf}$) are taken from our sampling technique, while the other

**Table 5.** Statistics of our pattern-aware staging approach

| Name | $R_{paf}$ | $R_{sf}$ | $R_{util}$ | $R_{write}$ | Estimated $T_{boost}/T_{copy} - 1.5$ | Measured $T_{boost}/T_{copy} - 1$ | Decision Correctness |
|------|-----------|----------|------------|-------------|-----------|----------|----------|
| RandomAccess | 0.0388 | 0.0620 | 8 | 0.5 | 22.4 (>0) | 20.3 (>0) | Correct |
| PTRANS | 0.00297 | 0.999 | 1 | 0 | 6.10 (>0) | 3.73 (>0) | Correct |
| FFT | 0.968 | 0.998 | 4.5 | 1 | 5.04 (>0) | 9.08 (>0) | Correct |
| Jacobi2D | 0.998 | 0.998 | 5 | 0 | 3.01 (>0) | 1.67 (>0) | Correct |
| Jacobi3D | 0.996 | 0.998 | 7 | 0 | 4.87 (>0) | 2.18 (>0) | Correct |
| IntegerSort | 0.691 | 0.687 | 6 | 0.5 | 10.2 (>0) | 10.6 (>0) | Correct |
| STREAM | 0.998 | 0.999 | 1 | 1 | −0.315 (<0) | −0.331 (<0) | Correct |
| ConjugateGradient | 0.368 | 0.0947 | 7 | 0 | 31.3 (> 0) | 17.8 (>0) | Correct |

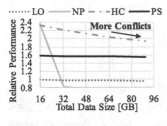

**Fig. 23.** Performance vs. data size (ConjugateGradient)

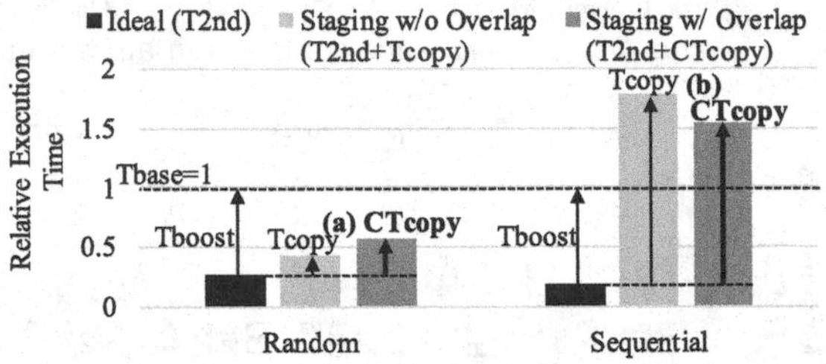

**Fig. 24.** Performance/overhead comparison

parameters ($R_{util}$, $R_{write}$) are acquired by manually counting the number of load/store instructions to the target array in the target loop. As for the decision makings, if $T_{boost} - T_{copy} - T_{th}$ is greater than zero, which is equal to $T_{boost}/T_{copy} - 1.5 > 0$ in our $T_{th}$ setting, we use the staging technique; otherwise not (see also Eq. (4) in Sect. 5.1). From this point of view, *as long as the **signs** of the estimated $T_{boost}/T_{copy} - 1.5$ and the measured $T_{boost}/T_{copy} - 1$ are the **same***, our *approach is correct,* and our approach is correct for all the workloads. Note that by adjusting $T_{th}$ based on the observation in Sect. 5.2, our approach successfully avoids slow down for STREAM unlike *HC*.

## 8   Discussions

***Applicability of the Approach:*** The most significant restriction to apply our approach to a kernel is that the data structure of a potential target array has to be transformable into a multi-dimensional array form (e.g., into a matrix or SoA). Note that several access optimization approaches, such as multi-pass gather/scatter [14], are useful to meet this requirement. For multi-dimensional arrays, we can choose a chunk by designating the indices for the higher dimensions, and at the same time, we can ensure the size of the chunk and the area of the accesses. After copying the chunk to the fast memory, the pointer to the data is replaced to go to the fast memory, while the remaining data stays in the large memory. With this, any complicated access pattern that includes accesses to both inside/outside of the chunked area are handled correctly, but the performance gain will be less if too many accesses don't hit the target chunk.

We assume the indices to choose the target chunk are manually assigned by the programmer just before the target loop by using a specific function to set them. However, it is not always easy for the programmer to set the right indices. One promising option to cope with this issue is providing a functionality to automatically choose the chunk that is most likely to be intensively accessed. We can support this option by extending our sampling and characterization approach to include additional filters to store the indices.

Our approach is applicable regardless of the number of arrays the target kernel accesses. In this work, we assume the programmer chooses one array by designating the variable in the directive shown in Fig. 8, and then the compiler generates a distilled version of the code that executes only the address generation path for the target while ignoring the others, which relies on the prior helper threading works [19,22,25,31]. However, our approach is extensible to multiple arrays: (1) listing them in the directive; (2) creating the address generation paths for all the targets; and (3) storing the addresses in their own unique filters separately. To this end, the decision making part needs several modifications (in both the decision function and the control structure after it).

When multiple different array/pointer variables are used in a kernel, pointer aliasing can potentially happen, i.e., different variables point to the same memory. Namely, even if a chunk is moved to the fast memory for a variable, another pointer may point to the old data stored on the large memory. One option to cope with this is applying our technique only when the programmer specifies that they are free from the aliasing by putting a keyword like *restrict* supported in C99. Such a keyword is widely utilized to allow compilers aggressive optimizations, and our approach can be considered one of them in a broad view.

***Overlapping and Pipelining:*** Pipelining is a well-known technique to hide the communication latency between components/nodes by overlapping computation and data transfer [28]. In our case, the second stage for one chunk and the first/third copy stages of other chunks can be overlapped (see also Sect. 2). However, we purposely do not consider this optimization in our approach due to *significant hardware contention* on the fast memory, as all of the stages access it intensively for *memory intensive tasks*.

We quantify the impact of the contention using the same environment and workloads as in Sect. 2.3, which clarifies that the performance benefit of overlapping is limited or even harmful (Fig. 24)[5]. This is due to the following reasons: the overlapping does not reduce the amount of traffic on the memory subsystem;

---

[5] * For "Staging w/ Overlap", we refer to the contention overhead as $C \times T_{copy}$, i.e., this approach is beneficial only when both $C < 1$ and $T_{boost} > CT_{copy}$ stand, which is **not the case in the figure: neither (a) nor (b).**
* "Ideal" or "Staging w/o Overlap" are executed by 64 threads, while for "Staging w/ Overlap", additional 64 copy threads also run in parallel and are distributed to all 64 cores to balance the loads. The contention in core resources does not matter as the memory is the bottleneck.

it can cause more conflicts on the memory resources (e.g., at row buffers [38]) for case (a) ; and the copy time is too large to hide for case (b).

***Interaction with Hardware Caching:*** In our evaluation, when applying our technique, we utilized the fast memory as a scratchpad region instead of a hardware cache. This is because the major benefit of our technique is *selectively* allocating a useful chunk on the fast memory, which should be *conflict free*, but the cache mode evicts data placed on the fast memory by automatically allocating the others (even more so for larger data, as demonstrated in Fig. 23).

***Application to Other Platforms:*** Our methodology is applicable to any hybrid memory systems including the configuration of DRAM+NVRAM [16,38]. This is because ours is based on the fundamental architectural principle: memories are optimized and thus operate significantly faster for sequential accesses [5,16,20,33,38] regardless of the memory cell implementation. Based on the above, our decision criterion estimates the impact of access pattern/types using several system-dependent coefficients. Thus, what we have to do when applying ours to different platforms is just updating the coefficients, i.e., the calibration process performed in Sect. 6.1, which is *needed only once for a system*.

***Automation:*** Although we quantify the effectiveness of our proposal, some parts, such as the sampling and the staging, are hand coded. In future work, we will automate them in the compilers/runtime tool chain such as LLVM [24] or the ROSE compiler [30], similar to previous software-based data management studies [22,28,31]. For this automation, our approach needs to obtain some parameters ($P$) at the code generation time or by using augmented codes at runtime as described in Sect. 5 (see the footnote). As for the staging part, existing compiler techniques to apply pipelining to CPU-GPU systems will be useful [28]. In addition, acquiring more parameters ($P_{else}$) at compilation or runtime and updating the scaling function $S()$ accordingly is a promising direction to cover more aspects in the decision making. One example for this is counting floating operations and memory access instructions in the target loops, calculating the arithmetic intensity based on the results, and tuning $S()$ following our existing models.

## 9   Related Work

Since hybrid memory systems have become a significant design choice recently, various software-based data placement techniques for them have been proposed. Due to their limited availabilities, we couldn't compare our approach with them quantitatively in the evaluation. However, our technique qualitatively has the following uniqueness/benefit compared with them: (1) ours does not require any application profiles; and thus (2) ours can detect the pattern of both input-dependent/independent memory accesses well, while the others cannot. Especially, when the pattern heavily depends on the input such as the problem settings, which is often the case for the scientific computing, our runtime pattern analysis approach becomes essential.

Data Tiering API provides a memory allocation interface that optimizes the page allocations automatically, but the decisions are based on the application statistics that depend on the inputs [13]. Unimem API provides a similar memory allocation interface and optimizes the placements at the granularity of data objects. However, it does not target the chunking except for sequential accesses [36]. A prior study proposed a compiler-based technique that attempts to optimize the initial data allocations, but it does not handle the data transfer and relies on a statical analysis [21]. Some runtime-based approaches target different programming model, such as task parallel programming [1,37], which is out of our scope. Other studies focus on application specific solutions [6,27], but ours aims at covering general applications. OS/HW-level page managements have been widely studied for hybrid memory systems, but they require hardware modifications [11,38]. A recently proposed page scheduler does not require such hardware, but needs a large number of profiles to work [12].

## 10 Conclusions

This paper proposed and made a case for a software-based data management technique called patten-aware staging to exploit both the high performance and the large capacity components of hybrid main memory systems. Our technique dynamically examines the pattern of memory accesses and, in case of irregular/sparse patterns, fetches chunks of data from large memories to fast memories, just before they are referenced. The experimental results using scientific codes on a real system show that our approach enables 300% improvements compared to using only large memory and still 41% compared to hardware caching.

**Acknowledgments.** We are grateful to all the reviewers of ISC'20, CGO'20, ICS'19, and IPDPS'19 for their valuable suggestions. In particular, we would like to express our sincere gratitude to our shepherd in ISC'20 for helping us with completing this work. Also, we would like to thank folks in CAPS at TU Munich, ITC at U Tokyo, and CASC at LLNL for their helpful comments to carry out this study. This work is partly supported by JSPS Grant-in-Aid for Research Activity Start-up (JP16H06677), JSPS Grant-in-Aid for Early-Career Scientists (JP18K18021), and Research on Processor Architecture, Power Management, System Software and Numerical Libraries for the Post K Computer System of RIKEN.

## References

1. Alvarez, L., et al.: Runtime-guided management of stacked DRAM memories in task parallel programs. In: ICS, pp. 218–228 (2018)
2. Bell, N., et al.: Implementing sparse matrix-vector multiplication on throughput-oriented processors. In: SC, pp. 18:1–18:11 (2009)
3. Benoit, A., et al.: A performance model to execute workflows on high-bandwidth-memory architectures. In: ICPP, pp. 36:1–36:10 (2018)

4. Bloom, B.H.: Space/time trade-offs in hash coding with allowable errors. Commun. ACM **13**(7), 422–426 (1970)
5. Burnett, G.J., et al.: A study of interleaved memory systems. In: AFIPS 1970 (Spring), pp. 467–474 (1970)
6. Butcher, N., et al.: Optimizing for KNL usage modes when data doesn't fit in MCDRAM. In: ICPP, pp. 37:1–37:10 (2018)
7. Cantalupo, C., et al.: User Extensible Heap Manager for Heterogeneous Memory Platforms and Mixed Memory Policies (2015)
8. Chatterjee, N., et al.: Architecting an energy-efficient dram system for GPUs. In: HPCA, pp. 73–84 (2017)
9. Consortium, H.M.C.: Hybrid Memory Cube Specification 2.1. Last Revision January (2015)
10. Davis, T.A., et al.: The university of Florida sparse matrix collection. ACM TOMS **38**(1), 1:1–1:25 (2011)
11. Dhiman, G., et al.: PDRAM: a Hybrid PRAM and DRAM main memory system. In: DAC, pp. 664–669 (2009)
12. Doudali, T.D., et al.: Kleio: a hybrid memory page scheduler with machine intelligence. In: HPDC, pp. 37–48 (2019)
13. Dulloor, S.R., et al.: Data tiering in heterogeneous memory systems. In: EuroSys (2016)
14. He, B., et al.: Efficient gather and scatter operations on graphics processors. In: SC, pp. 1–12 (2007)
15. Intel: Intel®Agilex™FPGA Advanced Information Brief: (Device Overview). INTEL (2019)
16. Izraelevitz, J., et al.: Basic performance measurements of the intel Optane DC persistent memory module. arXiv preprint arXiv:1903.05714 (2019)
17. Jeffers, J., et al.: Intel Xeon Phi Processor High Performance Programming: Knights, Landing edn. Morgan Kaufmann Publishers Inc., San Francisco (2016)
18. Jun, H.: HBM (High Bandwidth Memory) for 2.5D. SEMICON Taiwan (2015)
19. Kamruzzaman, M., et al.: Inter-core prefetching for multicore processors using migrating helper threads. In: ASPLOS, pp. 393–404 (2011)
20. Kaseridis, D., et al.: Minimalist open-page: a DRAM page-mode scheduling policy for the many-core era. In: MICRO, pp. 24–35 (2011)
21. Khaldi, D., et al.: Towards automatic HBM allocation using LLVM: a case study with knights landing. In: LLVM-HPC 2016, pp. 12–20 (2016)
22. Kim, D., et al.: Physical Experimentation with Prefetching Helper Threads on Intel's Hyper-Threaded Processors. In: CGO, p. 27 (2004)
23. Kim, J., et al.: HBM: memory solution for bandwidth-hungry processors. In: Hot Chips 26 Symposium (HCS), pp. 1–24 (2014)
24. Lattner, C., et al.: LLVM: a compilation framework for lifelong program analysis & transformation. In: CGO, p. 75 (2004)
25. Lee, J., et al.: Prefetching with helper threads for loosely coupled multiprocessor systems. IEEE TPDS **20**(9), 1309–1324 (2009)
26. Matsuoka, S., et al.: From FLOPS to BYTES: disruptive change in high-performance computing towards the post-moore eera. In: CF, pp. 274–281 (2016)
27. Miao, H., et al.: StreamBox-HBM: stream analytics on high bandwidth hybrid memory. In: ASPLOS, pp. 167–181 (2019)
28. Mokhtari, R., et al.: BigKernel - high performance CPU-GPU communication pipelining for big data-style applications. In: IPDPS, pp. 819–828 (2014)
29. Mutlu, O., et al.: Research problems and opportunities in memory systems. SUPERFRI **1**(3), 19–55 (2014)

30. Quinlan, D.: ROSE: compiler support for object-oriented frameworks. Parallel Process. Lett. **10**(02n03), 215–226 (2000)
31. Song, Y., et al.: Design and implementation of a compiler framework for helper threading on multi-core processors. In: PACT, pp. 99–109 (2005)
32. Stanley-Marbell, P., et al.: Pinned to the walls: impact of packaging and application properties on the memory and power walls. In: ISLPED, pp. 51–56 (2011)
33. Tang, X., et al.: Improving bank-level parallelism for irregular applications. In: MICRO, pp. 1–12 (2016)
34. Vetter, J.S., et al.: Opportunities for nonvolatile memory systems in extreme-scale high-performance computing. Comput. Sci. Eng. **17**(2), 73–82 (2015)
35. Vijayaraghavan, T., et al.: Design and analysis of an APU for exascale computing. In: HPCA, pp. 85–96 (2017)
36. Wu, K., et al.: UNIMEM: runtime data management on non-volatile memory-based heterogeneous main memory. In: SC, pp. 58:1–58:14 (2017)
37. Wu, K., et al.: Runtime data management on non-volatile memory-based heterogeneous memory for task-parallel programs. In: SC (2018)
38. Yoon, H., et al.: Row buffer locality aware caching policies for hybrid memories. In: ICCD, pp. 337–344 (2012)

# Simplifying Communication Overlap in OpenSHMEM Through Integrated User-Level Thread Scheduling

Md. Wasi-ur- Rahman[1]([✉]), David Ozog[2], and James Dinan[2]

[1] Intel Corporation, Austin, TX, USA
md.rahman@intel.com
[2] Intel Corporation, Hudson, MA, USA

**Abstract.** Overlap of communication with computation is a key optimization for high performance computing (HPC) applications. In this paper, we explore the usage of user-level threading to enable productive and efficient communication overlap and pipelining. We extend OpenSHMEM with integrated user-level thread scheduling, enabling applications to leverage fine-grain threading as an alternative to non-blocking communication. Our solution introduces communication-aware thread scheduling that utilizes the communication state of threads to minimize context switching overheads. We identify several patterns common to multi-threaded OpenSHMEM applications, leverage user-level threads to increase overlap of communication and computation, and explore the impact of different thread scheduling policies. Results indicate that user-level threading can enable blocking communication to meet the performance of highly-optimized, non-blocking, single-threaded codes with significantly lower application-level complexity. In one case, we observe a 28.7% performance improvement for the Smith-Waterman DNA sequence alignment benchmark.

## 1 Introduction

Communication latency hiding through pipelining and overlap with computation are key optimizations for High Performance Computing (HPC) applications. Popular communication middleware, such as MPI [22] and OpenSHMEM [24], facilitate these optimizations through non-blocking communication; however, managing asynchronous data movement can lead to significant application-level complexity. Multi-threaded programming can provide a simpler approach to enabling communication asynchrony, but the over-subscription required to reach effective pipelining depths can result in high context switching overheads in typical multi-threaded environments.

User-level threading and tasking models have been proposed as alternatives to conventional operating system (OS) scheduled threads. In contrast with OS threads, user-level threads reduce context switching overheads through cooperative, rather than preemptive, thread scheduling that is performed at the user level, without invoking the OS thread scheduler. Thus, relative to OS level multi-threading approaches, user-level threading enables a greater number of fine-grain operations to be in-flight. By reducing

The original version of this chapter was revised: The chapter was reverted to a regular, non-Open Access chapter. The correction to this chapter is available at https://doi.org/10.1007/978-3-030-50743-5_28

© Springer Nature Switzerland AG 2020, corrected publication 2020
P. Sadayappan et al. (Eds.): ISC High Performance 2020, LNCS 12151, pp. 496–516, 2020.
https://doi.org/10.1007/978-3-030-50743-5_25

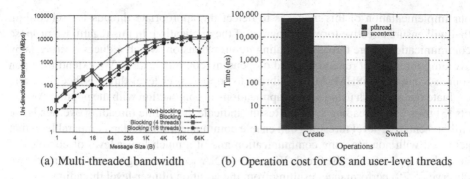

(a) Multi-threaded bandwidth          (b) Operation cost for OS and user-level threads

**Fig. 1.** Opportunities for user-level threads with OpenSHMEM applications

these overheads, user-level threading can make feasible multithreaded approaches to hiding communication latency.

Version 1.4 of the OpenSHMEM specification [24] was recently ratified and introduced threading support that allows OpenSHMEM programs with multi-threaded processes (PEs). This new feature enables hybrid programming with OpenSHMEM, which can be exploited to enable on-node shared memory programming and to enable trade-offs between the number of PEs and number of threads on a given node. However, in traditional usage, hybrid programming has avoided over-subscription, because of the overheads associated with context switching.

Figure 1(a) illustrates the performance challenges associated with multi-threading using a bandwidth experiment where 8 sender and receiver PEs are involved in measuring the uni-directional streaming bandwidth through the shmem_put operation. Further details of the experimental setup are available in Sect. 5. In this experiment, we use both blocking and non-blocking versions of the API and also launch the blocking API test with multiple OpenMP [6] threads. As shown in Fig. 1(a), while 4 OpenMP threads with blocking APIs improve the bandwidth achieved for several message sizes compared to the non-blocking API experiment, 16 OpenMP threads cause the performance to degrade relative to the blocking API experiment because of the over-subscription overheads.

A challenge to user-level threading is that such models require explicit, cooperative scheduling of threads and deadlock can occur if threads block in OpenSHMEM operations without first yielding. However, user-level control results in significantly lower overheads, as shown in Fig. 1(b), which compares user-level and OS thread creation and context switch operation costs. In this comparison, user-level threads are created using the Unix* ucontext [1] interface. The context switch overhead is measured by averaging a total of 100,000 context switches between two participating threads using a synthetic benchmark [8]. This experiment highlights that user-level threading can significantly reduce overheads.

In this work, we leverage these insights to design a generic thread scheduling extension to OpenSHMEM that integrates user-level threading with the OpenSHMEM middleware, enabling the runtime system to perform cooperative thread scheduling when threads become blocked in communication operations. One of the major challenges in our implementation of this model is to detect the appropriate threads for scheduling that will ensure effective forward progress of the application. In this regard, we propose communication-aware thread scheduling in our extension, which reduces overheads by avoiding threads that remain blocked on pending communication. We extend the open source Sandia OpenSHMEM [30] library to support user-level thread scheduling and evaluate our approach using several applications in conjunction with the popular Argobots [3] user-level threading system. Results indicate that, while threading overheads are still present, user-level threading can enable communication overlap comparable to that achieved with non-blocking communication and at a much lower level of complexity in application code. For the Smith-Waterman DNA sequence alignment benchmark, we observe 28.7% performance resulting from the addition of user-level threading.

## 2 Background and Related Work

We begin with a summary of the OpenSHMEM library specification, focusing on the recent developments that define multi-threaded interfaces, which are most relevant to this paper. For additional detail on the OpenSHMEM APIs, we refer the reader to the OpenSHMEM specification [24]. Next, we review user-level threading and prior approaches to thread integration.

### 2.1 OpenSHMEM

OpenSHMEM [24] is a community specification that defines a Partitioned Global Address Space (PGAS) parallel programming model. An OpenSHMEM application is comprised of multiple processes (PEs) running the same program, where each PE is parameterized with a unique integer identity in the range $0 \ldots npes - 1$. PEs expose a symmetric data segment and a symmetric heap for remote access. The values in memory at each PE differ; however, the layout of the symmetric segments is identical at all PEs, simplifying usage and providing opportunities for implementations to optimize performance. OpenSHMEM defines a library API that enables asynchronous, one-sided access to symmetric data at all PEs through put/get data transfers, atomic operations, and collective communication primitives.

The recently released OpenSHMEM 1.4 specification introduced support for multi-threaded communication with OpenSHMEM routines. Similar to multi-threading in MPI, OpenSHMEM provides an initialization routine, shmem_init_thread, which allows the user to specify a level of thread support required by the application. The most restrictive thread level is SHMEM_THREAD_SINGLE, for which there must *not* be any threads used by the application; and the least restrictive thread level supported is SHMEM_THREAD_MULTIPLE for which *any* thread may call an OpenSHMEM routine at any time. There is also a SHMEM_THREAD_FUNNELED model in which only a main thread invokes OpenSHMEM routines and a SHMEM_THREAD_SERIALIZED model, in which the application serializes OpenSHMEM calls made by any application thread.

OpenSHMEM 1.4 also introduced a communication *contexts* API, which facilitates better overlap of communication and computation by enabling applications to express streams of operations that can be synchronized and ordered independently. The contexts

API enables implementations to isolate groups of threads, reduce internal threading overheads, and more effectively manage underlying communication resources [14].

## 2.2 Sandia OpenSHMEM and OFI

We define a generic extension to OpenSHMEM to support an arbitrary user-level thread or task system focusing on the open source Sandia OpenSHMEM (SOS) implementation [30] that uses the OpenFabrics Interfaces (OFI) libfabric communication library [16] to support multiple popular HPC networks. Detailed descriptions of the implementation of SOS on OFI can be found in [31].

The OFI libfabric communication library provides a common, low-level interface to high-speed networks. OFI's design is focused on portable support for HPC communication, which requires low latency and high throughput. OFI defines a complete set of interfaces that enable one-sided and two-sided messaging, memory registration, communication event management, collective communication, and many other features. A primary focus of this work are OFI communication event counters that are used in SOS to track the number of communication operations pending on a given context.

## 2.3 User-Level Thread Libraries

User-level thread systems are similar to conventional OS threads; both models allow applications to create multiple threads to expose tasks that can be executed simultaneously. During execution, threads can yield when they become idle and when thread execution ends, threads join with a parent thread. OS threads are typically scheduled preemptively where the OS periodically interrupts the execution of threads to perform a context switch that exchanges the currently executing thread for another thread. The preemptive scheduling model guarantees that all OS threads make forward progress. User-level threads, on the other hand, are scheduled cooperatively where a thread either completes or executes a yield operation to enable another thread to execute. The cooperative scheduling model relies on threads to cooperatively yield in order for other threads to make forward progress.

A user-level threading yield operation may automatically choose the next thread to execute. Alternatively, the yielding thread can supply a context to specify the next thread, as is done with the Unix* ucontext and Boost [10] fcontext APIs. In such models, thread contexts are continuations that capture the state of a suspended thread and these models are commonly used as a lower layer by user-level threading and multitasking systems.

User-level thread and task execution models have been explored extensively in the context of HPC programming [11]. The Argobots [32] threading package used in this work provides a lightweight, user-level threading model that is similar to that of QThreads [35], MassiveThreads [23], Intel® Thread Building Blocks [28], and StackThreads [34]. Such user-level threading systems transparently map user level threads to one or more underlying OS threads. These OS-level threads provide the execution resource on which user-level threads are executed and are often referred to as shepherd threads. The parallel execution of these shepherd threads are, in turn, managed by the OS. While this mapping does allow for over-subscription, in HPC workloads, shepherds are typically not oversubscribed and are pinned to a specific processor core.

**Listing 1.** Proposed APIs for OpenSHMEM support of user-level thread scheduling

```
/* Register yield routine */
void shmemx_register_yield(void (*yield_fn)());

/* Optional routines to register user level thread info provider */
void shmemx_register_getultinfo(void (*get_ult_info_fn)(int *, uint64_t *));
void shmemx_register_getulthandle(void* (*get_ult_handle_fn)(void));

/* Optional scheduler initialize and finalize routines */
void shmemx_ult_scheduler_init(shmemx_scheduler_config conf);
void shmemx_ult_scheduler_finalize(void);

/* Optional routines for query and thread management within scheduler */
int shmemx_get_next_runnable_ult(void **next_ult);
int shmemx_get_registered_ult_count(void);
void shmemx_ult_unregister(void);
```

## 2.4  Integrated User-Level Threading

Lightweight threading has been extensively explored in the context of MPI applications. MPC-MPI [25] and FG-MPI [19] have explored supporting multiple MPI processes as threads within a single OS process. To increase overlapping between communication and computation, MPI/SMPS [21] proposed a hybrid environment of MPI and task based shared memory programming model [26] that allow the asynchronous communication among processes. Adaptive MPI [18] executes MPI processes as Charm++ tasks that can be adaptively scheduled. Castillo et al. [12,13] proposed to leverage MPI internal information to task-based runtime systems for making better scheduling decisions, whereas Sala et al. [29] utilized the external event information to pause and resume scheduled tasks. The most closely related research work to this work is MPI+ULT [20], which explored the usage of hybrid programming with MPI and user-level threads. As we explore in this work, the asynchronous, one-sided communication model provided by OpenSHMEM introduces unique challenges and opportunities to integration with user-level threading.

## 3  Enabling Thread Integration in OpenSHMEM

Supporting user-level threading effectively in an OpenSHMEM library requires integration of cooperative thread scheduling to prevent deadlock in scenarios where threads block or poll on updates to memory (e.g. in a call to shmem_wait or repeated calls to shmem_test) and to hide latency in scenarios where threads become blocked on communication (e.g. in a call to shmem_get). We propose several OpenSHMEM API extensions to register callbacks and provide query routines needed to support cooperative user-level thread scheduling in the OpenSHMEM library. The proposed API routines are shown in Listing 1 as OpenSHMEM extensions, prefixed by shmemx_*.

Among the proposed APIs, the only routine required to support user-level threading is shmemx_register_yield, which registers a callback that the OpenSHMEM library invokes to yield the current thread. In our proposed API, the yield function is defined to take no arguments and utilize the scheduling policies as defined by the application.

To enable deep integration of user-level threading with OpenSHMEM, we define two registration routines that register callbacks enabling OpenSHMEM implementations to collect user-level thread specific information, such as thread ID, shepherd ID, and thread handle. These optional routines enable the OpenSHMEM library to track the runnable state of threads that block on communication and use this information to optimize thread scheduling. To enable this usage model, we introduce an initialization API for setting up the thread scheduler before creating the threads. Through this initialization routine, the user can optionally provide a configuration argument that specifies the total number of shepherd threads and user-level threads. This configuration setting can also allow the user to customize the scheduler, for example to prioritize threads performing one RMA operation to another to optimize forward progress of the threads. For example, if an application is executing two sets of threads with one set executing a fetch operation and the other executing a put using the fetched content, the user can set the fetch operation priority higher so that the scheduler prioritizes those threads leading to improved communication overlap. The shmemx_ult_scheduler_finalize routine releases all resources and resets all the counters associated with the scheduler.

The optional routine shmemx_get_next_runnable_ult allows a user-level thread scheduler to query OpenSHMEM for a thread handle that is ready to be run. The library implementation can define its own policy on choosing the next runnable thread. The query routine shmemx_get_registered_ult_count returns the total number of registered user-level threads within the OpenSHMEM layer. This information will provide application flexibility to choose the next thread either from the already executing ones or from the ones that have not been started yet, if any. Finally, we provide a routine that unregisters a user-level thread from the OpenSHMEM library, removing it from the internal data structure that holds the thread information. A code example demonstrating the API usage is shown in Listing 2.

Through the optional APIs listed in Listing 1, we provide the user flexibility to control the scheduling policy as needed. An alternative approach will be to design the thread scheduling transparent to the user, without providing any control. While such a design approach would greatly reduce the complexity of using the APIs, it would require the OpenSHMEM library either to communicate with the underlying thread library that the user chooses or to implement the desired thread library functionalities within itself.

## 4   Design of OpenSHMEM with Integrated User-Level Threading

An architectural view of user-level threading integrated with OpenSHMEM is shown in Fig. 2(a). In this model, the application uses a user-level threading package to parallelize the workload within an OpenSHMEM PE and individual threads perform OpenSHMEM operations. In the OpenSHMEM 1.4 API, all point-to-point communication operations are associated with an application-level context and users can assign threads to different contexts to enable communication isolation.

We have extended the open source Sandia OpenSHMEM (SOS) library to support the proposed model, namely with the ability to yield and transfer execution among the user-level threads through callbacks registered by the application. By default, SOS

Listing 2. An example program in C highlighting the proposed API usage

```
void thread_func() {
  // execute thread parallel operations
  shmemx_ult_unregister();
}
void my_yield() {
  if (shmemx_get_registered_ult_count() == total_threads &&
      shmemx_get_next_runnable_ult(&next_thread))
    // yield directly to next_thread
  else
    // yield using default policy
}
void *my_get_thread_handle(void) { /* return current thread handle */ }
void my_get_ult_info(int *shepherd, uint64_t *tid) { /* return ult info */ }

int main(int argc, char* argv[]) {
  ...
  shmemx_register_yield(&my_yield);
  shmemx_register_getultinfo(&my_get_ult_info);
  shmemx_register_getulthandle(&my_get_thread_handle);

  ...
  shmemx_ult_scheduler_init(thread_conf);
  for (i = 0; i < num_threads; i++) { thread_create(..., thread_func, ...); }
  for (i = 0; i < num_threads; i++) { thread_join(...); }
  shmemx_ult_scheduler_finalize();
  ...
}
```

invokes the registered user-level threading yield function to participate in cooperative scheduling. A more advanced communication-aware thread scheduling module is also provided that tracks the communication state of individual threads to identify runnable threads from within the OpenSHMEM layer and avoid the overhead of switching to threads that are still blocked on OpenSHMEM operations. This module utilizes completion counters [14,27] associated with the OpenSHMEM contexts used by individual threads to track completions and identify runnable threads.

To hide latency associated with blocked one-sided communication operations, we extend the communication flows used by SOS as shown in Fig. 2(b). This figure shows the existing sequence of operations used to implement OpenSHMEM operations using the OpenFabrics Interfaces libfabric communication layer. In the existing approach, an OpenSHMEM blocking RMA operation relies on waiting on any update on the event counters provided by the OFI through invoking fi_cntr_wait. With our proposed changes, an RMA operation initiated by a user thread checks for completion, releases any locks, and yields to the next runnable thread if there is no update on the event counter associated with the given context. In this way, another thread can commence its execution while the original thread goes to a pending state and returns when the blocking operation gets completed.

### 4.1 Implementation of Communication Aware Thread Scheduling

Upon initialization by the application, the scheduler allocates a queue to hold thread data objects for threads blocked on OpenSHMEM operations. The thread data object stores thread ID, corresponding shepherd ID, thread handle, etc. It also contains the

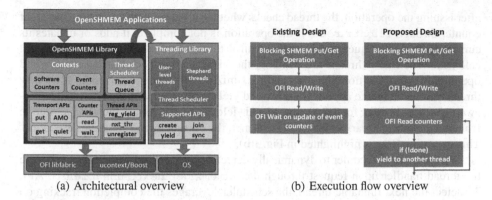

(a) Architectural overview          (b) Execution flow overview

**Fig. 2.** High-level overview for OpenSHMEM library integrated with user-level threads

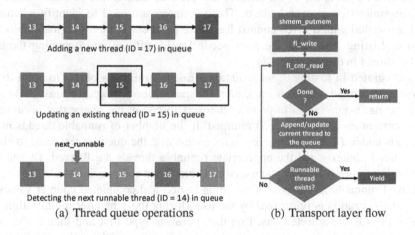

(a) Thread queue operations          (b) Transport layer flow

**Fig. 3.** Implementation details and the library usage of the thread scheduler

OpenSHMEM context that the thread is associated with along with the operation type (e.g. put, get) on which the thread is currently blocked. In addition, it maintains a flag indicating whether the thread is currently runnable. The queue data structure is used to support three basic operations as shown in Fig. 3(a):

*Append:* New threads are appended and remain in the queue until they are unregistered.

*Update:* Existing threads can be updated, e.g. when yielding in a blocking operation. An update operation moves the thread object to the end of the queue.

*Remove:* Upon completion, threads are removed from the queue. This is achieved at the application level by calling either shmemx_ult_unregister or shmemx_ult_scheduler_finalize.

After the scheduler is initialized, the library appends threads to the queue the first time a thread blocks on an RMA, AMO, or synchronization operation. Immediately after issuing the operation, the thread checks whether it is complete by reading the event counter through `fi_cntr_read`. If the operation is not complete, it adds or updates its current status to the queue and returns control to the application through the `yield` callback. When new threads are pending, the yield routine performs a generic yield operation to start additional threads and maximize communication overlap. If no new threads are pending, the application-provided yield routine queries the communication-aware thread scheduler for a ready thread and yields to it by invoking the *yield_to* routine from the threading library. If neither case is met, the current thread continues execution. This execution flow is highlighted in Fig. 3(b).

We design the scheduler to dynamically detect the next runnable thread and provide the thread handler upon request through the `shmemx_get_next_runnable_ult` API. To detect the next runnable thread, the scheduler leverages the completion tracking on individual OpenSHMEM contexts as described in [15]. In SOS, completion tracking is implemented by unsigned 64-bit integers that provide the number of issued and completed operations on a given context. These counters are used to identify whether a thread associated with a given context has made progress in their previously blocked operation. Listing 3 presents the pseudocode for identifying and obtaining the next runnable thread in our design.

As illustrated in Listing 3, we maintain a `next_runnable` object to point to the next runnable thread. On each invocation of `shmemx_get_next_runnable_ult`, we update the `next_runnable` to point to the next thread in the queue that is runnable and the current `next_runnable` is returned. If the number of runnable threads in the queue falls under a threshold `min_runnables_count`, the queue is traversed to check all the thread contexts and the appropriate runnable threads are flagged. During this check, for each thread context, the issued and completed counters are read. The threads are marked runnable in the case of matching issued and completed counter values. If a particular operation is prioritized by the user during the scheduler initialization, the runnable threads are selected based on the operation type first and then the counter values. For simplicity, we present the scheduler algorithm without the priority based selection in Listing 3.

## 4.2 Simplifying Communication Overlap

Our proposed extensions presented in Sect. 4.1 enable an application to be re-written with user-level threads using only blocking communication APIs. This simplifies the way a user achieves communication overlap in an application that is otherwise implemented with non-blocking APIs. While we present the performance comparisons between these two executions in Sect. 5, we highlight the application-level code changes in this section through an example.

Listing 4 shows the key exchange phase in parallel integer sorting application, ISx [17], with a single thread and non-blocking APIs. To achieve overlapping between the two communication operations, `shmem_fetch_add_nbi` and `shmem_put_nbi`, the code is split into two separate loops. Before invoking a put operation, we wait for the corresponding destination offset fetch operation to be complete, thus overlapping the remaining fetch operations with the put operations. Achieving communication overlap in this way requires careful consideration and manual interleaving of the APIs from the application developer's perspective.

**Listing 3.** Algorithm to detect and return the next runnable thread

```
procedure get_next_runnable()
  if next_runnable = NULL then
    if count_runnables ≤ min_runnables_count and find_next_runnables() = 0 then
      return NULL
    end
  end
  ret_object ← next_runnable
  update next_runnable with the next runnable thread in queue
  return ret_object

procedure find_next_runnables()
  count ← 0, curr_thread ← thread_queue
  while curr_thread ≠ NULL do
    if read_issued(curr_thread.ctx) = read_completed(curr_thread.ctx) then
      curr_thread.is_runnable ← true, count ← count + 1
      if next_runnable = NULL then
        next_runnable ← curr_thread
      end
    end
    curr_thread ← curr_thread.next
  done
  return count
```

**Listing 4.** Key exchange in ISx with single thread and non-blocking APIs

```
static long long bucket_offset = 0;
static int bucket_keys[BUCKET_SIZE];
...
long long dest_offsets = malloc(sizeof(long long) * shmem_n_pes());
for (int i = 0; i < shmem_n_pes(); i++) dest_offsets[i] = -1;
for (int i = 0; i < shmem_n_pes(); i++) {
  int dest_pe = peers_iter(i);
  shmem_longlong_atomic_fetch_add_nbi(&bucket_offset, bucket_sizes[dest_pe],
                                      &dest_offsets[dest_pe], dest_pe);
}
for (int i = 0; i < shmem_n_pes(); i++) {
  int dest_pe = peers_iter(i);
  shmem_longlong_wait_until(&dest_offsets[dest_pe], SHMEM_CMP_NE, -1);
  shmem_int_put_nbi(&bucket_keys[dest_offsets[dest_pe]], ..., dest_pe);
}
shmem_quiet();
```

On the other hand, our proposed extensions enable OpenSHMEM to efficiently schedule user-level threads that allow the same key exchange program to be re-written as shown in Listing 5. In this version, we use the blocking communication APIs, and the overlapping among different operations is achieved through the usage of user-level threads and communication-aware thread scheduling provided by the underlying implementation. As illustrated in Listing 5, this approach achieves operation overlapping from a single loop execution with load balanced across multiple threads using separate contexts, which reduces the level of code complexity.

**Listing 5.** Key exchange in ISx with user-level threads and blocking APIs

```
void thread_func(void *t_arg) {
  int tid = t_arg->id;
  shmem_ctx_t ctx;
  shmem_ctx_create(SHMEM_CTX_PRIVATE, &ctx);
  for (int i = 0; i < shmem_n_pes(); i++) {
    if (i % total_threads == tid) {
      int dest_pe = peers_iter(i);
      long long dest_offset = shmem_ctx_longlong_atomic_fetch_add(ctx, &offset,
                                                         ..., dest_pe);
      shmem_ctx_int_put(ctx, &dest_buffer[dest_offset], ..., dest_pe);
    }
  }
}
int main(int argc, char *argv[]) {
  ...
  for (i = 0; i < num_threads; i++) { thread_create(..., thread_func, ...); }
  ...
}
```

## 5  Experimental Results

We have extended Sandia OpenSHMEM (SOS) v1.4.4 with support for user-level threading integration. SOS was built using libfabric version 1.7.0 with the PSM2 [4] provider. SOS is configured with manual progress enabled with a progress interval of 1 us. We also disable bounce buffering to ensure consistent performance across different message sizes. We use the MPICH Hydra process launcher version 3.2 to execute all jobs and restrict processes to be bound to two CPU cores (--bind-to=core:2).

For the user-level thread library, we use Argobots [3,32] throughout our experiments. In our experiments, we analyze performance by utilizing both user-level threads and shepherd threads. A similar but alternative evaluation strategy would be to evaluate our proposed OpenSHMEM extensions in conjunction with BOLT [9], an OpenMP [6] based parallel library that utilizes Argobots for implementing the underlying threading mechanisms. As we provide the preliminary study on OpenSHMEM with user-level threads in this work, we plan to investigate an integration with other threading models in the future.

Results were gathered on a cluster with 8 compute nodes. Each compute node contains two Intel®Xeon®Platinum 8170 (Skylake) CPUs at 2.1 GHz and 192 GB of DDR4-2666 RAM. Each node contains one 100 Gbps Intel® Omni-Path Host Fabric Adapter 100 Series (Intel®OPA) and nodes are connected using an Intel® Omni-Path Edge Switch. Nodes are running Red Hat* Enterprise Linux Server release 7.5 (Maipo) with Linux* kernel 3.10.0-862.el7.x86_64.

### 5.1  Performance Analysis of Different Scheduler Policies

We first analyze the performance impact of different thread scheduling policies. We use either the round-robin (RR) or random policy for the Argobots thread scheduler to schedule uninitialized threads. Once registered with SOS, threads are scheduled by the integrated thread scheduler using a round-robin (RR), random, or communication aware policy. We conduct these experiments on 4 nodes with 4 PEs per node using the *Key*

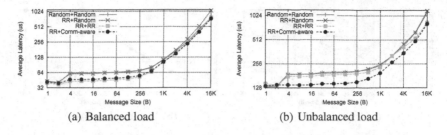

(a) Balanced load                          (b) Unbalanced load

**Fig. 4.** Performance impact of different scheduling policies with user-level threads

*Exchange* pattern introduced in Sect. 5.2, which performs an atomic fetch-add followed by a put operation. We evaluate cases where the workload is balanced and unbalanced across threads. Imbalance is introduced by creating additional threads that wait for and consume data as it arrives.

Figure 4 presents the results of these experiments, where the legend "A"+"B" indicates that thread library scheduler with policy "A" and OpenSHMEM thread scheduler with policy "B" is used. We present only one instance of the random scheduling for uninitialized threads used by the thread library scheduler as it has similar performance impact to the RR scheduling policy.

For balanced load experiments with 16 threads per PE presented in Fig. 4(a), we observe that our proposed communication-aware thread scheduler increases overhead, resulting in a 3–8% increase in latency compared to the default round-robin policy for message sizes up to 256 B. Larger message sizes incur higher latency, thus increasing the opportunity for communication-aware scheduling and achieving 3–5% performance improvement compared to the default round-robin policy. For the unbalanced load distribution with 64 threads per PE shown in Fig. 4(b), communication-aware thread scheduling uses the internal communication state to avoid scheduling blocked threads, improving performance by 23% across most message sizes. In both of these cases, random scheduling performs poorly because it ignores the current communication state, causing it to frequently select blocked threads for execution.

## 5.2   Micro-benchmark Case Studies

We identify several communication patterns that are commonly used in OpenSHMEM applications and create micro-benchmarks to analyze their performance with user-level threading. Our micro-benchmarks support both blocking and nonblocking communication and can be run with or without user-level threads. The resulting case studies provide a base case of potential communication performance improvement with user-level threading. A key area of inquiry is whether user-level threading can achieve communication performance similar to that of nonblocking communication, but with lower code complexity. We conduct each of these experiments on 4 nodes with 16 PEs per node. Latency is reported averaging 1000 iterations for each message size. For multi-threaded experiments, we run with one shepherd and 2, 8, or 32 user-level threads.

*Streaming:* This micro-benchmark performs a unidirectional streaming bandwidth test where a group of sender PEs send data to a group of receiver PEs using shmem_put

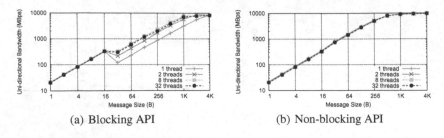

(a) Blocking API                      (b) Non-blocking API

**Fig. 5.** Performance impact of user-level threads for stream micro-benchmark

**Listing 6.** Case study 2 - All-to-all with shmem_put

```
for (int i = 0; i < shmem_n_pes(); i++) {
    int dest_pe = peers_iter(i);
    shmem_int_put(&dest_buffer[dest_offset], ..., dest_pe);
}
```

operations. Figure 5 show the bandwidth with 8 senders and 8 receiver PEs on two nodes. For cases with threads, we vary the number of user-level threads while keeping a single shepherd thread.

With blocking communication, shown in Fig. 5(a), we observe that user-level threads can improve the achieved bandwidth compared to that of single-threaded implementation. For 32 B–1 KB message size, 32 user-level threads provide 2.22x–2.64x more bandwidth compared to single-threaded execution. However, with non-blocking APIs, as presented in Fig. 5(b), user-level threads do not bring any additional benefits. Since this benchmark has only one operation, using non-blocking API for that operation yields the same performance between single and multiple user-level threads.

*Transpose:* In this study, we consider an all-to-all communication operation using shmem_put. Each PE runs a loop of all the PEs and use the loop index to construct the destination PE, sending different data to different PEs. This communication pattern represents a generic use-case in OpenSHMEM applications. For example, distributed matrix transpose, OpenSHMEM implementation of LAMMPS application [33], and distributed fast Fourier transform may utilize this communication pattern. Listing 6 presents this communication loop example with blocking API.

We develop a micro-benchmark for the communication pattern shown in Listing 6. When nonblocking shmem_int_put_nbi operations are used, we place a shmem_quiet after the loop to ensure completion of all the pending put operations. For multithreaded execution, we divide the loop across threads to assign each thread a set of destination PEs for the communication. We use separate contexts for each thread to avoid synchronization between threads. Figure 6 presents the results obtained from this experiment for up to 4 KB message size.

As shown in Fig. 6(a), user-level threading reduces latency with blocking communication by almost 42% with 8 threads for most message sizes (4 B–2 KB). In Fig. 6(b), we observe that with nonblocking communication user-level threads do not improve

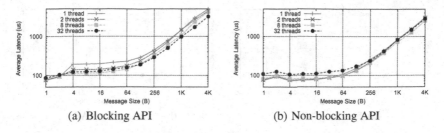

(a) Blocking API                    (b) Non-blocking API

**Fig. 6.** Performance impact of user-level threads for transpose micro-benchmark

**Listing 7.** Case study 3 - All-to-all with `shmem_fadd` and `shmem_put`

```
for (int i = 0; i < shmem_n_pes(); i++) {
    int dest_pe = peers_iter(i);
    long long dest_offset = shmem_longlong_atomic_fetch_add(&offset, ..., dest_pe);
    shmem_int_put(&dest_buffer[dest_offset], ..., dest_pe);
}
```

latency for sizes up to 32 B. For message sizes larger that 32 B, we observe a maximum performance improvement of 20% (for 2 KB message size) using 8 threads. In contrast to the blocking API, we observe performance degradation with 32 user-level threads for message sizes up to 128 B.

*Key exchange:* In this case study, we explore a communication pattern that is common to the key exchange phase of parallel sorting, similar to the pattern used by the Integer Sort (ISx) [17] benchmark. This communication pattern involves an atomic fetch-add operation followed by a put operation utilizing the fetched value. This pattern is used when different PEs append data to the same destination buffer on a remote PE and an atomic `fetch_add` to reserve buffer space at the destination PE. Listing 7 highlights this communication loop block with blocking APIs for `shmem_fetch_add` and `shmem_put`. For the non-blocking implementation, `shmem_fetch_add_nbi` and `shmem_put_nbi` are split into separate loops and a `shmem_quiet` operation is used to complete operations after each loop, as shown in Listing 4.

As shown in Fig. 7(a), we observe 46–52% performance improvement for message sizes up to 64 B and a maximum of 40% improvement for larger message sizes. With non-blocking APIs shown in Fig. 7(b), we observe a maximum of 27% improvement for 2 KB message size with 8 threads.

*Put with Signal:* Listing 8 shows the blocking version of commonly used Open-SHMEM communication loop that performs an all-to-all exchange where each iteration sends a message and then sets a signal flag at a given peer PE to notify that the data has arrived. For the non-blocking API, we use the nonblocking `shmem_put_signal_nbi` routine that performs the data transfer and subsequent signal flag update as a single operation. Put-with-signal has been ratified for OpenSHMEM 1.5 and is available in SOS.

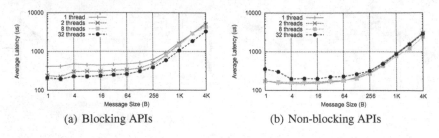

(a) Blocking APIs                    (b) Non-blocking APIs

**Fig. 7.** Performance impact of user-level threads for key exchange micro-benchmark

**Listing 8.** Case study 4 - All-to-all with `shmem_put` for data and signal

```
for (int i = 0; i < shmem_n_pes(); i++) {
    int dest_pe = peers_iter(i);
    shmem_long_put(&dest_buffer[dest_offset], ..., dest_pe);
    shmem_fence();
    shmem_uint64_put(&signal_addr, &signal_value, 1, dest_pe);
}
```

As shown in Fig. 8(a) and Fig. 8(b), we observe more than 40% performance benefit for both blocking and nonblocking APIs with the addition of user-level threads across all message sizes.

## 5.3   Application Case Studies

We analyze the application-level performance impact of integrated user-level thread scheduling using three benchmarks: Mandelbrot set generation, integer sort for exascale (ISx), and Smith-Waterman DNA sequence alignment.

*Mandelbrot:*  We use the OpenSHMEM implementation [2] of Mandelbrot set generator provided through the SOS repository and first introduced in [14]. We conduct two sets of experiments with this application. In the first set, we vary the total number of user-level threads per PE while keeping two shepherd threads for both default and modified implementation. We measure the speedup obtained with respect to total work rate compared to the default threaded implementation. We conduct this experiment on 8 nodes with 16 PEs per node. We use 8 K as the width and height of the Mandelbrot domain. We vary the number of user-level threads from 1 per PE (32 per node) to 64 per PE (2K per node). We compare the performance of user-level threading with two shepherds (2 pthreads) for the default implementation. Both cases use the same number of cores without OS thread oversubscription. We measure performance for three different communication variants provided by the benchmark: Blocking, Non-blocking, and Non-blocking pipelined (shown as NB-pipelined).

As shown in Fig. 9(a), with 16 user-level threads per PE, we observe 1.35× speedup for Blocking, 5% improvement for Non-blocking, and 1.57× speedup for Non-blocking with pipelining. These results demonstrate that the introduction of user-level threads can provide significant performance improvements without OS thread oversubscription. We further analyze the performance in the presence of OS thread oversubscription by using

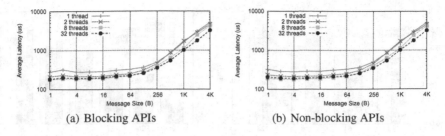

**Fig. 8.** Performance impact of user-level threads for put with signal micro-benchmark

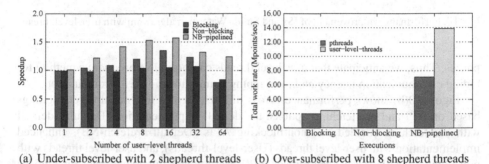

**Fig. 9.** Performance improvement of Mandelbrot benchmark with user-level threads

8 pthreads and shepherd threads for both the default and modified implementation of Mandelbrot, respectively. We use 8 user-level threads in this experiment and keep other settings same as the previous experiment. In Fig. 9(b), we report the total work rate and compare this between the two implementations. We observe similar performance benefits for all three settings: $1.21\times$ for Blocking, 5% for Non-blocking, and $1.94\times$ for Non-blocking with pipelined communication using contexts.

*ISx:* We conduct a weak scaling experiment with the Integer Sort (ISx) [17] benchmark on 8 nodes. As the current ISx implementation is single-threaded, we conduct this experiment with one shepherd thread and 64 user-level threads. We vary the total number of PEs from 4 per node to 16 per node with a fixed 64M keys per PE. We compare the performance with respect to average all-to-all time per PE reported by the benchmark. We measure this performance with the default setting of 1 warm-up and 1 test iteration. As shown in Fig. 10(a), we observe a maximum of 14.7% performance benefit for 96 PEs compared to the default non-threaded implementation.

*Smith-Waterman:* Smith-Waterman is a dynamic programming algorithm used for matching similarity between two DNA/RNA sequence, which locates regions in sequence with high levels of similarity. The OpenSHMEM implementation of this algorithm is first proposed in [7] and its open-source implementation is available in [5]. We observe that the OpenSHMEM Smith-Waterman benchmark performs a large number of RMA operations with complex interactions between communication and computation

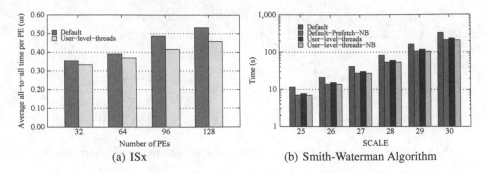

**Fig. 10.** Performance improvement of ISx and Smith-Waterman algorithm with user-level threads

phases. Thus, we anticipate that user-level threads can provide a productive method for hiding communication latency and overlapping communication with computation.

Figure 10(b) shows performance across different scales for four different settings based on API and pre-fetching options: the default implementation (Default), default with pre-fetching enabled and non-blocking APIs (Default-Prefetch-NB), enhanced implementation with user-level threads (User-level-threads), and user-level threads with non-blocking APIs (User-level-threads-NB). We conduct this experiment on 8 nodes with 4 PEs per node and 8 user-level threads per PE. We measure the time taken on kernel 1 execution of the implementation and compare the performance between the baseline user-level threaded versions. We observe that with user-level thread scheduling, performance of the algorithm improves by almost 28.74% compared to the baseline. With pre-fetching and non-blocking APIs, the algorithm performs slightly better compared to the user-level threaded implementation with blocking APIs. However, with non-blocking APIs and even without pre-fetching, user-level threaded implementation can out-perform the default best case by 1–3%.

To illustrate the additional overlap introduced by user-level threads, we utilize the performance counters [27] in SOS and analyze the number of pending communication operations for Smith-Waterman implementation. We conduct this experiment on 4 nodes with 4 PEs per node with a scale value of 25 and observe the differences between the default execution and user-level threaded execution. As presented in Fig. 11, user-level threads introduce better overlapping (increased number of pending operations in Fig. 11(b)) and thus, reduces the execution time.

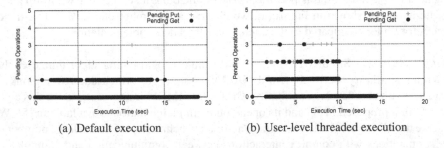

**Fig. 11.** Overlapping through performance counters for Smith-Waterman algorithm

# 6   Conclusion

This paper explores the usage of user user-level threading with OpenSHMEM as an effective method of exposing communication overlap, while maintaining the ease-ofprogramming provided by blocking communication interfaces We propose a generic OpenSHMEM API extension to enable cooperatively scheduled threads to safely use blocking OpenSHMEM interfaces. We further build on these concepts to introduce communication-aware thread scheduling for OpenSHMEM applications that leverages the OpenSHMEM runtime system's knowledge of multithreaded communication state to avoid scheduling blocked threads, thereby minimizing overheads.

Our experimental analysis indicates that user-level threading is effective at enabling communication overlap and pipelining. Microbenchmark results showed that blocking communication with user-level threading can provide performance comparable to optimized, single-threaded nonblocking communication. For example, in a majority of cases analyzed in Sect. 5.2, we observe that the blocking API implementation with user-level threads meets or exceeds the performance of single-threaded non-blocking implementations for message sizes larger than 128 B. Similar results were observed with the Mandelbrot and Smith-Waterman benchmarks presented in Figs. 9(a) and 10(b), respectively. We attribute overheads at smaller message sizes to threading inefficiencies that can be addressed with greater attention to threading support in the communication stack.

In this work, our proposed OpenSHMEM extensions define a generic infrastructure for building communication-aware schedulers. While the scheduler we have demonstrated is effective, this remains a broad area for further investigation and customization. Also, the usage of user-level threading in conjunction with the new OpenSHMEM features, such as the proposed teams interface, may provide new opportunities for performance optimization.

# References

1. Complete Context Control. https://www.gnu.org/software/libc/manual/html_node/System-V-contexts.htm
2. Mandelbrot in Sandia OpenSHMEM. https://github.com/Sandia-OpenSHMEM/SOS/blob/master/test/apps/mandelbrot.c
3. Official Argobots Repository. https://github.com/pmodels/argobots
4. OPA-PSM2. https://github.com/intel/opa-psm2
5. Smith-Waterman algorithm in SSCA1. https://github.com/ornl-languages/osb/tree/master/ssca1
6. The OpenMP API Specification. https://www.openmp.org/
7. Baker, M., Welch, A., Gorentla Venkata, M.: Parallelizing the smith-waterman algorithm using OpenSHMEM and MPI-3 one-sided interfaces. In: OpenSHMEM and Related Technologies. Experiences, Implementations, and Technologies, pp. 178–191 (2015)
8. Bendersky, E.: Measuring context switching and memory overheads for Linux threads. https://github.com/eliben/code-for-blog/tree/master/2018/threadoverhead
9. Bolt is openmp over light-weight threads. https://www.bolt-omp.org/
10. Boost c++ libraries. https://www.boost.org
11. Castelló, A., Peña, A.J., Seo, S., Mayo, R., Balaji, P., Quintana-Ort, E.S.: A review of lightweight thread approaches for high performance computing. In: IEEE International Conference on Cluster Computing (CLUSTER), pp. 471–480, September 2016
12. Castillo, E., et al.: Optimizing computation-communication overlap in asynchronous task-based programs. In: Eigenmann, R., Ding, C., McKee, S.A. (eds.) Proceedings of the ACM International Conference on Supercomputing, ICS 2019, Phoenix, AZ, USA, 26–28 June 2019, pp. 380–391 (2019)
13. Castillo, E., t al.: Optimizing computation-communication overlap in asynchronous task-based programs. In: Proceedings of the 24th Symposium on Principles and Practice of Parallel Programming, p. 415–416. PPoPP 19, New York, NY, USA (2019)
14. Dinan, J., Flajslik, M.: Contexts: a mechanism for high throughput communication in OpenSHMEM. In: Proceedings of the 8th International Conference on Partitioned Global Address Space Programming Models, pp. 10:1–10:9. New York, NY, USA (2014)
15. Grossman, M., Doyle, J., Dinan, J., Pritchard, H., Seager, K., Sarkar, V.: Implementation and evaluation of OpenSHMEM contexts using OFI libfabric. In: Gorentla Venkata, M., Imam, N., Pophale, S. (eds.) OpenSHMEM and Related Technologies. Big Compute and Big Data Convergence, pp. 19–34. Cham (2018)
16. Grun, P., et al.: A brief introduction to the OpenFabrics interfaces - a new network API for maximizing high performance application efficiency. In: 2015 IEEE 23rd Annual Symposium on High-Performance Interconnects, pp. 34–39, August 2015
17. Hanebutte, U., Hemstad, J.: ISx: a scalable integer sort for co-design in the exascale era. In: 9th International Conference on Partitioned Global Address Space Programming Models, pp. 102–104, September 2015
18. Huang, C., Lawlor, O., Kalé, L.V.: Adaptive MPI. In: Rauchwerger, L.(ed.) Languages and Compilers for Parallel Computing, pp. 306–322 (2004)

19. Kamal, H., Wagner, A.: FG-MPI: fine-grain MPI for multicore and clusters. In: IEEE International Symposium on Parallel Distributed Processing, Workshops and Ph.d. Forum (IPDPSW), pp. 1–8, April 2010
20. Lu, H., Seo, S., Balaji, P.: MPI+ULT: overlapping communication and computation with user-level threads. In: IEEE 17th International Conference on High Performance Computing and Communications, pp. 444–454, August 2015
21. Marjanović, V., Labarta, J., Ayguadé, E., Valero, M.: Overlapping communication and computation by using a hybrid MPI/SMPSS approach. In: Proceedings of the 24th ACM International Conference on Supercomputing, pp. 5–16. ICS 2010, NY, USA (2010)
22. MPI Forum: MPI: a message-passing interface standard version 3.1. Technical report, University of Tennessee, Knoxville, June 2015
23. Nakashima, J., Taura, K.: MassiveThreads: A Thread Library for High Productivity Languages, pp. 222–238. Heidelberg (2014)
24. OpenSHMEM application programming interface, version 1.4. http://www.openshmem.org, December 2017
25. Pérache, M., Jourdren, H., Namyst, R.: MPC: a unified parallel runtime for clusters of NUMA machines. In: Luque, E., Margalef, T., Benítez, D. (eds.) Euro-Par 2008 - Parallel Processing. pp. 78–88. Heidelberg (2008)
26. Perez, J.M., Badia, R.M., Labarta, J.: A dependency-aware task-based programming environment for multi-core architectures. In: 2008 IEEE International Conference on Cluster Computing, pp. 142–151, September 2008
27. Rahman, M.W.U., Ozog, D., Dinan, J.: Lightweight instrumentation and analysis using OpenSHMEM performance counters. In: OpenSHMEM and Related Technologies. OpenSHMEM in the Era of Extreme Heterogeneity. pp. 180–201 (2019)
28. Reinders, J.: Intel Threading Building Blocks. First edn, Sebastopol, CA, USA (2007)
29. Sala, K., et al.: Improving the interoperability between MPI and task-based programming models. In: Proceedings of the 25th European MPI Users Group Meeting. EuroMPI18, New York, NY, USA (2018)
30. Sandia OpenSHMEM (2018). https://github.com/Sandia-OpenSHMEM/SOS
31. Seager, K., Choi, S.E., Dinan, J., Pritchard, H., Sur, S.: Design and Implementation of OpenSHMEM Using OFI on the Aries Interconnect. In: Gorentla Venkata, M., Imam, N., Pophale, S., Mintz, T.M. (eds.) OpenSHMEM and Related Technologies. Enhancing OpenSHMEM for Hybrid Environments, pp. 97–113. Cham (2016)
32. Seo, S., et al.: Argobots: a lightweight low-level threading and tasking framework. IEEE Trans. Parallel Distrib. Syst. **29**(3), 512–526 (2018)
33. Tang, C., Bouteiller, A., Herault, T., Gorentla Venkata, M., Bosilca, G.: From MPI to OpenSHMEM: porting LAMMPS. In: OpenSHMEM and Related Technologies. Experiences, Implementations, and Technologies, pp. 121–137 (2015)

34. Taura, K., Tabata, K., Yonezawa, A.: Stackthreads/mp: Integrating futures into calling standards. In: ACM SIGPLAN Symposium Principles Practice Parallel Program (1999)
35. Wheeler, K.B., Murphy, R.C., Thain, D.: Qthreads: an API for programming with millions of lightweight threads. In: IEEE International Symposium on Parallel and Distributed Processing, pp. 1–8, April 2008

# Communication-Aware
# Hardware-Assisted MPI Overlap Engine

Mohammadreza Bayatpour[✉], Jahanzeb Hashmi Maqbool,
Sourav Chakraborty, Kaushik Kandadi Suresh,
Seyedeh Mahdieh Ghazimirsaeed, Bharath Ramesh, Hari Subramoni,
and Dhabaleswar K. Panda

Ohio State University, Columbus, OH 43210, USA
{bayatpour.1,hashmi.29,Chakraborty.52,kandadisuresh.1,ghazimirsaeed.3,
ramesh.113,subramoni.1,panda.2}@osu.edu

**Abstract.** Overlap of computation and communication is critical for good application-level performance. Modern high-performance networks offer Hardware-assisted tag matching and rendezvous offload to enable communication progress without involving the host CPU. However, hardware based offload cannot be used in many situations due to various hardware limitations and performance issues. Furthermore, hardware-based designs cannot provide good overlap for common communication patterns involving unexpected messages or non-contiguous datatypes. In this paper, we address these limitations by designing a communication-aware overlap engine for MPI that uses novel hardware-assisted and software-based solutions to extract overlap for both expected and unexpected messages. The proposed design adapts to the application's communication requirements including message size, datatype, and relative timing of processes using heuristics and history-driven predictions. We evaluate the proposed designs against state-of-the-art MPI libraries and show up to 41% and 22% reduction in latency for collective operations and stencil-based application kernels on 1024 and 128 nodes, respectively, as well as 23% improvement in communication performance of the P3DFFT application.

## 1 Introduction

The massive growth in the size and scale of supercomputing systems has been driven by the current trends in multi-/many-core architectures and the availability of RDMA-enabled, and high-performance interconnects such as InfiniBand (IB) and Omni-Path. The Message Passing Interface (MPI) [18] has been the de-facto programming model for developing high-performance parallel applications for the last couple of decades. One of the major features offered by modern high-performance network adapters (HCAs) is called 'RDMA' and it is the ability to

This research is supported in part by National Science Foundation grants #1931537, #1450440, #1664137, #1818253, and XRAC grant #NCR-130002.

© Springer Nature Switzerland AG 2020
P. Sadayappan et al. (Eds.): ISC High Performance 2020, LNCS 12151, pp. 517–535, 2020.
https://doi.org/10.1007/978-3-030-50743-5_26

read from and write data to remote memory locations without involving the host CPU. The MPI standard offers non-blocking communication primitives to take advantage of RDMA and enable overlap of communication and computation. Numerous studies have shown this overlap to be the critical factor for achieving good application performance and have proposed different solutions to address this [15,17,22].

There are generally two schemes in MPI to implement the point-to-point communications — 'Eager' and 'Rendezvous'. The eager protocol uses a set of pre-allocated and pre-registered buffers for the HCA to communicate asynchronously, without performing any handshake with peer processes. Upon receiving an eager message, this protocol involves one extra copy from pre-registered buffers into the application buffers, therefore, it is typically used for small messages. On the other hand, in Rendezvous protocol, the sending process first checks for the availability of the buffer in the receiver's side before transferring the actual message and it is used for medium and large message sizes. The Fig. 1(a) illustrates the RDMA read based rendezvous. The sender sends a control signal RTS to the receiver. The receiver after receiving the RTS issues an RDMA read signal which fetches the data from the sender without involving the sender's CPU. As it is seen in this figure, there is no overlap in communication with computation. In other words, the communication starts only after MPI wait is called by the application, after which the application is idle [25].

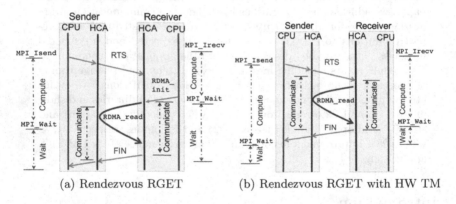

(a) Rendezvous RGET          (b) Rendezvous RGET with HW TM

Fig. 1. Comparison of RGET with and without HW Tag Matching [5].

To tackle this, modern HCAs such as Mellanox Infiniband ConnectX-5 and ConnectX-6 have included the ability to perform tag-matching in hardware and initiate RDMA operations without the involvement of the CPU on the receiver side [5,26]. This allows the MPI library to post a receive operation along with the address of its destination buffer to the HCA. If the posted receive request is expected, meaning that the time that the receive request has been posted ($t_{recv}$) is before the time that incoming Tag Mathing (TM) packet has arrived ($t_{arrive}$), ($t_{arrive} > t_{recv}$), a matching receive for an incoming RTS gets offloaded to the

HCA. Therefore, the HCA can perform an *RDMA_read* from the sender's buffer as soon as it gets the RTS without any involvement of the receiver process. Rendezvous offload using Hardware Tag Matching is depicted in Fig. 1(b).

While this feature enables the MPI library to extract more overlap in certain scenarios, it cannot be used as a universal solution due to various semantic limitations and performance bottlenecks [5]. For instance, when no matching receive is found for an incoming message (unexpected message), it cannot be handled by the HCA since it does not know the destination buffer. Similarly, small messages or non-contiguous messages may not be offloaded to the HCA due to performance reasons. Even for expected messages, existing hardware-assisted solutions [5, 26] do not provide the HCA peak bandwidth while the posted receive requests are offloaded. Furthermore, due to the semantic limitations of Hardware Tag Matching, these solutions do not provide reasonable overlap of communication and computation when the application uses a combination of 1) short and large or 2) contiguous and non-contiguous messages. These observations show that while hardware tag matching is useful in certain scenarios, MPI libraries need to address several challenges to mitigate its limited applicability as well as performance bottlenecks to provide a complete and high-performance solution.

## 2   Challenges

In this paper, our goal is to **design an overlap engine capable of adaptively utilizing advanced hardware and software-based schemes for progressing MPI operations for diverse application communication scenarios.** To achieve this, we need to answer the following five questions: **1)** What are the performance characteristics, benefits, and shortcomings of state-of-the-art hardware tag-matching and offload? **2)** Are the capabilities provided by the hardware sufficient or do they need to be augmented by software-based schemes? **3)** Which communication scenarios can be improved in terms of performance and overlap

**Table 1.** State-of-the-art designs and features to support efficient communication and computation overlap. In this table, we define the following design challenges for a high-performance overlap engine: C1) Adaptability to application communication requirements, C2) Efficient designs to extract overlap for unexpected messages, C3) Communication progress without receiver involvement, and C4) Efficient overlap for out-of-order messages

| Design challenges | State-of-the-art MPI libraries | | | | |
|---|---|---|---|---|---|
| | OpenMPI+ UCX with HW-TM | OpenMPI+ UCX | MVAPICH2 | MVAPICH2+ Async | Proposed |
| C1 [see the caption] | ✗ | ✗ | ✗ | ✗ | ✔ |
| C2 | ✗ | ✗ | ✗ | ✗ | ✔ |
| C3 | ✔ | ✗ | ✗ | ✔ | ✔ |
| C4 | ✗ | ✗ | ✗ | ✗ | ✔ |

by offloading to HW? **4)** Can we propose novel designs to extract overlap for unexpected messages? Can it be done without increasing the memory footprint of the MPI library? **5)** Can the proposed designs be combined so they can be adaptively applied to the application's communication requirements?

Table 1 shows an overview of the state-of-the-art solutions available in different MPI libraries to extract overlap. Four different representative open source solutions are considered - OpenMPI+UCX with and without support for hardware tag-matching [26]; and MVAPICH2 with and without software-based asynchronous progress [21]. As we can see, both hardware and software-based solutions enable communication progress without receiver involvement for expected messages. However, none of the solutions provide good overlap for unexpected messages. Furthermore, even for expected messages, existing hardware-assisted solutions do not provide good overlap when the application uses a combination of 1) short and large or 2) contiguous and non-contiguous messages. Similarly, existing designs do not efficiently handle out-of-order messages. These issues limit the performance and applicability of the existing solutions. To the best of our knowledge, a comprehensive solution that adaptively and efficiently handles different application scenarios has neither been proposed in literature nor available as a software product.

## 3   Contributions

In this paper, we tackle these questions and show that neither hardware nor software-based tag matching can provide the best performance and overlap for different communication scenarios. Thus, a hybrid design that can take advantage of both these approaches and adapt to the application's communication requirements is required. To this end, we propose a Communication-Aware Hardware-Assisted MPI Overlap Engine ("CHAMPION") that takes advantage of hardware and software features to provide high overlap of computation and communication for both expected and unexpected messages, and dynamically adapt to the application's communication requirements. To summarize, the paper makes the following contributions:

- In-depth characterization of state-of-the-art hardware tag-matching and offload schemes and identify regions of applicability for hardware tag matching and software-based solutions.
- Design a communication-aware Hardware Tag Matching offload mechanism that hides the performance overheads of the offload engine while maintaining the peak performance of this engine.
- Enable the processing of out-of-order messages in hardware, using a trace-based matching design to maximize the benefits of Hardware Tag Matching.
- Propose novel designs to extract overlap from unexpected rendezvous messages by efficient prefetching.
- Evaluate and analyze the proposed designs using various benchmarks and application kernels.

Compared to state-of-the-art MPI libraries, the proposed designs show up to 41% improvement for collectives on 1024 nodes, up to 23% reduction in latency, and up to 2× improvement in overlap for a stencil-based application kernel on 128 nodes and 23% improvement in communication performance of P3DFFT application.

# 4   Motivation

As the first step toward designing a high-performance and scalable overlap engine inside the MPI library using Hardware Tag Matching, we need to systematically analyze the key communication primitives and semantics in the MPI library. We consider the semantic challenges as well as performance challenges of state-of-the-art Hardware Tag Matching. To have a complete picture of the hardware improvements in this technology, we analyze Hardware Tag Matching in two latest models of Infiniband HCAs: ConnectX-5 EDR and ConnectX-6 HDR.

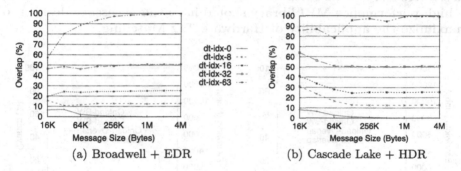

(a) Broadwell + EDR          (b) Cascade Lake + HDR

**Fig. 2.** Comparison of communication and computation overlap of Hardware Tag Matching with respect to the index of the inserted non-contiguous message in the window size of 64 on different architectures. This figure indicates that the receive requests which were posted after the non-contiguous receive request in the window are not getting offloaded, leading to underutilization of Hardware Tag Matching and lower overlap.

## 4.1   Semantic Challenges

In this section, to realize the impact of non-contiguous datatype on the overlap for medium to large messages, we modified the OMB [1] suite to insert a non-contiguous message in the window size of 64 and calculate the overlap and total latency. Figure 2 shows the impact of this insertion on the overlap. For instance, 'dt-idx-0' shows that insertion of non-contiguous message as the first transfer in the window leads to total overlap of almost 0%. On the other hand, 'dt-idx-63' which is the last transfer in the window almost has no impact on the expected overlap. These results indicate that posted receive messages that have been posted after the inserted non-contiguous message were not offloaded to the Hardware Tag Matching engine, leading to poor overlap and underutilization of Hardware Tag Matching. Such poor performance exists for both EDR as well as HDR models. MPI semantics mandate the MPI library to preserve the message ordering, i.e., consecutive messages with the same tag must match the posted receives in the same order they were posted. However, some of the posted receives cannot be offloaded to the HCA (such as unexpected messages or expected messages with non-contiguous datatypes) and need to be matched in software. In this scenario, the offloaded tag-matching handled by the HCA and software-based tag-matching handled by the CPU based communication progress in MPI library could lead to incorrect ordering. For instance, consider a scenario where the receiver posts two receives $r_1, r_2$, with the same tag $t$. However, due to some limitation $r_1$ cannot be offloaded to the HCA so only $r_2$ is offloaded. Now, the sender performs two sends $s_1$ and $s_2$ that should match with $r_1$ and $r_2$ respectively. However, the HCA will process the incoming message from $s_1$ first and match it to $r_2$, violating the MPI ordering semantics. Conversely, if the MPI library does not offload $r_2$ to prevent this scenario, it has to be progressed in software and benefits of hardware tag matching can not be obtained. **Thus, a high-performance MPI library should have the necessary designs to maximize the applicability of Hardware Tag Matching.**

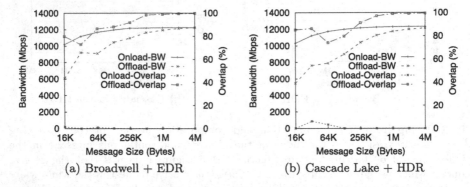

(a) Broadwell + EDR                    (b) Cascade Lake + HDR

**Fig. 3.** Comparison of bandwidth and overlap for different message sizes with and without hardware rendezvous offload on different architectures. As we observe here, Hardware Tag Matching is able to provide higher overlap compared to the software-based solutions for point-to-point communications. On the other hand, this feature is unable to maintain the peak bandwidth for message range less than 1 MB. HDR and EDR are showing similar behavior.

## 4.2   Performance Challenges

In this section, we compare the communication performance (bandwidth) and overlap achieved using point-to-point operations in Fig. 3. To measure overlap, we modified the osu_bw benchmark to calculate overlap similar to nonblocking collectives in OMB [1]. We call this benchmark osu_bw_overlap. To observe the effect of expected messages we introduce artificial delays at the sender to make sure that all the messages are expected and are handled by Hardware Tag Matching. As shown in Fig. 3, Hardware Tag Matching maintains the peak overlap of communication and computation in both EDR and HDR architectures. However, in the 'onload' scenario, there is no overlap of communication and computation. Here we assume that there is no asynchronous process/thread performing the communication progress on behalf of the main process. Therefore, RDMA Read is initiated only after application calls MPI_Wait, which happens after computation is done. On the other hand, by comparing the bandwidth of the 'offload' vs. 'onload', we can realize that Hardware Tag Matching performs worse compared to the CPU onloading. In the case of unexpected messages, RDMA Read is always initiated by CPU, therefore, the bandwidth is same for both 'onload' and 'offload' scenarios. Hardware tag matching requires pre-posting receives to HCA before the message has arrived at the receiver, so that the HCA can directly put the data into the application buffer. Clearly, this scheme cannot be applied to unexpected messages, where the message has already arrived but no matching receive operation has been posted to the HCA. As illustrated in Fig. 7(a), this scenario prevents overlap of computation and communication at the receiver. Also, the delayed receiver process may increase the communication progress and wait time at the sender side, leading to the propagation of a skew from the receiver process to the sender process. Furthermore, since the HCA is unable to process unexpected messages independent of the CPU, it disables hardware tag matching once an unexpected message arrives to avoid ordering issues. Further receives cannot be posted to the HCA until the unexpected message has been processed by the CPU. Since the process arrival pattern of HPC applications are often skewed [27], unexpected messages are a common scenario. **Thus, a high-performance Hardware Tag Matching assisted offload design in MPI must avoid performance degradation of hardware rendezvous offload while maintaining the peak overlap during the application runtime for both expected and unexpected messages.**

# 5   Proposed CHAMPION Design

A message in the MPI runtime can be classified as an expected or unexpected message. Each has its own challenges and requires different considerations to achieve better communication overlap. In view of the broad spectrum of MPI communication, we explore the design challenges and solutions for expected and unexpected messages. In the following sections, we show how our proposed designs for hardware tag-matching semantics augmented by software-based approaches are able to exploit better performance and overlap for various benchmarks and applications.

## 5.1   Communication-Aware and Adaptive Rendezvous HCA Offload

As we discussed in Sect. 4, rendezvous offload using Hardware Tag Matching has some performance degradations compared to the default version that all rendezvous protocol is initiated by host CPU. To address these limitations, we propose a communication aware design that tries to adaptively offload the MPI receive requests in an on-demand fashion. This design offloads only when an overlap opportunity is presented, otherwise, it avoids offloading to mitigate the overheads of the hardware tag-matching.

For expected messages, RDMA read needs to be performed as soon as the incoming RTS is received. To realize this in our opportunistic design, we employ a heuristic to find the frequency ($f$) of progress calls (MPI_Wait, MPI_Test) made during the runtime. The frequency $f$ is computed based on the difference between the time ($\delta$) when the receiver posts a receive request and when the actual RDMA operation is triggered. The frequency $f$ has an inverse relation to the offloading factor e.g., the higher the progress frequency, the less the number of offloaded tag-matching requests. This adaptive progress design is opportunistic in nature as it continuously looks for overlap opportunities on the receiver side.

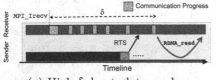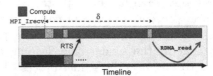
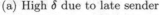

(a) High $\delta$ due to late sender

(b) High $\delta$ due to low frequency of communication progress

**Fig. 4.** In the proposed communication-aware Hardware Tag Matching design we consider high value of $\delta$ as indicator of the need for hardware offload. Here we show two different scenarios where $\delta$ can become high.

If $\delta$ is large enough (greater than a threshold $K$), then we try to offload the receive request for this process peer. $K$ depends on the number of outstanding rendezvous requests ($C_{rndv}$) and the average network latency of all outstanding rendezvous messages. To approximate the latency, we use the LogGP [2] model. $\alpha$ and $\beta$ are obtained in an offline fashion and they are architecture-specific.

$$K = (\frac{\sum_{i=1}^{C_{rndv}}(\alpha \times MSG_i + \beta)}{C_{rndv}}) \times C_{rndv} = \sum_{i=1}^{C_{rndv}}(\alpha \times MSG_i + \beta)$$

Large value of $\delta$ could be caused by either (or both) of the following cases: 1) Sender's RTS is posted later in time than the receiver has posted the receive-request. In this case, HW TM is needed to avoid the receiver to get blocked because of the late sender, leading to more overlap at the receiver side. Figure 4(a) depicts this scenario. 2) Receiver process does not progress the communication frequently enough and as a result, does not quickly poll the completion queue inside HCA to find the received RTS. In this scenario, HW TM is needed to take care of the handshake required for RGET based rendezvous protocol. This scenario is shown in Fig. 4(b). On the other hand, a small value of $\delta$

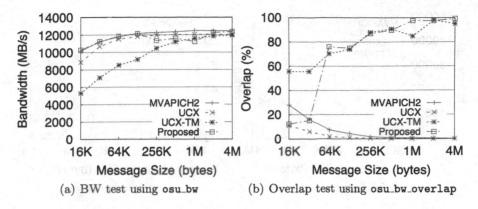

**Fig. 5.** Proposed communication-aware and adaptive HW-TM design on bandwidth and overlap benchmarks.

implies that there is no skew between the sender and the receiver processes. This means that the receiver process is frequently progressing the communication and there is no extra overlap gain from using HW TM, hence, we avoid offloading to the HCA. Our proposed communication-aware design further keeps track of the rate of canceled offloaded receive requests. If the cancelation rate passes a threshold during a period, our proposed design avoids offloading more receive requests until the next period. This is used to avoid the overheads of receive request cancelations.

Figures 5(a) and (b) show that our proposed design can correctly realize the lack of overlap opportunity in the osu_bw benchmark and adaptively avoids offloading receiver requests to the HCA. On the other hand, for osu_bw_overlap benchmark, it correctly offloads the receives to achieve maximum overlap. This benchmark is similar to osu_bw but it also calculates the overlap with the same formula as used in Nonblocking Collectives in OMB [1].

## 5.2 Trace-Based Matching

Scientific applications exhibit a wide variety of communication patterns involving a range of message sizes and datatype layouts. For instance, a sender is allowed to send a message with a derived datatype layout that cannot be offloaded, followed by a message with a contiguous datatype layout which can be offloaded. As discussed in Sect. 4, such variability in the message layouts limits the usability of the offloading if we only rely on HW TM semantics.

An MPI library must make sure that there are no messages offloaded to the network with the same tag to avoid the ordering issues which limit the usage of HW TM. To have such a capability, we add an additional variable to the tag-matching tuple of rank, tag, and context_id so that messages which have the same tag get differentiated. The new variable is unique and preserves the ordering of the messages for a sequence of messages with the same tag. To achieve this,

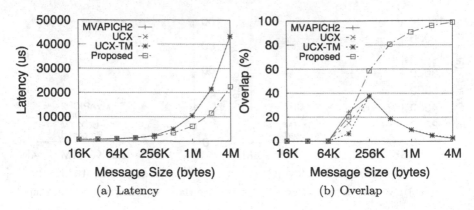

**Fig. 6.** Impact of proposed designs on variable memory layout communications. Out of 64 messages, all are using contiguous layouts while one is using MPI derived datatype.

two sequence numbers are added for each communicating peer. If an application uses more than one unique 'tag' when it calls MPI *Send* and *Recv* primitives, we allocate new sequence numbers for each new tag. Every communicator in the application has its own set of sequence numbers so that context_id remains same for all the sequence numbers within a communicator. Both the sequence numbers are used to keep track of corresponding *Send* and *Recv* MPI calls issued by the application for each unique combination of rank, tag, and context_id. Whenever an application issues these operations, the sequence numbers for that specific tag and peer are incremented, as there is always a matching *Recv* operation for a *Send* operation. Appending this sequence number within the 64-bit value of HW TM tag ensures that no two messages can have the same tag, while MPI ordering of the messages is preserved.

To evaluate our design, we analyze the same benchmark that we used in Sect. 4.1. As we mentioned before, the benchmark creates an MPI derived datatype and during the `window_size` number of transfers, it runs few iterations with derived datatypes by using the same tag as of other transfers in each iteration. By running this benchmark, when a software-based pending receive is available, MPI libraries such as OpenMPI+UCX stop offloading new incoming receives to the HCA until software takes care of the pending receives. Due to this limitation, the hardware cannot be exploited to its full potential to achieve maximum overlap. Figure 6 shows how our proposed trace-based matching design overcomes this limitation. As it can be seen, the presence of even a single non-contiguous datatype transfer can completely eliminate the benefits of naive hardware tag-matching design (refer to Sect. 4). However, our proposed trace-based matching design is able to address these limitations and offer better performance and overlap in comparison to other state-of-the-art solutions.

## 5.3   Improving the Overlap of Unexpected Messages

In this section, we discuss various design components for our overlap engine which are applicable to '*unexpected messages*' at the receiver side. We start with a speculative approach and move towards an optimized design. As we discussed in Sect. 4, Hardware Tag Matching does not provide any communication and computation overlap for unexpected messages. This is an expected behavior as upon receiving an unexpected RTS, receiver process has not yet posted the receive request and therefore, receiver HCA does not yet know where the destination buffer is. As illustrated in Fig. 7(a), this scenario prevents overlap of computation and communication at the receiver. Also, the delayed receiver process may increase the communication progress and wait time at the sender side, leading to the propagation of a skew from the receiver process to the sender process. Since the process arrival pattern of HPC applications are often skewed [27], unexpected messages are a common scenario.

In order to allow the sender to proceed without getting stuck on a late receiver process to post the receive request and perform the RDMA-Read, the receiver process selectively prefetches some of the unexpected rendezvous messages. To achieve this, we create a memory pool and register it with HCA during MPI_Init. Whenever an unexpected RTS is received at the receive side, we query the memory pool to see if there is a memory slot available to be used for prefetching. If a free slot is found, then based on the sender's information obtained from RTS packet, an RDMA read is issued to transfer the data from the sender's buffer. After the completion of the transfer, a FIN packet is sent to the sender indicating that the sender is free to mark the operation as complete. This design is illustrated in Fig. 7(b). To decide whether or not prefetch the incoming unexpected RTS, this design relies on the history of the previous prefetches and number of useful prefetches (ones that receiver process posted the receive request after the

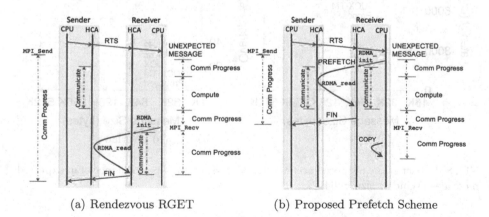

(a) Rendezvous RGET               (b) Proposed Prefetch Scheme

**Fig. 7.** The proposed design and default MVAPICH2 approaches in handling unexpected rendezvous messages. In the proposed design, the receiver process prefetches the unexpected rendezvous message, leading to better overlap and latency for sender and receiver as the sender does not get blocked by the late receiver.

prefetch is done) versus non-useful prefetches (ones that receiver process posted the receive request before prefetch is done, but obviously, after RTS is received).

To measure the impact of the proposed design for unexpected messages, we use a synthetic benchmark where we inject skew between the sender and the receiver to force the message to arrive as unexpected at the receiver. As it is shown in Fig. 8, closest in performance is the MVAPICH2-X library with asynchronous progress thread enabled—referred to as MVAPICH2+Async. In our proposed design, we also create a `tm-thread` that functions similar to how MVAPICH2+Async functions [21]. The proposed design improved overall runtime by up to 38% as well as achieved better overlap in comparison to MVAPICH2+Async design.

# 6  Performance Evaluation

In this section, we discuss the experimental results of our proposed designs and provide in-depth analyses. We implemented our proposed designs in a publicly available open-source version of MVAPICH2 [19]. To evaluate the proposed designs, we provide an in-depth comparison against the state-of-the-art designs employed by MPI libraries such as MVAPICH2-X v2.3rc2 (referred to as "MVAPICH2") and Open MPI v4.0.0 with UCX v1.4 (referred to as "Open-MPI+UCX"). All the reported numbers are an average of five runs. Microbenchmark evaluations ran for 1,000 iterations for each run and an average of five runs is reported. Furthermore, the standard deviation between these iterations is kept under 5%.

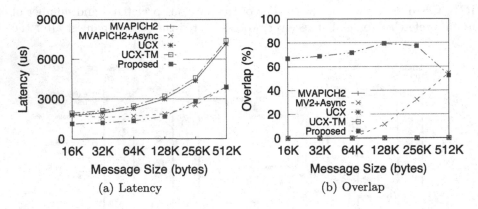

(a) Latency          (b) Overlap

**Fig. 8.** Impact of the proposed prefetch-based design on the performance of unexpected messages (Window size = 64)

## 6.1  Experimental Setup

We used the following clusters for our evaluation:

**Cluster-A**—Frontera cluster at the Texas Advanced Computing Center contains 8008 compute nodes equipped with the dual-socket Intel Xeon Platinum 8280 (Cascade Lake), 56-core processors (448,448 cores in total) operating at 2.70 GHz with 192 GB RAM. Each node is equipped with Mellanox HDR-100 ConnectX-6 HCAs (100 Gbps data rate).

**Cluster-B**—Pitzer cluster at the Ohio Supercomputing Center contains 260 compute nodes equipped with the Skylake Gold 6148 series of Xeon dual-socket, 20-core processors operating at 2.40 GHz with 128 GB RAM. Each node is equipped with Mellanox MT4119 EDR ConnectX-5 HCAs with PCI-Ex Gen3 interfaces. For some of the motivational numbers we used our local cluster which has similar details to this cluster but it has Broadwell series of Xeon dual-socket, 14-core processors operating at 2.40 GHz. All the results were obtained on Cluster-B except for the ones which are indicated that they were run on Cluster-A.

## 6.2   Impact of Proposed Designs on Collective Operations

In this section, we evaluate the performance of collective operations using the proposed designs.

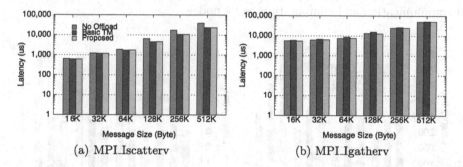

(a) MPI_Iscatterv                  (b) MPI_Igatherv

**Fig. 9.** Impact of proposed communication-aware design on collectives with 640 processes.

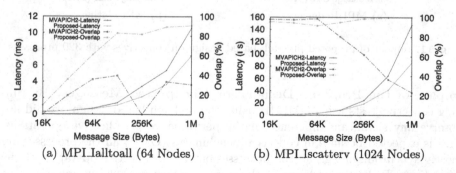

(a) MPI_Ialltoall (64 Nodes)          (b) MPI_Iscatterv (1024 Nodes)

**Fig. 10.** Performance impact of proposed designs on MPI_Ialltoall and MPI_Iscatterv running on cluster A

**Impact of Proposed Communication-Aware Hardware Tag Matching Design.** Figure 9(a) shows that by using the proposed design, MPI_Iscatterv performance increases by a factor of 1.6X. In MVAPICH2, MPI_Iscatterv uses a direct algorithm, meaning that the root process directly sends the data to all other non-root processes. Therefore, HW TM can provide nearly perfect overlap of communication and computation for this collective as only one receive request is issued by non-roots during the collective runtime and this receive request gets overlapped using HW TM. On the other hand, Fig. 9(b) shows that for MPI_Igatherv, basic TM design has around 10% to 15% degradation compared to default for medium messages but the proposed design can avoid this degradation. After profiling this test, we realized that even though Igatherv uses a direct algorithm, more than 90% of the offloaded receive requests at root are getting canceled, therefore, there will be no benefit from HW TM. Since our communication-aware design keeps track of the cancel rate of the offloaded receive requests, it avoids using HW TM for this benchmark during the runtime leading higher performance compared to basic HW TM design.

Figure 10 shows the impact of the proposed designs at large scale for Ialltoall and Iscatterv collectives. As it is shown in these figures, for iscatterv in 1024 node, there is up to 41% improvement in total latency while increasing the overlap up to 80%. On the other hand, Ialltoall also shows up to 33% improvement in total latency and up to 70% in overlap providing near-perfect overlap of communication and computation on 64 nodes.

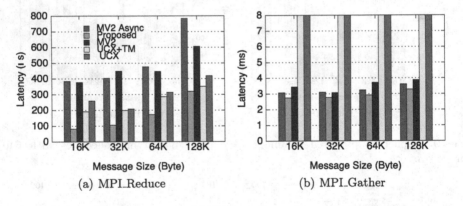

(a) MPI_Reduce    (b) MPI_Gather

**Fig. 11.** Impact of proposed prefetch-based design on collectives with 320 processes.

**Impact of the Proposed Designs for Unexpected Messages.** By running collective tests using OMB [1] using the prefetch-based design, we did not observe any significant difference in the performance of collective operations. This is expected because in collective benchmarks (OMB) all the processes are mostly synchronized e.g., all the processes enter the collective operation at the same time. To better understand the impact of our designs, we modify some benchmarks to insert skew for some of the processes as the real applications typically show skewed communication. We observed that the rooted collectives such as MPI_Gather and MPI_Reduce show benefits due to the prefetch design. This is due to the fact that the rooted collectives do not have any implicit barrier during the operation in contrast to dense collectives like MPI_Alltoall. For these communication patterns, the propagation of skew to other processes of the communicator can be avoided by efficiently prefetching the unexpected messages. Figure 11 conforms to our understanding where we see up to 55% improvement for MPI_Reduce and up to 17% improvement for MPI_Gather at 320 processes.

## 6.3 Impact of Proposed Designs on 3Dstencil Kernel

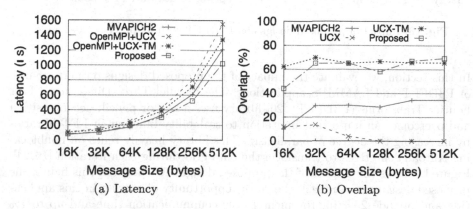

(a) Latency

(b) Overlap

**Fig. 12.** Performance of 3D-Stencil application kernel running on 128 nodes using proposed designs on cluster A

3DStencil is a common communication kernel that mimics the communication pattern of many stencil-based applications and Adaptive Mesh Refinement (AMR) kernels. This communication kernel performs 7-point stencil with neighboring processes using MPI non-blocking point-to-point primitives i.e., MPI_Isend and MPI_Irecv using contiguous datatypes. Figure 12 shows that proposed design achieve up to 2× increased overlap and up to 22% improved latency as compared to other MPI libraries running on 128 nodes. In this experiment, for all the message sizes, the Rendezvous protocol is getting used and our profiles showed in the proposed design, out of 579,365 receive requests that have been offloaded, 20,050 receive request has been canceled while 559,315 offload requests have been successful, having the offload rate of 96%. This results in more than 20% improvement in overall runtime compared to default MVAPICH2.

## 6.4   Application-Level Evaluations

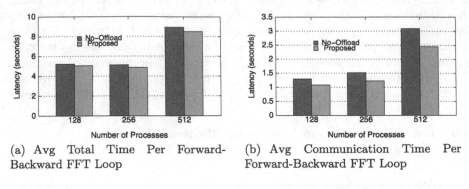

(a) Avg Total Time Per Forward-Backward FFT Loop

(b) Avg Communication Time Per Forward-Backward FFT Loop

**Fig. 13.** Impact of proposed designs on P3DFFT with 32 processes per node.

In this section, we evaluate the impact of the proposed designs on performance of P3DFFT and LAMMPS applications. The Parallel Three-Dimensional Fast Fourier Transforms (P3DFFT) [20] library uses a 2D, or pencil, decomposition and overcomes an important limitation to scalability inherent in FFT libraries by increasing the degree of parallelism. This library heavily relies on nonblocking Alltoall collectives to transform the data grid during each iteration [16,24]. Figure 13 shows the impact of the proposed design. As shown in this figure, the proposed design can correctly realize the opportunity of overlap in this application and provide 23% improvement in the communication time and up to 7% improvement in total application time.

Our second evaluation is on Large-scale Atomic/Molecular Massively Parallel Simulator (LAMMPS) [3] which is a molecular dynamics program developed in Sandia National Laboratories. This test runs on 32 nodes with 16 processes per node on Frontera cluster. On this configuration, we observed 3.58% improvement in total execution time compared to MVAPICH2. We further profile this application and realized that out of 266,896 rendezvous recieves, 216,517 receive requests have been successfully offloaded and matched in the Hardware Tag Matching engine and rest have been handled by software tag matching. This leads to 81% success rate in the tag matching offload and improved overlap in the application.

## 7   Related Work

Optimizing software-based MPI tag matching has been the interest of many researchers. Some of these proposals [8,9,11] consider static designs to improve tag matching operations, while others [4,10,12,13] propose adaptive and dynamic approaches. Offloading the communication progress to NICs for MPI point-to-point and collective operations has been explored in the past. For example, Researchers [28] explore the implementation of multicast in Myrinet based NICs. Graham et al. [14] explore the overlap of computation and communication in Mellanox ConnectX2 HCA. It uses the Core-Direct API to implement the barrier collective and study the improvements in the total time obtained due to Hardware offloading. Subramoni et al. [23] provide designs to effectively implement the collectives on the ConnectX2 HCA. Brightwell et al. [6] showed that eagerly sending large messages can improve latency for pre-posted receives. However, this scheme has to resend unexpected large messages in the presence of application skew, which does not affect our design. Chakraborty et al. [7] investigate different approaches to increase the overlap of intra-node communication and computation with inter-node communication. As we can see, no work exists in literature that can provide maximum overlap of computation and communication in a communication-aware fashion while taking advantage of state-of-the-art solutions in hardware and software in an adaptive fashion as "CHAMPION" is able to do.

## 8 Conclusion and Future Work

In this paper, we characterized the semantic and performance limitations of state-of-the-art hardware-based tag matching and rendezvous offload designs and showed that they cannot be applied to a number of scenarios. We also show that hardware tag-matching does not provide improved overlap for various common communication patterns such as unexpected or non-contiguous messages. We proposed an adaptive overlap engine for MPI that is cognizant of the application's communication requirements and can opportunistically offload receives to the network adapter based on factors like message size, datatype, as well as arrival patterns of the sender and the receiver process. The proposed design uses both hardware-assisted and history-driven software-based solutions to extract overlap for both expected and unexpected messages in different communication scenarios. We evaluated the efficacy of the proposed design against state-of-the-art hardware and software-based solutions using a variety of microbenchmarks and application kernels and showed up to 55% and 17% improvement for Reduce and Gather collectives with 320 processes. Furthermore, we showed that our designs can increase the performance of Iscatterv and Ialltoall up to 41% and 33% in 1024 and 64 nodes, respectively. We also show up to 2× increase in overlap and up to 22% reduction in overall runtime for stencil-based application kernels and 23% improvement in communication performance of P3DFFT. As the future work, we will work on proposing HW TM aware collectives as well as running more scientific applications to see the impact of proposed designs.

## References

1. Osu Micro-benchmarks (2017). http://mvapich.cse.ohio-state.edu/benchmarks

534    M. Bayatpour et al.

2. Alexandrov, A., Ionescu, M.F., Schauser, K.E., Scheiman, C.: LogGP: incorporating long messages into the LogP model – one step closer towards a realistic model for parallel computation. Tech. rep., Santa Barbara, CA, USA (1995)
3. Atomic, L.S., Simulator, M.M.P.: LAMMPS (2013). https://lammps.sandia.gov/
4. Bayatpour, M., Subramoni, H., Chakraborty, S., Panda, D.K.: Adaptive and dynamic design for MPI tag matching. In: 2016 IEEE International Conference on Cluster Computing (CLUSTER), pp. 1–10 (September 2016). https://doi.org/10.1109/CLUSTER.2016.69
5. Bayatpour, M., Ghazimirsaeed, S.M., Xu, S., Subramoni, H., Panda, D.K.: Design and characterization of infiniband hardware tag matching in MPI. In: 20th Annual IEEE/ACM International Symposium in Cluster, Cloud, and Grid Computing (Accepted to be published) (2020)
6. Brightwell, R., Underwood, K.: Evaluation of an eager protocol optimization for MPI. In: Dongarra, J., Laforenza, D., Orlando, S. (eds.) EuroPVM/MPI 2003. LNCS, vol. 2840, pp. 327–334. Springer, Heidelberg (2003). https://doi.org/10.1007/978-3-540-39924-7_46
7. Chakraborty, S., Bayatpour, M., Hashmi, J., Subramoni, H., Panda, D.K.: Cooperative rendezvous protocols for improved performance and overlap. In: SC18: International Conference for High Performance Computing, Networking, Storage and Analysis, pp. 361–373. IEEE (2018)
8. Dosanjh, M.G., et al.: The case for semi-permanent cache occupancy: understanding the impact of data locality on network processing. In: Proceedings of the 47th International Conference on Parallel Processing, p. 73. ACM (2018)
9. Dosanjh, M.G., Schonbein, W., Grant, R.E., Bridges, P.G., Ghazimirsaeed, S.M., Afsahi, A.: Fuzzy matching: hardware accelerated MPI communication middleware. In: 19th Annual IEEE/ACM International Symposium in Cluster, Cloud, and Grid Computing (CCGrid 2019) (2019)
10. Ghazimirsaeed, M., Grant, R., Afsahi, A.: A dynamic, unified design for dedicated message matching engines for collective and point-to-point communications. Parallel Comput. **89**, 102547 (2019)
11. Ghazimirsaeed, S.M., Afsahi, A.: Accelerating MPI message matching by a data clustering strategy. In: High Performance Computing Symposium (HPCS 2017). Kingston (2017)
12. Ghazimirsaeed, S.M., Grant, R.E., Afsahi, A.: A dedicated message matching mechanism for collective communications. In: Proceedings of the 47th International Conference on Parallel Processing Companion, p. 26. ACM (2018)
13. Ghazimirsaeed, S.M., Mirsadeghi, S.H., Afsahi, A.: Communication-aware message matching in MPI. Concurr. Comput.: Pract. Exp. **32**, e4862 (2019)
14. Graham, R.L., et al.: Overlapping computation and communication: barrier algorithms and ConnectX-2 Core-Direct capabilities. In: 2010 IEEE International Symposium on Parallel Distributed Processing, Workshops and PhD Forum (IPDPSW), pp. 1–8 (April 2010). https://doi.org/10.1109/IPDPSW.2010.5470854
15. Hoefler, T., Siebert, C., Lumsdaine, A.: Group operation assembly language - a flexible way to express collective communication. In: ICPP-2009 - The 38th International Conference on Parallel Processing. IEEE (September 2009)
16. Kandalla, K., Subramoni, H., Tomko, K., Pekurovsky, D., Sur, S., Panda, D.K.: High-performance and scalable non-blocking all-to-all with collective offload on infiniband clusters: a study with parallel 3D FFT. Comput. Sci.-Res. Dev. **26**(3–4), 237 (2011)

17. Venkata, M., et al.: ConnectX-2 CORE-Direct enabled asynchronous broadcast collective communications. In: Proceedings of the 25th IEEE International Parallel and Distributed Processing Symposium, Workshops (2011)
18. Message Passing Interface Forum: MPI: A Message-Passing Interface Standard (March 1994)
19. MVAPICH: MPI over InfiniBand, Omni-Path, Ethernet/iWARP, and RoCE (2017). http://mvapich.cse.ohio-state.edu/
20. Pekurovsky, D.: P3DFFT: a framework for parallel computations of fourier transforms in three dimensions. SIAM J. Sci. Comput. **34**(4), C192–C209 (2012)
21. Ruhela, A., Subramoni, H., Chakraborty, S., Bayatpour, M., Kousha, P., Panda, D.K.D.: Efficient design for MPI asynchronous progress without dedicated resources. Parallel Comput. **85**, 13–26 (2019)
22. Schneider, T., Eckelmann, S., Hoefler, T., Rehm, W.: Kernel-based offload of collective operations – implementation, evaluation and lessons learned. In: Jeannot, E., Namyst, R., Roman, J. (eds.) Euro-Par 2011. LNCS, vol. 6853, pp. 264–275. Springer, Heidelberg (2011). https://doi.org/10.1007/978-3-642-23397-5_26
23. Subramoni, H., Kandalla, K., Sur, S., Panda, D.K.: Design and evaluation of generalized collective communication primitives with overlap using ConnectX-2 offload engine. In: 2010 18th IEEE Symposium on High Performance Interconnects, pp. 40–49 (August 2010). https://doi.org/10.1109/HOTI.2010.22
24. Subramoni, H., et al.: Designing non-blocking personalized collectives with near perfect overlap for RDMA-enabled clusters. In: Kunkel, J.M., Ludwig, T. (eds.) ISC High Performance 2015. LNCS, vol. 9137, pp. 434–453. Springer, Cham (2015). https://doi.org/10.1007/978-3-319-20119-1_31
25. Subramoni, H., Chakraborty, S., Panda, D.K.: Designing dynamic and adaptive MPI point-to-point communication protocols for efficient overlap of computation and communication. In: Kunkel, J.M., Yokota, R., Balaji, P., Keyes, D. (eds.) ISC 2017. LNCS, vol. 10266, pp. 334–354. Springer, Cham (2017). https://doi.org/10.1007/978-3-319-58667-0_18
26. Unified Communication X (2019). http://www.openucx.org/
27. Venkatesh, A., et al.: A case for application-oblivious energy-efficient MPI runtime. In: Proceedings of the International Conference for High Performance Computing, Networking, Storage and Analysis, SC 2015, pp. 1–12. IEEE (2015)
28. Yu, W., Buntinas, D., Panda, D.K.: High performance and reliable NIC-based multicast over Myrinet/GM-2. In: Proceedings of 2003 International Conference on Parallel Processing, 2003, pp. 197–204 (October 2003). https://doi.org/10.1109/ICPP.2003.1240581

# Reinit++: Evaluating the Performance of Global-Restart Recovery Methods for MPI Fault Tolerance

Giorgis Georgakoudis[1]([✉]), Luanzheng Guo[2], and Ignacio Laguna[1]

[1] Center for Advanced Scientific Computing, Lawrence Livermore National Laboratory, Livermore, USA
{georgakoudis1,lagunaperalt1}@llnl.gov
[2] EECS, UC Merced, Merced, USA
lguo4@ucmerced.edu

**Abstract.** Scaling supercomputers comes with an increase in failure rates due to the increasing number of hardware components. In standard practice, applications are made resilient through checkpointing data and restarting execution after a failure occurs to resume from the latest checkpoint. However, re-deploying an application incurs overhead by tearing down and re-instating execution, and possibly limiting checkpointing retrieval from slow permanent storage.

In this paper we present Reinit++, a new design and implementation of the Reinit approach for global-restart recovery, which avoids application re-deployment. We extensively evaluate Reinit++ contrasted with the leading MPI fault-tolerance approach of ULFM, implementing global-restart recovery, and the typical practice of restarting an application to derive new insight on performance. Experimentation with three different HPC proxy applications made resilient to withstand process and node failures shows that Reinit++ recovers much faster than restarting, up to 6×, or ULFM, up to 3×, and that it scales excellently as the number of MPI processes grows.

## 1 Introduction

HPC system performance scales by increasing the number of computing nodes and by increasing the processing and memory elements of each node. Furthermore, electronics continue to shrink, thus are more susceptible to interference, such as radiation upsets or voltage fluctuations. Those trends increase the probability of a failure happening, either due to component failure or due to transient soft errors affecting electronics. Large HPC applications run for hours or days and use most, if not all, the nodes of a supercomputer, thus are vulnerable to failures, often leading to process or node crashes. Reportedly, the mean time between a node failure on petascale systems has been measured to be 6.7 h [24],

---

L. Guo—Work performed during internship at Lawrence Livermore National Laboratory

P. Sadayappan et al. (Eds.): ISC High Performance 2020, LNCS 12151, pp. 536–554, 2020.
https://doi.org/10.1007/978-3-030-50743-5_27

while worst-case projections [12] foresee that exascale systems may experience a failure even more frequently.

HPC applications often implement fault tolerance using checkpoints to restart execution, a method referred to as *Checkpoint-Restart* (CR). Applications periodically store checkpoints, e.g., every few iterations of an iterative computation, and when a failure occurs, execution aborts and restarts again to resume from the latest checkpoint. Most scalable HPC applications follow the Bulk Synchronous Parallel (BSP) paradigm, hence CR with global, backward, non-shrinking recovery [21], also known as *global-restart* naturally fits their execution. CR is straightforward to implement but requires re-deploying the whole application on a failure, re-spawning all processes on every node and re-initializing any application data structures. This method has significant overhead since a failure of few processes, even a single process failure, requires complete re-deployment, although most of the processes survived the failure.

By contrast, User-level Fault Mitigation (ULFM) [4] extends MPI with interfaces for handling failures at the application level without restarting execution. The programmer is required to use the ULFM extensions to detect a failure and repair communicators and either spawn new processes, for non-shrinking recovery, or continue execution with any survivor processes, for shrinking recovery. Although ULFM grants the programmer great flexibility to handle failures, it requires considerable effort to refactor the application for correctly and efficiently implementing recovery.

Alternatively, Reinit [11,22] has been proposed as an easier-to-program approach, but equally capable of supporting global-restart recovery. Reinit extends MPI with a function call that sets a rollback point in the application. It transparently implements MPI recovery, by spawning new processes and mending the world communicator at the MPI runtime level. Thus, Reinit transparently ensures a consistent, initial MPI state akin to the state after MPI initialization. However, the existing implementation of Reinit [11] is hard to deploy, since it requires modifications to the job scheduler, and difficult to compare with ULFM, which only requires extensions to the MPI library. Notably, both Reinit and ULFM approaches assume the application has checkpointing in place to resume execution at the application level.

Although there has been a large bibliography [4,5,9,11,16–18,21–23,26] discussing the programming model and prototypes of those approaches, no study has presented an in-depth performance evaluation of them –most previous works either focus on individual aspects of each approach or perform limited scale experiments. In this paper, we present an extensive evaluation using HPC proxy applications to contrast these two leading global-restart recovery approaches. Specifically, our contributions are:

- A new design and implementation of the Reinit approach, named Reinit$^{++}$, using the latest Open MPI runtime. Our design and implementation supports recovery from either process or node failures, is high performance, and deploys easily by extending the Open MPI library. Notably, we present a precise definition of the failures it handles and the scope of this design and implementation.

- An extensive evaluation of the performance of the possible recovery approaches (CR, Reinit$^{++}$, ULFM) using three HPC proxy applications (CoMD, LULESH, HPCCG), and including file and in-memory checkpointing schemes.
- New insight from the results of our evaluation which show that recovery under Reinit$^{++}$ is up to 6× faster than CR and up to 3× faster than ULFM. Compared to CR, Reinit$^{++}$ avoids the re-deployment overhead, while compared to UFLM, Reinit$^{++}$ avoids interference during fault-free application execution and has less recovery overhead.

## 2   Overview

This section presents an overview of the state-of-the-art approaches for MPI fault tolerance. Specifically, it provides an overview of the recovery models for applications and briefly discusses ULFM and Reinit, which represent the state-of-the-art in MPI fault tolerance.

### 2.1   Recovery Models for MPI Applications

There are several models for fault tolerance depending on the requirements of the application. Specifically, if all MPI processes must recover after a failure, recovery is *global*; otherwise if some, but not all, of the MPI processes need to recover then recovery is deemed as *local*. Furthermore, applications can either recover by rolling back computation at an earlier point in time, defined as *backward* recovery, or, if they can continue computation without backtracking, recovery is deemed as *forward*. Moreover, if recovery restores the number of MPI processes to resume execution, it is defined as *non-shrinking*, whereas if execution continues with whatever number of processes surviving the failure, then recovery is characterized as *shrinking*. *Global-restart* implements global, backward, non-shrinking recovery which fits most HPC applications that follow a bulk-synchronous paradigm where MPI processes have interlocked dependencies, thus it is the focus of this work.

### 2.2   Existing Approaches for MPI Fault Tolerance

**ULFM.** One of the state-of-the-art approaches for fault tolerance in MPI is User-level Fault Mitigation (ULFM) [4]. ULFM extends MPI to enable failure detection at the application level and provide a set of primitives for handling recovery. Specifically, ULFM taps to the existing error handling interface of MPI to implement user-level fault notification. Regarding its extensions to the MPI interface, we elaborate on communicators since their extensions are a superset of other communication objects (windows, I/O). Following, ULFM extends MPI with a *revoke* operation (`MPI_Comm_revoke(comm)`) to invalidate a communicator such that any subsequent operation on it raises an error. Also, it defines a *shrink* operation (`MPI_Comm_shrink(comm, newcomm)`) that creates a new communicator from an existing one after excluding any failed processes. Additionally, ULFM defines a collective *agreement* operation (`MPI_Comm_agree(comm,flag)`) which achieves consensus on the group of failed processes in a communicator and on the value of the integer variable `flag`.

Based on those extensions, MPI programmers are expected to implement their own recovery strategy tailored to their applications. ULFM operations are general enough to implement any type of recovery discussed earlier. However, this generality comes at the cost of complexity. Programmers need to understand the intricate semantics of those operations to correctly and efficiently implement recovery and restructure, possibly significantly, the application for explicitly handling failures. Although ULFM provides examples that prescribe the implementation of global-restart, the programmer must embed this in the code and refactor the application to function with the expectation that communicators may change during execution due to shrinking and merging, which is not ideal.

**Reinit.** Reinit [11,22] has been proposed as an alternative approach for implementing global-restart recovery, through a simpler interface compared to ULFM. The most recent implementation [11] of Reinit is limited in several aspects: (1) it requires modifying the job scheduler (SLURM), besides the MPI runtime, thus it is impractical to deploy and skews performance measurements due to crossing the interface between the job scheduler and the MPI runtime; (2) its implementation is not publicly available; (3) it bases on the MVAPICH2 MPI runtime, which makes comparisons with ULFM hard, since ULFM is implemented on the Open MPI runtime. Thus, we opt for a new design and implementation[1], named Reinit$^{++}$, which we present in detail in the next section.

## 3   Reinit$^{++}$

This section describes the programming interface of Reinit$^{++}$, the assumptions for application deployment, process and node failure detection, and the recovery algorithm for global-restart. We also define the semantics of MPI recovery for the implementation of Reinit$^{++}$ as well as discuss its specifics.

### 3.1   Design

**Programming Interface of Reinit$^{++}$.** Figure 1 presents the programming interface of Reinit$^{++}$ in the C language, while Fig. 2 shows sample usage of it. There is a single function call, `MPI_Reinit`, for the programmer to call to define the point in code to rollback and resume execution after a failure. This function must be called after `MPI_Init` so ensure the MPI runtime has been initialized. Its arguments imitate the parameters of `MPI_Init`, adding a parameter for a

---

[1] Available open-source at https://github.com/ggeorgakoudis/ompi/tree/reinit.

```
typedef enum {
  MPI_REINIT_NEW, MPI_REINIT_REINITED, MPI_REINIT_RESTARTED
} MPI_Reinit_state_t

typedef int
(*MPI_Restart_point)
  (int argc, char **argv, MPI_Reinit_state_t state);

int MPI_Reinit
  (int argc, char **argv, const MPI_Restart_point point);
```

**Fig. 1.** The programming interface of Reinit$^{++}$

```
int foo(int argc, char **argv, MPI_Reinit_state_t state)
{
  /* Load checkpoint if it exists */
  while(!done) {
    /* Do computation */
    /* Store checkpoint */
  }
}

int main(int argc, char **argv)
{
  MPI_Init(&argc, &argv);
  /* Application-specific initialization */
  // Entry point of the resilient function
  MPI_Reinit(&argc, &argv, foo);
  MPI_Finalize();
}
```

**Fig. 2.** Sample usage of the interface of Reinit$^{++}$

pointer to a user-defined function. Reinit$^{++}$ expects the programmer to encapsulate in this function the main computational loop of the application, which is restartable through checkpointing. Internally, `MPI_Reinit` passes the parameters `argc` and `argv` to this user-defined function, plus the parameter `state`, which indicates the MPI state of the process as values from the enumeration type `MPI_Reinit_state_t`. Specifically, the value `MPI_REINIT_NEW` designates a new process executing for the first time, the value `MPI_REINIT_REINITED` designates a survivor process that has entered the user-defined function after rolling back due to a failure, and the value `MPI_REINIT_RESTARTED` designates that the process has failed and has been re-spawned to resume execution. Note that this state variable describes only the MPI state of Reinit$^{++}$, thus has no semantics on the application state, such as whether to load a checkpoint or not.

**Application Deployment Model.** Reinit$^{++}$ assumes a logical, hierarchical topology of application deployment. Figure 3 shows a graphical representation of this deployment model. At the top level, there is a single *root* process that spawns and monitors *daemon* processes, one on each of the computing nodes

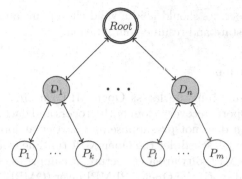

**Fig. 3.** Application deployment model

reserved for the application. Daemons spawn and monitor *MPI processes* local
to their nodes. The root communicates with daemons and keeps track of their
liveness, while daemons track the liveness of their children MPI processes. Based
on this execution and deployment model, Reinit$^{++}$ performs fault detection,
which we discuss next.

**Fault Detection.** Reinit$^{++}$ targets *fail-stop* failures of either MPI processes or
daemons. A daemon failure is deemed equivalent to a node failure. The causes
for those failures may be transient faults or hard faults of hardware components.

In the design of Reinit$^{++}$, the root manages the execution of the whole
applications, so any recovery decisions are taken by it, hence it is the focal point
for fault detection. Specifically, if an MPI process fails, its managing daemon is
notified of the failure and forwards this notification to the root, without taking
an action itself. If a daemon process fails, which means either the node failed or
the daemon process itself, the root directly detects the failure and also assumes
that the children MPI processes of that daemon are lost too. After detecting a
fault the root process proceeds with recovery, which we introduce in the following
section.

**MPI Recovery.** Reinit$^{++}$ recovery for both MPI process and daemon failures
is similar, except that on a daemon failure the root chooses a new host node to
re-instate failed MPI processes, since a daemon failure proxies a node failure. For
recovery, the root process broadcasts a *reinit* message to all daemons. Daemons
receiving that message roll back survivor processes and re-spawn failed ones.
After rolling back survivor MPI processes and spawning new ones, the semantics of MPI recovery are that only the world communicator is valid and any
previous MPI state (other communicators, windows, etc.) has been discarded.
This is similar to the MPI state available immediately after an application calls
`MPI_Init`. Next, the application restores its state, discussed in the following
section.

**Application Recovery.** Reinit$^{++}$ assumes that applications are responsible for
saving and restoring their state to resume execution. Hence, both survivor and

re-spawned MPI processes should load a valid checkpoint after MPI recovery to restore application state and resume computation.

## 3.2 Implementation

We implement Reinit$^{++}$ in the latest Open MPI runtime, version 4.0.0. The implementation supports recovery from both process and daemon (node) failures. This implementation does not presuppose any particular job scheduler, so it is compatible with any job scheduler the Open MPI runtime works with. Introducing briefly the Open MPI software architecture, it comprises of three frameworks of distinct functionality: (i) the OpenMPI MPI layer (OMPI), which implements the interface of the MPI specification used by the application developers; (ii) the OpenMPI Runtime Environment (ORTE), which implements runtime functions for application deployment, execution monitoring, and fault detection, and (iii) the Open Portability Access Layers (OPAL), which implements abstractions of OS interfaces, such as signal handling, process creation, etc.

Reinit$^{++}$ extends OMPI to provide the function `MPI_Reinit`. It extends ORTE to propagate fault notifications from daemons to the root and to implement the mechanism of MPI recovery on detecting a fault. Also, Reinit$^{++}$ extends OPAL to implement low-level process signaling for notifying survivor process to roll back. The following sections provide more details.

**Application Deployment.** Reinit$^{++}$ requires the application to deploy using the default launcher of Open MPI, `mpirun`. Note that using the launcher `mpirun` is compatible with any job scheduler and even uses optimized deployment interfaces, if the scheduler provides any. Physical application deployment in Open MPI closely follows the logical model of the design of Reinit$^{++}$. Specifically, Open MPI sets the root of the deployment at the process launching the `mpirun`, typically on a login node of HPC installations, which is deemed as the Head Node Process (HNP) in Open MPI terminology. Following, the root launches an ORTE daemon on each node allocated for the application. Daemons spawn the set of MPI processes in each node and monitor their execution. The root process communicates with each daemon over a channel of a reliable network transport and monitors the liveness of daemons through the existence of this channel.

Launching an application, the user specifies the number of MPI processes and optionally the number of nodes (or number of processes per node). To withstand process failures, this specification of deployment is sufficient, since Reinit$^{++}$ re-spawns failed processes on their original node of deployment. However, for node failures, the user must *over-provision* the allocated process slots for re-spawning the set of MPI processes lost due to a failed node. To do so, the most straightforward way is to allocate more nodes than required for fault-free operation, up to the maximum number of node failures to withstand.

**Fault Detection.** In Open MPI, a daemon is the parent of the MPI processes on its node. If an MPI process crashes, its parent daemon is notified, by trapping the signal `SIGCHLD`, in POSIX semantics. Implementing the fault detection

---

**Algorithm 1:** Root: HandleFailure

---

**Data:** $\mathcal{D}$: the set of daemons,
$Children(x)$: returns the set of children MPI processes of daemon $x$,
$Parent(x)$: returns the parent daemon of MPI process $x$
**Input:** The failed process $f$ (MPI process or daemon)
```
// failed process is a daemon
```
**if** $f \in \mathcal{D}$ **then**
$\quad$ $\mathcal{D} \leftarrow \mathcal{D} \setminus \{f\}$
$\quad$ $d' \leftarrow d \mid \underset{d \in \mathcal{D}}{\arg\min}\; Children(d)$
$\quad$ ``// broadcast REINIT to all daemons``
$\quad$ Broadcast $\mathcal{D}$ message $\langle$REINIT, $\{\, \langle d', c \rangle \mid \forall c \in Children(f)\,\}\,\rangle$
``// failed process is an MPI process``
**else**
$\quad$ Broadcast $\mathcal{D}$ message $\langle$REINIT, $\{\, \langle Parent(f), f \rangle \,\}\,\rangle$
**end**

---

requirements of Reinit$^{++}$, a daemon relays the fault notification to the root process for taking action. Regarding node failures, the root directly detects them proxied through daemon failures. Specifically, the root has an open communication channel with each daemon over some reliable transport, e.g., TCP. If the connection over that communication channel breaks, the root process is notified of the failure and regards the daemon at fault, thus assuming all its children MPI process lost and its host node is unavailable. For both types of failures (process and node), the root process initiates MPI recovery.

**MPI Recovery.** Algorithm 1 shows in pseudocode the operation of the root process when handling a failure. On detecting a failure, the root process distinguishes whether it is a faulty daemon or MPI process. For a node failure, the root selects the *least loaded node* in the resource allocation, that is the node with the fewest occupied process slots, and sets this node's daemon as the parent daemon for failed processes. For a process failure, the root selects the original parent daemon of the failed process to re-spawn that process. Next, the root process initiates recovery by broadcasting to all daemons a message with the REINIT command and the list of processes to spawn, along with their selected parent daemons. Following, when a daemon receives that message it signals its survivor, children MPI processes to roll back, and re-spawns any processes in the list that have this daemon as their parent. Algorithm 2 presents this procedure in pseudocode.

Regarding the asynchronous, signaling interface of Reinit$^{++}$, Algorithm 3 illustrates the internals of the Reinit$^{++}$ in pseudocode. When an MPI process executes MPI_Reinit, it installs a *signal handler* for the signal SIGREINIT, which aliases SIGUSR1 in our implementation. Also, MPI_Reinit sets a non-local goto point using the POSIX function setjmp(). The signal handler of SIGREINIT simply calls longjmp() to return execution of survivor processes to this goto point. Rolled back survivor processes discard any previous MPI state and block

---

**Algorithm 2:** Daemon $\hat{d}$: HandleReinit

**Data:** $Children(x)$: returns the set of children MPI processes of daemon $x$,
$Parent(x)$: returns the parent daemon of MPI process $x$
**Input:** List $\{\langle d_i, c_i \rangle, \cdots \}$
// Signal survivor MPI processes
for $c \in Children(\hat{d})$ do
   |  $c.state \leftarrow$ MPI_REINIT_REINITED
   |  Signal SIGREINIT to $c$
end
// Spawn new process if $\hat{d}$ is parent
foreach $\{\langle d_i, c_i \rangle, \cdots \}$ do
   |  if $\hat{d} == d_i$ then
   |     |  $Children(\hat{d}) \leftarrow Children(\hat{d}) \cup c_i$
   |     |  $c_i.state \leftarrow$ MPI_REINIT_RESTARTED
   |     |  Spawn $c_i$
   |  end
end

---

on a ORTE-level barrier. This barrier replicates the implicit barrier present in `MPI_Init` to synchronize with re-spawned processes joining the computation. After the barrier, survivor processes re-initialize the world communicator and call the function `foo` to resume computation. Re-spawned processes initialize the world communicator as part of the MPI initialization procedure of `MPI_Init` and go through `MPI_Reinit` to install the signal handler, set the goto point, and lastly call the user-defined function to resume computation.

**Application Recovery.** Application recovery includes the actions needed at the application-level to resume computation. Any additional MPI state besides the repaired world communicator, such as sub-communicators, must be re-created by the application's MPI processes. Also, it is expected that each process loads the latest consistent checkpoint to continue computing. Checkpointing lays within the responsibility of the application developer. In the next section, we discuss the scope and implications of our implementation.

**Discussion.** In this implementation, the scope of fault tolerance is to support recovery from failures *happening after* `MPI_Reinit` has been called by all MPI processes. This is because `MPI_Reinit` must install signal handlers and set the roll-back point on all MPI processes. This is sufficient for a large coverage of failures since execution time is dominated by the main computational loop. In the case a failure happens before the call to `MPI_Reinit`, the application falls back to the default action of aborting execution. Nevertheless, the design of Reinit[++] is not limited by this implementation choice. A possible approach instead of aborting, which we leave as future work, is to treat any MPI processes that have not called `MPI_Reinit` as if failed and re-execute them.

---

**Algorithm 3:** Reinit$^{++}$ internals

---

**Function** OnSignalReinit():
   | **goto** Rollback
**end**
**Function** MPI_Reinit(*argc, argv,* foo):
   | Install signal handler OnSignalReinit on SIGREINIT
Rollback:    | **if** *this.state == MPI_REINIT_REINITED* **then**
      | Discard MPI state
      | Wait on barrier
      | Re-initialize world communicator
   **end**
   | **return** foo *(argc, argv, this.state)*
**end**

---

Furthermore, signaling SIGREINIT for rolling back survivor MPI processes asynchronously interrupts execution. In our implementation, we render the MPI runtime library *signal and roll-back safe* by using masking to defer signal handling until a safe point, i.e., avoid interruption when locks are held or data structures are updating. Since application code is out of our control, Reinit$^{++}$ requires the application developer to program the application as signal and roll-back safe. A possible enhancement is to provide an interface for installing cleanup handlers, proposed in earlier designs of Reinit [21], so that application and library developers can install routines to reset application-level state on recovery. Another approach is to make recovery synchronous, by extending the Reinit$^{++}$ interface to include a function that tests whether a fault has been detected and trigger roll back. The developer may call this function at safe points during execution for recovery. We leave both those enhancements as future work, noting that the existing interface is sufficient for performing our evaluation.

# 4 Experimentation Setup

This section provides detailed information on the experimentation setup, the recovery approaches used for comparisons, the proxy applications and their configurations, and the measurement methodology.

**Table 1.** Proxy applications and their configuration

| Application | Input | No. ranks |
|---|---|---|
| CoMD | -i4 -j2 -k2 | 16, 32, 64, 128, 256, 512, 1024 |
|  | -x 80 -y 40 -z 40 -N 20 |  |
| HPCCG | 64 64 64 | 16, 32, 64, 128, 256, 512, 1024 |
| LULESH | -i 20 -s 48 | 8, 64, 512 |

**Recovery Approaches.** Experimentation includes the following recovery approaches:

- *CR*, which implements the typical approach of immediately restarting an application after execution aborts due to a failure.
- *ULFM*, by using its latest revision based on the Open MPI runtime v4.0.1 (4.0.1ulfm2.1rc1).
- *Reinit$^{++}$*, which is our own implementation of Reinit, based on OpenMPI runtime v4.0.0.

**Emulating Failures.** Failures are emulated through fault injection. We opt for random fault injection to emulate the occurrence of random faults, e.g., soft errors or failures of hardware components, that lead to a crash failure. Specifically, for process failures, we instrument applications so that at a random iteration of the main computational loop, a random MPI process suicides by raising the signal SIGKILL. The random selection of iteration and MPI process is the same for every recovery approach. For node failures, the method is similar, but instead of itself, the MPI process sends the signal SIGKILL to its parent daemon, thus kills the daemon and by extension all its children processes. In experimentation, we inject a *single* MPI process failure or a *single* node failure.

**Applications.** We experiment with three benchmark applications that represent different HPC domains: *CoMD* for molecular dynamics, *HPCCG* for iterative solvers, and *LULESH* for multi-physics computation. The motivation is to investigate global-restart recovery on a wide range of applications and evaluate any performance differences. Table 1 shows information on the proxy applications and scaling of their deployed number of ranks. Note *LULESH* requires a cube number of ranks, thus the trimmed down experimentation space. The deployment configuration has 16 ranks per node, so the smallest deployment comprises of one node while the largest one spans 64 nodes (1024 ranks). Application execute in *weak scaling* mode – for *CoMD* we show its input only 16 ranks and change it accordingly. We extend applications to implement global-restart with Reinit$^{++}$ or ULFM, to store a checkpoint after every iteration of their main computational loop and load the latest checkpoint upon recovery.

**Checkpointing.** For evaluation purposes, we implement our own, simple checkpointing library that supports saving and loading application data using in-memory and file checkpoints. Table 2 summarizes checkpointing per recovery approach and failure type. In detail, we implement two types of checkpointing: *file* and *memory*. For file checkpointing, each MPI process stores a checkpoint to globally accessible permanent storage, which is the networked, parallel filesystem Lustre available in our cluster. For memory checkpointing, an MPI process stores a checkpoint both locally in its own memory and remotely to the memory of a *buddy* [33,34] MPI process, which in our implementation is the (cyclically) next MPI process by rank. This memory checkpointing implementation is applicable only to single process failures since multiple process failures or a node failure can wipe out both local and buddy checkpoints for the failed MPI processes. CR necessarily uses file checkpointing since re-deploying the application requires permanent storage to retrieve checkpoints.

**Table 2.** Checkpointing per recovery and failure

| Failure | Recovery | | |
|---------|------|--------|--------|
| *process* | CR | ULFM | Reinit |
| | File | Memory | Memory |
| *node* | File | File | File |

**Statistical Evaluation.** For each proxy application and configuration we perform 10 independent measurements. Each measurement counts the total execution time of the application breaking it down to time needed for writing checkpoints, time spent during MPI recovery, time reading a checkpoint after a failure, and the pure application time executing the computation. Any confidence intervals shown correspond to a 95% confidence level and are calculated based on the t-distribution to avoid assumptions on the sampled population's distribution.

# 5 Evaluation

For the evaluation we compare CR, Reinit$^{++}$ and ULFM for both process and node failures. Results provide insight on the performance of each of those recovery approaches implementing global-restart and reveal the reasons for their performance differences.

## 5.1 Comparing Total Execution Time on a Process Failure

Figure 4 shows average total execution time for process failures using file checkpointing for CR and memory checkpointing for Reinit$^{++}$ and ULFM. The plot breaks down time to components of writing checkpoints, MPI recovery, and pure application time. Reading checkpoints occurs one-off after a failure and has negligible impact, in the order of tens of milliseconds, thus it is omitted.

The first observation is that Reinit$^{++}$ scales excellently compared to both CR and ULFM, across all programs. CR has the worse performance, increasingly so with more ranks. The reason is the limited scaling of writing checkpoints to the networked filesystem. By contrast, ULFM and Reinit$^{++}$ use memory checkpointing, spending minimal time writing checkpoints. Interestingly, ULFM scales worse than Reinit$^{++}$; we believe that the reason is that it inflates pure application execution time, which we illustrate in the next section. Further, in the following sections, we remove checkpointing overhead from the analysis to highlight the performance differences of the different recovering approaches.

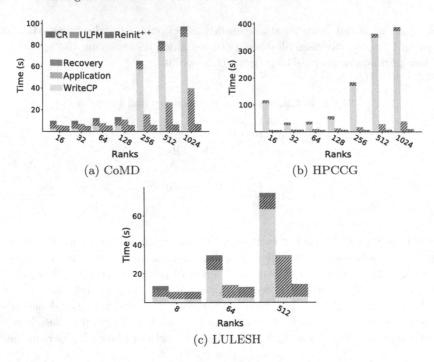

**Fig. 4.** Total execution time breakdown recovering from a process failure

## 5.2 Comparing Pure Application Time Under Different Recovery Approaches

Figure 5 shows the pure application time, without including reading/writing checkpoints or MPI recovery. We observe that application time is on par for CR and Reinit++, and that all applications scale weakly well on up to 1024 ranks. CR and Reinit++ do not interfere with execution, thus they have no impact on application time, which is on par to the fault-free execution time of the proxy applications. However, in ULFM, application time grows significantly as the number of ranks increases. ULFM extends MPI with an always-on, periodic heartbeat mechanism [8] to detect failures and also modifies communication primitives for fault tolerant operation. Following from our measurements, those

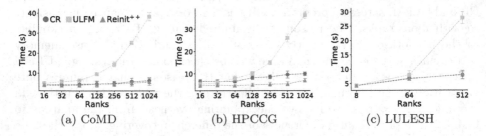

**Fig. 5.** Scaling of pure application time

extensions noticeably increase the original application execution time. However, it is inconclusive whether this is a result of the tested prototype implementation or a systemic trade-off. Next, we compare the MPI recovery times among all the approaches.

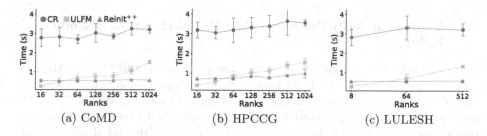

Fig. 6. Scaling of MPI recovery time recovering from a process failure

### 5.3  Comparing MPI Recovery Time Recovering from a Process Failure

Though checkpointing saves application's computation time, reducing MPI recovery time saves overhead from restarting. This overhead is increasingly important the larger the deployment and the higher the fault rate. In particular, Fig. 6 shows the scaling of time required for MPI recovery across all programs and recovery approaches, again removing any overhead for checkpointing to focus on the MPI recovery time. As expected, MPI recovery time depends only on the number of ranks, thus times are similar among different programs for the same recovery approach. Commenting on scaling, CR and Reinit$^{++}$ scale excellently, requiring almost constant time for MPI recovery regardless the number of ranks. However, CR is about 6× slower, requiring around 3 s to tear down execution and re-deploy the application, whereas Reinit$^{++}$ requires about 0.5 s to propagate the fault, re-initialize survivor processes and re-spawn the failed process. ULFM has on par recovery time with Reinit$^{++}$ up to 64 ranks, but then its time increases being up to 3× slower than Reinit$^{++}$ for 1024 ranks. ULFM

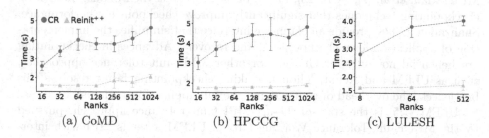

Fig. 7. Scaling of MPI recovery time recovering from a node failure

requires multiple collective operations among all MPI processes to implement global-restart (shrink the faulty communicator, spawn a new process, merge it to a new communicator). By contrast, Reinit$^{++}$ implements recovery at the MPI runtime layer requiring fewer operations and confining collective communication only between root and daemon processes.

### 5.4 Comparing MPI Recovery Time Recovering from a Node Failure

This comparison for a node failure includes only CR and Reinit$^{++}$, since the prototype implementation of ULFM faced robustness issues (hanging or crashing) and did not produce measurements. Also, since both CR and Reinit$^{++}$ use file checkpointing and do not interfere with pure application time, we present only results for MPI recovery times, shown in Fig. 7. Both CR and Reinit$^{++}$ scale very well with almost constant times, as they do for a process failure. However, in absolute values, Reinit$^{++}$ has a higher recovery time of about 1.5 s for a node failure compared to 0.5 s for a process failure. This is because recovering from a node failure requires extra work to select the least loaded node and spawn all the MPI processes of the failed node. Nevertheless, recovery with Reinit$^{++}$ is still about 2× faster than with CR.

## 6    Related Work

Checkpoint-Restart [1,2,10,15,20,27,29,32] is the most common approach to recover an MPI application after a failure. CR requires substantial development effort to identify which data to checkpoint and may have significant overhead. Thus, many efforts attempt to make checkpointing easier to adopt and render it fast and storage efficient. We briefly discuss them here.

Hargrove and Duell [15] implement the system-level CR library Berkeley Lab Checkpoint/Restart (BLCR) library to automatically checkpoint applications by extending the Linux kernel. Bosilca et al. [6] integrate an uncoordinated, distributed checkpoint/roll-back system in the MPICH runtime to automatically support fault tolerance for node failures. Furthermore. Sankaran et al. [27] integrate Berkeley Lab BLCR kernel-level C/R to the LAM implementation of MPI. Adam et al. [2], SCR [25], and FTI [3] propose asynchronous, multi-level checkpointing techniques that significantly improve checkpointing performance. Shahzad et al. [28] provide an extensive interface that simplifies the implementation of application-level checkpointing and recovery. Advances in checkpointing are beneficial not only for CR but for other MPI fault tolerance approaches, such as ULFM and Reinit. Though making checkpointing faster resolves this bottleneck, the overhead of re-deploying the full application remains.

ULFM [4,5] is the state-of-the-art MPI fault tolerance approach, pursued by the MPI Fault Tolerance Working Group. ULFM extends MPI with interfaces to shrink or revoke communicators, and fault-tolerant collective consensus. The application developer is responsible for implementing recovery using those operations, choosing the type of recovery best suited for its application. A collection of works on ULFM [9,16–18,21,23,26] has investigated the applicability of ULFM and benchmarked individual operations of it. Bosilca et al. [7,8] and Katti et al. [19] propose efficient fault detection algorithms to integrate with ULFM. Teranishi et al. [31] use spare processes to replace failed processes for local recovery so as to accelerate recovery of ULFM. Even though ULFM gives flexibility to developers to implement any type of recover, it requires significant developer effort to refactor the application. Also, implementing ULFM has been identified by previous work [14,31] to suffer from scalability issues, as our experimentation shows too. Fenix [13] provides a simplified abstraction layer atop ULFM to implement global-restart recovery. However, we choose to directly use ULFM since it already provides a straightforward, prescribed solution for implementing global-restart.

Reinit [11,22] is an alternative solution that supports only global-restart recovery and provide an easy to use interface to developers. Previous designs and implementations of Reinit have limited applicability because they require modifying the job scheduler and its interface with the MPI runtime. We present Reinit$^{++}$, a new design and implementation of Reinit using the latest Open MPI runtime and thoroughly evaluate it.

Lastly, Sultana et al. [30] propose MPI stages to reduce the overhead of global-restart recovery by checkpointing MPI state, so that rolling back does not have to re-create it. While this approach is interesting, it is still in proof-of-concept status. How to maintain consistent checkpoints of MPI state across all MPI processes, and doing so fast and efficiently, is still an open-problem.

# 7   Conclusion

We have presented Reinit$^{++}$, a new design and implementation of the global-restart approach of Reinit. Reinit$^{++}$ recovers from both process and node crash failures, by spawning new processes and mending the world communicator, requiring from the programmer only to provide a rollback point in execution and have checkpointing in place. Our extensive evaluation comparing with the state-of-the-art approaches Checkpoint-Restart (CR) and ULFM shows that Reinit$^{++}$ scales excellently as the number of ranks grows, achieving almost constant recovery time, being up to 6× faster than CR and up to 3× faster than ULFM. For future work, we plan to expand Reinit for supporting more recovery strategies besides global-restart, including shrinking recovery and forward recovery strategies, to maintain its implementation, and expand the experimentation with more applications and larger deployments.

**Acknowledgments.** The authors would like to thank the anonymous referees for their valuable comments and helpful suggestions. This work was performed under the auspices of the U.S. Department of Energy by Lawrence Livermore National Laboratory under contract DEAC52-07NA27344 (LLNL-CONF-800061).

# References

1. Adam, J., et al.: Transparent high-speed network checkpoint/restart in MPI. In: Proceedings of the 25th European MPI Users' Group Meeting, p. 12 (2018)
2. Adam, J., et al.: Checkpoint/restart approaches for a thread-based MPI runtime. Parallel Comput. **85**, 204–219 (2019)
3. Bautista-Gomez, L., Tsuboi, S., Komatitsch, D., Cappello, F., Maruyama, N., Matsuoka, S.: FTI: high performance fault tolerance interface for hybrid systems. In: SC 2011: Proceedings of 2011 International Conference for High Performance Computing, Networking, Storage and Analysis, pp. 1–12, November 2011. https://doi.org/10.1145/2063384.2063427
4. Bland, W., Bouteiller, A., Herault, T., Bosilca, G., Dongarra, J.: Post-failure recovery of MPI communication capability: design and rationale. Int. J. High Performance Comput. Appl. **27**(3), 244–254 (2013)
5. Bland, W., Lu, H., Seo, S., Balaji, P.: Lessons learned implementing user-level failure mitigation in mpich. In: 2015 15th IEEE/ACM International Symposium on Cluster, Cloud and Grid Computing (2015)
6. Bosilca, G., et al.: Mpich-v: toward a scalable fault tolerant MPI for volatile nodes. In: SC 2002: Proceedings of the 2002 ACM/IEEE Conference on Supercomputing, pp. 29–29. IEEE (2002)
7. Bosilca, G., et al.: Failure detection and propagation in HPC systems. In: SC 2016: Proceedings of the International Conference for High Performance Computing, Networking, Storage and Analysis, pp. 312–322 (2016)
8. Bosilca, G., et al.: A failure detector for HPC platforms. Int. J. High Performance Comput. Appl. **32**(1), 139–158 (2018). https://doi.org/10.1177/1094342017711505
9. Bouteiller, A., Bosilca, G., Dongarra, J.J.: Plan B: Interruption of ongoing MPI operations to support failure recovery. In: Proceedings of the 22nd European MPI Users' Group Meeting, p. 11 (2015)
10. Cao, J., et al.: System-level scalable checkpoint-restart for petascale computing. In: 2016 IEEE 22nd International Conference on Parallel and Distributed Systems (ICPADS) (2016)
11. Chakraborty, S., et al.: Ereinit: scalable and efficient fault-tolerance for bulk-synchronous MPI applications. Concurrency and Computation: Practice and Experience, e4863. https://doi.org/10.1002/cpe.4863, https://onlinelibrary.wiley.com/doi/abs/10.1002/cpe.4863, e4863 cpe.4863
12. Dongarra, J., et al.: The international exascale software project roadmap. Int. J. High Perform. Comput. Appl. **25**(1), 3–60 (2011). https://doi.org/10.1177/1094342010391989, http://dx.doi.org/10.1177/1094342010391989
13. Gamell, M., Katz, D.S., Kolla, H., Chen, J., Klasky, S., Parashar, M.: Exploring automatic, online failure recovery for scientific applications at extreme scales. In: Proceedings of the International Conference for High Performance Computing, Networking, Storage and Analysis, pp. 895–906. SC 2014, IEEE Press, Piscataway, NJ, USA (2014). https://doi.org/10.1109/SC.2014.78
14. Gamell, M., et al.: Local recovery and failure masking for stencil-based applications at extreme scales. In: SC 2015: Proceedings of the International Conference for High Performance Computing, Networking, Storage and Analysis, pp. 1–12 (2015)
15. Hargrove, P.H., Duell, J.C.: Berkeley lab checkpoint/restart (BLCR) for linux clusters. In: Journal of Physics: Conference Series. vol. 46, p. 494 (2006)

16. Herault, T., et al.: Practical scalable consensus for pseudo-synchronous distributed systems. In: SC 2015: Proceedings of the International Conference for High Performance Computing, Networking, Storage and Analysis, pp. 1–12 (2015)
17. Hori, A., Yoshinaga, K., Herault, T., Bouteiller, A., Bosilca, G., Ishikawa, Y.: Sliding substitution of failed nodes. In: Proceedings of the 22nd European MPI Users' Group Meeting, p. 14. ACM (2015)
18. Katti, A., Di Fatta, G., Naughton, T., Engelmann, C.: Scalable and fault tolerant failure detection and consensus. In: Proceedings of the 22nd European MPI Users' Group Meeting, p. 13 (2015)
19. Katti, A., Di Fatta, G., Naughton, T., Engelmann, C.: Epidemic failure detection and consensus for extreme parallelism. Int. J. High Performance Comput. Appl. **32**(5), 729–743 (2018)
20. Kohl, N., et al.: A scalable and extensible checkpointing scheme for massively parallel simulations. Int. J. High Performance Comput. Appl. **33**(4), 571–589 (2019)
21. Laguna, I., Richards, D.F., Gamblin, T., Schulz, M., de Supinski, B.R.: Evaluating user-level fault tolerance for MPI applications. In: Proceedings of the 21st European MPI Users' Group Meeting, pp. 57:57–57:62. EuroMPI/ASIA 2014, ACM, New York, NY, USA (2014). https://doi.org/10.1145/2642769.2642775, http://doi.acm.org/10.1145/2642769.2642775
22. Laguna, I., et al.: Evaluating and extending user-level fault tolerance in MPI applications. Int. J. High Performance Comput. Appl. **30**(3), 305–319 (2016). https://doi.org/10.1177/1094342015623623
23. Losada, N., Cores, I., Martín, M.J., González, P.: Resilient MPI applications using an application-level checkpointing framework and ULFM. The Journal of Supercomputing **73**(1) (2017)
24. Martino, C.D., Kalbarczyk, Z., Iyer, R.K., Baccanico, F., Fullop, J., Kramer, W.: Lessons learned from the analysis of system failures at petascale: The case of blue waters. In: 2014 44th Annual IEEE/IFIP International Conference on Dependable Systems and Networks. pp. 610–621, June 2014. https://doi.org/10.1109/DSN.2014.62
25. Mohror, K., Moody, A., Bronevetsky, G., de Supinski, B.R.: Detailed modeling and evaluation of a scalable multilevel checkpointing system. IEEE Trans. Parallel Distrib. Syst. **25**(9), 2255–2263 (2014). https://doi.org/10.1109/TPDS.2013.100
26. Pauli, S., Kohler, M., Arbenz, P.: A fault tolerant implementation of multi-level monte carlo methods. Parallel Comput. Acceler. Comput. Sci. Eng. (CSE) **25**, 471–480 (2014)
27. Sankaran, S., et al.: The lam/mpi checkpoint/restart framework: system-initiated checkpointing. JHPCA **19**(4), 479–493 (2005)
28. Shahzad, F., Thies, J., Kreutzer, M., Zeiser, T., Hager, G., Wellein, G.: Craft: a library for easier application-level checkpoint/restart and automatic fault tolerance. IEEE Trans. Parallel Distrib. Syst. **30**(3), 501–514 (2018)
29. Subasi, O., Martsinkevich, T., Zyulkyarov, F., Unsal, O., Labarta, J., Cappello, F.: Unified fault-tolerance framework for hybrid task-parallel message-passing applications. Int. J. High Performance Comput. Appl. **32**(5), 641–657 (2018)
30. Sultana, N., Rüfenacht, M., Skjellum, A., Laguna, I., Mohror, K.: Failure recovery for bulk synchronous applications with MPI stages. Parallel Comput. **84**, 1–14 (2019). https://doi.org/10.1016/j.parco.2019.02.007, http://www.sciencedirect.com/science/article/pii/S0167819118303260
31. Teranishi, K., Heroux, M.A.: Toward local failure local recovery resilience model using MPI-ULFM. In: Proceedings of the 21st European MPI Users' Group Meeting, p. 51 (2014)

32. Wang, Z., Gao, L., Gu, Y., Bao, Y., Yu, G.: A fault-tolerant framework for asynchronous iterative computations in cloud environments. IEEE Trans. Parallel Distrib. Syst. **29**(8), 1678–1692 (2018)
33. Zheng, G., Xiang N., Kalé, L.V.: A scalable double in-memory checkpoint and restart scheme towards exascale. In: IEEE/IFIP International Conference on Dependable Systems and Networks Workshops (DSN 2012), pp. 1–6, June 2012. https://doi.org/10.1109/DSNW.2012.6264677
34. Zheng, G., Huang, C., Kalé, L.V.: Performance evaluation of automatic checkpoint-based fault tolerance for ampi and charm++. SIGOPS Oper. Syst. Rev. **40**(2), 90–99 (2006). https://doi.org/10.1145/1131322.1131340, http://doi.acm.org/10.1145/1131322.1131340

# Correction to: High Performance Computing

Ponnuswamy Sadayappan, Bradford L. Chamberlain,
Guido Juckeland⦿, and Hatem Ltaief⦿

## Correction to:
**P. Sadayappan et al. (Eds.): *High Performance Computing*,
LNCS 12151, https://doi.org/10.1007/978-3-030-50743-5**

The original version of chapters 17 and 24 were previously published non-open access. They have now been made open access under a CC BY 4.0 license and the copyright holder has been changed to 'The Author(s).' The book has also been updated with the change.

The chapters 19 and 25 were inadvertently published open access. This has been corrected and the chapters are now non-open access.

---

The updated version of these chapters can be found at
https://doi.org/10.1007/978-3-030-50743-5_17
https://doi.org/10.1007/978-3-030-50743-5_19
https://doi.org/10.1007/978-3-030-50743-5_24
https://doi.org/10.1007/978-3-030-50743-5_25
https://doi.org/10.1007/978-3-030-50743-5

© Springer Nature Switzerland AG 2020
P. Sadayappan et al. (Eds.): ISC High Performance 2020, LNCS 12151, p. C1, 2020.
https://doi.org/10.1007/978-3-030-50743-5_28

# Author Index

Printed in the United States
by Baker & Taylor Publisher Services